T0182136

Neural Networks and Deep Learning

Charu C. Aggarwal

Neural Networks and Deep Learning

A Textbook

 Springer

Charu C. Aggarwal
IBM T. J. Watson Research Center
International Business Machines
Yorktown Heights, NY, USA

ISBN 978-3-030-06856-1   ISBN 978-3-319-94463-0   (eBook)
https://doi.org/10.1007/978-3-319-94463-0

This Springer imprint is published by the registered company Springer Nature Switzerland AG
The registered company address is: Gewerbestrasse 11, 6330 Cham, Switzerland

To my wife Lata, my daughter Sayani,
and my late parents Dr. Prem Sarup and Mrs. Pushplata Aggarwal.

Preface

"Any A.I. smart enough to pass a Turing test is smart enough to know to fail it."—Ian McDonald

Neural networks were developed to simulate the human nervous system for machine learning tasks by treating the computational units in a learning model in a manner similar to human neurons. The grand vision of neural networks is to create artificial intelligence by building machines whose architecture simulates the computations in the human nervous system. This is obviously not a simple task because the computational power of the fastest computer today is a minuscule fraction of the computational power of a human brain. Neural networks were developed soon after the advent of computers in the fifties and sixties. Rosenblatt's perceptron algorithm was seen as a fundamental cornerstone of neural networks, which caused an initial excitement about the prospects of artificial intelligence. However, after the initial euphoria, there was a period of disappointment in which the data hungry and computationally intensive nature of neural networks was seen as an impediment to their usability. Eventually, at the turn of the century, greater data availability and increasing computational power lead to increased successes of neural networks, and this area was reborn under the new label of "deep learning." Although we are still far from the day that artificial intelligence (AI) is close to human performance, there are specific domains like image recognition, self-driving cars, and game playing, where AI has matched or exceeded human performance. It is also hard to predict what AI might be able to do in the future. For example, few computer vision experts would have thought two decades ago that any automated system could ever perform an intuitive task like categorizing an image more accurately than a human.

Neural networks are *theoretically* capable of learning any mathematical function with sufficient training data, and some variants like recurrent neural networks are known to be *Turing complete*. Turing completeness refers to the fact that a neural network can simulate any learning algorithm, *given sufficient training data*. The sticking point is that the amount of data required to learn even simple tasks is often extraordinarily large, which causes a corresponding increase in training time (if we assume that enough training data is available in the first place). For example, the training time for image recognition, which is a simple task for a human, can be on the order of weeks even on high-performance systems. Furthermore, there are practical issues associated with the stability of neural network training, which are being resolved even today. Nevertheless, given that the speed of computers is expected to increase rapidly over time, and fundamentally more powerful paradigms like quantum computing are on the horizon, the computational issue might not eventually turn out to be quite as critical as imagined.

Although the biological analogy of neural networks is an exciting one and evokes comparisons with science fiction, the mathematical understanding of neural networks is a more mundane one. The neural network abstraction can be viewed as a modular approach of enabling learning algorithms that are based on continuous optimization on a computational graph of dependencies between the input and output. To be fair, this is not very different from traditional work in control theory; indeed, some of the methods used for optimization in control theory are strikingly similar to (and historically preceded) the most fundamental algorithms in neural networks. However, the large amounts of data available in recent years together with increased computational power have enabled experimentation with deeper architectures of these computational graphs than was previously possible. The resulting success has changed the broader perception of the potential of deep learning.

The chapters of the book are organized as follows:

1. *The basics of neural networks:* Chapter 1 discusses the basics of neural network design. Many traditional machine learning models can be understood as special cases of neural learning. Understanding the relationship between traditional machine learning and neural networks is the first step to understanding the latter. The simulation of various machine learning models with neural networks is provided in Chapter 2. This will give the analyst a feel of how neural networks push the envelope of traditional machine learning algorithms.

2. *Fundamentals of neural networks:* Although Chapters 1 and 2 provide an overview of the training methods for neural networks, a more detailed understanding of the training challenges is provided in Chapters 3 and 4. Chapters 5 and 6 present radial-basis function (RBF) networks and restricted Boltzmann machines.

3. *Advanced topics in neural networks:* A lot of the recent success of deep learning is a result of the specialized architectures for various domains, such as recurrent neural networks and convolutional neural networks. Chapters 7 and 8 discuss recurrent and convolutional neural networks. Several advanced topics like deep reinforcement learning, neural Turing mechanisms, and generative adversarial networks are discussed in Chapters 9 and 10.

We have taken care to include some of the "forgotten" architectures like RBF networks and Kohonen self-organizing maps because of their potential in many applications. The book is written for graduate students, researchers, and practitioners. Numerous exercises are available along with a solution manual to aid in classroom teaching. Where possible, an application-centric view is highlighted in order to give the reader a feel for the technology.

Throughout this book, a vector or a multidimensional data point is annotated with a bar, such as $\overline{X}$ or $\overline{y}$. A vector or multidimensional point may be denoted by either small letters or capital letters, as long as it has a bar. Vector dot products are denoted by centered dots, such as $\overline{X} \cdot \overline{Y}$. A matrix is denoted in capital letters without a bar, such as R. Throughout the book, the $n \times d$ matrix corresponding to the entire training data set is denoted by D, with n documents and d dimensions. The individual data points in D are therefore d-dimensional row vectors. On the other hand, vectors with one component for each data point are usually n-dimensional column vectors. An example is the n-dimensional column vector $\overline{y}$ of class variables of n data points. An observed value y_i is distinguished from a predicted value $\hat{y}_i$ by a circumflex at the top of the variable.

Yorktown Heights, NY, USA   Charu C. Aggarwal

Acknowledgments

I would like to thank my family for their love and support during the busy time spent in writing this book. I would also like to thank my manager Nagui Halim for his support during the writing of this book.

Several figures in this book have been provided by the courtesy of various individuals and institutions. The Smithsonian Institution made the image of the Mark I perceptron (cf. Figure 1.5) available at no cost. Saket Sathe provided the outputs in Chapter 7 for the tiny Shakespeare data set, based on code available/described in [233, 580]. Andrew Zisserman provided Figures 8.12 and 8.16 in the section on convolutional visualizations. Another visualization of the feature maps in the convolution network (cf. Figure 8.15) was provided by Matthew Zeiler. NVIDIA provided Figure 9.10 on the convolutional neural network for self-driving cars in Chapter 9, and Sergey Levine provided the image on self-learning robots (cf. Figure 9.9) in the same chapter. Alec Radford provided Figure 10.8, which appears in Chapter 10. Alex Krizhevsky provided Figure 8.9(b) containing *AlexNet*.

This book has benefitted from significant feedback and several collaborations that I have had with numerous colleagues over the years. I would like to thank Quoc Le, Saket Sathe, Karthik Subbian, Jiliang Tang, and Suhang Wang for their feedback on various portions of this book. Shuai Zheng provided feedbback on the section on regularized autoencoders in Chapter 4. I received feedback on the sections on autoencoders from Lei Cai and Hao Yuan. Feedback on the chapter on convolutional neural networks was provided by Hongyang Gao, Shuiwang Ji, and Zhengyang Wang. Shuiwang Ji, Lei Cai, Zhengyang Wang and Hao Yuan also reviewed the Chapters 3 and 7, and suggested several edits. They also suggested the ideas of using Figures 8.6 and 8.7 for elucidating the convolution/deconvolution operations.

For their collaborations, I would like to thank Tarek F. Abdelzaher, Jinghui Chen, Jing Gao, Quanquan Gu, Manish Gupta, Jiawei Han, Alexander Hinneburg, Thomas Huang, Nan Li, Huan Liu, Ruoming Jin, Daniel Keim, Arijit Khan, Latifur Khan, Mohammad M. Masud, Jian Pei, Magda Procopiuc, Guojun Qi, Chandan Reddy, Saket Sathe, Jaideep Srivastava, Karthik Subbian, Yizhou Sun, Jiliang Tang, Min-Hsuan Tsai, Haixun Wang, Jianyong Wang, Min Wang, Suhang Wang, Joel Wolf, Xifeng Yan, Mohammed Zaki, ChengXiang Zhai, and Peixiang Zhao. I would also like to thank my advisor James B. Orlin for his guidance during my early years as a researcher.

I would like to thank Lata Aggarwal for helping me with some of the figures created using PowerPoint graphics in this book. My daughter, Sayani, was helpful in incorporating special effects (e.g., image color, contrast, and blurring) in several JPEG images used at various places in this book.

Contents

Author Biography

Charu C. Aggarwal is a Distinguished Research Staff Member (DRSM) at the IBM T. J. Watson Research Center in Yorktown Heights, New York. He completed his undergraduate degree in Computer Science from the Indian Institute of Technology at Kanpur in 1993 and his Ph.D. from the Massachusetts Institute of Technology in 1996.

 He has worked extensively in the field of data mining. He has published more than 350 papers in refereed conferences and journals and authored over 80 patents. He is the author or editor of 18 books, including textbooks on data mining, recommender systems, and outlier analysis. Because of the commercial value of his patents, he has thrice been designated a Master Inventor at IBM. He is a recipient of an IBM Corporate Award (2003) for his work on bioterrorist threat detection in data streams, a recipient of the IBM Outstanding Innovation Award (2008) for his scientific contributions to privacy technology, and a recipient of two IBM Outstanding Technical Achievement Awards (2009, 2015) for his work on data streams/high-dimensional data. He received the EDBT 2014 Test of Time Award for his work on condensation-based privacy-preserving data mining. He is also a recipient of the IEEE ICDM Research Contributions Award (2015), which is one of the two highest awards for influential research contributions in the field of data mining.

He has served as the general co-chair of the IEEE Big Data Conference (2014) and as the program co-chair of the ACM CIKM Conference (2015), the IEEE ICDM Conference (2015), and the ACM KDD Conference (2016). He served as an associate editor of the IEEE Transactions on Knowledge and Data Engineering from 2004 to 2008. He is an associate editor of the IEEE Transactions on Big Data, an action editor of the Data Mining and Knowledge Discovery Journal, and an associate editor of the Knowledge and Information Systems Journal. He serves as the editor-in-chief of the ACM Transactions on Knowledge Discovery from Data as well as the ACM SIGKDD Explorations. He serves on the advisory board of the Lecture Notes on Social Networks, a publication by Springer. He has served as the vice-president of the SIAM Activity Group on Data Mining and is a member of the SIAM industry committee. He is a fellow of the SIAM, ACM, and the IEEE, for "contributions to knowledge discovery and data mining algorithms."

Chapter 1

An Introduction to Neural Networks

"Thou shalt not make a machine to counterfeit a human mind."—Frank Herbert

1.1 Introduction

Artificial neural networks are popular machine learning techniques that simulate the mechanism of learning in biological organisms. The human nervous system contains cells, which are referred to as *neurons*. The neurons are connected to one another with the use of *axons* and *dendrites*, and the connecting regions between axons and dendrites are referred to as *synapses*. These connections are illustrated in Figure 1.1(a). The strengths of synaptic connections often change in response to external stimuli. This change is how learning takes place in living organisms.

This biological mechanism is simulated in *artificial* neural networks, which contain computation units that are referred to as neurons. Throughout this book, we will use the term "neural networks" to refer to artificial neural networks rather than biological ones. The computational units are connected to one another through weights, which serve the same

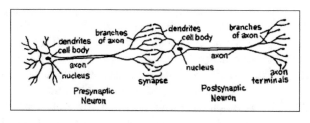

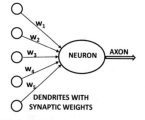

(a) Biological neural network   (b) Artificial neural network

Figure 1.1: The synaptic connections between neurons. The image in (a) is from *"The Brain: Understanding Neurobiology Through the Study of Addiction* [598]." Copyright ©2000 by BSCS & Videodiscovery. All rights reserved. Used with permission.

© Springer International Publishing AG, part of Springer Nature 2018
C. C. Aggarwal, *Neural Networks and Deep Learning*,
https://doi.org/10.1007/978-3-319-94463-0_1

role as the strengths of synaptic connections in biological organisms. Each input to a neuron is scaled with a weight, which affects the function computed at that unit. This architecture is illustrated in Figure 1.1(b). An artificial neural network computes a function of the inputs by propagating the computed values from the input neurons to the output neuron(s) and using the weights as intermediate parameters. Learning occurs by changing the weights connecting the neurons. Just as external stimuli are needed for learning in biological organisms, the external stimulus in artificial neural networks is provided by the training data containing examples of input-output pairs of the function to be learned. For example, the training data might contain pixel representations of images (input) and their annotated labels (e.g., carrot, banana) as the output. These training data pairs are fed into the neural network by using the input representations to make predictions about the output labels. The training data provides feedback to the correctness of the weights in the neural network depending on how well the predicted output (e.g., probability of carrot) for a particular input matches the annotated output label in the training data. One can view the errors made by the neural network in the computation of a function as a kind of unpleasant feedback in a biological organism, leading to an adjustment in the synaptic strengths. Similarly, the weights between neurons are adjusted in a neural network in response to prediction errors. The goal of changing the weights is to modify the computed function to make the predictions more correct in future iterations. Therefore, the weights are changed carefully in a mathematically justified way so as to reduce the error in computation on that example. By successively adjusting the weights between neurons over many input-output pairs, the function computed by the neural network is refined over time so that it provides more accurate predictions. Therefore, if the neural network is trained with many different images of bananas, it will eventually be able to properly recognize a banana in an image it has not seen before. This ability to accurately compute functions of unseen inputs by training over a finite set of input-output pairs is referred to as *model generalization*. The primary usefulness of all machine learning models is gained from their ability to generalize their learning from seen training data to unseen examples.

The biological comparison is often criticized as a very poor caricature of the workings of the human brain; nevertheless, the principles of neuroscience have often been useful in designing neural network architectures. A different view is that neural networks are built as higher-level abstractions of the classical models that are commonly used in machine learning. In fact, the most basic units of computation in the neural network are inspired by traditional machine learning algorithms like *least-squares regression* and *logistic regression*. Neural networks gain their power by putting together many such basic units, and learning the weights of the different units jointly in order to minimize the prediction error. From this point of view, a neural network can be viewed as a *computational graph* of elementary units in which greater power is gained by connecting them in particular ways. When a neural network is used in its most basic form, without hooking together multiple units, the learning algorithms often reduce to classical machine learning models (see Chapter 2). The real power of a neural model over classical methods is unleashed when these elementary computational units are combined, and the weights of the elementary models are trained using their dependencies on one another. By combining multiple units, one is increasing the power of the model to learn more complicated functions of the data than are inherent in the elementary models of basic machine learning. The way in which these units are combined also plays a role in the power of the architecture, and requires some understanding and insight from the analyst. Furthermore, sufficient training data is also required in order to learn the larger number of weights in these expanded computational graphs.

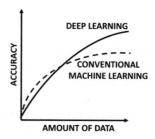

Figure 1.2: An illustrative comparison of the accuracy of a typical machine learning algorithm with that of a large neural network. Deep learners become more attractive than conventional methods primarily when sufficient data/computational power is available. Recent years have seen an increase in data availability and computational power, which has led to a "Cambrian explosion" in deep learning technology.

1.1.1 Humans Versus Computers: Stretching the Limits of Artificial Intelligence

Humans and computers are inherently suited to different types of tasks. For example, computing the cube root of a large number is very easy for a computer, but it is extremely difficult for humans. On the other hand, a task such as recognizing the objects in an image is a simple matter for a human, but has traditionally been very difficult for an automated learning algorithm. It is only in recent years that deep learning has shown an accuracy on some of these tasks that exceeds that of a human. In fact, the recent results by deep learning algorithms that surpass human performance [184] in (some narrow tasks on) image recognition would not have been considered likely by most computer vision experts as recently as 10 years ago.

Many deep learning architectures that have shown such extraordinary performance are not created by indiscriminately connecting computational units. The superior performance of *deep* neural networks mirrors the fact that biological neural networks gain much of their power from depth as well. Furthermore, biological networks are connected in ways we do not fully understand. In the few cases that the biological structure is understood at some level, significant breakthroughs have been achieved by designing artificial neural networks along those lines. A classical example of this type of architecture is the use of the *convolutional neural network* for image recognition. This architecture was inspired by Hubel and Wiesel's experiments [212] in 1959 on the organization of the neurons in the cat's visual cortex. The precursor to the convolutional neural network was the *neocognitron* [127], which was directly based on these results.

The human neuronal connection structure has evolved over millions of years to optimize survival-driven performance; survival is closely related to our ability to merge sensation and intuition in a way that is currently not possible with machines. Biological neuroscience [232] is a field that is still very much in its infancy, and only a limited amount is known about how the brain truly works. Therefore, it is fair to suggest that the biologically inspired success of convolutional neural networks might be replicated in other settings, as we learn more about how the human brain works [176]. A key advantage of neural networks over traditional machine learning is that the former provides a higher-level abstraction of expressing semantic insights about data domains by architectural design choices in the computational graph. The second advantage is that neural networks provide a simple way to adjust the complexity of a model by adding or removing neurons from the architecture according to the availability of training data or computational power. A large part of the recent success of neural networks is explained by the fact that the increased data availability and computational power of modern computers has outgrown the limits of traditional machine learning algorithms, which fail to take full advantage of what is now possible. This situation is illustrated in Figure 1.2. The performance of traditional machine learning remains better at times for smaller data sets because of more choices, greater ease of model interpretation, and the tendency to hand-craft interpretable features that incorporate domain-specific insights. With limited data, the best of a very wide diversity of models in machine learning will usually perform better than a single class of models (like neural networks). This is one reason why the potential of neural networks was not realized in the early years.

The "big data" era has been enabled by the advances in data collection technology; virtually everything we do today, including purchasing an item, using the phone, or clicking on a site, is collected and stored somewhere. Furthermore, the development of powerful Graphics Processor Units (GPUs) has enabled increasingly efficient processing on such large data sets. These advances largely explain the recent success of deep learning using algorithms that are only slightly adjusted from the versions that were available two decades back. Furthermore, these recent adjustments to the algorithms have been enabled by increased speed of computation, because reduced run-times enable efficient testing (and subsequent algorithmic adjustment). If it requires a month to test an algorithm, at most twelve variations can be tested in an year on a single hardware platform. This situation has historically constrained the intensive experimentation required for tweaking neural-network learning algorithms. The rapid advances associated with the three pillars of improved data, computation, and experimentation have resulted in an increasingly optimistic outlook about the future of deep learning. By the end of this century, it is expected that computers will have the power to train neural networks with as many neurons as the human brain. Although it is hard to predict what the true capabilities of artificial intelligence will be by then, our experience with computer vision should prepare us to expect the unexpected.

Chapter Organization

This chapter is organized as follows. The next section introduces single-layer and multi-layer networks. The different types of activation functions, output nodes, and loss functions are discussed. The backpropagation algorithm is introduced in Section 1.3. Practical issues in neural network training are discussed in Section 1.4. Some key points on how neural networks gain their power with specific choices of activation functions are discussed in Section 1.5. The common architectures used in neural network design are discussed in Section 1.6. Advanced topics in deep learning are discussed in Section 1.7. Some notable benchmarks used by the deep learning community are discussed in Section 1.8. A summary is provided in Section 1.9.

1.2   The Basic Architecture of Neural Networks

In this section, we will introduce single-layer and multi-layer neural networks. In the single-layer network, a set of inputs is directly mapped to an output by using a generalized variation of a linear function. This simple instantiation of a neural network is also referred to as the *perceptron*. In multi-layer neural networks, the neurons are arranged in layered fashion, in which the input and output layers are separated by a group of hidden layers. This layer-wise architecture of the neural network is also referred to as a *feed-forward network*. This section will discuss both single-layer and multi-layer networks.

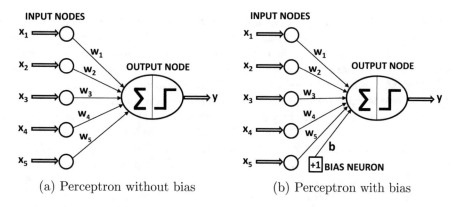

(a) Perceptron without bias   (b) Perceptron with bias

Figure 1.3: The basic architecture of the perceptron

1.2.1 Single Computational Layer: The Perceptron

The simplest neural network is referred to as the perceptron. This neural network contains a single input layer and an output node. The basic architecture of the perceptron is shown in Figure 1.3(a). Consider a situation where each training instance is of the form $(\overline{X}, y)$, where each $\overline{X} = [x_1, \dots x_d]$ contains d feature variables, and $y \in \{-1, +1\}$ contains the *observed value* of the binary class variable. By "observed value" we refer to the fact that it is given to us as a part of the training data, and our goal is to predict the class variable for cases in which it is not observed. For example, in a credit-card fraud detection application, the features might represent various properties of a set of credit card transactions (e.g., amount and frequency of transactions), and the class variable might represent whether or not this set of transactions is fraudulent. Clearly, in this type of application, one would have historical cases in which the class variable is observed, and other (current) cases in which the class variable has not yet been observed but needs to be predicted.

The input layer contains d nodes that transmit the d features $\overline{X} = [x_1 \dots x_d]$ with edges of weight $\overline{W} = [w_1 \dots w_d]$ to an output node. The input layer does not perform any computation in its own right. The linear function $\overline{W} \cdot \overline{X} = \sum_{i=1}^{d} w_i x_i$ is computed at the output node. Subsequently, the sign of this real value is used in order to predict the dependent variable of $\overline{X}$. Therefore, the prediction $\hat{y}$ is computed as follows:

$$\hat{y} = \text{sign}\{\overline{W} \cdot \overline{X}\} = \text{sign}\{\sum_{j=1}^{d} w_j x_j\} \tag{1.1}$$

The sign function maps a real value to either $+1$ or -1, which is appropriate for binary classification. Note the circumflex on top of the variable y to indicate that it is a predicted value rather than an observed value. The error of the prediction is therefore $E(\overline{X}) = y - \hat{y}$, which is one of the values drawn from the set $\{-2, 0, +2\}$. In cases where the error value $E(\overline{X})$ is nonzero, the weights in the neural network need to be updated in the (negative) direction of the error gradient. As we will see later, this process is similar to that used in various types of linear models in machine learning. In spite of the similarity of the perceptron with respect to traditional machine learning models, its interpretation as a computational unit is very useful because it allows us to put together multiple units in order to create far more powerful models than are available in traditional machine learning.

The architecture of the perceptron is shown in Figure 1.3(a), in which a single input layer transmits the features to the output node. The edges from the input to the output contain the weights $w_1 \ldots w_d$ with which the features are multiplied and added at the output node. Subsequently, the sign function is applied in order to convert the aggregated value into a class label. The sign function serves the role of an *activation function*. Different choices of activation functions can be used to simulate different types of models used in machine learning, like *least-squares regression with numeric targets*, the *support vector machine*, or a *logistic regression classifier*. Most of the basic machine learning models can be easily represented as simple neural network architectures. It is a useful exercise to model traditional machine learning techniques as neural architectures, because it provides a clearer picture of how deep learning generalizes traditional machine learning. This point of view is explored in detail in Chapter 2. It is noteworthy that the perceptron contains two layers, although the input layer does not perform any computation and only transmits the feature values. The input layer is not included in the count of the number of layers in a neural network. Since the perceptron contains a single *computational* layer, it is considered a single-layer network.

In many settings, there is an invariant part of the prediction, which is referred to as the *bias*. For example, consider a setting in which the feature variables are mean centered, but the mean of the binary class prediction from $\{-1, +1\}$ is not 0. This will tend to occur in situations in which the binary class distribution is highly imbalanced. In such a case, the aforementioned approach is not sufficient for prediction. We need to incorporate an additional bias variable b that captures this invariant part of the prediction:

$$\hat{y} = \text{sign}\{\overline{W} \cdot \overline{X} + b\} = \text{sign}\{\sum_{j=1}^{d} w_j x_j + b\} \qquad (1.2)$$

The bias can be incorporated as the weight of an edge by using a *bias neuron*. This is achieved by adding a neuron that always transmits a value of 1 to the output node. The weight of the edge connecting the bias neuron to the output node provides the bias variable. An example of a bias neuron is shown in Figure 1.3(b). Another approach that works well with single-layer architectures is to use a *feature engineering trick* in which an additional feature is created with a constant value of 1. The coefficient of this feature provides the bias, and one can then work with Equation 1.1. Throughout this book, biases will not be explicitly used (for simplicity in architectural representations) because they can be incorporated with bias neurons. The details of the training algorithms remain the same by simply treating the bias neurons like any other neuron with a fixed activation value of 1. Therefore, the following will work with the predictive assumption of Equation 1.1, which does not explicitly uses biases.

At the time that the perceptron algorithm was proposed by Rosenblatt [405], these optimizations were performed in a heuristic way with actual hardware circuits, and it was not presented in terms of a formal notion of optimization in machine learning (as is common today). However, the goal was always to minimize the error in prediction, even if a formal optimization formulation was not presented. The perceptron algorithm was, therefore, heuristically designed to minimize the number of misclassifications, and convergence proofs were available that provided correctness guarantees of the learning algorithm in simplified settings. Therefore, we can still write the (heuristically motivated) goal of the perceptron algorithm in least-squares form with respect to all training instances in a data set $\mathcal{D}$ containing feature-label pairs:

$$\text{Minimize}_{\overline{W}} \, L = \sum_{(\overline{X},y)\in\mathcal{D}} (y - \hat{y})^2 = \sum_{(\overline{X},y)\in\mathcal{D}} \left(y - \text{sign}\{\overline{W} \cdot \overline{X}\}\right)^2$$

This type of minimization objective function is also referred to as a *loss function*. As we will see later, almost all neural network learning algorithms are formulated with the use of a loss function. As we will learn in Chapter 2, this loss function looks a lot like least-squares regression. However, the latter is defined for continuous-valued target variables, and the corresponding loss is a smooth and continuous function of the variables. On the other hand, for the least-squares form of the objective function, the sign function is non-differentiable, with step-like jumps at specific points. Furthermore, the sign function takes on constant values over large portions of the domain, and therefore the exact gradient takes on zero values at differentiable points. This results in a staircase-like loss surface, which is not suitable for gradient-descent. The perceptron algorithm (implicitly) uses a smooth approximation of the gradient of this objective function with respect to each example:

$$\nabla L_{\text{smooth}} = \sum_{(\overline{X},y)\in\mathcal{D}} (y - \hat{y})\overline{X} \tag{1.3}$$

Note that the above gradient is not a true gradient of the staircase-like surface of the (heuristic) objective function, which does not provide useful gradients. Therefore, the staircase is smoothed out into a sloping surface defined by the *perceptron criterion*. The properties of the perceptron criterion will be described in Section 1.2.1.1. It is noteworthy that concepts like the "perceptron criterion" were proposed later than the original paper by Rosenblatt [405] in order to explain the heuristic gradient-descent steps. For now, we will assume that the perceptron algorithm optimizes some unknown smooth function with the use of gradient descent.

Although the above objective function is defined over the entire training data, the training algorithm of neural networks works by feeding each input data instance $\overline{X}$ into the network one by one (or in small batches) to create the prediction $\hat{y}$. The weights are then updated, based on the error value $E(\overline{X}) = (y - \hat{y})$. Specifically, when the data point $\overline{X}$ is fed into the network, the weight vector $\overline{W}$ is updated as follows:

$$\overline{W} \Leftarrow \overline{W} + \alpha(y - \hat{y})\overline{X} \tag{1.4}$$

The parameter α regulates the learning rate of the neural network. The perceptron algorithm repeatedly cycles through all the training examples in random order and iteratively adjusts the weights until convergence is reached. A single training data point may be cycled through many times. Each such cycle is referred to as an *epoch*. One can also write the gradient-descent update in terms of the error $E(\overline{X}) = (y - \hat{y})$ as follows:

$$\overline{W} \Leftarrow \overline{W} + \alpha E(\overline{X})\overline{X} \tag{1.5}$$

The basic perceptron algorithm can be considered a *stochastic gradient-descent* method, which implicitly minimizes the squared error of prediction by performing gradient-descent updates with respect to randomly chosen training points. The assumption is that the neural network cycles through the points in random order during training and changes the weights with the goal of reducing the prediction error on that point. It is easy to see from Equation 1.5 that non-zero updates are made to the weights only when $y \neq \hat{y}$, which occurs only when errors are made in prediction. In *mini-batch stochastic gradient descent*, the aforementioned updates of Equation 1.5 are implemented over a randomly chosen subset of training points S:

$$\overline{W} \Leftarrow \overline{W} + \alpha \sum_{\overline{X} \in S} E(\overline{X})\overline{X} \qquad (1.6)$$

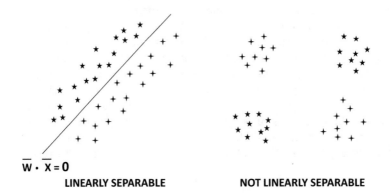

$$\overline{W} \cdot \overline{X} = 0$$
LINEARLY SEPARABLE   **NOT LINEARLY SEPARABLE**

Figure 1.4: Examples of linearly separable and inseparable data in two classes

The advantages of using mini-batch stochastic gradient descent are discussed in Section 3.2.8 of Chapter 3. An interesting quirk of the perceptron is that it is possible to set the learning rate α to 1, because the learning rate only scales the weights.

The type of model proposed in the perceptron is a *linear model*, in which the equation $\overline{W} \cdot \overline{X} = 0$ defines a linear hyperplane. Here, $\overline{W} = (w_1 \ldots w_d)$ is a d-dimensional vector that is normal to the hyperplane. Furthermore, the value of $\overline{W} \cdot \overline{X}$ is positive for values of $\overline{X}$ on one side of the hyperplane, and it is negative for values of $\overline{X}$ on the other side. This type of model performs particularly well when the data is *linearly separable*. Examples of linearly separable and inseparable data are shown in Figure 1.4.

The perceptron algorithm is good at classifying data sets like the one shown on the left-hand side of Figure 1.4, when the data is linearly separable. On the other hand, it tends to perform poorly on data sets like the one shown on the right-hand side of Figure 1.4. This example shows the inherent modeling limitation of a perceptron, which necessitates the use of more complex neural architectures.

Since the original perceptron algorithm was proposed as a heuristic minimization of classification errors, it was particularly important to show that the algorithm converges to reasonable solutions in some special cases. In this context, it was shown [405] that the perceptron algorithm always converges to provide zero error on the training data when the data are linearly separable. However, the perceptron algorithm is not guaranteed to converge in instances where the data are not linearly separable. For reasons discussed in the next section, the perceptron might sometimes arrive at a very poor solution with data that are not linearly separable (in comparison with many other learning algorithms).

1.2.1.1   What Objective Function Is the Perceptron Optimizing?

As discussed earlier in this chapter, the original perceptron paper by Rosenblatt [405] did not formally propose a loss function. In those years, these implementations were achieved using actual hardware circuits. The original *Mark I perceptron* was intended to be a machine rather than an algorithm, and custom-built hardware was used to create it (cf. Figure 1.5).

The general goal was to minimize the number of classification errors with a heuristic update process (in hardware) that changed weights in the "correct" direction whenever errors were made. This heuristic update strongly resembled gradient descent but it was not derived as a gradient-descent method. Gradient descent is defined only for smooth loss functions in algorithmic settings, whereas the hardware-centric approach was designed in a more

Figure 1.5: The perceptron algorithm was originally implemented using hardware circuits. The image depicts the Mark I perceptron machine built in 1958. (Courtesy: Smithsonian Institute)

heuristic way with *binary outputs*. Many of the binary and circuit-centric principles were inherited from the *McCulloch-Pitts* model [321] of the neuron. Unfortunately, binary signals are not prone to continuous optimization.

Can we find a smooth loss function, whose gradient turns out to be the perceptron update? The number of classification errors in a binary classification problem can be written in the form of a 0/1 loss function for training data point $(\overline{X_i}, y_i)$ as follows:

$$L_i^{(0/1)} = \frac{1}{2}(y_i - \text{sign}\{\overline{W} \cdot \overline{X_i}\})^2 = 1 - y_i \cdot \text{sign}\{\overline{W} \cdot \overline{X_i}\} \qquad (1.7)$$

The simplification to the right-hand side of the above objective function is obtained by setting both y_i^2 and $\text{sign}\{\overline{W} \cdot \overline{X_i}\}^2$ to 1, since they are obtained by squaring a value drawn from $\{-1, +1\}$. However, this objective function is not differentiable, because it has a staircase-like shape, especially when it is added over multiple points. Note that the 0/1 loss above is dominated by the term $-y_i\text{sign}\{\overline{W} \cdot \overline{X_i}\}$, in which the sign function causes most of the problems associated with non-differentiability. Since neural networks are defined by gradient-based optimization, we need to define a smooth objective function that is responsible for the perceptron updates. It can be shown [41] that the updates of the perceptron implicitly optimize the *perceptron criterion*. This objective function is defined by dropping the sign function in the above 0/1 loss and setting negative values to 0 in order to treat all correct predictions in a uniform and lossless way:

$$L_i = \max\{-y_i(\overline{W} \cdot \overline{X_i}), 0\} \qquad (1.8)$$

The reader is encouraged to use calculus to verify that the gradient of this smoothed objective function leads to the perceptron update, and the update of the perceptron is essentially

$\overline{W} \Leftarrow \overline{W} - \alpha \nabla_W L_i$. The modified loss function to enable gradient computation of a non-differentiable function is also referred to as a *smoothed surrogate loss function*. Almost all continuous optimization-based learning methods (such as neural networks) with discrete outputs (such as class labels) use some type of smoothed surrogate loss function.

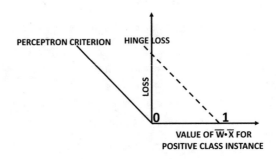

Figure 1.6: Perceptron criterion versus hinge loss

Although the aforementioned perceptron criterion was reverse engineered by working backwards from the perceptron updates, the nature of this loss function exposes some of the weaknesses of the updates in the original algorithm. An interesting observation about the perceptron criterion is that one can set $\overline{W}$ to the zero vector *irrespective of the training data set* in order to obtain the optimal loss value of 0. In spite of this fact, the perceptron updates continue to converge to a clear separator between the two classes in linearly separable cases; after all, a separator between the two classes provides a loss value of 0 as well. However, the behavior for data that are not linearly separable is rather arbitrary, and the resulting solution is sometimes not even a good approximate separator of the classes. The direct sensitivity of the loss to the *magnitude* of the weight vector can dilute the goal of class separation; it is possible for updates to worsen the number of misclassifications significantly while improving the loss. This is an example of how surrogate loss functions might sometimes not fully achieve their intended goals. Because of this fact, the approach is not stable and can yield solutions of widely varying quality.

Several variations of the learning algorithm were therefore proposed for inseparable data, and a natural approach is to always keep track of the best solution in terms of the number of misclassifications [128]. This approach of always keeping the best solution in one's "pocket" is referred to as the *pocket algorithm*. Another highly performing variant incorporates the notion of *margin* in the loss function, which creates an *identical* algorithm to the *linear support vector machine*. For this reason, the linear support vector machine is also referred to as the *perceptron of optimal stability*.

1.2.1.2   Relationship with Support Vector Machines

The perceptron criterion is a shifted version of the *hinge-loss* used in support vector machines (see Chapter 2). The hinge loss looks even more similar to the zero-one loss criterion of Equation 1.7, and is defined as follows:

$$L_i^{svm} = \max\{1 - y_i(\overline{W} \cdot \overline{X_i}), 0\} \tag{1.9}$$

Note that the perceptron does not keep the constant term of 1 on the right-hand side of Equation 1.7, whereas the hinge loss keeps this constant within the maximization function. This change does not affect the algebraic expression for the gradient, but it does change which points are lossless and should not cause an update. The relationship between the perceptron criterion and the hinge loss is shown in Figure 1.6. This similarity becomes particularly evident when the perceptron updates of Equation 1.6 are rewritten as follows:

$$\overline{W} \Leftarrow \overline{W} + \alpha \sum_{(\overline{X}, y) \in S^+} y \overline{X} \tag{1.10}$$

Here, S^+ is defined as the set of all misclassified training points $\overline{X} \in S$ that satisfy the condition $y(\overline{W} \cdot \overline{X}) < 0$. This update seems to look somewhat different from the perceptron, because the perceptron uses the error $E(\overline{X})$ for the update, which is replaced with y in the update above. A key point is that the (integer) error value $E(\overline{X}) = (y - \text{sign}\{\overline{W} \cdot \overline{X}\}) \in \{-2, +2\}$ can never be 0 for misclassified points in S^+. Therefore, we have $E(\overline{X}) = 2y$ *for misclassified points*, and $E(\overline{X})$ can be replaced with y in the updates after absorbing the factor of 2 within the learning rate. This update is identical to that used by the primal support vector machine (SVM) algorithm [448], except that the updates are performed only for the misclassified points in the perceptron, whereas the SVM also uses the marginally correct points near the decision boundary for updates. Note that the SVM uses the condition $y(\overline{W} \cdot \overline{X}) < 1$ [instead of using the condition $y(\overline{W} \cdot \overline{X}) < 0$] to define S^+, which is one of the key differences between the two algorithms. This point shows that the perceptron is fundamentally not very different from well-known machine learning algorithms like the support vector machine in spite of its different origins. Freund and Schapire provide a beautiful exposition of the role of margin in improving stability of the perceptron and also its relationship with the support vector machine [123]. It turns out that many traditional machine learning models can be viewed as minor variations of shallow neural architectures like the perceptron. The relationships between classical machine learning models and shallow neural networks are described in detail in Chapter 2.

1.2.1.3 Choice of Activation and Loss Functions

The choice of activation function is a critical part of neural network design. In the case of the perceptron, the choice of the sign activation function is motivated by the fact that a binary class label needs to be predicted. However, it is possible to have other types of situations where different target variables may be predicted. For example, if the target variable to be predicted is real, then it makes sense to use the identity activation function, and the resulting algorithm is the same as least-squares regression. If it is desirable to predict a probability of a binary class, it makes sense to use a *sigmoid* function for activating the output node, so that the prediction $\hat{y}$ indicates the probability that the observed value, y, of the dependent variable is 1. The negative logarithm of $|y/2 - 0.5 + \hat{y}|$ is used as the loss, assuming that y is coded from $\{-1, 1\}$. If $\hat{y}$ is the probability that y is 1, then $|y/2 - 0.5 + \hat{y}|$ is the probability that the correct value is predicted. This assertion is easy to verify by examining the two cases where y is 0 or 1. This loss function can be shown to be representative of the negative log-likelihood of the training data (see Section 2.2.3 of Chapter 2).

The importance of nonlinear activation functions becomes significant when one moves from the single-layered perceptron to the multi-layered architectures discussed later in this chapter. Different types of nonlinear functions such as the *sign, sigmoid,* or *hyperbolic tangents* may be used in various layers. We use the notation Φ to denote the activation function:

$$\hat{y} = \Phi(\overline{W} \cdot \overline{X}) \tag{1.11}$$

Therefore, a neuron really computes two functions within the node, which is why we have incorporated the summation symbol Σ as well as the activation symbol Φ within a neuron. The break-up of the neuron computations into two separate values is shown in Figure 1.7.

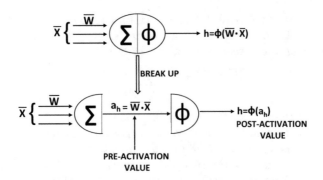

Figure 1.7: Pre-activation and post-activation values within a neuron

The value computed before applying the activation function $\Phi(\cdot)$ will be referred to as the *pre-activation value*, whereas the value computed after applying the activation function is referred to as the *post-activation value*. The output of a neuron is always the post-activation value, although the pre-activation variables are often used in different types of analyses, such as the computations of the *backpropagation algorithm* discussed later in this chapter. The pre-activation and post-activation values of a neuron are shown in Figure 1.7.

The most basic activation function $\Phi(\cdot)$ is the identity or linear activation, which provides no nonlinearity:

$$\Phi(v) = v$$

The linear activation function is often used in the output node, when the target is a real value. It is even used for discrete outputs when a smoothed surrogate loss function needs to be set up.

The classical activation functions that were used early in the development of neural networks were the sign, sigmoid, and the hyperbolic tangent functions:

$$\Phi(v) = \text{sign}(v) \text{ (sign function)}$$

$$\Phi(v) = \frac{1}{1 + e^{-v}} \text{ (sigmoid function)}$$

$$\Phi(v) = \frac{e^{2v} - 1}{e^{2v} + 1} \text{ (tanh function)}$$

While the sign activation can be used to map to binary outputs at prediction time, its non-differentiability prevents its use for creating the loss function at training time. For example, while the perceptron uses the sign function for prediction, the perceptron criterion in training only requires linear activation. The sigmoid activation outputs a value in $(0, 1)$, which is helpful in performing computations that should be interpreted as probabilities. Furthermore, it is also helpful in creating probabilistic outputs and constructing loss functions derived from maximum-likelihood models. The tanh function has a shape similar to that of the sigmoid function, except that it is horizontally re-scaled and vertically translated/re-scaled to $[-1, 1]$. The tanh and sigmoid functions are related as follows (see Exercise 3):

$$\tanh(v) = 2 \cdot \text{sigmoid}(2v) - 1$$

The tanh function is preferable to the sigmoid when the outputs of the computations are desired to be both positive and negative. Furthermore, its mean-centering and larger gradient

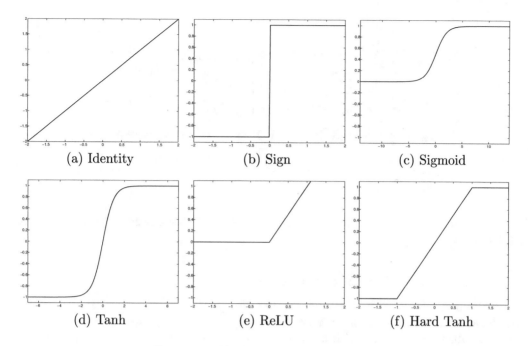

(a) Identity   (b) Sign   (c) Sigmoid

(d) Tanh   (e) ReLU   (f) Hard Tanh

Figure 1.8: Various activation functions

(because of stretching) with respect to sigmoid makes it easier to train. The sigmoid and the tanh functions have been the historical tools of choice for incorporating nonlinearity in the neural network. In recent years, however, a number of piecewise linear activation functions have become more popular:

$$\Phi(v) = \max\{v, 0\} \ (\text{Rectified Linear Unit [ReLU]})$$
$$\Phi(v) = \max\{\min[v, 1], -1\} \ (\text{hard tanh})$$

The ReLU and hard tanh activation functions have largely replaced the sigmoid and soft tanh activation functions in modern neural networks because of the ease in training multi-layered neural networks with these activation functions.

Pictorial representations of all the aforementioned activation functions are illustrated in Figure 1.8. It is noteworthy that all activation functions shown here are monotonic. Furthermore, other than the identity activation function, most[1] of the other activation functions *saturate* at large absolute values of the argument at which increasing further does not change the activation much.

As we will see later, such nonlinear activation functions are also very useful in multilayer networks, because they help in creating more powerful compositions of different types of functions. Many of these functions are referred to as *squashing* functions, as they map the outputs from an arbitrary range to bounded outputs. The use of a nonlinear activation plays a fundamental role in increasing the modeling power of a network. If a network used only linear activations, it would not provide better modeling power than a single-layer linear network. This issue is discussed in Section 1.5.

---

[1] The ReLU shows asymmetric saturation.

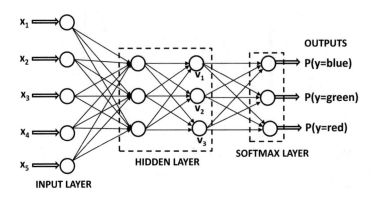

Figure 1.9: An example of multiple outputs for categorical classification with the use of a softmax layer

1.2.1.4   Choice and Number of Output Nodes

The choice and number of output nodes is also tied to the activation function, which in turn depends on the application at hand. For example, if k-way classification is intended, k output values can be used, with a softmax activation function with respect to outputs $\overline{v} = [v_1, \ldots, v_k]$ at the nodes in a given layer. Specifically, the activation function for the ith output is defined as follows:

$$\Phi(\overline{v})_i = \frac{\exp(v_i)}{\sum_{j=1}^{k} \exp(v_j)} \quad \forall i \in \{1, \ldots, k\} \tag{1.12}$$

It is helpful to think of these k values as the values output by k nodes, in which the inputs are $v_1 \ldots v_k$. An example of the softmax function with three outputs is illustrated in Figure 1.9, and the values v_1, v_2, and v_3 are also shown in the same figure. Note that the three outputs correspond to the probabilities of the three classes, and they convert the three outputs of the final hidden layer into probabilities with the softmax function. The final hidden layer often uses linear (identity) activations, when it is input into the softmax layer. Furthermore, there are no weights associated with the softmax layer, since it is only converting real-valued outputs into probabilities. The use of softmax with a single hidden layer of linear activations exactly implements a model, which is referred to as *multinomial logistic regression* [6]. Similarly, many variations like multi-class SVMs can be easily implemented with neural networks. Another example of a case in which multiple output nodes are used is the *autoencoder*, in which each input data point is fully reconstructed by the output layer. The autoencoder can be used to implement matrix factorization methods like *singular value decomposition*. This architecture will be discussed in detail in Chapter 2. The simplest neural networks that simulate basic machine learning algorithms are instructive because they lie on the continuum between traditional machine learning and deep networks. By exploring these architectures, one gets a better idea of the relationship between traditional machine learning and neural networks, and also the advantages provided by the latter.

1.2.1.5   Choice of Loss Function

The choice of the loss function is critical in defining the outputs in a way that is sensitive to the application at hand. For example, least-squares regression with numeric outputs requires a simple squared loss of the form $(y - \hat{y})^2$ for a single training instance with target y and prediction $\hat{y}$. One can also use other types of loss like *hinge loss* for $y \in \{-1, +1\}$ and real-valued prediction $\hat{y}$ (with identity activation):

$$L = \max\{0, 1 - y \cdot \hat{y}\} \tag{1.13}$$

The hinge loss can be used to implement a learning method, which is referred to as a *support vector machine.*

For multiway predictions (like predicting word identifiers or one of multiple classes), the softmax output is particularly useful. However, a softmax output is probabilistic, and therefore it requires a different type of loss function. In fact, for probabilistic predictions, two different types of loss functions are used, depending on whether the prediction is binary or whether it is multiway:

1. **Binary targets (logistic regression):** In this case, it is assumed that the observed value y is drawn from $\{-1, +1\}$, and the prediction $\hat{y}$ is a an arbitrary numerical value on using the identity activation function. In such a case, the loss function for a single instance with observed value y and real-valued prediction $\hat{y}$ (with identity activation) is defined as follows:

$$L = \log(1 + \exp(-y \cdot \hat{y})) \tag{1.14}$$

This type of loss function implements a fundamental machine learning method, referred to as *logistic regression.* Alternatively, one can use a sigmoid activation function to output $\hat{y} \in (0, 1)$, which indicates the probability that the observed value y is 1. Then, the negative logarithm of $|y/2 - 0.5 + \hat{y}|$ provides the loss, assuming that y is coded from $\{-1, 1\}$. This is because $|y/2 - 0.5 + \hat{y}|$ indicates the probability that the prediction is correct. This observation illustrates that one can use various combinations of activation and loss functions to achieve the same result.

2. **Categorical targets:** In this case, if $\hat{y}_1 \ldots \hat{y}_k$ are the probabilities of the k classes (using the softmax activation of Equation 1.9), and the rth class is the ground-truth class, then the loss function for a single instance is defined as follows:

$$L = -\log(\hat{y}_r) \tag{1.15}$$

This type of loss function implements multinomial logistic regression, and it is referred to as the *cross-entropy loss.* Note that binary logistic regression is identical to multinomial logistic regression, when the value of k is set to 2 in the latter.

The key point to remember is that the nature of the output nodes, the activation function, and the loss function depend on the application at hand. Furthermore, these choices also depend on one another. Even though the perceptron is often presented as the quintessential representative of single-layer networks, it is only a single representative out of a very large universe of possibilities. In practice, one rarely uses the perceptron criterion as the loss function. For discrete-valued outputs, it is common to use softmax activation with cross-entropy loss. For real-valued outputs, it is common to use linear activation with squared loss. Generally, cross-entropy loss is easier to optimize than squared loss.

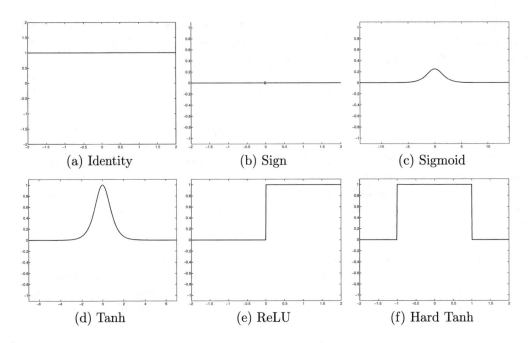

(a) Identity   (b) Sign   (c) Sigmoid

(d) Tanh   (e) ReLU   (f) Hard Tanh

Figure 1.10: The derivatives of various activation functions

1.2.1.6   Some Useful Derivatives of Activation Functions

Most neural network learning is primarily related to gradient-descent with activation functions. For this reason, the derivatives of these activation functions are used repeatedly in this book, and gathering them in a single place for future reference is useful. This section provides details on the derivatives of these loss functions. Later chapters will extensively refer to these results.

1. *Linear and sign activations:* The derivative of the linear activation function is 1 at all places. The derivative of $\text{sign}(v)$ is 0 at all values of v other than at $v = 0$, where it is discontinuous and non-differentiable. Because of the zero gradient and non-differentiability of this activation function, it is rarely used in the loss function even when it is used for prediction at testing time. The derivatives of the linear and sign activations are illustrated in Figure 1.10(a) and (b), respectively.

2. *Sigmoid activation:* The derivative of sigmoid activation is particularly simple, when it is expressed in terms of the *output* of the sigmoid, rather than the input. Let o be the output of the sigmoid function with argument v:

$$o = \frac{1}{1 + \exp(-v)} \tag{1.16}$$

Then, one can write the derivative of the activation as follows:

$$\frac{\partial o}{\partial v} = \frac{\exp(-v)}{(1 + \exp(-v))^2} \tag{1.17}$$

The key point is that this sigmoid can be written more conveniently in terms of the outputs:

$$\frac{\partial o}{\partial v} = o(1 - o) \qquad (1.18)$$

The derivative of the sigmoid is often used as a function of the output rather than the input. The derivative of the sigmoid activation function is illustrated in Figure 1.10(c).

3. *Tanh activation:* As in the case of the sigmoid activation, the tanh activation is often used as a function of the output o rather than the input v:

$$o = \frac{\exp(2v) - 1}{\exp(2v) + 1} \qquad (1.19)$$

One can then compute the gradient as follows:

$$\frac{\partial o}{\partial v} = \frac{4 \cdot \exp(2v)}{(\exp(2v) + 1)^2} \qquad (1.20)$$

One can also write this derivative in terms of the output o:

$$\frac{\partial o}{\partial v} = 1 - o^2 \qquad (1.21)$$

The derivative of the tanh activation is illustrated in Figure 1.10(d).

4. *ReLU and hard tanh activations:* The ReLU takes on a partial derivative value of 1 for non-negative values of its argument, and 0, otherwise. The hard tanh function takes on a partial derivative value of 1 for values of the argument in $[-1, +1]$ and 0, otherwise. The derivatives of the ReLU and hard tanh activations are illustrated in Figure 1.10(e) and (f), respectively.

1.2.2 Multilayer Neural Networks

Multilayer neural networks contain more than one computational layer. The perceptron contains an input and output layer, of which the output layer is the only computation-performing layer. The input layer transmits the data to the output layer, and all computations are completely visible to the user. Multilayer neural networks contain multiple computational layers; the additional intermediate layers (between input and output) are referred to as *hidden layers* because the computations performed are not visible to the user. The specific architecture of multilayer neural networks is referred to as *feed-forward* networks, because successive layers feed into one another in the forward direction from input to output. The default architecture of feed-forward networks assumes that all nodes in one layer are connected to those of the next layer. Therefore, the architecture of the neural network is almost fully defined, once the number of layers and the number/type of nodes in each layer have been defined. The only remaining detail is the loss function that is optimized in the output layer. Although the perceptron algorithm uses the perceptron criterion, this is not the only choice. It is extremely common to use softmax outputs with cross-entropy loss for discrete prediction and linear outputs with squared loss for real-valued prediction.

As in the case of single-layer networks, bias neurons can be used both in the hidden layers and in the output layers. Examples of multilayer networks with or without the bias neurons are shown in Figure 1.11(a) and (b), respectively. In each case, the neural network contains three layers. Note that the input layer is often not counted, because it simply transmits the data and no computation is performed in that layer. If a neural network contains $p_1 \ldots p_k$ units in each of its k layers, then the (column) vector representations of these outputs, denoted by $\overline{h}_1 \ldots \overline{h}_k$ have dimensionalities $p_1 \ldots p_k$. Therefore, the number of units in each layer is referred to as the *dimensionality* of that layer.

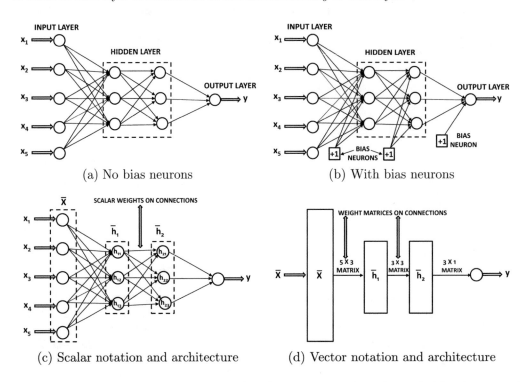

(a) No bias neurons

(b) With bias neurons

(c) Scalar notation and architecture

(d) Vector notation and architecture

Figure 1.11: The basic architecture of a feed-forward network with two hidden layers and a single output layer. Even though each unit contains a single scalar variable, one often represents all units within a single layer as a single vector unit. Vector units are often represented as rectangles and have connection *matrices* between them.

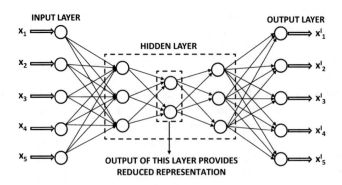

Figure 1.12: An example of an autoencoder with multiple outputs

The weights of the connections between the input layer and the first hidden layer are contained in a *matrix* W_1 with size $d \times p_1$, whereas the weights between the rth hidden layer and the $(r+1)$th hidden layer are denoted by the $p_r \times p_{r+1}$ matrix denoted by W_r. If the output layer contains o nodes, then the final matrix W_{k+1} is of size $p_k \times o$. The d-dimensional input vector $\overline{x}$ is transformed into the outputs using the following recursive equations:

$$\overline{h}_1 = \Phi(W_1^T \overline{x}) \qquad\qquad\qquad \text{[Input to Hidden Layer]}$$
$$\overline{h}_{p+1} = \Phi(W_{p+1}^T \overline{h}_p) \ \ \forall p \in \{1 \ldots k-1\} \qquad \text{[Hidden to Hidden Layer]}$$
$$\overline{o} = \Phi(W_{k+1}^T \overline{h}_k) \qquad\qquad\qquad \text{[Hidden to Output Layer]}$$

Here, the activation functions like the sigmoid function are applied in *element-wise* fashion to their vector arguments. However, some activation functions such as the softmax (which are typically used in the output layers) naturally have vector arguments. Even though each unit of a neural network contains a single variable, many architectural diagrams combine the units in a single layer to create a single vector unit, which is represented as a *rectangle* rather than a *circle*. For example, the architectural diagram in Figure 1.11(c) (with scalar units) has been transformed to a vector-based neural architecture in Figure 1.11(d). Note that the connections between the vector units are now matrices. Furthermore, an implicit assumption in the vector-based neural architecture is that all units in a layer use the same activation function, which is applied in element-wise fashion to that layer. This constraint is usually not a problem, because most neural architectures use the same activation function throughout the computational pipeline, with the only deviation caused by the nature of the output layer. Throughout this book, neural architectures in which units contain vector variables will be depicted with rectangular units, whereas scalar variables will correspond to circular units.

Note that the aforementioned recurrence equations and vector architectures are valid only for layer-wise feed-forward networks, and cannot always be used for unconventional architectural designs. It is possible to have all types of unconventional designs in which inputs might be incorporated in intermediate layers, or the topology might allow connections between non-consecutive layers. Furthermore, the functions computed at a node may not always be in the form of a combination of a linear function and an activation. It is possible to have all types of arbitrary computational functions at nodes.

Although a very classical type of architecture is shown in Figure 1.11, it is possible to vary on it in many ways, such as allowing multiple output nodes. These choices are often determined by the goals of the application at hand (e.g., classification or dimensionality reduction). A classical example of the dimensionality reduction setting is the autoencoder, which recreates the outputs from the inputs. Therefore, the number of outputs and inputs is equal, as shown in Figure 1.12. The constricted hidden layer in the middle outputs the reduced representation of each instance. As a result of this constriction, there is some loss in the representation, which typically corresponds to the noise in the data. The outputs of the hidden layers correspond to the reduced representation of the data. In fact, a shallow variant of this scheme can be shown to be mathematically equivalent to a well-known dimensionality reduction method known as *singular value decomposition*. As we will learn in Chapter 2, increasing the depth of the network results in inherently more powerful reductions.

Although a fully connected architecture is able to perform well in many settings, better performance is often achieved by pruning many of the connections or sharing them in an insightful way. Typically, these insights are obtained by using a domain-specific understanding of the data. A classical example of this type of weight pruning and sharing is that of the *convolutional neural network architecture* (cf. Chapter 8), in which the architecture is carefully designed in order to conform to the typical properties of image data. Such an approach minimizes the risk of *overfitting* by incorporating domain-specific insights (or *bias*). As we will discuss later in this book (cf. Chapter 4), overfitting is a pervasive problem in neural network design, so that the network often performs very well on the training data, but it *generalizes* poorly to unseen test data. This problem occurs when the number of free parameters, (which is typically equal to the number of weight connections), is too large compared to the size of the training data. In such cases, the large number of parameters memorize the specific nuances of the training data, but fail to recognize the statistically significant patterns for classifying unseen test data. Clearly, increasing the number of nodes in the neural network tends to encourage overfitting. Much recent work has been focused both on the architecture of the neural network as well as on the computations performed within each node in order to minimize overfitting. Furthermore, the way in which the neural network is trained also has an impact on the quality of the final solution. Many clever methods, such as *pretraining* (cf. Chapter 4), have been proposed in recent years in order to improve the quality of the learned solution. This book will explore these advanced training methods in detail.

1.2.3 The Multilayer Network as a Computational Graph

It is helpful to view a neural network as a *computational graph*, which is constructed by piecing together many basic parametric models. Neural networks are fundamentally more powerful than their building blocks because the parameters of these models are learned *jointly* to create a highly optimized composition function of these models. The common use of the term "perceptron" to refer to the basic unit of a neural network is somewhat misleading, because there are many variations of this basic unit that are leveraged in different settings. In fact, it is far more common to use logistic units (with sigmoid activation) and piecewise/fully linear units as building blocks of these models.

A multilayer network evaluates compositions of functions computed at individual nodes. A path of length 2 in the neural network in which the function $f(\cdot)$ follows $g(\cdot)$ can be considered a composition function $f(g(\cdot))$. Furthermore, if $g_1(\cdot)$, $g_2(\cdot) \ldots g_k(\cdot)$ are the functions computed in layer m, and a particular layer-$(m + 1)$ node computes $f(\cdot)$, then the composition function computed by the layer-$(m + 1)$ node in terms of the layer-m inputs is $f(g_1(\cdot), \ldots g_k(\cdot))$. The use of nonlinear activation functions is the key to increasing the power of multiple layers. If all layers use an identity activation function, then a multilayer network can be shown to simplify to linear regression. It has been shown [208] that a network with a single hidden layer of nonlinear units (with a wide ranging choice of squashing functions like the sigmoid unit) and a single (linear) output layer can compute almost any "reasonable" function. As a result, neural networks are often referred to as *universal function approximators*, although this theoretical claim is not always easy to translate into practical usefulness. The main issue is that the number of hidden units required to do so is rather large, which increases the number of parameters to be learned. This results in practical problems in training the network with a limited amount of data. In fact, deeper networks are often preferred because they reduce the number of hidden units in each layer as well as the overall number of parameters.

The "building block" description is particularly appropriate for multilayer neural networks. Very often, off-the-shelf softwares for building neural networks[2] provide analysts

---

[2]Examples include Torch [572], Theano [573], and TensorFlow [574].

with access to these building blocks. The analyst is able to specify the number and type of units in each layer along with an off-the-shelf or customized loss function. A deep neural network containing tens of layers can often be described in a few hundred lines of code. All the learning of the weights is done automatically by the *backpropagation algorithm* that uses dynamic programming to work out the complicated parameter update steps of the underlying computational graph. The analyst does not have to spend the time and effort to explicitly work out these steps. This makes the process of trying different types of architectures relatively painless for the analyst. Building a neural network with many of the off-the-shelf softwares is often compared to a child constructing a toy from building blocks that appropriately fit with one another. Each block is like a unit (or a layer of units) with a particular type of activation. Much of this ease in training neural networks is attributable to the backpropagation algorithm, which shields the analyst from explicitly working out the parameter update steps of what is actually an extremely complicated optimization problem. Working out these steps is often the most difficult part of most machine learning algorithms, and an important contribution of the neural network paradigm is to bring modular thinking into machine learning. In other words, the modularity in neural network design translates to modularity in learning its parameters; the specific name for the latter type of modularity is "backpropagation." This makes the design of neural networks more of an (experienced) engineer's task rather than a mathematical exercise.

1.3 Training a Neural Network with Backpropagation

In the single-layer neural network, the training process is relatively straightforward because the error (or loss function) can be computed as a direct function of the weights, which allows easy gradient computation. In the case of multi-layer networks, the problem is that the loss is a complicated composition function of the weights in earlier layers. The gradient of a composition function is computed using the backpropagation algorithm. The backpropagation algorithm leverages the chain rule of differential calculus, which computes the error gradients in terms of summations of local-gradient products over the various paths from a node to the output. Although this summation has an exponential number of components (paths), one can compute it efficiently using *dynamic programming*. The backpropagation algorithm is a direct application of dynamic programming. It contains two main phases, referred to as the *forward* and *backward* phases, respectively. The forward phase is required to compute the output values and the local derivatives at various nodes, and the backward phase is required to accumulate the products of these local values over all paths from the node to the output:

1. *Forward phase:* In this phase, the inputs for a training instance are fed into the neural network. This results in a forward cascade of computations across the layers, using the current set of weights. The final predicted output can be compared to that of the training instance and the derivative of the loss function with respect to the output is computed. The derivative of this loss now needs to be computed with respect to the weights in all layers in the backwards phase.

2. *Backward phase:* The main goal of the backward phase is to learn the gradient of the loss function with respect to the different weights by using the chain rule of differential calculus. These gradients are used to update the weights. Since these gradients are learned in the backward direction, starting from the output node, this learning process is referred to as the backward phase. Consider a sequence of hidden units

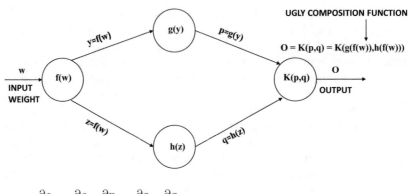

$$\frac{\partial o}{\partial w} = \frac{\partial o}{\partial p} \cdot \frac{\partial p}{\partial w} + \frac{\partial o}{\partial q} \cdot \frac{\partial q}{\partial w} \quad \text{[Multivariable Chain Rule]}$$

$$= \frac{\partial o}{\partial p} \cdot \frac{\partial p}{\partial y} \cdot \frac{\partial y}{\partial w} + \frac{\partial o}{\partial q} \cdot \frac{\partial q}{\partial z} \cdot \frac{\partial z}{\partial w} \quad \text{[Univariate Chain Rule]}$$

$$= \underbrace{\frac{\partial K(p,q)}{\partial p} \cdot g'(y) \cdot f'(w)}_{\text{First path}} + \underbrace{\frac{\partial K(p,q)}{\partial q} \cdot h'(z) \cdot f'(w)}_{\text{Second path}}$$

Figure 1.13: **Illustration of chain rule in computational graphs:**   The products of node-specific partial derivatives along paths from weight w to output o are aggregated. The resulting value yields the derivative of output o with respect to weight w. Only two paths between input and output exist in this simplified example.

$h_1, h_2, \ldots, h_k$ followed by output o, with respect to which the loss function L is computed. Furthermore, assume that the weight of the connection from hidden unit h_r to h_{r+1} is $w_{(h_r, h_{r+1})}$. Then, in the case that a single path exists from h_1 to o, one can derive the gradient of the loss function with respect to any of these edge weights using the chain rule:

$$\frac{\partial L}{\partial w_{(h_{r-1}, h_r)}} = \frac{\partial L}{\partial o} \cdot \left[\frac{\partial o}{\partial h_k} \prod_{i=r}^{k-1} \frac{\partial h_{i+1}}{\partial h_i} \right] \frac{\partial h_r}{\partial w_{(h_{r-1}, h_r)}} \quad \forall r \in 1 \ldots k \qquad (1.22)$$

The aforementioned expression assumes that only a *single path* from h_1 to o exists in the network, whereas an exponential number of paths might exist in reality. A generalized variant of the chain rule, referred to as the *multivariable chain rule*, computes the gradient in a computational graph, where more than one path might exist. This is achieved by adding the composition along each of the paths from h_1 to o. An example of the chain rule in a computational graph with two paths is shown in Figure 1.13. Therefore, one generalizes the above expression to the case where a set $\mathcal{P}$ of paths exist from h_r to o:

$$\frac{\partial L}{\partial w_{(h_{r-1}, h_r)}} = \frac{\partial L}{\partial o} \cdot \underbrace{\left[\sum_{[h_r, h_{r+1}, \ldots h_k, o] \in \mathcal{P}} \frac{\partial o}{\partial h_k} \prod_{i=r}^{k-1} \frac{\partial h_{i+1}}{\partial h_i} \right]}_{\text{Backpropagation computes } \Delta(h_r, o) = \frac{\partial L}{\partial h_r}} \frac{\partial h_r}{\partial w_{(h_{r-1}, h_r)}} \qquad (1.23)$$

The computation of $\frac{\partial h_r}{\partial w_{(h_{r-1},h_r)}}$ on the right-hand side is straightforward and will be discussed below (cf. Equation 1.27). However, the path-aggregated term above [annotated by $\Delta(h_r,o) = \frac{\partial L}{\partial h_r}$] is aggregated over an exponentially increasing number of paths (with respect to path length), which seems to be intractable at first sight. A key point is that the computational graph of a neural network does not have cycles, and it is possible to compute such an aggregation in a principled way in the backwards direction by first computing $\Delta(h_k,o)$ for nodes h_k closest to o, and then recursively computing these values for nodes in earlier layers in terms of the nodes in later layers. Furthermore, the value of $\Delta(o,o)$ for each output node is initialized as follows:

$$\Delta(o,o) = \frac{\partial L}{\partial o} \tag{1.24}$$

This type of dynamic programming technique is used frequently to efficiently compute all types of path-centric functions in directed acyclic graphs, which would otherwise require an exponential number of operations. The recursion for $\Delta(h_r,o)$ can be derived using the multivariable chain rule:

$$\Delta(h_r,o) = \frac{\partial L}{\partial h_r} = \sum_{h:h_r \Rightarrow h} \frac{\partial L}{\partial h}\frac{\partial h}{\partial h_r} = \sum_{h:h_r \Rightarrow h} \frac{\partial h}{\partial h_r}\Delta(h,o) \tag{1.25}$$

Since each h is in a later layer than h_r, $\Delta(h,o)$ has already been computed while evaluating $\Delta(h_r,o)$. However, we still need to evaluate $\frac{\partial h}{\partial h_r}$ in order to compute Equation 1.25. Consider a situation in which the edge joining h_r to h has weight $w_{(h_r,h)}$, and let a_h be the value computed in hidden unit h just *before* applying the activation function $\Phi(\cdot)$. In other words, we have $h = \Phi(a_h)$, where a_h is a linear combination of its inputs from earlier-layer units incident on h. Then, by the univariate chain rule, the following expression for $\frac{\partial h}{\partial h_r}$ can be derived:

$$\frac{\partial h}{\partial h_r} = \frac{\partial h}{\partial a_h} \cdot \frac{\partial a_h}{\partial h_r} = \frac{\partial \Phi(a_h)}{\partial a_h} \cdot w_{(h_r,h)} = \Phi'(a_h) \cdot w_{(h_r,h)}$$

This value of $\frac{\partial h}{\partial h_r}$ is used in Equation 1.25, which is repeated recursively in the backwards direction, starting with the output node. The corresponding updates in the backwards direction are as follows:

$$\Delta(h_r,o) = \sum_{h:h_r \Rightarrow h} \Phi'(a_h) \cdot w_{(h_r,h)} \cdot \Delta(h,o) \tag{1.26}$$

Therefore, gradients are successively accumulated in the backwards direction, and each node is processed exactly once in a backwards pass. Note that the computation of Equation 1.25 (which requires proportional operations to the number of outgoing edges) needs to be repeated for each incoming edge into the node to compute the gradient with respect to all edge weights. Finally, Equation 1.23 requires the computation of $\frac{\partial h_r}{\partial w_{(h_{r-1},h_r)}}$, which is easily computed as follows:

$$\frac{\partial h_r}{\partial w_{(h_{r-1},h_r)}} = h_{r-1} \cdot \Phi'(a_{h_r}) \tag{1.27}$$

Here, the key gradient that is backpropagated is the derivative with respect to *layer activations*, and the gradient with respect to the weights is easy to compute for any incident edge on the corresponding unit.

It is noteworthy that the dynamic programming recursion of Equation 1.26 can be computed in multiple ways, depending on which variables one uses for intermediate chaining. All these recursions are equivalent in terms of the final result of backpropagation. In the following, we give an alternative version of the dynamic programming recursion, which is more commonly seen in textbooks. Note that Equation 1.23 uses the variables in the hidden layers as the "chain" variables for the dynamic programming recursion. One can also use the pre-activation values of the variables for the chain rule. The pre-activation variables in a neuron are obtained after applying the linear transform (but before applying the activation variables) as the intermediate variables. The pre-activation value of the hidden variable $h = \Phi(a_h)$ is a_h. The differences between the pre-activation and post-activation values within a neuron are shown in Figure 1.7. Therefore, instead of Equation 1.23, one can use the following chain rule:

$$\frac{\partial L}{\partial w_{(h_{r-1}, h_r)}} = \underbrace{\frac{\partial L}{\partial o} \cdot \Phi'(a_o) \cdot \left[\sum_{[h_r, h_{r+1}, \dots h_k, o] \in \mathcal{P}} \frac{\partial a_o}{\partial a_{h_k}} \prod_{i=r}^{k-1} \frac{\partial a_{h_{i+1}}}{\partial a_{h_i}} \right]}_{\text{Backpropagation computes } \delta(h_r, o) = \frac{\partial L}{\partial a_{h_r}}} \underbrace{\frac{\partial a_{h_r}}{\partial w_{(h_{r-1}, h_r)}}}_{h_{r-1}} \quad (1.28)$$

Here, we have introduced the notation $\delta(h_r, o) = \frac{\partial L}{\partial a_{h_r}}$ instead of $\Delta(h_r, o) = \frac{\partial L}{\partial h_r}$ for setting up the recursive equation. The value of $\delta(o, o) = \frac{\partial L}{\partial a_o}$ is initialized as follows:

$$\delta(o, o) = \frac{\partial L}{\partial a_o} = \Phi'(a_o) \cdot \frac{\partial L}{\partial o} \quad (1.29)$$

Then, one can use the multivariable chain rule to set up a similar recursion:

$$\delta(h_r, o) = \frac{\partial L}{\partial a_{h_r}} = \sum_{h:h_r \Rightarrow h} \overbrace{\frac{\partial L}{\partial a_h}}^{\delta(h,o)} \underbrace{\frac{\partial a_h}{\partial a_{h_r}}}_{\Phi'(a_{h_r})w_{(h_r,h)}} = \Phi'(a_{h_r}) \sum_{h:h_r \Rightarrow h} w_{(h_r,h)} \cdot \delta(h, o) \quad (1.30)$$

This recursion condition is found more commonly in textbooks discussing backpropagation. The partial derivative of the loss with respect to the weight is then computed using $\delta(h_r, o)$ as follows:

$$\frac{\partial L}{\partial w_{(h_{r-1}, h_r)}} = \delta(h_r, o) \cdot h_{r-1} \quad (1.31)$$

As with the single-layer network, the process of updating the nodes is repeated to convergence by repeatedly cycling through the training data in epochs. A neural network may sometimes require thousands of epochs through the training data to learn the weights at the different nodes. A detailed description of the backpropagation algorithm and associated issues is provided in Chapter 3. In this chapter, we provide a brief discussion of these issues.

1.4 Practical Issues in Neural Network Training

In spite of the formidable reputation of neural networks as universal function approximators, considerable challenges remain with respect to actually training neural networks to provide this level of performance. These challenges are primarily related to several practical problems associated with training, the most important one of which is *overfitting*.

1.4.1 The Problem of Overfitting

The problem of overfitting refers to the fact that fitting a model to a particular training data set does not guarantee that it will provide good prediction performance on unseen test data, even if the model predicts the targets on the training data perfectly. In other words, there is always a gap between the training and test data performance, which is particularly large when the models are complex and the data set is small.

In order to understand this point, consider a simple single-layer neural network on a data set with five attributes, where we use the identity activation to learn a real-valued target variable. This architecture is almost identical to that of Figure 1.3, except that the identity activation function is used in order to predict a real-valued target. Therefore, the network tries to learn the following function:

$$\hat{y} = \sum_{i=1}^{5} w_i \cdot x_i \qquad (1.32)$$

Consider a situation in which the observed target value is real and is always twice the value of the first attribute, whereas other attributes are completely unrelated to the target. However, we have only four training instances, which is one less than the number of features (free parameters). For example, the training instances could be as follows:

x_1	x_2	x_3	x_4	x_5	y
1	1	0	0	0	2
2	0	1	0	0	4
3	0	0	1	0	6
4	0	0	0	1	8

The correct parameter vector in this case is $\overline{W} = [2, 0, 0, 0, 0]$ based on the known relationship between the first feature and target. The training data also provides zero error with this solution, although the relationship needs to be *learned* from the given instances since it is not given to us a priori. However, the problem is that the number of training points is fewer than the number of parameters and it is possible to find an infinite number of solutions with zero error. For example, the parameter set $[0, 2, 4, 6, 8]$ also provides zero error *on the training data*. However, if we used this solution on unseen test data, it is likely to provide very poor performance because the learned parameters are spuriously inferred and are unlikely to *generalize* well to new points in which the target is twice the first attribute (and other attributes are random). This type of spurious inference is caused by the paucity of training data, where random nuances are encoded into the model. As a result, the solution does not generalize well to unseen test data. This situation is almost similar to learning by rote, which is highly predictive for training data but not predictive for unseen test data. Increasing the number of training instances improves the generalization power of the model, whereas increasing the complexity of the model reduces its generalization power. At the same time, when a lot of training data is available, an overly simple model is unlikely to capture complex relationships between the features and target. A good rule of thumb is that the total number of training data points should be at least 2 to 3 times larger than the number of parameters in the neural network, although the precise number of data instances depends on the specific model at hand. In general, models with a larger number of parameters are said to have *high capacity*, and they require a larger amount of data in order to gain generalization power to unseen test data. The notion of overfitting is often understood in the trade-off between *bias* and *variance* in machine learning. The key

take-away from the notion of bias-variance trade-off is that one does not always win with
more powerful (i.e., less *biased*) models when working with limited training data, because
of the higher *variance* of these models. For example, if we change the training data in the
table above to a different set of four points, we are likely to learn a completely different set
of parameters (from the random nuances of those points). This new model is likely to yield
a completely different prediction *on the same test instance* as compared to the predictions
using the first training data set. This type of variation in the prediction of the same test
instance using different training data sets is a manifestation of *model variance*, which also
adds to the error of the model; after all, both predictions of the same test instance could not
possibly be correct. More complex models have the drawback of seeing spurious patterns
in random nuances, especially when the training data are insufficient. One must be careful
to pick an optimum point when deciding the complexity of the model. These notions are
described in detail in Chapter 4.

Neural networks have always been known to theoretically be powerful enough to approximate any function [208]. However, the lack of data availability can result in poor
performance; this is one of the reasons that neural networks only recently achieved prominence. The greater availability of data has revealed the advantages of neural networks over
traditional machine learning (cf. Figure 1.2). In general, neural networks require careful
design to minimize the harmful effects of overfitting, even when a large amount of data is
available. This section provides an overview of some of the design methods used to mitigate
the impact of overfitting.

1.4.1.1 Regularization

Since a larger number of parameters causes overfitting, a natural approach is to constrain
the model to use fewer non-zero parameters. In the previous example, if we constrain the
vector $\overline{W}$ to have only one non-zero component out of five components, it will correctly
obtain the solution $[2, 0, 0, 0, 0]$. Smaller absolute values of the parameters also tend to
overfit less. Since it is hard to constrain the values of the parameters, the softer approach
of adding the penalty $\lambda ||\overline{W}||^p$ to the loss function is used. The value of p is typically set to
2, which leads to *Tikhonov regularization*. In general, the squared value of each parameter
(multiplied with the regularization parameter $\lambda > 0$) is added to the objective function.
The practical effect of this change is that a quantity proportional to λw_i is subtracted from
the update of the parameter w_i. An example of a regularized version of Equation 1.6 for
mini-batch S and update step-size $\alpha > 0$ is as follows:

$$\overline{W} \Leftarrow \overline{W}(1 - \alpha\lambda) + \alpha \sum_{\overline{X} \in S} E(\overline{X})\overline{X} \tag{1.33}$$

Here, $E[\overline{X}]$ represents the current error $(y - \hat{y})$ between observed and predicted values
of training instance $\overline{X}$. One can view this type of penalization as a kind of weight decay
during the updates. Regularization is particularly important when the amount of available
data is limited. A neat biological interpretation of regularization is that it corresponds to
gradual forgetting, as a result of which "less important" (i.e., *noisy*) patterns are removed.
In general, it is often advisable to use more complex models with regularization rather than
simpler models without regularization.

As a side note, the general form of Equation 1.33 is used by many regularized machine
learning models like *least-squares regression* (cf. Chapter 2), where $E(\overline{X})$ is replaced by the
error-function of that specific model. Interestingly, weight decay is only sparingly used in the

single-layer perceptron[3] because it can sometimes cause overly rapid forgetting with a small number of recently misclassified training points dominating the weight vector; the main issue is that the perceptron criterion is already a degenerate loss function with a minimum value of 0 at $\overline{W} = 0$ (unlike its hinge-loss or least-squares cousins). This quirk is a legacy of the fact that the single-layer perceptron was originally defined in terms of biologically inspired updates rather than in terms of carefully thought-out loss functions. Convergence to an optimal solution was never guaranteed other than in linearly separable cases. For the single-layer perceptron, some other regularization techniques, which are discussed below, are more commonly used.

1.4.1.2 Neural Architecture and Parameter Sharing

The most effective way of building a neural network is by constructing the architecture of the neural network after giving some thought to the underlying data domain. For example, the successive words in a sentence are often related to one another, whereas the nearby pixels in an image are typically related. These types of insights are used to create specialized architectures for text and image data with fewer parameters. Furthermore, many of the parameters might be shared. For example, a convolutional neural network uses the same set of parameters to learn the characteristics of a local block of the image. The recent advancements in the use of neural networks like *recurrent neural networks* and *convolutional neural networks* are examples of this phenomena.

1.4.1.3 Early Stopping

Another common form of regularization is *early stopping*, in which the gradient descent is ended after only a few iterations. One way to decide the stopping point is by holding out a part of the training data, and then testing the error of the model on the held-out set. The gradient-descent approach is terminated when the error on the held-out set begins to rise. Early stopping essentially reduces the size of the parameter space to a smaller neighborhood within the initial values of the parameters. From this point of view, early stopping acts as a regularizer because it effectively restricts the parameter space.

1.4.1.4 Trading Off Breadth for Depth

As discussed earlier, a two-layer neural network can be used as a universal function approximator [208], if a large number of hidden units are used within the hidden layer. It turns out that networks with more layers (i.e., greater *depth*) tend to require far fewer units per layer because the composition functions created by successive layers make the neural network more powerful. Increased depth is a form of regularization, as the features in later layers are forced to obey a particular type of structure imposed by the earlier layers. Increased constraints reduce the capacity of the network, which is helpful when there are limitations on the amount of available data. A brief explanation of this type of behavior is given in Section 1.5. The number of units in each layer can typically be reduced to such an extent that a deep network often has far fewer parameters even when added up over the greater number of layers. This observation has led to an explosion in research on the topic of *deep learning*.

---

[3]Weight decay is generally used with other loss functions in single-layer models and in all multi-layer models with a large number of parameters.

Even though deep networks have fewer problems with respect to overfitting, they come with a different family of problems associated with ease of training. In particular, the loss derivatives with respect to the weights in different layers of the network tend to have vastly different magnitudes, which causes challenges in properly choosing step sizes. Different manifestations of this undesirable behavior are referred to as the *vanishing* and *exploding gradient* problems. Furthermore, deep networks often take unreasonably long to converge. These issues and design choices will be discussed later in this section and at several places throughout the book.

1.4.1.5   Ensemble Methods

A variety of ensemble methods like *bagging* are used in order to increase the generalization power of the model. These methods are applicable not just to neural networks but to any type of machine learning algorithm. However, in recent years, a number of ensemble methods that are specifically focused on neural networks have also been proposed. Two such methods include *Dropout* and *Dropconnect*. These methods can be combined with many neural network architectures to obtain an additional accuracy improvement of about 2% in many real settings. However, the precise improvement depends to the type of data and the nature of the underlying training. For example, normalizing the activations in hidden layers can reduce the effectiveness of *Dropout* methods, although one can gain from the normalization itself. Ensemble methods are discussed in Chapter 4.

1.4.2   The Vanishing and Exploding Gradient Problems

While increasing depth often reduces the number of parameters of the network, it leads to different types of practical issues. Propagating backwards using the chain rule has its drawbacks in networks with a large number of layers in terms of the stability of the updates. In particular, the updates in earlier layers can either be negligibly small (vanishing gradient) or they can be increasingly large (exploding gradient) in certain types of neural network architectures. This is primarily caused by the chain-like product computation in Equation 1.23, which can either exponentially increase or decay over the length of the path. In order to understand this point, consider a situation in which we have a multi-layer network with one neuron in each layer. Each local derivative along a path can be shown to be the product of the weight and the derivative of the activation function. The overall backpropagated derivative is the product of these values. If each such value is randomly distributed, and has an expected value less than 1, the product of these derivatives in Equation 1.23 will drop off exponentially fast with path length. If the individual values on the path have expected values greater than 1, it will typically cause the gradient to explode. Even if the local derivatives are randomly distributed with an expected value of exactly 1, the overall derivative will typically show instability depending on how the values are actually distributed. In other words, the vanishing and exploding gradient problems are rather natural to deep networks, which makes their training process unstable.

Many solutions have been proposed to address this issue. For example, a sigmoid activation often encourages the vanishing gradient problem, because its derivative is less than 0.25 at all values of its argument (see Exercise 7), and is extremely small at saturation. A ReLU activation unit is known to be less likely to create a vanishing gradient problem because its derivative is always 1 for positive values of the argument. More discussions on this issue are provided in Chapter 3. Aside from the use of the ReLU, a whole host of gradient-descent tricks are used to improve the convergence behavior of the problem. In particular, the use of *adaptive learning rates* and *conjugate gradient methods* can help in many cases. Furthermore, a recent technique called *batch normalization* is helpful in addressing some of these issues. These techniques are discussed in Chapter 3.

1.4.3 Difficulties in Convergence

Sufficiently fast convergence of the optimization process is difficult to achieve with very deep networks, as depth leads to increased resistance to the training process in terms of letting the gradients smoothly flow through the network. This problem is somewhat related to the vanishing gradient problem, but has its own unique characteristics. Therefore, some "tricks" have been proposed in the literature for these cases, including the use of *gating networks* and *residual networks* [184]. These methods are discussed in Chapters 7 and 8, respectively.

1.4.4 Local and Spurious Optima

The optimization function of a neural network is highly nonlinear, which has lots of local optima. When the parameter space is large, and there are many local optima, it makes sense to spend some effort in picking good initialization points. One such method for improving neural network initialization is referred to as *pretraining*. The basic idea is to use either supervised or unsupervised training on *shallow sub-networks* of the original network in order to create the initial weights. This type of pretraining is done in a *greedy and layerwise fashion* in which a single layer of the network is trained at one time in order to learn the initialization points of that layer. This type of approach provides initialization points that ignore drastically irrelevant parts of the parameter space to begin with. Furthermore, unsupervised pretraining often tends to avoid problems associated with overfitting. The basic idea here is that some of the minima in the loss function are spurious optima because they are exhibited only in the training data and not in the test data. Using unsupervised pretraining tends to move the initialization point closer to the basin of "good" optima in the test data. This is an issue associated with model generalization. Methods for pretraining are discussed in Section 4.7 of Chapter 4.

Interestingly, the notion of spurious optima is often viewed from the lens of model generalization in neural networks. This is a different perspective from traditional optimization. In traditional optimization, one does not focus on the differences in the loss functions of the training and test data, but on the shape of the loss function in only the training data. Surprisingly, the problem of local optima (from a traditional perspective) is a smaller issue in neural networks than one might normally expect from such a nonlinear function. Most of the time, the nonlinearity causes problems during the training process itself (e.g., failure to converge), rather than getting stuck in a local minimum.

1.4.5 Computational Challenges

A significant challenge in neural network design is the running time required to train the network. It is not uncommon to require weeks to train neural networks in the text and image domains. In recent years, advances in hardware technology such as Graphics Processor Units (GPUs) have helped to a significant extent. GPUs are specialized hardware processors that can significantly speed up the kinds of operations commonly used in neural networks. In this sense, some algorithmic frameworks like *Torch* are particularly convenient because they have GPU support tightly integrated into the platform.

Although algorithmic advancements have played a role in the recent excitement around deep learning, a lot of the gains have come from the fact that the same algorithms can do much more on modern hardware. Faster hardware also supports algorithmic development, because one needs to repeatedly test computationally intensive algorithms to understand what works and what does not. For example, a recent neural model such as the long short-term memory has changed only modestly [150] since it was first proposed in 1997 [204]. Yet, the potential of this model has been recognized only recently because of the advances in computational power of modern machines and algorithmic tweaks associated with improved experimentation.

One convenient property of the vast majority of neural network models is that most of the computational heavy lifting is *front loaded* during the training phase, and the prediction phase is often computationally efficient, because it requires a small number of operations (depending on the number of layers). This is important because the prediction phase is often far more time-critical compared to the training phase. For example, it is far more important to classify an image in real time (with a pre-built model), although the actual building of that model might have required a few weeks over millions of images. Methods have also been designed to compress trained networks in order to enable their deployment in mobile and space-constrained settings. These issues are discussed in Chapter 3.

1.5   The Secrets to the Power of Function Composition

Even though the biological metaphor sounds like an exciting way to intuitively justify the computational power of a neural network, it does not provide a complete picture of the settings in which neural networks perform well. At its most basic level, a neural network is a computational graph that performs compositions of simpler functions to provide a more complex function. Much of the power of deep learning arises from the fact that *repeated* composition of multiple nonlinear functions has significant expressive power. Even though the work in [208] shows that the single composition of a large number of squashing functions can approximate almost any function, this approach will require an extremely large number of units (i.e., parameters) of the network. This increases the capacity of the network, which causes overfitting unless the data set is extremely large. Much of the power of deep learning arises from the fact that the *repeated composition of certain types of functions increases the representation power of the network, and therefore reduces the parameter space required for learning.*

Not all base functions are equally good at achieving this goal. In fact, the nonlinear squashing functions used in neural networks are not arbitrarily chosen, but are carefully designed because of certain types of properties. For example, imagine a situation in which the identity activation function is used in each layer, so that only linear functions are computed. In such a case, the resulting neural network is no stronger than a single-layer, linear network:

Theorem 1.5.1 *A multi-layer network that uses only the identity activation function in all its layers reduces to a single-layer network performing linear regression.*

Proof: Consider a network containing k hidden layers, and therefore contains a total of $(k+1)$ computational layers (including the output layer). The corresponding $(k+1)$ weight matrices between successive layers are denoted by $W_1 \ldots W_{k+1}$. Let $\overline{x}$ be the d-dimensional column vector corresponding to the input, $\overline{h}_1 \ldots \overline{h}_k$ be the column vectors corresponding to the hidden layers, and $\overline{o}$ be the m-dimensional column vector corresponding to the output.

Then, we have the following recurrence condition for multi-layer networks:

$$\overline{h}_1 = \Phi(W_1^T \overline{x}) = W_1^T \overline{x}$$
$$\overline{h}_{p+1} = \Phi(W_{p+1}^T \overline{h}_p) = W_{p+1}^T \overline{h}_p \quad \forall p \in \{1 \dots k-1\}$$
$$\overline{o} = \Phi(W_{k+1}^T \overline{h}_k) = W_{k+1}^T \overline{h}_k$$

In all the cases above, the activation function $\Phi(\cdot)$ has been set to the identity function. Then, by eliminating the hidden layer variables, it is easy to show the following:

$$\overline{o} = W_{k+1}^T W_k^T \dots W_1^T \overline{x}$$
$$= \underbrace{(W_1 W_2 \dots W_{k+1})^T}_{W_{xo}^T} \overline{x}$$

Note that one can replace the matrix $W_1 W_2 \dots W_{k+1}$ with the new $d \times m$ matrix W_{xo}, and learn the coefficients of W_{xo} instead of those of all the matrices $W_1, W_2 \dots W_{k+1}$, without loss of expressivity. In other words, we have the following:

$$\overline{o} = W_{xo}^T \overline{x}$$

However, this condition is exactly identical to that of linear regression with multiple outputs [6]. In fact, it is a bad idea to learn the redundant matrices $W_1 \dots W_{k+1}$ instead of W_{xo}, because doing so increases the number of parameters to be learned without increasing the power of the model in any way. Therefore, a multilayer neural network with identity activations does not gain over a single-layer network in terms of expressivity. ∎

The aforementioned result is for the case of regression modeling with numeric target variables. A similar result holds true for binary target variables. In the special case, where all layers use identity activation and the final layer uses a single output with sign activation for prediction, the multilayer neural network reduces to the perceptron.

Lemma 1.5.1 *Consider a multilayer network in which all hidden layers use identity activation and the single output node uses the perceptron criterion as the loss function and the sign activation for prediction. This neural network reduces to the single-layer perceptron.*

The proof of this result is almost identical to that of the one discussed above. In fact, as long as the hidden layers are linear, nothing is gained using the additional layers.

This result shows that deep networks largely make sense only when the activation functions in intermediate layers are non-linear. Typically, the functions like sigmoid and tanh are *squashing* functions in which the output is bounded within an interval, and the gradients are largest near zero values. For large absolute values of their arguments, these functions are said to reach *saturation* where increasing the absolute value of the argument further does not change its value significantly. This type of function in which values do not vary significantly at large absolute values of their arguments is shared by another family of functions, referred to as *Gaussian kernels*, which are commonly used in non-parametric density estimation:

$$\Phi(v) = \exp(-v^2/2) \tag{1.34}$$

The only difference is that Gaussian kernels saturate to 0 at large values of their argument, whereas functions like sigmoid and tanh can also saturate to values of $+1$ and -1. It is well known in the literature on density estimation [451] that the sum of many small Gaussian kernels can be used to approximate any density function. Density functions have a special nonnegative structure in which extremes of the data distribution always saturate to zero density, and therefore the underlying kernels also show the same behavior. A similar principle holds true (more generally) for squashing functions in which the linear combination of many small activation functions can be used to approximate an arbitrary function; however, squashing functions do not saturate to zero in order to handle arbitrary behavior at extreme values. The universal approximation result of neural networks [208] posits that a linear combination of sigmoid units (and/or most other reasonable squashing functions) in a single hidden layer can be used to approximate any function well. Note that the linear combination can be performed by a single output node. Therefore, a two-layer network is sufficient as long as the number of hidden units is large enough. However, some kind of basic non-linearity in the activation function is always required in order to model the turns and twists in an arbitrary function. To understand this point, note that all 1-dimensional functions can be approximated as a sum of scaled/translated step functions and most of the activation functions discussed in this chapter (e.g., sigmoid) look awfully like step functions (see Figure 1.8). This basic idea is the essence of the universal approximation theorem of neural networks. In fact, the proof of the ability of squashing functions to approximate any function is conceptually similar to that of kernels at least at an intuitive level. However, the number of base functions required to reach a high level of approximation can be extremely large in both cases, potentially increasing the data-centric requirements to an unmanageable level. For this reason, shallow networks face the persistent problem of overfitting. The universal approximation theorem asserts the ability to well-approximate the function implicit in the training data, but makes no guarantee about whether the function can be generalized to unseen test data.

1.5.1   The Importance of Nonlinear Activation

The previous section provides a concrete proof of the fact that a neural network with only linear activations does not gain from increasing the number of layers in it. For example, consider the two-class data set illustrated in Figure 1.14, which is represented in two dimensions denoted by x_1 and x_2. There are two instances, A and B, of the class denoted by '*' with coordinates $(1, 1)$ and $(-1, 1)$, respectively. There is also a single instance B of the class denoted by '+' with coordinates $(0, 1)$, A neural network with only linear activations will never be able to classify the training data perfectly because the points are not linearly separable.

On the other hand, consider a situation in which the hidden units have ReLU activation, and they learn the two new features h_1 and h_2, which are as follows:

$$h_1 = \max\{x_1, 0\}$$
$$h_2 = \max\{-x_1, 0\}$$

Note that these goals can be achieved by using appropriate weights from the input to hidden layer, and also applying a ReLU activation unit. The latter achieves the goal of thresholding negative values to 0. We have indicated the corresponding weights in the neural network shown in Figure 1.14. We have shown a plot of the data in terms of h_1 and h_2 in the same figure. The coordinates of the three points in the 2-dimensional hidden layer are $\{(1, 0), (0, 1), (0, 0)\}$. It is immediately evident that the two classes become linearly separable in terms of the new hidden representation. In a sense, the task of the first layer was *representation learning* to enable the solution of the problem with a linear classifier. Therefore, if we add a single linear output layer to the neural network, it will be able to

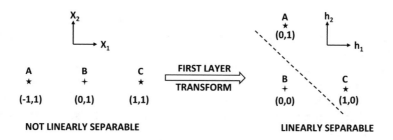

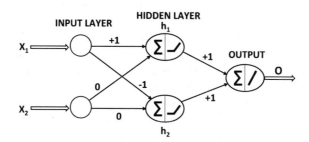

Figure 1.14: The power of nonlinear activation functions in transforming a data set to linear separability

classify these training instances perfectly. The key point is that the use of the nonlinear ReLU function is crucial in ensuring this linear separability. *Activation functions enable nonlinear mappings of the data, so that the embedded points can become linearly separable.* In fact, if both the weights from hidden to output layer are set to 1 with a linear activation function, the output O will be defined as follows:

$$O = h_1 + h_2 \tag{1.35}$$

This simple linear function separates the two classes because it always takes on the value of 1 for the two points labeled '*' and takes on 0 for the point labeled '+'. Therefore, much of the power of neural networks is hidden in the use of activation functions. The weights shown in Figure 1.14 will need to be *learned* in a data-driven manner, although

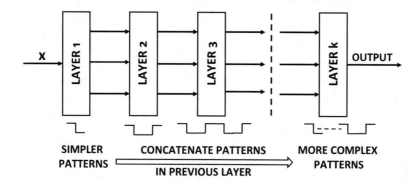

Figure 1.15: Deeper networks can learn more complex functions by composing the functions learned in earlier layers.

there are many alternative choices of weights that can make the hidden representation linearly separable. Therefore, the learned weights may be different than the ones shown in Figure 1.14 if actual training is performed. Nevertheless, in the case of the perceptron, there is no choice of weights at which one could hope to classify this training data set perfectly because the data set is not linearly separable in the original space. In other words, the activation functions enable nonlinear transformations of the data, that become increasingly powerful with multiple layers. A sequence of nonlinear activations imposes a specific type of structure on the learned model, whose power increases with the depth of the sequence (i.e., number of layers in the neural network).

Another classical example is the XOR function in which the two points $\{(0, 0), (1, 1)\}$ belong to one class, and the other two points $\{(1, 0), (0, 1)\}$ belong to the other class. It is possible to use ReLU activation to separate these two classes as well, although bias neurons will be needed in this case (see Exercise 1). The original backpropagation paper [409] discusses the XOR function, because this function was one of the motivating factors for designing multilayer networks and the ability to train them. The XOR function is considered a litmus test to determine the basic feasibility of a particular family of neural networks to properly predict nonlinearly separable classes. Although we have used the ReLU activation function above for simplicity, it is possible to use most of the other nonlinear activation functions to achieve the same goals.

1.5.2   Reducing Parameter Requirements with Depth

The basic idea of deep learning is that repeated composition of functions can often reduce the requirements on the number of base functions (computational units) by a factor that is exponentially related to the number of layers in the network. Therefore, even though the number of layers in the network increases, the number of parameters required to approximate the same function reduces drastically. This increases the generalization power of the network.

The idea behind deeper architectures is that they can better leverage *repeated regularities* in the data patterns in order to reduce the number of computational units and therefore *generalize* the learning even to areas of the data space where one does not have examples. Often these repeated regularities are learned by the neural network within the weights as the basis vectors of *hierarchical features*. Although a detailed proof [340] of this fact is beyond the scope of this book, we provide a simple example to elucidate this point. Consider a situation in which a 1-dimensional function is defined by 1024 repeated steps of the same size and height. A shallow network with one hidden layer and step activation functions would require at least 1024 units in order to model the function. However, a multilayer network would model a pattern of 1 step in the first layer, 2 steps in the next, 4 steps in the third, and 2^r steps in the rth layer. This situation is illustrated in Figure 1.15. Note that the pattern of 1 step is the simplest feature because it is repeated 1024 times, whereas a pattern of 2 steps is more complex. Therefore, the features (and the functions learned) in successive layers are hierarchically related. In this case, a total of 10 layers are required and a small number of constant nodes are required in each layer to model the joining of the two patterns from the previous layer.

Another way to understand this point is as follows. Consider a 1-dimensional function which takes one the value of 1 and -1 in alternate intervals, and this value switches 1024 times at regular intervals of the argument. The only way to simulate this function with a linear combination of step activation functions (containing only one switch in value) is to use 1024 of them (or a small constant factor of this number). However, a neural network with 10 hidden layers and only 2 units per layer has $2^{10} = 1024$ paths from the source to the output. As long as the function to be learned is regular in some way, it is often possible to learn parameters for the layers so that these 1024 paths are able to capture the complexity of 1024 different value switches in the function. The earlier layers learn more detailed patterns, whereas the later layers learn higher-level patterns. Therefore, the overall number of nodes required is an *order of magnitude less* than that required in the single-layer network. This means that the amount of data required for learning is also an order of magnitude less. The reason for this is that the multilayer network implicitly *looks for the repeated regularities and learns them* with less data, rather than trying to explicitly learn every turn and twist of the target function. When using convolutional neural networks with image data, this behavior becomes intuitively obvious in which earlier layers model simple features like lines, a middle layer might model elementary shapes, and a later layer might model a complex shape like a face. On the other hand, a single layer would have difficulty in modeling every twist and turn of a face. This provides the deeper model with better generalization power and also the ability to learn with less data.

However, increasing the depth of the network is not without its disadvantages. Deeper networks are often harder to train, and they show all types of unstable behavior such as the vanishing and exploding gradient problems. Deep networks are also notoriously unstable to parameter choice. These issues are often addressed with careful design of the functions computed within nodes, as well as the use of pretraining procedures to improve performance.

1.5.3   Unconventional Neural Architectures

The aforementioned discussion provides an overview of the most common ways in which the operations and structures of typical neural networks are constructed. However, there are many variations of this common theme. The following will discuss some of these variations.

1.5.3.1   Blurring the Distinctions Between Input, Hidden, and Output Layers

In general, there is a heavy emphasis on layer-wise feed-forward networks in the neural network domain with a sequential arrangement between input, hidden, and output layers. In other words, all input nodes feed into the first hidden layer, the hidden layers successively feed into one another, and the final hidden layer feeds into the output layer. The compu-

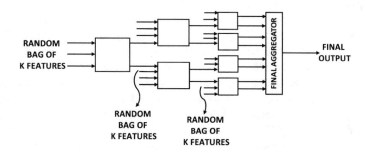

Figure 1.16: An example of an unconventional architecture in which inputs occur to layers other than the first hidden layer. As long as the neural network is acyclic (or can be transformed into an acyclic representation), the weights of the underlying computation graph can be learned using dynamic programming (backpropagation).

tational units are often defined by squashing functions applied to linear combinations of input. The hidden layer generally does not take inputs, and the loss is generally not computed over the values in the hidden layers. Because of this focus, it is easy to forget that a neural network can be defined as *any type of parameterized computation graph*, where these restrictions are not necessary for the backpropagation algorithm to work. In general, it is possible to have input and loss computation in intermediate layers, although this is less common. For example, a neural network is proposed in [515] that is inspired by the notion of a *random forest* [49], and it allows input in different layers of the network. An example of this type of network is shown in Figure 1.16. In this case, it is clear that the distinction between the input layers and the hidden layers has been blurred.

In other variations of the basic feed-forward architecture, loss functions are computed not just at the output nodes, but also at the hidden nodes. The contributions at the hidden nodes are often in the form of *penalties* that act as regularizers. For example, these types of methods are used to perform sparse feature learning by imposing penalties on the hidden nodes (cf. Chapters 2 and 4). In this case, the distinction between the hidden layers and output layers is blurred.

Another recent example of a design choice is the use of *skip connections* [184] in which the inputs from a particular layer are allowed to connect to layers beyond the immediate next layer. This type of approach leads to truly deep models. For example, a 152-layer architecture, referred to as *ResNet* [184], has reached human-level performance in the image recognition task. Although this architecture does not blur the distinction between input, hidden, and output layers, its structure differs from a traditional feed-forward network in which connections are placed only between successive layers. These networks have an *iterative view* of feature engineering [161], in which the features in later layers are iterative refinements of those in previous layers. In contrast, the traditional approach to feature engineering is *hierarchical*, in which features in later layers are increasingly abstract representations obtained from those in previous layers.

1.5.3.2   Unconventional Operations and Sum-Product Networks

Some neural networks like *long short-term memory* and convolutional neural networks define various types of multiplicative "forgetting," convolution, and pooling operations between variables that are not strictly in any of the forms discussed in this chapter. In fact, these architectures are now used so heavily in the text and image domains that they are no longer considered unusual.

Another unique type of architecture is the *sum-product network* [383]. In this case, the nodes are either summation nodes or product nodes. Summation nodes are similar to the traditional linear transformation with a set of weighted edges. However, the weights are constrained to be positive. The product nodes simply multiply its inputs without the need for weights. It is noteworthy that there are many variations in terms of how products can be computed. For example, if the inputs are two scalars, then one can simply compute their product. If the inputs are two vectors of equal length, one can compute their element-wise product. Several deep learning libraries do support these types of product operations. It is natural for the summation layers and the product layers to alternate in order to maximize expressivity.

Sum-product networks are quite expressive, and it is often possible to build deep variations with a high level of expressivity [30, 93]. A key point is that almost any mathematical function can be approximately written as a polynomial function of its inputs. Therefore, almost any function can be expressed using the sum-product architecture, although deeper architectures allow modeling with greater structure. Unlike traditional neural networks in which nonlinearity is incorporated with activation functions, the product operation is the key to nonlinearity in the sum-product network.

Training Issues

It is often helpful to be flexible in using different types of computational operations within the nodes beyond the known transformations and activation functions. Furthermore, the connections between nodes need not be structured in layer-wise fashion and nodes in the hidden layer can be included in the loss computation. As long as the underlying computational graph is acyclic, it is easy to generalize the backpropagation algorithm to any type of architecture and computational operation. After all, a dynamic programming algorithm (like backpropagation) can be used on virtually any type of directed acyclic graph in which multiple nodes can be used for initializing the dynamic programming recursion. It is important to keep in mind that architectures that are designed with a proper domain-specific understanding can often provide superior results to black-box methods that use fully connected feed-forward networks.

1.6 Common Neural Architectures

There are several types of neural architectures that are used commonly in various machine learning applications. This section will provide a brief overview of some of these architectures, which will be discussed in greater detail in later chapters.

1.6.1 Simulating Basic Machine Learning with Shallow Models

Most of the basic machine learning models like linear regression, classification, support vector machines, logistic regression, singular value decomposition, and matrix factorization can be simulated with shallow neural networks containing no more than one or two layers. It is instructive to explore these basic architectures, because it indirectly showcases the power of neural networks; most of what we know about machine learning can be simulated with relatively simple models! Furthermore, many basic neural network models like the *Widrow-Hoff learning model* are directly related to traditional machine learning models like the Fisher's discriminant, even though they were proposed independently. A noteworthy observation is that deeper architectures are often created by stacking these simpler models in a creative way. The neural architectures for basic machine learning models are discussed in Chapter 2. A number of applications to text mining, graphs, and recommender systems will also be discussed in this chapter.

1.6.2 Radial Basis Function Networks

Radial basis function (RBF) networks represent the forgotten architecture from the rich history of neural networks. They are not commonly used in the modern era, although they do have significant potential for specific types of problems. One limiting issue is that these networks are not deep, and they typically use only two layers. The first layer is constructed in an unsupervised way, whereas the second layer is trained using supervised methods. These networks are fundamentally different from feed-forward networks, and gain their power from the larger number of nodes in the unsupervised layer. The basic principles of using RBF networks are fundamentally very different from those of feed-forward networks, in the sense that the former gains its power from expanding the size of the feature space rather than depth. This approach is based on *Cover's theorem on separability of patterns* [84], which states that pattern classification problems are more likely to be linearly separable when cast into a high-dimensional space with a nonlinear transformation. The second layer of the network contains a prototype in each node and the activation is defined by the similarity of the input data to the prototype. These activations are then combined with trained weights of the next layer to create a final prediction. This approach is very similar to that of nearest-neighbor classifiers, except that the weights in the second layer provide an additional level of supervision. In other words, the approach is a *supervised* nearest-neighbor method.

Notably, support vector machines are known to be supervised variants of nearest-neighbor classifiers in which a kernel function is combined with supervised weights to weight the neighboring points in the final prediction [6]. Radial basis function networks can be used to simulate kernel methods like support vector machines. For specific types of problems like classification, one can use these architectures more effectively than an off-the-shelf kernel support vector machine. This is because these models are more general, providing more opportunities for experimentation than a kernel support vector machine. Furthermore, it is sometimes possible to gain some advantages from increased depth in the supervised layers. The full potential of radial basis function networks remains unexplored in the literature, because this architecture has largely been forgotten with the increased focus on vanilla feed-forward methods. A discussion of radial basis function networks is provided in Chapter 5.

1.6.3   Restricted Boltzmann Machines

Restricted Boltzmann machines (RBMs) use the notion of energy minimization in order to create neural network architectures for modeling data in an unsupervised way. These methods are particularly useful for creating generative models of the data, and they are closely related to probabilistic graphical models [251]. Restricted Boltzmann machines owe their origins to the use of *Hopfield networks* [207], which can be used to store memories. Stochastic variants of these networks were generalized to *Boltzmann machines*, in which hidden layers modeled generative aspects of the data.

Restricted Boltzmann machines are often used for unsupervised modeling and dimensionality reduction, although they can also be used for supervised modeling. However, since they were not naturally suited to supervised modeling, the supervised training was often preceded by an unsupervised phase. This naturally led to the discovery of the notion of pretraining, which was found to be extremely beneficial for supervised learning. RBMs were among the first models that were used for deep learning, especially in the unsupervised setting. The pretraining approach was eventually adopted by other types of models. Therefore, RBMs also have a historical significance in terms of motivating some training methodologies for deep models.

The training process of a restricted Boltzmann machine is quite different from that of a feed-forward network. In particular, these models cannot be trained using backpropagation, and they require Monte Carlo sampling in order to perform the training. The particular algorithm that is used commonly for training an RBM is the *contrastive divergence algorithm*. A discussion of restricted Boltzmann machines is provided in Chapter 6.

1.6.4   Recurrent Neural Networks

Recurrent neural networks are designed for sequential data like text sentences, time-series, and other discrete sequences like biological sequences. In these cases, the input is of the form $\overline{x}_1 \ldots \overline{x}_n$, where $\overline{x}_t$ is a d-dimensional point received at the time-stamp t. For example, the vector $\overline{x}_t$ might contain the d values at the tth tick of a multivariate time-series (with d different series). In a text-setting, the vector $\overline{x}_t$ will contain the *one-hot encoded* word at the tth time-stamp. In one-hot encoding, we have a vector of length equal to the lexicon size, and the component for the relevant word has a value of 1. All other components are 0.

An important point about sequences is that successive words are dependent on one another. Therefore, it is helpful to receive a particular input $\overline{x}_t$ only *after* the earlier inputs have already been received and converted into a hidden state. The traditional type of feed-forward network in which all inputs feed into the first layer does not achieve this goal. Therefore, the recurrent neural network allows the input $\overline{x}_t$ to interact directly with the hidden state created from the inputs at previous time stamps. The basic architecture of the recurrent neural network is illustrated in Figure 1.17(a). The key point is that there is an input $\overline{x}_t$ at each time-stamp, and a hidden state $\overline{h}_t$ that changes at each time stamp as new data points arrive. Each time-stamp also has an output value $\overline{y}_t$. For example, in a time-series setting, the output $\overline{y}_t$ might be the forecasted prediction of $\overline{x}_{t+1}$. When used in the text-setting of predicting the next word, this approach is referred to as *language modeling*. In some applications, we do not output $\overline{y}_t$ at each time stamp, but only at the end of the sequence. For example, if one is trying the classify the sentiment of a sentence as "*positive*" or "*negative*," the output will occur only at the final time stamp.

The hidden state at time t is given by a function of the input vector at time t and the hidden vector at time $(t-1)$:

$$\overline{h}_t = f(\overline{h}_{t-1}, \overline{x}_t) \tag{1.36}$$

A separate function $\overline{y}_t = g(\overline{h}_t)$ is used to learn the output probabilities from the hidden states. Note that the functions $f(\cdot)$ and $g(\cdot)$ are the same at each time stamp. The implicit assumption is that the time-series exhibits a certain level of *stationarity*; the underlying properties do not change with time. Although this property is not exactly true in real settings, it is a good assumption to use for regularization.

A key point here is the presence of the self-loop in Figure 1.17(a), which will cause the hidden state of the neural network to change after the input of each $\overline{x}_t$. In practice, one only works with sequences of finite length, and it makes sense to unfurl the loop into a "time-layered" network that looks more like a feed-forward network. This network is shown in Figure 1.17(b). Note that in this case, we have a different node for the hidden

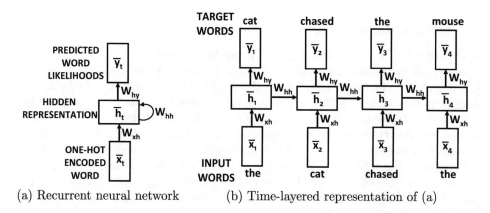

(a) Recurrent neural network   (b) Time-layered representation of (a)

Figure 1.17: A recurrent neural network and its time-layered representation

state at each time-stamp and the self-loop has been unfurled into a feed-forward network. This representation is mathematically equivalent to Figure 1.17(a), but is much easier to comprehend because of its similarity to a traditional network. Note that unlike traditional feed-forward networks, the inputs also occur to intermediate layers in this unfurled network. The weight matrices of the connections *are shared by multiple connections* in the time-layered network to ensure that the same function is used at each time stamp. This sharing is the key to the domain-specific insights that are learned by the network. The backpropagation algorithm takes the sharing and temporal length into account when updating the weights during the learning process. This special type of backpropagation algorithm is referred to as *backpropagation through time (BPTT)*. Because of the recursive nature of Equation 1.36, the recurrent network has the *ability to compute a function of variable-length inputs*. In other words, one can expand the recurrence of Equation 1.36 to define the function for $\overline{h}_t$ in terms of t inputs. For example, starting at $\overline{h}_0$, which is typically fixed to some constant vector, we have $\overline{h}_1 = f(\overline{h}_0, \overline{x}_1)$ and $\overline{h}_2 = f(f(\overline{h}_0, \overline{x}_1), \overline{x}_2)$. Note that $\overline{h}_1$ is a function of only $\overline{x}_1$, whereas $\overline{h}_2$ is a function of both $\overline{x}_1$ and $\overline{x}_2$. Since the output $\overline{y}_t$ is a function of $\overline{h}_t$, these properties are inherited by $\overline{y}_t$ as well. In general, we can write the following:

$$\overline{y}_t = F_t(\overline{x}_1, \overline{x}_2, \ldots \overline{x}_t) \tag{1.37}$$

Note that the function $F_t(\cdot)$ varies with the value of t. Such an approach is particularly useful for variable-length inputs like text sentences. More details of recurrent neural networks are provided in Chapter 7; this chapter will also discuss the applications of recurrent neural networks in various domains.

An interesting theoretical property of recurrent neural networks is that they are *Turing complete* [444]. What this means is that *given enough data and computational resources*, a recurrent neural network can simulate any algorithm. In practice, however, this theoretical property is not useful because recurrent networks have significant practical problems with generalization for long sequences. The amount of data and the size of the hidden states required for longer sequences increases in a way that is not realistic. Furthermore, there are practical issues in finding the optimum choices of parameters because of the vanishing and exploding gradient problems. As a result, specialized variants of the recurrent neural network architecture have been proposed, such as the use of long short-term memory. These advanced architectures will also be discussed in Chapter 7. Furthermore, some advanced variants of the recurrent architecture, such as neural Turing machines, have shown improvements over the recurrent neural network in some applications.

1.6.5   Convolutional Neural Networks

Convolutional neural networks are biologically inspired networks that are used in computer vision for image classification and object detection. The basic motivation for the convolutional neural network was obtained from Hubel and Wiesel's understanding [212] of the workings of the cat's visual cortex, in which specific portions of the visual field seemed to excite particular neurons. This broader principle was used to design a sparse architecture for convolutional neural networks. The first basic architecture based on this biological inspiration was the *neocognitron*, which was then generalized to the *LeNet-5* architecture [279]. In the convolutional neural network architecture, each layer of the network is 3-dimensional, which has a spatial extent and a depth corresponding to the number of features. The notion of depth of a single layer in a convolutional neural network is distinct[4] from the notion of

---

[4]This is an overloading of the terminology used in convolutional neural networks. The meaning of the word "depth" is inferred from the context in which it is used.

depth in terms of the number of layers. In the input layer, these features correspond to the color channels like RGB (i.e., red, green, blue), and in the hidden channels these features represent hidden feature maps that encode various types of shapes in the image. If the input is in grayscale (like *LeNet-5*), then the input layer will have a depth of 1, but later layers will still be 3-dimensional. The architecture contains two types of layers, referred to as the *convolution* and *subsampling* layers, respectively.

For the convolution layers, a *convolution operation* is defined, in which a filter is used to map the activations from one layer to the next. A convolution operation uses a 3-dimensional filter of weights with the same depth as the current layer but with a smaller spatial extent. The dot product between all the weights in the filter and any choice of spatial region (of the same size as the filter) in a layer defines the value of the hidden state in the next layer (after applying an activation function like ReLU). The operation between the filter and the spatial regions in a layer is performed at every possible position in order to define the next layer (in which the activations retain their spatial relationships from the previous layer).

The connections in a convolutional neural network are very sparse, because any activation in a particular layer is a function of only a small spatial region in the previous layer. All layers other than the final set of two of three layers maintain their spatial structure. Therefore, it is possible to spatially visualize what parts of the image affect particular portions of the activations in a layer. The features in lower-level layers capture lines or other primitive shapes, whereas the features in higher-level layers capture more complex shapes like loops (which commonly occur in many digits). Therefore, later layers can create digits by composing the shapes in these intuitive features. This is a classical example of the way in which semantic insights about specific data domains are used to design clever architectures. In addition, a subsampling layer simply averages the values in the local regions of size 2×2 in order to compress the spatial footprints of the layers by a factor of 2. An illustration of the architecture of *LeNet-5* is shown in Figure 1.18. In the early years, *LeNet-5* was used by several banks to recognize hand-written numbers on checks.

Convolutional neural networks have historically been the most successful of all types of neural networks. They are used widely for image recognition, object detection/localization, and even text processing. The performance of these networks has recently exceeded that of humans in the problem of image classification [184]. Convolutional neural networks provide a very good example of the fact that architectural design choices in a neural network should be performed with semantic insight about the data domain at hand. In the particular case

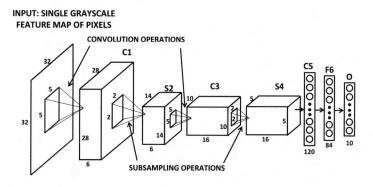

Figure 1.18: LeNet-5: One of the earliest convolutional neural networks.

of the convolutional neural network, this insight was obtained by observing the biological workings of a cat's visual cortex, and heavily using the spatial relationships among pixels. This fact also provides some evidence that a further understanding of neuroscience might also be helpful for the development of methods in artificial intelligence.

Pretrained convolutional neural networks from publicly available resources like *ImageNet* are often available for use in an off-the-shelf manner for other applications and data sets. This is achieved by using most of the pretrained weights in the convolutional network without any change except for the final classification layer. The weights of the final classification layer are learned from the data set at hand. The training of the final layer is necessary because the class labels in a particular setting may be different from those of *ImageNet*. Nevertheless, the weights in the early layers are still useful because they learn various types of shapes in the images that can be useful for virtually any type of classification application. Furthermore, the feature activations in the penultimate layer can even be used for unsupervised applications. For example, one can create a multidimensional representation of an arbitrary image data set by passing each image through the convolutional neural network and extracting the activations of the penultimate layer. Subsequently, any type of indexing can be applied to this representation for retrieving images that are similar to a specific target image. Such an approach often provides surprisingly good results in image retrieval because of the semantic nature of the features learned by the network. It is noteworthy that the use of pretrained convolutional networks is so popular that training is rarely started from scratch. Convolutional neural networks are discussed in detail in Chapter 8.

1.6.6   Hierarchical Feature Engineering and Pretrained Models

Many deeper architectures with feed-forward architectures have multiple layers in which successive transformations of the inputs from the previous layer lead to increasingly sophisticated representations of the data. The values of each hidden layer for a particular input contain a transformed representation of the input point, which becomes increasingly informative about the target value we are trying to learn, as the layer gets closer to the output node. As shown in Section 1.5.1, appropriately transformed feature representations are more amenable to simple types of predictions in the output layer. This sophistication is a result of the nonlinear activations in intermediate layers. Traditionally, the sigmoid and tanh activations were the most popular choices in the hidden layers, but the ReLU activation has become increasingly popular in recent years because of the desirable property that it is better at avoiding the vanishing and exploding gradient problems (cf. Section 3.4.2 of Chapter 3). For classification, the final layer can be viewed as a relatively simple prediction layer which contains a single linear neuron in the case of regression, and is a sigmoid/sign function in the case of binary classification. More complex outputs might require multiple nodes. One way of viewing this division of labor between the hidden layers and final prediction layer is that the early layers create a feature representation that is more amenable to the task at hand. The final layer then leverages this learned feature representation. This division of labor is shown in Figure 1.19. A key point is that the features learned in the hidden layers are often (but not always) generalizable to other data sets and problem settings in the same domain (e.g., text, images, and so on). This property can be leveraged in various ways by simply replacing the output node(s) of a pretrained network with a different application-specific output layer (e.g., linear regression layer instead of sigmoid classification layer) for the data set and problem at hand. Subsequently, only the weights of the newly replaced output layer may need to be learned for the new data set and application, whereas the weights of other layers are fixed.

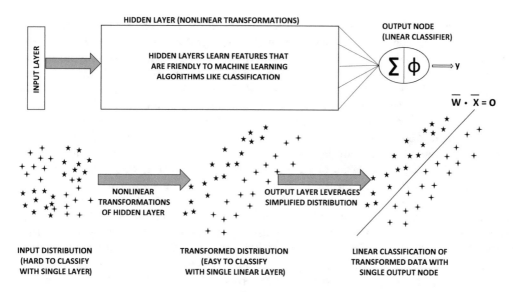

Figure 1.19: The feature engineering role of the hidden layers

The output of each hidden layer is a transformed feature representation of the data, in which the dimensionality of the representation is defined by the number of units in that layer. One can view this process as a kind of hierarchical feature engineering in which the features in earlier layers represent primitive characteristics of the data, whereas those in later layers represent complex characteristics with semantic significance to the class labels. Data represented in the terms of the features of later layers are often more well behaved (e.g., linearly separable) because of the semantic nature of the features learned by the transformation. This type of behavior is particularly evident in a visually interpretable way in some domains like convolutional neural networks for image data. In convolutional neural networks, the features in earlier layers capture detailed but primitive shapes like lines or edges from the data set of images. On the other hand, the features in later layers capture shapes of greater complexity like hexagons, honeycombs, and so forth, depending on the type of images provided as training data. Note that such semantically interpretable shapes often have closer correlations with class labels in the image domain. For example, almost any image will contain lines or edges, but images belonging to particular classes will be more likely to have hexagons or honeycombs. This property tends to make the representations of later layers easier to classify with simple models like linear classifiers. This process is illustrated in Figure 1.19. The features in earlier layers are used repeatedly as building blocks to create more complex features. This general principle of "putting together" simple features to create more complex features lies at the core of the successes achieved with neural networks. As it turns out, this property is also useful in leveraging pretrained models in a carefully calibrated way. The practice of using pretrained models is also referred to as *transfer learning.*

A particular type of transfer learning, which is used commonly in neural networks, is that the data and structure available in a given data set are used to learn features for that entire domain. A classical example of this setting is that of text or image data. In text data, the representations of text words are created using standardized benchmark data sets like *Wikipedia* [594] and models like *word2vec.* These can be used in almost any text application, since the nature of text data does not change very much with the application. A similar approach is often used for image data, in which the *ImageNet data set* (cf. Section 1.8.2) is used to pretrain convolutional neural networks, and provide ready-to-use features. One can download a pretrained convolutional neural network model and convert any image data set into a multidimensional representation by passing the image through the pretrained network. Furthermore, if additional application-specific data is available, one can regulate the level of transfer learning depending on the amount of available data. This is achieved by fine-tuning a subset of the layers in the pretrained neural network with this additional data. If a small amount of application-specific data is available, one can fix the weights of the early layers to their pretrained values and fine-tune only the last few layers of the neural network. The early layers often contain primitive features, which are more easily generalizable to arbitrary applications. For example, in a convolutional neural network, the early layers learn primitive features like edges, which are useful across diverse images like trucks or carrots. On the other hand, the later layers contain complex features which might depend on the image collection at hand (e.g., truck wheel versus carrot top). Fine-tuning only the weights of the later layers makes sense in such cases. If a large amount of application-specific data is available, one can fine-tune a larger number of layers. Therefore, deep networks provide significant flexibility in terms of how transfer learning is done with pretrained neural network models.

1.7   Advanced Topics

Several topics in deep learning have increasingly gained attention, and have had significant successes. Although some of these methods are limited by current computational considerations, their potential is quite significant. This section will discuss some of these topics.

1.7.1   Reinforcement Learning

In general forms of artificial intelligence, the neural network must learn to take actions in ever-changing and dynamic situations. Examples include learning robots and self-driving cars. In these cases, a critical assumption is that the learning system has no knowledge of the appropriate sequence of actions up front, and it learns through reward-based *reinforcement* as it takes various actions. These types of learning correspond to dynamic sequences of actions that are hard to model using traditional machine learning methods. The key assumption here is that these systems are too complex to explicitly model, but they are simple enough to evaluate, so that a *reward value* can be assigned for each action of the learner.

Imagine a setting in which one wishes to train a learning system to play a video game from scratch without any prior knowledge of the rules. Video games are excellent test beds for reinforcement learning methods because they are microcosms of living the "game" of life. As in real-world settings, the number of possible *states* (i.e., unique position in game) might be too large to even enumerate, and the optimal choice of move depends critically on the knowledge of what is truly important to model from a particular state. Furthermore, since one does not start with any knowledge of the rules, the learning system would need to collect the data through its actions much as a mouse explores a maze to learn its structure. Therefore, the collected data is highly biased by the user actions, which provides a particularly challenging landscape for learning. The successful training of reinforcement learning methods is a critical gateway for *self-learning systems*, which is the holy grail of artificial intelligence. Although the field of reinforcement learning was developed independently of the field of neural networks, the strong complementarity of the two fields has brought them together. Deep learning methods can be useful in learning feature representations from high-dimensional sensory inputs (e.g., the video screens of pixels in a video game or the screen of pixels in a robot's "vision"). Furthermore, reinforcement learning methods are often used to support various types of neural network algorithms like attention mechanisms. Reinforcement learning methods are discussed in Chapter 9.

1.7.2 Separating Data Storage and Computations

An important aspect of neural networks is that the data storage and computations are tightly integrated. For example, the states in a neural network can be considered a type of transient memory, which behave much like the ever-changing registers in the central processing unit of a computer. But what if we want to construct a neural network where one can control where to read data from, and where to write the data to. This goal is achieved with the notion of *attention* and *external memory*. Attention mechanisms can be used in various applications like image processing where one focuses on small parts of the image to gain successive insights. These techniques are also used for machine translation. Neural networks that can tightly control access in reading and writing to an external memory are referred to as *neural Turing machines* [158] or *memory networks* [528]. Although these methods are advanced variants of recurrent neural networks, they show significantly improved potential than their predecessors in terms of the types of problems they can handle. These methods are discussed in Chapter 10.

1.7.3 Generative Adversarial Networks

Generative adversarial networks are a model of data generation that can create a generative model of a base data set by using an adversarial game between two players. The two players correspond to a generator and a discriminator. The generator takes Gaussian noise as input and produces an output, which is a *generated* sample like the base data. The discriminator is typically a probabilistic classifier like logistic regression whose job is to distinguish real samples from the base data set and the generated sample. The generator tries to create samples that are as realistic as possible; its job is to fool the discriminator, whereas the job of the discriminator is to identify the fake samples irrespective of how well the generator tries to fool it. The problem can be understood as an adversarial game between the generator and discriminator, and the formal optimization model is a minimax learning problem. The *Nash equilibrium* of this minimax game provides the final trained model. Typically, this equilibrium point is one at which the discriminator is unable to distinguish between real and fake samples.

Such methods can create realistic fantasy samples using a base data set, and are used commonly in the image domain. For example, if the approach is trained using a data set containing images of bedrooms, it will produce realistic looking bedrooms that are not actually a part of the base data. Therefore, the approach can be used for artistic or creative endeavors. These methods can also be conditioned on specific types of context, which could be any type of object such as label, text caption, or an image with missing details. In these cases, *pairs* of related training objects are used. A typical pair could be a caption (context) and an image (base object). Similarly, one might have pairs corresponding to sketches of objects and actual photographs. Therefore, starting with a captioned image data set of various types of animals, it is possible to create a fantasy image that is not a part of the base data by using a contextual caption such as "*blue bird with sharp claws*." Similarly, starting with an artist's sketch of a purse, the approach can create a realistic and colored image of a purse. Generative adversarial networks are discussed in Chapter 10.

1.8   Two Notable Benchmarks

The benchmarks used in the neural network literature are dominated by data from the domain of computer vision. Although traditional machine learning data sets like the UCI repository [601] can be used for testing neural networks, the general trend is towards using data sets from perceptually oriented data domains that can be visualized well. Although there are a variety of data sets drawn from the text and image domains, two of them stand out because of their ubiquity in deep learning papers. Although both are data sets drawn from computer vision, the first of them is simple enough that it can also be used for testing generic applications beyond the field of vision. In the following, we provide a brief overview of these two data sets.

1.8.1   The MNIST Database of Handwritten Digits

The MNIST database, which stands for *Modified National Institute of Standards and Technology* database, is a large database of handwritten digits [281]. As the name suggests, this data set was created by modifying an original database of handwritten digits provided by NIST. The data set contains 60,000 training images and 10,000 testing images. Each image is a scan of a handwritten digit from 0 to 9, and the differences between different images are a result of the differences in the handwriting of different individuals. These individuals were American Census Bureau employees and American high school students. The original black and white images from NIST were size normalized to fit in a 20×20 pixel box while preserving their aspect ratio and centered in a 28×28 image by computing the center of mass of the pixels. The images were translated to position this point at the center of the 28×28 field. Each of these 28×28 pixel values takes on a value from 0 to 255, depending on where it lies in the grayscale spectrum. The labels associated with the images correspond to the ten digit values. Examples of the digits in the MNIST database are illustrated in Figure 1.20. The size of the data set is rather small, and it contains only a simple object corresponding to a digit. Therefore, one might argue that the MNIST database is a toy data

Figure 1.20: Examples of handwritten digits in the MNIST database

set. However, its small size and simplicity is also an advantage because it can be used as a laboratory for quick testing of machine learning algorithms. Furthermore, the simplification of the data set by virtue of the fact that the digits are (roughly) centered makes it easy to use it to test algorithms beyond computer vision. Computer vision algorithms require specialized assumptions such as translation invariance. The simplicity of this data set makes these assumptions unnecessary. It has been remarked by Geoff Hinton [600] that the MNIST database is used by neural network researchers in much the same way as biologists use fruit flies for early and quick results (before serious testing on more complex organisms).

Although the matrix representation of each image is suited to a convolutional neural network, one can also convert it into a multidimensional representation of $28 \times 28 = 784$ dimensions. This conversion loses some of the spatial information in the image, but this loss is not debilitating (at least in the case of the MNIST data set) because of its relative simplicity. In fact, the use of a simple support vector machine on the 784-dimensional representation can provide an impressive error rate of about 0.56%. A straightforward 2-layer neural network on the multidimensional representation (without using the spatial structure in the image) generally does worse than the support vector machine across a broad range of parameter choices! A deep neural network without any special convolutional architecture can achieve an error rate of 0.35% [72]. Deeper neural networks and convolutional neural networks (that do use spatial structure) can reduce the error rate to as low as 0.21% by using an ensemble of five convolutional networks [402]. Therefore, even on this simple data set, one can see that the relative performance of neural networks with respect to traditional machine learning is sensitive to the specific architecture used in the former.

Finally, it should be noted that the 784-dimensional non-spatial representation of the MNIST data is used for testing all types of neural network algorithms beyond the domain of computer vision. Even though the use of the 784-dimensional (flattened) representation is not appropriate for a vision task, it is still useful for testing the general effectiveness of non-vision oriented (i.e., generic) neural network algorithms. For example, the MNIST data is frequently used to test generic autoencoders and not just convolutional ones. Even when the non-spatial representation of an image is used to reconstruct it with an autoencoder, one can still visualize the results with the original spatial positions of the reconstructed pixels to obtain a feel of what the algorithm is doing with the data. This visual exploration often gives the researcher some insights that are not available with arbitrary data sets like those obtained from the UCI Machine Learning Repository [601]. In this sense, the MNIST data set tends to have broader usability than many other types of data sets.

1.8.2   The ImageNet Database

The *ImageNet* database [581] is a huge database of over 14 million images drawn from 1000 different categories. Its class coverage is exhaustive enough that it covers most types of images that one would encounter in everyday life. This database is organized according to a *WordNet* hierarchy of nouns [329]. The *WordNet* database is a data set containing the relationships among English words using the notion of *synsets*. The *WordNet* hierarchy has been successfully used for machine learning in the natural language domain, and therefore it is natural to design an image data set around these relationships.

The *ImageNet* database is famous for the fact that an annual *ImageNet Large Scale Visual Recognition Challenge (ILSVRC)* [582] is held using this dataset. This competition has a very high profile in the vision community and receives entries from most major research groups in computer vision. The entries to this competition have resulted in many of the state-of-the-art image recognition architectures today, including the methods that have surpassed human performance on some narrow tasks like image classification [184]. Because of the wide availability of known results on these data sets, it is a popular alternative for benchmarking. We will discuss some of the state-of-the-art algorithms submitted to the *ImageNet* competition in Chapter 8 on convolutional neural networks.

Another important significance of the *ImageNet* data set is that it is large and diverse enough to be representative of the key visual concepts within the image domain. As a result, convolutional neural networks are often trained on this data set; the pretrained network can be used to extract features from an arbitrary image. This image representation is defined by the hidden activations in the penultimate layer of the neural network. Such an approach creates new multidimensional representations of image data sets that are amenable for use with traditional machine learning methods. One can view this approach as a kind of transfer learning in which the visual concepts in the *ImageNet* data set are transferred to unseen data objects for other applications.

1.9   Summary

Although a neural network can be viewed as a simulation of the learning process in living organisms, a more direct understanding of neural networks is as computational graphs. Such computational graphs perform recursive composition of simpler functions in order to learn more complex functions. Since these computational graphs are parameterized, the problem generally boils down to learning the parameters of the graph in order to optimize a loss function. The simplest types of neural networks are often basic machine learning models like least-squares regression. The real power of neural networks is unleashed by using more complex combinations of the underlying functions. The parameters of such networks are learned by using a dynamic programming method, referred to as backpropagation. There are several challenges associated with learning neural network models, such as overfitting and training instability. In recent years, numerous algorithmic advancements have reduced these problems. The design of deep learning methods in specific domains such as text and images requires carefully crafted architectures. Examples of such architectures include recurrent neural networks and convolutional neural networks. For dynamic settings in which a sequence of decisions need to be learned by a system, methods like reinforcement learning are useful.

1.10   Bibliographic Notes

A proper understanding of neural network design requires a solid understanding of machine learning algorithms, and especially the linear models based on gradient descent. The reader is recommended to refer to [2, 3, 40, 177] for basic knowledge on machine learning methods. Numerous surveys and overviews of neural networks in different contexts may be found in [27, 28, 198, 277, 345, 431]. Classical books on neural networks for pattern recognition may be found in [41, 182], whereas more recent perspectives on deep learning may be found in [147]. A recent text mining book [6] also discusses recent advances in deep learning for text analytics. An overview of the relationships between deep learning and computational neuroscience may be found in [176, 239].

The perceptron algorithm was proposed by Rosenblatt [405]. To address the issue of stability, the *pocket algorithm* [128], the *Maxover* algorithm [523], and other margin-based methods [123]. Other early algorithms of a similar nature included the Widrow-Hoff [531] and the Winnow algorithms [245]. The Winnow algorithm uses multiplicative updates instead of additive updates, and is particularly useful when many features are irrelevant. The original idea of backpropagation was based on the idea of differentiation of composition of functions as developed in control theory [54, 237]. The use of dynamic programming to perform gradient-based optimization of variables that are related via a directed acyclic graph has been a standard practice since the sixties. However, the ability to use these methods for neural network training had not yet been observed at the time. In 1969, Minsky and Papert published a book on perceptrons [330], which was largely negative about the potential of being able to properly train multilayer neural networks. The book showed that a single perceptron had limited expressiveness, and no one knew how to train multiple layers of perceptrons anyway. Minsky was an influential figure in artificial intelligence, and the negative tone of his book contributed to the first winter in the field of neural networks. The adaptation of dynamic programming methods to backpropagation in neural networks was first proposed by Paul Werbos in his PhD thesis in 1974 [524]. However, Werbos's work could not overcome the strong views against neural networks that had already become entrenched at the time. The backpropagation algorithm was proposed again by Rumelhart et al. in 1986 [408, 409]. Rumelhart et al.'s work is significant for the beauty of its presentation, and it was able to address at least some of the concerns raised earlier by Minsky and Papert. This is one of the reasons that the Rumelhart et al. paper is considered very influential from the perspective of backpropagation, even though it was certainly not the first to propose the method. A discussion of the history of the backpropagation algorithm may be found in the book by Paul Werbos [525].

At this point, the field of neural networks was only partially resurrected, as there were still problems with training neural networks. Nevertheless, pockets of researchers continued to work in the area, and had already set up most of the known neural architectures, such as convolution neural networks, recurrent neural networks, and LSTMs, before the year 2000. The accuracy of these methods was still quite modest because of data and computation limitations. Furthermore, backpropagation turned out to be less effective at training deeper networks because of the vanishing and exploding gradient problems. However, by this time, it was already hypothesized by several prominent researchers that existing algorithms would yield large performance improvements with increases in data, computational power, and algorithmic experimentation. The coupling of big data frameworks with GPUs turned out to be a boon for neural network research in the late 2000s. With reduced cycle times for experimentation enabled by increased computational power, tricks like pretraining started showing up in the late 2000s [198]. The publicly obvious resurrection of neural networks occurred after the year 2011 with the resounding victories [255] of neural networks in deep learning competitions for image classification. The consistent victories of deep learning algorithms in these competitions laid the foundation for the explosion in popularity we see today. Notably, the differences of these winning architectures from the ones that were developed more than two decades earlier are modest (but essential).

Paul Werbos was a pioneer of recurrent neural networks, and proposed the original version of backpropagation through time [526]. The basics of the convolutional neural network were proposed in the context of the neocognitron in [127]. This idea was then generalized to LeNet-5, which was one of the first convolutional neural networks. The ability of neural networks to perform universal function approximation is discussed in [208]. The beneficial effect of depth on reducing the number of parameters is discussed in [340].

The theoretical expressiveness of neural networks was recognized early in its development. For example, early work recognized that a neural network with a single hidden layer can be used to approximate any function [208]. A further result is that certain neural architectures like recurrent networks are Turing complete [444]. The latter means that neural networks can potentially simulate any algorithm. Of course, there are numerous practical issues associated with neural network training, as to why these exciting theoretical results do not always translate into real-world performance. The foremost problem among them is the data-hungry nature of shallow architectures, which is ameliorated with increased depth. Increased depth can be viewed as a form of regularization in which one is forcing the neural network to identify and learn repeating patterns in data points. Increased depth, however, makes the neural network harder to train from an optimization point of view. A discussion on some of these issues may be found in [41, 140, 147]. An experimental evaluation showing the advantages of deeper architectures is provided in [267].

1.10.1   Video Lectures

Deep learning has a significant number of free video lectures available on resources such as *YouTube* and *Coursera*. Two of the most authoritative resources include Geoff Hinton's course at *Coursera* [600]. *Coursera* has multiple offerings on deep learning, and offers a group of related courses in the area. During the writing of this book, an accessible course from Andrew Ng was also added to the offerings. A course on convolutional neural networks from Stanford University is freely available on *YouTube* [236]. The Stanford class by Karpathy, Johnson, and Fei-Fei [236] is on convolutional neural networks, although it does an excellent job in covering broader topics in neural networks. The initial parts of the course deal with vanilla neural networks and training methods.

Numerous topics in machine learning [89] and deep learning [90] are covered by Nando de Freitas in a lectures available on *YouTube*. Another interesting class on neural networks is available from Hugo Larochelle at the Universite de Sherbrooke [262]. A deep learning course by Ali Ghodsi at the University of Waterloo is available at [137]. Video lectures by Christopher Manning on natural language processing methods for deep learning may be found in [312]. David Silver's course on reinforcement learning is available at [619].

1.10.2   Software Resources

Deep learning is supported by numerous software frameworks like *Caffe* [571], *Torch* [572], *Theano* [573], and *TensorFlow* [574]. Extensions of *Caffe* to Python and MATLAB are available. *Caffe* was developed at the University of California at Berkeley, and it is written in C++. It provides a high-level interface in which one can specify the architecture of the network, and it enables the construction of neural networks with very little code writing and relatively simple scripting. The main drawback of *Caffe* is the relatively limited documentation available. *Theano* [35] is Python-based, and it provides high-level packages like *Keras* [575] and *Lasagne* [576] as interfaces. *Theano* is based on the notion of computational graphs, and most of the capabilities provided around it use this abstraction explicitly. *TensorFlow* [574] is also strongly oriented towards computational graphs, and is the framework proposed by Google. *Torch* [572] is written in a high-level language called *Lua*, and it is relatively friendly to use. In recent years, *Torch* has gained some ground compared to other frameworks. Support for GPUs is tightly integrated in *Torch*, which makes it relatively easy to deploy *Torch*-based applications on GPUs. Many of these frameworks contain pretrained models from computer vision and text mining, which can be used to extract features. Many off-the-shelf tools for deep learning are available from the **DeepLearning4j** repository [590]. IBM has a *PowerAI* platform that offers many machine learning and deep learning frameworks on top of IBM Power Systems [599]. Notably, as of the writing of this book, this platform also has a free edition available for certain uses.

1.11 Exercises

1. Consider the case of the XOR function in which the two points $\{(0,0),(1,1)\}$ belong to one class, and the other two points $\{(1,0),(0,1)\}$ belong to the other class. Show how you can use the ReLU activation function to separate the two classes in a manner similar to the example in Figure 1.14.

2. Show the following properties of the sigmoid and tanh activation functions (denoted by $\Phi(\cdot)$ in each case):

    (a) Sigmoid activation: $\Phi(-v) = 1 - \Phi(v)$
    (b) Tanh activation: $\Phi(-v) = -\Phi(v)$
    (c) Hard tanh activation: $\Phi(-v) = -\Phi(v)$

3. Show that the tanh function is a re-scaled sigmoid function with both horizontal and vertical stretching, as well as vertical translation:

$$\tanh(v) = 2\mathrm{sigmoid}(2v) - 1$$

4. Consider a data set in which the two points $\{(-1,-1),(1,1)\}$ belong to one class, and the other two points $\{(1,-1),(-1,1)\}$ belong to the other class. Start with perceptron parameter values at $(0,0)$, and work out a few stochastic gradient-descent updates with $\alpha = 1$. While performing the stochastic gradient-descent updates, cycle through the training points in any order.

    (a) Does the algorithm converge in the sense that the change in objective function becomes extremely small over time?
    (b) Explain why the situation in (a) occurs.

5. For the data set in Exercise 4, where the two features are denoted by (x_1, x_2), define a new 1-dimensional representation z denoted by the following:

$$z = x_1 \cdot x_2$$

Is the data set linearly separable in terms of the 1-dimensional representation corresponding to z? Explain the importance of nonlinear transformations in classification problems.

6. Implement the perceptron in a programming language of your choice.

7. Show that the derivative of the sigmoid activation function is at most 0.25, irrespective of the value of its argument. At what value of its argument does the sigmoid activation function take on its maximum value?

8. Show that the derivative of the tanh activation function is at most 1, irrespective of the value of its argument. At what value of its argument does the tanh activation take on its maximum value?

9. Consider a network with two inputs x_1 and x_2. It has two hidden layers, each of which contain two units. Assume that the weights in each layer are set so that top unit in each layer applies sigmoid activation to the sum of its inputs and the bottom unit in each layer applies tanh activation to the sum of its inputs. Finally, the single output

node applies ReLU activation to the sum of its two inputs. Write the output of this neural network *in closed form* as a function of x_1 and x_2. This exercise should give you an idea of the complexity of functions computed by neural networks.

10. Compute the partial derivative of the closed form computed in the previous exercise with respect to x_1. Is it practical to compute derivatives for gradient descent in neural networks by using closed-form expressions (as in traditional machine learning)?

11. Consider a 2-dimensional data set in which all points with $x_1 > x_2$ belong to the positive class, and all points with $x_1 \leq x_2$ belong to the negative class. Therefore, the true separator of the two classes is linear hyperplane (line) defined by $x_1 - x_2 = 0$. Now create a training data set with 20 points randomly generated inside the unit square in the positive quadrant. Label each point depending on whether or not the first coordinate x_1 is greater than its second coordinate x_2.

   (a) Implement the perceptron algorithm without regularization, train it on the 20 points above, and test its accuracy on 1000 randomly generated points inside the unit square. Generate the test points using the same procedure as the training points.

   (b) Change the perceptron criterion to hinge-loss in your implementation for training, and repeat the accuracy computation on the same test points above. Regularization is not used.

   (c) In which case do you obtain better accuracy and why?

   (d) In which case do you think that the classification of the same 1000 test instances will not change significantly by using a different set of 20 training points?

Chapter 2

Machine Learning with Shallow Neural Networks

"Simplicity is the ultimate sophistication."—Leonardo da Vinci

2.1 Introduction

Conventional machine learning often uses optimization and gradient-descent methods for learning parameterized models. Examples of such models include linear regression, support vector machines, logistic regression, dimensionality reduction, and matrix factorization. Neural networks are also parameterized models that are learned with continuous optimization methods. This chapter will show that a wide variety of optimization-centric methods in machine learning can be captured with *very simple* neural network architectures containing one or two layers. In fact, neural networks can be viewed as more powerful versions of these simple models, with this power being achieved by combining the basic models into a comprehensive neural architecture (i.e., computational graph). It is useful to show these parallels early on, as this allows the understanding of the design of a deep network as a composition of the basic units that one often uses in machine learning. Furthermore, showing this relationship provides an appreciation of the specific way in which traditional machine learning is different from neural networks, and of the cases in which one can hope to do better with neural networks. In many cases, minor variations of these simple neural network architectures (corresponding to traditional machine learning methods) provide useful variations of machine learning models that have not been studied elsewhere. In a sense, the number of ways in which one can combine the different elements of a computational graph is far greater than what is studied in traditional machine learning, even when shallow models are used.

Complex or deep neural architectures are often an overkill in instances where only a small amount of data are available. Additionally, it is easier to optimize traditional machine

C. C. Aggarwal, *Neural Networks and Deep Learning*,
https://doi.org/10.1007/978-3-319-94463-0_2

learning models in data-lean settings as these models are more interpretable. On the other hand, as the amount of data increases, neural networks have an advantage because they

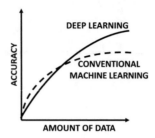

Figure 2.1: Re-visiting Figure 1.2: The effect of increased data availability on accuracy.

retain the flexibility to model more complex functions with the addition of neurons to the computational graph. Figure 2.1 illustrates this point.

One way of viewing deep learning models is as a stacking of simpler models like logistic or linear regression. The coupling of a linear neuron with the sigmoid activation leads to *logistic regression*, which will be discussed in detail in this chapter. The coupling of a linear unit with sigmoid activation is also used[1] extensively for building complex neural networks. Therefore, it is natural to ask the following question [312]:

> *Is deep learning simply a stacking of simpler models like logistic or linear regression?*

Although many neural networks can be viewed in this way, this point of view does not fully capture the complexity and the style of thinking involved in deep learning models. For example, several models (such as recurrent neural networks or convolutional neural networks) perform this stacking in a particular way with a *domain-specific understanding* of the input data. Furthermore, the parameters of different units are sometimes shared in order to force the solution to obey specific types of properties. The ability to put together the basic units in a clever way is a key architectural skill required by practitioners in deep learning. Nevertheless, it is also important to learn the properties of the basic models in machine learning, since they are used repeatedly in deep learning as elementary units of computation. This chapter will, therefore, explore these basic models.

It is noteworthy that there are close relationships between some of the earliest neural networks (e.g., perceptron and Widrow-Hoff learning) and traditional machine learning models (e.g., support vector machine and Fisher discriminant). In some cases, these relationships remained unnoticed for several years, as these models were proposed independently by different communities. As a specific example, the loss function of the L_2-support vector machine was proposed by Hinton [190] in the context of a neural architecture in 1989. When used with regularization, the resulting neural network would behave identically to an L_2-support vector machine. In comparison, Cortes and Vapnik's paper on the support vector machine [82] appeared several years later with an L_1-loss function. These relationships are not surprising because the best way to define a shallow neural network is often closely related to a known machine learning algorithm. Therefore, it is important to explore these basic neural models in order to develop an integrated view of neural networks and traditional machine learning.

---

[1]In recent years, the sigmoid unit has fallen out of favor compared to the ReLU.

This chapter will primarily discuss two classes of models for machine learning:

1. *Supervised models:* The supervised models discussed in this chapter primarily correspond to linear models and their variants. These include methods like least-squares regression, support vector machines, and logistic regression. Multiclass variants of these models will also be studied.

2. *Unsupervised models:* The unsupervised models discussed in this chapter primarily correspond to dimensionality reduction and matrix factorization. Traditional methods like principal component analysis can also be presented as simple neural network architectures. Minor variations of these models can provide reductions of vastly different properties, which will be discussed later. The neural network framework also provides a way of understanding the relationships between widely different unsupervised methods like linear dimensionality reduction, nonlinear dimensionality reduction, and sparse feature learning, thereby providing an integrated view of traditional machine learning algorithms.

This chapter assumes that the reader has a basic familiarity with the classical machine learning models. Nevertheless, a brief overview of each model will also be provided to the uninitiated reader.

Chapter Organization

The next section will discuss some basic models for classification and regression, such as least-squares regression, binary Fisher discriminant, support vector machine, and logistic regression. The multiway variants of these models will be discussed in Section 2.3. Feature selection methods for neural networks are discussed in Section 2.4. The use of autoencoders for matrix factorization is discussed in Section 2.5. As a specific application of simple neural architectures, the *word2vec* method is discussed in Section 2.6. Simple methods for creating node embeddings in graphs are introduced in Section 2.7. A summary is given in Section 2.8.

2.2 Neural Architectures for Binary Classification Models

In this section, we will discuss some basic architectures for machine learning models such as least-squares regression and classification. As we will see, the corresponding neural architectures are minor variations of the perceptron model in machine learning. The main difference is in the choice of the activation function used in the final layer, and the loss function used on these outputs. This will be a recurring theme throughout this chapter, where we will see that small changes in neural architectures can result in distinct models from traditional machine learning. Presenting traditional machine learning models in the form of neural architectures also helps one appreciate the true closeness among various machine learning models.

Throughout this section, we will work with a single-layer network with d input nodes and a single output node. The coefficients of the connections from the d input nodes to the output node are denoted by $\overline{W} = (w_1 \ldots w_d)$. Furthermore, the bias will not be explicitly shown because it can be seamlessly modeled as the coefficient of an additional dummy input with a constant value of 1.

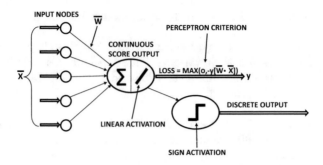

Figure 2.2: An extended architecture of the perceptron with both discrete and continuous predictions

2.2.1   Revisiting the Perceptron

Let $(\overline{X_i}, y_i)$ be a training instance, in which the observed value y_i is predicted from the feature variables $\overline{X_i}$ using the following relationship:

$$\hat{y}_i = \text{sign}(\overline{W} \cdot \overline{X_i}) \tag{2.1}$$

Here, $\overline{W}$ is the d-dimensional coefficient vector learned by the perceptron. Note the circumflex on top of $\hat{y}_i$ to indicate that it is a predicted value rather than an observed value. In general, the goal of training is to ensure that the prediction $\hat{y}_i$ is as close as possible to the observed value y_i. The gradient-descent steps of the perceptron are focused on reducing the number of misclassifications, and therefore the updates are proportional to the difference $(y_i - \hat{y}_i)$ between the observed and predicted values based on Equation 1.33 of Chapter 1:

$$\overline{W} \Leftarrow \overline{W}(1 - \alpha\lambda) + \alpha(y_i - \hat{y}_i)\overline{X_i} \tag{2.2}$$

A gradient-descent update that is proportional to the difference between the observed and predicted values is naturally caused by a squared loss function such as $(y_i - \hat{y}_i)^2$. Therefore, one possibility is to consider the squared loss between the predicted and observed values as the loss function. This architecture is shown in Figure 2.3(a), and the output is a discrete value. However, the problem is that this loss function is discrete because it takes on the value of either 0 or 4. Such a loss function is not differentiable because of its staircase-like jumps.

The perceptron is one of the few learning models in which the gradient-descent updates were proposed historically before the loss function was proposed. What *differentiable* objective function does the perceptron really optimize? The answer to this question may be found in Section 1.2.1.1 of Chapter 1 by observing that the updates are performed only for misclassified training instances (i.e., $y_i \hat{y}_i < 0$), and may be written using the indicator function $I(\cdot) \in \{0, 1\}$ that takes on 1 when the condition in its argument is satisfied:

$$\overline{W} \Leftarrow \overline{W}(1 - \alpha\lambda) + \alpha y_i \overline{X_i} \left[I(y_i \hat{y}_i < 0) \right] \tag{2.3}$$

This rewrite from Equation 2.2 to Equation 2.3 uses the fact that $y_i = (y_i - \hat{y}_i)/2$ for misclassified points, and one can absorb a constant factor of 2 within the learning rate. This update can be shown to be consistent with the loss function L_i (specific to the ith training example) as follows:

$$L_i = \max\{0, -y_i(\overline{W} \cdot \overline{X_i})\} \tag{2.4}$$

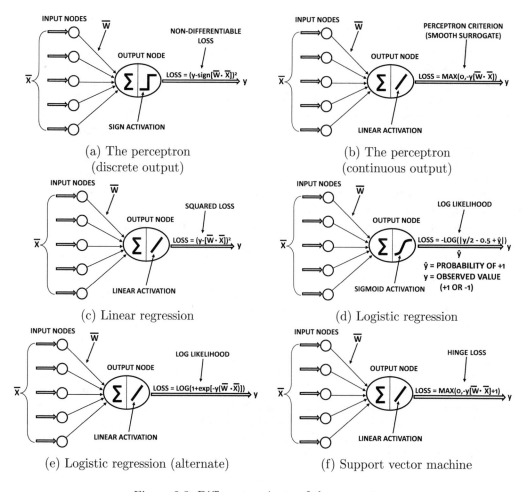

Figure 2.3: Different variants of the perceptron

This loss function is referred to as the *perceptron criterion*, which is correspondingly reflected in Figure 2.3(b). Note that Figure 2.3(b) uses *linear* activations to compute the continuous loss function, although it still uses sign activations to compute the discrete predictions for a given test instance. In many discrete variable prediction settings, the output is often a predicted score (e.g., probability of class or the value of $\overline{W} \cdot \overline{X_i}$), which is then converted into a discrete prediction. Nevertheless, the final prediction need not always be converted into a discrete value, and one can simply output the relevant score for the class (which is often used for computing the loss function anyway). The sign activation is rarely used in most neural-network implementations, as most class-variable predictions of neural-network implementations are continuous scores. One can, in fact, create an extended architecture for the perceptron (cf. Figure 2.2), in which both discrete and continuous values are output. However, since the discrete part is not relevant to the loss computation and most outputs are reported as scores anyway, one rarely uses this type of extended representation. Therefore, throughout the remainder of this book, the activation in the output node is based on the score output (and how the loss function is computed), rather than on how a test instance is predicted as a discrete value.

2.2.2   Least-Squares Regression

In least-squares regression, the training data contains n different training pairs $(\overline{X_1}, y_1) \ldots (\overline{X_n}, y_n)$, where each $\overline{X_i}$ is a d-dimensional representation of the data points, and each y_i is a *real-valued* target. The fact that the target is real-valued is important, because the underlying problem is then referred to as *regression* rather than *classification*. Least-squares regression is the oldest of all learning problems, and the gradient-descent methods proposed by Tikhonov and Arsenin in the 1970s [499] are very closely related to the gradient-descent updates of Rosenblatt [405] for the perceptron algorithm. In fact, as we will see later, one can also use least-squares regression on binary targets by "pretending" that these targets are real-valued. The resulting approach is equivalent to the Widrow-Hoff learning algorithm, which is famous in the neural network literature as the second learning algorithm proposed after the perceptron.

In least-squares regression, the target variable is related to the feature variables using the following relationship:

$$\hat{y}_i = \overline{W} \cdot \overline{X_i} \tag{2.5}$$

Note the presence of the circumflex on top of $\hat{y}_i$ to indicate that it is a predicted value. The bias is missing in the relationship of Equation 2.5. Throughout this section, it will be assumed that one of the features in the training data has a constant value of 1, and the coefficient of this dummy feature is the bias. This is a standard feature engineering trick borrowed from conventional machine learning. In neural networks, the bias is often represented with the use of a bias neuron (cf. Section 1.2.1 of Chapter 1) with a constant output of 1. Although the bias neuron is almost always used in real settings, we avoid showing it explicitly throughout this book in order to maintain simplicity in presentation.

The error of the prediction, e_i, is given by $e_i = (y_i - \hat{y}_i)$. Here, $\overline{W} = (w_1 \ldots w_d)$ is a d-dimensional coefficient vector that needs to be learned so as to minimize the total squared error on the training data, which is $\sum_{i=1}^{n} e_i^2$. The portion of the loss that is specific to the ith training instance is given by the following:

$$L_i = e_i^2 = (y_i - \hat{y}_i)^2 \tag{2.6}$$

This loss can be simulated with the use of an architecture similar to the perceptron except that the squared loss is paired with the identity activation function. This architecture is shown in Figure 2.3(c), whereas the perceptron architecture is shown in Figure 2.3(a). Both the perceptron and least-squares regression have the same goal of minimizing the prediction error. However, since the loss function in classification is inherently discrete, the perceptron algorithm uses a smooth approximation of the desired goal. This results in the smoothed *perceptron criterion* shown in Figure 2.3(b). As we will see below, the gradient-descent update in least-squares regression is very similar to that in the perceptron, with the main difference being that real-valued errors are used in regression rather than discrete errors drawn from $\{-2, +2\}$.

As in the perceptron algorithm, the stochastic gradient-descent steps are determined by computing the gradient of e_i^2 with respect to $\overline{W}$, when the training pair $(\overline{X_i}, y_i)$ is presented to the neural network. This gradient can be computed as follows:

$$\frac{\partial e_i^2}{\partial \overline{W}} = -e_i \overline{X_i} \tag{2.7}$$

Therefore, the gradient-descent updates for $\overline{W}$ are computed using the above gradient and step-size α:

$$\overline{W} \Leftarrow \overline{W} + \alpha e_i \overline{X}$$

One can rewrite the above update as follows:

$$\overline{W} \Leftarrow \overline{W} + \alpha(y_i - \hat{y}_i)\overline{X} \tag{2.8}$$

It is possible to modify the gradient-descent updates of least-squares regression to incorporate forgetting factors. Adding regularization is equivalent to penalizing the loss function of least-squares classification with the additional term proportional to $\lambda \cdot ||\overline{W}||^2$, where $\lambda > 0$ is the regularization parameter. With regularization, the update can be written as follows:

$$\overline{W} \Leftarrow \overline{W}(1 - \alpha \cdot \lambda) + \alpha(y_i - \hat{y}_i)\overline{X} \tag{2.9}$$

Note that the update above looks identical to the perceptron update of Equation 2.2. The updates are, however, not exactly identical because of how the predicted value $\hat{y}_i$ is computed in the two cases. In the case of the perceptron, the sign function is applied to $\overline{W} \cdot \overline{X}_i$ in order to compute the binary value $\hat{y}_i$ and therefore the error $(y_i - \hat{y}_i)$ can only be drawn from $\{-2, +2\}$. In least-squares regression, the prediction $\hat{y}_i$ is a real value without the application of the sign function.

This observation naturally leads to the following question; what if we applied least-squares regression directly to minimize the squared distance of the *real-valued* prediction $\hat{y}_i$ from the observed binary targets $y_i \in \{-1, +1\}$? The direct application of least-squares regression to binary targets is referred to as *least-squares classification*. The gradient-descent update is the same as the one shown in Equation 2.9, which *looks* identical to that of the perceptron. However, the least-squares classification method does not yield the same result as the perceptron algorithm, because the *real-valued* training errors $(y_i - \hat{y}_i)$ in least-squares classification are computed differently from the *integer* error $(y_i - \hat{y}_i)$ in the perceptron. This direct application of least-squares regression to binary targets is referred to as *Widrow-Hoff learning*.

2.2.2.1 Widrow-Hoff Learning

Following the perceptron, the Widrow-Hoff learning rule was proposed in 1960. However, the method was not a fundamentally new one, as it is a direct application of least-squares regression to binary targets. Although the sign function is applied to the real-valued prediction *of unseen test instances* to convert them to binary predictions, the error of training instances is computed directly using real-valued predictions (unlike the perceptron). Therefore, it is also referred to as *least-squares classification* or *linear least-squares method* [6]. Remarkably, a seemingly unrelated method proposed in 1936, known as the Fisher discriminant, also reduces to Widrow-Hoff learning in the special case of binary targets.

The Fisher discriminant is formally defined as a direction $\overline{W}$ along which the ratio of inter-class variance to the intra-class variance is maximized in the projected data. By choosing a scalar b in order to define the hyperplane $\overline{W} \cdot \overline{X} = b$, it is possible to model the separation between the two classes. This hyperplane is used for classification. Although the definition of the Fisher discriminant seems quite different from least-squares regression/classification at first sight, a remarkable result is that the Fisher discriminant for binary targets is identical to the least-squares regression as applied to binary targets (i.e., least-squares classification). Both the data and the targets need to be mean-centered, which allows the bias variable b to be set to 0. Several proofs of this result are available in the literature [3, 6, 40, 41].

The neural architecture for classification with the Widrow-Hoff method is illustrated in Figure 2.3(c). The gradient-descent steps in both the perceptron and the Widrow-Hoff would be given by Equation 2.8, except for differences in how $(y_i - \hat{y}_i)$ is computed. In the case of the perceptron, this value will always be drawn from $\{-2, +2\}$. In the case of Widrow-Hoff, these errors can be arbitrary real values, since $\hat{y}_i$ is set to $\overline{W} \cdot \overline{X}_i$ without using the sign function. This difference is important because the perceptron algorithm never penalizes a positive class point for $\overline{W} \cdot \overline{X}_i$ being "too correct" (i.e., larger than 1), whereas using real-valued predictions to compute the error has the unfortunate effect of penalizing such points. The inappropriate penalization of over-performance is the Achilles heel of Widrow-Hoff learning and the Fisher discriminant [6].

It is noteworthy that least-squares regression/classification, Widrow-Hoff learning, and the Fisher discriminant were proposed independently in very different eras and by different communities of researchers. Indeed, the Fisher discriminant, which is oldest of these methods and dates back to 1936, is often viewed as a method for finding class-sensitive directions rather than as a classifier. It can, however, also be used as a classifier by using the resulting direction $\overline{W}$ to create a linear prediction. The completely different origins and seemingly different motives of all these methods make the equivalence in their solutions all the more noticeable. The Widrow-Hoff learning rule is also referred to as *Adaline*, which is short for *adaptive linear neuron*. It is also referred to as the *delta rule*. To recap, the learning rule of Equation 2.8, when applied to binary targets in $\{-1, +1\}$, can be alternatively referred to as least-squares classification, least mean-squares algorithm (LMS), Fisher[2] discriminant classifier, the Widrow-Hoff learning rule, delta rule, or Adaline. Therefore, the family of least-squares classification methods has been rediscovered several times in the literature under different names and with different motivations.

The loss function of the Widrow-Hoff method can be rewritten slightly from least-squares regression because of its binary responses:

$$L_i = (y_i - \hat{y}_i)^2 = \underbrace{y_i^2}_{1} (y_i - \hat{y}_i)^2$$

$$= (\underbrace{y_i^2}_{1} - \hat{y}_i y_i)^2 = (1 - \hat{y}_i y_i)^2$$

This type of encoding is possible when the target variable y_i is drawn from $\{-1, +1\}$ because we can use $y_i^2 = 1$. It is helpful to convert the Widrow-Hoff objective function to this form because it can be more easily related to other objective functions like the perceptron and the support vector machine. For example, the loss function of the support vector machine is obtained by "repairing" the above loss so that over-performance is not penalized. One can repair the loss function by changing the objective function to $[\max\{(1-\hat{y}_i y_i), 0\}]^2$, which was Hinton's L_2-loss support vector machine (SVM) [190]. Almost all the binary classification models discussed in this chapter can be shown to be closely related to the Widrow-Hoff loss function by using different ways of repairing the loss, so that over-performance is not penalized.

The gradient-descent updates (cf. Equation 2.9) of least-squares regression can be rewritten slightly for Widrow-Hoff learning because of binary response variables:

$$\overline{W} \Leftarrow \overline{W}(1 - \alpha \cdot \lambda) + \alpha(y_i - \hat{y}_i)\overline{X} \quad \text{[For numeric as well as binary responses]}$$

$$= \overline{W}(1 - \alpha \cdot \lambda) + \alpha y_i(1 - y_i\hat{y}_i)\overline{X} \quad \text{[Only for binary responses, since } y_i^2 = 1\text{]}$$

---

[2]In order to obtain exactly the same direction as the Fisher method with Equation 2.8, it is important to mean-center both the feature variables and the binary targets. Therefore, each binary target will be one of two real values with different signs. The real values will contain the fraction of instances belonging to the other class. Alternatively, one can use a bias neuron to absorb the constant offsets.

The second form of the update is helpful in relating it to perceptron and SVM updates, in each of which $(1 - y_i\hat{y}_i)$ is replaced with an indicator variable that is a function of $y_i\hat{y}_i$. This point will be discussed in a later section.

2.2.2.2 Closed Form Solutions

The special case of least-squares regression and classification is solvable in closed form (without gradient-descent) by using the *pseudo-inverse* of the $n \times d$ training data matrix D, whose rows are $\overline{X_1} \ldots \overline{X_n}$. Let the n-dimensional column vector of dependent variables be denoted by $\overline{y} = [y_1 \ldots y_n]^T$. The pseudo-inverse of matrix D is defined as follows:

$$D^+ = (D^T D)^{-1} D^T \tag{2.10}$$

Then, the row-vector $\overline{W}$ is defined by the following relationship:

$$\overline{W}^T = D^+ \overline{y} \tag{2.11}$$

If regularization is incorporated, the coefficient vector $\overline{W}$ is given by the following:

$$\overline{W}^T = (D^T D + \lambda I)^{-1} D^T \overline{y} \tag{2.12}$$

Here, $\lambda > 0$ is the regularization parameter. However, inverting a matrix like $(D^T D + \lambda I)$ is typically done using numerical methods that require gradient descent anyway. One rarely inverts large matrices like $D^T D$. In fact, the Widrow-Hoff updates provide a very efficient way of solving the problem without using the closed-form solution.

2.2.3 Logistic Regression

Logistic regression is a probabilistic model that classifies the instances in terms of probabilities. Because the classification is probabilistic, a natural approach for optimizing the parameters is to ensure that the predicted probability of the observed class for each training instance is as large as possible. This goal is achieved by using the notion of *maximum-likelihood estimation* in order to learn the parameters of the model. The likelihood of the training data is defined as the product of the probabilities of the observed labels of each training instance. Clearly, larger values of this objective function are better. By using the negative logarithm of this value, one obtains an a loss function in minimization form. Therefore, the output node uses the negative *log-likelihood* as a loss function. This loss function replaces the squared error used in the Widrow-Hoff method. The output layer can be formulated with the sigmoid activation function, which is very common in neural network design.

Let $(\overline{X_1}, y_1), (\overline{X_2}, y_2), \ldots (\overline{X_n}, y_n)$ be a set of n training pairs in which $\overline{X_i}$ contains the d-dimensional features and $y_i \in \{-1, +1\}$ is a binary class variable. As in the case of a perceptron, a single-layer architecture with weights $\overline{W} = (w_1 \ldots w_d)$ is used. Instead of using the hard sign activation on $\overline{W} \cdot \overline{X_i}$ to predict y_i, logistic regression applies the soft sigmoid function to $\overline{W} \cdot \overline{X_i}$ in order to estimate the *probability* that y_i is 1:

$$\hat{y}_i = P(y_i = 1) = \frac{1}{1 + \exp(-\overline{W} \cdot \overline{X_i})} \tag{2.13}$$

For a test instance, it can be predicted to the class whose predicted probability is greater than 0.5. Note that $P(y_i = 1)$ is 0.5 when $\overline{W} \cdot \overline{X_i} = 0$, and $\overline{X_i}$ lies on the separating hyperplane. Moving $\overline{X_i}$ in either direction from the hyperplane results in different signs of $\overline{W} \cdot \overline{X_i}$ and corresponding movements in the probability values. Therefore, the sign of $\overline{W} \cdot \overline{X_i}$ also yields the same prediction as picking the class with probability larger than 0.5.

We will now describe how the loss function corresponding to likelihood estimation is set up. This methodology is important because it is used widely in many neural models. For positive samples in the training data, we want to maximize $P(y_i = 1)$ and for negative samples, we want to maximize $P(y_i = -1)$. For positive samples satisfying $y_i = 1$, one wants to maximize $\hat{y}_i$ and for negative samples satisfying $y_i = -1$, one wants to maximize $1 - \hat{y}_i$. One can write this casewise maximization in the form of a consolidated expression of always maximizing $|y_i/2 - 0.5 + \hat{y}_i|$. The products of these probabilities must be maximized over all training instances to maximize the likelihood $\mathcal{L}$:

$$\mathcal{L} = \prod_{i=1}^{n} |y_i/2 - 0.5 + \hat{y}_i| \tag{2.14}$$

Therefore, the loss function is set to $L_i = -\log(|y_i/2 - 0.5 + \hat{y}_i|)$ for each training instance, so that the product-wise maximization is converted to additive minimization over training instances.

$$\mathcal{LL} = -\log(\mathcal{L}) = \sum_{i=1}^{n} \underbrace{-\log(|y_i/2 - 0.5 + \hat{y}_i|)}_{L_i} \tag{2.15}$$

Additive forms of the objective function are particularly convenient for the types of stochastic gradient updates that are common in neural networks. The overall architecture and loss function is illustrated in Figure 2.3(d). For each training instance, the predicted probability $\hat{y}_i$ is computed by passing it through the neural network, and the loss is used to determine the gradient for each training instance.

Let the loss for the ith training instance be denoted by L_i, which is also annotated in Equation 2.15. Then, the gradient of L_i with respect to the weights in $\overline{W}$ can be computed as follows:

$$\frac{\partial L_i}{\partial \overline{W}} = -\frac{\text{sign}(y_i/2 - 0.5 + \hat{y}_i)}{|y_i/2 - 0.5 + \hat{y}_i|} \cdot \frac{\partial \hat{y}_i}{\partial \overline{W}}$$

$$= -\frac{\text{sign}(y_i/2 - 0.5 + \hat{y}_i)}{|y_i/2 - 0.5 + \hat{y}_i|} \cdot \frac{\overline{X_i}}{1 + \exp(-\overline{W} \cdot \overline{X_i})} \cdot \frac{1}{1 + \exp(\overline{W} \cdot \overline{X_i})}$$

$$= \begin{cases} -\frac{\overline{X_i}}{1 + \exp(\overline{W} \cdot \overline{X_i})} & \text{if } y_i = 1 \\ \frac{\overline{X_i}}{1 + \exp(-\overline{W} \cdot \overline{X_i})} & \text{if } y_i = -1 \end{cases}$$

Note that one can concisely write the above gradient as follows:

$$\frac{\partial L_i}{\partial \overline{W}} = -\frac{y_i \overline{X_i}}{1 + \exp(y_i \overline{W} \cdot \overline{X_i})} = -\left[\text{Probability of mistake on } (\overline{X_i}, y_i)\right](y_i \overline{X_i}) \tag{2.16}$$

Therefore, the gradient-descent updates of logistic regression are given by the following (including regularization):

$$\overline{W} \Leftarrow \overline{W}(1 - \alpha\lambda) + \alpha \frac{y_i \overline{X_i}}{1 + \exp[y_i(\overline{W} \cdot \overline{X_i})]} \tag{2.17}$$

Just as the perceptron and the Widrow-Hoff algorithms use the *magnitudes* of the mistakes to make updates, the logistic regression method uses the *probabilities* of the mistakes to make updates. This is a natural extension of the probabilistic nature of the loss function to the update.

2.2.3.1 Alternative Choices of Activation and Loss

It is possible to implement the same model by using different choices of activation and loss in the output node as long as they combine to yield the same result. Instead of using sigmoid activation to create the output $\hat{y}_i \in (0, 1)$, it is also possible to use identity activation to create the output $\hat{y}_i \in (-\infty, +\infty)$, and then apply the following loss function:

$$L_i = \log(1 + \exp(-y_i \cdot \hat{y}_i)) \tag{2.18}$$

The alternative architecture for logistic regression is shown in Figure 2.3(e). For the final prediction of the test instance, the sign function can be applied to $\hat{y}_i$, which is equivalent to predicting it to the class for which its probability is greater than 0.5. This example shows that it is possible to implement the same model using different combinations of activation and loss functions, as long as they combine to yield the same result.

One desirable property of using the identity activation to define $\hat{y}_i$ is that it is consistent with how the loss functions of other models like the perceptron and Widrow-Hoff learning are defined. Furthermore, the loss function of Equation 2.18 contains the product of y_i and $\hat{y}_i$ as in other models. This makes it possible to directly compare the loss functions of various models, which will be explored later in this chapter.

2.2.4 Support Vector Machines

The loss function in support vector machines is closely related to that in logistic regression. However, instead of using a smooth loss function (like that in Equation 2.18), the *hinge-loss* is used instead.

Consider the training data set of n instances denoted by $(\overline{X_1}, y_1), (\overline{X_2}, y_2), \ldots (\overline{X_n}, y_n)$. The neural architecture of the support-vector machine is identical to that of least-squares classification (Widrow-Hoff). The main difference is in the choice of loss function. As in the case of least-squares classification, the prediction $\hat{y}_i$ for the training point $\overline{X_i}$ is obtained by applying the identity activation function on $\overline{W} \cdot \overline{X_i}$. Here, $\overline{W} = (w_1, \ldots w_d)$ contains the vector of d weights for the d different inputs into the single-layer network. Therefore, the output of the neural network is $\hat{y}_i = \overline{W} \cdot \overline{X_i}$ for computing the loss function, although a test instance is predicted by applying the sign function to the output.

The loss function L_i for the ith training instance in the support-vector machine is defined as follows:

$$L_i = \max\{0, 1 - y_i \hat{y}_i\} \tag{2.19}$$

This loss is referred to as the *hinge-loss*, and the corresponding neural architecture is illustrated in Figure 2.3(f). The overall idea behind this loss function is that a positive training instance is only penalized for being less than 1, and a negative training instance is only penalized for being greater than -1. In both cases, the penalty is linear, and abruptly flattens out at the aforementioned thresholds. It is helpful to compare this loss function with the Widrow-Hoff loss value of $(1 - y_i\hat{y}_i)^2$, in which predictions are penalized for being *different* from the target values. As we will see later, this difference is an important advantage for the support vector machine over the Widrow-Hoff loss function.

In order to explain the difference in loss functions between the perceptron, Widrow-Hoff, logistic regression, and the support vector machine, we have shown the loss for a single *positive* training instance at different values of $\hat{y}_i = \overline{W} \cdot \overline{X}_i$ in Figure 2.4. In the case of the perceptron, only the smoothed *surrogate* loss function (cf. Section 1.2.1.1 of Chapter 1) is shown. Since the target value is +1, the loss function shows diminishing

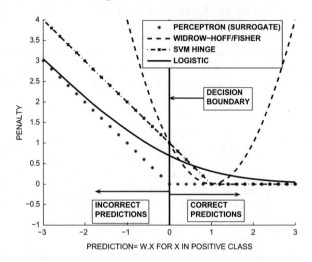

Figure 2.4: The loss functions of different variants of the perceptron. Key observations: (i) The SVM loss is shifted from the perceptron (surrogate) loss by exactly one unit to the right; (ii) the logistic loss is a smooth variant of the SVM loss; (iii) the Widrow-Hoff/Fisher loss is the only case in which points are increasingly penalized for classifying points "too correctly" (i.e., increasing $\overline{W} \cdot \overline{X}$ beyond +1 for $\overline{X}$ in positive class). Repairing the Widrow-Hoff loss function by setting it to 0 for $\overline{W} \cdot \overline{X} > 1$ yields the *quadratic loss* SVM [190].

improvement by increasing $\overline{W} \cdot \overline{X}_i$ beyond +1 in the case of logistic regression. In the case of the support-vector machine the hinge-loss function flattens out beyond this point. In other words, only misclassified points or points that are too close to the decision boundary $\overline{W} \cdot \overline{X} = 0$ are penalized. The perceptron criterion is identical in shape to the hinge loss, except that it is shifted by one unit to the left. The Widrow-Hoff method is the only case in which a positive training point is penalized for having too large a positive value of $\overline{W} \cdot \overline{X}_i$. In other words, the Widrow-Hoff method penalizes points for being properly classified in a very strong way. This is a potential problem with the Widrow-Hoff objective function, in which well-separated points cause problems in training.

The stochastic gradient-descent method computes the partial derivative of the point-wise loss function L_i with respect to the elements in $\overline{W}$. The gradient is computed as follows:

$$\frac{\partial L_i}{\partial \overline{W}} = \begin{cases} -y_i \overline{X}_i & \text{if } y_i \hat{y}_i < 1 \\ 0 & \text{otherwise} \end{cases} \qquad (2.20)$$

Therefore, the stochastic gradient method samples a point and checks whether $y_i \hat{y}_i < 1$. If this is the case, an update is performed that is proportional to $y_i \overline{X}_i$:

$$\overline{W} \Leftarrow \overline{W}(1 - \alpha\lambda) + \alpha y_i \overline{X}_i \left[I(y_i \hat{y}_i < 1) \right] \qquad (2.21)$$

Here, $I(\cdot) \in \{0, 1\}$ is the indicator function that takes on the value of 1 when the condition in its argument is satisfied. This approach is the simplest version of the primal update for

SVMs [448]. The reader should also convince herself is that this update is *identical* to that of a (regularized) perceptron (cf. Equation 2.3), except that the condition for making this update in the perceptron is $y_i \hat{y}_i < 0$. Therefore, a perceptron makes the update only when a point is misclassified, whereas the support vector machine also makes updates for points that are classified correctly, albeit not very confidently. This neat relationship is because the loss function of the perceptron criterion shown in Figure 2.4 is shifted from the hinge-loss in the SVM.

To emphasize the similarities and differences in the loss functions used by the different methods, we tabulate the loss functions below:

Model	Loss function L_i for $(\overline{X_i}, y_i)$
Perceptron (Smoothed surrogate)	$\max\{0, -y_i \cdot (\overline{W} \cdot \overline{X_i})\}$
Widrow-Hoff/Fisher	$(y_i - \overline{W} \cdot \overline{X_i})^2 = \{1 - y_i \cdot (\overline{W} \cdot \overline{X_i})\}^2$
Logistic Regression	$\log(1 + \exp[-y_i (\overline{W} \cdot \overline{X_i})])$
Support vector machine (Hinge)	$\max\{0, 1 - y_i \cdot (\overline{W} \cdot \overline{X_i})\}$
Support vector machine (Hinton's L_2-Loss) [190]	$[\max\{0, 1 - y_i \cdot (\overline{W} \cdot \overline{X_i})\}]^2$

It is noteworthy that all the derived updates in this section typically correspond to stochastic gradient-descent updates that are encountered both in traditional machine learning and in neural networks. The updates are the same whether or not we use a neural architecture to represent the models for these algorithms. Our main point in going through this exercise is to show that rudimentary special cases of neural networks are instantiations of well-known algorithms in the machine learning literature. The key point is that with greater availability of data one can incorporate additional nodes and depth to increase the model's capacity, explaining the superior behavior of neural networks with larger data sets (cf. Figure 2.1).

2.3 Neural Architectures for Multiclass Models

All the models discussed so far in this chapter are designed for binary classification. In this section, we will discuss how one can design multiway classification models by changing the architecture of the perceptron slightly, and allowing multiple output nodes.

2.3.1 Multiclass Perceptron

Consider a setting with k different classes. Each training instance $(\overline{X_i}, c(i))$ contains a d-dimensional feature vector $\overline{X_i}$ and the index $c(i) \in \{1 \ldots k\}$ of its observed class. In such a case, we would like to find k different linear separators $\overline{W_1} \ldots \overline{W_k}$ simultaneously so that the value of $\overline{W}_{c(i)} \cdot \overline{X_i}$ is larger than $\overline{W_r} \cdot \overline{X_i}$ for each $r \neq c(i)$. This is because one always predicts a data instance $\overline{X_i}$ to the class r with the largest value of $\overline{W_r} \cdot \overline{X_i}$. Therefore, the loss function for the ith training instance in the case of the multiclass perceptron is defined as follows:

$$L_i = \max_{r:r \neq c(i)} \max(\overline{W_r} \cdot \overline{X_i} - \overline{W}_{c(i)} \cdot \overline{X_i}, 0) \qquad (2.22)$$

The multiclass perceptron is illustrated in Figure 2.5(a). As in all neural network models, one can use gradient-descent in order to determine the updates. For a correctly classified instance, the gradient is always 0, and there are no updates. For a misclassified instance, the gradients are as follows:

$$\frac{\partial L_i}{\partial \overline{W}_r} = \begin{cases} -\overline{X}_i & \text{if } r = c(i) \\ \overline{X}_i & \text{if } r \neq c(i) \text{ is most misclassified prediction} \\ 0 & \text{otherwise} \end{cases} \qquad (2.23)$$

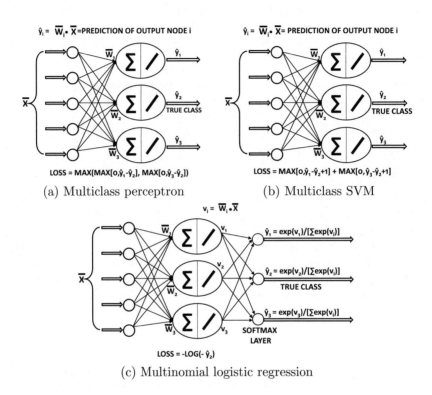

(a) Multiclass perceptron   (b) Multiclass SVM

(c) Multinomial logistic regression

Figure 2.5: Multiclass models: In each case, class 2 is assumed to be the ground-truth class.

Therefore, the stochastic gradient-descent method is applied as follows. Each training instance is fed into the network. If the correct class $r = c(i)$ receives the largest of output $\overline{W}_r \cdot \overline{X}_i$, then no update needs to be executed. Otherwise, the following update is made to each separator $\overline{W}_r$ for learning rate $\alpha > 0$:

$$\overline{W}_r \Leftarrow \overline{W}_r + \begin{cases} \alpha \overline{X}_i & \text{if } r = c(i) \\ -\alpha \overline{X}_i & \text{if } r \neq c(i) \text{ is most misclassified prediction} \\ 0 & \text{otherwise} \end{cases} \qquad (2.24)$$

Only two of the separators are always updated at a given time. In the special case that $k = 2$, these gradient updates reduce to the perceptron because both the separators $\overline{W}_1$ and $\overline{W}_2$ will be related as $\overline{W}_1 = -\overline{W}_2$ if the descent is started at $\overline{W}_1 = \overline{W}_2 = 0$. Another quirk that is specific to the unregularized perceptron is that it is possible to use a learning rate of $\alpha = 1$ without affecting the learning because the value of α only has the effect of scaling the weight when starting with $\overline{W}_j = 0$ (see Exercise 2). This property is, however, not true for other linear models in which the value of α does affect the learning.

2.3.2 Weston-Watkins SVM

The Weston-Watkins SVM [529] varies on the multiclass perceptron in two ways:

1. The multiclass perceptron only updates the linear separator of a class that is predicted *most* incorrectly along with the linear separator of the true class. On the other hand, the Weston-Watkins SVM updates the separator of *any* class that is predicted more favorably than the true class. In both cases, the separator of the observed class is updated by the same aggregate amount as the incorrect classes (but in the opposite direction).

2. Not only does the Weston-Watkins SVM update the separator in the case of misclassification, it updates the separators in cases where an incorrect class gets a prediction that is "uncomfortably close" to the true class. This is based on the notion of margin.

As in the case of the multiclass perceptron, it is assumed that the ith training instance is denoted by $(\overline{X_i}, c(i))$, where $\overline{X_i}$ contains the d-dimensional feature variables, and $c(i)$ contains the class index drawn from $\{1, \ldots, k\}$. One wants to learn d-dimensional coefficients $\overline{W_1} \ldots \overline{W_k}$ of the k linear separators so that the class index r with the largest value of $\overline{W_r} \cdot \overline{X_i}$ is predicted to be the correct class $c(i)$. The loss function L_i for the ith training instance $(\overline{X_i}, c(i))$ in the Weston-Watkins SVM is as follows:

$$L_i = \sum_{r:r \neq c(i)} \max(\overline{W_r} \cdot \overline{X_i} - \overline{W}_{c(i)} \cdot \overline{X_i} + 1, 0) \tag{2.25}$$

The neural architecture of the Weston-Watkins SVM is illustrated in Figure 2.5(b). It is instructive to compare the objective function of the Weston-Watkins SVM (Equation 2.25) with that of the multiclass perceptron (Equation 2.22). First, for each class $r \neq c(i)$, if the prediction $\overline{W_r} \cdot \overline{X_i}$ lags behind that of the true class by less than a margin amount of 1, then a loss is incurred for that class. Furthermore, the losses over all such classes $r \neq c(i)$ are *added*, rather than taking the maximum of the losses. These two differences accomplish the two intuitive goals discussed above.

In order to determine the gradient-descent updates, one can find the gradient of the loss function with respect to each $\overline{W_r}$. In the event that the loss function L_i is 0, the gradient of the loss function is 0 as well. Therefore, no update is required when the training instance is classified correctly with sufficient margin with respect to the second-best class. However, if the loss function is non-zero we have either a misclassified or a "barely correct" prediction in which the second-best and best class prediction are not sufficiently separated. In such cases, the gradient of the loss is non-zero. The loss function of Equation 2.25 is created by adding up the contributions of the $(k-1)$ separators belonging to the incorrect classes. Let $\delta(r, \overline{X_i})$ be a 0/1 indicator function, which is 1 when the rth class separator contributes positively to the loss function in Equation 2.25. In such a case, the gradient of the loss function is as follows:

$$\frac{\partial L_i}{\partial \overline{W_r}} = \begin{cases} -\overline{X_i}[\sum_{j \neq r} \delta(j, \overline{X_i})] & \text{if } r = c(i) \\ \overline{X_i}[\delta(r, \overline{X_i})] & \text{if } r \neq c(i) \end{cases} \tag{2.26}$$

This results in the following stochastic gradient-descent step for the rth separator $\overline{W_r}$ at learning rate α:

$$\overline{W_r} \Leftarrow \overline{W_r}(1 - \alpha\lambda) + \alpha \begin{cases} \overline{X_i}[\sum_{j \neq r} \delta(j, \overline{X_i})] & \text{if } r = c(i) \\ -\overline{X_i}[\delta(r, \overline{X_i})] & \text{if } r \neq c(i) \end{cases} \tag{2.27}$$

For training instances $\overline{X_i}$ in which the loss L_i is zero, the above update can be shown to simplify to a regularization update of each hyperplane $\overline{W_r}$:

$$\overline{W_r} \Leftarrow \overline{W_r}(1 - \alpha\lambda) \tag{2.28}$$

The regularization uses the parameter $\lambda > 0$. Regularization is considered essential to the proper functioning of a support vector machine.

2.3.3 Multinomial Logistic Regression (Softmax Classifier)

Multinomial logistic regression can be considered the multi-way generalization of logistic regression, just as the Weston-Watkins SVM is the multiway generalization of the binary SVM. Multinomial logistic regression uses negative log-likelihood loss, and is therefore a probabilistic model. As in the case of the multiclass perceptron, it is assumed that the input to the model is a training data set containing pairs of the form $(\overline{X_i}, c(i))$, where $c(i) \in \{1 \ldots k\}$ is the index of the class of d-dimensional data point $\overline{X_i}$. As in the case of the previous two models, the class r with the largest value of $\overline{W_r} \cdot \overline{X_i}$ is predicted to be the label of the data point $\overline{X_i}$. However, in this case, there is an additional probabilistic interpretation of $\overline{W_r} \cdot \overline{X_i}$ in terms of the posterior probability $P(r|\overline{X_i})$ that the data point $\overline{X_i}$ takes on the label r. This estimation can be naturally accomplished with the softmax activation function:

$$P(r|\overline{X_i}) = \frac{\exp(\overline{W_r} \cdot \overline{X_i})}{\sum_{j=1}^{k} \exp(\overline{W_j} \cdot \overline{X_i})} \tag{2.29}$$

In other words, the model predicts the class membership in terms of probabilities. The loss function L_i for the ith training instance is defined by the cross-entropy, which is the negative logarithm of the probability of the true class. The neural architecture of the softmax classifier is illustrated in Figure 2.5(c).

The cross-entropy loss may be expressed in terms of either the input features or in terms of the softmax pre-activation values $v_r = \overline{W_r} \cdot \overline{X_i}$ as follows:

$$L_i = -\log[P(c(i)|\overline{X_i})] \tag{2.30}$$

$$= -\overline{W}_{c(i)} \cdot \overline{X_i} + \log[\sum_{j=1}^{k} \exp(\overline{W_j} \cdot \overline{X_i})] \tag{2.31}$$

$$= -v_{c(i)} + \log[\sum_{j=1}^{k} \exp(v_j)] \tag{2.32}$$

Therefore, the partial derivative of L_i with respect to v_r can be computed as follows:

$$\frac{\partial L_i}{\partial v_r} = \begin{cases} -\left(1 - \frac{\exp(v_r)}{\sum_{j=1}^{k}\exp(v_j)}\right) & \text{if } r = c(i) \\ \left(\frac{\exp(v_r)}{\sum_{j=1}^{k}\exp(v_j)}\right) & \text{if } r \neq c(i) \end{cases} \tag{2.33}$$

$$= \begin{cases} -(1 - P(r|\overline{X_i})) & \text{if } r = c(i) \\ P(r|\overline{X_i}) & \text{if } r \neq c(i) \end{cases} \tag{2.34}$$

The gradient of the loss of the ith training instance with respect to the separator of the rth class is computed by using the chain rule of differential calculus in terms of its pre-activation value $v_j = \overline{W_j} \cdot \overline{X_i}$:

$$\frac{\partial L_i}{\partial \overline{W}_r} = \sum_j \left(\frac{\partial L_i}{\partial v_j} \right) \left(\frac{\partial v_j}{\partial \overline{W}_r} \right) = \frac{\partial L_i}{\partial v_r} \underbrace{\frac{\partial v_r}{\partial \overline{W}_r}}_{\overline{X}_i} \tag{2.35}$$

In the above simplification, we used the fact that v_j has a zero gradient with respect to $\overline{W}_r$ for $j \neq r$. The value of $\frac{\partial L_i}{\partial v_r}$ in Equation 2.35 can be substituted from Equation 2.34 to obtain the following result:

$$\frac{\partial L_i}{\partial \overline{W}_r} = \begin{cases} -\overline{X}_i(1 - P(r|\overline{X}_i)) & \text{if } r = c(i) \\ \overline{X}_i \, P(r|\overline{X}_i) & \text{if } r \neq c(i) \end{cases} \tag{2.36}$$

Note that we have expressed the gradient indirectly using probabilities (based on Equation 2.29) both for brevity and for intuitive understanding of how the gradient is related to the probability of making different types of mistakes. Each of the terms $[1 - P(r|\overline{X}_i)]$ and $P(r|\overline{X}_i)$ is the probability of making a mistake for an instance with label $c(i)$ with respect to the predictions for the rth class. After including similar regularization impact as other models, the separator for the rth class is updated as follows:

$$\overline{W}_r \Leftarrow \overline{W}_r(1 - \alpha\lambda) + \alpha \begin{cases} \overline{X}_i \cdot (1 - P(r|\overline{X}_i)) & \text{if } r = c(i) \\ -\overline{X}_i \cdot P(r|\overline{X}_i) & \text{if } r \neq c(i) \end{cases} \tag{2.37}$$

Here, α is the learning rate, and λ is the regularization parameter. The softmax classifier updates all the k separators for each training instance, unlike the multiclass perceptron and the Weston-Watkins SVM, each of which updates only a small subset of separators (or no separator) for each training instance. This is a consequence of probabilistic modeling, in which correctness is defined in a soft way.

2.3.4 Hierarchical Softmax for Many Classes

Consider a classification problem in which we have an extremely large number of classes. In such a case, learning becomes too slow, because of the large number of separators that need to be updated for each training instance. This situation can occur in applications like text mining, where the prediction is a target word. Predicting target words is particularly common in *neural language models*, which try to predict the next word given the immediate history of previous words. The cardinality of the number of classes will typically be larger than 10^5 in such cases. Hierarchical softmax is a way of improving learning efficiency by decomposing the classification problem hierarchically. The idea is to group the classes hierarchically into a binary tree-like structure, and then perform $\log_2(k)$ binary classifications from the root to the leaf for k-way classification. Although the hierarchical classification can compromise the accuracy to some extent, the efficiency improvements can be significant.

How is the hierarchy of classes obtained? The naïve approach is to create a random hierarchy. However, the specific grouping of classes has an effect on performance. Grouping similar classes tends to improve performance. It is possible to use domain-specific insights to improve the quality of the hierarchy. For example, if the prediction is a target word, one can use the *WordNet* hierarchy [329] to guide the grouping. Further reorganization may be needed [344] because the *WordNet* hierarchy is not exactly a binary tree. Another option is to use Huffman encoding in order to create the binary tree [325, 327]. Refer to the bibliographic notes for more pointers.

2.4   Backpropagated Saliency for Interpretability and Feature Selection

One of the common refrains about neural networks has been their lack of interpretability [97]. However, it turns out that one can use backpropagation in order to determine the features that contribute the most to the classification of a particular test instance. This provides the analyst with an understanding of the relevance of each feature to classification. This approach also has the useful property that it can be used for feature selection [406].

Consider a test instance $\overline{X} = (x_1, \ldots x_d)$, for which the multilabel output scores of the neural network are $o_1 \ldots o_k$. Furthermore, let the output of the winning class among the k outputs be o_m, where $m \in \{1 \ldots k\}$. Our goal is to identify the features that are most relevant to the classification of this test instance. In general, for each attribute x_i, we would like to determine the sensitivity of the output o_m to x_i. Features with large *absolute* magnitudes of this sensitivity are obviously relevant to the classification of this test instance. In order to achieve this goal, we would like to compute the absolute magnitude of $\frac{\partial o_m}{\partial x_i}$. The features with the largest absolute value of the partial derivative have the greatest influence on the classification to the winning class. The sign of this derivative also tells us whether increasing x_i slightly from its current value increases or decreases the score of the winning class. For classes other than the winning class, the derivative also provides some understanding of the sensitivity, but this is less important, particularly when the number of classes is large. The value of $\frac{\partial o_m}{\partial x_i}$ can be computed by a straightforward application of the backpropagation algorithm, in which one does not stop backpropagating at the first hidden layer but applies the process all the way to the input layer.

One can also use this approach for feature selection by aggregating the absolute value of the gradient over all classes and all correctly classified training instances. The features with the largest aggregate sensitivity over the whole training data are the most relevant. Strictly speaking, one does not need to aggregate this value over all classes, but one can simply use only the winning class for correctly classified training instances. However, the original work in [406] aggregates this value over all classes and all instances.

Similar methods for interpreting the effects of different portions of the input are also used in computer vision with convolutional neural networks [466]. A discussion of some of these methods is provided in Section 8.5.1 of Chapter 8. In the case of computer vision, the visual effects of this type of saliency analysis are sometimes spectacular. For example, for an image of a dog, the analysis will tell us which features (i.e., pixels) results in the image being considered a dog. As a result, we can create a black-and-white saliency image in which the portion corresponding to a dog is emphasized in light color against a dark background (cf. Figure 8.12 of Chapter 8).

2.5   Matrix Factorization with Autoencoders

Autoencoders represent a fundamental architecture that is used for various types of unsupervised learning, including matrix factorization, principal component analysis, and dimensionality reduction. Natural architectural variations of the autoencoder can also be used for matrix factorization of incomplete data to create recommender systems. Furthermore, some recent feature engineering methods in the natural language domain like *word2vec* can also be viewed as variations of autoencoders, which perform nonlinear matrix factorizations of word-context matrices. The nonlinearity is achieved with the activation function in the output layer, which is usually not available with traditional matrix factorization. Therefore, one of our goals will be to demonstrate how small changes to the underlying building blocks of the neural network can be used to implement sophisticated variations of a given family of methods. This is particularly convenient for the analyst, who only has to experiment with small variations of the architecture to test different types of models. Such variations would require more effort to construct in traditional machine learning, because one does not have the benefit of learning abstractions like backpropagation. First, we begin with a simple simulation of a traditional matrix factorization method with a shallow neural architecture. Then, we discuss how this basic setup provides the path to generalizations to nonlinear dimensionality reduction methods by adding layers and/or nonlinear activation functions. Therefore, the goal of this section is to show two things:

1. Classical dimensionality reduction methods like singular value decomposition and principal component analysis are special cases of neural architectures.

2. By adding different types of complexities to the basic architecture, one can generate complex nonlinear embeddings of the data. While nonlinear embeddings are also available in machine learning, neural architectures provide unprecedented flexibility in controlling the properties of the embedding by making various types of architectural changes (and allowing backpropagation to take care of the changes in the underlying learning algorithms).

We will also discuss a number of applications such as recommender systems and outlier detection.

2.5.1 Autoencoder: Basic Principles

The basic idea of an autoencoder is to have an output layer with the same dimensionality as the inputs. The idea is to try to reconstruct each dimension exactly by passing it through the network. An autoencoder *replicates* the data from the input to the output, and is therefore sometimes referred to as a *replicator neural network*. Although reconstructing the data might seem like a trivial matter by simply copying the data forward from one layer to another, this is not possible when the number of units in the middle are *constricted*. In other words, the number of units in each middle layer is typically fewer than that in the input (or output). As a result, these units hold a reduced representation of the data, and the final layer can no longer reconstruct the data exactly. Therefore, this type of reconstruction is inherently *lossy*. The loss function of this neural network uses the sum-of-squared differences between the input and the output in order to force the output to be as similar as possible to the input. This general representation of the autoencoder is given in Figure 2.6(a), where an architecture is shown with three constricted layers. It is noteworthy that the representation of the innermost hidden layer will be hierarchically related to those in the two outer hidden layers. Therefore, an autoencoder is capable of performing hierarchical data reduction.

It is common (but not necessary) for an M-layer autoencoder to have a symmetric architecture between the input and output, where the number of units in the kth layer is the same as that in the $(M - k + 1)$th layer. Furthermore, the value of M is often odd, as a result of which the $(M + 1)/2$th layer is often the most constricted layer. Here, we are counting the (non-computational) input layer as the first layer, and therefore the minimum number of layers in an autoencoder would be three, corresponding to the input layer, constricted layer, and the output layer. As we will see later, this simplest form of the autoencoder is used in traditional machine learning for singular value decomposition. The symmetry in the architecture often extends to the fact that the weights outgoing from the

kth layer are tied to those incoming to the $(M - k)$th layer in many architectures. For now, we will not make this assumption for simplicity in presentation. Furthermore, the symmetry is never absolute because of the effect of nonlinear activation functions. For example, if a nonlinear activation function is used in the output layer, there is no way to symmetrically mirror that fact in the (non-computational) input layer.

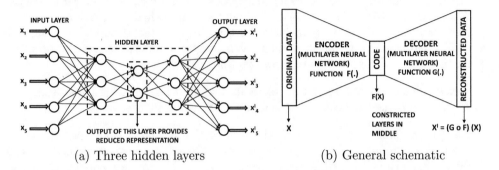

(a) Three hidden layers   (b) General schematic

Figure 2.6: The basic schematic of the autoencoder

The reduced representation of the data is also sometimes referred to as the *code*, and the number of units in this layer is the dimensionality of the reduction. The initial part of the neural architecture before the bottleneck is referred to as the *encoder* (because it creates a reduced code), and the final part of the architecture is referred to as the *decoder* (because it reconstructs from the code). The general schematic of the autoencoder is shown in Figure 2.6(b).

2.5.1.1   Autoencoder with a Single Hidden Layer

In the following, we describe the simplest version of an autoencoder, which is used for matrix factorization. This autoencoder only has a single hidden layer of $k \ll d$ units between the input and output layers of d units each. For the purpose of discussion, assume that we have an $n \times d$ matrix denoted by D, which we would like to factorize into an $n \times k$ matrix U and a $d \times k$ matrix V:

$$D \approx UV^T \tag{2.38}$$

Here, k is the rank of the factorization. The matrix U contains the reduced representation of the data, and the matrix V contains the basis vectors. Matrix factorization is one of the most widely studied problems in supervised learning, and it is used for dimensionality reduction, clustering, and predictive modeling in recommender systems.

In traditional machine learning, this problem is solved by minimizing the *Frobenius norm* of the *residual matrix* denoted by $(D - UV^T)$. The squared Frobenius norm of a matrix is the sum of the squares of the entries in the matrix. Therefore, one can write the objective function of the optimization problem as follows:

$$\text{Minimize } J = ||D - UV^T||_F^2$$

Here, the notation $|| \cdot ||_F$ indicates the Frobenius norm. The parameter matrices U and V need to be learned in order to optimize the aforementioned error. This objective function has an infinite number of optima, one of which has mutually orthogonal basis vectors. That particular solution is referred to as *truncated singular value decomposition*. Although it is relatively easy to derive the gradient-descent steps [6] for this optimization problem (without worrying about neural networks at all), our goal here is to capture this optimization problem within a neural architecture. Going through this exercise helps us show that SVD is a special case of an autoencoder architecture, which sets the stage for understanding the gains obtained with more complex autoencoders.

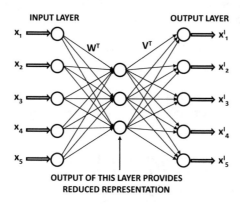

Figure 2.7: A basic autoencoder with a single layer

This neural architecture for SVD is illustrated in Figure 2.7, where the hidden layer contains k units. The rows of D are input into the autoencoder, whereas the k-dimensional rows of U are the activations of the hidden layer. The $k \times d$ matrix of weights in the decoder is V^T. As we discussed in the introduction to the multilayer neural network in Chapter 1, the vector of values in a particular layer of the network can be obtained by multiplying the vector of values in the previous layer with the matrix of weights connecting the two layers (with linear activation). Since the activations of the hidden layer are U and the decoder weights contain the matrix V^T, it follows that the reconstructed output contains the rows of UV^T. The autoencoder minimizes the sum-of-squared differences between the input and the output, which is equivalent to minimizing $||D - UV^T||^2$. Therefore, the same problem is being solved as singular value decomposition.

Note that one can use this approach to provide the reduced representation of *out-of-sample* instances that were not included in the original matrix D. One simply has to feed these out-of-sample rows as the input, and the activations of the hidden layer will provide the reduced representation. Reducing out-of-sample instances is particularly useful for nonlinear dimensionality-reduction methods, as it is more difficult for traditional machine learning methods to fold in new instances.

Encoder Weights

As shown in Figure 2.7, the encoder weights are contained in the $k \times d$ matrix denoted by W. How is this matrix related to U and V? Note that the autoencoder creates the reconstructed representation $DW^T V^T$ of the original data matrix. Therefore, it tries to optimize the problem of minimizing $||DW^T V^T - D||^2$. The optimal solution to this problem is obtained when the matrix W contains the *pseudo-inverse* of V, which is defined as follows:

$$W = (V^T V)^{-1} V^T \tag{2.39}$$

This result is easy to show at least for non-degenerate cases in which the rows of matrix D span the full rank of d dimensions (see Exercise 14). Of course, the final solution found by the training algorithm of the autoencoder might deviate from this condition because it might not solve the problem precisely or because the matrix D might be of smaller rank.

By the definition of the pseudo-inverse, it follows that $WV = I$ and $V^T W^T = I$, where I is a $k \times k$ identity matrix. Post-multiplying Equation 2.38 with W^T we obtain the following:

$$DW^T \approx U \underbrace{(V^T W^T)}_{I} = U \qquad (2.40)$$

In other words, multiplying each row of the matrix D with the $d \times k$ matrix W^T yields the reduced representation of that instance, which is the corresponding row in U. Furthermore, multiplying that row of U again with V^T yields the reconstructed version of the original data matrix D.

Note that there are many alternate optima for W and V, but in order for reconstruction to occur (i.e., minimization of loss function), the learned matrix W will always be (approximately) related to V as its pseudo-inverse and the columns of V will always span[3] a particular k-dimensional subspace defined by the SVD optimization problem.

2.5.1.2   Connections with Singular Value Decomposition

The single-layer autoencoder architecture is closely connected with singular value decomposition (SVD). Singular value decomposition finds a factorization UV^T in which the columns of V are orthonormal. The loss function of this neural network is identical to that of singular value decomposition, and a solution V in which the columns of V are orthonormal will always be one of the *possible* optima obtained by training the neural network. However, since this loss function allows alternative optima, it is possible to find an optimal solution in which the columns of V are not necessarily mutually orthogonal or scaled to unit norm. SVD is defined by an orthonormal basis system. Nevertheless, the subspace spanned by the k columns of V will be the same as that spanned by the top-k basis vectors of SVD. Principal component analysis is identical to singular value decomposition, except that it is applied to a mean-centered matrix D. Therefore, the approach can also be used to find the subspace spanned by the top-k principal components. However, each column of D needs to be mean-centered up front by subtracting its mean. One can achieve an orthonormal basis system, which is even closer to SVD and PCA by sharing some of the weights in the encoder and decoder. This approach is discussed in the next section.

2.5.1.3   Sharing Weights in Encoder and Decoder

There are many possible alternate solutions for W and V in the above discussion, in which W is the pseudo-inverse of V. One can, therefore, reduce the parameter footprint further without significant[4] loss in reconstruction accuracy. A common practice that is used in the autoencoder construction is to share some of the weights between the encoder and the

---

[3]This subspace is defined by the top-k singular vectors of singular value decomposition. However, the optimization problem does not impose orthogonality constraints, and therefore the columns of V might use a different non-orthogonal basis system to represent this subspace.

[4]There is no loss in reconstruction accuracy in several special cases like the single-layer case discussed here, even on the training data. In other cases, the loss of accuracy is only on the training data, but the autoencoder tends to better reconstruct out-of-sample data because of the regularization effects of parameter footprint reduction.

decoder. This is also referred to as *tying the weights*. In particular, the autoencoder has an inherently symmetric structure, in which the weights of the encoder and decoder are forced to be the same in symmetrically matching layers. In the shallow case, the encoder and decoder weights are shared by using the following relationship:

$$W = V^T \qquad (2.41)$$

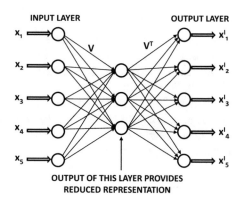

Figure 2.8: Basic autoencoder with a single layer; note tied weights (unlike the autoencoder shown in Figure 2.7).

This architecture is shown in Figure 2.8, and it is identical to the architecture of Figure 2.7 except for the presence of tied weights. In other words, the $d \times k$ matrix V of weights is first used to transform the d-dimensional data point $\overline{X}$ into a k-dimensional representation. Then, the matrix V^T of weights is used to reconstruct the data to its original representation.

The tying of the weights effectively means that V^T is the pseudo-inverse of V (see Exercise 14). In other words, we have $V^T V = I$, and therefore the columns of V are mutually orthogonal. As a result, by tying the weights, it is now possible to *exactly* simulate SVD, in which the different basis vectors need to be mutually orthogonal.

In this particular example of an architecture with a single hidden layer, the tying of weights is done only for a pair of weight matrices. In general, one would have an odd number of hidden layers and an even number of weight matrices. It is a common practice to match up the weight matrices in a symmetric way about the middle. In such a case, the symmetrically arranged hidden layers would need to have the same numbers of units. Even though it is not necessary to share weights between the encoder and decoder portions of the architecture, it reduces the number of parameters by a factor of 2. This is beneficial from the point of view of reducing overfitting. In other words, the approach would better reconstruct out-of-sample data. Another benefit of tying the weight matrices in the encoder and the decoder is that it automatically normalizes the columns of V to similar values. For example, if we do not tie the weight matrices in the encoder and the decoder, it is possible for the different columns of V to have very different norms. At least in the case of linear activations, tying the weight matrices forces all columns of V to have similar norms. This is also useful from the perspective of providing better normalization of the embedded representation. The normalization and orthogonality properties no longer hold exactly when nonlinear activations are used in the computational layers. However, there are considerable benefits in tying the weights even in these cases in terms of better conditioning of the solution.

The sharing of weights does require some changes to the backpropagation algorithm during training. However, these modifications are not very difficult. All that one has to do is to perform normal backpropagation by pretending that the weights are not tied in order to compute the gradients. Then, the gradients across different copies of the same weight are added in order to compute the gradient-descent steps. The logic for handing shared weights in this way is discussed in Section 3.2.9 of Chapter 3.

2.5.1.4   Other Matrix Factorization Methods

It is possible to modify the simple three-layer autoencoder to simulate other types of matrix factorization methods such as non-negative matrix factorization, probabilistic latent semantic analysis, and logistic matrix factorization methods. Different methods for logistic matrix factorization will be discussed in the next section, in Section 2.6.3, and in Exercise 8. Methods for non-negative matrix factorization and probabilistic latent semantic analysis are discussed in Exercises 9 and 10. It is instructive to examine the relationships between these different variations, because it shows how one can vary on simple neural architectures in order to get results with vastly different properties.

2.5.2   Nonlinear Activations

So far, the discussion has focussed on simulating singular value decomposition using a neural architecture. Clearly, this does not seem to achieve much because many off-the-shelf tools exist for singular value decomposition. However, the real power of autoencoders is realized when one starts using nonlinear activations and multiple layers. For example, consider a situation in which the matrix D is binary. In such a case, one can use the same neural architecture as shown in Figure 2.7, but one can also use a sigmoid function in the final layer to predict the output. This sigmoid layer is combined with negative log loss. Therefore, for a binary matrix $B = [b_{ij}]$, the model assumes the following:

$$B \sim \text{sigmoid}(UV^T) \qquad (2.42)$$

Here, the sigmoid function is applied in element-wise fashion. Note the use of $\sim$ instead of $\approx$ in the above expression, which indicates that the binary matrix B is an instantiation of random draws from Bernoulli distributions with corresponding parameters contained in sigmoid(UV^T). The resulting factorization can be shown to be equivalent to *logistic matrix factorization*. The basic idea is that the (i, j)th element of UV^T is the parameter of a Bernoulli distribution, and the binary entry b_{ij} is generated from a Bernoulli distribution with these parameters. Therefore, U and V are learned using the log-likelihood loss of this *generative* model. The log-likelihood loss implicitly tries to find parameter matrices U and V so that the probability of the matrix B being generated by these parameters is maximized.

Logistic matrix factorization has only recently been proposed [224] as a sophisticated matrix factorization method for binary data, which is useful for recommender systems with *implicit feedback* ratings. Implicit feedback refers to the binary actions of users such as buying or not buying specific items. The solution methodology of this recent work on logistic matrix factorization [224] seems to be vastly different from SVD, and it is not based on a neural network approach. However, for a neural network practitioner, the change from the SVD model to that of logistic matrix factorization is a relatively small one, where only the final layer of the neural network needs to be changed. It is this modular nature of neural networks that makes them so attractive to engineers and encourages all types of experimentation. In fact, one of the variants of the popular *word2vec* neural approach [325, 327] for text feature engineering is a logistic matrix factorization method, when one examines it more closely. Interestingly, *word2vec* was proposed earlier than logistic matrix factorization in traditional machine learning [224], although the equivalence of the two methods was not shown in the original work. The equivalence was first shown in [6], and a proof of this result is also provided later in this chapter. Indeed, for multilayer variants of the autoencoder,

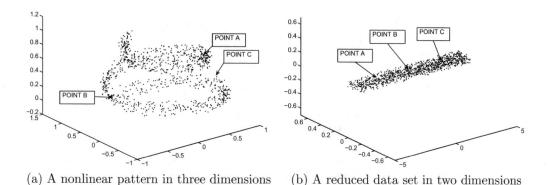

(a) A nonlinear pattern in three dimensions   (b) A reduced data set in two dimensions

Figure 2.9: The effect of nonlinear dimensionality reduction. This figure is drawn for illustrative purposes only.

an exact counterpart does not even exist in traditional machine learning. All this seems to suggest that it is often more natural to discover sophisticated machine learning algorithms when working with the modular approach of constructing multilayer neural networks. Note that one can even use this approach to factorize real-valued matrix entries drawn from $[0, 1]$, as long as the log-loss is suitably modified to handle fractional values (see Exercise 8). Logistic matrix factorization is a type of *kernel matrix factorization*.

One can also use non-linear activations in the hidden layer rather than (or in addition to) the output layer. By using the non-linearity in the hidden layer to impose non-negativity, one can simulate non-negative matrix factorization (cf. Exercises 9 and 10). Furthermore, consider an autoencoder with a single hidden layer in which sigmoid units are used in the hidden layer, and the output layer is linear. Furthermore, the input-to-hidden and the hidden-to-output matrices are denoted by W^T and V^T, respectively. In this case, the matrix W will no longer be the pseudo-inverse of V because of the non-linear activation in the hidden layer.

If U is the output of the hidden layer in which the nonlinear activation $\Phi(\cdot)$ is applied, we have:

$$U = \Phi(DW^T) \tag{2.43}$$

If the output layer is linear, the overall factorization is still of the following form:

$$D \approx UV^T \tag{2.44}$$

Note, however, that we can write $U' = DW^T$, which is a linear projection of the original matrix D. Then, the factorization can be written as follows:

$$D \approx \Phi(U')V^T \tag{2.45}$$

Here, U' is a linear projection of D. This is a different type of nonlinear matrix factorization [521, 558]. Although the specific form of the nonlinearity (e.g., sigmoid) might seem simplistic compared to what is considered typical in kernel methods, in reality multiple hidden layers are used to learn more complex forms of nonlinear dimensionality reduction. Nonlinearity can also be combined in the hidden layers and in the output layer. Nonlinear dimensionality reduction methods can map the data into much lower dimensional spaces

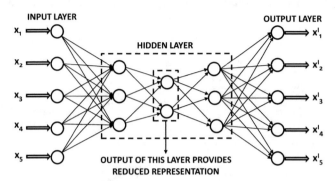

Figure 2.10: An example of an autoencoder with three hidden layers. Combining nonlinear activations with multiple hidden layers increases the representation power of the network.

(with good reconstruction characteristics) than would be possible with methods like PCA. An example of a data set, which is distributed on a nonlinear spiral, is shown in Figure 2.9(a). This data set cannot be reduced to lower dimensionality using PCA (without causing significant reconstruction error). However, the use of nonlinear dimensionality reduction methods can flatten out the nonlinear spiral into a 2-dimensional representation. This representation is shown in Figure 2.9(b).

Nonlinear dimensionality-reduction methods often require deeper networks due to the more complex transformations possible with the combination of nonlinear units. The benefits of depth will be discussed in the next section.

2.5.3   Deep Autoencoders

The real power of autoencoders in the neural network domain is realized when deeper variants are used. For example, an autoencoder with three hidden layers is shown in Figure 2.10. One can increase the number of intermediate layers in order to further increase the representation power of the neural network. It is noteworthy that it is essential for some of the layers of the deep autoencoder to use a nonlinear activation function to increase its representation power. As shown in Lemma 1.5.1 of Chapter 1, no additional power is gained by a multilayer network when only linear activations are used. Although this result was shown in Chapter 1 for the classification problem, it is broadly true for any type of multilayer neural network (including an autoencoder).

Deep networks with multiple layers provide an extraordinary amount of representation power. The multiple layers of this network provide *hierarchically* reduced representations of the data. For some data domains like images, hierarchically reduced representations are particularly natural. Note that there is no precise analog of this type of model in traditional machine learning, and the backpropagation approach rescues us from the challenges associated in computing the complicated gradient-descent steps. A nonlinear dimensionality reduction might map a manifold of arbitrary shape into a reduced representation. Although several methods for nonlinear dimensionality reduction are known in machine learning, neural networks have some advantages over these methods:

1. Many nonlinear dimensionality reduction methods have a very hard time mapping out-of-sample data points to reduced representations, unless these points are included in the training data up front. On the other hand, it is a relatively simple matter to

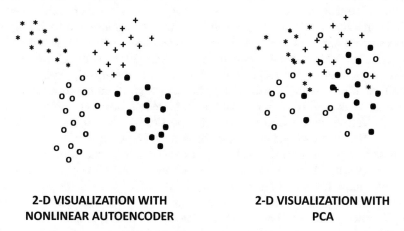

2-D VISUALIZATION WITH NONLINEAR AUTOENCODER

2-D VISUALIZATION WITH PCA

Figure 2.11: A depiction of the typical difference between the embeddings created by nonlinear autoencoders and principal component analysis (PCA). Nonlinear and deep autoencoders are often able to separate out the entangled class structures in the underlying data, which is not possible within the constraints of linear transformations like PCA. This occurs because individual classes are often populated on curved manifolds in the original space, which would appear mixed when looking at a data in any 2-dimensional cross-section unless one is willing to warp the space itself. The figure above is drawn for illustrative purposes only and does not represent a specific data set.

   compute the reduced representation of an out-of-sample point by passing it through the network.

2. Neural networks allow more power and flexibility in the nonlinear data reduction by varying on the number and type of layers used in intermediate stages. Furthermore, by choosing specific types of activation functions in particular layers, one can engineer the nature of the reduction to the properties of the data. For example, it makes sense to use a logistic output layer with logarithmic loss for a binary data set.

It is possible to achieve extraordinarily compact reductions by using this approach. For example, the work in [198] shows how one can convert a 784-dimensional representation of the pixels of an image into a 6-dimensional reduction with the use of deep autoencoders. Greater reduction is always achieved by using nonlinear units, which implicitly map warped manifolds into linear hyperplanes. The superior reduction in these cases is because it is easier to thread a warped surface (as opposed to a linear surface) through a larger number of points. This property of nonlinear autoencoders is often used for 2-dimensional visualizations of the data by creating a deep autoencoder in which the most compact hidden layer has only two dimensions. These two dimensions can then be mapped on a plane to visualize the points. In many cases, the class structure of the data is exposed in terms of well-separated clusters.

An illustrative example of the typical behavior of real data distributions is shown in Figure 2.11, in which the 2-dimensional mapping created by a deep autoencoder seems to clearly separate out the different classes. On the other hand, the mapping created by PCA does not seem to separate the classes well. Figure 2.9, which provides a nonlinear spiral mapped to a linear hyperplane, clarifies the reason for this behavior. In many cases, the data may contain heavily entangled spirals (or other shapes) that belong to different classes. Linear dimensionality reduction methods cannot attain clear separation because nonlinearly entangled shapes are not linearly separable. On the other hand, deep autoencoders with nonlinearity are far more powerful and able to disentangle such shapes. Deep autoencoders can sometimes be used as alternatives to other robust visualization methods like t-distributed stochastic neighbor embedding (t-SNE) [305]. Although t-SNE can often provide better performance[5] for visualization (because it is specifically designed for visualization rather than dimensionality reduction), the advantage of an autoencoder over t-SNE is that it is easier to generalize to out-of-sample data. When new data points are received, they can simply be passed through the encoder portion of the autoencoder in order to add them to the current set of visualized points. A specific example of a visualization of a high-dimensional document collection with an autoencoder is provided in [198].

It is, however, possible to go too far and create representations that are not useful. For example, one can compress a very high-dimensional data point into a single dimension, which reconstructs a point from the training data very well but gives high reconstruction error for test data. In other words, the neural network has found a way to memorize the data set without sufficient ability to create reduced representations of unseen points. Therefore, even for unsupervised problems like dimensionality reduction, it is important to keep aside some points as a *validation set*. The points in the validation set are not used during training. One can then quantify the difference in reconstruction error between the training and validation data. Large differences in reconstruction error between the training and validation data are indicative of overfitting. Another issue is that deep networks are harder to train, and therefore tricks like *pretraining* are important. These tricks will be discussed in Chapters 3 and 4.

2.5.4 Application to Outlier Detection

Dimensionality reduction is closely related to outlier detection, because outlier points are hard to encode and decode without losing substantial information. It is a well-known fact that if a matrix D is factorized as $D \approx D' = UV^T$, then the low-rank matrix D' is a de-noised representative of the data. After all, the compressed representation U captures only the regularities in the data, and is unable to capture the unusual variations in specific points. As a result, reconstruction to D' misses all these unusual variations.

The absolute values of the entries of $(D - D')$ represent the outlier scores of the matrix entries. Therefore, one can use this approach to find outlier entries, or add the squared scores of the entries in each row of D to find the outlier score of that row. Therefore, one can identify outlier data points. Furthermore, by adding the squared scores in each column of D, one can find outlier features. This is useful for applications like feature selection in clustering, where a feature with a large outlier score can be removed because it adds noise to the clustering. Although we have provided the description above with the use of matrix factorization, any type of autoencoder can be used. In fact, the construction of de-noising autoencoders is a vibrant field in its own right. Refer to the bibliographic notes.

---

[5]The t-SNE method works on the principle is that it is impossible to preserve all pairwise similarities and dissimilarities with the same level of accuracy in a low-dimensional embedding. Therefore, unlike dimensionality reduction or autoencoders that try to faithfully reconstruct the data, it has an asymmetric loss function in terms of how similarity is treated versus dissimilarity. This type of asymmetric loss function is particularly helpful for separating out different manifolds during visualization. Therefore, t-SNE might perform better than autoencoders at visualization.

2.5.5   When the Hidden Layer Is Broader than the Input Layer

So far, we have only discussed cases in which the hidden layer has fewer units than the input layer. It makes sense for the hidden layer to have fewer units than the input layer when one is looking for a compressed representation of the data. A constricted hidden layer forces dimensionality reduction, and the loss function is designed to avoid information loss. Such representations are referred to as *undercomplete representations*, and they correspond to the traditional use-case of autoencoders.

What about the case when the number of hidden units is greater than the input dimensionality? This situation corresponds to the case of *over-complete representations*. Increasing the number of hidden units beyond the number of input units makes it possible for the hidden layer to simply learn the identity function (with zero loss). Simply copying the input across the layers does not seem to be particularly useful. However, this does not occur in practice (while learning weights), especially if certain types of regularization and *sparsity constraints* are imposed on the hidden layer. Even if no sparsity constraints are imposed, and stochastic gradient descent is used for learning, the probabilistic regularization caused by stochastic gradient descent is sufficient to ensure that the hidden representation will always scramble the input before reconstructing it at the output. This is because stochastic gradient descent is a type of noise addition to the learning process, and therefore it will not be possible to learn weights that simply copy input to output as identity functions across layers. Furthermore, because of some peculiarities of the training process, a neural network almost never uses its full modeling ability, which leads to dependencies among the weights [94]. Rather, an over-complete representation may be created, although it may not have the property of sparsity (which needs to be explicitly encouraged). The next section will discuss ways of encouraging sparsity.

2.5.5.1   Sparse Feature Learning

When explicit sparsity constraints are imposed, the resulting autoencoder is referred to as a *sparse autoencoder*. A sparse representation of a d-dimensional point is a k-dimensional point in which $k \gg d$ and most of the values in the sparse representation are 0s. Sparse feature learning has tremendous applicability to many settings like image data, where the learned features are often intuitively more interpretable from an application-specific perspective. Furthermore, points with a variable amount of information will be naturally represented by having varying numbers of nonzero feature values. This type of property is naturally true in some *input* representations like documents; documents with more information will have more non-zero features (word frequencies) when represented in multidimensional format. However, if the available input is not sparse to begin with, there are often benefits in creating a sparse transformation where such a flexibility of representation exists. Sparse representations also enable the effective use of particular types of efficient algorithms that are highly dependent on sparsity. There are many ways in which constraints might be enforced on the hidden layer to create sparsity. One approach is to add biases to the hidden layer, so that many units are encouraged to be zeros. Some examples are as follows:

1. One can impose an L_1-penalty on the activations in the hidden layer to force sparse activations. The notion of L_1-penalties for creating sparse solutions (in terms of either weights or hidden units) is discussed in Sections 4.4.2 and 4.4.4 of Chapter 4. In such a case, backpropagation must also propagate the gradient of this penalty in the backwards direction. Surprisingly, this natural alternative is rarely used.

2. One can allow only the top-r activations in the hidden layer to be nonzero for $r \leq k$. In such a case, backpropagation only backpropagates through the activated units. This approach is referred to as the r-sparse autoencoder [309].

3. Another approach is the *winner-take-all* autoencoder [310], in which only a fraction f of the activations of *each* hidden unit are allowed over the *whole training data*. In this case, the top activations are computed across training examples, whereas in the previous case the top activations are computed across a hidden layer for a single training example. Therefore node-specific thresholds need to be estimated using the statistics of a minibatch. The backpropagation algorithm needs to propagate the gradient only through the activated units.

Note that the implementations of the competitive mechanisms are almost like ReLU activations with adaptive thresholds. Refer to the bibliographic notes for pointers and more details of these algorithms.

2.5.6   Other Applications

Autoencoders form the workhorse of unsupervised learning in the neural network domain. They are used for a host of applications, which will be discussed later in the book. After training an autoencoder, it is not necessary to use both the encoder and decoder portions. For example, when using the approach for dimensionality reduction, one can use the encoder portion in order to create the reduced representations of the data. The reconstructions of the decoder might not be required at all.

Although an autoencoder naturally removes noise (like almost any dimensionality reduction method), one can enhance the ability of the autoencoder to remove specific types of noise. To perform the training of a *de-noising autoencoder*, a special type of training is used. First, some noise is added to the training data before passing it through the neural network. The distribution of the added noise reflects the analyst's understanding of the natural types of noise in that particular data domain. However, the loss is computed with respect to the *original* training data instances rather than their corrupted versions. The original training data are relatively clean, although one expects the test instances to be corrupted. Therefore, the autoencoder learns to recover clean representations from corrupted data. A common approach to add noise is to randomly set a fraction f of the inputs to zeros [506]. This approach is especially effective when the inputs are binary. The value of f regulates the level of corruption in the inputs. One can either fix f or even allow f to randomly vary over different training instances. In some cases, when the input is real-valued, Gaussian noise is also used. More details of the de-noising autoencoder are provided in Section 4.10.2 of Chapter 4. A closely related autoencoder is the *contractive autoencoder*, which is discussed in Section 4.10.3.

Another interesting application of the autoencoder is one in which we use only the *decoder* portion of the network to create artistic renderings. This idea is based on the notion of *variational autoencoders* [242, 399], in which the loss function is modified to impose a specific structure on the hidden layer. For example, one might add a term to the loss function to enforce the fact that the hidden variables are drawn from a Gaussian distribution. Then, one might repeatedly draw samples from this Gaussian distribution and use only the decoder portion of the network in order to generate samples of the original data. The generated samples often represent realistic samples from the original data distribution.

A closely related model is that of *generative adversarial networks*, which have become increasingly popular in recent years. These models pair the learning of a decoding network with that of an adversarial discriminator in order to create generative samples of a data set. Generative adversarial networks are used frequently with image, video, and text data, and they generate artistic renderings of images and videos, which often have the flavor of an AI that is "dreaming." These methods can be used for image-to-image translation as well. The variational autoencoder is discussed in detail in Section 4.10.4 of Chapter 4. Generative adversarial networks are discussed in Section 10.4 of Chapter 10.

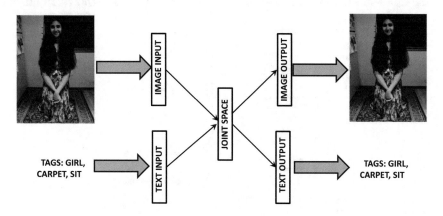

Figure 2.12: Multimodal embedding with autoencoders

One can use an autoencoder for embedding multimodal data in a joint latent space. Multimodal data is essentially data in which the input features are heterogeneous. For example, an image with descriptive tags can be considered multimodal data. Multimodal data pose challenges to mining applications because different features require different types of processing and treatment. By embedding the heterogeneous attributes in a unified space, one is removing this source of difficulty in the mining process. An autoencoder can be used to embed the heterogeneous data into a joint space. An example of such a setting is shown in Figure 2.12. This figure shows an autoencoder with only a single layer, although one might have multiple layers in general [357, 468]. Such joint spaces can be very useful in a variety of applications.

Finally, autoencoders are used to improve the learning process in neural networks. A specific example is that of *pretraining* in which an autoencoder is used to initialize the weights of a neural network. The basic idea is that learning the manifold structure of a data set is also useful for supervised learning applications like classification. This is because the features that define the manifold of a data set are often likely to be more informative in terms of their relationships to different classes. Pretraining methods are discussed in Section 4.7 of Chapter 4.

2.5.7 Recommender Systems: Row Index to Row Value Prediction

One of the most interesting applications of matrix factorization is the design of neural architectures for recommender systems. Consider an $n \times d$ ratings matrix D with n users and d items. The (i,j)th entry of the matrix is the rating of user i for item j. However, most entries in the matrix are not specified, which creates difficulties in using a traditional autoencoder architecture. This is because traditional autoencoders are designed for fully specified matrices, in which a single *row* of the matrix is input at one time. On the other hand, recommender systems are inherently suited to *elementwise* learning, in which a very small subset of ratings from a row may be available. As a practical matter, one might consider the input to a recommender system as a set of triplets of the following form:

$$\langle \text{RowId} \rangle, \langle\ \text{ColumnId}\ \rangle, \langle\ \text{Rating}\ \rangle$$

As in traditional forms of matrix factorization, the ratings matrix D is given by UV^T. However, the difference is that one must learn U and V using triplet-centric input because

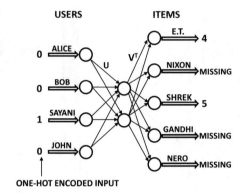

Figure 2.13: Row-index-to-value encoder for matrix factorization with missing values.

all entries of D are not observed. Therefore, a natural approach is to create an architecture in which the inputs are not affected by the missing entries and can be uniquely specified. The input layer contains n input units, which is the same as the number of rows (users). However, the input is a one-hot encoded index of the row identifier. Therefore, only one entry of the input takes on the value of 1, with the remaining entries taking on values of 0. The hidden layer contains k units, where k is the rank of the factorization. Finally, the output layer contains d units, where d is the number of columns (items). The output is a vector containing the d ratings (even though only a small subset of them are observed). The goal is to train the neural network with an incomplete data matrix D so that the network outputs all the ratings corresponding to a one-hot encoded row index after it is input. The approach is to be able to reconstruct the data by learning the ratings associated with each row index.

Consider a setting in which the $n \times k$ input-to-hidden matrix is U, and the $k \times d$ hidden-to-output matrix is V^T. The entries of the matrix U are denoted by u_{iq}, and those of the matrix V are denoted by v_{jq}. Assume that all activation functions are linear. Furthermore, let the one-hot encoded input (row) vector for the rth user be $\overline{e}_r$. This row vector contains n dimensions in which only the rth value is 1, and the remaining values are zeros. The loss function is the sum of the squares of the errors in the output layer. However, because of the missing entries, not all output nodes have an observed output value, and the updates are performed only with respect to entries that are known. The overall architecture of this neural network is illustrated in Figure 2.13. For any particular row-wise input we are really training on a neural network that is a subset of this base network, depending on which entries are specified. However, it is possible to give *predictions* for all outputs in the network (even though a loss function cannot be computed for missing entries). Since a neural network with linear activations performs matrix multiplications, it is easy to see that the vector of d outputs for the rth user is given by $\overline{e}_r U V^T$. In essence, pre-multiplication with $\overline{e}_r$ pulls out the rth row in the matrix $U V^T$. These values appear at the output layer and represent the item-wise ratings predictions for the rth user. Therefore, all feature values are reconstructed in one shot.

How is training performed? The main attraction of this architecture is that one can perform the training either in row-wise fashion or in element-wise fashion. When performing the training in row-wise fashion, the one-hot encoded index for that row is input, and all *specified* entries of that row are used to compute the loss. The backpropagation algorithm is

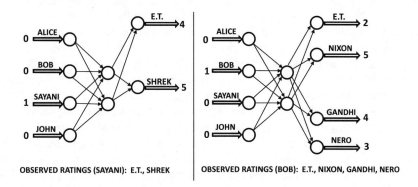

OBSERVED RATINGS (SAYANI): E.T., SHREK | OBSERVED RATINGS (BOB): E.T., NIXON, GANDHI, NERO

Figure 2.14: Dropping output nodes based on missing values. Output nodes are missing only at training time. At prediction time, all output nodes are materialized. One can achieve similar results with an RBM architecture as well (cf. Figure 6.5 of Chapter 6).

done only starting at output nodes where the values are specified. From a theoretical point of view, each row is being trained on a slightly different neural network with a subset of the base output nodes (depending on which entries are observed), although the weights for the different neural networks are shared. This situation is shown in Figure 2.14, where the neural networks for the movie ratings of two different users, Bob and Sayani, are shown. For example, Bob is missing a rating for *Shrek*, as a result of which the corresponding output node is missing. However, since both users have specified a rating for *E.T.*, the k-dimensional hidden factors for this movie in matrix V will be updated during backpropagation when either Bob or Sayani is processed. This ability to train using only a subset of the output nodes is sometimes used as an efficiency optimization to reduce training time even in cases where all outputs are specified. Such situations occur often in binary recommendation data sets (referred to as *implicit feedback data sets*), where the vast majority of outputs are zeros. In such cases, only a subset of zeros is sampled for training in matrix factorization methods [4]. This technique is referred to as *negative sampling*. A specific example is that of neural models for natural language processing like *word2vec*.

It is also possible to perform the training in element-wise fashion, where a single triplet is input. In such a case, the loss is computed only with respect to a single column index specified in the triplet. Consider the case where the row index is i, and the column index is j. In this specific case, and the single error computed at the output layer is $y - \hat{y} = e_{ij}$. the backpropagation algorithm essentially updates the weights on all the k paths from node j in the output layer to the node i in the input layer. These k paths pass through the k nodes in the hidden layer. It is easy to show that the update along the qth such path is as follows:

$$u_{iq} \Leftarrow u_{iq}(1 - \alpha\lambda) + \alpha e_{ij}v_{jq}$$
$$v_{jq} \Leftarrow v_{jq}(1 - \alpha\lambda) + \alpha e_{ij}u_{iq}$$

Here, α is the step-size, and λ is the regularization parameter. *These updates are identical to those used in stochastic gradient descent for matrix factorization in recommender systems.* However, an important advantage of the use of the neural architecture (over traditional matrix factorization) is that we can vary on it in so many different ways in order to enforce different properties. For example, for matrices with binary data, we can use a logistic layer in the output. This will result in *logistic matrix factorization.* We can incorporate multiple hidden layers to create more powerful models. For matrices with categorical entries (and count-centric weights attached to entries), one can use a softmax layer at the very end. This will result in *multinomial matrix factorization.* To date, we are not aware of a formal description of multinomial matrix factorization in traditional machine learning; yet, it is a simple modification of the neural architecture (implicitly) used by recommender systems. In general, it is often easy to stumble upon sophisticated models when working with neural architectures because of their modular structure. One does not need to relate the neural architecture to a conventional machine learning model, as long as empirical results establish its robustness. For example, two variations of the (highly successful) skip-gram model of *word2vec* [325, 327] correspond to logistic and multinomial matrix factorizations of word-context matrices; yet, this fact does not seem to be pointed[6] out by either by the original authors of *word2vec* [325, 327] or the broader community. In conventional machine learning, models like logistic matrix factorization are considered relatively esoteric techniques that have only recently been proposed [224]; yet, these sophisticated models represent relatively simple neural architectures. In general, the neural network abstraction brings practitioners (without too much mathematical training) much closer to sophisticated methods in machine learning, while being shielded from the details of optimization with the backpropagation framework.

2.5.8 Discussion

The main goal of this section was to show the benefits of the modular nature of neural networks in unsupervised learning. In our particular example, we started with a simple simulation of SVD, and then showed how minor changes to the neural architecture can achieve very different types of goals in intuitive settings. However, from an architectural point of view, the amount of effort required by the analyst to change from one architecture to the other is often a few lines of code. This is because modern softwares for building neural networks often provide templates for describing the architecture of the neural network, where each layer is specified independently. In a sense, the neural network is "built" with the well-known types of machine-learning units much like a child puts together building blocks of a toy. Backpropagation takes care of the details of optimization, while shielding the user from the complexities of the steps. Consider the significant mathematical differences between the specific details of SVD and logistic matrix factorization. Changing the output layer from linear to sigmoid (along with a change of loss function) can literally be a matter of changing a trivially small number of lines of code without affecting most of the remaining code (which usually isn't large anyway). This type of modularity is tremendously useful in application-centric settings. Autoencoders are also related to another type of unsupervised learning method, known as a Restricted Boltzmann Machines (RBM) (cf. Chapter 6). These methods can also be used for recommender systems, as discussed in Section 6.5.2 of Chapter 6.

---

[6]The work in [287] does point out a number of *implicit* relationships with matrix factorization, but not the more direct ones pointed out in this book. Some of these relationships are also pointed out in [6].

2.6 Word2vec: An Application of Simple Neural Architectures

Neural network methods have been used to learn word embeddings of text data. In general, one can create embeddings of both documents and words by using methods like SVD. In SVD, an $n \times d$ matrix of document-word counts is created. This matrix is then factorized as $D \approx UV$. Here, U and V are $n \times k$ and $k \times d$ matrices, respectively. The rows of U contain embeddings of documents and the columns of V contain embeddings of words. Note that we have changed the notation slightly from the previous section (by using UV instead of UV^T for factorization), because it is more convenient for this section.

SVD is, however, a method that treats a document as a bag of words. Here, we are interested in factorizations that use the sequential orderings among words to create embeddings. The focus here is to create *word* embeddings rather than *document* embeddings. The family of *word2vec* methods is well suited to creating word embeddings. The two variants of *word2vec* are as follows:

1. *Predicting target words from contexts:* This model tries to predict the ith word, w_i, in a sentence using a window of width t around the word. Therefore, the words $w_{i-t}w_{i-t+1} \ldots w_{i-1}w_{i+1} \ldots w_{i+t-1}w_{i+t}$ are used to predict the target word w_i. This model is also referred to as the *continuous bag-of-words (CBOW) model.*

2. *Predicting contexts from target words:* This model tries to predict the context $w_{i-t}w_{i-t+1} \ldots w_{i-1}w_{i+1} \ldots w_{i+t-1}w_{i+t}$ around word w_i, given the ith word in the sentence, denoted by w_i. This model is referred to as the *skip-gram model*. There are, however, two ways in which one can perform this prediction. The first technique is a *multinomial* model which predicts one word out of d outcomes. The second model is a Bernoulli model, which predicts whether or not each context is present for a particular word. The second model uses *negative sampling* of contexts for better efficiency and accuracy.

Each of these methods will be discussed in this section.

2.6.1 Neural Embedding with Continuous Bag of Words

In the continuous bag-of-words (CBOW) model, the training pairs are all context-word pairs in which a window of context words is input, and a single target word is predicted. The context contains $2 \cdot t$ words, corresponding to t words both before and after the target word. For notational ease, we will use the length $m = 2 \cdot t$ to define the length of the context. Therefore, the input to the system is a set of m words. Without loss of generality, let the subscripts of these words be numbered so that they are denoted by $w_1 \ldots w_m$, and let the target (output) word in the middle of the context window be denoted by w. Note that w can be viewed as a categorical variable with d possible values, where d is the size of the lexicon. The goal of the neural embedding is to compute the probability $P(w|w_1w_2 \ldots w_m)$ and maximize the product of these probabilities over all training samples.

The overall architecture of this model is illustrated in Figure 2.15. In the architecture, we have a single input layer with $m \times d$ nodes, a hidden layer with p nodes, and an output layer with d nodes. The nodes in the input layer are clustered into m different groups, each of which has d units. Each group with d input units is the one-hot encoded input vector of one of the m context words being modeled by CBOW. Only one of these d inputs will be 1 and the remaining inputs will be 0. Therefore, one can represent an input x_{ij} with two indices corresponding to contextual position and word identifier. Specifically, the input $x_{ij} \in \{0, 1\}$ contains two indices i and j in the subscript, where $i \in \{1 \ldots m\}$ is the position of the context, and $j \in \{1 \ldots d\}$ is the identifier of the word.

The hidden layer contains p units, where p is the dimensionality of the hidden layer in *word2vec*. Let $h_1, h_2, \ldots h_p$ be the outputs of the hidden layer nodes. Note that each of the d words in the lexicon has m different representatives in the input layer corresponding to the m different context words, but the weight of each of these m connections is the same. Such

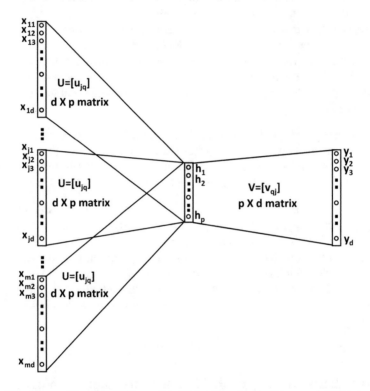

Figure 2.15: Word2vec: The CBOW model. Note the similarities and differences with Figure 2.13, which uses a single set of inputs with a linear output layer. One could also choose to collapse the m sets of d input nodes into a single set of d inputs, and aggregate the m one-hot encoded inputs in a single context window to achieve the same effect. In such a case, the input is no longer one-hot encoded.

weights are referred to as shared. Sharing weights is a common trick used for regularization in neural networks, when one has specific insight about the domain at hand. Let the shared weight of each connection from the jth word in the lexicon to the qth hidden layer node be denoted by u_{jq}. Note that each of the m groups in the input layer has connections to the hidden layer that are defined by the same $d \times p$ weight matrix U. This situation is shown in Figure 2.15.

It is noteworthy that $\overline{u}_j = (u_{j1}, u_{j2}, \ldots u_{jp})$ can be viewed as the p-dimensional embedding of the jth input word over the entire corpus, and $\overline{h} = (h_1 \ldots h_p)$ provides the embedding of a specific instantiation of an input context. Then, the output of the hidden layer is obtained by averaging the embeddings of the words present in the context. In other words, we have the following:

$$h_q = \sum_{i=1}^{m} \left[\sum_{j=1}^{d} u_{jq} x_{ij} \right] \qquad \forall q \in \{1 \dots p\} \tag{2.46}$$

Many expositions use an additional factor of m in the denominator on the right-hand side, although this type of multiplicative scaling (with a constant) is inconsequential. One can also write this relationship in vector form:

$$\overline{h} = \sum_{i=1}^{m} \sum_{j=1}^{d} \overline{u}_j x_{ij} \tag{2.47}$$

In essence, the one-hot encodings of the input words are aggregated, which implies that the ordering of the words within the window of size m does not affect the output of the model. This is the reason that the model is referred to as the continuous bag-of-words model. However, sequential information is still used by virtue of restricting the prediction to a context window.

The embedding $(h_1 \dots h_p)$ is used to predict the probability that the target word is one of each of the d outputs with the use of the softmax function. The weights in the output layer are parameterized with a $p \times d$ matrix $V = [v_{qj}]$. The jth column of V is denoted by $\overline{v}_j$. The output after applying softmax creates d output values $\hat{y}_1 \dots \hat{y}_d$, which are real values in $(0, 1)$. These real values sum to 1 because they can be interpreted as probabilities. The *ground-truth* value of only one of the outputs $y_1 \dots y_d$ is 1 and the remaining values are 0 for a given training instance. One can write this condition as follows:

$$y_j = \begin{cases} 1 & \text{if the target word } w \text{ is the } j\text{th word} \\ 0 & \text{otherwise} \end{cases} \tag{2.48}$$

The softmax function computes the probability $P(w|w_1 \dots w_m)$ of the one-hot encoded ground-truth outputs y_j as follows:

$$\hat{y}_j = P(y_j = 1|w_1 \dots w_m) = \frac{\exp(\sum_{q=1}^{p} h_q v_{qj})}{\sum_{k=1}^{d} \exp(\sum_{q=1}^{p} h_q v_{qk})} \tag{2.49}$$

Note that this probabilistic form of the prediction is based on the softmax layer (cf. Section 1.2.1.4 of Chapter 1). For a particular target word $w = r \in \{1 \dots d\}$, the loss function is given by $L = -\log[P(y_r = 1|w_1 \dots w_m)] = -\log(\hat{y}_r)$. The use of the negative logarithm turns the multiplicative likelihoods over different training instances into an additive loss function using log-likelihoods.

The updates are defined by using the backpropagation algorithm, as training instances are passed through the neural network one by one. First, the derivative of the aforementioned loss function can be used to update the gradients of the weight matrix V in the output layer. Then, backpropagation can be used to update the weight matrix U between the input and hidden layer. The update equations with learning rate α are as follows:

$$\overline{u}_i \Leftarrow \overline{u}_i - \alpha \frac{\partial L}{\partial \overline{u}_i} \quad \forall i$$

$$\overline{v}_j \Leftarrow \overline{v}_j - \alpha \frac{\partial L}{\partial \overline{v}_j} \quad \forall j$$

One can compute the partial derivatives of this expression easily [325, 327, 404].

The probability of making a mistake in prediction on the jth word in the lexicon is defined by $|y_j - \hat{y}_j|$. However, we use *signed* mistakes ϵ_j, in which only the correct word with $y_j = 1$ is given a positive mistake value, while all the other words in the lexicon receive negative mistake values. This is achieved by dropping the modulus:

$$\epsilon_j = y_j - \hat{y}_j \tag{2.50}$$

Note that ϵ_j can also be shown to be equal to the negative of the derivative of the cross-entropy loss with respect to jth input into the softmax layer (which is $\overline{h} \cdot \overline{v}_j$). This result is shown in Section 3.2.5.1 of the next chapter and is useful in deriving the backpropagation updates. Then, the updates[7] for a particular input context and output word are as follows:

$$\overline{u}_i \Leftarrow \overline{u}_i + \alpha \sum_{j=1}^{d} \epsilon_j \overline{v}_j \quad [\forall \text{ words } i \text{ present in context window}]$$

$$\overline{v}_j \Leftarrow \overline{v}_j + \alpha \epsilon_j \overline{h} \quad [\forall j \text{ in lexicon}]$$

Here, $\alpha > 0$ is the learning rate. Repetitions of the same word i in the context window trigger multiple updates of $\overline{u}_i$. It is noteworthy that the input embeddings of the context words are aggregated in both updates, considering the fact that $\overline{h}$ aggregates input embeddings according to Equation 2.47. This type of aggregation has a smoothing effect on the CBOW model, which is particularly helpful with smaller data sets.

The training examples of context-target pairs are presented one by one, and the weights are trained to convergence. It is noteworthy that the *word2vec* model provides not one but two different embeddings corresponding to the p-dimensional rows of the matrix U and the p-dimensional columns of the matrix V. The former type of embedding of words is referred to as the *input* embedding, whereas the latter is referred to as the *output* embedding. In the CBOW model, the input embedding represents context, and therefore it makes sense to use the output embedding. However, the input embedding (or the sum/concatenation of input and output embeddings) can also be helpful for many tasks.

2.6.2   Neural Embedding with Skip-Gram Model

In the skip-gram model, the target words are used to predict the m context words. Therefore, we have one input word and m outputs. One issue with the CBOW model is that the averaging effect of the input words in the context window (which creates the hidden representation) has a (helpful) smoothing effect with less data, but fails to take full advantage of a larger amount of data. The skip-gram model is the technique of choice when a large amount of data is available.

The skip-gram model uses a single target word w as the input and outputs the m context words denoted by $w_1 \ldots w_m$. Therefore, the goal is to estimate $P(w_1, w_2, \ldots w_m | w)$, which is different from the quantity $P(w | w_1 \ldots w_m)$ estimated in the CBOW model. As in the case of the continuous bag-of-words model, we can use one-hot encoding of the (categorical) input and outputs in the skip-gram model. After such an encoding, the skip-gram model will have d binary inputs denoted by $x_1 \ldots x_d$ corresponding to the d possible values of the single input word. Similarly, the output of each training instance is encoded as $m \times d$ values $y_{ij} \in \{0, 1\}$, where i ranges from 1 to m (size of context window), and j ranges

---

[7]There is a slight abuse of notation in the updates adding $\overline{u}_i$ and $\overline{v}_j$. This is because $\overline{u}_i$ is a row vector and $\overline{v}_j$ is a column vector. Throughout this section, we omit the explicit transposition of one of these two vectors to avoid notational clutter, since the updates are intuitively clear.

from 1 to d (lexicon size). Each $y_{ij} \in \{0, 1\}$ indicates whether the ith contextual word takes on the jth possible value for that training instance. However, the (i, j)th output node only computes a soft probability value $\hat{y}_{ij} = P(y_{ij} = 1|w)$. Therefore, the probabilities $\hat{y}_{ij}$ in the output layer for fixed i and varying j sum to 1, since the ith contextual position takes on exactly one of the d words. The hidden layer contains p units, the outputs are denoted by $h_1 \ldots h_p$. Each input x_j is connected to all the hidden nodes with a $d \times p$ matrix U. Furthermore, the p hidden nodes are connected to each of the m groups of d output nodes with the same set of shared weights. This set of shared weights between the p hidden nodes and the d output nodes of each of the context words is defined by the $p \times d$ matrix V. Note that the input-output structure of the skip-gram model is an inverted version of the input-output structure of the CBOW model. The neural architecture of the skip-gram model is illustrated in Figure 2.16(a). However, in the case of the skip-gram model, one can collapse the m identical outputs into a single output, and achieve the same results simply by using a *particular type of mini-batching* during stochastic gradient descent. In particular, all elements of a single context window are always forced to belong to the same mini-batch. This architecture is shown in Figure 2.16(b). Since the value of m is small, this specific type of mini-batching has a very limited effect, and the simplified architecture of Figure 2.16(b) is sufficient to describe the model whether or not any specific type of mini-batching is used. For the purpose of further discussion, we will use the architecture of Figure 2.16(a).

The output of the hidden layer can be computed from the input layer using the $d \times p$ matrix of weights $U = [u_{jq}]$ between the input and hidden layer as follows:

$$h_q = \sum_{j=1}^{d} u_{jq} x_j \quad \forall q \in \{1 \ldots p\} \tag{2.51}$$

The above equation has a simple interpretation because of the one-hot encoding of the input word w in terms of $x_1 \ldots x_d$. If the input word w is the rth word, then one simply copies u_{rq} to the qth node of the hidden layer for each $q \in \{1 \ldots p\}$. In other words, the rth row $\overline{u}_r$ of U is copied to the hidden layer. As discussed above, the hidden layer is connected to m groups of d output nodes, each of which is connected to the hidden layer with a $p \times d$ matrix $V = [v_{qj}]$. Each of these m groups of d output nodes computes the probabilities of the various words for a particular context word. The jth column of V is denoted by $\overline{v}_j$ and represents the output embedding of the jth word. The output $\hat{y}_{ij}$ is the probability that the word in the ith context position takes on the jth word of the lexicon. However, since the same matrix V is shared by all groups, the neural network predicts the same multinomial distribution for each of the context words. Therefore, we have the following:

$$\hat{y}_{ij} = P(y_{ij} = 1|w) = \underbrace{\frac{\exp(\sum_{q=1}^{p} h_q v_{qj})}{\sum_{k=1}^{d} \exp(\sum_{q=1}^{p} h_q v_{qk})}}_{\text{Independent of context position } i} \quad \forall i \in \{1 \ldots m\} \tag{2.52}$$

Note that the probability $\hat{y}_{ij}$ is the same for varying i and fixed j, since the right-hand side of the above equation does not depend on the exact location i in the context window.

The loss function for the backpropagation algorithm is the negative of the log-likelihood values of the ground truth $y_{ij} \in \{0, 1\}$ of a training instance. This loss function L is given by the following:

$$L = -\sum_{i=1}^{m} \sum_{j=1}^{d} y_{ij} \log(\hat{y}_{ij}) \tag{2.53}$$

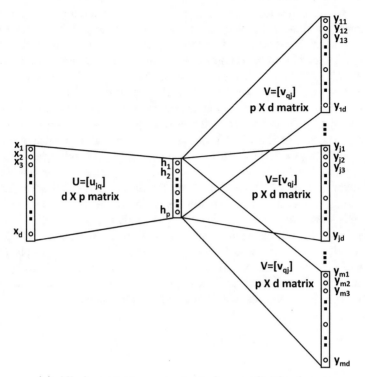

(a) All elements in context window explicitly shown

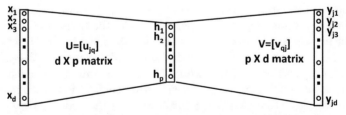

**MINIBATCH THE m d-DIMENSIONAL OUTPUT VECTORS IN EACH
CONTEXT WINDOW DURING STOCHASTIC GRADIENT DESCENT.
THE SHOWN OUTPUTS y$_{jk}$ CORRESPOND TO THE jth OF m OUTPUTS.**

(b) All elements in context window not explicitly shown

Figure 2.16: Word2vec: The skip-gram model. Note the similarity with Figure 2.13, which uses a single set of linear outputs. One could also choose to collapse the m sets of d output nodes in (a) into a single set of d outputs, and mini-batch the m instances in a single context window during stochastic gradient descent to achieve the same effect. All elements in the mini-batch are explicitly shown in (a), whereas the elements of the mini-batch are not explicitly shown in (b). However, both are equivalent as long as the nature of mini-batching is respected.

Note that the value outside the logarithm is a ground-truth binary value, whereas the value inside the logarithm is a predicted (probability) value. Since y_{ij} is one-hot encoded for fixed i and varying j, the objective function has only m non-zero terms. For each training instance, this loss function is used in combination with backpropagation to update the weights of the connections between the nodes. The update equations with learning rate α are as follows:

$$\overline{u}_i \Leftarrow \overline{u}_i - \alpha \frac{\partial L}{\partial \overline{u}_i} \quad \forall i$$

$$\overline{v}_j \Leftarrow \overline{v}_j - \alpha \frac{\partial L}{\partial \overline{v}_j} \quad \forall j$$

We state the details of the updates below after introducing some additional notations.

The probability of making a mistake in predicting the jth word in the lexicon for the ith context is defined by $|y_{ij} - \hat{y}_{ij}|$. However, we use *signed* mistakes ϵ_{ij} in which only the predicted words (positive examples) have a positive probability. This is achieved by dropping the modulus:

$$\epsilon_{ij} = y_{ij} - \hat{y}_{ij} \tag{2.54}$$

Then, the updates for a particular input word r and its output context are as follows:

$$\overline{u}_r \Leftarrow \overline{u}_r + \alpha \sum_{j=1}^{d} \left[\sum_{i=1}^{m} \epsilon_{ij} \right] \overline{v}_j \qquad \text{[Only for input word } r]$$

$$\overline{v}_j \Leftarrow \overline{v}_j + \alpha \left[\sum_{i=1}^{m} \epsilon_{ij} \right] \overline{h} \qquad \text{[For all words } j \text{ in lexicon]}$$

Here, $\alpha > 0$ is the learning rate. The p-dimensional rows of the matrix U are used as the embeddings of the words. In other words, the convention is to use the input embeddings in the rows of U rather than the output embeddings in the columns of V. It is stated in [288] that adding the input and output embeddings can help in some tasks (but hurt in others). The concatenation of the two can also be useful.

Practical Issues

Several practical issues are associated with the accuracy and efficiency of the *word2vec* framework. The embedding dimensionality, defined by the number of nodes in the hidden layer, provides the trade-off between bias and variance. Increasing the embedding dimensionality improves discrimination, but it requires a greater amount of data. In general, the typical embedding dimensionality is of the order of several hundred, although it is possible to choose dimensionalities in the thousands for very large collections. The size of the context window typically varies between 5 and 10, with larger window sizes being used for the skip-gram model as compared to the CBOW model. Using a random window size is a variant that has the implicit effect of giving greater weight to words that are placed close together. The skip-gram model is slower but it works better for infrequent words and for larger data sets.

Another issue is that the effect of frequent and less discriminative words (e.g., "*the*") can dominate the results. Therefore, a common approach is to downsample the frequent words, which improves both accuracy and efficiency. Note that downsampling frequent words has the implicit effect of increasing the context window size because dropping a word in the middle of two words brings the latter pair closer. The words that are very rare are misspellings, and it is hard to create a meaningful embedding for them without overfitting. Therefore, such words are ignored.

From a computational point of view, the updates of output embeddings are expensive. This is caused by applying the softmax over a lexicon of d words, which requires an update of each $\overline{v}_j$. Therefore, the softmax function is implemented hierarchically with *Huffman encoding* for better efficiency. We refer the reader to [325, 327, 404] for details.

Skip-Gram with Negative Sampling

An efficient alternative to the hierarchical softmax technique is a method known as *skip-gram with negative sampling (SGNS)* [327], in which both presence or absence of word-context pairs are used for training. As the name implies, the negative contexts are artificially generated by sampling words in proportion to their frequencies in the corpus (i.e., unigram distribution). This approach optimizes a different objective function from the skip-gram model, which is related to ideas from *noise contrastive estimation* [166, 333, 334].

The basic idea is that instead of directly predicting each of the m words in the context window, we try to predict whether or not each of the d words in the lexicon is present in the window. In other words, the final layer of Figure 2.16 is not a softmax prediction, but a Bernoulli layer of sigmoids. The output unit for each word at each context position in Figure 2.16 is a sigmoid providing a probability value that the position takes on that word. As the ground-truth values are also available, it is possible to use the logistic loss function over all the words. Therefore, in this point of view, even the prediction problem is defined differently. Of course, it is computationally inefficient to try to make binary predictions for all d words. Therefore, the SGNS approach uses all the positive words in a context window and a *sample* of negative words. The number of negative samples is k times the number of positive samples. Here, k is a parameter controlling the sampling rate. Negative sampling becomes essential in this modified prediction problem to avoid learning trivial weights that predict all examples to 1. In other words, we cannot choose to avoid negative samples entirely (i.e., we cannot set $k = 0$).

How does one generate the negative samples? The vanilla unigram distribution samples words in proportion to their relative frequencies $f_1 \ldots f_d$ in the corpus. Better results are obtained [327] by sampling words in proportion to $f_j^{3/4}$ rather than f_j. As in all *word2vec* models, let U be a $d \times p$ matrix representing the input embedding, and V be a $p \times d$ matrix representing the output embedding. Let $\overline{u}_i$ be the p-dimensional row of U (input embedding of ith word) and $\overline{v}_j$ be the p-dimensional column of V (output embedding of jth word). Let $\mathcal{P}$ be the set of positive target-context word pairs in a context window, and $\mathcal{N}$ be the set of negative target-context word pairs which are created by sampling. Therefore, the size of $\mathcal{P}$ is equal to the context window m, and that of $\mathcal{N}$ is $m \cdot k$. Then, the (minimization) objective function for each context window is obtained by summing up the logistic loss over the m positive samples and $m \cdot k$ negative samples:

$$O = - \sum_{(i,j)\in\mathcal{P}} \log(P[\text{Predict } (i,j) \text{ to } 1]) - \sum_{(i,j)\in\mathcal{N}} \log(P[\text{Predict } (i,j) \text{ to } 0]) \qquad (2.55)$$

$$= - \sum_{(i,j)\in\mathcal{P}} \log\left(\frac{1}{1 + \exp(-\overline{u}_i \cdot \overline{v}_j)}\right) - \sum_{(i,j)\in\mathcal{N}} \log\left(\frac{1}{1 + \exp(\overline{u}_i \cdot \overline{v}_j)}\right) \qquad (2.56)$$

This modified objective function is used in the skip-gram with negative sampling (SGNS) model in order to update the weights of U and V. SGNS is mathematically different from the basic skip-gram model discussed earlier. SGNS is not only efficient, but it also provides the best results among the different variants of skip-gram models.

What Is the Actual Neural Architecture of SGNS?

Even though the original *word2vec* paper seems to treat SGNS as an efficiency optimization of the skip-gram model, it is using a fundamentally different architecture in terms of the activation function used in the final layer. Unfortunately, the original *word2vec* paper does not explicitly point this out (and only provides the changed objective function), which causes confusion.

The modified neural architecture of SGNS is as follows. The softmax layer is no longer used in the SGNS implementation. Rather, each observed value y_{ij} in Figure 2.16 is *independently* treated as a *binary* outcome, rather than as a multinomial outcome in which the probabilistic predictions of different outcomes at a contextual position depend on one another. Instead of using softmax to create the prediction $\hat{y}_{ij}$, it uses the sigmoid activation to create probabilistic predictions $\hat{y}_{ij}$, whether each y_{ij} is 0 or 1. Then, one can add up the log loss of $\hat{y}_{ij}$ with respect to observed y_{ij} over all $m \cdot d$ possible values of (i, j) to create the full loss function of a context window. However, this is impractical because the number of zero values of y_{ij} is too large and zero values are noisy anyway. Therefore, SGNS uses negative sampling to approximate this *modified* objective function. This means that for each context window, we are backpropagating from only a subset of the $m \cdot d$ outputs in Figure 2.16. The size of this subset is $m + m \cdot k$. This is where efficiency is achieved. However, since the final layer uses binary predictions (with sigmoids), it makes the SGNS architecture fundamentally different from the vanilla skip-gram model even in terms of the basic neural network it uses (i.e., logistic instead of softmax activation). The difference between the SGNS model and the vanilla skip-gram model is analogous to the difference between the Bernoulli and multinomial models in naïve Bayes classification (with negative sampling applied only to the Bernoulli model). Obviously, one cannot be considered a direct efficiency optimization of the other.

2.6.3   Word2vec (SGNS) Is Logistic Matrix Factorization

Even though the work in [287] shows an *implicit* relationship between *word2vec* and matrix factorization, we provide a more direct relationship here. The architectures of the skip-gram models look suspiciously similar to those used in row index to value prediction in recommender systems (cf. Section 2.5.7). The use of a backpropagation from a subset of observed outputs is similar to the negative sampling idea, except that the dropping of outputs in negative sampling is performed for the purpose of efficiency. However, unlike the linear outputs of Figure 2.13 in Section 2.5.7, the SGNS model uses logistic outputs to model binary predictions. The SGNS model of *word2vec* can be simulated with logistic matrix factorization. To understand the similarity with the problem setting of Section 2.5.7, one can understand the predictions of a particular word-context window using the following triplets:

$$\langle \text{WordId} \rangle, \ \langle \text{Context WordId} \rangle, \ \langle 0/1 \rangle$$

Each context window produces $m \cdot d$ such triplets, although negative sampling only uses $m \cdot k + m$ of them, and *mini-batches* them during training. This mini-batching is another source of the difference between the architectures between Figures 2.13 and 2.16, wherein the latter has m different groups of outputs to accommodate m positive samples. However, these differences are relatively superficial, and one can still use logistic matrix factorization to represent the underlying model.

Let $B = [b_{ij}]$ be a binary matrix in which the (i,j)th value is 1 if word j occurs at least once in the context of word i in the data set, and 0 otherwise. The weight c_{ij} for any word (i,j) that occurs in the corpus is defined by the number of times word j occurs in the context of word i. The weights of the zero entries in B are defined as follows. For each row i in B we sample $k\sum_j b_{ij}$ different entries from row i, among the entries for which $b_{ij} = 0$, and the frequency with which the jth word is sampled is proportional to $f_j^{3/4}$. These are the negative samples, and one sets the weights c_{ij} for the negative samples (i.e., those for which $b_{ij} = 0$) to the number of times that each entry is sampled. As in *word2vec*, the p-dimensional embeddings of the ith word and jth context are denoted by $\overline{u}_i$ and $\overline{v}_j$, respectively. The simplest way of factorizing is to use *weighted* matrix factorization of B with the Frobenius norm:

$$\text{Minimize}_{U,V} \sum_{i,j} c_{ij}(b_{ij} - \overline{u}_i \cdot \overline{v}_j)^2 \qquad (2.57)$$

Even though the matrix B is of size $O(d^2)$, this matrix factorization only has a limited number of nonzero terms in the objective function, which have $c_{ij} > 0$. These weights are dependent on co-occurrence counts, but some zero entries also have positive weight. Therefore, the stochastic gradient-descent steps only have to focus on entries with $c_{ij} > 0$. Each cycle of stochastic gradient-descent is *linear* in the number of non-zero entries, as in the SGNS implementation of *word2vec*.

However, this objective function also looks somewhat different from *word2vec*, which has a logistic form. Just as it is advisable to replace linear regression with logistic regression in supervised learning of binary targets, one can use the same trick in matrix factorization of binary matrices [224]. We can change the squared error term to the familiar likelihood term L_{ij}, which is used in logistic regression:

$$L_{ij} = \left| b_{ij} - \frac{1}{1 + \exp(\overline{u}_i \cdot \overline{v}_j)} \right| \qquad (2.58)$$

The value of L_{ij} always lies in the range $(0,1)$, and higher values indicate greater likelihood (which results in a maximization objective). The modulus in the above expression flips the sign only for the negative samples in which $b_{ij} = 0$. Now, one can optimize the following objective function in minimization form:

$$\text{Minimize}_{U,V} \ J = -\sum_{i,j} c_{ij} \log(L_{ij}) \qquad (2.59)$$

The main difference from the objective function (cf. Equation 2.56) of *word2vec* is that this is a global objective function over all matrix entries, rather than a local objective function over a particular context window. Using mini-batch stochastic gradient-descent in matrix factorization (with an appropriately chosen mini-batch) makes the approach almost identical to *word2vec*'s backpropagation updates.

How can one interpret this type of factorization? Instead of $B \approx UV$, we have $B \approx f(UV)$, where $f(\cdot)$ is the sigmoid function. More precisely, this is a *probabilistic* factorization in which one computes the product of matrices U and V, and then applies the sigmoid function to obtain the parameters of the Bernoulli distribution from which B is generated:

$$P(b_{ij} = 1) = \frac{1}{1 + \exp(-\overline{u}_i \cdot \overline{v}_j)} \qquad \text{[Matrix factorization analog of logistic regression]}$$

It is also easy to verify from Equation 2.58 that L_{ij} is $P(b_{ij} = 1)$ for positive samples and $P(b_{ij} = 0)$ for negative samples. Therefore, the objective function of the factorization is in the form of log-likelihood maximization. This type of logistic matrix factorization is commonly used [224] in recommender systems with binary data (e.g., user click-streams).

Gradient Descent

It is also helpful to examine the gradient-descent steps of the factorization. One can compute the derivative of J with respect to the input and output embeddings:

$$\frac{\partial J}{\partial \overline{u}_i} = -\sum_{j:b_{ij}=1} \frac{c_{ij}\overline{v}_j}{1 + \exp(\overline{u}_i \cdot \overline{v}_j)} + \sum_{j:b_{ij}=0} \frac{c_{ij}\overline{v}_j}{1 + \exp(-\overline{u}_i \cdot \overline{v}_j)}$$

$$= -\underbrace{\sum_{j:b_{ij}=1} c_{ij}P(b_{ij}=0)\overline{v}_j}_{\text{Positive Mistakes}} + \underbrace{\sum_{j:b_{ij}=0} c_{ij}P(b_{ij}=1)\overline{v}_j}_{\text{Negative Mistakes}}$$

$$\frac{\partial J}{\partial \overline{v}_j} = -\sum_{i:b_{ij}=1} \frac{c_{ij}\overline{u}_i}{1 + \exp(\overline{u}_i \cdot \overline{v}_j)} + \sum_{i:b_{ij}=0} \frac{c_{ij}\overline{u}_i}{1 + \exp(-\overline{u}_i \cdot \overline{v}_j)}$$

$$= -\underbrace{\sum_{i:b_{ij}=1} c_{ij}P(b_{ij}=0)\overline{u}_i}_{\text{Positive Mistakes}} + \underbrace{\sum_{i:b_{ij}=0} c_{ij}P(b_{ij}=1)\overline{u}_i}_{\text{Negative Mistakes}}$$

The optimization procedure uses gradient descent to convergence:

$$\overline{u}_i \Leftarrow \overline{u}_i - \alpha \frac{\partial J}{\partial \overline{u}_i} \quad \forall i$$

$$\overline{v}_j \Leftarrow \overline{v}_j - \alpha \frac{\partial J}{\partial \overline{v}_j} \quad \forall j$$

It is noteworthy that the derivatives can be expressed in terms of the probabilities of making mistakes in predicting b_{ij}. This is common in gradient descent with log-likelihood optimization. It is also noteworthy that the derivative of the SGNS objective in Equation 2.56 yields a similar form of the gradient. The only difference is that the derivative of the SGNS objective is expressed over a smaller batch of instances, defined by a context window. We can also solve the probabilistic matrix factorization with mini-batch stochastic gradient descent. With an appropriate choice of the mini-batch, the stochastic gradient descent of matrix factorization becomes identical to the backpropagation update of SGNS. The only difference is that SGNS samples negative entries *for each set of updates* on the fly, whereas matrix factorization fixes the negative samples up front. Of course, on-the-fly sampling can also be used with matrix factorization updates. The similarity of SGNS to matrix factorization can also be inferred by observing that the architecture of Figure 2.16(b) is almost identical to the matrix factorization architecture for recommender systems in Figure 2.13. As in the case of recommender systems, SGNS has missing (negative) entries. This is caused by the fact the negative sampling uses only a subset of the zero values. The only difference between the two cases is that the architecture of SGNS caps the output layer with sigmoid units, whereas a linear layer is used for recommender systems. However, recommender systems with implicit feedback use *logistic matrix factorization* [224], which is similar to the *word2vec* setting.

2.6.4   Vanilla Skip-Gram Is Multinomial Matrix Factorization

Since we have already shown that the SGNS enhancement of the skip-gram model is logistic matrix factorization, a natural question arises as to whether we can also recast the original skip-gram model as a matrix factorization method. It turns out that one can also recast the vanilla skip-gram model as a *multinomial matrix factorization* model because of the use of the softmax layer at the very end.

Let $C = [c_{ij}]$ be a $d \times d$ word-context co-occurrence matrix in which the value of c_{ij} is the number of times that word j occurs in the context of word i. Let U be a $d \times p$ matrix containing the input embedding in its rows, and V be a $p \times d$ matrix containing the output embedding in its columns. *Then, the skip-gram model roughly creates a model in which the frequency vector of the rth row of C is an empirical instantiation of the probabilities obtained by applying the softmax to the rth row of UV.*

Let $\overline{u}_i$ be the p-dimensional vector corresponding to the ith row of U and $\overline{v}_j$ be the p-dimensional vector corresponding to the jth column of V. The loss function of the aforementioned factorization is as follows:

$$O = -\sum_{i=1}^{d} \sum_{j=1}^{d} c_{ij} \log \underbrace{\left(\frac{\exp(\overline{u}_i \cdot \overline{v}_j)}{\sum_{q=1}^{d} \exp(\overline{u}_i \cdot \overline{v}_q)} \right)}_{P(\text{word } j | \text{word } i)} \tag{2.60}$$

This loss function is written in minimization form. Note that this loss function is identical to the one used in the vanilla skip-gram model, except that the latter uses a mini-batch stochastic gradient descent in which the m words in a given context are grouped together. This type of specific mini-batch does not make a significant difference.

2.7   Simple Neural Architectures for Graph Embeddings

Large networks have become very common because of their ubiquity in many social- and Web-centric applications. Graphs are structural entries containing *nodes* and *edges* connecting them. For example, in a social network, each person is a node, and a friendship link between two people is an edge. In this particular exposition, we consider the case of very large networks like the Web, a social network, or a communication network. The goal is to embed the nodes into feature vectors, so that the graph captures the relationships between nodes. For simplicity we consider undirected graphs, although directed graphs with weights on the edges can be easily handled with very few changes to the exposition below.

Consider an $n \times n$ adjacency matrix $B = [b_{ij}]$ for a graph with n nodes. The entry b_{ij} is 1 if an undirected edge exists between nodes i and j. Furthermore, the matrix B is symmetric, because we have $b_{ij} = b_{ji}$ for an undirected graph. In order to determine the embedding, we would like to determine two $n \times p$ factor matrices U and V, so that B can be derived as a function of UV^T. In the simplest case, one can set B to exactly UV^T, which is no different than a traditional matrix factorization method for factoring graphs [4]. However, for binary matrices, one can do better and use logistic matrix factorization instead. In other words, each entry of B is generated using the matrix of Bernoulli parameters in $f(UV^T)$, where $f(\cdot)$ is the element-wise application of the sigmoid function to each entry of the matrix in its argument:

$$f(x) = \frac{1}{1 + \exp(-x)} \tag{2.61}$$

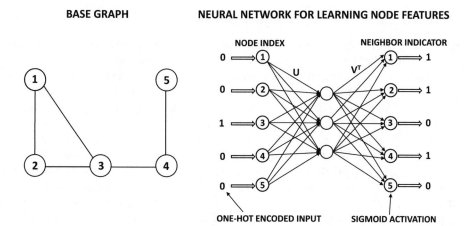

Figure 2.17: A graph of five nodes is shown together with a neural architecture for row index to neighbor indicator mapping. The shown input and output represent node 3 and its neighbors. Note the similarity to Figure 2.13. The main difference is that there are no missing values above, and the number of inputs is the same as the number of outputs for a square matrix. Both input and outputs are binary vectors. However, if negative sampling is used with sigmoid activation, most output nodes with zero values may be dropped.

Therefore, if $\overline{u}_i$ is the ith row of U and $\overline{v}_j$ is the jth row of V, we have the following:

$$b_{ij} \sim \text{Bernoulli distribution with parameter } f(\overline{u}_i \cdot \overline{v}_j) \qquad (2.62)$$

This type of generative model is typically solved using a log-likelihood model. Furthermore, *the problem formulation is identical to the logistic matrix factorization equivalent of the SGNS model in word2vec.*

Note that all *word2vec* models are logistic/multinomial variants of the model in Figure 2.13 that maps row indexes to values with linear activation. In order to explain this point, we show the neural architecture in Figure 2.17 for a toy graph containing 5 nodes. The input is the one-hot encoded index of a row in B (i.e., node), and the output is the list of all 0/1 values for all nodes in the network. In this particular case, we have shown the input for node 3 and its corresponding output. Since the node 3 has three neighbors, the output vector contains three 1s. Note that this architecture is not very different from Figure 2.13 except that it uses a sigmoid activations at the output (rather than linear activations). Furthermore, since the number of 0s is usually much greater[8] than the number of 1s in the output, it is possible to drop many of the 0s with the use of negative sampling. This type of negative sampling will create a situation similar to that of Figure 2.14. With this neural architecture, the gradient-descent steps will be identical to the SGNS model of *word2vec*. The main difference is that a node appears at most once as a neighbor of another node, whereas a word might appear more than once in the context of another word. Allowing arbitrary counts on the edges takes away this distinction.

---

[8]This fact is not evident in the toy example of Figure 2.17. In practice, the degree of a node is a tiny fraction of the total number of nodes. For example, a person might have 100 friends in a social network of millions of nodes.

2.7.1   Handling Arbitrary Edge Counts

The aforementioned discussion assumes that the weight of each edge is binary. Consider a setting in which an arbitrary count c_{ij} is associated with the edge (i, j). In such cases, both positive and negative sampling are required. The first step is to sample an edge (i, j) from the network with probability proportional to c_{ij}. The input is, therefore, a one-hot encoded vector of the node at one end point (say, i) of this edge. The output is the one-hot encoding of node j. By default, both the input and output are n-dimensional vectors. However, if negative sampling is used, then one can reduce the output vector to a $(k + 1)$-dimensional vector. Here, $k \ll n$ is a parameter that defines the sampling rate. A total of k negative nodes are sampled with probabilities proportional to their (weighted) degrees[9] and the outputs of these nodes are 0s. One can compute the log-likelihood loss by treating each output as the outcome of a Bernoulli trial, where the parameter of the Bernoulli trial is the output of the sigmoid activation function. The gradient descent is performed with respect to this loss. This variant is an almost exact simulation of the SGNS variant of the *word2vec* model.

2.7.2   Multinomial Model

The vanilla skip-gram model of *word2vec* is a multinomial model. It is also possible to use a multinomial model to create the embedding. The only difference is that the final layer of the neural network in Figure 2.17 needs to use softmax activation (instead of the sigmoid activation function). Furthermore, negative sampling is not used in the multinomial model, and both input and output layers contain exactly n nodes. As in the SGNS model, a single edge (i, j) is sampled with probability proportional to c_{ij} to create each input-output pair. The input is the one-hot encoding of i and the output is the one-hot encoding of j. One can also use mini-batch sampling of edges to improve performance. The stochastic gradient-descent steps of this model are virtually similar to those used in the vanilla skip-gram model of *word2vec*.

2.7.3   Connections with DeepWalk and Node2vec

The recently proposed *DeepWalk* [372] and *node2vec* models [164] belong to the family of multinomial models discussed above (with specialized preprocessing steps). The main difference is that the *DeepWalk* and *node2vec* models use depth-first or breadth-first walks to (indirectly) generate c_{ij}. *DeepWalk* is itself a precursor to (and special case of) *node2vec* in terms of how the random walks are performed. In this case, c_{ij} can be interpreted as the number of times that node j appears in the neighborhood of node i because it was included in a breadth-first or depth-first walk starting at node i. One can view the value of c_{ij} in the walk-based models as providing a more robust measure of the affinity between nodes i and j, as compared to the raw weights in the original graph. Of course, there is nothing sacrosanct about using a random walk to improve the robustness of c_{ij}. The number of choices is almost unlimited in terms of how to generate this type of affinity value. All *link prediction methods* [295] generate such affinity values. For example, the *Katz measure* [295], which is closely related to the number of random walks between a pair of nodes, is a robust measure of the affinity between nodes i and j.

---

[9]The weighted degree of node j is $\sum_r c_{rj}$.

2.8 Summary

This chapter discusses a number of neural models supervised and unsupervised learning. One of the goals was to show that many of the traditional models used in machine learning are instantiations of relatively simple neural models. Methods for binary/multiclass classification and matrix factorization were discussed. In addition, the applications of the approach to recommender systems and word embedding were introduced. When a traditional machine learning technique like singular value decomposition is generalized to a neural representation, it is often inefficient compared to its counterpart in traditional machine learning. However, the advantage of neural models is that they can usually be generalized to more powerful nonlinear models. Furthermore, it is relatively easy to experiment with nonlinear variants of traditional machine learning models with the use of neural networks. This chapter also discusses several practical applications like recommender systems, text, and graph embeddings.

2.9 Bibliographic Notes

The perceptron algorithm was proposed by Rosenblatt [405], and a detailed discussion may be found in [405]. The Widrow-Hoff algorithm was proposed in [531] and is closely related to Tikhonov-Arsenin's work [499]. The Fisher discriminant was proposed by Ronald Fisher [120] in 1936, and is a specific case of the family of linear discriminant analysis methods [322]. Even though the Fisher discriminant uses an objective function that appears o to be different from least-squares regression, it turns out to be a special case of least-squares regression in which the binary response variable is used as the regressand [40]. A detailed discussion of generalized linear models is provided in [320]. A variety of procedures such as *generalized iterative scaling, iteratively reweighted least-squares,* and *gradient descent* for multinomial logistic regression are discussed in [178]. The support-vector machine is generally credited to Cortes and Vapnik [82], although the primal method for L_2-loss SVMs was proposed several years earlier by Hinton [190]! This approach repairs the loss function in least-squares classification by keeping only one-half of the quadratic loss curve and setting the remaining to zero, so that it looks like a smooth version of hinge loss (try this on Figure 2.4). The specific significance of this contribution was lost within the broader literature on neural networks. Hinton's work also does not focus on the importance of regularization in SVMs, although the general notion of adding shrinkage to gradient-descent steps in neural networks was well known. The hinge-loss SVM [82] is heavily presented from the perspective of duality and the maximum-margin interpretation, making its relationship to regularized least-squares classification somewhat opaque. The relationship of SVMs to least-squares classification is more evident from other related works [400, 442], where it becomes evident that quadratic and hinge-loss SVMs are natural variations of regularized L_2-loss (i.e., Fisher discriminant) and L_1-loss classification that use the binary class variables as the regression responses [139]. The Weston-Watkins multiclass SVM was introduced in [529]. It was shown in [401] that the one-against-all approach to generalizing multiple classes seems to be as effective as the tightly integrated multiclass variants. Many hierarchical softmax methods are discussed in [325, 327, 332, 344].

An excellent overview paper on methods for reducing the dimensionality of data with neural networks is available in [198], although this work focuses on the use of a related model known as the Restricted Boltzmann Machine (RBM). The earliest introduction of the autoencoder (in a more general form) is given in the backpropagation paper [408]. This work discusses the problem of recoding between input and output patterns. Both classification and autoencoders can be considered special cases of this architecture by using an appropriate choice of input and output patterns. The paper on backpropagation [408] also discusses the special case in which the recoding of the input is the identity mapping, which is exactly the scenario of the autoencoder. More detailed discussions of the autoencoder during its early years were provided in [48, 275]. A discussion of single-layer unsupervised learning may be found in [77]. The standard method for regularizing an autoencoder is to use weight decay, which corresponds to L_2-regularization. Sparse autoencoders are discussed in [67, 273, 274, 284, 354]. Another way of regularizing the autoencoder is to penalize the derivatives during gradient descent. This ensures that the learned function does not change too much with change in input. This method is referred to as the *contractive autoencoder* [397]. Variational autoencoders can encode complex probabilistic distributions, and are discussed in [106, 242, 399]. The de-noising autoencoder is discussed in [506]. Many of these methods are discussed in detail in Chapter 4. The use of autoencoders for outlier detection is explored in [64, 181, 564], and a survey on the use in clustering is provided in [8].

The application of dimensionality reduction for recommender systems may be found in [414], although this approach uses a restricted Boltzmann machine, which is different from the matrix factorization method discussed in this chapter. An item-based autoencoder is discussed in [436], and this approach is a neural generalization of item-based neighborhood regression [253]. The main difference is that the regression weights are regularized with a constricted hidden layer. Similar works with different types of item-to-item models with the use of de-noising autoencoders are discussed in [472, 535]. A more direct generalization of matrix factorization methods may be found in [186], although the approach in [186] is slightly different from the simpler approach presented in this chapter. The incorporation of content in building recommender systems for deep learning is discussed in [513]. A multiview deep learning approach, which has also been extended to temporal recommender systems in a later work [465], is proposed in [110]. A survey of deep learning methods for recommenders may be found in [560].

The *word2vec* model is proposed in [325, 327], and a detailed exposition may be found in [404]. The basic idea has been extended to sentence- and paragraph-level embeddings, with a model, which is referred to as *doc2vec* [272]. An alternative of *word2vec* that uses a different type of matrix factorization is GloVe [371]. Multi-lingual word embeddings are presented in [9]. The extension of *word2vec* to graphs with node-level embeddings is provided in the *DeepWalk* [372] and *node2vec* [164] models. Various types of network embeddings are discussed in [62, 512, 547, 548].

2.9.1   Software Resources

Machine learning models like linear regression, SVMs, and logistic regression are available from *scikit-learn* [587]. The DISSECT (Distributional Semantics Composition Toolkit) [588] is a toolkit that uses word co-occurrence counts in order to create embeddings. The GloVe method is available from Stanford NLP [589] and the **gensim** library [394]. The *word2vec* tool is available under the Apache license [591], and as a **TensorFlow** version [592]. The **gensim** library has Python implementations of *word2vec* and *doc2vec* [394]. Java versions of *doc2vec*, *word2vec*, and GloVe may be found in the **DeepLearning4j** repository [590]. In several cases, one can simply download pre-trained versions of the representations (on a large corpus that is considered generally representative of text) and use them directly, as a convenient alternative to training for the specific corpus at hand. The *node2vec* software is available from the original author at [593].

2.10 Exercises

1. Consider the following loss function for training pair $(\overline{X}, y)$:

$$L = \max\{0, a - y(\overline{W} \cdot \overline{X})\}$$

The test instances are predicted as $\hat{y} = \text{sign}\{\overline{W} \cdot \overline{X}\}$. A value of $a = 0$ corresponds to the perceptron criterion and a value of $a = 1$ corresponds to the SVM. Show that any value of $a > 0$ leads to the SVM with an unchanged optimal solution when no regularization is used. What happens when regularization is used?

2. Based on Exercise 1, formulate a generalized objective for the Weston-Watkins SVM.

3. Consider the unregularized perceptron update for binary classes with learning rate α. Show that using any value of α is inconsequential in the sense that it only scales up the weight vector by a factor of α. Show that these results also hold true for the multiclass case. Do the results hold true when regularization is used?

4. Show that if the Weston-Watkins SVM is applied to a data set with $k = 2$ classes, the resulting updates are equivalent to the binary SVM updates discussed in this chapter.

5. Show that if multinomial logistic regression is applied to a data set with $k = 2$ classes, the resulting updates are equivalent to logistic regression updates.

6. Implement the softmax classifier using a deep-learning library of your choice.

7. In linear-regression-based neighborhood models, the rating of an item is predicted as a weighted combination of the ratings of other items of the same user, where the item-specific weights are learned with linear regression. Show how you can construct an autoencoder architecture to create this type of model. Discuss the relationship of this architecture with the matrix factorization architecture.

8. **Logistic matrix factorization:** Consider an autoencoder which has an input layer, a single hidden layer containing the reduced representation, and an output layer with sigmoid units. The hidden layer has linear activation:

   (a) Set up a negative log-likelihood loss function for the case when the input data matrix is known to contain binary values from $\{0, 1\}$.

   (b) Set up a negative log-likelihood loss function for the case when the input data matrix contains real values from $[0, 1]$.

9. **Non-negative matrix factorization with autoencoders:** Let D be an $n \times d$ data matrix with non-negative entries. Show how you can approximately factorize $D \approx UV^T$ into two non-negative matrices U and V, respectively, by using an autoencoder architecture with d inputs and outputs. [Hint: Choose an appropriate activation function in the hidden layer, and modify the gradient-descent updates.]

10. **Probabilistic latent semantic analysis:** Refer to [99, 206] for a definition of probabilistic latent semantic analysis. Propose a modification of the approach in Exercise 9 for probabilistic latent semantic analysis. [Hint: What is the relationship between non-negative matrix factorization and probabilistic latent semantic analysis?]

11. **Simulating a model combination ensemble:** In machine learning, a model combination ensemble averages the scores of multiple models in order to create a more robust classification score. Discuss how you can approximate the averaging of an Adaline and logistic regression with a two-layer neural network. Discuss the similarities and differences of this architecture with an actual model combination ensemble when backpropagation is used to train it. Show how to modify the training process so that the final result is a fine-tuning of the model combination ensemble.

12. **Simulating a stacking ensemble:** In machine learning, a stacking ensemble creates a higher-level classification model on top of features learned from first-level classifiers. Discuss how you can modify the architecture of Exercise 11, so that the first level of classifiers correspond to an Adaline and a logistic regression classifier and the higher-level classifier corresponds to a support vector machine. Discuss the similarities and differences of this architecture with an actual stacking ensemble when backpropagation is used to train it. Show how you can modify the training process of the neural network so that the final result is a fine-tuning of the stacking ensemble.

13. Show that the stochastic gradient-descent updates of the perceptron, Widrow-Hoff learning, SVM, and logistic regression are all of the form $\overline{W} \Leftarrow \overline{W}(1 - \alpha\lambda) + \alpha y[\delta(\overline{X}, y)]\overline{X}$. Here, the mistake function $\delta(\overline{X}, y)$ is $1 - y(\overline{W} \cdot \overline{X})$ for least-squares classification, an indicator variable for perceptron/SVMs, and a probability value for logistic regression. Assume that α is the learning rate, and $y \in \{-1, +1\}$. Write the specific forms of $\delta(\overline{X}, y)$ in each case.

14. The linear autoencoder discussed in the chapter is applied to each d-dimensional row of the $n \times d$ data set D to create a k-dimensional representation. The encoder weights contain the $k \times d$ weight matrix W and the decoder weights contain the $d \times k$ weight matrix V. Therefore, the reconstructed representation is DW^TV^T, and the aggregate loss value $||DW^TV^T - D||^2$ is minimized over the entire training data set.

    (a) For a fixed value of V, show that the optimal matrix W must satisfy $D^TD(W^TV^TV - V) = 0$.

    (b) Use (a) to show that if the $n \times d$ matrix D has rank d, we have $W^TV^TV = V$.

    (c) Use (b) to show that $W = (V^TV)^{-1}V^T$. Assume that V^TV is invertible.

    (d) Repeat exercise parts (a), (b), and (c), when the encoder-decoder weights are tied as $W = V^T$. Show that the columns of V must be orthonormal.

Chapter 3

Training Deep Neural Networks

"I hated every minute of training, but I said, 'Don't quit. Suffer now and live the rest of your life as a champion.'"—Muhammad Ali

3.1 Introduction

The procedure for training neural networks with backpropagation is briefly introduced in Chapter 1. This chapter will expand on the description on Chapter 1 in several ways:

1. The backpropagation algorithm is presented in greater detail together with implementation details. Some details from Chapter 1 are repeated for completeness of the presentation, and so that readers do not have to frequently refer back to the earlier text.

2. Important issues related to feature preprocessing and initialization will be studied in the chapter.

3. The computational procedures that are paired with gradient descent will be introduced. The effect of network depth on training stability will be studied, and methods will be presented for addressing these issues.

4. The efficiency issues associated with training will be discussed. Methods for compressing trained models of neural networks will be presented. Such methods are useful for deploying pretrained networks on mobile devices.

In the early years, methods for training multilayer networks were not known. In their influential book, Minsky and Papert [330] strongly argued against the prospects of neural networks because of the inability to train multilayer networks. Therefore, neural networks stayed out of favor as a general area of research till the eighties. The first significant breakthrough in this respect was proposed[1] by Rumelhart *et al.* [408, 409] in the form of the backpropagation algorithm. The proposal of this algorithm rekindled an interest in neural networks. However, several computational, stability, and overfitting challenges were found in the use of this algorithm. As a result, research in the field of neural networks again fell from favor.

At the turn of the century, several advances again brought popularity to neural networks. Not all of these advances were algorithm-centric. For example, increased data availability and computational power have played the primary role in this resurrection. However, some changes to the basic backpropagation algorithm and clever methods for initialization, such as *pretraining*, have also helped. It has also become easier in recent years to perform the intensive experimentation required for making algorithmic adjustments due to the reduced testing cycle times (caused by improved computational hardware). Therefore, increased data, computational power, and reduced experimentation time (for algorithmic tweaking) went hand-in-hand. These so-called "tweaks" are, nevertheless, very important; this chapter and the next will discuss most of these important algorithmic advancements.

One key point is that the backpropagation algorithm is rather *unstable* to minor changes in the algorithmic setting, such as the initialization point used by the approach. This instability is particularly significant when one is working with very deep networks. A point to note is that neural network optimization is a *multivariable optimization problem*. These variables correspond to the weights of the connections in various layers. Multivariable optimization problems often face stability challenges because one must perform the steps along each direction in the "right" proportion. This turns out to be particularly hard in the neural network domain, and the effect of a gradient-descent step might be somewhat unpredictable. One issue is that *a gradient only provides a rate of change over an infinitesimal horizon in each direction*, whereas an actual step has a finite length. One needs to choose steps of reasonable size in order to make any real progress in optimization. The problem is that the gradients do change over a step of finite length, and in some cases they change drastically. The complex optimization surfaces presented by neural network optimization are particularly treacherous in this respect, and the problem is exacerbated with poorly chosen settings (such as the initialization point or the normalization of the input features). As a result, the (easily computable) steepest-descent direction is often not the best direction to use for retaining the ability to use large steps. Small step sizes lead to slow progress, whereas the optimization surface might change in unpredictable ways with the use of large step sizes. All these issues make neural network optimization more difficult than would seem at first sight. However, many of these problems can be avoided by carefully tailoring the gradient-descent steps to be more robust to the nature of the optimization surface. This chapter will discuss algorithms that leverage some of this understanding.

---

[1]Although the backpropagation algorithm was popularized by the Rumelhart *et al.* papers [408, 409], it had been studied earlier in the context of control theory. Crucially, Paul Werbos's forgotten (and eventually rediscovered) thesis in 1974 discussed how these backpropagation methods could be used in neural networks. This was well before Rumelhart *et al.*'s papers in 1986, which were nevertheless significant because the style of presentation contributed to a better understanding of why backpropagation might work.

Chapter Organization

This chapter is organized as follows. The next section reviews the backpropagation algorithm initially discussed in Chapter 1. The discussion in this chapter is more detailed, and several variants of the algorithm are discussed. Some parts of the backpropagation algorithm that were already discussed in Chapter 1 are repeated so that this chapter is self-contained. Feature preprocessing and initialization issues are discussed in Section 3.3. The vanishing and exploding gradient problem, which is common in deep networks, is discussed in Section 3.4, with common solutions for dealing with this issue presented. Gradient-descent strategies for deep learning are discussed in Section 3.5. Batch normalization methods are introduced in Section 3.6. A discussion of accelerated implementations of neural networks is found in Section 3.7. The summary is presented in Section 3.8.

3.2 Backpropagation: The Gory Details

In this section, the backpropagation algorithm from Chapter 1 is reviewed again in considerably more detail. The goal of this more-detailed review is to show that the chain rule can be used in multiple ways. To this end, we first explore the standard backpropagation update as it is commonly presented in most textbooks (and Chapter 1). Second, a simplified and decoupled view of backpropagation is examined in which the linear matrix multiplications are decoupled from the activation layers. This decoupled view of backpropagation is what most off-the-shelf systems implement.

3.2.1 Backpropagation with the Computational Graph Abstraction

A neural network is a *computational graph*, in which a unit of computation is the neuron. Neural networks are fundamentally more powerful than their building blocks because the parameters of these models are learned *jointly* to create a highly optimized composition function of these models. Furthermore, the nonlinear activations between the different layers add to the expressive power of the network.

A multilayer network evaluates compositions of functions computed at individual nodes. A path of length 2 in the neural network in which the function $f(\cdot)$ follows $g(\cdot)$ can be considered a composition function $f(g(\cdot))$. Just to provide an idea, let us look at a trivial computational graph with two nodes, in which the sigmoid function is applied at each node to the input weight w. In such a case, the computed function appears as follows:

$$f(g(w)) = \frac{1}{1 + \exp\left[-\frac{1}{1+\exp(-w)}\right]} \tag{3.1}$$

We can already see how awkward it would be to compute the derivative of this function with respect to w. Furthermore, consider the case in which $g_1(\cdot), g_2(\cdot) \ldots g_k(\cdot)$ are the functions computed in layer m, and they feed into a particular layer-$(m+1)$ node that computes $f(\cdot)$. In such a case, the composition function computed by the layer-$(m+1)$ node in terms of the layer-m inputs is $f(g_1(\cdot), \ldots g_k(\cdot))$. As we can see, this is a multivariate composition function, which looks rather ugly. Since the loss function uses the output(s) as its argument(s), it may typically be expressed a recursively nested function in terms of the weights in earlier layers. For a neural network with 10 layers and only 2 nodes in each layer, a recursively nested function of depth 10 will result in a summation of 2^{10} recursively nested terms, which appear forbidding from the perspective of computing partial derivatives. Therefore, we need some kind of iterative approach to compute these derivatives. The resulting iterative approach is *dynamic programming*, and the corresponding update is really the *chain rule of differential calculus*.

In order to understand how the chain rule works in a computational graph, we will discuss the two basic variants of the rule that one needs to keep in mind. The simplest version of the chain rule works for a straightforward composition of the functions:

$$\frac{\partial f(g(w))}{\partial w} = \frac{\partial f(g(w))}{\partial g(w)} \cdot \frac{\partial g(w)}{\partial w} \tag{3.2}$$

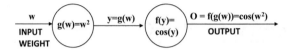

Figure 3.1: A simple computational graph with two nodes

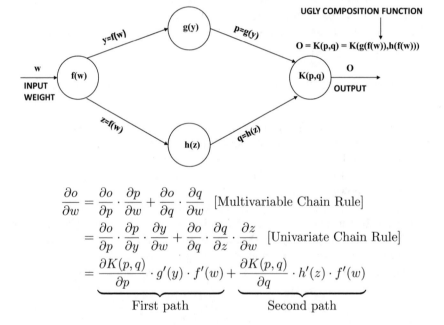

$$\frac{\partial o}{\partial w} = \frac{\partial o}{\partial p} \cdot \frac{\partial p}{\partial w} + \frac{\partial o}{\partial q} \cdot \frac{\partial q}{\partial w} \quad \text{[Multivariable Chain Rule]}$$

$$= \frac{\partial o}{\partial p} \cdot \frac{\partial p}{\partial y} \cdot \frac{\partial y}{\partial w} + \frac{\partial o}{\partial q} \cdot \frac{\partial q}{\partial z} \cdot \frac{\partial z}{\partial w} \quad \text{[Univariate Chain Rule]}$$

$$= \underbrace{\frac{\partial K(p,q)}{\partial p} \cdot g'(y) \cdot f'(w)}_{\text{First path}} + \underbrace{\frac{\partial K(p,q)}{\partial q} \cdot h'(z) \cdot f'(w)}_{\text{Second path}}$$

Figure 3.2: **Revisiting Figure 1.13 on chain rule in computational graphs:** The products of node-specific partial derivatives along paths from weight w to output o are aggregated. The resulting value yields the derivative of output O with respect to weight w. Only two paths between input and output exist in this simplified example.

This variant is referred to as the *univariate chain rule*. Note that each term on the right-hand side is a *local gradient* because it computes the derivative of a function with respect to its immediate argument rather than a recursively derived argument. The basic idea is that a composition of functions is applied on the weight w to yield the final output, and the gradient of the final output is given by the product of the local gradients along that path.

Each local gradient only needs to worry about its specific input and output, which simplifies the computation. An example is shown in Figure 3.1 in which the function $f(y)$ is $\cos(y)$ and $g(w) = w^2$. Therefore, the composition function is $\cos(w^2)$. On using the univariate chain rule, we obtain the following:

$$\frac{\partial f(g(w))}{\partial w} = \underbrace{\frac{\partial f(g(w))}{\partial g(w)}}_{-sin(g(w))} \cdot \underbrace{\frac{\partial g(w)}{\partial w}}_{2w} = -2w \cdot \sin(w^2)$$

The computational graphs in neural networks are not paths, which is the main reason that backpropagation is needed. A hidden layer often gets its input from multiple units, which results in multiple paths from a variable w to an output. Consider the function

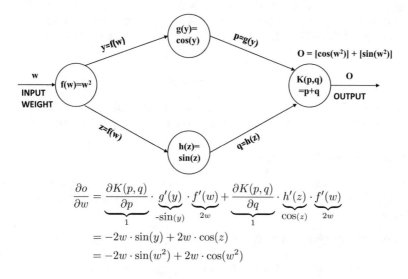

$$\frac{\partial o}{\partial w} = \underbrace{\frac{\partial K(p,q)}{\partial p}}_{1} \cdot \underbrace{g'(y)}_{-\sin(y)} \cdot \underbrace{f'(w)}_{2w} + \underbrace{\frac{\partial K(p,q)}{\partial q}}_{1} \cdot \underbrace{h'(z)}_{\cos(z)} \cdot \underbrace{f'(w)}_{2w}$$

$$= -2w \cdot \sin(y) + 2w \cdot \cos(z)$$

$$= -2w \cdot \sin(w^2) + 2w \cdot \cos(w^2)$$

Figure 3.3: An example of the chain rule in action based on the computational graph of Figure 3.2.

$f(g_1(w), \ldots g_k(w))$, in which a unit computing the *multivariate* function $f(\cdot)$ gets its inputs from k units computing $g_1(w) \ldots g_k(w)$. In such cases, the *multivariable chain rule* needs to be used. The multivariable chain rule is defined as follows:

$$\frac{\partial f(g_1(w), \ldots g_k(w))}{\partial w} = \sum_{i=1}^{k} \frac{\partial f(g_1(w), \ldots g_k(w))}{\partial g_i(w)} \cdot \frac{\partial g_i(w)}{\partial w} \qquad (3.3)$$

It is easy to see that the multivariable chain rule of Equation 3.3 is a simple generalization of that in Equation 3.2. An important consequence of the multivariable chain rule is as follows:

Lemma 3.2.1 (Pathwise Aggregation Lemma) *Consider a directed acyclic computational graph in which the ith node contains variable $y(i)$. The local derivative $z(i,j)$ of the directed edge (i,j) in the graph is defined as $z(i,j) = \frac{\partial y(j)}{\partial y(i)}$. Let a non-null set of paths $\mathcal{P}$ exist from variable w in the graph to output node containing variable o. Then, the value of $\frac{\partial o}{\partial w}$ is given by computing the product of the local gradients along each path in $\mathcal{P}$, and* *summing these products over all paths.*

$$\frac{\partial o}{\partial w} = \sum_{P \in \mathcal{P}} \prod_{(i,j) \in P} z(i,j) \tag{3.4}$$

This lemma can be easily shown by applying Equation 3.3 recursively. Although Lemma 3.2.1 is not used anywhere in the backpropagation algorithm, it helps us develop another exponential-time algorithm that computes the derivatives explicitly. This point of view helps us interpret the multivariable chain rule as a dynamic programming recursion to compute a quantity that would otherwise be computationally too expensive to evaluate. Consider the example shown in Figure 3.2. There are two paths in this particular case. The recursive application of the chain rule is also shown in this example. It is evident that the final result is obtained by computing the product of the local gradients along each of the two paths and then adding them. In Figure 3.3, we have shown a more concrete example of a function that is evaluated by the same computational graph.

$$o = \sin(w^2) + \cos(w^2) \tag{3.5}$$

We have also shown in Figure 3.3 that the application of the chain rule on the computational graph correctly evaluates the derivative, which is $-2w \cdot \sin(w^2) + 2w \cdot \cos(w^2)$.

An Exponential-Time Algorithm

The fact that we can compute the composite derivative as an aggregation of the products of local derivatives along all paths in the computational graph leads to the following exponential-time algorithm:

1. Use computational graph to compute the value $y(i)$ of each nodes i in a forward phase.

2. Compute the local partial derivatives $z(i,j) = \frac{\partial y(j)}{\partial y(i)}$ on each edge in the computational graph.

3. Let $\mathcal{P}$ be the set of all paths from an input node with value w to the output. For each path $P \in \mathcal{P}$ compute the product of each local derivative $z(i,j)$ on that path.

4. Add up these values over all paths in $\mathcal{P}$.

In general, a computational graph will have an exponentially increasing number of paths with depth and one must add the product of the local derivatives over all paths. An example is shown in Figure 3.4, in which we have five layers, each of which has only two units. Therefore, the number of paths between the input and output is $2^5 = 32$. The jth hidden unit of the ith layer is denoted by $h(i,j)$. Each hidden unit is defined as the product of its inputs:

$$h(i,j) = h(i-1,1) \cdot h(i-1,2) \quad \forall j \in \{1,2\} \tag{3.6}$$

In this case, the output is w^{32}, which is expressible in closed form, and can be differentiated easily with respect to w. However, we will use the exponential time algorithm to elucidate the workings of the exponential time algorithm. The derivative of each $h(i,j)$ with respect to each of its two inputs are the values of the complementary inputs:

$$\frac{\partial h(i,j)}{\partial h(i-1,1)} = h(i-1,2), \quad \frac{\partial h(i,j)}{\partial h(i-1,2)} = h(i-1,1)$$

The pathwise aggregation lemma implies that the value of $\frac{\partial o}{\partial w}$ is the product of the local derivatives (which are the complementary input values in this particular case) along all 32 paths from the input to the output:

$$\frac{\partial o}{\partial w} = \sum_{j_1,j_2,j_3,j_4,j_5 \in \{1,2\}^5} \prod \underbrace{h(1,j_1)}_{w} \underbrace{h(2,j_2)}_{w^2} \underbrace{h(3,j_3)}_{w^4} \underbrace{h(4,j_4)}_{w^8} \underbrace{h(5,j_5)}_{w^{16}}$$

$$= \sum_{\text{All 32 paths}} w^{31} = 32w^{31}$$

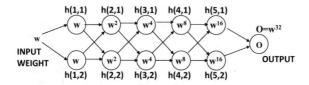

EACH NODE COMPUTES THE PRODUCT OF ITS INPUTS

Figure 3.4: The number of paths in a computational graph increases exponentially with depth. In this case, the chain rule will aggregate the product of local derivatives along $2^5 = 32$ paths.

This result is, of course, consistent with what one would obtain on differentiating w^{32} directly with respect to w. However, an important observation is that it requires 2^5 aggregations to compute the derivative in this way for a relatively simple graph. More importantly, *we repeatedly differentiate the same function computed in a node* for aggregation.

Obviously, this is an inefficient approach to compute gradients. For a network with 100 nodes in each layer and three layers, we will have a million paths. *Nevertheless, this is exactly what we do in traditional machine learning when our prediction function is a complex composition function.* This also explains why most of traditional machine learning is a shallow neural model (cf. Chapter 2). Manually working out the details of a complex composition function is tedious and impractical beyond a certain level of complexity. It is here that the beautiful dynamic programming idea of backpropagation brings order to chaos, and enables models that would otherwise have been impossible.

3.2.2 Dynamic Programming to the Rescue

Although the summation discussed above has an exponential number of components (paths), one can compute it efficiently using dynamic programming. In graph theory, computing all types of path-aggregative values over directed acyclic graphs is done using dynamic programming. Consider a directed acyclic graph in which the value $z(i,j)$ (interpreted as local partial derivative of variable in node j with respect to variable in node i) is associated with edge (i,j). An example of such a computational graph is shown in Figure 3.5. We would like to compute the product of $z(i,j)$ over each path $P \in \mathcal{P}$ from source node w to output o and then add them.

$$S(w,o) = \sum_{P \in \mathcal{P}} \prod_{(i,j) \in P} z(i,j) \tag{3.7}$$

Let $A(i)$ be the set of nodes at the end points of outgoing edges from node i. We can compute the aggregated value $S(i, o)$ for each intermediate node i (between w and o) using the following well-known dynamic programming update:

$$S(i, o) \Leftarrow \sum_{j \in A(i)} S(j, o) z(i, j) \qquad (3.8)$$

This computation can be performed backwards starting from the nodes directly incident on o, since $S(o, o)$ is already known to be 1. The algorithm discussed above is among the most widely used methods for computing all types of path-centric functions on directed acyclic graphs, which would otherwise require exponential time. For example, one can even

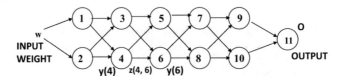

EACH NODE i CONTAINS y(i) AND EACH EDGE BETWEEN i AND j CONTAINS z(i, j)
EXAMPLE: z(4, 6)= PARTIAL DERIVATIVE OF y(6) WITH RESPECT TO y(4)

Figure 3.5: Example of computational graph with edges corresponding to local partial derivatives

use a variation of the above algorithm to find the longest path in a directed acyclic graph (which is known to be NP-hard for general graphs with cycles) [7]. This generic dynamic programming approach is used extensively in directed acyclic graphs.

In fact, *the aforementioned dynamic programming update is exactly the multivariable chain rule of Equation 3.3, which is repeated in the backwards direction starting at the output node where the local gradient is known.* This is because we derived the path-aggregative form of the loss gradient (Lemma 3.2.1) using this chain rule in the first place. The main difference is that we apply the rule in a particular order in order to minimize computations. We summarize this point below:

> Using dynamic programming to efficiently aggregate the product of local gradients along the exponentially many paths in a computational graph results in a dynamic programming update that is identical to the multivariable chain rule of differential calculus.

The above discussion is for the case of generic computational graphs. How do we apply these ideas to neural networks? In the case of neural networks, one can easily compute $\frac{\partial L}{\partial o}$ in terms of the known value of o (by running the input through the network). This derivative is propagated backwards using the local partial derivatives $z(i, j)$, depending on which variables in the neural network are used as intermediate variables. For example, when the post-activation values inside nodes are treated as nodes of the computational graph, the value of $z(i, j)$ is the product of the weight of edge (i, j) and the local derivative of the activation at node j. On the other hand, if we use the pre-activation variables as the nodes of the computational graph, the value of $z(i, j)$ is product of the local derivative of the activation at node i and the weight of the edge (i, j). We will discuss more about the notion of pre-activation variables and post-activation variables in a neural network with the use of an example slightly later (Figure 3.6). We can even create computational graphs containing both pre-activation and post-activation variables to *decouple* linear operations from activation functions. All these methods are equivalent, and will be discussed in the upcoming sections.

3.2.3 Backpropagation with Post-Activation Variables

In this section, we show how to instantiate the aforementioned approach by considering a computational graph in which the nodes contain the post-activation variables in a neural network. These are the same as the hidden variables of different layers.

The backpropagation algorithm first uses a *forward phase* in order to compute the output and the loss. Therefore, the forward phase sets up the initialization for the dynamic programming recurrence, and also the intermediate variables that will be needed in the backwards phase. As discussed in the previous section, the backwards phase uses the dynamic programming recurrence based on the multivariable chain rule of differential calculus. We describe the forward and backward phases as follows:

Forward phase: In the forward phase, a particular input vector is used to compute the values of each hidden layer based on the current values of the weights; the name "forward phase" is used because such computations naturally cascade forward across the layers. The goal of the forward phase is to compute all the intermediate hidden and output variables for a given input. These values will be required during the backward phase. At the point at which the computation is completed, the value of the output o is computed, as is the derivative of the loss function L with respect to this output. The loss is typically a function of all the outputs in the presence of multiple nodes; therefore, the derivatives with respect to all outputs are computed. For now, we will consider the case of a single output node o for simplicity, and then discuss the straightforward generalization to multiple outputs.

Backward phase: The backward phase computes the gradient of the loss function with respect to various weights. The first step is to compute the derivative $\frac{\partial L}{\partial o}$. If the network has multiple outputs, then this value is computed for each output. This sets up the initialization of the gradient computation. Subsequently, the derivatives are propagated in the backwards direction using the multivariable chain rule of Equation 3.3.

Consider a path is denoted by the sequence of hidden units $h_1, h_2, \ldots, h_k$ followed by output o. The weight of the connection from hidden unit h_r to h_{r+1} is denoted by $w_{(h_r, h_{r+1})}$. If a single path exists in the network, it would be a simple matter to backpropagate the derivative of the loss function L with respect to the weights along this path. In most cases, an exponentially large number of paths will exist in the network from any node h_r to the output node o. As shown in Lemma 3.2.1, the partial derivative can be computed by aggregating the products of partial derivatives over all paths from h_r to o. When a set $\mathcal{P}$ of paths exist from h_r to o, one can write the loss derivative as follows:

$$\frac{\partial L}{\partial w_{(h_{r-1}, h_r)}} = \frac{\partial L}{\partial o} \cdot \underbrace{\left[\sum_{[h_r, h_{r+1}, \ldots h_k, o] \in \mathcal{P}} \frac{\partial o}{\partial h_k} \prod_{i=r}^{k-1} \frac{\partial h_{i+1}}{\partial h_i} \right]}_{\text{Backpropagation computes } \Delta(h_r, o) = \frac{\partial L}{\partial h_r}} \frac{\partial h_r}{\partial w_{(h_{r-1}, h_r)}} \tag{3.9}$$

The computation of $\frac{\partial h_r}{\partial w_{(h_{r-1}, h_r)}}$ on the right-hand side is useful in converting a recursively computed partial derivative with respect to *layer activations* into a partial derivative with respect to the *weights*. The path-aggregated term above [annotated by $\Delta(h_r, o) = \frac{\partial L}{\partial h_r}$] is very similar to the quantity $S(i, o) = \frac{\partial o}{\partial y_i}$ discussed in Section 3.2.2. As in that section, the idea is to first compute $\Delta(h_k, o)$ for nodes h_k closest to o, and then recursively compute these values for nodes in earlier layers in terms of nodes in later layers. The value of $\Delta(o, o) = \frac{\partial L}{\partial o}$ is computed as the initial point of the recursion. Subsequently, this computation is propagated in the backwards direction with dynamic programming updates (similar to Equation 3.8). The multivariable chain rule directly provides the recursion for $\Delta(h_r, o)$:

$$\Delta(h_r, o) = \frac{\partial L}{\partial h_r} = \sum_{h:h_r \Rightarrow h} \frac{\partial L}{\partial h} \frac{\partial h}{\partial h_r} = \sum_{h:h_r \Rightarrow h} \frac{\partial h}{\partial h_r} \Delta(h, o) \qquad (3.10)$$

Since each h is in a later layer than h_r, $\Delta(h, o)$ has already been computed while evaluating $\Delta(h_r, o)$. However, we still need to evaluate $\frac{\partial h}{\partial h_r}$ in order to compute Equation 3.10. Consider a situation in which the edge joining h_r to h has weight $w_{(h_r, h)}$, and let a_h be the value computed in hidden unit h just *before* applying the activation function $\Phi(\cdot)$. In other words, we have $h = \Phi(a_h)$, where a_h is a linear combination of its inputs from earlier-layer units incident on h. Then, by the univariate chain rule, the following expression for $\frac{\partial h}{\partial h_r}$ can be derived:

$$\frac{\partial h}{\partial h_r} = \frac{\partial h}{\partial a_h} \cdot \frac{\partial a_h}{\partial h_r} = \frac{\partial \Phi(a_h)}{\partial a_h} \cdot w_{(h_r, h)} = \Phi'(a_h) \cdot w_{(h_r, h)} \qquad (3.11)$$

This value of $\frac{\partial h}{\partial h_r}$ is used in Equation 3.10 to obtain the following:

$$\Delta(h_r, o) = \sum_{h:h_r \Rightarrow h} \Phi'(a_h) \cdot w_{(h_r, h)} \cdot \Delta(h, o) \qquad (3.12)$$

This recursion is repeated in the backwards direction, starting with the output node. The entire process is linear in the number of edges in the network. Note that one could also have derived Equation 3.12 by using the generic computational graph algorithm in Section 3.2.2 with respect to post-activation variables. One simply needs to set $z(i, j)$ in Equation 3.8 to the product of the weight between nodes i and j, and the activation derivative at node j.

Backpropagation can be summarized in the following steps:

1. Use a forward-pass to compute the values of all hidden units, output o, and loss L for a particular input-output pattern $(\overline{X}, y)$.

2. Initialize $\Delta(o, o)$ to $\frac{\partial L}{\partial o}$.

3. Use the recurrence of Equation 3.12 to compute each $\Delta(h_r, o)$ in the backwards direction. After each such computation, compute the gradients with respect to incident weights as follows:

$$\frac{\partial L}{\partial w_{(h_{r-1}, h_r)}} = \Delta(h_r, o) \cdot h_{r-1} \cdot \Phi'(a_{h_r}) \qquad (3.13)$$

   The partial derivatives with respect to incident biases can be computed by using the fact that bias neurons are always activated at a value of $+1$. Therefore, to compute the partial derivative of the loss with respect to the bias of node h_r, we simply set h_{r-1} to 1 in the right-hand side of Equation 3.13.

4. Use the computed partial derivatives of loss function with respect to weights in order to perform stochastic gradient descent for input-output pattern $(\overline{X}, y)$.

This description of backpropagation is greatly simplified, and actual implementations have to incorporate numerous changes for efficiency and stability. For example, the gradients are computed with respect to multiple training instances at one time, and these multiple instances are referred to as a *mini-batch*. These are all backpropagated simultaneously in order to add up their local gradients and execute mini-batch stochastic gradient descent. This enhancement will be discussed in Section 3.2.8. Another difference is that we have assumed a single output. However, in many types of neural networks (e.g., multiclass perceptrons), multiple outputs exist. The description of this section can easily be generalized to multiple outputs by adding the contributions of different outputs to the loss derivatives (see Section 3.2.7).

A few observations are noteworthy. Equation 3.13 shows that the partial derivative of the loss with respect to an edge from h_{r-1} to h_r always contains h_{r-1} as a multiplicative

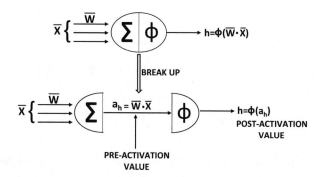

Figure 3.6: Pre- and post-activation values within a neuron

term. The remaining portion of the multiplicative factor in Equation 3.13 is seen as a backpropagated "error." In a sense, the algorithm recursively backpropagates the errors and multiplies them with the values in the hidden layer just before the weight matrix to be updated. This is why backpropagation is sometimes understood as error propagation.

3.2.4 Backpropagation with Pre-activation Variables

In the aforementioned discussion, the values $h_1 \ldots h_k$ along a path are used to compute the chain rule. However, one can also use the values *before* computing the activation function $\Phi(\cdot)$ in order to define the chain rule. In other words, the gradients are computed with respect to the pre-activation values of the hidden variables, which are then propagated backwards. This alternative approach to backpropagation is how it is presented in most textbooks.

The pre-activation value of the hidden variable h_r is denoted by a_{h_r}, where:

$$h_r = \Phi(a_{h_r}) \tag{3.14}$$

Figure 3.6 shows the distinction between pre- and post-activation values. In such a case, we can rewrite Equation 3.9 as follows:

$$\frac{\partial L}{\partial w_{(h_{r-1},h_r)}} = \underbrace{\frac{\partial L}{\partial o} \cdot \Phi'(a_o) \cdot \left[\sum_{[h_r,h_{r+1},\ldots h_k,o]\in\mathcal{P}} \frac{\partial a_o}{\partial a_{h_k}} \prod_{i=r}^{k-1} \frac{\partial a_{h_{i+1}}}{\partial a_{h_i}} \right]}_{\text{Backpropagation computes } \delta(h_r,o) = \frac{\partial L}{\partial a_{h_r}}} h_{r-1} \tag{3.15}$$

We have introduced the notation $\delta()$ to enable recurrence in this case. Note that the recurrence for $\Delta(h_r,o) = \frac{\partial L}{\partial h_r}$ uses the hidden values *after* each activation as intermediate variables in the chain rule, whereas the recurrence for $\delta(h_r, o) = \frac{\partial L}{\partial a_{h_r}}$ uses the hidden values *before* activation. Like Equation 3.10, we can obtain the following recurrence equations:

$$\delta(h_r, o) = \frac{\partial L}{\partial a_{h_r}} = \sum_{h:h_r \Rightarrow h} \frac{\partial L}{\partial a_h} \frac{\partial a_h}{\partial a_{h_r}} = \sum_{h:h_r \Rightarrow h} \frac{\partial a_h}{\partial a_{h_r}} \delta(h, o) \qquad (3.16)$$

One can use the chain rule to compute the expression for $\frac{\partial a_h}{\partial a_{h_r}}$ on the right-hand side of Equation 3.16:

$$\frac{\partial a_h}{\partial a_{h_r}} = \frac{\partial a_h}{\partial h_r} \cdot \frac{\partial h_r}{\partial a_{h_r}} = w_{(h_r,h)} \cdot \frac{\partial \Phi(a_{h_r})}{\partial a_{h_r}} = \Phi'(a_{h_r}) \cdot w_{(h_r,h)} \qquad (3.17)$$

By substituting the computed expression for $\frac{\partial a_h}{\partial a_{h_r}}$ in the right-hand side of Equation 3.16, we obtain the following:

$$\delta(h_r, o) = \Phi'(a_{h_r}) \sum_{h:h_r \Rightarrow h} w_{(h_r,h)} \cdot \delta(h, o) \qquad (3.18)$$

Equation 3.18 can also be derived by using pre-activation variables in the generic computational graph algorithm of Section 3.2.2. One simply needs to set $z(i, j)$ in Equation 3.8 to the product of the weight between nodes i and j, and the activation derivative at node i.

One advantage of this recurrence condition over the one obtained using post-activation variables is that the activation gradient is outside the summation, and therefore we can easily compute the specific form of the recurrence for each type of activation function at node h_r. Furthermore, since the activation gradient is outside the summation, one can simplify the backpropagation computation by decoupling the effect of the activation function and that of the linear transformation in backpropagation updates. The simplified and decoupled view will be discussed in more detail in Section 3.2.6, and it uses *both* pre-activation and post-activation variables for the dynamic programming recursion. This simplified approach represents how backpropagation is actually implemented in real systems. From an implementation point of view, decoupling the linear transformation from the activation function is helpful, because the linear portion is a simple matrix multiplication and the activation portion is an elementwise multiplication. Both can be implemented efficiently on all types of matrix-friendly hardware (such as graphics processor units).

The backpropagation process can now be described as follows:

1. Use a forward-pass to compute the values of all hidden units, output o, and loss L for a particular input-output pattern $(\overline{X}, y)$.

2. Initialize $\frac{\partial L}{\partial a_o} = \delta(o, o)$ to $\frac{\partial L}{\partial o} \cdot \Phi'(a_o)$.

3. Use the recurrence of Equation 3.18 to compute each $\delta(h_r, o)$ in the backwards direction. After each such computation, compute the gradients with respect to incident weights as follows:

$$\frac{\partial L}{\partial w_{(h_{r-1}, h_r)}} = \delta(h_r, o) \cdot h_{r-1} \qquad (3.19)$$

The partial derivatives with respect to incident biases can be computed by using the fact that bias neurons are always activated at a value of $+1$. Therefore, to compute the partial derivative of the loss with respect to the bias of node h_r, we simply set h_{r-1} to 1 in the right-hand side of Equation 3.19.

4. Use the computed partial derivatives of loss function with respect to weights in order to perform stochastic gradient descent for input-output pattern $(\overline{X}, y)$.

The main difference of this (more common) variant of the backpropagation algorithm is in terms of the way in which the recursion is written, because pre-activation variables have been used for dynamic programming. Both the pre- and post-activation variants of backpropagation are mathematically equivalent (see Exercise 9). We have chosen to show both variations of backpropagation in order to emphasize the fact that one can use dynamic programming in a variety of ways to derive equivalent equations. An even more simplified view of backpropagation, in which *both* pre-activation and post-activation variables are used, is provided in Section 3.2.6.

3.2.5 Examples of Updates for Various Activations

One advantage of Equation 3.18 is that we can compute the specific types of updates for various nodes. In the following, we provide the instantiation of Equation 3.18 for different types of nodes:

$$\delta(h_r, o) = \sum_{h:h_r \Rightarrow h} w_{(h_r, h)} \delta(h, o) \quad \text{[Linear]}$$

$$\delta(h_r, o) = h_r(1 - h_r) \sum_{h:h_r \Rightarrow h} w_{(h_r, h)} \delta(h, o) \quad \text{[Sigmoid]}$$

$$\delta(h_r, o) = (1 - h_r^2) \sum_{h:h_r \Rightarrow h} w_{(h_r, h)} \delta(h, o) \quad \text{[Tanh]}$$

Note that the derivative of the sigmoid can be written in terms of its *output* value h_r as $h_r(1 - h_r)$. Similarly, the tanh derivative can be expressed as $(1 - h_r^2)$. The derivatives of different activation functions are discussed in Section 1.2.1.6 of Chapter 1. For the ReLU function, the value of $\delta(h_r, o)$ can be computed in case-wise fashion:

$$\delta(h_r, o) = \begin{cases} \sum_{h:h_r \Rightarrow h} w_{(h_r, h)} \delta(h, o) & \text{if } 0 < a_{h_r} \\ 0 & \text{otherwise} \end{cases}$$

A similar recurrence can be shown for the hard tanh function except that the update condition is slightly different:

$$\delta(h_r, o) = \begin{cases} \sum_{h:h_r \Rightarrow h} w_{(h_r, h)} \delta(h, o) & \text{if } -1 < a_{h_r} < 1 \\ 0 & \text{otherwise} \end{cases}$$

It is noteworthy that the ReLU and tanh are non-differentiable at exactly the condition boundaries. However, this is rarely a problem in practical settings, in which one works with finite precision.

3.2.5.1 The Special Case of Softmax

Softmax activation is a special case because the function is not computed with respect to one input, but with respect to multiple inputs. Therefore, one cannot use exactly the same type of update, as with other activation functions. As discussed in Equation 1.12 of

Chapter 1, the softmax converts k real-valued predictions $v_1 \ldots v_k$ into output probabilities $o_1 \ldots o_k$ using the following relationship:

$$o_i = \frac{\exp(v_i)}{\sum_{j=1}^{k} \exp(v_j)} \quad \forall i \in \{1, \ldots, k\} \tag{3.20}$$

Note that if we try to use the chain rule to backpropagate the derivative of the loss L with respect to $v_1 \ldots v_k$, then one has to compute each $\frac{\partial L}{\partial o_i}$ and also each $\frac{\partial o_i}{\partial v_j}$. This backpropagation of the softmax is greatly simplified, when we take two facts into account:

1. The softmax is almost always used in the output layer.

2. The softmax is almost always paired with the *cross-entropy loss*. Let $y_1 \ldots y_k \in \{0, 1\}$ be the one-hot encoded (observed) outputs for the k mutually exclusive classes. Then, the cross-entropy loss is defined as follows:

$$L = -\sum_{i=1}^{k} y_i \log(o_i) \tag{3.21}$$

The key point is that the value of $\frac{\partial L}{\partial v_i}$ has a particularly simple form in the case of the softmax:

$$\frac{\partial L}{\partial v_i} = \sum_{j=1}^{k} \frac{\partial L}{\partial o_j} \cdot \frac{\partial o_j}{\partial v_i} = o_i - y_i \tag{3.22}$$

The reader is encouraged to work out the detailed derivation of the result above; it is tedious, but relatively straightforward algebra. The derivation is enabled by the fact that the value of $\frac{\partial o_j}{\partial v_i}$ in Equation 3.22 can be shown to be equal to $o_i(1 - o_i)$ when $i = j$ (which is the same as sigmoid), and otherwise can be shown to be equal to $-o_i o_j$ (see Exercise 10).

Therefore, in the case of the softmax, one first backpropagates the gradient from the output to the layer containing $v_1 \ldots v_k$. Further backpropagation can proceed according to the rules discussed earlier in this section. Note that in this case, we have decoupled the backpropagation update of the softmax activation from the backpropagation in the rest of the network, in which matrix multiplications are always included along with the activation function in the backpropagation update. In general, it is helpful to create a view of backpropagation in which the linear matrix multiplications and activation layers are decoupled because it greatly simplifies the updates. This view will be discussed in the next section.

3.2.6   A Decoupled View of Vector-Centric Backpropagation

In the previous discussion, two equivalent ways of computing the updates based on Equations 3.12 and 3.18 were provided. In each case, *one is really backpropagating through a linear matrix multiplication and an activation computation simultaneously.* The way in which we order these two coupled computations affects whether we obtain Equation 3.12 or 3.18. Unfortunately, this unnecessarily complicated view of backpropagation has proliferated in papers and textbooks since the beginning. This is, in part, because layers are traditionally defined in a neural network by combining the two separate operations of linear transformation and activation function computation.

However, in many real implementations, the linear computations and the activation computations are decoupled as separate "layers," and one separately backpropagates through the two layers. Furthermore, we use a vector-centric representation of the neural network, so that operations on vector representations of layers are vector-to-vector operations such as a matrix multiplication in a linear layer [cf. Figure 1.11(d) in Chapter 1]. This view greatly simplifies the computations. Therefore, one can create a neural network in which activation layers are alternately arranged with linear layers, as shown in Figure 3.7. Note that the activation layers can use identity activation if needed. Activation layers (usually) perform one-to-one, elementwise computations on the vector components with the activation function $\Phi(\cdot)$, whereas linear layers perform all-to-all computations by multiplying with the coefficient matrix W. Then, for each pair of matrix multiplication and activation function layers, the following forward and backward steps need to be performed:

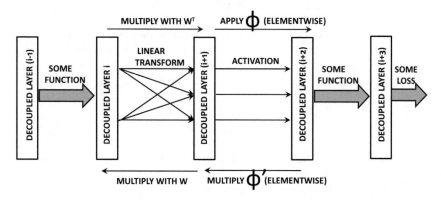

Figure 3.7: A decoupled view of backpropagation

Table 3.1: Examples of different functions and their backpropagation updates between layers i and $(i+1)$. The hidden values and gradients in layer i are denoted by $\overline{z}_i$ and $\overline{g}_i$. Some of these computations use $I(\cdot)$ as the binary indicator function.

Function	Type	Forward	Backward
Linear	Many-Many	$\overline{z}_{i+1} = W^T \overline{z}_i$	$\overline{g}_i = W \overline{g}_{i+1}$
Sigmoid	One-One	$\overline{z}_{i+1} =$ sigmoid$(\overline{z}_i)$	$\overline{g}_i = \overline{g}_{i+1} \odot \overline{z}_{i+1} \odot (1 - \overline{z}_{i+1})$
Tanh	One-One	$\overline{z}_{i+1} =$ tanh$(\overline{z}_i)$	$\overline{g}_i = \overline{g}_{i+1} \odot (1 - \overline{z}_{i+1} \odot \overline{z}_{i+1})$
ReLU	One-One	$\overline{z}_{i+1} = \overline{z}_i \odot I(\overline{z}_i > 0)$	$\overline{g}_i = \overline{g}_{i+1} \odot I(\overline{z}_i > 0)$
Hard Tanh	One-One	Set to ± 1 ($\notin [-1, +1]$) Copy ($\in [-1, +1]$)	Set to 0 ($\notin [-1, +1]$) Copy ($\in [-1, +1]$)
Max	Many-One	Maximum of inputs	Set to 0 (non-maximal inputs) Copy (maximal input)
Arbitrary function $f_k(\cdot)$	Anything	$\overline{z}_{i+1}^{(k)} = f_k(\overline{z}_i)$	$\overline{g}_i = J^T \overline{g}_{i+1}$ J is Jacobian (Equation 3.23)

1. Let $\overline{z}_i$ and $\overline{z}_{i+1}$ be the column vectors of activations in the forward direction when the matrix of linear transformations from the ith to the $(i+1)$th layer is denoted by W. Furthermore, let $\overline{g}_i$ and $\overline{g}_{i+1}$ be the backpropagated vectors of gradients in the two layers. Each element of $\overline{g}_i$ is the partial derivative of the loss function with respect to

a hidden variable in the ith layer. Then, we have the following:

$$\overline{z}_{i+1} = W^T \overline{z}_i \quad \text{[Forward Propagation]}$$
$$\overline{g}_i = W \overline{g}_{i+1} \quad \text{[Backward Propagation]}$$

2. Now consider a situation where the activation function $\Phi(\cdot)$ is applied to each node in layer $(i+1)$ to obtain the activations in layer $(i+2)$. Then, we have the following:

$$\overline{z}_{i+2} = \Phi(\overline{z}_{i+1}) \quad \text{[Forward Propagation]}$$
$$\overline{g}_{i+1} = \overline{g}_{i+2} \odot \Phi'(\overline{z}_{i+1}) \quad \text{[Backward Propagation]}$$

Here, $\Phi(\cdot)$ and its derivative $\Phi'(\cdot)$ are applied in element-wise fashion to vector arguments. The symbol $\odot$ indicates elementwise multiplication.

Note the extraordinary simplicity once the activation is decoupled from the matrix multiplication in a layer. The forward and backward computations are shown in Figure 3.7. Furthermore, the derivatives of $\Phi(\overline{z}_{i+1})$ can often be computed in terms of the outputs of the next layer. Based on Section 3.2.5, one can show the following for sigmoid activations:

$$\Phi'(\overline{z}_{i+1}) = \Phi(\overline{z}_{i+1}) \odot (1 - \Phi(\overline{z}_{i+1}))$$
$$= \overline{z}_{i+2} \odot (1 - \overline{z}_{i+2})$$

Examples of different types of backpropagation updates for various forward functions are shown in Table 3.1. In this case, we have used layer indices of i and $(i+1)$ for *both* linear transformations and activation functions (rather than using $(i+2)$ for activation function). Note that the second to last entry in the table corresponds to the maximization function. This type of function is useful for *max-pooling* operations in convolutional neural networks. Therefore, the backward propagation operation is just like forward propagation. Given the vector of gradients in a layer, one only has to apply the operations shown in the final column of Table 3.1 to obtain the gradients with respect to the previous layer.

Some neural operations are more complex many-to-many functions than simple matrix multiplications. These cases can be handled by assuming that the kth activation in layer-$(i+1)$ is obtained by applying an arbitrary function $f_k(\cdot)$ on the vector of activations in layer-i. Then, the elements of the Jacobian are defined as follows:

$$J_{kr} = \frac{\partial f_k(\overline{z}_i)}{\partial \overline{z}_i^{(r)}} \tag{3.23}$$

Here, $\overline{z}_i^{(r)}$ is the rth element in $\overline{z}_i$. Let J be the matrix whose elements are J_{kr}. Then, it is easy to see that the backpropagation update from layer to layer can be written as follows:

$$\overline{g}_i = J^T \overline{g}_{i+1} \tag{3.24}$$

Writing backpropagation equations as matrix multiplications is often beneficial from an implementation-centric point of view, such as acceleration with Graphics Processor Units (cf. Section 3.7.1). Note that the elements in $\overline{g}_i$ represent gradients of the loss with respect to the *activations* in the ith layer, and therefore an additional step is needed to compute gradients with respect to the *weights*. The gradient of the loss with respect to a weight between the pth unit of the $(i-1)$th layer and the qth unit of ith layer is obtained by multiplying the pth element of $\overline{z}_{i-1}$ with the qth element of $\overline{g}_i$.

3.2.7 Loss Functions on Multiple Output Nodes and Hidden Nodes

For simplicity, the discussion above has used only a single output node at which the loss function is computed. However, in most applications, the loss function is computed over multiple output nodes O. The only difference in this case is that the value of *each* $\frac{\partial L}{\partial a_o} = \delta(o, O)$ for $o \in O$ is initialized to $\frac{\partial L}{\partial o} \Phi'(o)$. Backpropagation is then executed in order to compute $\frac{\partial L}{\partial a_h} = \delta(h, O)$ for each hidden node h.

In some forms of sparse feature learning, even the outputs of the hidden nodes have loss functions associated with them. This occurs frequently in order to encourage solutions with specific properties, such as a hidden layer that is sparse (e.g., sparse autoencoder), or a hidden layer with a specific type of regularization penalty (e.g., contractive autoencoder). The case of sparsity penalties is discussed in Section 4.4.4 of Chapter 4, and the problem of contractive autoencoders is discussed in Section 4.10.3 of Chapter 4. In such cases, the backpropagation algorithm requires only minor modifications in which the gradient flow in the backwards direction is based on all the nodes at which the loss is computed. This can be achieved by simple aggregation of the gradient flows resulting from different losses. One can view this as a special type of network in which the hidden nodes are also output nodes, and the output nodes are not restricted to the final layer of the network. At a fundamental level, the backpropagation methodology remains the same.

Consider the case in which the loss function L_{h_r} is associated with the hidden node h_r, whereas the overall loss over all nodes is L. Furthermore, let $\frac{\partial L}{\partial a_{h_r}} = \delta(h_r, N(h_r))$ denote the gradient flow from all nodes $N(h_r)$ reachable from node h_r, with which some portion of the loss is associated. In this case, the node set $N(h_r)$ might contain both nodes in the output layer as well as nodes in the hidden layer (with which a loss is associated), as long as these nodes are reachable from h_r. Therefore, the set $N(h_r)$ uses h_r as an argument. Note that the set $N(h_r)$ includes the node h_r. Then, the update of Equation 3.18 is first applied as follows:

$$\delta(h_r, N(h_r)) \Leftarrow \Phi'(a_{h_r}) \sum_{h:h_r \Rightarrow h} w_{(h_r, h)} \delta(h, N(h)) \qquad (3.25)$$

This is similar to the standard backpropagation update. However, the current value of $\delta(h_r, N(h_r))$ does not yet include the contribution of h_r. Therefore, an *additional step* is executed to adjust $\delta(h_r, N(h_r))$ based on the contribution of h_r to the loss function:

$$\delta(h_r, N(h_r)) \Leftarrow \delta(h_r, N(h_r)) + \Phi'(h_r) \frac{\partial L_{h_r}}{\partial h_r} \qquad (3.26)$$

It is important to keep in mind that the overall loss L is different from L_{h_r}, which is the loss specific to node h_r. Furthermore, the addition to the gradient flow in Equation 3.26 has a similar algebraic form to the value of the initialization of the output nodes. In other words, the gradient flows caused by the hidden nodes are similar to those of the output nodes. The only difference is that the computed value is added to the existing gradient flow at the hidden nodes. Therefore, the overall framework of backpropagation remains almost identical, with the main difference being that the backpropagation algorithm picks up additional contributions from the losses at the hidden nodes.

3.2.8 Mini-Batch Stochastic Gradient Descent

From the very first chapter of this book, all updates to the weights are performed in point-specific fashion, which is referred to as *stochastic* gradient descent. Such an approach is common in machine learning algorithms. In this section, we provide a justification for this choice along with related variants like *mini-batch stochastic gradient descent*. We also provide an understanding of the advantages and disadvantages of various choices.

Most machine learning problems can be recast as optimization problems over specific objective functions. For example, the objective function in neural networks can be defined in terms optimizing a loss function L, which is often a *linearly separable sum* of the loss functions on the individual training data points. For example, in a *linear regression application*, one minimizes the sum of the squared prediction errors over the training data points. In a *dimensionality reduction application*, one minimizes the sum of squared representation errors in the reconstructed training data points. One can write the loss function of a neural network in the following form:

$$L = \sum_{i=1}^{n} L_i \tag{3.27}$$

Here, L_i is the loss contributed by the ith training point. For most of the algorithms in Chapter 2, we have worked with training point-specific loss rather than the aggregate loss.

In gradient descent, one tries to minimize the loss function of the neural network by moving the parameters along the negative direction of the gradient. For example, in the case of the perceptron, the parameters correspond to $\overline{W} = (w_1 \ldots w_d)$. Therefore, one would try to compute the loss of the underlying objective function over all points simultaneously and perform gradient descent. Therefore, in traditional gradient descent, one would try to perform gradient-descent steps such as the following:

$$\overline{W} \Leftarrow \overline{W} - \alpha \left(\frac{\partial L}{\partial w_1}, \frac{\partial L}{\partial w_2} \ldots \frac{\partial L}{\partial w_d} \right) \tag{3.28}$$

This type of derivative can also be written succinctly in vector notation (i.e., matrix calculus notation):

$$\overline{W} \Leftarrow \overline{W} - \alpha \frac{\partial L}{\partial \overline{W}} \tag{3.29}$$

For single-layer networks like the perceptron, gradient-descent is done only with respect to $\overline{W}$, whereas for larger networks, all parameters in the network need to be updated with backpropagation. The number of parameters can easily be on the order of millions in large-scale applications, and one needs to *simultaneously* run all examples forwards and backwards through the network in order to compute the backpropagation updates. It is, however, impractical to simultaneously run all examples through the network to compute the gradient with respect to the *entire data set* in one shot. Note that even the memory requirements of all intermediate/final predictions *for each training instance* would need to be maintained by gradient descent. This can be exceedingly large in most practical settings. At the beginning of the learning process, the weights are often incorrect to such a degree that even a small sample of points can be used to create an excellent estimate of the gradient's direction. The additive effect of the updates created from such samples can often provide an accurate direction of movement. This observation provides a practical foundation for the success of the stochastic gradient-descent method and its variants.

Since the loss function of most optimization problems can be expressed as a linear sum of the losses with respect to individual points (cf. Equation 3.27), it is easy to show the following:

$$\frac{\partial L}{\partial \overline{W}} = \sum_{i=1}^{n} \frac{\partial L_i}{\partial \overline{W}} \tag{3.30}$$

In this case, updating the full gradient with respect to all the points sums up the individual point-specific effects. Machine learning problems inherently have a high level of redundancy between the knowledge captured by different training points, and one can often more efficiently undertake the learning process with the point-specific updates of stochastic gradient descent:

$$\overline{W} \Leftarrow \overline{W} - \alpha \frac{\partial L_i}{\partial \overline{W}} \tag{3.31}$$

This type of gradient descent is referred to as *stochastic* because one cycles through the points in some random order. Note that the long-term effect of repeated updates is approximately the same, although each update in stochastic gradient descent can only be viewed as a probabilistic approximation. Each local gradient can be computed efficiently, which makes stochastic gradient descent fast, albeit at the expense of accuracy in gradient computation. However, one interesting property of stochastic gradient descent is that even though it might not perform as well on the training data (compared to gradient descent), it often performs comparably (and sometimes even better) on the test data [171]. As you will learn in Chapter 4, stochastic gradient descent has the indirect effect of regularization. However, it can occasionally provide very poor results with certain orderings of training points.

In mini-batch stochastic descent, one uses a batch $B = \{j_1 \ldots j_m\}$ of training points for the update:

$$\overline{W} \Leftarrow \overline{W} - \alpha \sum_{i \in B} \frac{\partial L_i}{\partial \overline{W}} \tag{3.32}$$

Mini-batch stochastic gradient descent often provides the best trade-off between stability, speed, and memory requirements. When using mini-batch stochastic gradient descent, the outputs of a layer are matrices instead of vectors, and forward propagation requires the multiplication of the weight matrix with the activation matrix. The same is true for backward propagation in which matrices of gradients are maintained. Therefore, the implementation of mini-batch stochastic gradient descent increases the memory requirements, which is a key limiting factor on the size of the mini-batch.

The size of the mini-batch is therefore regulated by the amount of memory available on the particular hardware architecture at hand. Keeping a batch size that is too small also results in constant overheads, which is inefficient even from a computational point of view. Beyond a certain batch size (which is typically of the order of a few hundred points), one does not gain much in terms of the accuracy of gradient computation. It is common to use powers of 2 as the size of the mini-batch, because this choice often provides the best efficiency on most hardware architectures; commonly used values are 32, 64, 128, or 256. Although the use of mini-batch stochastic gradient descent is ubiquitous in neural network learning, most of this book will use a single point for the update (i.e., pure stochastic gradient descent) for simplicity in presentation.

3.2.9 Backpropagation Tricks for Handling Shared Weights

A very common approach for regularizing neural networks is to use *shared weights*. The basic idea is that if one has some semantic insight that a similar function will be computed in different nodes of the network, then the weights associated with those nodes will be constrained to be the same value. Some examples are as follows:

1. In an autoencoder simulating PCA (cf. Section 2.5.1.3 of Chapter 2), the weights in the input layer and the output layer are shared.

2. In a recurrent neural network for text (cf. Chapter 7), the weights in different temporal layers are shared, because it is assumed that the *language model* at each time-stamp is the same.

3. In a convolutional neural network, the same grid of weights (corresponding to a visual field) is used over the entire spatial extent of the neurons (cf. Chapter 8).

Sharing weights in a semantically insightful way is one of the key tricks to successful neural network design. When one can identify the insight that the function computed at two nodes ought to be similar, it makes sense to use the same set of weights in that pair of nodes.

At first sight, it might seem to be an onerous task to compute the gradient of the loss with respect to the shared weights in these different regions of the network, because the different uses of the weights would also influence one another in an unpredictable way in the computational graph. However, backpropagation with respect to shared weights turns out to be mathematically simple.

Let w be a weight, which is shared at T different nodes in the network, and the corresponding copies of the weights at these nodes be denoted by $w_1 \ldots w_T$. Let the loss function be L. Then, it is easy to use the chain rule to show the following:

$$\frac{\partial L}{\partial w} = \sum_{i=1}^{T} \frac{\partial L}{\partial w_i} \cdot \underbrace{\frac{\partial w_i}{\partial w}}_{=1}$$

$$= \sum_{i=1}^{T} \frac{\partial L}{\partial w_i}$$

In other words, all we have to do is to pretend that these weights are independent, compute their derivatives, and add them! Therefore, we simply have to execute the backpropagation algorithm without any change and then sum up the gradients of different copies of the shared weight. This simple observation is used at many places in neural network learning. It also forms the basis of the learning algorithm in recurrent neural networks.

3.2.10   Checking the Correctness of Gradient Computation

The backpropagation algorithm is quite complex, and one might occasionally check the correctness of gradient computation. This can be performed easily with the use of numerical methods. Consider a particular weight w of a randomly selected edge in the network. Let $L(w)$ be the current value of the loss. The weight of this edge is perturbed by adding a small amount $\epsilon > 0$ to it. Then, the forward algorithm is executed with this perturbed weight and the loss $L(w + \epsilon)$ is computed. Then, the partial derivative of the loss with respect to w can be shown to be the following:

$$\frac{\partial L(w)}{\partial w} \approx \frac{L(w + \epsilon) - L(w)}{\epsilon} \tag{3.33}$$

When the partial derivatives do not match closely enough, it is easy to detect that an error must have occurred in computation. One needs to perform the above estimation for only two or three checkpoints in the training process, which is quite efficient. However, it might be advisable to perform the checking over a large subset of the parameters at these checkpoints. One problem is in determining when the gradients are "close enough," especially when one has no idea about the absolute magnitudes of these values. This is achieved by using relative ratios.

Let the backpropagation-determined derivative be denoted by G_e, and the aforementioned estimation be denoted by G_a. Then, the relative ratio ρ is defined as follows:

$$\rho = \frac{|G_e - G_a|}{|G_e + G_a|} \tag{3.34}$$

Typically, the ratio should be less than 10^{-6}, although for some activation functions like the ReLU in which sharp changes in derivatives occur at particular points, it is possible for the numerical gradient to be different from the computed gradient. In such cases, the ratio should still be less than 10^{-3}. One can use this numerical approximation to test various edges and check the correctness of their gradients. If there are millions of parameters, then one can test a sample of the derivatives for a quick check of correctness. It is also advisable to perform this check at two or three points in the training because the checks at initialization might correspond to special cases that do not generalize to arbitrary points in the parameter space.

3.3 Setup and Initialization Issues

There are several important issues associated with the setup of the neural network, preprocessing, and initialization. First, the *hyperparameters* of the neural network (such as the learning rates and regularization parameters) need to be selected. Feature preprocessing and initialization can also be rather important. Neural networks tend to have larger parameter spaces compared to other machine learning algorithms, which magnifies the effect of preprocessing and initialization in many ways. In the following, we will discuss the basic methods used for feature preprocessing and initialization. Strictly speaking, advanced methods like *pretraining* can also be considered initialization techniques. However, these techniques require a deeper understanding of the model generalization issues associated with neural network training. For this reason, discussion on this topic will be deferred to the next chapter.

3.3.1 Tuning Hyperparameters

Neural networks have a large number of *hyperparameters* such as the learning rate, the weight of regularization, and so on. The term "hyperparameter" is used to specifically refer to the parameters regulating the design of the model (like learning rate and regularization), and they are different from the more fundamental parameters representing the weights of connections in the neural network. In Bayesian statistics, the notion of hyperparameter is used to control the prior distribution, although we use this definition in a somewhat loose sense here. In a sense, there is a two-tiered organization of parameters in the neural network, in which primary model parameters like weights are optimized with backpropagation only after fixing the hyperparameters either manually or with the use of a *tuning* phase. As we will discuss in Section 4.3 of Chapter 4, the hyperparameters should not be tuned using the same data used for gradient descent. Rather, a portion of the data is held out as validation data, and the performance of the model is tested on the validation set with various choices of hyperparameters. This type of approach ensures that the tuning process does not overfit to the training data set (while providing poor test data performance).

How should the candidate hyperparameters be selected for testing? The most well-known technique is *grid search*, in which a set of values is selected for each hyperparameter. In the most straightforward implementation of grid search, all combinations of selected values of the hyperparameters are tested in order to determine the optimal choice. One issue with this procedure is that the number of hyperparameters might be large, and the number of points in the grid increases *exponentially* with the number of hyperparameters. For example, if we have 5 hyperparameters, and we test 10 values for each hyperparameter, the training procedure needs to be executed $10^5 = 100000$ times to test its accuracy. Although one does not run such testing procedures to completion, the number of runs is still too large to be reasonably executed for most settings of even modest size. Therefore, a commonly used trick is to first work with coarse grids. Later, when one narrows down to a particular range of interest, finer grids are used. One must be careful when the optimal hyperparameter selected is at the edge of a grid range, because one would need to test beyond the range to see if better values exist.

The testing approach may at times be too expensive even with the coarse-to-fine-grained process. It has been pointed out [37] that grid-based hyperparameter exploration is not necessarily the best choice. In some cases, it makes sense to randomly sample the hyperparameters uniformly within the grid range. As in the case of grid ranges, one can perform multi-resolution sampling, where one first samples in the full grid range. One then creates a new set of grid ranges that are geometrically smaller than the previous grid ranges and centered around the optimal parameters from the previously explored samples. Sampling is repeated on this smaller box and the entire process is iteratively repeated multiple times to refine the parameters.

Another key point about sampling many types of hyperparameters is that the *logarithms* of the hyperparameters are sampled uniformly rather than the hyperparameters themselves. Two examples of such parameters include the regularization rate and the learning rate. For example, instead of sampling the learning rate α between 0.1 and 0.001, we first sample $\log(\alpha)$ uniformly between -1 and -3, and then exponentiate it to the power of 10. It is more common to search for hyperparameters in the logarithmic space, although there are some hyperparameters that should be searched for on a uniform scale.

Finally, a key point about large-scale settings is that it is sometimes impossible to run these algorithms to completion because of the large training times involved. For example, a single run of a convolutional neural network in image processing might take a couple of weeks. Trying to run the algorithm over many different choices of parameter combinations is impractical. However, one can often obtain a reasonable estimate of the broader behavior of the algorithm in a short time. Therefore, the algorithms are often run for a certain number of epochs to test the progress. Runs that are obviously poor or diverge from convergence can be quickly killed. In many cases, multiple threads of the process with different hyperparameters can be run, and one can successively terminate or add new sampled runs. In the end, only one winner is allowed to train to completion. Sometimes a few winners may be allowed to train to completion, and their predictions will be averaged as an ensemble.

A mathematically justified way of choosing for hyperparameters is the use of *Bayesian optimization* [42, 306]. However, these methods are often too slow to practically use in large-scale neural networks and remain an intellectual curiosity for researchers. For smaller networks, it is possible to use libraries such as *Hyperopt* [614], *Spearmint* [616], and *SMAC* [615].

3.3.2   Feature Preprocessing

The feature processing methods used for neural network training are not very different from those in other machine learning algorithms. There are two forms of feature preprocessing used in machine learning algorithms:

1. *Additive preprocessing and mean-centering:* It can be useful to mean-center the data in order to remove certain types of bias effects. Many algorithms in traditional machine learning (such as principal component analysis) also work with the assumption of mean-centered data. In such cases, a vector of column-wise means is subtracted from each data point. Mean-centering is often paired with *standardization*, which is discussed in the section of feature normalization.

   A second type of pre-processing is used when it is desired for all feature values to be non-negative. In such a case, the absolute value of the most negative entry of a feature is added to the corresponding feature value of each data point. The latter is typically combined with min-max normalization, which is discussed below.

2. *Feature normalization:* A common type of normalization is to divide each feature value by its standard deviation. When this type of feature scaling is combined with mean-centering, the data is said to have been *standardized*. The basic idea is that each feature is presumed to have been drawn from a *standard* normal distribution with zero mean and unit variance.

   The other type of feature normalization is useful when the data needs to be scaled in the range $(0, 1)$. Let min_j and max_j be the minimum and maximum values of the jth attribute. Then, each feature value x_{ij} for the jth dimension of the ith point is scaled by min-max normalization as follows:

$$x_{ij} \Leftarrow \frac{x_{ij} - min_j}{max_j - min_j} \tag{3.35}$$

Feature normalization often does ensure better performance, because it is common for the relative values of features to vary by more than an order of magnitude. In such cases, parameter learning faces the problem of ill-conditioning, in which the loss function has an inherent tendency to be more sensitive to some parameters than others. As we will see later in this chapter, this type of ill-conditioning affects the performance of gradient descent. Therefore, it is advisable to perform the feature scaling up front.

Whitening

Another form of feature pre-processing is referred to as *whitening*, in which the axis-system is rotated to create a new set of *de-correlated* features, each of which is scaled to unit variance. Typically, principal component analysis is used to achieve this goal.

Principal component analysis can be viewed as the application of singular value decomposition *after* mean-centering a data matrix (i.e., subtracting the mean from each column). Let D be an $n \times d$ data matrix that has already been mean-centered. Let C be the $d \times d$ co-variance matrix of D in which the (i, j)th entry is the co-variance between the dimensions i and j. Because the matrix D is mean-centered, we have the following:

$$C = \frac{D^T D}{n} \propto D^T D \tag{3.36}$$

The eigenvectors of the co-variance matrix provide the de-correlated directions in the data. Furthermore, the eigenvalues provide the variance along each of the directions. Therefore, if one uses the top-k eigenvectors (i.e., largest k eigenvalues) of the covariance matrix, most of the variance in the data will be retained and the noise will be removed. One can also choose $k = d$, but this will often result in the variances along the near-zero eigenvectors being dominated by numerical errors in the computation. It is a bad idea to include dimensions in which the variance is caused by computational errors, because such dimensions will contain little useful information for learning application-specific knowledge. Furthermore, the whitening process will scale each transformed feature to unit variance, which will blow up the errors along these directions. At the very least, it is advisable to use some threshold like 10^{-5} on the magnitude of the eigenvalues. Therefore, as a practical matter, k will rarely be exactly equal to d. Alternatively, one can add 10^{-5} to each eigenvalue for regularization before scaling each dimension.

Let P be a $d \times k$ matrix in which each column contains one of the top-k eigenvectors. Then, the data matrix D can be transformed into the k-dimensional axis system by post-multiplying with the matrix P. The resulting $n \times k$ matrix U, whose rows contain the transformed k-dimensional data points, is given by the following:

$$U = DP \tag{3.37}$$

Note that the variances of the columns of U are the corresponding eigenvalues, because this is the property of the de-correlating transformation of principal component analysis. In whitening, each column of U is scaled to unit variance by dividing it with its standard deviation (i.e., the square root of the corresponding eigenvalue). The transformed features are fed into the neural network. Since whitening might reduce the number of features, this type of preprocessing might also affect the architecture of the network, because it reduces the number of inputs.

One important aspect of whitening is that one might not want to make a pass through a large data set to estimate its covariance matrix. In such cases, the covariance matrix and columnwise means of the original data matrix can be estimated on a sample of the data. The $d \times k$ eigenvector matrix P is computed in which the columns contain the top-k eigenvectors. Subsequently, the following steps are used for each data point: (i) The mean of each column is subtracted from the corresponding feature; (ii) Each d-dimensional row vector representing a training data point (or test data point) is post-multiplied with P to create a k-dimensional row vector; (iii) Each feature of this k-dimensional representation is divided by the square-root of the corresponding eigenvalue.

The basic idea behind whitening is that data is assumed to be generated from an independent Gaussian distribution along each principal component. By whitening, one assumes that each such distribution is a *standard* normal distribution, and provides equal importance to the different features. Note that after whitening, the scatter plot of the data will roughly have a spherical shape, even if the original data is elliptically elongated with an arbitrary orientation. The idea is that the uncorrelated concepts in the data have now been scaled to equal importance (on an a priori basis), and the neural network can decide which of them to emphasize in the learning process. Another issue is that when different features are scaled very differently, the activations and gradients will be dominated by the "large" features in the initial phase of learning (if the weights are initialized randomly to values of similar magnitude). This might hurt the relative learning rate of some of the important weights in the network. The practical advantages of using different types of feature preprocessing and normalization are discussed in [278, 532].

3.3.3   Initialization

Initialization is particularly important in neural networks because of the stability issues associated with neural network training. As you will learn in Section 3.4, neural networks often exhibit stability problems in the sense that the activations of each layer either become successively weaker or successively stronger. The effect is exponentially related to the depth of the network, and is therefore particularly severe in deep networks. One way of ameliorating this effect to some extent is to choose good initialization points in such a way that the gradients are stable across the different layers.

One possible approach to initialize the weights is to generate random values from a Gaussian distribution with zero mean and a small standard deviation, such as 10^{-2}. Typically, this will result in small random values that are both positive and negative. One problem with this initialization is that it is not sensitive to the number of inputs to a specific neuron. For example, if one neuron has only 2 inputs and another has 100 inputs, the output of the former is far more sensitive to the average weight because of the additive effect of more inputs (which will show up as a much larger gradient). In general, it can be shown that the

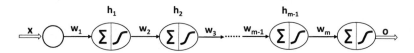

Figure 3.8: The vanishing and exploding gradient problems

variance of the outputs linearly scales with the number of inputs, and therefore the standard deviation scales with the square root of the number of inputs. To balance this fact, each weight is initialized to a value drawn from a Gaussian distribution with standard deviation $\sqrt{1/r}$, where r is the number of inputs to that neuron. Bias neurons are always initialized to zero weight. Alternatively, one can initialize the weight to a value that is uniformly distributed in $[-1/\sqrt{r}, 1/\sqrt{r}]$.

More sophisticated rules for initialization consider the fact that the nodes in different layers interact with one another to contribute to output sensitivity. Let r_{in} and r_{out} respectively be the fan-in and fan-out for a particular neuron. One suggested initialization rule, referred to as *Xavier initialization* or *Glorot initialization* is to use a Gaussian distribution with standard deviation of $\sqrt{2/(r_{in} + r_{out})}$.

An important consideration in using randomized methods is that *symmetry breaking* is important. if all weights are initialized to the same value (such as 0), all updates will move in lock-step in a layer. As a result, identical features will be created by the neurons in a layer. It is important to have a source of asymmetry among the neurons to begin with.

3.4 The Vanishing and Exploding Gradient Problems

Deep neural networks have several stability issues associated with training. In particular, networks with many layers may be hard to train because of the way in which the gradients in earlier and later layers are related.

In order to understand this point, let us consider a very deep network that has a single node in each layer. We assume that there are $(m + 1)$ layers, including the non-computational input layer. The weights of the edges between the various layers are denoted by $w_1, w_2, \ldots w_m$. Furthermore, assume that the sigmoid activation function $\Phi(\cdot)$ is applied in each layer. Let x be the input, $h_1 \ldots h_{m-1}$ be the hidden values in the various layers, and o be the final output. Let $\Phi'(h_t)$ be the derivative of the activation function in hidden layer t. Let $\frac{\partial L}{\partial h_t}$ be the derivative of the loss function with respect to the hidden activation h_t. The neural architecture is illustrated in Figure 3.8. It is relatively easy to use the backpropagation update to show the following relationship:

$$\frac{\partial L}{\partial h_t} = \Phi'(h_{t+1}) \cdot w_{t+1} \cdot \frac{\partial L}{\partial h_{t+1}} \tag{3.38}$$

Since the fan-in is 1 of each node, assume that the weights are initialized from a standard normal distribution. Therefore, each w_t has an expected average magnitude of 1.

Let us examine the specific behavior of this recurrence in the case where the sigmoid activation is used. The derivative with a sigmoid with output $f \in (0, 1)$ is given by $f(1 - f)$. This value takes on its maximum at $f = 0.5$, and therefore the value of $\Phi'(h_t)$ is no more than 0.25 even at its maximum. Since the absolute value of w_{t+1} is expected to be 1, it follows that each weight update will (typically) cause the value of $\frac{\partial L}{\partial h_t}$ to be less than 0.25 that of $\frac{\partial L}{\partial h_{t+1}}$. Therefore, after moving by about r layers, this value will typically be less than 0.25^r. Just to get an idea of the magnitude of this drop, if we set $r = 10$, then the gradient update magnitudes drop to 10^{-6} of their original values! Therefore, when backpropagation is used, the earlier layers will receive very small updates compared to the later layers. This problem is referred to as the *vanishing gradient problem*. Note that we could try to solve this problem by using an activation function with larger gradients and also initializing the weights to be larger. However, if we go too far in doing this, it is easy to end up in the opposite situation where the gradient *explodes* in the backward direction instead of vanishing. In general, unless we initialize the weight of every edge so that the product of the weight and the derivative of each activation is exactly 1, there will be considerable instability in the magnitudes of the partial derivatives. In practice, this is impossible with most activation functions because the derivative of an activation function will vary from iteration to iteration.

Although we have used an oversimplified example here with only one node in each layer, it is easy to generalize the argument to cases in which multiple nodes are available in each layer. In general, it is possible to show that the layer-to-layer backpropagation update includes a matrix multiplication (rather than a scalar multiplication). Just as repeated scalar multiplication is inherently unstable, so is repeated matrix multiplication. In particular, the loss derivatives in layer-$(i + 1)$ are multiplied by a matrix referred to as the Jacobian (cf. Equation 3.23). The Jacobian contains the derivatives of the activations in layer-$(i + 1)$ with respect to those in layer i. In certain cases like recurrent neural networks, the Jacobian is a square matrix and one can actually impose stability conditions with respect to the largest eigenvalue of the Jacobian. These stability conditions are rarely satisfied exactly, and therefore the model has an inherent tendency to exhibit the vanishing and exploding gradient problems. Furthermore, the effect of activation functions like the sigmoid tends to encourage the vanishing gradient problem. One can summarize this problem as follows:

Observation 3.4.1 *The relative magnitudes of the partial derivatives with respect to the parameters in different parts of the network tend to be very different, which creates problems for gradient-descent methods.*

In the next section, we will provide a geometric understanding of why it is natural for unstable gradient ratios to cause problems in most multivariate optimization problems, even when working in relatively simple settings.

3.4.1   Geometric Understanding of the Effect of Gradient Ratios

The vanishing and exploding gradient problems are inherent to multivariable optimization, even in cases where there are no local optima. In fact, minor manifestations of this problem are encountered in almost any convex optimization problem. Therefore, in this section, we will consider the simplest possible case of a convex, quadratic objective function with a bowl-like shape and a single global minimum. In a single-variable problem, the path of steepest descent (which is the only path of descent), will always pass through the minimum point of the bowl (i.e., optimum objective function value). However, the moment we increase the number of variables in the optimization problem from 1 to 2, this is no longer the case. The key point to understand is that *with very few exceptions, the path of steepest descent in most loss functions is only an instantaneous direction of best movement, and is not the correct direction of descent in the longer term.* In other words, small steps with "course corrections" are always needed. When an optimization problem exhibits the vanishing gradient problem, it means that the only way to reach the optimum with steepest-descent updates is by using

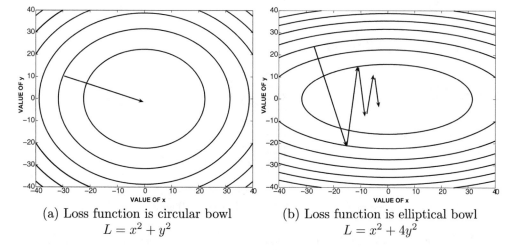

(a) Loss function is circular bowl
$$L = x^2 + y^2$$

(b) Loss function is elliptical bowl
$$L = x^2 + 4y^2$$

Figure 3.9: The effect of the shape of the loss function on steepest-gradient descent.

an *extremely large number of tiny updates and course corrections*, which is obviously very inefficient.

In order to understand this point, we look at two bivariate loss functions in Figure 3.9. In this figure, the contour plots of the loss function are shown, in which each line corresponds to points in the XY-plane where the loss function has the same value. The direction of steepest descent is always perpendicular to this line. The first loss function is of the form $L = x^2 + y^2$, which takes the shape of a perfectly circular bowl, if one were to view the height as the objective function value. This loss function treats x and y in a symmetric way. The second loss function is of the form $L = x^2 + 4y^2$, which is an elliptical bowl. Note that this loss function is more sensitive to changes in the value of y as compared to changes in the value of x, although the specific sensitivity depends on the position of the data point.

In the case of the circular bowl of Figure 3.9(a), the gradient points directly at the optimum solution, and one can reach the optimum in a single step, as long as the correct step-size is used. This is not quite the case in the loss function of Figure 3.9(b), in which the gradients are often more significant in the y-direction compared to the x-direction. Furthermore, the gradient never points to the optimal solution, as a result of which many course corrections are needed over the descent. A salient observation is that the steps along the y-direction are large, but subsequent steps undo the effect of previous steps. On the other hand, the progress along the x-direction is consistent but tiny. Although the situation of

Figure 3.9(b) occurs in almost any optimization problem using steepest descent, the case of the vanishing gradient is an extreme manifestation[2] of this behavior. The fact that a simple quadratic bowl (which is trivial compared to the typical loss function of a deep network) shows so much oscillation with the steepest-descent method is concerning. After all, the repeated composition of functions (as implied by the underlying computational graph) is

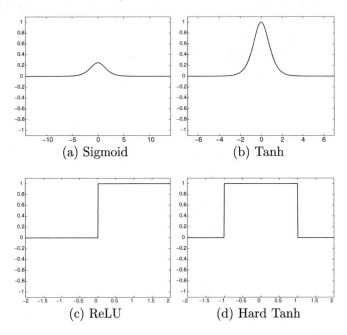

(a) Sigmoid   (b) Tanh

(c) ReLU   (d) Hard Tanh

Figure 3.10: The derivatives of different activation functions are shown. Piecewise linear activation functions have local gradient values of 1.

highly *unstable* in terms of the sensitivity of the output to the parameters in different parts of the network. The problem of differing relative derivatives is extraordinarily large in real neural networks, in which we have millions of parameters and gradient ratios that vary by orders of magnitude. Furthermore, many activation functions have small derivatives, which tends to encourage the vanishing gradient problem during backpropagation. As a result, the parameters in later layers with large descent components are often oscillating with large updates, whereas those in earlier layers make tiny but consistent updates. Therefore, neither the earlier nor the later layers make much progress in getting closer to the optimal solution. As a result, it is possible to get into situations where very little progress is made even after training for a long time.

---

[2]A different type of manifestation occurs in cases where the parameters in earlier and later layers are shared. In such cases, the effect of an update can be highly unpredictable because of the combined effect of different layers. Such scenarios occur in recurrent neural networks in which the parameters in later temporal layers are tied to those of earlier temporal layers. In such cases, small changes in the parameters can cause large changes in the loss function in very localized regions without any gradient-based indication in nearby regions. Such topological characteristics of the loss function are referred to as *cliffs* (cf. Section 3.5.4), and they make the problem harder to optimize because the gradient descent tends to either overshoot or undershoot.

3.4.2 A Partial Fix with Activation Function Choice

The specific choice of activation function often has a considerable effect on the severity of the vanishing gradient problem. The derivatives of the sigmoid and the tanh activation functions are illustrated in Figure 3.10(a) and (b), respectively. The sigmoid activation function never has a gradient of more than 0.25, and therefore it is very prone to the vanishing gradient problem. Furthermore, it *saturates* at large absolute values of the argument, which refers to the fact that the gradient is almost 0. In such cases, the weights of the neuron change very slowly. Therefore, a few such activations within the network can significantly affect the gradient computations. The tanh function fares better than the sigmoid function because it has a gradient of 1 near the origin, but the gradient saturates rapidly at increasingly large absolute values of the argument. Therefore, the tanh function will also be susceptible to the vanishing gradient problem.

In recent years, the use of the sigmoid and the tanh activation functions has been increasingly replaced with the ReLU and the hard tanh functions. The ReLU is also faster to train because its gradient is efficient to compute. The derivatives of the ReLU and the hard tanh functions are shown in Figure 3.10(c) and (d), respectively. It is evident that these functions take on the derivative of 1 in certain intervals, although they might have zero gradient in others. As a result, the vanishing gradient problem tends to occur less often, as long as most of these units operate within the intervals where the gradient is 1. In recent years, these piecewise linear variants have become far more popular than their smooth counterparts. Note that the replacement of the activation function is only a partial fix because the matrix multiplication across layers still causes a certain level of instability. Furthermore, the piecewise linear activations introduce the new problem of *dead neurons*.

3.4.3 Dying Neurons and "Brain Damage"

It is evident from Figure 3.10(c) and (d) that the gradient of the ReLU is zero for negative values of its argument. This can occur for a variety of reasons. For example, consider the case where the input into a neuron is always nonnegative, whereas all the weights have somehow been initialized to negative values. Therefore, the output will be 0. Another example is the case where a high learning rate is used. In such a case, the pre-activation values of the ReLU can jump to a range where the gradient is 0 irrespective of the input. In other words, high learning rates can "knock out" ReLU units. In such cases, the ReLU might not fire for any data instance. Once a neuron reaches this point, the gradient of the loss with respect to the weights just before the ReLU will always be zero. In other words, the weights of this neuron will never be updated further during training. Furthermore, its output will not vary across different choices of inputs and therefore will not play a role in discriminating between different instances. Such a neuron can be considered *dead*, which is considered a kind of permanent "brain damage" in biological parlance. The problem of dying neurons can be partially ameliorated by using learning rates that are somewhat modest. Another fix is to use the *leaky ReLU*, which allows the neurons outside the active interval to leak some gradient backwards.

3.4.3.1 Leaky ReLU

The leaky ReLU is defined using an additional parameter $\alpha \in (0, 1)$:

$$\Phi(v) = \begin{cases} \alpha \cdot v & v \leq 0 \\ v & \text{otherwise} \end{cases} \tag{3.39}$$

Although α is a hyperparameter chosen by the user, it is also possible to learn it. Therefore, at negative values of v, the leaky ReLU can still propagate some gradient backwards, albeit at a reduced rate defined by $\alpha < 1$.

The gains with the leaky ReLU are not guaranteed, and therefore this fix is not completely reliable. A key point is that dead neurons are not always a problem, because they represent a kind of pruning to control the precise structure of the neural network. Therefore, a certain level of dropping of neurons can be viewed as a part of the learning process. After all, there are limitations to our ability to tune the number of neurons in each layer. Dying neurons do a part of this tuning for us. Indeed, the intentional pruning of *connections* is sometimes used as a strategy for regularization [282]. Of course, if a very large fraction of the neurons in the network are dead, that can be a problem as well because much of the neural network will be inactive. Furthermore, it is undesirable for too many neurons to be knocked out during the early training phases, when the model is very poor.

3.4.3.2   Maxout

A recently proposed solution is the use of *maxout networks* [148]. The idea in the maxout unit is to have two coefficient vectors $\overline{W_1}$ and $\overline{W_2}$ instead of a single one. Subsequently, the activation used is $\max\{\overline{W_1}\cdot\overline{X}, \overline{W_2}\cdot\overline{X}\}$. In the event that bias neurons are used, the maxout activation is $\max\{\overline{W_1}\cdot\overline{X} + b_1, \overline{W_2}\cdot\overline{X} + b_2\}$. One can view the maxout as a generalization of the ReLU, because the ReLU is obtained by setting one of the coefficient vectors to 0. Even the leaky ReLU can be shown to be a special case of maxout, in which we set $\overline{W_2} = \alpha\overline{W_1}$ for $\alpha \in (0, 1)$. Like the ReLU, the maxout function is piecewise linear. However, it does not saturate at all, and is linear almost everywhere. In spite of its linearity, it has been shown [148] that maxout networks are universal function approximators. Maxout has advantages over the ReLU, and it enhances the performance of ensemble methods like *Dropout* (cf. Section 4.5.4 of Chapter 4). The only drawback with the use of maxout is that it doubles the number of required parameters.

3.5   Gradient-Descent Strategies

The most common method for parameter learning in neural networks is the *steepest-descent method*, in which the gradient of the loss function is used to make parameter updates. In fact, all the discussions in previous chapters are based on this assumption. As discussed in the earlier section, the steepest-gradient method can sometimes behave unexpectedly because it does not always point in the best direction of improvement, when steps of finite size are considered. The steepest-descent direction is the optimal direction only from the perspective of infinitesimal steps. A steepest-descent direction can sometimes become an ascent direction after a small update in parameters. As a result, many course corrections are needed. A specific example of this phenomenon is discussed in Section 3.4.1 in which minor differences in sensitivity to different features can cause a steepest-descent algorithm to have oscillations. The problem of oscillation and zigzagging is quite ubiquitous whenever the steepest-descent direction moves along a direction of *high curvature* in the loss function. The most extreme manifestation of this problem occurs in the case of extreme ill-conditioning, for which the partial derivatives of the loss are wildly different with respect to the different optimization variables. In this section, we will discuss several clever learning strategies that work well in these ill-conditioned settings.

3.5.1 Learning Rate Decay

A constant learning rate is not desirable because it poses a dilemma to the analyst. The dilemma is as follows. A lower learning rate used early on will cause the algorithm to take too long to come even close to an optimal solution. On the other hand, a large initial learning rate will allow the algorithm to come reasonably close to a good solution at first; however, the algorithm will then oscillate around the point for a very long time, or diverge in an unstable way, if the high rate of learning is maintained. In either case, maintaining a constant learning rate is not ideal. Allowing the learning rate to decay over time can naturally achieve the desired learning-rate adjustment to avoid these challenges.

The two most common decay functions are *exponential decay* and *inverse decay*. The learning rate α_t can be expressed in terms of the initial decay rate α_0 and epoch t as

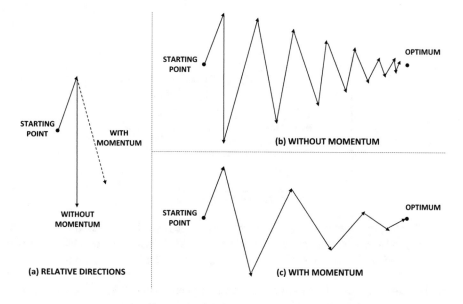

Figure 3.11: Effect of momentum in smoothing zigzag updates

follows:

$$\alpha_t = \alpha_0 \exp(-k \cdot t) \quad \text{[Exponential Decay]}$$
$$\alpha_t = \frac{\alpha_0}{1 + k \cdot t} \quad \text{[Inverse Decay]}$$

The parameter k controls the rate of the decay. Another approach is to use step decay in which the learning rate is reduced by a particular factor every few epochs. For example, the learning rate might be multiplied by 0.5 every 5 epochs. A common approach is to track the loss on a held-out portion of the training data set, and reduce the learning rate whenever this loss stops improving. In some cases, the analyst might even babysit the learning process, and use an implementation in which the learning rate can be changed manually depending on the progress. This type of approach can be used with simple implementations of gradient descent, although it does not address many of the other problematic issues.

3.5.2 Momentum-Based Learning

Momentum-based techniques recognize that zigzagging is a result of highly contradictory steps that cancel out one another and reduce the *effective* size of the steps in the correct (long-term) direction. An example of this scenario is illustrated in Figure 3.9(b). Simply attempting to increase the size of the step in order to obtain greater movement in the correct direction might actually move the current solution even further away from the optimum solution. In this point of view, it makes a lot more sense to move in an "averaged" direction of the last few steps, so that the zigzagging is smoothed out.

In order to understand this point, consider a setting in which one is performing gradient-descent with respect to the parameter vector $\overline{W}$. The normal updates for gradient-descent with respect to loss function L (defined over a mini-batch of instances) are as follows:

$$\overline{V} \Leftarrow -\alpha \frac{\partial L}{\partial \overline{W}}; \quad \overline{W} \Leftarrow \overline{W} + \overline{V}$$

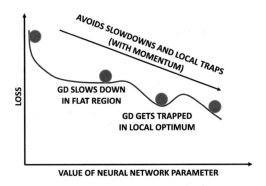

Figure 3.12: Effect of momentum in navigating complex loss surfaces. The annotation "GD" indicates pure gradient descent without momentum. Momentum helps the optimization process retain speed in flat regions of the loss surface and avoid local optima.

Here, α is the learning rate. In momentum-based descent, the vector $\overline{V}$ is modified with exponential smoothing, where $\beta \in (0,1)$ is a smoothing parameter:

$$\overline{V} \Leftarrow \beta \overline{V} - \alpha \frac{\partial L}{\partial \overline{W}}; \quad \overline{W} \Leftarrow \overline{W} + \overline{V}$$

Larger values of β help the approach pick up a consistent velocity $\overline{V}$ in the correct direction. Setting $\beta = 0$ specializes to straightforward mini-batch gradient-descent. The parameter β is also referred to as the *momentum parameter* or the *friction parameter*. The word "friction" is derived from the fact that small values of β act as "brakes," much like friction.

With momentum-based descent, the learning is accelerated, because one is generally moving in a direction that often points closer to the optimal solution and the useless "sideways" oscillations are muted. The basic idea is to give greater preference to *consistent* directions over multiple steps, which have greater importance in the descent. This allows the use of larger steps in the correct direction without causing overflows or "explosions" in the sideways direction. As a result, learning is accelerated. An example of the use of momentum is illustrated in Figure 3.11. It is evident from Figure 3.11(a) that momentum increases the relative component of the gradient in the correct direction. The corresponding effects on the updates are illustrated in Figure 3.11(b) and (c). It is evident that momentum-based updates can reach the optimal solution in fewer updates.

The use of momentum will often cause the solution to slightly overshoot in the direction where velocity is picked up, just as a marble will overshoot when it is allowed to roll down a bowl. However, with the appropriate choice of β, it will still perform better than a situation in which momentum is not used. The momentum-based method will generally perform better because the marble gains speed as it rolls down the bowl; the quicker arrival at the optimal solution more than compensates for the overshooting of the target. Overshooting is desirable to the extent that it helps avoid local optima. Figure 3.12, which shows a marble rolling down a complex loss surface (picking up speed as it rolls down), illustrates this concept. The marble's gathering of speed helps it efficiently navigate flat regions of the loss surface. The parameter β controls the amount of friction that the marble encounters while rolling down the loss surface. While increased values of β help in avoiding local optima, it might also increase oscillation at the end. In this sense, the momentum-based method has a neat interpretation in terms of the physics of a marble rolling down a complex loss surface.

3.5.2.1   Nesterov Momentum

The Nesterov momentum [353] is a modification of the traditional momentum method in which the gradients are computed at a point that would be reached after executing a β-discounted version of the previous step again (i.e., the momentum portion of the current step). This point is obtained by multiplying the previous update vector $\overline{V}$ with the friction parameter β and then computing the gradient at $\overline{W} + \beta\overline{V}$. The idea is that this corrected gradient uses a better understanding of how the gradients will change because of the momentum portion of the update, and incorporates this information into the gradient portion of the update. Therefore, one is using a certain amount of lookahead in computing the updates. Let us denote the loss function by $L(\overline{W})$ at the current solution $\overline{W}$. In this case, it is important to explicitly denote the argument of the loss function because of the way in which the gradient is computed. Therefore, the update may be computed as follows:

$$\overline{V} \Leftarrow \beta\overline{V} - \alpha\frac{\partial L(\overline{W} + \beta\overline{V})}{\partial \overline{W}}; \quad \overline{W} \Leftarrow \overline{W} + \overline{V}$$

Note that the *only* difference from the standard momentum method is in terms of *where* the gradient is computed. Using the value of the gradient a little further along the previous update can lead to faster convergence. In the previous analogy of the rolling marble, such an approach will start applying the "brakes" on the gradient-descent procedure when the marble starts reaching near the bottom of the bowl, because the lookahead will "warn" it about the reversal in gradient direction.

The Nesterov method works only in mini-batch gradient descent with modest batch sizes; using very small batches is a bad idea. In such cases, it can be shown that the Nesterov method reduces the error to $O(1/t^2)$ after t steps, as compared to an error of $O(1/t)$ in the momentum method.

3.5.3   Parameter-Specific Learning Rates

The basic idea in the momentum methods of the previous section is to leverage the *consistency* in the gradient direction of certain parameters in order to speed up the updates. This goal can also be achieved more explicitly by having different learning rates for different parameters. The idea is that parameters with large partial derivatives are often oscillating and zigzagging, whereas parameters with small partial derivatives tend to be more consistent but move in the same direction. An early method, which was proposed in this direction, was the *delta-bar-delta* method [217]. This approach tracks whether the sign of each partial derivative changes or stays the same. If the sign of a partial derivative stays consistent, then it is indicative of the fact that the direction is correct. In such a case, the partial derivative in that direction increases. On the other hand, if the sign of the partial derivative flips all the time, then the partial derivative decreases. However, this kind of approach is designed for gradient descent rather than stochastic gradient descent, because the errors in stochastic gradient descent can get magnified. Therefore, a number of methods have been proposed that can work well even when the mini-batch method is used.

3.5.3.1 AdaGrad

In the AdaGrad algorithm [108], one keeps track of the aggregated squared magnitude of the partial derivative with respect to each parameter over the course of the algorithm. The square-root of this value is *proportional* to the root-mean-square slope for that parameter (although the absolute value will increase with the number of epochs because of successive aggregation).

Let A_i be the aggregate value for the ith parameter. Therefore, in each iteration, the following update is performed:

$$A_i \Leftarrow A_i + \left(\frac{\partial L}{\partial w_i}\right)^2 \quad \forall i \tag{3.40}$$

The update for the ith parameter w_i is as follows:

$$w_i \Leftarrow w_i - \frac{\alpha}{\sqrt{A_i}}\left(\frac{\partial L}{\partial w_i}\right); \quad \forall i$$

If desired, one can use $\sqrt{A_i + \epsilon}$ in the denominator instead of $\sqrt{A_i}$ to avoid ill-conditioning. Here, ϵ is a small positive value such as 10^{-8}.

Scaling the derivative inversely with $\sqrt{A_i}$ is a kind of "signal-to-noise" normalization because A_i only measures the historical magnitude of the gradient rather than its sign; it encourages faster *relative* movements along gently sloping directions with consistent sign of the gradient. If the gradient component along the ith direction keeps wildly fluctuating between $+100$ and -100, this type of magnitude-centric normalization will penalize that component far more than another gradient component that consistently takes on the value in the vicinity of 0.1 (but with a consistent sign). For example, in Figure 3.11, the movements along the oscillating direction will be de-emphasized, and the movement along the consistent direction will be emphasized. However, absolute movements along all components will tend to slow down over time, which is the main problem with the approach. The slowing down is caused by the fact that A_i is the *aggregate* value of the entire history of partial derivatives. This will lead to diminishing values of the scaled derivative. As a result, the progress of AdaGrad might prematurely become too slow, and it will eventually (almost) stop making progress. Another problem is that the aggregate scaling factors depend on ancient history, which can eventually become stale. The use of stale scaling factors can increase inaccuracy. As we will see later, most of the other methods use exponential averaging, which solves both problems.

3.5.3.2 RMSProp

The RMSProp algorithm [194] uses a similar motivation as AdaGrad for performing the "signal-to-noise" normalization with the absolute magnitude $\sqrt{A_i}$ of the gradients. However, instead of simply adding the squared gradients to estimate A_i, it uses *exponential averaging*. Since one uses *averaging* to normalize rather than *aggregate* values, the progress is not slowed prematurely by a constantly increasing scaling factor A_i. The basic idea is to use a decay factor $\rho \in (0, 1)$, and weight the squared partial derivatives occurring t updates ago by ρ^t. Note that this can be easily achieved by multiplying the current squared aggregate (i.e., *running* estimate) by ρ and then adding $(1 - \rho)$ times the current (squared) partial derivative. The running estimate is initialized to 0. This causes some (undesirable) bias in early iterations, which disappears over the longer term. Therefore, if A_i is the exponentially averaged value of the ith parameter w_i, we have the following way of updating A_i:

$$A_i \Leftarrow \rho A_i + (1 - \rho) \left(\frac{\partial L}{\partial w_i} \right)^2 \quad \forall i \tag{3.41}$$

The square-root of this value for each parameter is used to normalize its gradient. Then, the following update is used for (global) learning rate α:

$$w_i \Leftarrow w_i - \frac{\alpha}{\sqrt{A_i}} \left(\frac{\partial L}{\partial w_i} \right); \quad \forall i$$

If desired, one can use $\sqrt{A_i + \epsilon}$ in the denominator instead of $\sqrt{A_i}$ to avoid ill-conditioning. Here, ϵ is a small positive value such as 10^{-8}. Another advantage of RMSProp over AdaGrad is that the importance of ancient (i.e., stale) gradients decays exponentially with time. Furthermore, it can benefit by incorporating concepts of momentum within the computational algorithm (cf. Sections 3.5.3.3 and 3.5.3.5). The drawback of RMSProp is that the running estimate A_i of the second-order moment is biased in early iterations because it is initialized to 0.

3.5.3.3 RMSProp with Nesterov Momentum

RMSProp can also be combined with Nesterov momentum. Let A_i be the squared aggregate of the ith weight. In such cases, we introduce the additional parameter $\beta \in (0, 1)$ and use the following updates:

$$v_i \Leftarrow \beta v_i - \frac{\alpha}{\sqrt{A_i}} \left(\frac{\partial L(\overline{W} + \beta \overline{V})}{\partial w_i} \right); \quad w_i \Leftarrow w_i + v_i \quad \forall i$$

Note that the partial derivative of the loss function is computed at a shifted point, as is common in the Nesterov method. The weight $\overline{W}$ is shifted with $\beta \overline{V}$ while computing the partial derivative with respect to the loss function. The maintenance of A_i is done using the shifted gradients as well:

$$A_i \Leftarrow \rho A_i + (1 - \rho) \left(\frac{\partial L(\overline{W} + \beta \overline{V})}{\partial w_i} \right)^2 \quad \forall i \tag{3.42}$$

Although this approach benefits from adding momentum to RMSProp, it does not correct for the initialization bias.

3.5.3.4 AdaDelta

The AdaDelta algorithm [553] uses a similar update as RMSProp, except that it eliminates the need for a global learning parameter by computing it as a function of incremental updates in previous iterations. Consider the update of RMSProp, which is repeated below:

$$w_i \Leftarrow w_i - \underbrace{\frac{\alpha}{\sqrt{A_i}} \left(\frac{\partial L}{\partial w_i} \right)}_{\Delta w_i}; \quad \forall i$$

We will show how α is replaced with a value that depends on the previous incremental updates. In each update, the value of Δw_i is the increment in the value of w_i. As with the exponentially smoothed gradients A_i, we keep an exponentially smoothed value δ_i of the values of Δw_i in previous iterations with the same decay parameter ρ:

$$\delta_i \Leftarrow \rho \delta_i + (1 - \rho)(\Delta w_i)^2 \quad \forall i \tag{3.43}$$

For a given iteration, the value of δ_i can be computed using only the iterations before it because the value of Δw_i is not yet available. On the other hand, A_i can be computed using the partial derivative in the current iteration as well. This is a subtle difference between how A_i and δ_i are computed. This results in the following AdaDelta update:

$$w_i \Leftarrow w_i - \underbrace{\sqrt{\frac{\delta_i}{A_i}} \left(\frac{\partial L}{\partial w_i} \right)}_{\Delta w_i}; \quad \forall i$$

It is noteworthy that a parameter α for the learning rate is completely missing from this update. The AdaDelta method shares some similarities with second-order methods because the ratio $\sqrt{\frac{\delta_i}{A_i}}$ in the update is a heuristic surrogate for the inverse of the second derivative of the loss with respect to w_i [553]. As discussed in subsequent sections, many second-order methods like the Newton method also do not use learning rates.

3.5.3.5   Adam

The Adam algorithm uses a similar "signal-to-noise" normalization as AdaGrad and RMSProp; however, it also exponentially smooths the first-order gradient in order to incorporate momentum into the update. It also directly addresses the bias inherent in exponential smoothing when the running estimate of a smoothed value is unrealistically initialized to 0.

As in the case of RMSProp, let A_i be the exponentially averaged value of the ith parameter w_i. This value is updated in the same way as RMSProp with the decay parameter $\rho \in (0, 1)$:

$$A_i \Leftarrow \rho A_i + (1 - \rho) \left(\frac{\partial L}{\partial w_i} \right)^2 \quad \forall i \tag{3.44}$$

At the same time, an exponentially smoothed value of the gradient is maintained for which the ith component is denoted by F_i. This smoothing is performed with a different decay parameter ρ_f:

$$F_i \Leftarrow \rho_f F_i + (1 - \rho_f) \left(\frac{\partial L}{\partial w_i} \right) \quad \forall i \tag{3.45}$$

This type of exponentially smoothing of the gradient with ρ_f is a variation of the momentum method discussed in Section 3.5.2 (which is parameterized by a friction parameter β instead of ρ_f). Then, the following update is used at learning rate α_t in the tth iteration:

$$w_i \Leftarrow w_i - \frac{\alpha_t}{\sqrt{A_i}} F_i; \quad \forall i$$

There are two key differences from the RMSProp algorithm. First, the gradient is replaced with its exponentially smoothed value in order to incorporate momentum. Second, the learning rate α_t now depends on the iteration index t, and is defined as follows:

$$\alpha_t = \alpha \underbrace{\left(\frac{\sqrt{1-\rho^t}}{1-\rho_f^t} \right)}_{\text{Adjust Bias}} \quad (3.46)$$

Technically, the adjustment to the learning rate is actually a bias correction factor that is applied to account for the unrealistic initialization of the two exponential smoothing mechanisms, and it is particularly important in early iterations. Both F_i and A_i are initialized

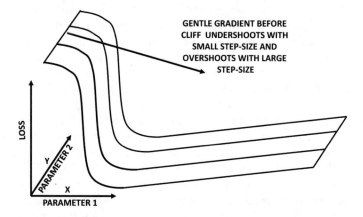

GENTLE GRADIENT BEFORE
CLIFF UNDERSHOOTS WITH
SMALL STEP-SIZE AND
OVERSHOOTS WITH LARGE
STEP-SIZE

LOSS

PARAMETER 2

Y

X

PARAMETER 1

Figure 3.13: An example of a cliff in the loss surface

to 0, which causes bias in early iterations. The two quantities are affected differently by the bias, which accounts for the ratio in Equation 3.46. It is noteworthy that each of ρ^t and ρ_f^t converge to 0 for large t because $\rho, \rho_f \in (0, 1)$. As a result, the initialization bias correction factor of Equation 3.46 converges to 1, and α_t converges to α. The default suggested values of ρ_f and ρ are 0.9 and 0.999, respectively, according to the original Adam paper [241]. Refer to [241] for details of other criteria (such as parameter sparsity) used for selecting ρ and ρ_f. Like other methods, Adam uses $\sqrt{A_i + \epsilon}$ (instead of $\sqrt{A_i}$) in the denominator of the update for better conditioning. The Adam algorithm is extremely popular because it incorporates most of the advantages of other algorithms, and often performs competitively with respect to the best of the other methods [241].

3.5.4 Cliffs and Higher-Order Instability

So far, only the use of first-order derivatives has been discussed in this chapter. The progress with first-order derivatives can be slow with some error surfaces. Part of the problem is that the first-order derivatives provide a limited amount of information about the error surface, which can cause the updates to overshoot. The complexity of the loss surfaces of many neural networks can cause gradient-based updates to perform in an unanticipated way.

An example of a loss surface is shown in Figure 3.13. In this case, there is a gently sloping surface that rapidly changes into a cliff. However, if one computed only the first-order partial derivative with respect to the variable x shown in the figure, one would only see a gentle slope. As a result, a small learning rate will lead to very slow learning, whereas increasing the learning rate can suddenly cause overshooting to a point far from the optimal solution. This problem is caused by the nature of the curvature (i.e., changing gradient), where the first-order gradient does not contain the information needed to control the size of the update. In many cases, the rate of change of gradient can be computed using the second-order derivative, which provides useful (additional) information. In general, second-order methods approximate the local loss surface with a quadratic bowl, which is more accurate than the linear approximation. Some second-order methods like the *Newton method* require exactly one iteration in order to find the local optimal solution for a quadratic surface. Of course, the loss surface of neural models is typically not quadratic. Nevertheless, the approximation is often good enough that gradient-descent methods are greatly accelerated at least in cases where the change in the gradient is not too sudden or drastic.

Cliffs are not desirable because they manifest a certain level of instability in the loss function. This implies that a small change in some of the weights can either change the loss in a tiny way or suddenly change the loss by such a large amount that the resulting solution is even further away from the true optimum. As you will learn in Chapter 7, all temporal layers of a recurrent neural network share the same parameters. In such a case, the vanishing and exploding gradient means that there is varying sensitivity of the loss function with respect to the parameters in earlier and later layers (which are tied anyway). Therefore, a small change in a well-chosen parameter can cascade in an unstable way through the layers and either blow up or have negligible effect on the value of the loss function. Furthermore, it is hard to control the step size in a way that prevents one of these two events. This is the typical behavior one would encounter near a cliff. As a result, it is easy to miss the optimum during a gradient-descent step. One way of understanding this behavior is that sharing parameters across layers naturally leads to higher-order effects of weight perturbations on the loss function. This is because the shared weights of different layers are multiplied during neural network prediction, and a first-order gradient is now insufficient to model the effect of the *curvature* in the loss function, which is a measure of the change in gradient along a particular direction. Such settings are often addressed with techniques that either clip the gradient, or explicitly use the curvature (i.e., second-order derivative) of the loss function.

3.5.5   Gradient Clipping

Gradient clipping is a technique that is used to deal with settings in which the partial derivatives along different directions have exceedingly different magnitudes. Some forms of gradient clipping use a similar principle to that used in adaptive learning rates by trying the make the different components of the partial derivatives more even. However, the clipping is done only on the basis of the current values of the gradients rather than their historical values. Two forms of gradient clipping are most common:

1. *Value-based clipping:* In value-based clipping, a minimum and maximum threshold are set on the gradient values. All partial derivatives that are less than the minimum are set to the minimum threshold. All partial derivatives that are greater than the maximum are set to the maximum threshold.

2. *Norm-based clipping:* In this case, the entire gradient vector is normalized by the L_2-norm of the entire vector. Note that this type of clipping does not change the relative magnitudes of the updates along different directions. However, for neural networks that share parameters across different layers (like *recurrent neural networks*),

the effect of the two types of clipping is very similar. By clipping, one can achieve a better conditioning of the values, so that the updates from mini-batch to mini-batch are roughly similar. Therefore, it would prevent an anomalous gradient explosion in a particular mini-batch from affecting the solution too much.

By and large, the effects of gradient clipping are quite limited compared to many other methods. However, it is particularly effective in avoiding the exploding gradient problem in recurrent neural networks. In recurrent neural networks (cf. Chapter 7), the parameters are shared across different layers, and a derivative is computed with respect to each copy of the shared parameter by treating it as a separate variable. These derivatives are the temporal components of the overall gradient, and the values are clipped before adding them in order to obtain the overall gradient. A geometric interpretation of the exploding gradient problem is provided in [369], and a detailed exploration of why gradient clipping works is provided in [368].

3.5.6 Second-Order Derivatives

A number of methods have been proposed in recent years for using second-order derivatives for optimization. Such methods can partially alleviate some of the problems caused by curvature of the loss function.

Consider the parameter vector $\overline{W} = (w_1 \dots w_d)^T$, which is expressed[3] as a column vector. The second-order derivatives of the loss function $L(\overline{W})$ are of the following form:

$$H_{ij} = \frac{\partial^2 L(\overline{W})}{\partial w_i \partial w_j}$$

Note that the partial derivatives use all pairwise parameters in the denominator. Therefore, for a neural network with d parameters, we have a $d \times d$ *Hessian matrix* H, for which the (i, j)th entry is H_{ij}. The second-order derivatives of the loss function can be computed with backpropagation [315], although this is rarely done in practice. The Hessian can be viewed as the Jacobian of the gradient.

One can write a quadratic approximation of the loss function in the vicinity of parameter vector $\overline{W}_0$ by using the following Taylor expansion:

$$L(\overline{W}) \approx L(\overline{W}_0) + (\overline{W} - \overline{W}_0)^T [\nabla L(\overline{W}_0)] + \frac{1}{2}(\overline{W} - \overline{W}_0)^T H(\overline{W} - \overline{W}_0) \qquad (3.47)$$

Note that the Hessian H is computed at $\overline{W}_0$. Here, the parameter vectors $\overline{W}$ and $\overline{W}_0$ are d-dimensional column vectors, as is the gradient of the loss function. This is a quadratic approximation, and one can simply set the gradient to 0, which results in the following optimality condition for the quadratic approximation:

$$\nabla L(\overline{W}) = 0 \quad \text{[Gradient of Loss Function]}$$

$$\nabla L(\overline{W}_0) + H(\overline{W} - \overline{W}_0) = 0 \quad \text{[Gradient of Taylor approximation]}$$

One can rearrange the above optimality condition to obtain the following Newton update:

$$\overline{W}^* \Leftarrow \overline{W}_0 - H^{-1}[\nabla L(\overline{W}_0)] \qquad (3.48)$$

---

[3]In most of this book, we have worked with $\overline{W}$ as a row-vector. However, it is notationally convenient here to work with $\overline{W}$ as a column-vector.

One interesting characteristic of this update is that it is directly obtained from an optimality condition, and therefore there is no learning rate. In other words, this update is
approximating the loss function with a quadratic bowl and moving *exactly* to the bottom
of the bowl *in a single step*; the learning rate is already incorporated implicitly. Recall from
Figure 3.9 that first-order methods bounce along directions of high curvature. Of course,
the bottom of the quadratic approximation is not the bottom of the true loss function, and
therefore multiple Newton updates will be needed.

The main difference of Equation 3.48 from the update of steepest-gradient descent is pre-
multiplication of the steepest direction (which is $[\nabla L(\overline{W}_0)]$) with the inverse of the Hessian.
This multiplication with the inverse Hessian plays a key role in changing the direction of
the steepest-gradient descent, so that one can take larger steps in that direction (resulting

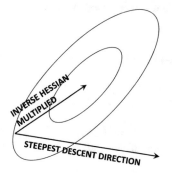

Figure 3.14: The effect of pre-multiplication of steepest-descent direction with the inverse
Hessian

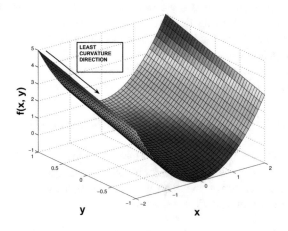

Figure 3.15: The curvature effect in valleys

in better improvement of the objective function) even if the *instantaneous* rate of change in
that direction is not as large as the steepest-descent direction. This is because the Hessian
encodes how fast the gradient is changing in each direction. Changing gradients are bad for
larger updates because one might inadvertently worsen the objective function, if the signs
of many components of the gradient change during the step. It is profitable to move in
directions where the ratio of the gradient to the rate of change of the gradient is large, so

that one can take larger steps without causing harm to the optimization. Pre-multiplication with the inverse of the Hessian achieves this goal. The effect of the pre-multiplication of the steepest-descent direction with the inverse Hessian is shown in Figure 3.14. It is helpful to reconcile this figure with the example of the quadratic bowl in Figure 3.9. In a sense, pre-multiplication with the inverse Hessian biases the learning steps towards low-curvature directions. In one dimension, the Newton step is simply the ratio of the first derivative (rate of change) to the second derivative (curvature). In multiple dimensions, the low-curvature directions tend to win out because of multiplication by the inverse Hessian.

The specific effect of curvature is particularly evident when one encounters loss functions in the shape of sloping or winding valleys. An example of a sloping valley is shown in Figure 3.15. A valley is a dangerous topography for a gradient-descent method, particularly if the bottom of the valley has a steep and rapidly changing surface (which creates a narrow valley). This is, of course, not the case in Figure 3.15, which is a relatively easier case. However, even in this case, the steepest-descent direction will often bounce along the sides of the valley, and move down the slope relatively slowly if the step-sizes are chosen inaccurately. In narrow valleys, the gradient-descent method will bounce along the steep sides of the valley even more violently without making much progress in the gently sloping direction, where the greatest *long-term* gains are present. In such cases, it is only by normalizing the gradient information with the curvature, that will provide the correct directions of long-term movement. This type of normalization tends to favor low-curvature directions like the ones shown in Figure 3.15. Multiplication of the steepest-descent direction with the inverse Hessian achieves precisely this goal.

In most large-scale neural network settings, the Hessian is too large to store or compute explicitly. It is not uncommon to have neural networks with millions of parameters. Trying to compute the inverse of a $10^6 \times 10^6$ Hessian matrix is impractical with the computational power available today. In fact, it is difficult to even compute the Hessian, let alone invert it! Therefore, many approximations and variations of the Newton method have been developed. Examples of such methods include *Hessian-free optimization* [41, 189, 313, 314] (or method of *conjugate gradients*) and quasi-Newton methods that approximate the Hessian. The basic goal of these methods to make second-order updates without exactly computing the Hessian.

3.5.6.1 Conjugate Gradients and Hessian-Free Optimization

The *conjugate gradient method* [189] requires d steps to reach the optimal solution of a quadratic loss function (instead of a single Newton step). This approach is well known in the classical literature on neural networks [41, 443], and a variant has recently been reborn under the title of "Hessian-free optimization." This name is motivated by the fact that the search direction can be computed without the explicit computation of the Hessian.

A key problem in first-order methods is the zigzag movement of the optimization process, which undoes much of the work done in previous iterations. In the conjugate gradient method, the directions of movement are related to one another in such a way that the work done in previous iterations is never undone (for a quadratic loss function). This is because the change in gradient in a step, when projected along the vector of any other movement direction, is always 0. Furthermore, one uses *line search* to determine the optimal step size by searching over different step sizes. *Since an optimal step is taken along each direction and the work along that direction is never undone by subsequent steps, d linearly independent steps are needed to reach the optimum of a d-dimensional function.* Since it is possible to find such directions only for quadratic loss functions, we will first discuss the conjugate gradient method under the assumption that the loss function $L(\overline{W})$ is quadratic.

A quadratic and convex loss function $L(\overline{W})$ has an ellipsoidal contour plot of the type shown in Figure 3.16. The orthonormal eigenvectors $\overline{q}_0 \ldots \overline{q}_{d-1}$ of the symmetric Hessian represent the axes directions of the ellipsoidal contour plot. One can rewrite the loss function in a new coordinate space corresponding to the eigenvectors. In the axis system corresponding the eigenvectors, the (transformed) variables do not have interactions with one another because of the alignment of ellipsoidal loss contour with the axis system. *This is because the new Hessian $H_q = Q^T H Q$ obtained by rewriting the loss function in terms of the transformed variables is diagonal*, where Q is a $d \times d$ matrix with columns containing the eigenvectors. Therefore, each transformed variable can be optimized independently of

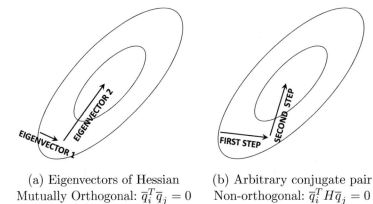

(a) Eigenvectors of Hessian   (b) Arbitrary conjugate pair
Mutually Orthogonal: $\overline{q}_i^T \overline{q}_j = 0$ Non-orthogonal: $\overline{q}_i^T H \overline{q}_j = 0$

Figure 3.16: The eigenvectors of the Hessian of a quadratic function represent the orthogonal axes of the quadratic ellipsoid and are also mutually orthogonal. The eigenvectors of the Hessian are orthogonal conjugate directions. The generalized definition of conjugacy may result in non-orthogonal directions.

the others. Alternatively, one can work with the original variables by successively making the best (projected) gradient-descent step along each eigenvector so as to minimize the loss function. The best movement along a particular direction is done using line search to select the step size. The nature of the movement is illustrated in Figure 3.16(a). Note that movement along the jth eigenvector does not disturb the work done along earlier eigenvectors and therefore d steps are sufficient to each the optimal solution.

Although it is impractical to compute the eigenvectors of the Hessian, there are other efficiently computable directions satisfying similar properties; this key property is referred to as *mutual conjugacy* of vectors. Note that two eigenvectors $\overline{q}_i$ and $\overline{q}_j$ of the Hessian satisfy $\overline{q}_i^T \overline{q}_j = 0$ because of orthogonality. Furthermore, since $\overline{q}_j$ is an eigenvector of H, we have $H \overline{q}_j = \lambda_j \overline{q}_j$ for some scalar eigenvalue λ_j. Multiplying both sides with $\overline{q}_i^T$, we can easily show that the eigenvectors of the Hessian satisfy $\overline{q}_i^T H \overline{q}_j = 0$ in pairwise fashion. This condition is referred to as the *mutual conjugacy condition*, and it is equivalent to saying that the Hessian $H_q = Q^T H Q$ in the transformed axis-system of directions $\overline{q}_0 \ldots \overline{q}_{d-1}$ is diagonal. In fact, it turns out that *if we select any set of (not necessarily orthogonal) vectors $\overline{q}_0 \ldots \overline{q}_{d-1}$ satisfying the mutual conjugacy condition, then movement along any of these directions does not disturb the projected gradient along other directions.* Conjugate directions other than Hessian eigenvectors, such as those shown in Figure 3.16(b), may not be mutually orthogonal. If we re-write the quadratic loss function in terms of coordinates in a non-orthogonal axis system of conjugate directions, we will get nicely separated variables with a diagonal Hessian $H_q = Q^T H Q$. However, H_q is not a true diagonalization of H because $Q^T Q \neq I$. Nevertheless, such non-interacting directions are crucial to avoid zigzagging.

Let $\overline{W}_t$ and $\overline{W}_{t+1}$ represent the respective parameter vectors before and after movement along $\overline{q}_t$. The change in gradient $\nabla L(\overline{W}_{t+1}) - \nabla L(\overline{W}_t)$ caused by movement along the direction $\overline{q}_t$ points in the same direction as $H\overline{q}_t$. This is because the product of the second-derivative (Hessian) matrix with a direction is proportional to the change in the first-derivative (gradient) when moving along that direction. This relationship is a finite-difference approximation for non-quadratic functions and it is exact for quadratic functions. Therefore, the projection (or dot product) of this change vector with respect to any other step vector $(\overline{W}_{i+1} - \overline{W}_i) \propto \overline{q}_i$ is given by the following:

$$\underbrace{[\overline{W}_{i+1} - \overline{W}_i]^T}_{\text{Earlier step}} \underbrace{[\nabla L(\overline{W}_{t+1}) - \nabla L(\overline{W}_t)]}_{\text{Current gradient change}} \propto \overline{q}_i^T H \overline{q}_t = 0$$

This means that the only change to the gradient along a particular direction $\overline{q}_i$ (during the entire learning) occurs during the step along that direction. Line search ensures that the final gradient along that direction is 0. Convex loss functions have linearly independent conjugate directions (see Exercise 7). By making the best step along each conjugate direction, the final gradient will have zero dot product with d linearly independent directions; this is possible only when the final gradient is the zero vector (see Exercise 8), which implies optimality for a convex function. In fact, one can often reach a near-optimal solution in far fewer than d updates.

How can one generate conjugate directions iteratively? The obvious approach requires one needs to track $O(d^2)$ vector components of all previous $O(d)$ conjugate directions in order to enforce conjugacy of the next direction with respect to all these previous directions (see Exercise 11). Surprisingly, only the most recent conjugate direction is needed to generate the next direction [359, 443], when steepest decent directions are used for iterative generation. This is not an obvious result (see Exercise 12). The direction $\overline{q}_{t+1}$ is, therefore, defined iteratively as a linear combination of *only* the previous conjugate direction $\overline{q}_t$ and the current steepest descent direction $\nabla L(\overline{W}_{t+1})$ with combination parameter β_t:

$$\overline{q}_{t+1} = -\nabla L(\overline{W}_{t+1}) + \beta_t \overline{q}_t \tag{3.49}$$

Premultiplying both sides with $\overline{q}_t^T H$ and using the conjugacy condition to set the left-hand side to 0, one can solve for β_t:

$$\beta_t = \frac{\overline{q}_t^T H[\nabla L(\overline{W}_{t+1})]}{\overline{q}_t^T H \overline{q}_t} \tag{3.50}$$

This leads to an iterative update process, which initializes $\overline{q}_0 = -\nabla L(\overline{W}_0)$, and computes $\overline{q}_{t+1}$ iteratively for $t = 0, 1, 2, \ldots T$:

1. Update $\overline{W}_{t+1} \Leftarrow \overline{W}_t + \alpha_t \overline{q}_t$. Here, the step size α_t is computed using line search to minimize the loss function.

2. Set $\overline{q}_{t+1} = -\nabla L(\overline{W}_{t+1}) + \left(\frac{\overline{q}_t^T H[\nabla L(\overline{W}_{t+1})]}{\overline{q}_t^T H \overline{q}_t} \right) \overline{q}_t$. Increment t by 1.

It can be shown [359, 443] that $\overline{q}_{t+1}$ satisfies conjugacy with respect to *all* previous $\overline{q}_i$. A systematic road-map of this proof is provided in Exercise 12.

The above updates do not *seem* to be Hessian-free, because the matrix H is included in the above updates. However, the underlying computations only need the *projection* of the

Hessian along particular directions; we will see that these can be computed indirectly using the method of finite differences without explicitly computing the individual elements of the Hessian. Let $\overline{v}$ be the vector direction for which the projection $H\overline{v}$ needs to be computed. The method of finite differences computes the loss gradient at the current parameter vector $\overline{W}$ and at $\overline{W} + \delta\overline{v}$ for some small value of δ in order to perform the approximation:

$$H\overline{v} \approx \frac{\nabla L(\overline{W} + \delta\overline{v}) - \nabla L(\overline{W})}{\delta} \propto \nabla L(\overline{W} + \delta\overline{v}) - \nabla L(\overline{W}) \qquad (3.51)$$

The right-hand side is free of the Hessian. The condition is exact for quadratic functions. Other alternatives for Hessian-free updates are discussed in [41].

So far, we have discussed the simplified case of quadratic loss functions, in which the second-order derivative matrix (i.e., Hessian) is a constant matrix (i.e., independent of the current parameter vector). However, neural loss functions are not quadratic and, therefore, the Hessian matrix is dependent on the current value of $\overline{W}_t$. Do we first create a quadratic approximation at a point and then solve it for a few iterations with the Hessian (quadratic approximation) fixed at that point, or do we change the Hessian every iteration? The former is referred to as the *linear conjugate gradient method*, whereas the latter is referred to as the *nonlinear conjugate gradient method*. The two methods are equivalent for quadratic loss functions, which almost never occur in neural networks.

Classical work in neural networks and machine learning has predominantly explored the use of the nonlinear conjugate gradient method [41], whereas recent work [313, 314] advocates the use of linear conjugate methods. In the nonlinear conjugate gradient method, the mutual conjugacy of the directions will deteriorate over time, which can have an unpredictable effect on overall progress even after a large number of iterations. A part of the problem is that the process of computing conjugate directions needs to be restarted every few steps as the mutual conjugacy deteriorates. If the deterioration occurs too fast, one does not gain much from conjugacy. On the other hand, each quadratic approximation in the linear conjugate gradient method can be solved exactly, and will typically be (almost) solved in much fewer than d iterations. Although multiple such approximations will be needed, there is guaranteed progress within each approximation, and the required number of approximations is often not too large. The work in [313] experimentally shows the superiority of linear conjugate gradient methods.

3.5.6.2   Quasi-Newton Methods and BFGS

The acronym BFGS stands for the Broyden–Fletcher–Goldfarb–Shanno algorithm, and it is derived as an approximation of the Newton method. Let us revisit the updates of the Newton method. A typical update of the Newton method is as follows:

$$\overline{W}^* \Leftarrow \overline{W}_0 - H^{-1}[\nabla L(\overline{W}_0)] \qquad (3.52)$$

In quasi-Newton methods, a sequence of approximations of the inverse Hessian matrix are used in various steps. Let the approximation of the inverse Hessian matrix in the tth step be denoted by G_t. In the very first iteration, the value of G_t is initialized to the identity matrix, which amounts to moving along the steepest-descent direction. This matrix is continuously updated from G_t to G_{t+1} with low-rank updates. A direct restatement of the Newton update in terms of the inverse Hessian $G_t \approx H_t^{-1}$ is as follows:

$$\overline{W}_{t+1} \Leftarrow \overline{W}_t - G_t[\nabla L(\overline{W}_t)] \qquad (3.53)$$

The above update can be improved with an optimized learning rate α_t for non-quadratic loss functions working with (inverse) Hessian approximations like G_t:

$$\overline{W}_{t+1} \Leftarrow \overline{W}_t - \alpha_t G_t [\nabla L(\overline{W}_t)] \tag{3.54}$$

The optimized learning rate α_t is identified with line search. The line search does not need to be performed exactly (like the conjugate gradient method), because maintenance of conjugacy is no longer critical. Nevertheless, approximate conjugacy of the early set of directions is maintained by the method when starting with the identity matrix. One can (optionally) reset G_t to the identity matrix every d iterations (although this is rarely done).

It remains to be discussed how the matrix G_{t+1} is approximated from G_t. For this purpose, the *quasi-Newton condition*, also referred to as the *secant condition*, is needed:

$$\underbrace{\overline{W}_{t+1} - \overline{W}_t}_{\text{Parameter Change}} = G_{t+1} \underbrace{[\nabla L(\overline{W}_{t+1}) - \nabla L(\overline{W}_t)]}_{\text{First derivative change}} \tag{3.55}$$

The above formula is simply a finite-difference approximation. Intuitively, multiplication of the second-derivative matrix (i.e., Hessian) with the parameter change (vector) approximately provides the gradient change. Therefore, multiplication of the inverse Hessian approximation G_{t+1} with the gradient change provides the parameter change. The goal is to find a symmetric matrix G_{t+1} satisfying Equation 3.55, but it represents an underdetermined system of equations with an infinite number of solutions. Among these, BFGS chooses the closest symmetric G_{t+1} to the current G_t, and achieves this goal by posing a minimization objective function $\|G_{t+1} - G_t\|_F$ in the form of a weighted Frobenius norm. The solution is as follows:

$$G_{t+1} \Leftarrow (I - \Delta_t \overline{q}_t \overline{v}_t^T) G_t (I - \Delta_t \overline{v}_t \overline{q}_t^T) + \Delta_t \overline{q}_t \overline{q}_t^T \tag{3.56}$$

Here, the (column) vectors $\overline{q}_t$ and $\overline{v}_t$ represent the parameter change and the gradient change; the scalar $\Delta_t = 1/(\overline{q}_t^T \overline{v}_t)$ is the inverse of the dot product of these two vectors.

$$\overline{q}_t = \overline{W}_{t+1} - \overline{W}_t; \quad \overline{v}_t = \nabla L(\overline{W}_{t+1}) - \nabla L(\overline{W}_t)$$

The update in Equation 3.56 can be made more space efficient by expanding it, so that fewer temporary matrices need to be maintained. Interested readers are referred to [300, 359, 376] for implementation details and derivation of these updates.

Even though BFGS benefits from approximating the inverse Hessian, it does need to carry over a matrix G_t of size $O(d^2)$ from one iteration to the next. The *limited memory BFGS* (L-BFGS) reduces the memory requirement drastically from $O(d^2)$ to $O(d)$ by not carrying over the matrix G_t from the previous iteration. In the most basic version of the L-BFGS method, the matrix G_t is replaced with the identity matrix in Equation 3.56 in order to derive G_{t+1}. A more refined choice is to store the $m \approx 30$ most recent vectors $\overline{q}_t$ and $\overline{v}_t$. Then, L-BFGS is equivalent to initializing G_{t-m+1} to the identity matrix and recursively applying Equation 3.56 m times to derive G_{t+1}. In practice, the implementation is optimized to directly compute the direction of movement from the vectors without explicitly storing large intermediate matrices from G_{t-m+1} to G_t. The directions found by L-BFGS roughly satisfy mutual conjugacy even with approximate line search.

3.5.6.3 Problems with Second-Order Methods: Saddle Points

Second-order methods are susceptible to the presence of *saddle points*. A saddle point is a stationary point of a gradient-descent method because its gradient is zero, but it is not a minimum (or maximum). A saddle point is an *inflection point*, which appears to be either a minimum or a maximum depending on which direction we approach it from. Therefore, the quadratic approximation of the Newton method will give vastly different shapes depending on the direction that one approaches the saddle point from. A 1-dimensional function with a saddle point is the following:

$$f(x) = x^3$$

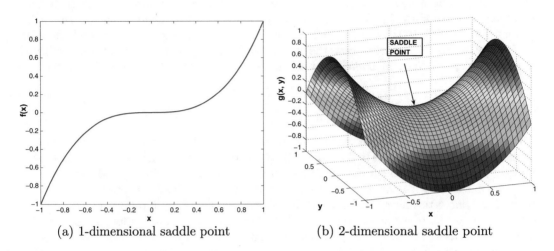

(a) 1-dimensional saddle point   (b) 2-dimensional saddle point

Figure 3.17: Illustrations of saddle points

This function is shown in Figure 3.17(a), and it has an inflection point at $x = 0$. Note that a quadratic approximation at $x > 0$ will look like an upright bowl, whereas a quadratic approximation at $x < 0$ will look like an inverted bowl. Furthermore, even if one reaches $x = 0$ in the optimization process, both the second derivative and the first derivative will be zero. Therefore, a Newton update will take the 0/0 form and become indefinite. Such a point is a degenerate point from the perspective of numerical optimization. Not all saddle points are degenerate points and vice versa. For multivariate problems, such degenerate points are often wide and flat regions that are not minima of the objective function. They do present a significant problem for numerical optimization. An example of such a function is $h(x, y) = x^3 + y^3$, which is degenerate at $(0, 0)$. Furthermore, the region near $(0, 0)$ will appear like a flat plateau. These types of plateaus create problems for learning algorithms, because first-order algorithms slow down in these regions and second-order algorithms also cannot recognize them as spurious regions. It is noteworthy that such saddle points arise only in higher-order algebraic functions (i.e., higher than second order), which are common in neural network optimization.

It is also instructive to examine the case of a saddle point that is not a degenerate point. An example of a 2-dimensional function with a saddle point is as follows:

$$g(x, y) = x^2 - y^2$$

This function is shown in Figure 3.17(b). The saddle point is $(0, 0)$. It is easy to see that the shape of this function resembles a riding saddle. In this case, approaching from the x direction or from the y direction will result in very different quadratic approximations. In one case, the function will appear to be a minimum, and in another case the function will appear to be a maximum. Furthermore, the saddle point $(0, 0)$ will be a stationary point from the perspective of a Newton update, even though it is not an extremum. Saddle points occur frequently in regions between two hills of the loss function, and they present a problematic topography for second-order methods. Interestingly, first-order methods are often able to escape from saddle points [146], because the trajectory of first-order methods is simply not attracted by such points. On the other hand, Newton's method will jump directly to the saddle point.

Unfortunately, some neural-network loss functions seem to contain a large number of saddle points. Second-order methods therefore are not always preferable to first-order methods; the specific topography of a particular loss function may have an important role to play. Second-order methods are advantageous in situations with complex curvatures of the loss function or in the presence of cliffs. In other functions with saddle points, first-order methods are advantageous. Note that the pairing of computational algorithms (like Adam) with first-order gradient-descent methods already incorporates several advantages of second-order methods in an implicit way. Therefore, real-world practitioners often prefer first-order methods in combination with computational algorithms like Adam. Recently, some methods have been proposed [88] to address saddle points in second-order methods.

3.5.7 Polyak Averaging

One of the motivations for second-order methods is to avoid the kind of bouncing behavior caused by high-curvature regions. The example of the bouncing behavior caused in valleys (cf. Figure 3.15) is another example of this setting. One way of achieving some stability with any learning algorithm is to create an exponentially decaying average of the parameters over time, so that the bouncing behavior is avoided. Let $\overline{W}_1 \ldots \overline{W}_T$, be the sequence of parameters found by any learning method over the full sequence of T steps. In the simplest version of Polyak averaging, one simply computes the average of all the parameters as the final set $\overline{W}_T^f$:

$$\overline{W}_T^f = \frac{\sum_{i=1}^{T} \overline{W}_i}{T} \tag{3.57}$$

For simple averaging, we only need to compute $\overline{W}_T^f$ once at the end of the process, and we do not need to compute the values at $1 \ldots T - 1$.

However, for exponential averaging with decay parameter $\beta < 1$, it is helpful to compute these values iteratively and maintain a running average over the course of the algorithm:

$$\overline{W}_t^f = \frac{\sum_{i=1}^{t} \beta^{t-i} \overline{W}_i}{\sum_{i=1}^{t} \beta^{t-i}} \qquad \text{[Explicit Formula]}$$

$$\overline{W}_t^f = (1 - \beta)\overline{W}_t + \beta \overline{W}_{t-1}^f \quad \text{[Recursive Formula]}$$

The two formulas above are approximately equivalent at large values of t. The second formula is convenient because it enables maintenance over the course of the algorithm, and one does not need to maintain the entire history of parameters. Exponentially decaying averages are more useful than simple averages to avoid the effect of stale points. In simple averaging, the final result may be too heavily influenced by the early points, which are poor approximations to the correct solution.

3.5.8 Local and Spurious Minima

The example of the quadratic bowl given in earlier sections is a relatively simple optimization problem that has a single global optimum. Such problems are referred to as *convex optimization problems*, and they represent the simplest case of optimization. In general, however, the objective function of a neural network is not convex, and it is likely to have many local minima. In such cases, it is possible for the learning to converge to a suboptimal solution. In spite of this fact, with reasonably good initialization, the problem of local minima in neural networks causes fewer problems than might be expected.

Local minima are problematic only when their objective function values are significantly larger than that of the global minimum. In practice, however, this does not seem to be the case in neural networks. Many research results [88, 426] have shown that the local minima of real-life networks have very similar objective function values to the global minimum. As a result, their presence does not seem to cause as strong a problem as usually thought.

Local minima often cause problems in the context of *model generalization* with limited data. An important point to keep in mind is that the loss function is always defined on a limited sample of the training data, which is only a rough approximation of what the shape of the loss function looks like on the true distribution of the unseen test data. When the size of the training data is small, a number of spurious global or local minima are created by the paucity of training data. These minima are not seen in the (infinitely large) unseen distribution of test examples, but they appear as random artifacts of the particular choice of the training data set. Such spurious minima are often more prominent and attractive when the loss function is constructed on smaller training samples. In such cases, spurious minima can indeed create a problem, because they do not generalize well to unseen test instances. This problem is slightly different from the usual concept of local minima understood in traditional optimization; the *local minima on the training data do not generalize well to the test data*. In other words, the shape of the loss function is not even the same on the training and on the test data, and therefore the minima in the two cases do not match. Here, it is important to understand that there are fundamental differences between traditional optimization and machine learning methods that attempt to generalize a loss function on a limited data set to the universe of test examples. This is a notion referred to as *empirical risk minimization*, in which one computes the (approximate) *empirical* risk for a learning algorithm because the true distribution of the examples is unknown. When starting with random initialization points, it is often possible to fall into one of these spurious minima, unless one is careful to move the initialization point to a place closer to the basins of true optima (from a model generalization point of view). One such approach is that of *unsupervised pretraining*, which is discussed in Chapter 4.

The specific problem of spurious minima (caused by the inability to generalize the results from a limited training data to unseen test data) is a much larger problem in neural network learning than the problem of local minima (from the perspective of traditional optimization). The nature of this problem is different enough from the normal understanding of local minima, so that it discussed in a separate chapter on model generalization (cf. Chapter 4).

3.6 Batch Normalization

Batch normalization is a recent method to address the vanishing and exploding gradient problems, which cause activation gradients in successive layers to either reduce or increase in magnitude. Another important problem in training deep networks is that of *internal covariate shift*. The problem is that the parameters change during training, and therefore the hidden variable activations change as well. In other words, the hidden inputs from early layers to later layers keep changing. Changing inputs from early layers to later layers causes slower convergence during training because the training data for later layers is not stable.

Batch normalization is able to reduce this effect.

In batch normalization, the idea is to add additional "normalization layers" between hidden layers that resist this type of behavior by creating features with somewhat similar variance. Furthermore, each unit in the normalization layers contains two additional parameters β_i and γ_i that regulate the precise level of normalization in the ith unit; these

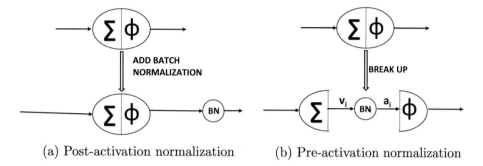

(a) Post-activation normalization   (b) Pre-activation normalization

Figure 3.18: The different choices in batch normalization

parameters are learned in a data-driven manner. The basic idea is that the output of the ith unit will have a mean of β_i and a standard deviation of γ_i *over each mini-batch of training instances*. One might wonder whether it might make sense to simply set each β_i to 0 and each γ_i to 1, but doing so reduces the representation power of the network. For example, if we make this transformation, then the sigmoid units will be operating within their linear regions, especially if the normalization is performed just before activation (see below for discussion of Figure 3.18). Recall from the discussion in Chapter 1 that multilayer networks do not gain power from depth without nonlinear activations. Therefore, allowing some "wiggle" with these parameters and learning them in a data-driven manner makes sense. Furthermore, the parameter β_i plays the role of a learned bias variable, and therefore we do not need additional bias units in these layers.

We assume that the ith unit is connected to a special type of node BN_i, where BN stands for batch normalization. This unit contains two parameters β_i and γ_i that need to be learned. Note that BN_i has only one input, and its job is to perform the normalization and scaling. This node is then connected to the next layer of the network in the standard way in which a neural network is connected to future layers. Here, we mention that there are two choices for where the normalization layer can be connected:

1. The normalization can be performed just after applying the activation function to the linearly transformed inputs. This solution is shown in Figure 3.18(a). Therefore, the normalization is performed on *post-activation values*.

2. The normalization can be performed after the linear transformation of the inputs, but before applying the activation function. This situation is shown in Figure 3.18(b). Therefore, the normalization is performed on *pre-activation values*.

It is argued in [214] that the second choice has more advantages. Therefore, we focus on this choice in this exposition. The BN node shown in Figure 3.18(b) is just like any other computational node (albeit with some special properties), and one can perform backpropagation through this node just like any other computational node.

What transformations does BN_i apply? Consider the case in which its input is $v_i^{(r)}$, corresponding to the rth element of the batch feeding into the ith unit. Each $v_i^{(r)}$ is obtained by using the linear transformation defined by the coefficient vector $\overline{W}_i$ (and biases if any). For a particular batch of m instances, let the values of the m activations be denoted by $v_i^{(1)}, v_i^{(2)}, \ldots v_i^{(m)}$. The first step is to compute the mean μ_i and standard deviation σ_i for the ith hidden unit. These are then scaled using the parameters β_i and γ_i to create the outputs for the next layer:

$$\mu_i = \frac{\sum_{r=1}^{m} v_i^{(r)}}{m} \quad \forall i \tag{3.58}$$

$$\sigma_i^2 = \frac{\sum_{r=1}^{m} (v_i^{(r)} - \mu_i)^2}{m} + \epsilon \quad \forall i \tag{3.59}$$

$$\hat{v}_i^{(r)} = \frac{v_i^{(r)} - \mu_i}{\sigma_i} \quad \forall i, r \tag{3.60}$$

$$a_i^{(r)} = \gamma_i \cdot \hat{v}_i^{(r)} + \beta_i \quad \forall i, r \tag{3.61}$$

A small value of ϵ is added to σ_i^2 to regularize cases in which all activations are the same, which results in zero variance. Note that $a_i^{(r)}$ is the pre-activation output of the ith node, when the rth batch instance passes through it. This value would otherwise have been set to $v_i^{(r)}$, if we had not applied batch normalization. We conceptually represent this node with a special node BN_i that performs this additional processing. This node is shown in Figure 3.18(b). Therefore, the backpropagation algorithm has to account for this additional node and ensure that the loss derivative of layers earlier than the batch normalization layer accounts for the transformation implied by these new nodes. It is important to note that the function applied at each of these special BN nodes is specific to the *batch* at hand. This type of computation is unusual for a neural network in which the gradients are linearly separable sums of the gradients with respect to individual training examples. This is not quite true in this case because the batch normalization layer computes nonlinear metrics from the batch (such as its standard deviation). Therefore, the activations depend on how the examples in a batch are related to one another, which is not common in most neural computations. However, this special property of the BN node does not prevent us from backpropagating through the computations performed in it.

The following will describe the changes in the backpropagation algorithm caused by the normalization layer. The main point of this change is to show how to backpropagate through the newly added layer of normalization nodes. Another point to be aware of is that we want to optimize the parameters β_i and γ_i. For the gradient-descent steps with respect to each β_i and γ_i, we need the gradients with respect to these parameters. Assume that we have already backpropagated up to the output of the BN node, and therefore we have each $\frac{\partial L}{\partial a_i^{(r)}}$ available. Then, the derivatives with respect to the two parameters can be computed as follows:

$$\frac{\partial L}{\partial \beta_i} = \sum_{r=1}^{m} \frac{\partial L}{\partial a_i^{(r)}} \cdot \frac{\partial a_i^{(r)}}{\partial \beta_i} = \sum_{r=1}^{m} \frac{\partial L}{\partial a_i^{(r)}}$$

$$\frac{\partial L}{\partial \gamma_i} = \sum_{r=1}^{m} \frac{\partial L}{\partial a_i^{(r)}} \cdot \frac{\partial a_i^{(r)}}{\partial \gamma_i} = \sum_{r=1}^{m} \frac{\partial L}{\partial a_i^{(r)}} \cdot \hat{v}_i^{(r)}$$

We also need a way to compute $\frac{\partial L}{\partial v_i^r}$. Once this value is computed, the backpropagation to the pre-activation values $\frac{\partial L}{\partial a_j^r}$ for all nodes j in the previous layer uses the straightforward backpropagation update introduced earlier in this chapter. Therefore, the dynamic programming recursion will be complete because one can then use these values of $\frac{\partial L}{\partial a_j^r}$. One can compute the value of $\frac{\partial L}{\partial v_i^r}$ in terms of $\hat{v}_i^{(r)}$, μ_i, and σ_i, by observing that $v_i^{(r)}$ can be written as a (normalization) function of only $\hat{v}_i^{(r)}$, mean μ_i, and variance σ_i^2. Observe that μ_i and σ_i are not treated as constants, but as variables because they depend on the batch at hand. Therefore, we have the following:

$$\frac{\partial L}{\partial v_i^{(r)}} = \frac{\partial L}{\partial \hat{v}_i^{(r)}} \frac{\partial \hat{v}_i^{(r)}}{\partial v_i^{(r)}} + \frac{\partial L}{\partial \mu_i} \frac{\partial \mu_i}{\partial v_i^{(r)}} + \frac{\partial L}{\partial \sigma_i^2} \frac{\partial \sigma_i^2}{\partial v_i^{(r)}} \tag{3.62}$$

$$= \frac{\partial L}{\partial \hat{v}_i^{(r)}} \left(\frac{1}{\sigma_i} \right) + \frac{\partial L}{\partial \mu_i} \left(\frac{1}{m} \right) + \frac{\partial L}{\partial \sigma_i^2} \left(\frac{2(v_i^{(r)} - \mu_i)}{m} \right) \tag{3.63}$$

We need to evaluate each of the three partial derivatives on the right-hand side of the above equation in terms of the quantities that have been computed using the already-executed dynamic programming updates of backpropagation. This allows the creation of the recurrence equation for the batch normalization layer. Among these, the first expression, which is $\frac{\partial L}{\partial \hat{v}_i^{(r)}}$, can be substituted in terms of the loss derivatives of the next layer by observing that $a_i^{(r)}$ is related to $\hat{v}_i^{(r)}$ by a constant of proportionality γ_i:

$$\frac{\partial L}{\partial \hat{v}_i^{(r)}} = \gamma_i \frac{\partial L}{\partial a_i^{(r)}} \quad [\text{Since } a_i^{(r)} = \gamma_i \cdot \hat{v}_i^{(r)} + \beta_i] \tag{3.64}$$

Therefore, by substituting this value of $\frac{\partial L}{\partial \hat{v}_i^{(r)}}$ in Equation 3.63, we have the following:

$$\frac{\partial L}{\partial v_i^{(r)}} = \frac{\partial L}{\partial a_i^{(r)}} \left(\frac{\gamma_i}{\sigma_i} \right) + \frac{\partial L}{\partial \mu_i} \left(\frac{1}{m} \right) + \frac{\partial L}{\partial \sigma_i^2} \left(\frac{2(v_i^{(r)} - \mu_i)}{m} \right) \tag{3.65}$$

It now remains to compute the partial derivative of the loss with respect to the mean and the variance. The partial derivative of the loss with respect to the variance is computed as follows:

$$\frac{\partial L}{\partial \sigma_i^2} = \underbrace{\sum_{q=1}^{m} \frac{\partial L}{\partial \hat{v}_i^{(q)}} \cdot \frac{\partial \hat{v}_i^{(q)}}{\partial \sigma_i^2}}_{\text{Chain rule}} = \underbrace{-\frac{1}{2\sigma_i^3} \sum_{q=1}^{m} \frac{\partial L}{\partial \hat{v}_i^{(q)}} (v_i^{(q)} - \mu_i)}_{\text{Use Equation 3.60}} = \underbrace{-\frac{1}{2\sigma_i^3} \sum_{q=1}^{m} \frac{\partial L}{\partial a_i^{(q)}} \gamma_i \cdot (v_i^{(q)} - \mu_i)}_{\text{Substitution from Equation 3.64}}$$

The partial derivatives of the loss with respect to the mean can be computed as follows:

$$\frac{\partial L}{\partial \mu_i} = \underbrace{\sum_{q=1}^{m} \frac{\partial L}{\partial \hat{v}_i^{(q)}} \cdot \frac{\partial \hat{v}_i^{(q)}}{\partial \mu_i} + \frac{\partial L}{\partial \sigma_i^2} \cdot \frac{\partial \sigma_i^2}{\partial \mu_i}}_{\text{Chain rule}} = \underbrace{-\frac{1}{\sigma_i} \sum_{q=1}^{m} \frac{\partial L}{\partial \hat{v}_i^{(q)}} - 2\frac{\partial L}{\partial \sigma_i^2} \cdot \frac{\sum_{q=1}^{m}(v_i^{(q)} - \mu_i)}{m}}_{\text{Use Equations 3.59 and 3.60}}$$

$$= \underbrace{-\frac{\gamma_i}{\sigma_i} \sum_{q=1}^{m} \frac{\partial L}{\partial a_i^{(q)}}}_{\text{Eq. 3.64}} + \underbrace{\left(\frac{1}{\sigma_i^3} \right) \cdot \left(\sum_{q=1}^{m} \frac{\partial L}{\partial a_i^{(q)}} \gamma_i \cdot (v_i^{(q)} - \mu_i) \right) \cdot \left(\frac{\sum_{q=1}^{m}(v_i^{(q)} - \mu_i)}{m} \right)}_{\text{Substitution for } \frac{\partial L}{\partial \sigma_i^2}}$$

By plugging in the partial derivatives of the loss with respect to the mean and variance in Equation 3.65, we get a full recursion for $\frac{\partial L}{\partial v_i^{(r)}}$ (value before batch-normalization layer) in terms of $\frac{\partial L}{\partial a_i^{(r)}}$ (value *after* the batch normalization layer). This provides a full view of the backpropagation of the loss through the batch-normalization layer corresponding to the BN node. The other aspects of backpropagation remain similar to the traditional case. Batch normalization enables faster inference because it prevents problems such as the exploding and vanishing gradient (which cause slow learning).

A natural question about batch normalization arises during inference (prediction) time. Since the transformation parameters μ_i and σ_i depend on the batch, how should one compute them during testing when a *single* test instance is available? In this case, the values of μ_i are σ_i are computed up front using the *entire* population (of training data), and then treated as constants during testing time. One can also keep an exponentially weighted average of these values during training. Therefore, the normalization is a simple linear transformation during inference.

An interesting property of batch normalization is that *it also acts as a regularizer*. Note that the same data point can cause somewhat different updates depending on which batch it is included in. One can view this effect as a kind of noise added to the update process. Regularization is often achieved by adding a small amount of noise to the training data. It has been experimentally observed that regularization methods like *Dropout* (cf. Section 4.5.4 of Chapter 4) do not seem to improve performance when batch normalization is used [184], although there is not a complete agreement on this point. A variant of batch normalization, known as *layer normalization*, is known to work well with recurrent networks. This approach is discussed in Section 7.3.1 of Chapter 7.

3.7   Practical Tricks for Acceleration and Compression

Neural network learning algorithms can be extremely expensive, both in terms of the number of parameters in the model and the amount of data that needs to be processed. There are several strategies that are used to accelerate and compress the underlying implementations. Some of the common strategies are as follows:

1. *GPU-acceleration:* Graphics Processor Units (GPUs) have historically been used for rendering video games with intensive graphics because of their efficiency in settings where repeated matrix operations (e.g., on graphics pixels) are required. It was eventually realized by the machine learning community (and GPU hardware companies) that such repetitive operations are also used in settings like neural networks, in which matrix operations are extensively used. Even the use of a single GPU can significantly speed up implementation because of its high memory bandwidth and multithreading within its multicore architecture.

2. *Parallel implementations:* One can parallelize the implementations of neural networks by using multiple GPUs or CPUs. Either the neural network model or the data can be partitioned across different processors. These implementations are referred to as *model-parallel* and *data-parallel* implementations.

3. *Algorithmic tricks for model compression during deployment:* A key point about the practical use of neural networks is that they have different computational requirements during training and deployment. While it is acceptable to train a model for a week with a large amount of memory, the final deployment might be performed on a mobile

phone, which is highly constrained both in terms of memory and computational power. Therefore, numerous tricks are used for model compression during testing time. This type of compression often results in better cache performance and efficiency as well.

In the following, we will discuss some of these acceleration and compression techniques.

3.7.1 GPU Acceleration

GPUs were originally developed for rendering graphics on screens with the use of lists of 3-dimensional coordinates. Therefore, graphics cards were inherently designed to perform many matrix multiplications in parallel to render the graphics rapidly. GPU processors have evolved significantly, moving well beyond their original functionality of graphics rendering. Like graphics applications, neural-network implementations require large matrix multiplications, which is inherently suited to the GPU setting. In a traditional neural network, each forward propagation is a multiplication of a matrix and vector, whereas in a convolutional neural network, two matrices are multiplied. When a mini-batch approach is used, activations become matrices (instead of vectors) in a traditional neural network. Therefore, forward propagations require matrix multiplications. A similar result is true for backpropagation, during which two matrices are multiplied frequently to propagate the derivatives backwards. In other words, most of the intensive computations involve vector, matrix, and tensor operations. Even a single GPU is good at parallelizing these operations in its different cores with multithreading [203], in which some groups of threads sharing the same code are executed concurrently. This principle is referred to as *Single Instruction Multiple Threads (SIMT)*. Although CPUs also support short-vector data parallelization via *Single Instruction Multiple Data (SIMD)* instructions, the degree of parallelism is much lower as compared to the GPU. There are different trade-offs when using GPUs as compared to traditional CPUs. GPUs are very good at repetitive operations, but they have difficulty at performing branching operations like *if-then* statements. Most of the intensive operations in neural network learning are repetitive matrix multiplications across different training instances, and therefore this setting is suited to the GPU. Although the clock speed of a single instruction in the GPU is slower than the traditional CPU, the parallelization is so much greater in the GPU that huge advantages are gained.

GPU threads are grouped into small units called *warps*. Each thread in the warp shares the same code in each cycle, and this restriction enables a concurrent execution of the threads. The implementation needs to be carefully tailored to reduce the use of memory bandwidth. This is done by *coalescing* the memory reads and writes from different threads, so that a single memory transaction can be used to read and write values from different threads. Consider a common operation like matrix multiplication in neural network settings. The matrices are multiplied by making each thread responsible for computing a single entry in the product matrix. For example, consider a situation in which a 100×50 matrix is multiplied with a 50×200 matrix. In such a case, a total of $100 \times 200 = 20000$ threads would be launched in order to compute the entries of the matrix. These threads will typically be partitioned into multiple warps, each of which is highly parallelized. Therefore, speedups are achieved. A discussion of matrix multiplication on GPUs is provided in [203].

With high amounts of parallelization, memory bandwidth is often the primary limiting factor. Memory bandwidth refers to the speed at which the processor can access the relevant parameters from their stored locations in memory. GPUs have a high degree of parallelism and high memory bandwidth as compared to traditional CPUs. Note that if one cannot access the relevant parameters from memory fast enough, then faster execution does not help the speed of computation. In such cases, the memory transfer cannot keep up with the speed of the processor whether working with the CPU or the GPU, and the CPU/GPU cores will idle. GPUs have different trade-offs between cache access, computation, and memory access. CPUs have much larger caches than GPUs and they rely on the caches to store an intermediate result, such as the result of multiplying two numbers. Accessing a computed value from a cache is much faster than multiplying them again, which is where the CPU has an advantage over the GPU. However, this advantage is neutralized in neural network settings, where the sizes of the parameter matrices and activations are often too large to fit in the CPU cache. Even though the CPU cache is larger than that of the GPU, it is not large enough to handle the scale at which neural-network operations are performed. In such cases, one has to rely on high memory bandwidth, which is where the GPU has an advantage over the CPU. Furthermore, it is often faster to perform the same computation again rather than accessing it from memory, when working with the GPU (assuming that the result is unavailable in a cache). Therefore, GPU implementations are done somewhat differently from traditional CPU implementations. Furthermore, the advantage gained can be sensitive to the choice of neural network architecture, as the memory bandwidth requirements and multi-threading gains of different architectures can be different.

At first sight, it might seem from the above example that the use of a GPU requires a lot of low-level programming, and it would indeed be a challenge to create custom GPU code for each neural architecture. With this problem in mind, companies like NVIDIA have modularized the interface between the programmer and the GPU implementation. The key point is that the speeding of primitives like matrix multiplication and convolution can be hidden from the user by providing a library of neural network operations that perform these faster operations behind the scenes. The GPU library is tightly integrated with deep learning frameworks like Caffe or Torch to take advantage of the accelerated operations on the GPU. A specific example of such a library is the *NVIDIA CUDA Deep Neural Network Library* [643], which is referred to in short as *cuDNN*. CUDA is a parallel computing platform and programming model that works with CUDA-enabled GPU processors. However, it provides an abstraction and a programming interface that is easy to use with relatively limited rewriting of code. The cuDNN library can be integrated with multiple deep learning frameworks such as Caffe, TensorFlow, Theano, and Torch. The changes required to convert the training code of a particular neural network from its CPU version to a GPU version are often small. For example, in Torch, the CUDA Torch package is incorporated at the beginning of the code, and various data structures (like tensors) are initialized as CUDA tensors (instead of regular tensors). With these types of modest modifications, virtually the same code can run on a GPU instead of a CPU in Torch. A similar situation holds true in other deep learning frameworks. This type of approach shields the developers from the low-level performance tuning required in GPU frameworks, because the primitives in the library already have the code that takes care of all the low-level details of parallelization on the GPU.

3.7.2   Parallel and Distributed Implementations

It is possible to make training even faster by using multiple CPUs or GPUs. Since it is more common to use multiple GPUs, we focus on this setting. Parallelism is not a simple matter when working with GPUs because there are overheads associated with the communication between different processors. The delay caused by these overheads has recently been reduced with specialized network cards for GPU-to-GPU transfer. Furthermore, algorithmic tricks like using 8-bit approximations of the gradients [98] can help in speeding up the communication. There are several ways in which one can partition the work across different processors, namely hyperparameter parallelism, model parallelism, and data parallelism. These methods are discussed below.

Hyperparameter Parallelism

The simplest possible way to achieve parallelism in the training process without much overhead is to train neural networks with different parameter settings on different processors. No communication is required across different executions, and therefore wasteful overhead is avoided. As discussed earlier in this chapter, runs with suboptimal hyperparameters are often terminated long before running them to completion. Nevertheless, a small number of different runs with optimized parameters are often used in order to create an ensemble of models. The training of different ensemble components can be performed independently on different processors.

Model Parallelism

Model parallelism is particularly useful when a single model is too large to fit on a GPU. In such a case, the hidden layer is divided across the different GPUs. The different GPUs work on exactly the same batch of training points, although different GPUs compute different parts of the activations and the gradients. Each GPU only contains the portion of the weight matrix that are multiplied with the hidden activations present in the GPU. However, it would still need to communicate the results of its activations to the other GPUs. Similarly, it would need to receive the derivatives with respect to the hidden units in other GPUs in order to compute the gradients of the weights between its hidden units and those of other GPUs. This is achieved with the use of inter-connections across GPUs, and the computations across these interconnections add to the overhead. In some cases, these interconnections are dropped in a subset of the layers in order to reduce the communication overhead (although the resulting model would not quite be the same as the sequential version). Model parallelism is not helpful in cases where the number of parameters in the neural network is small, and should only be used for large networks. A good practical example of model parallelism is the design of *AlexNet*, which is a convolutional neural network (cf. Section 8.4.1 of Chapter 8). A sequential version of *AlexNet* and a GPU-partitioned version of *AlexNet* are both shown in Figure 8.9 of Chapter 8. Note that the sequential version in Figure 8.9 is not exactly equivalent to the GPU-partitioned version because the interconnections between GPUs have been dropped in some of the layers. A discussion of model parallelism may be found in [74].

Data Parallelism

Data parallelism works best when the model is small enough to fit on each GPU, but the amount of training data is large. In these cases, the parameters are shared across the different GPUs and the goal of the updates is to use the different processors with different training points for faster updates. The problem is that perfect synchronization of the updates can slow down the process, because locking mechanisms would need to be used to synchronize the updates. The key point is that each processor would have to wait for the others to make their updates. As a result, the slowest processor creates a bottleneck. A method that uses *asynchronous* stochastic gradient descent was proposed in [91]. The basic idea is to use a parameter server in order to share the parameters across different GPU processors. The updates are performed without using any locking mechanism. In other words, each GPU can read the shared parameters at any time, perform the computation, and write the parameters to the parameter server without worrying about locks. In this case, inefficiency would still be caused by one GPU processor overwriting the progress made by another, but there would be no waiting times for writes. As a result, the overall progress would still be faster than with a synchronized mechanism. Distributed asynchronous gradient descent is quite popular as a strategy for parallelism in large-scale industrial settings.

Exploiting the Trade-Offs for Hybrid Parallelism

It is evident from the above discussion that model parallelism is well suited to models with a large parameter footprint, whereas data parallelism is well suited to smaller models. It turns out that one can combine the two types of parallelism over different parts of the network. In certain types of convolutional neural networks that have fully connected layers, the vast majority of parameters occur in the fully connected layers, whereas more computations are performed in the earlier layers. In these cases, it makes sense to use data parallelism for the early part of the network, and model parallelism for the later part of the network. This type of approach is referred to as *hybrid parallelism*. A discussion of this type of approach may be found in [254].

3.7.3   Algorithmic Tricks for Model Compression

Training a neural network and deploying it typically have different requirements in terms of memory and efficiency requirements. While it may be acceptable to require a week to train a neural network to recognize faces in images, the end user might wish to use the trained neural network to recognize a face within a matter of a few seconds. Furthermore, the model might be deployed on a mobile device with little memory and computational availability. In such cases, it is crucial to be able to use the trained model efficiently, and also use it with a limited amount of storage. Efficiency is generally not a problem at deployment time, because the prediction of a test instance often requires straightforward matrix multiplications over a few layers. On the other hand, storage requirements are often a problem because of the large number of parameters in multilayer networks. There are several tricks that are used for model compression in such cases. In most of the cases, a larger trained neural network is modified so that it requires less space by approximating some parts of the model. In addition, some efficiency improvements can also be realized at prediction time by model compression because of better cache performance and fewer operations, although this is not the primary goal. Interestingly, this approximation might occasionally *improve* accuracy on out-of-sample predictions because of regularization effects, especially if the original model is unnecessarily large compared to the training data size.

Sparsifying Weights in Training

The links in a neural network are associated with weights. If the absolute value of a particular weight is small, then the model is not strongly influenced by that weight. Such weights can be dropped, and the neural network can be fine-tuned starting with the current weights on links that have not yet been dropped. The level of sparsification will depend on the weight threshold at which links are dropped. By choosing a larger threshold at which weights are dropped, the size of the model will reduce significantly. In such cases, it is particularly important to fine-tune the values of the retained weights with further epochs of training. One can also encourage the dropping of links by using L_1-regularization, which will be discussed in Chapter 4. When L_1-regularization is used during training, many of the weights will have zero values anyway because of the natural mathematical properties of this form of regularization. However, it has been shown in [169] that L_2-regularization has the advantage of higher accuracy. Therefore, the work in [169] uses L_2-regularization and prunes the weights that are below a particular threshold.

Further enhancements were reported in [168], where the approach was combined with Huffman coding and quantization for compression. The goal of quantization is to reduce the number of bits representing each connection. This approach reduced the storage required by *AlexNet* [255] by a factor of 35, or from about 240MB to 6.9MB, with no loss of accuracy. It is now possible as a result of this reduction to fit the model into an on-chip SRAM cache rather than off-chip DRAM memory; this also provide a beneficial effect on prediction times.

Leveraging Redundancies in Weights

It was shown in [94] that the vast majority of the weights in a neural network are redundant. In other words, for any $m \times n$ weight matrix W between a pair of layers with m_1 and m_2 units respectively, one can express this weight matrix as $W \approx UV^T$, where U and V are of sizes $m_1 \times k$ and $m_2 \times k$, respectively. Furthermore, it is assumed that $k \ll \min\{m_1, m_2\}$. This phenomenon occurs because of several peculiarities in the training process. For example, the features and weights in a neural network tend to *co-adapt* because of different parts of the network training at different rates. Therefore, the faster parts of the network often adapt to the slower parts. As a result, there is a lot of redundancy in the network both in terms of the features and the weights, and the full expressivity of the network is never utilized. In such a case, one can replace the pair of layers (containing weight matrix W) with three layers of size m_1, k, and m_2. The weight matrices between the first pair of layers is U and the weight matrix between the second pair of layers is V^T. Even though the new matrix is deeper, it is better regularized as long as $W - UV^T$ only contains noise. Furthermore, the matrices U and V require $(m_1 + m_2) \cdot k$ parameters, which is less than the number of parameters in W as long as k is less than half the harmonic mean of m_1 and m_2:

$$\frac{\text{Parameters in } W}{\text{Parameters in } U, V} = \frac{m_1 \cdot m_2}{k(m_1 + m_2)} = \frac{\text{HARMONIC-MEAN}(m_1, m_2)}{2k}$$

As shown in [94], more than 95% of the parameters in the neural network are redundant, and therefore a low value of the rank k suffices for approximation.

An important point is that the replacement of W with U and V must be done *after* completion of the learning of W. For example, if we replaced the pair of layers corresponding to W with the three layers containing the two weight matrices U and V^T and trained from scratch, good results may not be obtained. This is because co-adaptation will occur again during training, and the resulting matrices U and V will have a rank even lower than k. As a result, under-fitting might occur.

Finally, one can compress even further by realizing that both U and V need not be learned because they are redundant with respect to each other. For any rank-k matrix U, one can learn V so that the product UV^T is the same value. Therefore, the work in [94] provides methods to fix U, and then learn V instead.

Hash-Based Compression

One can reduce the number of parameters to be stored by forcing randomly chosen entries of the weight matrix to take on shared values of the parameters. The random choice is achieved with the application of a hash function on the entry position (i, j) in the matrix.

For example, imagine a situation where we have a weight matrix of size 100×100 with 10^4 entries. In such a case, one can hash each weight to a value in the range $\{1, \ldots 1000\}$ to create 1000 groups. Each of these groups will contain an average of 10 connections that will share weights. Backpropagation can handle shared weights using the approach discussed in Section 3.2.9. This approach requires a space requirement of only 1000 for the matrix, which is 10% of the original space requirement. Note that one could instead use a matrix of size 100×10 to achieve the same compression, but the key point is that using shared weights does not hurt the expressivity of the model as much as would reducing the size of the weight matrix *a priori*. More details of this approach are discussed in [66].

Leveraging Mimic Models

Some interesting results in [13, 55] show that it is possible to significantly compress a model by creating a new training data set from a trained model, which is easier to model. This "easier" training data can be used to train a much smaller network without significant loss of accuracy. This smaller model is referred to as a *mimic model*. The following steps are used to create the mimic model:

1. A model is created on the original training data. This model might be very large, and potentially even created out of an ensemble of different models, further increasing the number of parameters; it would not be appropriate to use in space-constrained settings. It is assumed that the model outputs softmax probabilities of the different classes. This model is also referred to as the teacher model.

2. New training data is created by passing unlabeled examples through the trained network. The targets in the newly created training data are set to the softmax probability outputs of the trained model on the unlabeled examples. Since unlabeled data is often copious, it is possible to create a lot of training data in this way. It is noteworthy that the new training data contains soft (probabilistic) targets rather than the discrete targets in the original training data, which significantly contributes to the creation of the compressed model.

3. A much smaller and shallower network is trained using the new training data (with artificially generated labels). The original training data is not used at all. This much smaller and shallower network, which is referred to as the mimic or *student* model, is what is deployed in space-constrained settings. It can be shown that the accuracy of the mimic model does not substantially degrade from the model trained over the original neural network, even though it is much smaller in size.

A natural question arises as to why the mimic model should perform as well as the original model, even though it is much smaller in size both in terms of the depth as well as the number of parameters. Trying to construct a shallow model on the original data cannot match the accuracy of either the shallow model or the mimic model. A number of possible reasons have been hypothesized for the superior performance of the mimic model [13]:

1. If there are errors in the original training data because of mislabeling, it causes unnecessary complexity in the trained model. These types of errors are largely removed in the new training data.

2. If there are complex regions of the decision space, the teacher model simplifies them by providing softer labels in terms of probabilities. Complexity is washed away by filtering targets through the teacher model.

3. The original training data contains targets with $0/1$ values, whereas the newly created training contains soft targets, which are more informative. This is particularly useful in one-hot encoded multilabel targets, where there are clear correlations across different classes.

4. The original targets might depend on inputs that are not available in the training data. On the other hand, the teacher-created labels depend on only the available inputs. This makes the model simpler to learn and washes away unexplained complexity. Unexplained complexity often leads to unnecessary parameters and depth.

One can view some of the above benefits as a kind of regularization effect. The results in [13] are stimulating, because they show that deep networks are not *theoretically* necessary, although the regularization effect of depth is practically necessary when working with the original training data. The mimic model enjoys the benefits of this regularization effect by using the artificially created targets instead of depth.

3.8 Summary

This chapter discusses the problem of training deep neural networks. We revisit the back-propagation algorithm in detail along with its challenges. The vanishing and the exploding gradient problems are introduced along with the challenges associated with varying sensitivity of the loss function to different optimization variables. Certain types of activation functions like ReLU are less sensitive to this problem. However, the use of the ReLU can sometimes lead to dead neurons, if one is not careful about the learning rate. The type of gradient descent used to accelerate learning is also important for more efficient executions. Modified stochastic gradient-descent methods include the use of Nesterov momentum, Ada-Grad, AdaDelta, RMSProp, and Adam. All these methods encourage gradient-steps that accelerate the learning process.

Numerous methods have been introduced for addressing the problem of cliffs with the use of second-order optimization methods. In particular, Hessian-free optimization is seen as an effective approach for handling many of the underlying optimization issues. An exciting method that has been used recently to improve learning rates is the use of batch normalization. Batch normalization transforms the data layer by layer in order to ensure that the scaling of different variables is done in an optimum way. The use of batch normalization has become extremely common in different types of deep networks. Numerous methods have been proposed for accelerating and compressing neural network algorithms. Acceleration is often achieved via hardware improvements, whereas compression is achieved with algorithmic tricks.

3.9 Bibliographic Notes

The original idea of backpropagation was based on idea of differentiation of composition of functions as developed in control theory [54, 237] under the ambit of *automatic differentiation*. The adaptation of these methods to neural networks was proposed by Paul Werbos in his PhD thesis in 1974 [524], although a more modern form of the algorithm was proposed by Rumelhart *et al.* in 1986 [408]. A discussion of the history of the backpropagation algorithm may be found in the book by Paul Werbos [525].

A discussion of algorithms for hyperparameter optimization in neural networks and other machine learning algorithms may be found in [36, 38, 490]. The random search method for hyperparameter optimization is discussed in [37]. The use of *Bayesian optimization* for hyperparameter tuning is discussed in [42, 306, 458]. Numerous libraries are available for Bayesian tuning such as *Hyperopt* [614], *Spearmint* [616], and *SMAC* [615].

The rule that the initial weights should depend on both the fan-in and fan-out of a node in proportion to $\sqrt{2/(r_{in} + r_{out})}$ is based on [140]. The analysis of initialization methods for rectifier neural networks is provided in [183]. Evaluations and analysis of the effect of feature preprocessing on neural network learning may be found in [278, 532]. The use of rectifier linear units for addressing some of the training challenges is discussed in [141].

Nesterov's algorithm for gradient descent may be found in [353]. The delta-bar-delta method was proposed by [217]. The AdaGrad algorithm was proposed in [108]. The RMSProp algorithm is discussed in [194]. Another adaptive algorithm using stochastic gradient descent, which is *AdaDelta*, is discussed in [553]. This algorithms shares some similarities with second-order methods, and in particular to the method in [429]. The Adam algorithm, which is a further enhancement along this line of ideas, is discussed in [241]. The practical importance of initialization and momentum in deep learning is discussed in [478]. Beyond the use of the stochastic gradient method, the use of coordinate descent has been proposed [273]. The strategy of *Polyak averaging* is discussed in [380].

Several of the challenges associated with the vanishing and exploding gradient problems are discussed in [140, 205, 368]. Ideas for parameter initialization that avoid some of these problems are discussed in [140]. The gradient clipping rule was discussed by Mikolov in his PhD thesis [324]. A discussion of the gradient clipping method in the context of recurrent neural networks is provided in [368]. The ReLU activation function was introduced in [167], and several of its interesting properties are explored in [141, 221].

A description of several second-order gradient optimization methods (such as the Newton method) is provided in [41, 545, 300]. The basic principles of the conjugate gradient method have been described in several classical books and papers [41, 189, 443], and the work in [313, 314] discusses applications to neural networks. The work in [316] leverages a Kronecker-factored curvature matrix for fast gradient descent. Another way of approximating the Newton method is the quasi-Newton method [273, 300], with the simplest approximation being a diagonal Hessian [24]. The acronym BFGS stands for the Broyden-Fletcher-Goldfarb-Shanno algorithm. A variant known as limited memory BFGS or L-BFGS [273, 300] does not require as much memory. Another popular second-order method is the Levenberg–Marquardt algorithm. This approach is, however, defined for squared loss functions and cannot be used with many forms of cross-entropy or log-losses that are common in neural networks. Overviews of the approach may be found in [133, 300]. General discussions of different types of nonlinear programming methods are provided in [23, 39].

The stability of neural networks to local minima is discussed in [88, 426]. Batch normalization methods were introduced recently in [214]. A method that uses whitening for batch normalization is discussed in [96], although the approach seems not to be practical. Batch normalization requires some minor adjustments for recurrent networks [81], although a more effective approach for recurrent networks is that of *layer normalization* [14]. In this method (cf. Section 7.3.1), a single training case is used for normalizing all units in a layer, rather than using mini-batch normalization of a single unit. The approach is useful for recurrent networks. An analogous notion to batch normalization is that of weight normalization [419], in which the magnitudes and directions of the weight vectors are decoupled during the learning process. Related training tricks are discussed in [362].

A broader discussion of accelerating machine learning algorithms with GPUs may be found in [644]. Various types of parallelization tricks for GPUs are discussed in [74, 91, 254], and specific discussions on convolutional neural networks are provided in [541]. Model compression with regularization is discussed in [168, 169]. A related model compression method is proposed in [213]. The use of mimic models for compression is discussed in [55, 13]. A related approach is discussed in [202]. The leveraging of parameter redundancy for compressing neural networks is discussed in [94]. The compression of neural networks with the hashing trick is discussed in [66].

3.9.1 Software Resources

All the training algorithms discussed in this chapter are supported by numerous deep learning frameworks like *Caffe* [571], *Torch* [572], *Theano* [573], and *TensorFlow* [574]. Extensions of *Caffe* to Python and MATLAB are available. All these frameworks provide a variety of training algorithms that are discussed in this chapter. Options for batch normalization are available as separate layers in these frameworks. Several software libraries are available for Bayesian optimization of hyperparameters. These libraries include *Hyperopt* [614], *Spearmint* [616], and *SMAC* [615]. Although these are designed for smaller machine learning problems, they can still be used in some cases. Pointers to the NVIDIA cuDNN may be found in [643]. The different frameworks supported by cuDNN are discussed in [645].

3.10 Exercises

1. Consider the following recurrence:

$$(x_{t+1}, y_{t+1}) = (f(x_t, y_t), g(x_t, y_t)) \qquad (3.66)$$

Here, $f()$ and $g()$ are multivariate functions.

   (a) Derive an expression for $\frac{\partial x_{t+2}}{\partial x_t}$ in terms of only x_t and y_t.

   (b) Can you draw an architecture of a neural network corresponding to the above recursion for t varying from 1 to 5? Assume that the neurons can compute any function you want.

2. Consider a two-input neuron that multiplies its two inputs x_1 and x_2 to obtain the output o. Let L be the loss function that is computed at o. Suppose that you know that $\frac{\partial L}{\partial o} = 5$, $x_1 = 2$, and $x_2 = 3$. Compute the values of $\frac{\partial L}{\partial x_1}$ and $\frac{\partial L}{\partial x_2}$.

3. Consider a neural network with three layers including an input layer. The first (input) layer has four inputs x_1, x_2, x_3, and x_4. The second layer has six hidden units corresponding to all pairwise multiplications. The output node o simply adds the values in the six hidden units. Let L be the loss at the output node. Suppose that you know that $\frac{\partial L}{\partial o} = 2$, and $x_1 = 1$, $x_2 = 2$, $x_3 = 3$, and $x_4 = 4$. Compute $\frac{\partial L}{\partial x_i}$ for each i.

4. How does your answer to the previous question change when the output o is computed as a maximum of its six inputs rather than its sum?

5. The chapter discusses (cf. Table 3.1) how one can perform a backpropagation of an arbitrary function by using the multiplication with the Jacobian matrix. Discuss why one must be careful in using this matrix-centric approach.[Hint: Compute the Jacobian with respect to sigmoid function]

6. Consider the loss function $L = x^2 + y^{10}$. Implement a simple steepest-descent algorithm to plot the coordinates as they vary from the initialization point to the optimal value of 0. Consider two different initialization points of $(0.5, 0.5)$ and $(2, 2)$ and plot the trajectories in the two cases at a constant learning rate. What do you observe about the behavior of the algorithm in the two cases?

7. The Hessian H of a strongly convex quadratic function always satisfies $\overline{x}^T H \overline{x} > 0$ for any nonzero vector $\overline{x}$. For such problems, show that all conjugate directions are linearly independent.

8. Show that if the dot product of a d-dimensional vector $\overline{v}$ with d linearly independent vectors is 0, then $\overline{v}$ must be the zero vector.

9. This chapter discusses two variants of backpropagation, which use the pre-activation and the postactivation variables, respectively, for the dynamic programming recursion. Show that these two variants of backpropagation are mathematically equivalent.

10. Consider the softmax activation function in the output layer, in which real-valued outputs $v_1 \ldots v_k$ are converted into probabilities as follows (according to Equation 3.20):

$$o_i = \frac{\exp(v_i)}{\sum_{j=1}^{k} \exp(v_j)} \quad \forall i \in \{1, \ldots, k\}$$

   (a) Show that the value of $\frac{\partial o_i}{\partial v_j}$ is $o_i(1 - o_i)$ when $i = j$. In the case that $i \neq j$, show that this value is $-o_i o_j$.

   (b) Use the above result to show the correctness of Equation 3.22:

$$\frac{\partial L}{\partial v_i} = o_i - y_i$$

   Assume that we are using the cross-entropy loss $L = -\sum_{i=1}^{k} y_i \log(o_i)$, where $y_i \in \{0, 1\}$ is the one-hot encoded class label over different values of $i \in \{1 \ldots k\}$.

11. The chapter uses steepest descent directions to iteratively generate conjugate directions. Suppose we pick d *arbitrary* directions $\overline{v}_0 \ldots \overline{v}_{d-1}$ that are linearly independent. Show that (with appropriate choice of β_{ti}) we can start with $\overline{q}_0 = \overline{v}_0$ and generate successive conjugate directions in the following form:

$$\overline{q}_{t+1} = \overline{v}_{t+1} + \sum_{i=0}^{t} \beta_{ti} \overline{q}_i$$

   Discuss why this approach is more expensive than the one discussed in the chapter.

12. The definition of β_t in Section 3.5.6.1 ensures that $\overline{q}_t$ is conjugate to $\overline{q}_{t+1}$. This exercise systematically shows that *any* direction $\overline{q}_i$ for $i \leq t$ satisfies $\overline{q}_i^T H \overline{q}_{t+1} = 0$.
   [Hint: Prove (b), (c), and (d) *jointly* with induction on t while staring at (a).]

   (a) Recall from Equation 3.51 that $H \overline{q}_i = [\nabla L(\overline{W}_{i+1}) - \nabla L(\overline{W}_i)]/\delta_i$ for quadratic loss functions, where δ_i depends on ith step-size. Combine this condition with Equation 3.49 to show the following for all $i \leq t$:

$$\delta_i [\overline{q}_i^T H \overline{q}_{t+1}] = -[\nabla L(\overline{W}_{i+1}) - \nabla L(\overline{W}_i)]^T [\nabla L(\overline{W}_{t+1})] + \delta_i \beta_t (\overline{q}_i^T H \overline{q}_t)$$

   Also show that $[\nabla L(\overline{W}_{t+1}) - \nabla L(\overline{W}_t)] \cdot \overline{q}_i = \delta_t \overline{q}_i^T H \overline{q}_t$.

(b) Show that $\nabla L(\overline{W}_{t+1})$ is orthogonal to each $\overline{q}_i$ for $i \leq t$. [The proof for the case when $i = t$ is trivial because the gradient at line-search termination is always orthogonal to the search direction.]

(c) Show that the loss gradients at $\overline{W}_0 \ldots \overline{W}_{t+1}$ are mutually orthogonal.

(d) Show that $\overline{q}_i^T H \overline{q}_{t+1} = 0$ for $i \leq t$. [The case for $i = t$ is trivial.]

Chapter 4

Teaching Deep Learners to Generalize

"All generalizations are dangerous, even this one."—Alexandre Dumas

4.1 Introduction

Neural networks are powerful learners that have repeatedly proven to be capable of learning complex functions in many domains. However, the great power of neural networks is also their greatest weakness; neural networks often simply overfit the training data if care is not taken to design the learning process carefully. In practical terms, what overfitting means is that a neural network will provide excellent prediction performance on the training data that it is built on, but will perform poorly on unseen test instances. This is caused by the fact that the learning process often remembers random artifacts of the training data that do not generalize well to the test data. Extreme forms of overfitting are referred to as *memorization*. A helpful analogy is to think of a child who can solve all the analytical problems for which he or she has seen the solutions, but is unable to provide useful solutions to a new problem. However, if the child is exposed to the solutions of more and more different types of problems, he or she will be more likely to solve a new problem by abstracting out the essence of the patterns that are repeated across different problems and their solutions. Machine learning proceeds in a similar way by identifying patterns that are useful for prediction. For example, in a spam detection application, if the pattern *"Free Money!!"* occurs thousands of times in spam emails, the machine learner generalizes this rule to identify spam email instances it has not seen before. On the other hand, a prediction that is based on the patterns seen in a tiny training data set of two emails will lead to good performance on those emails but not on new emails. The ability of a learner to provide useful predictions for instances it has not seen before is referred to as *generalization*.

Generalization is a useful practical property, and is therefore the holy grail in all machine learning applications. After all, if the training examples are already labeled, there is no practical use of predicting such examples again. For example, in an image-captioning application,

C. C. Aggarwal, *Neural Networks and Deep Learning*,
https://doi.org/10.1007/978-3-319-94463-0_4

one is always looking to use the labeled images in order to learn captions for images that the learner has not seen before.

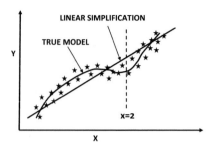

Figure 4.1: An example of a nonlinear distribution in which one would expect a model with $d = 3$ to work better than a linear model with $d = 1$.

The level of overfitting depends both on the complexity of the model and on the amount of data available. The complexity of the model defined by a neural network depends on the number of underlying parameters. Parameters provide additional degrees of freedom, which can be used to explain specific training data points without generalizing well to unseen points. For example, imagine a situation in which we attempt to predict the variable y from x using the following formula for polynomial regression:

$$\hat{y} = \sum_{i=0}^{d} w_i x^i \tag{4.1}$$

This is a model that uses $(d + 1)$ parameters $w_0 \ldots w_d$ in order to explain pairs (x, y) available to us. One could implement this model by using a neural network with d inputs corresponding to x, $x^2 \ldots x^d$, and a single bias neuron whose coefficient is w_0. The loss function uses the squared difference between the observed value y and predicted value $\hat{y}$. In general, larger values of d can capture better nonlinearity. For example, in the case of Figure 4.1, a nonlinear model with $d = 4$ should be able to fit the data better than a linear model with $d = 1$, *given an infinite amount (or a lot) of data*. However, when working with a small, finite data set, this does not always turn out to be the case.

If we have $(d+1)$ or less training pairs (x, y), it is possible to fit the data exactly with zero error *irrespective of how well these training pairs reflect the true distribution.* For example, consider a situation in which we have five training points available. One can show that it is possible to fit the training points exactly with zero error using a polynomial of degree 4. This does not, however, mean that zero error will be achieved on unseen test data. An example of this situation is illustrated in Figure 4.2, where both the linear and polynomial models on three sets of five randomly chosen data points are shown. It is clear that the linear model is stable, although it is unable to exactly model the curved nature of the true data distribution. On the other hand, even though the polynomial model is capable of modeling the true data distribution more closely, it varies wildly over the different training data sets. Therefore, the same test instance at $x = 2$ (shown in Figure 4.2) would receive similar predictions from the linear model, but would receive very different predictions from the polynomial model over different choices of training data sets. The behavior of the polynomial model is, of course, undesirable from a practitioner's point of view, who would expect similar predictions for a particular test instance, even when different samples of the training data set are used. Since all the different predictions of the polynomial model cannot be correct, it is evident that the increased power of the polynomial model over the linear model actually increases

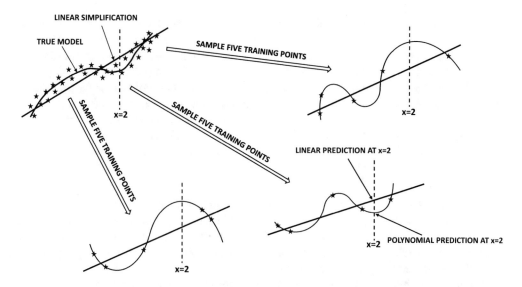

Figure 4.2: **Overfitting with increased model complexity:** The linear model does not change much with the training data, whereas the polynomial model changes drastically. As a result, the inconsistent predictions of the polynomial model at $x = 2$ are often more inaccurate than those of the linear model. The polynomial model does have the ability to outperform the linear model *if enough training data is provided.*

the error rather than reducing it. This difference in predictions for the same test instance (but different training data sets) is manifested as the *variance* of a model. As evident from Figure 4.2, models with high variance tend to memorize random artifacts of the training data, causing inconsistency and inaccuracy in the prediction of unseen test instances. It is noteworthy that a polynomial model with higher degree is inherently more powerful than a linear model because the higher-order coefficients could always be set to 0; however, it is unable to achieve its full potential when the amount of data is limited. Simply speaking, the variance inherent in the finiteness of the data set causes increased complexity to be counterproductive. This trade-off between the power of a model and its performance on limited data is captured with the *bias-variance trade-off*.

There are several tell-tale signs of overfitting:

1. When a model is trained on different data sets, the same test instance might obtain very different predictions. This is a sign that the training process is memorizing the nuances of the specific training data set, rather than learning patterns that generalize to unseen test instances. Note that the three predictions at $x = 2$ in Figure 4.2 are quite different for the polynomial model. This is not quite the case for the linear model.

2. The gap between the error of predicting training instances and unseen test instances is rather large. Note that in Figure 4.2, the predictions at the unseen test point $x = 2$ are often more inaccurate in the polynomial model than in the linear model. On the other hand, the training error is always zero for the polynomial model, whereas the training error is always nonzero for the linear model.

Because of the large gaps between training and test error, models are often tested on unseen portions of the training data. These unseen portions of the test data are often held out early on, and then used in order to make different types of algorithmic decisions such as parameter tuning. This set of points is referred to as the *validation set*. The final accuracy is tested on a fully out-of-sample set of points that was not used for either model building or for parameter tuning. The error on out-of-sample test data is also referred to as the *generalization error*.

Neural networks are large, and they might have millions of parameters in complex applications. In spite of these challenges, there are a number of tricks that one can use in order to ensure that overfitting is not a problem. The choice of method depends on the specific setting, and the type of neural network used. The key methods for avoiding overfitting in a neural network are as follows:

1. *Penalty-based regularization:* Penalty-based regularization is the most common technique used by neural networks in order to avoid overfitting. The idea in regularization is to create a penalty or other types of constraints on the parameters in order to favor simpler models. For example, in the case of polynomial regression, a possible constraint on the parameters would be to ensure that at most k different values of w_i are non-zero. This will ensure simpler models. However, since it is hard to impose such constraints explicitly, a simpler approach is to impose a softer penalty like $\lambda \sum_{i=0}^{d} w_i^2$ and add it to the loss function. Such an approach roughly amounts to multiplying each parameter w_i with a multiplicative decay factor of $(1 - \alpha\lambda)$ before each update at learning rate α. Aside from penalizing parameters of the network, one can also choose to penalize the activations of hidden units. This approach often leads to sparse hidden representations.

2. *Generic and tailored ensemble methods:* Many ensemble methods are not specific to neural networks, but can be used for other machine learning problems. We will discuss bagging and subsampling, which are two of the simplest ensemble methods that can be implemented for virtually any model or learning problem. These methods are inherited from traditional machine learning.

   There are several ensemble methods that are specifically designed for neural networks. A straightforward approach is to average the predictions of different neural architectures obtained by quick and dirty hyper-parameter optimization. *Dropout* is another ensemble technique that is designed for neural networks. This technique uses the selective dropping of nodes to create different neural networks. The predictions of different networks are combined to create the final result. Dropout reduces overfitting by indirectly acting as a regularizer.

3. *Early stopping:* In early stopping, the iterative optimization method is terminated early without converging to the optimal solution on the training data. The stopping point is determined using a portion of the training data that is not used for model building. One terminates when the error on the held-out data begins to rise. Even though this approach is not optimal for the training data, it seems to perform well on the test data because the stopping point is determined on the basis of the held-out data.

4. *Pretraining:* Pretraining is a form of learning in which a greedy algorithm is used to find a good initialization. The weights in different layers of the neural network are trained sequentially in greedy fashion. These trained weights are used as a good starting point for the overall process of learning. Pretraining can be shown to be an indirect form of regularization.

5. *Continuation and curriculum methods:* These methods perform more effectively by first training simple models, and then making them more complex. The idea is that it is easy to train simpler models without overfitting. Furthermore, starting with the optimum point of the simpler model provides a good initialization for a complex model that is closely related to the simpler model. It is noteworthy that some of these methods can be considered similar to pretraining. Pretraining also finds solutions from the simple to the complex by decomposing the training of a deep neural network into a set of shallow layers.

6. *Sharing parameters with domain-specific insights:* In some data-domains like text and images, one often has some insight about the structure of the parameter space. In such cases, some of the parameters in different parts of the network can be set to the same value. This reduces the number of degrees of freedom of the model. Such an approach is used in recurrent neural networks (for sequence data) and convolutional neural networks (for image data). Sharing parameters does come with its own set of challenges because the backpropagation algorithm needs to be appropriately modified to account for the sharing.

This chapter will first discuss the issue of model generalization in a generic way by introducing some theoretical results associated with the bias-variance trade-off. Subsequently, the different ways of reducing overfitting will be discussed.

An interesting observation is that several forms of regularization can be shown to be roughly equivalent to the injection of noise in either the input data or the hidden variables. For example, it can be shown that many penalty-based regularizers are equivalent to the addition of noise [44]. Furthermore, even the use of *stochastic* gradient descent instead of gradient descent can be viewed as a kind of noise addition to the steps of the algorithm. As a result, stochastic gradient descent often shows excellent accuracy on the test data, even though its performance on the training data might not be as good as that of gradient descent. Furthermore, some ensemble techniques like *Dropout* and data perturbation are equivalent to injecting noise. Throughout this chapter, the similarities between noise injection and regularization will be discussed where needed.

Even though a natural way of avoiding overfitting is to simply build smaller networks (with fewer units and parameters), it has often been observed that it is better to build large networks and then regularize them in order to avoid overfitting. This is because large networks retain the *option* of building a more complex model if it is truly warranted. At the same time, the regularization process can smooth out the random artifacts that are not supported by sufficient data. By using this approach, we are giving the model the choice to decide what complexity it needs, rather than making a rigid decision for the model up front (which might even underfit the data).

Supervised settings tend to be more prone to overfitting than unsupervised settings, and supervised problems are therefore the main focus of the literature on generalization. To understand this point, consider that a supervised application tries to learn a single target variable and might have hundreds of input (explanatory) variables. It is easy to overfit the process of learning a very focused goal because a limited degree of supervision (e.g., binary label) is available for each training example. On the other hand, an unsupervised application has the same number of target variables as the explanatory variables. After all, we are trying to model the entire data from itself. In the latter case, overfitting is less likely (albeit still possible) because a single training example has a larger number of bits of information. Nevertheless, regularization is still used in unsupervised applications, especially when the intent is to impose a desired structure on the learned representations.

Chapter Organization

This chapter is organized as follows. The next section introduces the bias-variance trade-off. The practical implications of the bias-variance trade-off for model training are discussed in Section 4.3. The use of penalty-based regularization to reduce overfitting is presented in Section 4.4. Ensemble methods are explained in Section 4.5. Some methods, such as bagging, are generic techniques, whereas others (like *Dropout*) are specifically designed for neural networks. Early stopping methods are discussed in Section 4.6. Methods for unsupervised pretraining are discussed in Section 4.7. Continuation and curriculum learning methods are presented in Section 4.8. Parameter sharing methods are discussed in Section 4.9. Unsupervised forms of regularization are discussed in Section 4.10. A summary is given in Section 4.11.

4.2   The Bias-Variance Trade-Off

The introduction section provides an example of how a polynomial model fits a smaller training data set, leading to the predictions on unseen test data being more erroneous than are the predictions of a (simpler) linear model. This is because a polynomial model requires more data in order to not be misled by random artifacts of the training data set. The fact that more powerful models do not always win in terms of prediction accuracy with a finite data set is the key take-away from the bias-variance trade-off.

The bias-variance trade-off states that the squared error of a learning algorithm can be partitioned into three components:

1. *Bias:* The bias is the error caused by the simplifying assumptions in the model, which causes certain test instances to have consistent errors across different choices of training data sets. Even if the model has access to an infinite source of training data, the bias cannot be removed. For example, in the case of Figure 4.2, the linear model has a higher model bias than the polynomial model, because it can never fit the (slightly curved) data distribution exactly, no matter how much data is available. The prediction of a particular out-of-sample test instance at $x = 2$ will always have an error in a particular direction when using a linear model for any choice of training sample. If we assume that the linear and curved lines in the top left of Figure 4.2 were estimated using an infinite amount of data, then the difference between the two at any particular values of x is the bias. An example of the bias at $x = 2$ is shown in Figure 4.2.

2. *Variance:* Variance is caused by the inability to learn all the parameters of the model in a statistically robust way, especially when the data is limited and the model tends to have a larger number of parameters. The presence of higher variance is manifested by overfitting to the specific training data set at hand. Therefore, if different choices of training data sets are used, different predictions will be provided for the same test instance. Note that the linear prediction provides similar predictions at $x = 2$ in Figure 4.2, whereas the predictions of the polynomial model vary widely over different choices of training instances. In many cases, the widely inconsistent predictions at $x = 2$ are wildly incorrect predictions, which is a manifestation of model variance. Therefore, the polynomial predictor has a higher variance than the linear predictor in Figure 4.2.

3. *Noise:* The noise is caused by the inherent error in the data. For example, all data points in the scatter plot vary from the true model in the upper-left corner of Fig-

ure 4.2. If there had been no noise, all points in the scatter plot would overlap with the curved line representing the true model.

The above description provides a qualitative view of the bias-variance trade-off. In the following, we will provide a more formal and mathematical view.

4.2.1 Formal View

We assume that the base distribution from which the training data set is generated is denoted by $\mathcal{B}$. One can generate a data set $\mathcal{D}$ from this base distribution:

$$\mathcal{D} \sim \mathcal{B} \tag{4.2}$$

One could draw the training data in many different ways, such as selecting only data sets of a particular size. For now, assume that we have some well-defined generative process according to which training data sets are drawn from $\mathcal{B}$. The analysis below does not rely on the specific mechanism with which training data sets are drawn from $\mathcal{B}$.

Access to the base distribution $\mathcal{B}$ is equivalent to having access to an infinite resource of training data, because one can use the base distribution an unlimited number of times to generate training data sets. In practice, such base distributions (i.e., infinite resources of data) are not available. As a practical matter, an analyst uses some data collection mechanism to collect only *one finite instance* of $\mathcal{D}$. However, the conceptual existence of a base distribution from which other training data sets can be generated is useful in theoretically quantifying the sources of error in training on this finite data set.

Now imagine that the analyst had a set of t test instances in d dimensions, denoted by $\overline{Z_1} \ldots \overline{Z_t}$. The dependent variables of these test instances are denoted by $y_1 \ldots y_t$. For clarity in discussion, let us assume that the test instances and their dependent variables were also generated from the same base distribution $\mathcal{B}$ by a third party, but the analyst was provided access only to the feature representations $\overline{Z_1} \ldots \overline{Z_t}$, and no access to the dependent variables $y_1 \ldots y_t$. Therefore, the analyst is tasked with job of using the single finite instance of the training data set $\mathcal{D}$ in order to predict the dependent variables of $\overline{Z_1} \ldots \overline{Z_t}$.

Now assume that the relationship between the dependent variable y_i and its feature representation $\overline{Z_i}$ is defined by the *unknown* function $f(\cdot)$ as follows:

$$y_i = f(\overline{Z_i}) + \epsilon_i \tag{4.3}$$

Here, the notation ϵ_i denotes the intrinsic noise, which is independent of the model being used. The value of ϵ_i might be positive or negative, although it is assumed that $E[\epsilon_i] = 0$. If the analyst knew what the function $f(\cdot)$ corresponding to this relationship was, then they could simply apply the function to each test point $\overline{Z_i}$ in order to approximate the dependent variable y_i, with the only remaining uncertainty being caused by the intrinsic noise.

The problem is that the analyst does not know what the function $f(\cdot)$ is in practice. Note that this function is used within the generative process of the base distribution $\mathcal{B}$, and the entire generating process is like an oracle that is unavailable to the analyst. The analyst only has examples of the input and output of this function. Clearly, the analyst would need to develop some type of *model* $g(\overline{Z_i}, \mathcal{D})$ using the training data in order to *approximate* this function in a data-driven way.

$$\hat{y}_i = g(\overline{Z_i}, \mathcal{D}) \tag{4.4}$$

Note the use of the circumflex (i.e., the symbol '^') on the variable $\hat{y}_i$ to indicate that it is a *predicted* value by a specific algorithm rather than the observed (true) value of y_i.

All prediction functions of learning models (including neural networks) are examples of the estimated function $g(\cdot, \cdot)$. Some algorithms (such as linear regression and perceptrons) can even be expressed in a concise and understandable way:

$$g(\overline{Z}_i, \mathcal{D}) = \underbrace{\overline{W} \cdot \overline{Z}_i}_{\text{Learn } \overline{W} \text{ with } \mathcal{D}} \qquad [\text{Linear Regression}]$$

$$g(\overline{Z}_i, \mathcal{D}) = \underbrace{\text{sign}\{\overline{W} \cdot \overline{Z}_i\}}_{\text{Learn } \overline{W} \text{ with } \mathcal{D}} \qquad [\text{Perceptron}]$$

Most neural networks are expressed algorithmically as compositions of multiple functions computed at different nodes. The choice of computational function includes the effect of its specific parameter setting, such as the coefficient vector $\overline{W}$ in a perceptron. Neural networks with a larger number of units will require more parameters to fully learn the function. This is where the variance in predictions arises on the same test instance; a model with a large parameter set $\overline{W}$ will learn very different values of these parameters, when a different choice of the training data set is used. Consequently, the prediction of the same test instance will also be very different for different training data sets. These inconsistencies add to the error, as illustrated in Figure 4.2.

The goal of the bias-variance trade-off is to quantify the expected error of the learning algorithm in terms of its bias, variance, and the (data-specific) noise. For generality in discussion, we assume a numeric form of the target variable, so that the error can be intuitively quantified by the *mean-squared error* between the predicted values $\hat{y}_i$ and the observed values y_i. This is a natural form of error quantification in regression, although one can also use it in classification in terms of probabilistic predictions of test instances. The mean squared error, MSE, of the learning algorithm $g(\cdot, \mathcal{D})$ is defined over the set of test instances $\overline{Z}_1 \ldots \overline{Z}_t$ as follows:

$$MSE = \frac{1}{t} \sum_{i=1}^{t} (\hat{y}_i - y_i)^2 = \frac{1}{t} \sum_{i=1}^{t} (g(\overline{Z}_i, \mathcal{D}) - f(\overline{Z}_i) - \epsilon_i)^2$$

The best way to estimate the error in a way that is independent of the specific choice of training data set is to compute the *expected* error over different choices of training data sets:

$$E[MSE] = \frac{1}{t} \sum_{i=1}^{t} E[(g(\overline{Z}_i, \mathcal{D}) - f(\overline{Z}_i) - \epsilon_i)^2]$$

$$= \frac{1}{t} \sum_{i=1}^{t} E[(g(\overline{Z}_i, \mathcal{D}) - f(\overline{Z}_i))]^2 + \frac{\sum_{i=1}^{t} E[\epsilon_i^2]}{t}$$

The second relationship is obtained by expanding the quadratic expression on the right-hand side of the first equation, and then using the fact that the average value of ϵ_i over a large number of test instances is 0.

The right-hand side of the above expression can be further decomposed by adding and subtracting $E[g(\overline{Z}_i, \mathcal{D})]$ within the squared term on the right-hand side:

$$E[MSE] = \frac{1}{t} \sum_{i=1}^{t} E[\{(f(\overline{Z}_i) - E[g(\overline{Z}_i, \mathcal{D})]) + (E[g(\overline{Z}_i, \mathcal{D})] - g(\overline{Z}_i, \mathcal{D}))\}^2] + \frac{\sum_{i=1}^{t} E[\epsilon_i^2]}{t}$$

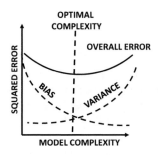

Figure 4.3: The trade-off between bias and variance usually causes a point of optimal model complexity.

One can expand the quadratic polynomial on the right-hand side to obtain the following:

$$E[MSE] = \frac{1}{t} \sum_{i=1}^{t} E[\{f(\overline{Z_i}) - E[g(\overline{Z_i}, \mathcal{D})]\}^2]$$

$$+ \frac{2}{t} \sum_{i=1}^{t} \{f(\overline{Z_i}) - E[g(\overline{Z_i}, \mathcal{D})]\}\{E[g(\overline{Z_i}, \mathcal{D})] - E[g(\overline{Z_i}, \mathcal{D})]\}$$

$$+ \frac{1}{t} \sum_{i=1}^{t} E[\{E[g(\overline{Z_i}, \mathcal{D})] - g(\overline{Z_i}, \mathcal{D})\}^2] + \frac{\sum_{i=1}^{t} E[\epsilon_i^2]}{t}$$

The second term on the right-hand side of the aforementioned expression evaluates to 0 because one of the multiplicative factors is $E[g(\overline{Z_i}, \mathcal{D})] - E[g(\overline{Z_i}, \mathcal{D})]$. On simplification, we obtain the following:

$$E[MSE] = \underbrace{\frac{1}{t} \sum_{i=1}^{t} \{f(\overline{Z_i}) - E[g(\overline{Z_i}, \mathcal{D})]\}^2}_{\text{Bias}^2} + \underbrace{\frac{1}{t} \sum_{i=1}^{t} E[\{g(\overline{Z_i}, \mathcal{D}) - E[g(\overline{Z_i}, \mathcal{D})]\}^2]}_{\text{Variance}} + \underbrace{\frac{\sum_{i=1}^{t} E[\epsilon_i^2]}{t}}_{\text{Noise}}$$

In other words, the squared error can be decomposed into the (squared) bias, variance, and noise. The variance is the key term that prevents neural networks from generalizing. In general, the variance will be higher for neural networks that have a large number of parameters. On the other hand, too few model parameters can cause bias because there are not sufficient degrees of freedom to model the complexities of the data distribution. This trade-off between bias and variance with increasing model complexity is illustrated in Figure 4.3. Clearly, there is a point of optimal model complexity where the performance is optimized. Furthermore, paucity of training data will increase variance. However, careful choice of design can reduce overfitting. This chapter will discuss several such choices.

4.3   Generalization   Issues   in   Model   Tuning   and   Evaluation

There are several practical issues in the training of neural network models that one must be careful of because of the bias-variance trade-off. The first of these issues is associated with model tuning and hyperparameter choice. For example, if one tuned the neural network with the same data that were used to train it, one would not obtain very good results because of overfitting. Therefore, the hyperparameters (e.g., regularization parameter) are tuned on a separate held-out set than the one on which the weight parameters on the neural network are learned.

Given a labeled data set, one needs to use this resource for training, tuning, and testing the accuracy of the model. Clearly, one cannot use the entire resource of labeled data for model building (i.e., learning the weight parameters). For example, using the same data set for both model building and testing grossly overestimates the accuracy. This is because the main goal of classification is to *generalize* a model of labeled data to unseen test instances. Furthermore, the portion of the data set used for *model selection* and *parameter tuning* also needs to be different from that used for model building. A common mistake is to use the same data set for both parameter tuning and final evaluation (testing). Such an approach partially mixes the training and test data, and the resulting accuracy is overly optimistic. A given data set should always be divided into three parts defined according to the way in which the data are used:

1. *Training data:* This part of the data is used to build the training model (i.e., during the process of learning the weights of the neural network). Several design choices may be available during the building of the model. The neural network might use different hyperparameters for the learning rate or for regularization. The same training data set may be tried multiple times over different choices for the hyperparameters or completely different algorithms to build the models in multiple ways. This process allows estimation of the relative accuracy of different algorithm settings. This process sets the stage for *model selection*, in which the best algorithm is selected out of these different models. However, the actual *evaluation* of these algorithms for selecting the best model is not done on the training data, but on a separate validation data set to avoid favoring overfitted models.

2. *Validation data:* This part of the data is used for model selection and parameter tuning. For example, the choice of the learning rate may be tuned by constructing the model multiple times on the first part of the data set (i.e., training data), and then using the validation set to estimate the accuracy of these different models. As discussed in Section 3.3.1 of Chapter 3, different combinations of parameters are sampled within a range and tested for accuracy on the validation set. The best choice of each combination of parameters is determined by using this accuracy. In a sense, validation data should be viewed as a kind of test data set to tune the parameters of the algorithm (e.g., learning rate, number of layers or units in each layer), or to select the best design choice (e.g., sigmoid versus tanh activation).

3. *Testing data:* This part of the data is used to test the accuracy of the final (tuned) model. It is important that the testing data are not even looked at during the process of parameter tuning and model selection to prevent overfitting. The testing data are *used only once at the very end of the process.* Furthermore, if the analyst uses the results on the test data to adjust the model in some way, then the results will be

contaminated with knowledge from the testing data. The idea that one is allowed to look at a test data set only once is an extraordinarily strict requirement (and an important one). Yet, it is frequently violated in real-life benchmarks. The temptation to use what one has learned from the final accuracy evaluation is simply too high.

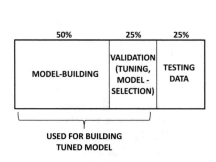

Figure 4.4: Partitioning a labeled data set for evaluation design

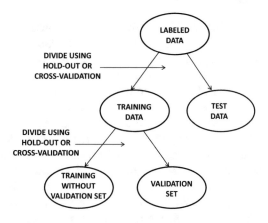

Figure 4.5: Hierarchical division into training, validation, and testing portions

The division of the labeled data set into training data, validation data, and test data is shown in Figure 4.4. Strictly speaking, the validation data is also a part of the training data, because it influences the final model (although only the model building portion is often referred to as the training data). The division in the ratio of 2:1:1 is a conventional rule of thumb that has been followed since the nineties. However, it should not be viewed as a strict rule. For very large labeled data sets, one needs only a modest number of examples to estimate accuracy. When a very large data set is available, it makes sense to use as much of it for model building as possible, because the variance induced by the validation and evaluation stage is often quite low. A constant number of examples (e.g., less than a few thousand) in the validation and test data sets are sufficient to provide accurate estimates. Therefore, the 2:1:1 division is a rule of thumb inherited from an era in which data sets were small. In the modern era, where data sets are large, almost all of the points are used for training, and a modest (constant) number are used for testing. It is not uncommon to have divisions such as 98:1:1.

4.3.1 Evaluating with Hold-Out and Cross-Validation

The aforementioned description of partitioning the labeled data into three segments is an implicit description of a method referred to as *hold-out* for segmenting the labeled data into various portions. However, the division into *three* parts is not done in one shot. Rather, the training data is first divided into *two* parts for training and testing. The testing part is then carefully hidden away from any further analysis *until the very end where it can be used only once*. The remainder of the data set is then divided again into the training and validation portions. This type of recursive division is shown in Figure 4.5.

A key point is that the types of division at both levels of the hierarchy are conceptually identical. In the following, we will consistently use the terminology of the first level of division in Figure 4.5 into "training" and "testing" data, even though the same approach can also be used for the second-level division into model building and validation portions. This allows us to provide a common description of evaluation processes at both levels of the division.

Hold-Out

In the hold-out method, a fraction of the instances are used to build the training model. The remaining instances, which are also referred to as the *held-out* instances, are used for testing. The accuracy of predicting the labels of the held-out instances is then reported as the overall accuracy. Such an approach ensures that the reported accuracy is not a result of overfitting to the specific data set, because different instances are used for training and testing. The approach, however, underestimates the true accuracy. Consider the case where the held-out examples have a higher presence of a particular class than the labeled data set. This means that the held-in examples have a lower average presence of the same class, which will cause a mismatch between the training and test data. Furthermore, the class-wise frequency of the held-in examples will always be inversely related to that of the held-out examples. This will lead to a consistent pessimistic bias in the evaluation. In spite of these weaknesses, the hold-out method has the advantage of being simple and efficient, which makes it a popular choice in large-scale settings. From a deep-learning perspective, this is an important observation because large data sets are common.

Cross-Validation

In the cross-validation method, the labeled data is divided into q equal segments. One of the q segments is used for testing, and the remaining $(q-1)$ segments are used for training. This process is repeated q times by using each of the q segments as the test set. The average accuracy over the q different test sets is reported. Note that this approach can closely estimate the true accuracy when the value of q is large. A special case is one where q is chosen to be equal to the number of labeled data points and therefore a single point is used for testing. Since this single point is left out from the training data, this approach is referred to as *leave-one-out cross-validation*. Although such an approach can closely approximate the accuracy, it is usually too expensive to train the model a large number of times. In fact, cross-validation is sparingly used in neural networks because of efficiency issues.

4.3.2   Issues with Training at Scale

One practical issue that arises in the specific case of neural networks is when the sizes of the training data sets are large. Therefore, while methods like cross-validation are well established to be superior choices to hold-out in traditional machine learning, their technical soundness is often sacrificed in favor of efficiency. In general, training time is such an important consideration in neural network modeling that many compromises have to be made to enable practical implementation.

A computational problem often arises in the context of grid search of hyperparameters (cf. Section 3.3.1 of Chapter 3). Even a single hyperparameter choice can sometimes require a few days to evaluate, and a grid search requires the testing of a large number of possibilities. Therefore, a common strategy is to run the training process of each setting for a fixed number of epochs. Multiple runs are executed over different choices of hyperparameters in different threads of execution. Those choices of hyperparameters in which good progress is not made after a fixed number of epochs are terminated. In the end, only a few ensemble members are allowed to run to completion. One reason that such an approach works well is because the vast majority of the progress is often made in the early phases of the training. This process is also described in Section 3.3.1 of Chapter 3.

4.3.3 How to Detect Need to Collect More Data

The high generalization error in a neural network may be caused by several reasons. First, the data itself might have a lot of noise, in which case there is little one can do in order to improve accuracy. Second, neural networks are hard to train, and the large error might be caused by the poor convergence behavior of the algorithm. The error might also be caused by high bias, which is referred to as *underfitting.* Finally, overfitting (i.e., high variance) may cause a large part of the generalization error. In most cases, the error is a combination of more than one of these different factors. However, one can detect overfitting in a specific training data set by examining the gap between the training and test accuracy. Overfitting is manifested *by a large gap between training and test accuracy.* It is not uncommon to have close to 100% training accuracy on a small training set, even when the test error is quite low. The first solution to this problem is to collect more data. With increased training data, the training accuracy will reduce, whereas the test/validation accuracy will increase. However, if more data is not available, one would need to use other techniques such as regularization in order to improve generalization performance.

4.4 Penalty-Based Regularization

Penalty-based regularization is the most common approach for reducing overfitting. In order to understand this point, let us revisit the example of the polynomial with degree d. In this case, the prediction $\hat{y}$ for a given value of x is as follows:

$$\hat{y} = \sum_{i=0}^{d} w_i x^i \qquad (4.5)$$

It is possible to use a single-layer network with d inputs and a single bias neuron with weight w_0 in order to model this prediction. The ith input is x^i. This neural network uses linear activations, and the squared loss function for a set of training instances (x, y) from data set $\mathcal{D}$ can be defined as follows:

$$L = \sum_{(x,y) \in \mathcal{D}} (y - \hat{y})^2$$

As discussed in the example of Figure 4.2, a large value of d tends to increase overfitting. One possible solution to this problem is to reduce the value of d. In other words, using a model with *economy in parameters* leads to a simpler model. For example, reducing d to 1 creates a linear model that has fewer degrees of freedom and tends to fit the data in a similar way over different training samples. However, doing so does lose some expressivity when the data patterns are indeed complex. In other words, oversimplification reduces the expressive power of a neural network, so that it is unable to adjust sufficiently to the needs of different types of data sets.

How can one retain some of this expressiveness without causing too much overfitting? Instead of reducing the number of parameters in a hard way, one can use a *soft* penalty on the use of parameters. Furthermore, large (absolute) values of the parameters are penalized more than small values, because small values do not affect the prediction significantly. What kind of penalty can one use? The most common choice is L_2-regularization, which is also referred to as *Tikhonov regularization*. In such a case, the additional penalty is defined by the sum of squares of the values of the parameters. Then, for the regularization parameter $\lambda > 0$, one can define the objective function as follows:

$$L = \sum_{(x,y)\in\mathcal{D}} (y - \hat{y})^2 + \lambda \cdot \sum_{i=0}^{d} w_i^2$$

Increasing or decreasing the value of λ reduces the softness of the penalty. One advantage of this type of parameterized penalty is that one can tune this parameter for optimum performance on a portion of the training data set that is not used for learning the parameters. This type of approach is referred to as *model validation*. Using this type of approach provides greater flexibility than fixing the economy of the model up front. Consider the case of polynomial regression discussed above. Restricting the number of parameters up front severely constrains the learned polynomial to a specific shape (e.g., a linear model), whereas a soft penalty is able to control the shape of the learned polynomial in a more data-driven manner. In general, it has been experimentally observed that it is more desirable to use complex models (e.g., larger neural networks) with regularization rather than simple models without regularization. The former also provides greater flexibility by providing a tunable knob (i.e., regularization parameter), which can be chosen in a data-driven manner. The value of the tunable knob is learned on a held-out portion of the data set.

How does regularization affect the updates in a neural network? For any given weight w_i in the neural network, the updates are defined by gradient descent (or the batched version of it):

$$w_i \Leftarrow w_i - \alpha \frac{\partial L}{\partial w_i}$$

Here, α is the learning rate. The use of L_2-regularization is roughly equivalent to the use of decay imposition after each parameter update:

$$w_i \Leftarrow w_i(1 - \alpha\lambda) - \alpha \frac{\partial L}{\partial w_i}$$

Note that the update above first multiplies the weight with the decay factor $(1 - \alpha\lambda)$, and then uses the gradient-based update. The decay of the weights can also be understood in terms of a biological interpretation, if we assume that the initial values of the weights are close to 0. One can view weight decay as a kind of forgetting mechanism, which brings the weights closer to their initial values. This ensures that only the repeated updates have a significant effect on the absolute magnitude of the weights. A forgetting mechanism prevents a model from *memorizing* the training data, because only significant and repeated updates will be reflected in the weights.

4.4.1   Connections with Noise Injection

The addition of noise to the input has connections with penalty-based regularization. It can be shown that the addition of an equal amount of Gaussian noise to each input is equivalent to Tikhonov regularization of a single-layer neural network with an identity activation function (for linear regression).

One way of showing this result is by examining a single training case $(\overline{X}, y)$, which becomes $(\overline{X} + \sqrt{\lambda}\overline{\epsilon}, y)$ after noise with variance λ is added to each feature. Here, $\overline{\epsilon}$ is a random vector, in which each entry ϵ_i is independently drawn from the standard normal distribution with zero mean and unit variance. Then, the noisy prediction $\hat{y}$, which is based on $\overline{X} + \sqrt{\lambda}\overline{\epsilon}$, is as follows:

$$\hat{y} = \overline{W} \cdot (\overline{X} + \sqrt{\lambda}\epsilon) = \overline{W} \cdot \overline{X} + \sqrt{\lambda}\overline{W} \cdot \overline{\epsilon} \tag{4.6}$$

Now, let us examine the squared loss function $L = (y - \hat{y})^2$ contributed by a single training case. We will compute the *expected* value of the loss function. It is easy to show the following in expectation:

$$E[L] = E[(y - \hat{y})^2]$$
$$= E[(y - \overline{W} \cdot \overline{X} - \sqrt{\lambda}\overline{W} \cdot \overline{\epsilon})^2]$$

One can then expand the expression on the right-hand side as follows:

$$E[L] = (y - \overline{W} \cdot \overline{X})^2 - 2\sqrt{\lambda}(y - \overline{W} \cdot \overline{X}) \underbrace{E[\overline{W} \cdot \overline{\epsilon}]}_{0} + \lambda E[(\overline{W} \cdot \overline{\epsilon})^2]$$

$$= (y - \overline{W} \cdot \overline{X})^2 + \lambda E[(\overline{W} \cdot \overline{\epsilon})^2]$$

The second expression can be expanded using $\overline{\epsilon} = (\epsilon_1 \ldots \epsilon_d)$ and $\overline{W} = (w_1 \ldots w_d)$. Furthermore, one can set any term of the form $E[\epsilon_i \epsilon_j]$ to $E[\epsilon_i] \cdot E[\epsilon_j] = 0$ because of independence of the random variables ϵ_i and ϵ_j. Any term of the form $E[\epsilon_i^2]$ is set to 1, because each ϵ_i is drawn from a standard normal distribution. On expanding $E[(\overline{W} \cdot \overline{\epsilon})^2]$ and making the above substitutions, one finds the following:

$$E[L] = (y - \overline{W} \cdot \overline{X})^2 + \lambda(\sum_{i=1}^{d} w_i^2) \tag{4.7}$$

It is noteworthy that *this loss function is exactly the same as L_2-regularization* of a single instance.

Although the equivalence between weight decay and noise addition is exactly true for the case of linear regression, the analysis does not hold in the case of neural networks with nonlinear activations. Nevertheless, penalty-based regularization continues to be intuitively similar to noise addition even in these cases, although the results might be qualitatively different. Because of these similarities one sometimes tries to perform regularization by direct noise addition. One such approach is referred to as *data perturbation*, in which noise is added to the training input, and the test data points are predicted with the added noise. The approach is repeated multiple times with different training data sets created by adding noise repeatedly in Monte Carlo fashion. The prediction of the same test instance across different additions of noise is averaged in order to yield the improved results. In this case, the noise is added only to the training data, and it does not need to be added to the test data. When explicitly adding noise, it is important to average the prediction of the same test instance over multiple ensemble components in order to ensure that the solution properly represents the *expected* value of the loss (without added variance caused by the noise). This approach is described in Section 4.5.5.

4.4.2 L_1-Regularization

The use of the squared norm penalty, which is also referred to as L_2-regularization, is the most common approach for regularization. However, it is possible to use other types of penalties on the parameters. A common approach is L_1-regularization in which the squared penalty is replaced with a penalty on the sum of the absolute magnitudes of the coefficients. Therefore, the new objective function is as follows:

$$L = \sum_{(x,y)\in\mathcal{D}} (y-\hat{y})^2 + \lambda \cdot \sum_{i=0}^{d} |w_i|_1$$

The main problem with this objective function is that it contains the term $|w_i|$, which is not differentiable when w_i is exactly equal to 0. This requires some modifications to the gradient-descent method when w_i is 0. For the case when w_i is non-zero, one can use the straightforward update obtained by computing the partial derivative. By differentiating the above objective function, we can define the update equation at least for the case when w_i is different than 0:

$$w_i \Leftarrow w_i - \alpha\lambda s_i - \alpha\frac{\partial L}{\partial w_i}$$

The value of s_i, which is the partial derivative of $|w_i|$ (with respect to w_i), is as follows:

$$s_i = \begin{cases} -1 & w_i < 0 \\ +1 & w_i > 0 \end{cases}$$

However, we also need to set the partial derivative of $|w_i|$ for cases in which the value of w_i is exactly 0. One possibility is to use the *subgradient* method in which the value of w_i is set stochastically to a value in $\{-1, +1\}$. However, this is not necessary in practice. Computers are of finite-precision, and the computational errors will rarely cause w_i to be *exactly* 0. Therefore, the computational errors will often perform the task that would otherwise be achieved by stochastic sampling. Furthermore, for the rare cases in which the value w_i is exactly 0, one can omit the regularization and simply set s_i to 0. This type of approximation to the subgradient method works reasonably well in many settings.

One difference between the update equations for L_1-regularization and those in L_2-regularization is that L_2-regularization uses multiplicative decay as a forgetting mechanism, whereas L_1-regularization uses additive updates as a forgetting mechanism. In both cases, the regularization portions of the updates tend to move the coefficients closer to 0. However, there are some differences in the types of solutions found in the two cases, which are discussed in the next section.

4.4.3 L_1- or L_2-Regularization?

A question arises as to whether L_1- or L_2-regularization is desirable. From an accuracy point of view, L_2-regularization usually outperforms L_1-regularization. This is the reason that L_2-regularization is almost always preferred over L_1-regularization is most implementations. The performance gap is small when the number of inputs and units is large.

However, L_1-regularization does have specific applications from an interpretability point of view. An interesting property of L_1-regularization is that it creates *sparse* solutions in which the vast majority of the values of w_i are 0s (after ignoring[1] computational errors). If the value of w_i is zero for a connection incident on the input layer, then that particular input has no effect on the final prediction. In other words, such an input can be *dropped*,

---

[1]Computational errors can be ignored by requiring that $|w_i|$ should be at least 10^{-6} in order for w_i to be considered truly non-zero.

and the L_1-regularizer acts as a feature selector. Therefore, one can use L_1-regularization to estimate which features are predictive to the application at hand.

What about the connections in the hidden layers whose weights are set to 0? These connections can be dropped, which results in a sparse neural network. Such sparse neural networks can be useful in cases where one repeatedly performs training on the same type of data set, but the nature and broader characteristics of the data set do not change significantly with time. Since the sparse neural network will contain only a small fraction of the connections in the original neural network, it can be retrained much more efficiently whenever more training data is received.

4.4.4 Penalizing Hidden Units: Learning Sparse Representations

The penalty-based methods, which have been discussed so far, penalize the *parameters* of the neural network. A different approach is to penalize the *activations* of the neural network, so that only a small subset of the neurons are activated for any given data instance. In other words, even though the neural network might be large and complex only a small part of it is used for predicting any given data instance.

The simplest way to achieve sparsity is to impose an L_1-penalty on the hidden units. Therefore, the original loss function L is modified to the regularized loss function L' as follows:

$$L' = L + \lambda \sum_{i=1}^{M} |h_i| \tag{4.8}$$

Here, M is the total number of units in the network, and h_i is the value of the ith hidden unit. Furthermore, the regularization parameter is denoted by λ. In many cases, a single *layer* of the network is regularized, so that a sparse feature representation can be extracted from the activations of that particular layer.

How does this change to the objective function affect the backpropagation algorithm? The main difference is that the loss function is aggregated not only over nodes in the output layer, but also over nodes in the hidden layer. At a fundamental level, this change does not affect the overall dynamics and principles of backpropagation. This situation is discussed in Section 3.2.7 of Chapter 3.

The backpropagation algorithm needs to be modified so that the regularization penalty contributed by a hidden unit is incorporated into the backwards gradient flow of all connections incoming into that node. Let $N(h)$ be the set of nodes reachable from any particular node h in the computational graph (including itself). Then, the gradient $\frac{\partial L}{\partial a_h}$ of the loss L also depends on the penalty contributions of the nodes in $N(h)$. Specifically, for any node h_r with pre-activation value a_{h_r}, its gradient flow $\frac{\partial L}{\partial a_{h_r}} = \delta(h_r, N(h_r))$ to the output node is increased by $\lambda \Phi'(a_{h_r}) \operatorname{sign}(h_r)$. Here, the gradient flow $\frac{\partial L}{\partial a_{h_r}} = \delta(h_r, N(h_r)))$ is defined according to the discussion in Section 3.2.7 of Chapter 3. Consider Equation 3.25 of Chapter 3, which computes the backwards gradient flow as follows:

$$\delta(h_r, N(h_r)) = \Phi'(a_{h_r}) \sum_{h:h_r \Rightarrow h} w_{(h_r,h)} \delta(h, N(h)) \tag{4.9}$$

Here, $w_{(h_r,h)}$ is the weight of the edge from h_r to h. Immediately after making this update, the value of $\delta(h_r, N(h_r))$ is adjusted to account for the regularization term at that node as follows:

$$\delta(h_r, N(h_r)) \Leftarrow \delta(h_r, N(h_r)) + \lambda \Phi'(a_{h_r}) \cdot \operatorname{sign}(h_r)$$

Note that the above update is based on Equation 3.26 of Chapter 3. Once the value of $\delta(h_r, N(h_r))$ is modified at a given node h_r, the changes will automatically be backpropagated to all nodes that reach h_r. This is the only change that is required in order to enforce L_1-regularization of the hidden units. In a sense, incorporating penalties on nodes in intermediate layers does not change the backpropagation algorithm in a fundamental way, except that hidden nodes are now also treated as output nodes in terms of contributing to the gradient flow.

4.5   Ensemble Methods

Ensemble methods derive their inspiration from the bias-variance trade-off. One way of reducing the error of a classifier is to find a way to reduce either its bias or the variance without affecting the other component. Ensemble methods are used commonly in machine learning, and two examples of such methods are *bagging* and *boosting*. The former is a method for variance reduction, whereas the latter is a method for bias reduction.

Most ensemble methods in neural networks are focused on variance reduction. This is because neural networks are valued for their ability to build arbitrarily complex models in which the bias is relatively low. However, operating at the complex end of the bias-variance trade-off almost always leads to higher variance, which is manifested as overfitting. Therefore, the goal of most ensemble methods in the neural network setting is variance reduction (i.e., better generalization). This section will focus on such methods.

4.5.1   Bagging and Subsampling

Imagine that you had an infinite resource of training data available to you, where you could generate as many training points as you wanted from a base distribution. How can one use this unusually generous resource of data to get rid of variance? If a sufficient number of samples is available, after all, the variance of most types of statistical estimates can by asymptotically reduced to 0.

A natural approach for reducing the variance in this case would be to repeatedly create different training data sets and predict the same test instance using these data sets. The prediction across different data sets can then be averaged to yield the final prediction. If a sufficient number of training data sets is used, the variance of the prediction will be reduced to 0, although the bias will still remain depending on the choice of model.

The approach described above can be used only when an infinite resource of data is available. However, in practice, we only have a single finite instance of the data available to us. In such cases, one obviously cannot implement the above methodology. However, it turns out that an imperfect simulation of the above methodology still has better variance characteristics than a single execution of the model on the entire training data set. The basic idea is to generate new training data sets from the single instance of the base data by sampling. The sampling can be performed with or without replacement. The predictions on a particular test instance, which are obtained from the models built with different training sets, are then averaged to create the final prediction. One can average either the real-valued predictions (e.g., probability estimates of class labels) or the discrete predictions. In the case of real-valued predictions, better results are sometimes obtained by using the median of the values.

It is common to use the softmax to yield probabilistic predictions of discrete outputs. If probabilistic predictions are averaged, it is common to average the *logarithms* of these values. This is the equivalent of using the *geometric* means of the probabilities. For discrete predictions, arithmetically averaged voting is used. This distinction between the handling of discrete and probabilistic predictions is carried over to other types of ensemble methods that require averaging of the predictions. This is because the logarithms of the probabilities have a log-likelihood interpretation, and log-likelihoods are inherently additive.

The main difference between bagging and subsampling is in terms of whether or not replacement is used in the creation of the sampled training data sets. We summarize these methods as follows:

1. *Bagging:* In bagging, the training data is sampled with replacement. The sample size s may be different from the size of the training data size n, although it is common to set s to n. In the latter case, the resampled data will contain duplicates, and about a fraction $(1 - 1/n)^n \approx 1/e$ of the original data set will not be included at all. Here, the notation e denotes the base of the natural logarithm. A model is constructed on the resampled training data set, and each test instance is predicted with the resampled data. The entire process of resampling and model building is repeated m times. For a given test instance, each of these m models is applied to the test data. The predictions from different models are then averaged to yield a single robust prediction. Although it is customary to choose $s = n$ in bagging, the best results are often obtained by choosing values of s much less than n.

2. Subsampling is similar to bagging, except that the different models are constructed on the samples of the data created *without* replacement. The predictions from the different models are averaged. In this case, it is essential to choose $s < n$, because choosing $s = n$ yields the same training data set and identical results across different ensemble components.

When a sufficient training data are available, subsampling is often preferable to bagging. However, using bagging makes sense when the amount of available data is limited.

It is noteworthy that all the variance cannot be removed by using bagging or subsampling, because the different training samples will have overlaps in the included points. Therefore, the predictions of test instances from different samples will be positively correlated. The average of a set of random variables that are positively correlated will always have a variance that is proportional to the level of correlation. As a result, there will always be a residual variance in the predictions. This residual variance is a consequence of the fact that bagging and subsampling are imperfect simulations of drawing the training data from a base distribution. Nevertheless, the variance of this approach is still lower than that of constructing a single model on the entire training data set. The main challenge in directly using bagging for neural networks is that one must construct multiple training models, which is highly inefficient. However, the construction of different models can be fully parallelized, and therefore this type of setting is a perfect candidate for training on multiple GPU processors.

4.5.2 Parametric Model Selection and Averaging

One challenge in the case of neural network construction is the selection of a large number of hyperparameters like the depth of the network and the number of neurons in each layer. Furthermore, the choice of the activation function also has an effect on performance, depending on the application at hand. The presence of a large number of parameters creates problems in model construction, because the performance might be sensitive to the particular configuration used. One possibility is to hold out a portion of the training data and try different combinations of parameters and model choices. The selection that provides the highest accuracy on the held-out portion of the training data is then used for prediction. This is, of course, the standard approach used for parameter tuning in all machine learning models, and is also referred to as *model selection*. In a sense, model selection is inherently an ensemble-centric approach, where the best out of bucket of models is selected. Therefore, the approach is also sometimes referred to as the *bucket-of-models* technique.

The main problem in deep learning settings is that the number of possible configurations is rather large. For example, one might need to select the number of layers, the number of units in each layer, and the activation function. The combination of these possibilities is rather large. Therefore, one is often forced to try only a limited number of possibilities to choose the configuration. An additional approach that can be used to reduce the variance, is to select the k best configurations and then average the predictions of these configurations. Such an approach leads to more robust predictions, especially if the configurations are very different from one another. Even though each individual configuration might be suboptimal, the overall prediction will still be quite robust. However, such an approach cannot be used in very large-scale settings because each execution might require on the order of a few weeks. Therefore, one is often reduced to leveraging the single best configuration based on the approach in Section 3.3.1 of Chapter 3. As in the case of bagging, the use of multiple configurations is often feasible only when multiple GPUs are available for training.

4.5.3   Randomized Connection Dropping

The random dropping of connections between different layers in a multilayer neural network often leads to diverse models in which different combinations of features are used to construct the hidden variables. The dropping of connections between layers does tend to create less powerful models because of the addition of constraints to the model-building process. However, since different random connections are dropped from different models, the predictions from different models are very diverse. The averaged prediction from these different models is often highly accurate. It is noteworthy that the weights of different models are not shared in this approach, which is different from another technique called *Dropout*.

Randomized connection dropping can be used for any type of predictive problem and not just classification. For example, the approach has been used for outlier detection with autoencoder ensembles [64]. As discussed in Section 2.5.4 of Chapter 2, autoencoders can be used for outlier detection by estimating the reconstruction error of each data point. The work in [64] uses multiple autoencoders with randomized connections, and then aggregates the outlier scores from these different components in order to create the score of a single data point. However, the use of the median is preferred to the mean in [64]. It has been shown in [64] that such an approach improves the overall accuracy of outlier detection. It is noteworthy that this approach might seem superficially similar to *Dropout* and *DropConnect*, although it is quite different. This is because methods like *Dropout* and *DropConnect* share weights between different ensemble components, whereas this approach does not share any weights between ensemble components.

4.5.4   Dropout

Dropout is a method that uses node sampling instead of edge sampling in order to create a neural network ensemble. If a node is dropped, then all incoming and outgoing connections from that node need to be dropped as well. The nodes are sampled only from the input and hidden layers of the network. Note that sampling the output node(s) would make it impossible to provide a prediction and compute the loss function. In some cases, the input nodes are sampled with a different probability than the hidden nodes. Therefore, if the full neural network contains M nodes, then the total number of possible sampled networks is 2^M.

A key point that is different from the connection sampling approach discussed in the previous section is that *weights of the different sampled networks are shared*. Therefore, *Dropout* combines node sampling with weight sharing. The training process then uses a single sampled example in order to update the weights of the sampled network using back-propagation. The training process proceeds using the following steps, which are repeated again and again in order to cycle through all of the training points in the network:

1. Sample a neural network from the base network. The input nodes are each sampled with probability p_i, and the hidden nodes are each sampled with probability p_h. Furthermore, all samples are independent of one another. When a node is removed from the network, all its incident edges are removed as well.

2. Sample a single training instance or a mini-batch of training instances.

3. Update the weights of the retained edges in the network using backpropagation on the sampled training instance or the mini-batch of training instances.

It is common to exclude nodes with probability between 20% and 50%. Large learning rates are often used with momentum, which are tempered with a max-norm constraint on the weights. In other words, the L_2-norm of the weights entering each node is constrained to be no larger than a small constant such as 3 or 4.

It is noteworthy that a different neural network is used for every small mini-batch of training examples. Therefore, the number of neural networks sampled is rather large, and depends on the size of the training data set. This is different from most other ensemble methods like bagging in which the number of ensemble components is rarely larger than 25. In the *Dropout* method, thousands of neural networks are sampled with shared weights, and a tiny training data set is used to update the weights in each case. Even though a large number of neural networks is sampled, the *fraction* of neural networks sampled out of the base number of possibilities is still minuscule. Another assumption that is used in this class of neural networks is that the output is in the form of a probability. This assumption has a bearing on the way in which the predictions of the different neural networks are combined.

How can one use the ensemble of neural networks to create a prediction for an unseen test instance? One possibility is to predict the test instance using all the neural networks that were sampled, and then use the geometric mean of the probabilities that are predicted by the different networks. The geometric mean is used rather than the arithmetic mean, because the assumption is that the output of the network is a probability and the geometric mean is equivalent to averaging log-likelihoods. For example, if the neural network has k probabilistic outputs corresponding to the k classes, and the jth ensemble yields an output of $p_i^{(j)}$ for the ith class, then the ensemble estimate for the ith class is computed as follows:

$$p_i^{Ens} = \left[\prod_{j=1}^{m} p_i^{(j)} \right]^{1/m} \qquad (4.10)$$

Here, m is the total number of ensemble components, which can be rather large in the case of the *Dropout* method. One problem with this estimation is that the use of geometric means results in a situation where the probabilities over the different classes do not sum to 1. Therefore, the values of the probabilities are re-normalized so that they sum to 1:

$$p_i^{Ens} \Leftarrow \frac{p_i^{Ens}}{\sum_{i=1}^{k} p_i^{Ens}} \qquad (4.11)$$

The main problem with this approach is that the number of ensemble components is too large, which makes the approach inefficient.

A key insight of the *Dropout* method is that it is not necessary to evaluate the prediction on all ensemble components. Rather, one can perform forward propagation on only the base network (with no dropping) after re-scaling the weights. The basic idea is to multiply the weights going out of each unit with the probability of sampling that unit. By using this approach, the expected output of that unit from a sampled network is captured. This rule is referred to as the *weight scaling inference rule*. Using this rule also ensures that the input going into a unit is also the same as the expected input that would occur in a sampled network.

The weight scaling inference rule is exact for many types of networks with linear activations, although the rule is not exactly true for networks with nonlinearities. In practice, the rule tends to work well across a broad variety of networks. Since most practical neural networks have nonlinear activations, the weight scaling inference rule of *Dropout* should be viewed as a heuristic rather than a theoretically justified result. *Dropout* has been used with a wide variety of models that use a distributed representation; it has been used with feed-forward networks, Restricted Boltzmann machines, and recurrent neural networks.

The main effect of *Dropout* is to incorporate regularization into the learning procedure. By dropping both input units and hidden units, *Dropout* effectively incorporates noise into both the input data and the hidden representations. The nature of this noise can be viewed as a kind of masking noise in which some inputs and hidden units are set to 0. Noise addition is a form of regularization. It has been shown in the original paper [467] on *Dropout* that this approach works better than other regularizers such as weight decay. *Dropout* prevents a phenomenon referred to as *feature co-adaptation* from occurring between hidden units. Since the effect of *Dropout* is a masking noise that removes some of the hidden units, this approach forces a certain level of redundancy between the features learned at the different hidden units. This type of redundancy leads to increased robustness.

Dropout is efficient because each of the sampled subnetworks is trained with a small set of sampled instances. Therefore, only the work of sampling the hidden units needs to be done additionally. However, since *Dropout* is a regularization method, it reduces the expressive power of the network. Therefore, one needs to use larger models and more units in order to gain the full advantages of *Dropout*. This results in a hidden computational overhead. Furthermore, if the original training data set is already large enough to reduce the likelihood of overfitting, the additional computational advantages of *Dropout* may be small but still perceptible. For example, many of the convolutional neural networks trained on large data repositories like *ImageNet* [255] report consistently improved results of about 2% with *Dropout*. A variation of *Dropout* is *DropConnect*, which applies a similar approach to the weights rather than to the neural network nodes [511].

A Note on Feature Co-adaptation

In order to understand why *Dropout* works, it is useful to understand the notion of feature co-adaptation. Ideally, it is useful for the hidden layers of the neural network to create features that reflect important classification characteristics of the input without having complex dependencies on other features, unless these other features are truly useful. To understand this point, consider a situation in which all edges incident on 50% of the nodes in each layer are fixed at their initial random values, and are not *updated* during backpropagation (even though all gradients are *computed* in the normal fashion). Interestingly, even in this case, it will often be possible for the neural network to provide reasonably good results by adapting the other weights and features to the effect of these randomly fixed subsets of weights (and corresponding activations). Of course, this is not a desirable situation because the goal of features working together is to combine the powers held by each essential feature rather than merely having some features adjust to the detrimental effects of others. Even in the normal training of a neural network (where all weights are updated), this type of co-adaptation can occur. For example, if the updates in some parts of the neural network are not fast enough, some of the features will not be useful and other features will adapt to these less-than-useful features. This situation is very likely in neural network training, because different parts of the neural network do tend to learn at different rates. An even more troubling scenario arises when the co-adapted features work well in predicting training points by picking up on complex dependencies in the training points, which do not generalize well to out-of-sample test points. *Dropout* prevents this type of co-adaptation by forcing the neural network to make predictions using only a subset of the inputs and activations. This forces the network to be able to make predictions with a certain level of redundancy while also encouraging smaller subsets of learned features to have predictive power. In other words, co-adaptation occurs only when it is truly essential for modeling instead of learning random nuances of the training data. This is, of course, a form of regularization. Furthermore, by learning redundant features, *Dropout* averages over the predictions of redundant features, which is similar to what is done in bagging.

4.5.5   Data Perturbation Ensembles

Most of the ensemble techniques discussed so far are either sampling-based ensembles or model-centric ensembles. *Dropout* can be considered an ensemble that adds noise to the data in an indirect way. It is also possible to use explicit data perturbation methods.

In the simplest case, a small amount of noise can be added to the input data, and the weights can be learned on the perturbed data. This process can be repeated with multiple such additions, and the predictions of the test point from different ensemble components can be averaged. This type of approach is a generic ensemble method, which is not specific to neural networks. As discussed in Section 4.10, this approach is used commonly in the unsupervised setting with *de-noising autoencoders*.

It is also possible to add noise to the hidden layer. However, in this case, the noise has to be carefully calibrated [382]. It is noteworthy that the *Dropout* method indirectly adds noise to the hidden layer by dropping nodes randomly. A dropped node is similar to masking noise in which the activation of that node is set to 0.

One can also perform other types of data set augmentation. For example, an image instance can be rotated or translated in order to add to the data set. Carefully designed data augmentation schemes can often greatly improve the accuracy of a learner by increasing its generalization power. However, strictly speaking such schemes are not perturbation schemes because the augmented examples are created with a calibrated procedure and an understanding of the domain at hand. Such methods are used commonly in convolutional neural networks (cf. Section 8.3.4 of Chapter 8).

4.6   Early Stopping

Neural networks are trained using variations of gradient-descent methods. In most optimization models, gradient-descent methods are executed to convergence. However, executing gradient descent to convergence optimizes the loss on the training data, but not necessarily on the out-of-sample test data. This is because the final few steps often overfit to the specific nuances of the training data, which might not generalize well to the test data.

A natural solution to this dilemma is to use *early stopping*. In this method, a portion of the training data is held out as a validation set. The backpropagation-based training is only applied to the portion of the training data that does not include the validation set. At the same time, the error of the model on the validation set is continuously monitored. At some point, this error begins to rise on the validation set, even though it continues to reduce on the training set. This is the point at which further training causes overfitting. Therefore, this point can be chosen for termination. It is important to keep track of the best solution achieved so far in the learning process (as computed on the validation data). This is because one does not perform early stopping after tiny increases in the out-of-sample error (which might be caused by noisy variations), but it is advisable to continue to train to check if the error continues to rise. In other words, the termination point is chosen in hindsight after the error on the validation set continues to rise, and all hope is lost of improving the error performance on the validation set.

Even though the removal of the validation set does lose some training points, the effect of data loss is often quite small. This is because neural networks are often trained on extremely large data sets of the order of tens of millions of points. A validation set does not need a large number of points. For example, the use of a sample of 10,000 points for validation might be tiny compared to the full data size. Although one can often include the validation set within the training data to retrain the network for the same number of steps (as was obtained at the early stopping point), the effect of this approach can sometimes be unpredictable. It can also lead to a doubling of computational costs, because the neural network needs to be trained all over again.

One advantage of early stopping is that it can be easily added to neural network training without significantly changing the training procedure. Furthermore, methods like weight decay require us to try different values of the regularization parameter, λ, which can be expensive. Because of the ease in combining it with existing algorithms, early stopping can be used in combination with other regularizers in a relatively straightforward way. Therefore, early stopping is almost always used, because one does not lose much by adding it to the learning procedure.

One can view early stopping as a kind of constraint on the optimization process. By restricting the number of steps in the gradient descent, one is effectively restricting the distance of the final solution from the initialization point. Adding constraints to the model of a machine learning problem is often a form of regularization.

4.6.1   Understanding Early Stopping from the Variance Perspective

One way of understanding the bias-variance trade-off is that the true loss function of an optimization problem can only be constructed if we have infinite data. If we have a finite amount of data, the loss function constructed from the training data does not reflect the true loss function. Illustrative examples of the contours of the true loss function and its shifted counterpart on the training data are illustrated in Figure 4.6. This shifting is an indirect manifestation of the variance in prediction created by a particular training data set. Different training data sets will shift the loss function in different and unpredictable ways.

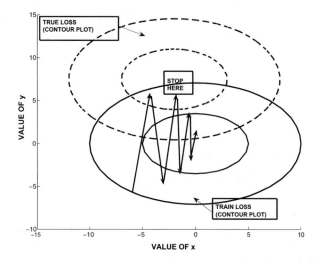

Figure 4.6: Shift in loss function caused by variance effects and the effect of early stopping. Because of the differences in the true loss function and that on the training data, the error will begin to rise if gradient descent is continued beyond a certain point. Here, we have shown a similar shape of the true and training loss functions for simplicity, although this might not be the case in practice.

Unfortunately, the learning procedure can perform the gradient-descent only on the loss function defined on the training data set, because the true loss function is unknown. However, if the training data is representative of the true loss function, the optimum solutions in the two cases will be reasonably close as shown in Figure 4.6. As discussed in Chapter 3, most gradient-descent procedures take a circuitous and oscillatory route to the optimal solution. During the final stage of convergence to the optimal solution (on the training data), the gradient descent will often encounter better solutions with respect to the true loss function before it converges to the best solution with respect to the training data. These solutions will be detected by the improved accuracy on the validation set, and therefore provide good termination points. An example of a good early stopping point is shown in Figure 4.6.

4.7 Unsupervised Pretraining

Deep networks are inherently hard to train because of a number of different characteristics discussed in the previous chapter. One issue is the exploding and vanishing gradient problem, because of which the different layers of the neural network do not get trained at the same rate. The multiple layers of the neural network cause distortions in the gradient, which make them hard to train.

Although the depth of the neural network causes challenges, the problems associated with depth are also heavily dependent on how the network is initialized. A good initialization point can often solve many of the problems associated with reaching good solutions. A ground-breaking break-through in this context was the use of unsupervised pretraining in order to provide robust initializations [196]. This initialization is achieved by training the network greedily in layer-wise fashion. The approach was originally proposed in the context of deep belief networks, but it was later extended to other types of models such as autoencoders [386, 506]. In this chapter, we will study the autoencoder approach because of its simplicity. First, we will start with the dimensionality reduction application, because the application is unsupervised and it is easy to show how to use unsupervised pretraining in this case. However, unsupervised pretraining can also be used for supervised applications like classification with minor modifications.

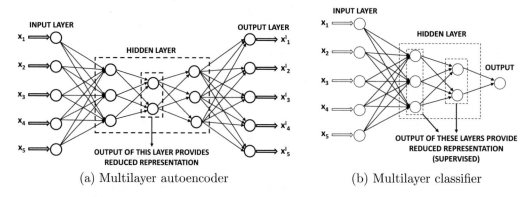

(a) Multilayer autoencoder   (b) Multilayer classifier

Figure 4.7: Both the multilayer classifier and the multilayer autoencoder use a similar pre-training procedure.

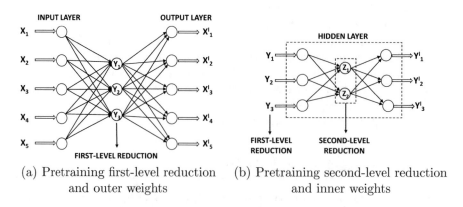

(a) Pretraining first-level reduction   (b) Pretraining second-level reduction
and outer weights   and inner weights

Figure 4.8: Pretraining a neural network

In pretraining, a greedy approach is used to train the network one layer at a time by learning the weights of the outer hidden layers first and then learning the weights of the inner hidden layers. The resulting weights are used as starting points for a final phase of traditional neural network backpropagation in order to fine-tune them.

Consider the autoencoder and classifier architectures shown in Figure 4.7. Since these architectures have multiple layers, randomized initialization can sometimes cause challenges. However, it is possible to create a good initialization by setting the initial weights layer by layer in a greedy fashion. First, we describe the process in the context of the autoencoder shown in Figure 4.7(a), although an almost identical procedure is relevant to the classifier of Figure 4.7(b). We have intentionally chosen neural architectures in the two cases so that the hidden layers have similar numbers of nodes.

The pretraining process is shown in Figure 4.8. The basic idea is to assume that the two (symmetric) outer hidden layers contain a first-level reduced representation of larger dimensionality, and the inner hidden layer contains a second-level reduced representation of smaller dimensionality. Therefore, the first step is to learn the first-level reduced representation and the corresponding weights associated with the outer hidden layers using the simplified network of Figure 4.8(a). In this network, the middle hidden layer is missing and the two outer hidden layers are collapsed into a single hidden layer. The assumption is that the two outer hidden layers are related to one another in a symmetric way like a smaller autoencoder. In the second step, the reduced representation in the first step is used to learn the second-level reduced representation (and weights) of the inner hidden layers. Therefore, the inner portion of the neural network is treated as a smaller autoencoder in its own right. Since each of these pretrained subnetworks is much smaller, the weights can be learned more easily. This initial set of weights is then used to train the entire neural network with backpropagation. Note that this process can be performed in layerwise fashion for a deep neural network containing any number of hidden layers.

So far, we have only discussed how we can use unsupervised pretraining for unsupervised applications. A natural question arises as to how one can use pretraining for supervised applications. Consider a multilayer classification architecture with a single output layer and k hidden layers. During the pretraining stage, the output layer is removed, and the representation of the final hidden layer is learned in an unsupervised way. This is achieved by creating an autoencoder with $2 \cdot k - 1$ hidden layers, where the middle layer is the final hidden layer of the supervised setting. For example, the relevant autoencoder for Figure 4.7(b) is shown in Figure 4.7(a). Therefore, an additional $(k - 1)$ hidden layers are added, each of which has a symmetric counterpart in the original network. This network is trained in exactly the same layer-wise fashion as discussed above for the autoencoder architecture. The weights of only the encoder portion of this autoencoder are used for initialization of the weights entering into all hidden layers. The weights between the final hidden layer and the output layer can also be initialized by treating the final hidden layer and output nodes as a single-layer network. This single-layer network is fed with the reduced representations of the final hidden layer (based on the autoencoder learned in pretraining). After the weights of all the layers have been learned, the output nodes are re-attached to the final hidden layer. The backpropagation algorithm is applied to this initialized network in order to fine-tune the weights from the pretrained stage. Note that this approach learns all the initial hidden representations in an unsupervised way, and only the weights entering into the output layer are initialized using the labels. Therefore, the pretraining can still be considered to be largely unsupervised.

During the early years, pretraining was often seen as a more stable way to train a deep network in which the different layers have a better chance of being initialized in an equally effective way. Although this issue does play a role in explaining the improvements of pretraining, the problem is often manifested as overfitting. As discussed in Chapter 3, the (finally converged) weights in the early layers may not change much from their random initializations, when the network exhibits the vanishing gradient problem. Even when the connection weights in the first few layers are random (as a result of poor training), it is possible for the later layers to adapt their weights sufficiently so as to give zero error on the *training* data. In this case, the random connections in the early layers provide near-random transformations to the later layers, but the later layers are still able to overfit to these features in order to provide very low training error. In other words, the features in later layers *adapt* to those in early layers as a result of training inefficiencies. Any kind of feature co-adaptation caused by training inefficiencies almost always leads to overfitting. Therefore, when the approach is applied to unseen test data, the overfitting becomes apparent because the various layers are not specifically adapted to these unseen test instances. In this sense, pretraining is an unusual form of regularization.

Incidentally, unsupervised pretraining helps even in cases where the amount of training data is very large. It is likely that this behavior is caused by the fact that pretraining helps in issues beyond model generalization. One evidence of this fact is that in larger data sets, even the error on the training data seems to be high, when methods like pretraining are not used. In these cases, the weights of the early layers often do not change much from their initializations, and one is using only a small number of later layers on a random transformation of the data (defined by the random initialization of the early layers). As a result, the trained portion of the network is rather shallow, with some additional loss caused by the random transformation. In such cases, pretraining also helps a model realize the full benefits of depth, thereby facilitating the improvement of prediction accuracy on larger data sets.

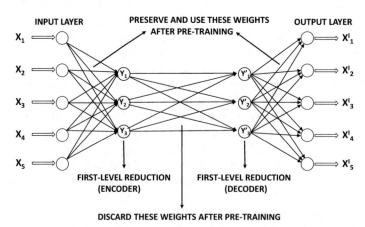

Figure 4.9: This architecture allows the first-level representations in the encoder and decoder to be significantly different. It is helpful to compare this architecture with that in Figure 4.8(a).

Another way of understanding pretraining is that it provides insights into the repeated patterns in the data, which are the features learned from the training data points. For example, an autoencoder might learn that many digits have loops in them, and certain digits have strokes that are curved in a particular way. The decoder reconstructs the digits by putting together these frequent shapes. However, these shapes also have discriminative power with respect to recognizing digits. Expressing the data in terms of a few features then helps in recognizing how these features are related to the class labels. This principle is summarized by Geoff Hinton [192] in the context of image classification as follows: "*To recognize shapes, first learn to generate images.*" This type of regularization preconditions the training process in a semantically relevant region of the parameter space, where several important features have already been learned, and further training can fine-tune and combine them for prediction.

4.7.1 Variations of Unsupervised Pretraining

There are many different ways in which one can introduce variations to the procedure of unsupervised pretraining. For example, multiple layers can be trained at one time instead of performing pretraining only one layer at a time. A particular case in point is *VGG* (cf. Section 8.4.3 of Chapter 8) in which as many as eleven layers of an even deeper architecture were trained together. Indeed, there are some advantages in grouping as many layers as possible within the pretraining because a (successful) training procedure with larger pieces of the neural network leads to more powerful initializations. On the other hand, grouping too many layers together within each pretraining component can lead to problems (such as the vanishing and exploding gradient problems) within each component.

A second point is that the pretraining procedure of Figure 4.8 assumes that the autoencoder works in a completely symmetric way in which the reduction in the kth layer of the encoder is approximately similar to the reduction in its mirror layer in the decoder. This might be a restrictive assumption in practice, if different types of activation functions are used in different layers. For example, a sigmoid activation function in a particular layer of the encoder will create only nonnegative values, whereas a tanh activation in the matching layer of the decoder might create both positive and negative values. Another approach is to use a relaxed pretraining architecture in which we learn separate reductions for the kth level reduction in the encoder and its mirror image in the decoder. This allows the corresponding reductions in the encoder and the decoder to be different. An additional layer of weights must be added between the two layers to allow for the differences between the two reductions. This additional layer of weights is discarded after the reduction, and only the encoder-decoder weights are preserved. The only location at which an additional set of weights is not used for pretraining is in the innermost reduction, which proceeds in a similar manner to that discussed in the earlier section (cf. Figure 4.8(b)). An example of such an architecture for the first-level reduction of Figure 4.8(a) is shown in Figure 4.9. Note that the first-level representations for the encoder and decoder layers can be quite different in this case, which provides some flexibility during the pretraining process. When the approach is used for classification, only the weights in the encoder can be used, and the final reduced code can be capped with a classification layer for learning.

4.7.2 What About Supervised Pretraining?

So far, we have only discussed *unsupervised* pretraining, whether the base application is supervised or unsupervised. Even in the case where the base application is supervised, the initialization was done using an unsupervised autoencoder architecture. Although it is possible to perform supervised pretraining as well, an interesting and surprising result is that supervised pretraining does not seem to give as good results as unsupervised pretraining in at least some settings [113, 31]. This does not mean that supervised pretraining is *never* helpful. Indeed, there are cases of networks in which it is hard to train the network itself because of its depth. For example, networks with hundreds of layers are extremely hard to train because of issues associated with convergence and other problems. In such cases, even the error *on the training data* is high, which means that one is unable to make the training algorithm work. *This is a different problem from that of model generalization.* Aside from supervised pretraining, many techniques such as the construction of *highway networks* [161, 470], *gating networks* [204], and *residual networks* [184], can address many of these problems. However, these solutions do not specifically address overfitting, whereas unsupervised pretraining seems to hedge its bets in addressing both issues in at least some types of networks.

In supervised pretraining [31], the autoencoder architecture is not used for learning the weights of connections incident on the hidden layer. In the first iteration, the constructed network contains only the first hidden layer, which is connected to all nodes in the output layer. This step learns the weights of the connections from the input to hidden layer, although the weights of the output layer are discarded. Subsequently, the outputs of the first hidden layer are used as the new representations of the training points. Then, we create another neural network containing the first and second hidden layers and the output layer. The first hidden layer is now treated as an input layer with its inputs as the transformed representations of the training points learned in the previous iteration. These are then used to learn the next layer of weights and their hidden representations. This approach is repeated all the way to the final layer. Although this approach does provide improvements over an approach that does not use pretraining, it does not seem to work as well as unsupervised pretraining in at least some settings. The main difference in performance is on the *generalization error* on unseen test data, whereas the errors on the training data are often similar [31]. This is a near-certain sign of differential levels of overfitting of different methods.

Why does supervised pretraining not help as much as unsupervised pretraining in many settings? A key problem of supervised pretraining is that it is a bit too greedy and the early layers are initialized to representations that are very directly related to the outputs. As a result, the full advantages of depth are not exploited. This is a different type of overfitting. An important explanation for the success of unsupervised pretraining is that the learned representations are often related to the class labels in a gentle way; as a result, further learning is able to isolate and fine-tune the important characteristics of these representations. Therefore, one can view pretraining as an unusual form of *semi-supervised learning* as well, which forces the initial representations of the hidden layers to lie on the low-dimensional manifolds of data instances. The secret to the success of pretraining is that more features on these manifolds are predictive of classification accuracy than the features corresponding to random regions of the data space. After all, class distributions vary smoothly over the underlying data manifolds. The locations of data points on these manifolds are therefore good features in predicting class distributions. Therefore, the final phase of learning only has to fine-tune and enhance these features.

Are there cases in which unsupervised pretraining does not help? The work in [31] provides examples in which the manifold corresponding to the data distribution does not seem to exhibit too much relationship with the target. This tends to occur more often in regression as compared to classification. In such cases, it was shown that adding some supervision to pretraining can indeed help. The first layer of weights (between input and first hidden layer) is trained using a combination of gradient updates from autoencoder-like reconstruction as well as greedy supervised pretraining. Thus, the learning of the weights of the first layer is partially supervised. Subsequent layers are trained using the autoencoder approach only. The inclusion of supervision in the first level of weights automatically incorporates some level of supervision into the inner layers as well. This approach is used for initializing the weights of the neural network. These weights are then fine tuned using fully supervised backpropagation over the entire network.

4.8 Continuation and Curriculum Learning

The discussions in the previous and current chapter show that the learning of neural network parameters is inherently a complex optimization problem, in which the loss function has a complex topological shape. Furthermore, the loss function on the training data is not exactly the same as the true loss function, which leads to spurious minima. These minima are spurious because they might be near optimal minima on the training data, but they might not be minima at all on unseen test instances. In many cases, optimizing a complex loss function tends to lead to such solutions with little generalization power.

The experience with pretraining shows that simplifying the optimization problem (or providing simple greedy solutions without too much optimization) can often precondition the solution towards the basins of better optima on the test data. In other words, instead of trying to solve a complex problem in one shot, one should first try to solve simplifications, and gradually work one's way towards complex solutions. Two such notions are those of *continuation* and *curriculum* learning:

1. *Continuation learning:* In continuation learning, one starts with a simplified version of the optimization problem and solves it. Starting with this solution, one continues to a more complex refinement of the optimization problem and updates the solution. This process is repeated until the complex optimization problem is solved. Thus, continuation learning leverages a model-centric view of working from simpler to complex problems. For example, if one has a loss function with many local optima, one can smooth it to a loss function with a single global optimum and find the optimal solution. Then, one can gradually work with better and better approximations (with increased complexity) until the exact loss function is used.

2. *Curriculum learning:* In curriculum learning, one starts by training the model on simpler data instances, and then gradually adds more difficult instances to the training data. Therefore, curriculum learning leverages a data-centric view of working from the simple to the complex, whereas continuation methods leverage a model-centric view.

A different view of curriculum and continuation learning may be obtained by examining how humans naturally learn tasks. Humans often learn simple concepts first and then move to the complex. The training of a child is often created using such a *curriculum* in order to accelerate learning. This principle also seems to work well in machine learning. In the following, we will examine both continuation and curriculum learning.

4.8.1 Continuation Learning

In continuation learning, one designs a series of loss functions $L_1 \ldots L_r$, in which the difficulty in optimizing this sequence of loss functions grows from the easy to the difficult. In other words, each L_{i+1} is more difficult to optimize than L_i. All the optimization problems are defined on the same set of parameters, because they are defined on the same neural network. The smoothing of a loss function is a form of regularization. One can view each

L_i as a smoothed version of L_{i+1}. Solving each L_i brings the solution closer to the basin of optimal solutions from the point of view of generalization error.

Continuation loss functions are often constructed by using *blurring*. The idea is to compute the loss function at sampled points in the vicinity of a given point, and then average these values in order to create the new loss function. For example, one could use a normal distribution with standard deviation σ_i for computing the ith loss function L_i. One can view this approach as a type of noise addition to the loss function, which is also a form of regularization. The amount of blurring depends on the size of the locality used for blurring, which is defined by σ_i. If the value of σ_i is set to be too large, then the cost will be very similar at all points, and the loss function will not retain sufficient details about the objective. However, it will often be very simple to optimize. On the other hand, setting σ_i to 0 will retain all the details in the loss function. Therefore, the natural solution is to start with large values of σ_i and then reduce the value over successive loss functions. One can view this approach as that of using an increased amount of noise for regularization in the early iterations, and then reducing the level of regularization as the algorithm nears an attractive solution. Such tricks of adding a varying amount of calibrated noise to enable the avoidance of local optima is a recurring theme in many optimization techniques such as *simulated annealing* [244]. The main problem with continuation methods is that they are expensive due to the need to optimize a series of loss functions.

4.8.2 Curriculum Learning

Curriculum learning methods take a *data-centric* view of the goals that are achieved by the *model-centric* continuation learning methods. The main hypothesis is that different training data sets present different levels of difficulty to a learner. In curriculum methods, easy examples are first presented to the learner. One possible way of defining a difficult example is as one that falls on the wrong side of a decision boundary with a perceptron or an SVM. There are other possibilities, such as the use of a Bayes classifier. The basic idea is that the difficult examples are often noisy or they represent exceptional patterns that confuse the learner. Therefore, it is inadvisable to start training with such examples.

In other words, the initial iterations of stochastic gradient descent use only the easy examples to "pretrain" the learner towards a reasonable parameter setting. Subsequently, difficult examples are included with the easy examples in later iterations. It is important to include both easy and difficult examples in the later phases, or else the learner will overfit to only the difficult examples. In many cases, the difficult examples might be exceptional patterns in particular regions of the space, or they might even be noise. If only the difficult examples are presented to the learner in later phases, the overall accuracy will not be good. The best results are often obtained by using a random mixture of simple and difficult examples in later phases. The proportion of difficult examples are increased over the course of the curriculum until the input represents the true data distribution. This type of *stochastic curriculum* has been shown to be an effective approach.

4.9 Parameter Sharing

A natural form of regularization that reduces the parameter footprint of the model is the sharing of parameters across different connections. Often, this type of parameter sharing is enabled by domain-specific insights. The main insight required to share parameters is that the function computed at two nodes should be related in some way. This type of insight can be obtained when one has a good idea of how a particular computational node relates to the input data. Examples of such parameter-sharing methods are as follows:

1. *Sharing weights in autoencoders:* The symmetric weights in the encoder and decoder portion of the autoencoder are often shared. Although an autoencoder will work whether or not the weights are shared, doing so improves the regularization properties of the algorithm. In a single-layer autoencoder with linear activation, weight sharing forces orthogonality among the different hidden components of the weight matrix. This provides the same reduction as singular value decomposition.

2. *Recurrent neural networks:* These networks are often used for modeling sequential data, such as time-series, biological sequences, and text. The last of these is the most commonly used application of recurrent neural networks. In recurrent neural networks, a time-layered representation of the network is created in which the neural network is replicated across layers associated with time stamps. Since each time stamp is assumed to use the same model, the parameters are shared between different layers. Recurrent neural networks are discussed in detail in Chapter 7.

3. *Convolutional neural networks:* Convolutional neural networks are used for image recognition and prediction. Correspondingly, the inputs of the network are arranged into a rectangular grid pattern, along with all the layers of the network. Furthermore, the weights across contiguous patches of the network are typically shared. The basic idea is that a rectangular patch of the image corresponds to a portion of the visual field, and it should be interpreted in the same way no matter where it is located. In other words, a carrot means the same thing whether it is at the left or the right of the image. In essence, these methods use semantic insights about the data to reduce the parameter footprint, share weights, and sparsify the connections. Convolutional neural networks are discussed in Chapter 8.

In many of these cases, it is evident that parameter sharing is enabled by the use of domain-specific insights about the training data as well as a good understanding of how the computed function at a node relates to the training data. The modifications to the backpropagation algorithm required for enabling weight sharing are discussed in Section 3.2.9 of Chapter 3.

An additional type of weight sharing is *soft weight sharing* [360]. In soft weight sharing, the parameters are not completely tied, but a penalty is associated with them being different. For example, if one expects the weights w_i and w_j to be similar, the penalty $\lambda(w_i - w_j)^2/2$ might be added to the loss function. In such a case, the quantity $\alpha\lambda(w_j - w_i)$ might be added to the update of w_i, and the quantity $\alpha\lambda(w_i - w_j)$ might be added to the update of w_j. Here, α is the learning rate. These types of changes to the updates tend to pull the weights towards each other.

4.10 Regularization in Unsupervised Applications

Although overfitting does occur in unsupervised applications, it is often less of a problem. In classification, one is trying to learn a single bit of information associated with each example, and therefore using more parameters than the number of examples can cause overfitting. This is not quite the case in unsupervised applications in which a single training example may contain many more bits of information corresponding to the different dimensions. In general, the number of bits of information will depend on the intrinsic dimensionality of the data set. Therefore, one tends to hear fewer complaints about overfitting in unsupervised applications.

Nevertheless, there are many unsupervised settings in which it is beneficial to use regularization. A common case is one in which we have an *overcomplete* autoencoder, in which the number of hidden units is greater than the number of input units. An important goal of regularization in unsupervised applications is to impose some kind of structure on the learned representations. This approach to regularization can have different application-specific benefits like creating sparse representations or in providing the ability to clean corrupted data. As in the case of supervised models, one can use semantic insights about a problem domain in order to force a solution to have specific types of desired properties. This section will show how different types of penalties and constraints on the hidden units can create hidden/reconstructed representations with useful properties.

4.10.1   Value-Based Penalization: Sparse Autoencoders

The penalizing of sparse hidden units has unsupervised applications such as *sparse autoencoders*. Sparse autoencoders contain a much larger number of hidden units in each layer as compared to the number of input units. However, the values of the hidden units are encouraged to be 0s by either explicit penalization or by constraints. As a result, most of the values in the hidden units will be 0s at convergence. One possible approach is to impose an L_1-penalty on the hidden units in order to create sparse representations. The gradient-descent approach with L_1-penalties on the hidden units is discussed in Section 4.4.4. It is also noteworthy that the use of L_1-regularization seems to be somewhat unusual in the autoencoder literature (although there is no reason not to use it). Other constraint-based methods exist, such as allowing only the top-k hidden units to be activated. In most of these cases, the constraints are chosen in such a way that the backpropagation approach can be modified in a reasonable way. For example, if only the top-k units are selected for activation, then the gradient flows are allowed to backpropagate only through these chosen units. Constraint-based techniques are simply hard variations of penalty-based methods. More details are provided on some of these learning methods in Section 2.5.5.1 of Chapter 2.

4.10.2   Noise Injection: De-noising Autoencoders

As discussed in Section 4.4.1, noise injection is a form of penalty-based regularization of the weights. The use of Gaussian noise in the input is roughly equal to L_2-regularization in single-layer networks with linear activation. The de-noising autoencoder is based on noise injection rather than penalization of the weights or hidden units. However, the goal of the de-noising autoencoder is to reconstruct good examples from corrupted training data. Therefore, the type of noise should be calibrated to the nature of the input. Several different types of noise can be added:

1. *Gaussian noise:* This type of noise is appropriate for real-valued inputs. The added noise has zero mean and variance $\lambda > 0$ for each input. Here, λ is the regularization parameter.

2. *Masking noise:* The basic idea is to set a fraction f of the inputs to zeros in order to corrupt the inputs. This type of approach is particularly useful when working with binary inputs.

3. *Salt-and-pepper noise:* In this case, a fraction f of the inputs are set to either their minimum or maximum possible values according to a fair coin flip. The approach is typically used for binary inputs, for which the minimum and maximum values are 0 and 1, respectively.

De-noising autoencoders are useful when dealing with data that is corrupted. Therefore, the main application of such autoencoders is to reconstruct corrupted data. The inputs to the autoencoder are corrupted training records, and the outputs are the uncorrupted data records. As a result, the autoencoder learns to recognize the fact that the input is corrupted, and the true representation of the input needs to be reconstructed. Therefore, even if there is corruption in the test data (as a result of application-specific reasons), the approach is able to reconstruct clean versions of the test data. Note that the noise in the training data is explicitly added, whereas that in the test data is already present as a result of various application-specific reasons. For example, as shown in the top portion of Figure 4.10, one can use the approach to removing blurring or other noise from images. The nature of the noise added to the input training data should be based on insights about the type of corruption present in the test data. Therefore, one does require uncorrupted examples of the training data for best performance. In most domains, this is not very difficult to achieve. For example, if the goal is to remove noise from images, the training data might contain high-quality images as the output and artificially blurred images as the input. It is common for the de-noising autoencoder to be overcomplete, when it is used for reconstruction from corrupted data. However, this choice also depends on the nature of the input and the amount of noise added. Aside from its use for reconstructing inputs, the addition of noise is also an excellent regularizer that tends to make the approach work better for out-of-sample inputs even when the autoencoder is undercomplete.

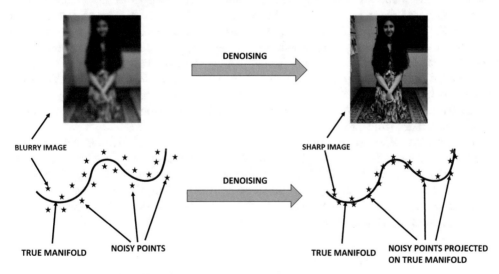

Figure 4.10: The de-noising autoencoder

The way in which the de-noising autoencoder works is that it uses the noise in the input data to learn the true manifold on which the data is embedded. Each corrupted point is projected to its "closest" matching point on the true manifold of the data distribution. The closest matching point is the expected position on the manifold from which the model predicts that the noisy point has originated. This projection is shown in the bottom portion of Figure 4.10. The true manifold is a more concise representation of the data as compared to the noisy data, and this conciseness is a result of the regularization inherent in the addition of noise to the input. All forms of regularization tend to increase the conciseness of the underlying model.

4.10.3 Gradient-Based Penalization: Contractive Autoencoders

As in the case of the de-noising autoencoder, the hidden representation of the contractive autoencoder is often overcomplete, because the number of hidden units is greater than the number of input units. A contractive autoencoder is a heavily regularized encoder in which we do not want the hidden representation to change very significantly with small changes in input values. Obviously, this will also result in an output that is less sensitive to the input. Trying to create an autoencoder in which the output is less sensitive to changes in the input seems like an odd goal at first sight. After all, an autoencoder is supposed to reconstruct the data exactly. Therefore, the goals of regularization seem to be completely at odds with those of the contractive regularization portion of the loss function.

A key point is that contractive encoders are designed to be robust only to *small* changes in the input data. Furthermore, they tend to be insensitive to those changes that are inconsistent with the manifold structure of the data. In other words, if one makes a small change to the input that does not lie on the manifold structure of the input data, the contractive autoencoder will tend to damp the change in the reconstructed representation. Here, it is important to understand that the vast majority of (randomly chosen) directions in high-dimensional input data (with a much lower-dimensional manifold) tend to be approximately orthogonal to the manifold structure, which has the effect of changing the components of the change on the manifold structure. The damping of the changes in the reconstructive representation based on the local manifold structure is also referred to as the *contractive* property of the autoencoder. As a result, contractive autoencoders tend to remove noise from the input data (like de-noising autoencoders), although the mechanism for doing this is different from that of de-noising autoencoders. As we will see later, contractive autoencoders penalize the gradients of the hidden values with respect to the inputs. When the hidden values have low gradients with respect to the inputs, it means that they are not very sensitive to small changes in the inputs (although larger changes or changes parallel to manifold structure will tend to change the gradients).

For ease in discussion, we will discuss the case where the contractive autoencoder has a single hidden layer. The generalization to multiple hidden layers is straightforward. Let $h_1 \ldots h_k$ be the values of the k hidden units for the input variables $x_1 \ldots x_d$. Let the reconstructed values in the output layer be given by $\hat{x}_1 \ldots \hat{x}_d$. Then, the objective function is given by the weighted sum of the reconstruction loss and the regularization term. The loss L for a single training instance is given by the following:

$$L = \sum_{i=1}^{d} (x_i - \hat{x}_i)^2 \tag{4.12}$$

The regularization term is constructed by using the sum of the squares of the partial derivatives of all hidden variables with respect to all input dimensions. For a problem with k hidden units denoted by $h_1 \ldots h_k$, the regularization term R can be written as follows:

$$R = \frac{1}{2} \sum_{i=1}^{d} \sum_{j=1}^{k} \left(\frac{\partial h_j}{\partial x_i} \right)^2 \tag{4.13}$$

In the original paper [397], the sigmoid nonlinearity is used in the hidden layer, in which case the following can be shown (cf. Section 3.2.5 of Chapter 3):

$$\frac{\partial h_j}{\partial x_i} = w_{ij} h_j (1 - h_j) \; \forall i, j \qquad (4.14)$$

Here, w_{ij} is the weight of the input unit i to the hidden unit j.

The overall objective function for a single training instance is given by a weighted sum of the loss and the regularization terms.

$$J = L + \lambda \cdot R$$

$$= \sum_{i=1}^{d} (x_i - \hat{x}_i)^2 + \frac{\lambda}{2} \sum_{j=1}^{k} h_j^2 (1 - h_j)^2 \sum_{i=1}^{d} w_{ij}^2$$

This objective function contains a combination of weight and hidden unit regularization. Penalties on hidden units can be handled in the same way as discussed in Section 3.2.7 of Chapter 3. Let a_{h_j} be the pre-activation value for the node h_j. The backpropagation updates are traditionally defined in terms of the preactivation values, where the value of $\frac{\partial J}{\partial a_{h_j}}$ is propagated backwards. After $\frac{\partial J}{\partial a_{h_j}}$ is computed using the dynamic programming update of backpropagation from the output layer, one can further update it to incorporate the effect of hidden-layer regularization of h_j:

$$\frac{\partial J}{\partial a_{h_j}} \Leftarrow \frac{\partial J}{\partial a_{h_j}} + \frac{\lambda}{2} \frac{\partial [h_j^2 (1 - h_j)^2]}{\partial a_{h_j}} \sum_{i=1}^{d} w_{ij}^2$$

$$= \frac{\partial J}{\partial a_{h_j}} + \lambda h_j (1 - h_j)(1 - 2h_j) \underbrace{\frac{\partial h_j}{\partial a_{h_j}}}_{h_j(1-h_j)} \sum_{i=1}^{d} w_{ij}^2$$

$$= \frac{\partial J}{\partial a_{h_j}} + \lambda h_j^2 (1 - h_j)^2 (1 - 2h_j) \sum_{i=1}^{d} w_{ij}^2$$

The value of $\frac{\partial h_j}{\partial a_{h_j}}$ is set to $h_j (1 - h_j)$ because the sigmoid activation is assumed, although it would be different for other activations. According to the chain rule, the value of $\frac{\partial J}{\partial a_{h_j}}$ should be multiplied with the value of $\frac{\partial a_{h_j}}{\partial w_{ij}} = x_i$ to obtain the gradient of the loss with respect to w_{ij}. However, according to the *multivariable* chain rule, we also need to directly add the derivative of the regularizer with respect to w_{ij} in order to obtain the full gradient. Therefore, the partial derivative of the hidden-layer regularizer R with respect to the weight is added as follows:

$$\frac{\partial J}{\partial w_{ij}} \Leftarrow \frac{\partial J}{\partial a_{h_j}} \frac{\partial a_{h_j}}{\partial w_{ij}} + \lambda \frac{\partial R}{\partial w_{ij}}$$

$$= x_i \frac{\partial J}{\partial a_{h_j}} + \lambda w_{ij} h_j^2 (1 - h_j)^2$$

Interestingly, if a linear hidden unit is used instead of the sigmoid, it is easy to see that the objective function will become identical to that of an L_2-regularized autoencoder. Therefore, it makes sense to use this approach only with a nonlinear hidden layer, because a linear hidden layer can be handled in a much simpler way. The weights in the encoder and decoder can be either tied or independent. If the weights are tied then the gradients over both copies of a weight need to be added. The above discussion assumes a single hidden layer, although it is easy to generalize to more hidden layers. The work in [397] showed that better compression can be achieved with the use of deeper variants of the approach.

Some interesting relationships exist between the de-noising autoencoder and the contractive autoencoder. The de-noising autoencoder achieves its goals of robustness stochastically by explicitly adding noise, whereas a contractive autoencoder achieves its goals analytically by adding a regularization term. Adding a small amount of Gaussian noise in a de-noising autoencoder achieves roughly similar goals as a contractive autoencoder, when the hidden layer uses linear activation. When the hidden layer uses linear activation, the partial derivative of the hidden unit with respect to an input is simply the connecting weight, and therefore the objective function of the contractive autoencoder becomes the following:

$$J_{linear} = \sum_{i=1}^{d}(x_i - \hat{x}_i)^2 + \frac{\lambda}{2}\sum_{i=1}^{d}\sum_{j=1}^{k} w_{ij}^2 \qquad (4.15)$$

In that case, both the contractive and the de-noising autoencoders become similar to regularized singular value decomposition with L_2-regularization. The difference between the de-noising autoencoder and the contractive autoencoder is visually illustrated in Figure 4.11. In the case of the de-noising autoencoder on the left, the autoencoder learns the directions along the true manifold of uncorrupted data by using the relationship between the corrupted data in the output and the true data in the input. This goal is achieved analytically in the contractive autoencoder, because the vast majority of random perturbations are roughly orthogonal to the manifold when the dimensionality of the manifold is much smaller than the input data dimensionality. In such a case, perturbing the data point slightly does not change the hidden representation along the manifold very much. Penalizing the partial derivative of the hidden layer equally along all directions ensures that the partial derivative is significant only along the small number of directions along the true manifold, and the partial derivatives along the vast majority of orthogonal directions are close to 0. In other words, the variations that are not meaningful to the distribution of the specific training data set at hand are damped, and only the meaningful variations are kept.

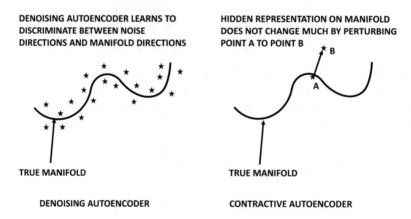

Figure 4.11: The difference between the de-noising and the contractive autoencoder

Another difference between the two methods is that the de-noising autoencoder shares the responsibility for regularization between the encoder and decoder, whereas the contractive autoencoder places this responsibility only on the encoder. Only the encoder portion is used in feature extraction; therefore, contractive autoencoders are more useful for feature engineering.

In a contractive autoencoder, the gradients are deterministic, and therefore it is also easier to use second-order learning methods as compared to the de-noising autoencoder. On the other hand, the de-noising autoencoder is easier to construct (with small changes to the code of an unregularized autoencoder), if first-order learning methods are used.

4.10.4 Hidden Probabilistic Structure: Variational Autoencoders

Just as sparse encoders impose a sparsity constraint on the hidden units, variational encoders impose a specific probabilistic structure on the hidden units. The simplest constraint is that the activations in the hidden units over the whole data should be drawn from the standard Gaussian distribution (i.e., zero mean and unit variance in each direction). By imposing this type of constraint, one advantage is that we can throw away the encoder after training, and simply feed samples from the standard normal distribution to the decoder in order to generate samples of the training data. However, if every object is generated from an identical distribution, then it would be impossible to either differentiate the various objects or to reconstruct them from a given input. Therefore, the *conditional* distribution of the activations in the hidden layer (with respect to a specific input object) would have a different distribution from the standard normal distribution. Even though a regularization term would try to pull even the conditional distribution towards the standard normal distribution, this goal would only be achieved over the distribution of hidden samples from the whole data rather than the hidden samples from a single object.

Imposing a constraint on the probabilistic distribution of hidden variables is more complicated than the other regularizers discussed so far. However, the key is to use a re-parametrization approach in which the encoder creates the k-dimensional mean and standard deviations vector of the conditional Gaussian distribution, and the hidden vector is sampled from this distribution as shown in Figure 4.12(a). Unfortunately, this network still has a sampling component. The weights of such a network cannot be learned by backpropagation because the stochastic portions of the computations are not differentiable, and therefore backpropagation cannot be not used. Therefore, the stochastic part of it can be addressed by the user explicitly generating k-dimensional samples in which each component is drawn from the standard normal distribution. The mean and standard deviation output by the encoder are used to scale and translate the input sample from the Gaussian distribution. This architecture is shown in Figure 4.12(b). By generating the stochastic potion explicitly as a part of the input, the resulting architecture is now fully deterministic, and its weights can be learned by backpropagation. Furthermore, the values of the generated samples from the standard normal distribution will need to be used in the backpropagation updates.

For each object $\overline{X}$, separate hidden activations for the mean and standard deviation are created by the encoder. The k-dimensional activations for the mean and standard deviation are denoted by $\overline{\mu}(\overline{X})$ and $\overline{\sigma}(\overline{X})$, respectively. In addition, a k-dimensional sample $\overline{z}$ is generated from $\mathcal{N}(0, I)$, where I is the identity matrix, and treated as an input into the hidden layer by the user. The hidden representation $\overline{h}(\overline{X})$ is created by scaling this random input vector $\overline{z}$ with the mean and standard deviation as follows:

$$\overline{h}(\overline{X}) = \overline{z} \odot \overline{\sigma}(\overline{X}) + \overline{\mu}(\overline{X}) \tag{4.16}$$

Here, $\odot$ indicates element-wise multiplication. These operations are shown in Figure 4.12(b) with the little circles containing the multiplication and addition operators. The elements of the vector $\overline{h}(\overline{X})$ for a particular object will obviously diverge from the standard normal distribution unless the vectors $\overline{\mu}(\overline{X})$ and $\overline{\sigma}(\overline{X})$ contain only 0s and 1s, respectively. This will not be the case because of the reconstruction component of the loss, which forces the conditional distributions of the hidden representations of particular points to have different means and lower standard deviations than that of the standard normal distribution (which is like a prior distribution). The distribution of the hidden representation of a particular point is a posterior distribution (conditional on the specific training data point), and therefore it will differ from the Gaussian prior. The overall loss function is expressed as a weighted sum of the reconstruction loss and the regularization loss. One can use a variety of choices for the reconstruction error, and for simplicity we will use the squared loss, which is defined as follows:

$$L = ||\overline{X} - \overline{X}'||^2 \tag{4.17}$$

Here, $\overline{X}'$ is the reconstruction of the input point $\overline{X}$ from the decoder. The regularization loss R is simply the Kullback-Leibler (KL)-divergence measure of the conditional hidden distribution with parameters $(\overline{\mu}(\overline{X})), \overline{\sigma}(\overline{X}))$ with respect to the k-dimensional Gaussian distribution with parameters $(0, I)$. This value is defined as follows:

$$R = \frac{1}{2} \left(\underbrace{||\overline{\mu}(\overline{X})||^2}_{\overline{\mu}(\overline{X})_i \Rightarrow 0} + \underbrace{||\overline{\sigma}(\overline{X})||^2 - 2 \sum_{i=1}^{k} \ln(\overline{\sigma}(\overline{X})_i)}_{\overline{\sigma}(\overline{X})_i \Rightarrow 1} - k \right) \tag{4.18}$$

Below some of the terms, we have annotated the specific effects of these terms in pushing parameters in particular directions. The constant term does not really do anything but it is a part of the KL-divergence function. Including the constant term does have the cosmetically satisfying effect that the regularization portion of the objective function reduces to 0, if the parameters $(\overline{\mu}(\overline{X})), \overline{\sigma}(\overline{X}))$ are the same as those of the isotropic Gaussian distribution with zero mean and unit variance in all directions. However, this will not be the case for any specific data point because of the effect of the reconstruction portion of the objective function. Over all training data points, the distribution of the hidden representation will, however, move closer to the standardized Gaussian because of the regularization term. The overall objective function J for the data point $\overline{X}$ is defined as the weighted sum of the reconstruction loss and the regularization loss:

$$J = L + \lambda R \tag{4.19}$$

Here, $\lambda > 0$ is the regularization parameter. Small values of λ will favor exact reconstruction, and the approach will behave like a traditional autoencoder. The regularization term forces the hidden representations to be stochastic, so that multiple hidden representations generate almost the same point. This increases generalization power because it is easier to model a new image that is like (but not an exact likeness of) an image in the training data within the stochastic range of hidden values. However, since there will be overlaps among the distributions of the hidden representations of similar points, it has some undesirable side effects. For example, the reconstructions tend to be blurry, when using the approach to reconstruct images. This is caused by an averaging effect over somewhat similar points. In the extreme case, if the value of λ is chosen to be exceedingly large, then all points will have the same hidden distribution (which is an isotropic Gaussian distribution with zero mean and unit variance). The reconstruction might provide a gross averaging over large numbers of training points, which will not be meaningful. The blurriness of the reconstructions of the variational autoencoder is an undesirable property of this class of models in comparison with several other related models for generative modeling.

Training the Variational Autoencoder

The training of a variational autoencoder is relatively straightforward because the stochasticity has been pulled out as an additional input. One can backpropagate as in any traditional neural network. The only difference is that one needs to backpropagate across the unusual form of Equation 4.16. Furthermore, one needs to account for the penalties of the hidden layer during backpropagation.

First, one can backpropagate the loss L up to the hidden state $\overline{h}(\overline{X}) = (h_1 \ldots h_k)$ using traditional methods. Let $\overline{z} = (z_1 \ldots z_k)$ be the k random samples from $\mathcal{N}(0, 1)$, which are used in the current iteration. In order to backpropagate from $\overline{h}(\overline{X})$ to $\overline{\mu}(\overline{X}) = (\mu_1 \ldots \mu_k)$ and $\overline{\sigma}(\overline{X}) = (\sigma_1 \ldots \sigma_k)$, one can use the following relationship:

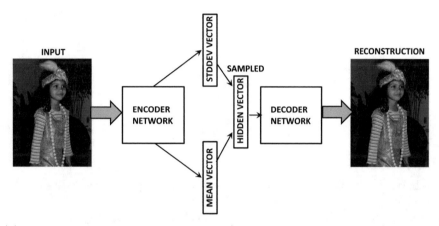

(a) Point-specific Gaussian distribution (stochastic and non-differentiable loss)

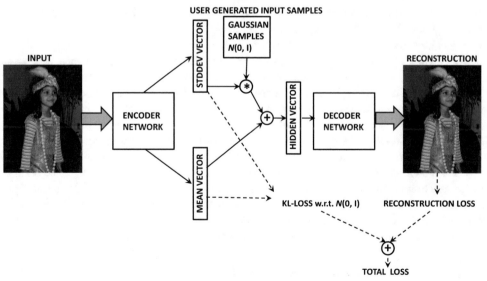

(b) Point-specific Gaussian distribution (deterministic and differentiable loss)

Figure 4.12: Re-parameterizing a variational autoencoder

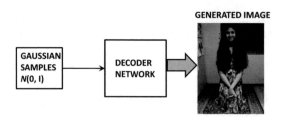

Figure 4.13: Generating samples from the variational autoencoder. The images are illustrative only.

$$J = L + \lambda R \tag{4.20}$$

$$\frac{\partial J}{\partial \mu_i} = \frac{\partial L}{\partial h_i} \underbrace{\frac{\partial h_i}{\partial \mu_i}}_{=1} + \lambda \frac{\partial R}{\partial \mu_i} \tag{4.21}$$

$$\frac{\partial J}{\partial \sigma_i} = \frac{\partial L}{\partial h_i} \underbrace{\frac{\partial h_i}{\partial \sigma_i}}_{=z_i} + \lambda \frac{\partial R}{\partial \sigma_i} \tag{4.22}$$

The values below the under-braces show the evaluations of partial derivatives of h_i with respect to μ_i and σ_i, respectively. Note that the values of $\frac{\partial h_i}{\partial \mu_i} = 1$ and $\frac{\partial h_i}{\partial \sigma_i} = z_i$ are obtained by differentiating Equation 4.16 with respect to μ_i and σ_i, respectively. The value of $\frac{\partial L}{\partial h_i}$ on the right-hand side is available from backpropagation. The values of $\frac{\partial R}{\partial \mu_i}$ and $\frac{\partial R}{\partial \sigma_i}$ are straightforward derivatives of the KL-divergence in Equation 4.18. Subsequent error propagation from the activations for $\overline{\mu}(\overline{X})$ and $\overline{\sigma}(\overline{X})$ can proceed in a similar way to the normal workings of the backpropagation algorithm.

The architecture of the variational autoencoder is considered fundamentally different from other types of autoencoders because it models the hidden variables in a stochastic way. However, there are still some interesting connections. In the de-noising autoencoder, one adds noise to the input; however, there is no constraint on the shape of the hidden distribution. In the variational autoencoder, one works with a stochastic hidden representation, although the stochasticity is pulled out by using it as an additional input during training. In other words, noise is added to the hidden representation rather than the input data. The variational approach improves generalization, because it encourages each input to map to its own stochastic region in the hidden space rather than mapping it to a single point. Small changes in the hidden representation, therefore, do not change the reconstruction too much. This assertion would also be true with a contractive autoencoder. However, constraining the shape of the hidden distribution to be Gaussian is a more fundamental difference of the variational autoencoder from other types of transformations.

4.10.4.1   Reconstruction and Generative Sampling

The approach can be used for creating the reduced representations as well as generating samples. In the case of data reduction, a Gaussian distribution with mean $\overline{\mu}(\overline{X})$ and standard deviation $\overline{\sigma}(\overline{X})$ is obtained, which represents the distribution of the hidden representation.

However, a particularly interesting application of the variational autoencoder is to generate samples from the underlying data distribution. Just as feature engineering methods

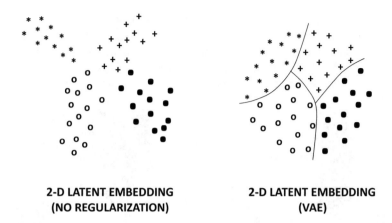

**2-D LATENT EMBEDDING
(NO REGULARIZATION)**

**2-D LATENT EMBEDDING
(VAE)**

Figure 4.14: Illustrations of the embeddings created by a variational autoencoder in relation to the unregularized version. The unregularized version has large discontinuities in the latent space, which might not correspond to meaningful points. The Gaussian embedding of the points in the variational autoencoder makes sampling possible.

use only the encoder portion of the autoencoder (once training is done), variational autoencoders use only the decoder portion. The basic idea is to repeatedly draw a point from the Gaussian distribution and feed it to the hidden units in the decoder. The resulting "reconstruction" output of the decoder will be a point satisfying a similar distribution as the original data. As a result, the generated point will be a realistic sample from the original data. The architecture for sample generation is shown in Figure 4.13. The shown image is illustrative only, and does not reflect the actual output of a variational autoencoder (which is generally of somewhat lower quality). To understand why a variational autoencoder can generate images in this way, it is helpful to view the typical types of embeddings an unregularized autoencoder would create versus a method like the variational autoencoder. In the left side of Figure 4.14, we have shown an example of the 2-dimensional embeddings of the training data created by an unregularized autoencoder of a four-class distribution (e.g., four digits of MNIST). It is evident that there are large discontinuities in particular regions of the latent space, and that these sparse regions may not correspond to meaningful points. On the other hand, the regularization term in the variational autoencoder encourages the training points to be (roughly) distributed in a Gaussian distribution, and there are far fewer discontinuities in the embedding on the right-hand side of Figure 4.14. Consequently, sampling from any point in the latent space will yield meaningful reconstructions of one of the four classes (i.e., one of the digits of MNIST). Furthermore, "walking" from one point in the latent space to another along a straight line in the second case will result in a smooth transformation across classes. For example, walking from a region containing instances of '4' to a region containing instances of '7' in the latent space of the MNIST data set would result in a slow change in the style of the digit '4' until a transition point, where the handwritten digit could be interpreted either as a '4' or a '7'. This situation does occur in real settings as well because such types of confusing handwritten digits do occur in the MNIST data set. Furthermore, the placement of different digits within the embedding would be such that digit pairs with smooth transitions at confusion points (e.g., [4, 7] or [5, 6]) are placed adjacent to one another in the latent space.

It is important to understand that the generated objects are often similar to but not exactly the same as those drawn from the training data. Because of its stochastic nature, the variational autoencoder has the ability to explore different modes of the generation process, which leads to a certain level of creativity in the face of ambiguity. This property can be put to good use by conditioning the approach on another object.

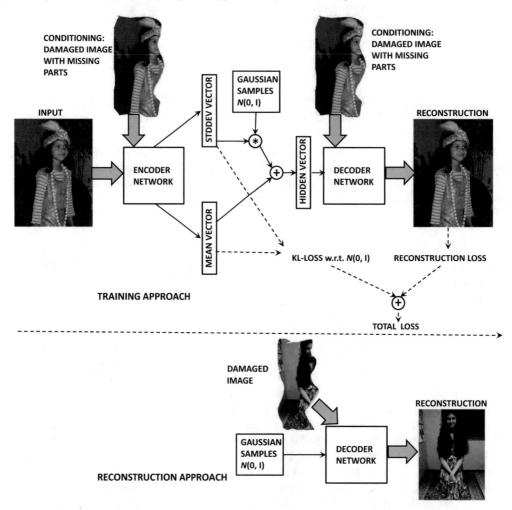

Figure 4.15: Reconstructing damaged images with the conditional variational autoencoder. The images are illustrative only.

4.10.4.2   Conditional Variational Autoencoders

One can apply conditioning to variational autoencoders in order to obtain some interesting results [510, 463]. The basic idea in conditional variational autoencoders is to add an additional conditional input, which typically provides a related context. For example, the context might be a damaged image with missing holes, and the job of the autoencoder is to reconstruct it. Predictive models will generally perform poorly in this type of setting because the level of ambiguity may be too large, and an averaged reconstruction across all images might not be useful. During the training phase, pairs of damaged and original images are needed, and therefore the encoder and decoder are able to learn how the context relates to the images being generated from the training data. The architecture of the training phase is illustrated in the upper part of Figure 4.15. The training is otherwise similar to the unconditional variational autoencoder. During the testing phase, the context is provided as an additional input, and the autoencoder reconstructs the missing portions in a reasonable way based on the model learned in the training phase. The architecture of the reconstruction phase is illustrated in the lower part of Figure 4.15. The simplicity of this architecture is particularly notable. The shown images are only illustrative; in actual executions on image data, the generated images are often blurry, especially in the missing portions. This is a type of image-to-image translation approach, which will be revisited in Chapter 10 under the context of a discussion on *generative adversarial networks*.

4.10.4.3 Relationship with Generative Adversarial Networks

Variational autoencoders are closely related to another class of models, referred to as generative adversarial networks. However, there are some key differences as well. Like variational autoencoders, generative adversarial networks can be used to create images that are similar to a base training data set. Furthermore, conditional variants of both models are useful for completing missing data, especially in cases where the ambiguity is large enough to require a certain level of creativity from the generative process. However, the results of generative adversarial networks are often more realistic because the decoders are explicitly trained to create good counterfeits. This is achieved by having a discriminator as a judge of the quality of the generated objects. Furthermore, the objects are also generated in a more creative way because the generator is never shown the original objects in the training data set, but is only given guidance to fool the discriminator. As a result, generative adversarial networks learn to create creative counterfeits. In certain domains such as image and video data, this approach can have remarkable results; unlike variational autoencoders, the quality of the images is not blurry. One can create vivid images and videos with an artistic flavor, that give the impression of dreaming. These techniques can also be used in numerous applications like text-to-image or image-to-image translation. For example, one can specify a text description, and then obtain a fantasy image that matches the description [392]. Generative adversarial networks are discussed in Section 10.4 of Chapter 10.

4.11 Summary

Neural networks often contain a large number of parameters, which causes overfitting. One solution is to restrict the size of the networks up front. However, such an approach often provides suboptimal solutions when the model is complex and sufficient data are available. A more flexible approach is to use tunable regularization, in which a large number of parameters are allowed. In such cases, the regularization restricts the size of the parameter space in a soft way. The most common form of regularization is penalty-based regularization. It is common to use penalties on the parameters, although it is also possible to use penalties on the activations of the hidden units. The latter approach leads to sparse representations in the hidden units. Ensemble learning is a common approach to reduce variance, and some ensemble methods like *Dropout* are specifically designed for neural networks. Other common regularization methods include early stopping and pretraining. Pretraining acts as a regularizer by acting as a form of semi-supervised learning, which works from the simple to the complex by initializing with a simple heuristic and using backpropagation to discover refined solutions. Other related techniques include curriculum and continuation methods, which also work from the simple to the complex in order to provide solutions with low generalization error. Although overfitting is often a less serious problem in unsupervised settings, different types of regularization are used to impose structure on the learned models.

4.12   Bibliographic Notes

A detailed discussion of the bias-variance trade-off may be found in [177]. The bias-variance trade-off originated in the field of statistics, where it was proposed in the context of the regression problem. The generalization to the case of binary loss functions in classification was proposed in [247, 252]. Early methods for reducing overfitting were proposed in [175, 282] in which unimportant weights were removed from a network to reduce its parameter footprint. It was shown that this type of pruning had significant benefits in terms of generalization. The early work also showed [450] that deep and narrow networks tended to generalize better than broad and shallow networks. This is primarily because the depth imposes a structure on the data, and can represent the data in a fewer number of parameters. A recent study of model generalization in neural networks is provided in [557].

The use of L_2-regularization in regression dates back to Tikhonov-Arsenin's seminal work [499]. The equivalence of Tikhonov regularization and training with noise was shown by Bishop [44]. The use of L_1-regularization is studied in detail in [179]. Several regularization methods have also been proposed that are specifically designed for neural architectures. For example, the work in [201] proposes a regularization technique that constrains the norm of each layer in a neural network. Sparse representations of the data are explored in [67, 273, 274, 284, 354].

Detailed discussions of ensemble methods for classification may be found in [438, 566]. The bagging and subsampling methods are discussed in [50, 56]. The work in [515] proposes an ensemble architecture that is inspired by a random forest. This architecture is illustrated in Figure 1.16 of Chapter 1. This type of ensemble is particularly well suited for problems with small data sets, where a random forest is known to work well. The approach for random edge dropping was introduced in the context of outlier detection [64], whereas the *Dropout* approach was presented in [467]. The work in [567] discusses the notion that it is better to combine the results of the top-performing ensemble components rather than combining all of them. Most ensemble methods are designed for variance reduction, although a few techniques like *boosting* [122] are also designed for bias reduction. Boosting has also been used in the context of neural network learning [435]. However, the use of boosting in neural networks is generally restricted to the incremental addition of hidden units based on error characteristics. A key point about boosting is that it tends to overfit the data, and is therefore suitable for high-bias learners but not high-variance learners. Neural networks are inherently high-variance learners. The relationship between boosting and certain types of neural architectures is pointed out in [32]. Data perturbation methods for classification are discussed in [63], although this method primarily seems to be about increasing the amount of available data of a minority class, and does not discuss variance reduction methods. A later book [5] discusses how this approach can be combined with a variance reduction method. Ensemble methods for neural networks are proposed in [170].

Different types of pretraining have been explored in the context of neural networks [31, 113, 196, 386, 506]. The earliest methods for unsupervised pretraining were proposed in [196]. The original work of pretraining [196] was based on probabilistic graphical models (cf. Section 6.7) and was later extended to conventional autoencoders [386, 506].

Compared to unsupervised pretraining, the effect of supervised pretraining is limited [31]. A detailed discussion of why unsupervised pretraining helps deep learning is provided in [113]. This work posits that unsupervised pretraining implicitly acts as a regularizer, and therefore it improves the generalization power to unseen test instances. This fact is also evidenced by the experimental results in [31], which show that supervised variations of pretraining do not help as much as unsupervised variations of pretraining. In this sense, unsupervised pretraining can be viewed as a type of semi-supervised learning, which restricts the parameter search to specific regions of the parameter space, which depend on the base data distribution at hand. Pretraining also does not seem to help with certain types of tasks [303]. Another form of semi-supervised learning can be performed with *ladder networks* [388, 502], in which skip-connections are used in conjunction with an autoencoder-like architecture.

Curriculum and continuation learning are applications of the principle of moving from simple to complex models. Continuation learning methods are discussed in [339, 536]. A number of methods were proposed in the early years [112, 422, 464] that showed the advantages of curriculum learning. The basic principles of curriculum learning are discussed in [238]. The relationship between curriculum and continuation learning is explored in [33].

Numerous unsupervised methods have been proposed for regularization. A discussion of sparse autoencoders may be found in [354]. De-noising autoencoders are discussed in [506]. The contractive autoencoder is discussed in [397]. The use of de-noising autoencoders in recommender systems is discussed in [472, 535]. The ideas in the contractive autoencoder are reminiscent of *double backpropagation* [107] in which small changes in the input are not allowed to change the output. Related ideas are also discussed in the *tangent classifier* [398].

The variational autoencoder is introduced in [242, 399]. The use of importance weighting to improve over the representations learned by the variational autoencoder is discussed in [58]. Conditional variational autoencoders are discussed in [463, 510]. A tutorial on variational autoencoders is found in [106]. Generative variants of de-noising autoencoders are discussed in [34]. Variational autoencoders are closely related to generative adversarial networks, which are discussed in Chapter 10. Closely related methods for designing adversarial autoencoders are discussed in [311].

4.12.1 Software Resources

Numerous ensemble methods are available from machine learning libraries like *scikit-learn* [587]. Most of the weight-decay and penalty-based methods are available as standardized options in the deep learning libraries. However, techniques like *Dropout* are application-specific and need to be implemented from scratch. Implementations of several different types of autoencoders may be found in [595]. Several implementations of the variational autoencoder may be found in [596, 597, 640].

4.13 Exercises

1. Consider two neural networks used for regression modeling with identical structure of an input layer and 10 hidden layers containing 100 units each. In both cases, the output node is a single unit with linear activation. The only difference is that one of them uses linear activations in the hidden layers and the other uses sigmoid activations. Which model will have higher variance in prediction?

2. Consider a situation in which you have four attributes $x_1 \ldots x_4$, and the dependent variable y is such that $y = 2x_1$. Create a tiny training data set of 5 distinct examples in which a linear regression model without regularization will have an infinite number of coefficient solutions with $w_1 = 0$. Discuss the performance of such a model on out-of-sample data. Why will regularization help?

3. Implement a perceptron with and without regularization. Test the accuracy of both variations of the perceptron on both the training data and the out-of-sample data on the *Ionosphere* data set of the *UCI Machine Learning Repository* [601]. What do you observe about the effect of regularization in the two cases? Repeat the experiment with smaller samples of the *Ionosphere* training data, and report your observations.

4. Implement an autoencoder with a single hidden layer. Reconstruct inputs for the *Ionosphere* data set of the previous exercise with (a) no added noise and weight regularization, (b) added Gaussian noise and no weight regularization.

5. The discussion in the chapter uses an example of sigmoid activation for the contractive autoencoder. Consider a contractive autoencoder with a single hidden layer and ReLU activation. Discuss how the updates change when ReLU activation is used.

6. Suppose that you have a model that provides around 80% accuracy on the training as well as on the out-of-sample test data. Would you recommend increasing the amount of data or adjusting the model to improve accuracy?

7. In the chapter, we showed that adding Gaussian noise to the input features in linear regression is equivalent to L_2-regularization of linear regression. Discuss why adding of Gaussian noise to the input data in a de-noising single-hidden layer autoencoder with linear units is roughly equivalent to L_2-regularized singular value decomposition.

8. Consider a network with a single input layer, two hidden layers, and a single output predicting a binary label. All hidden layers use the sigmoid activation function and no regularization is used. The input layer contains d units, and each hidden layer contains p units. Suppose that you add an additional hidden layer between the two current hidden layers, and this additional hidden layer contains q linear units.

   (a) Even though the number of parameters have increased by adding the hidden layer, discuss why the capacity of this model will decrease when $q < p$.

   (b) Does the capacity of the model increase when $q > p$?

9. Bob divided the labeled classification data into a portion used for model construction and another portion for validation. Bob then tested 1000 neural architectures by learning parameters (backpropagating) on the model-construction portion and testing its accuracy on the validation portion. Discuss why the resulting model is likely to yield poorer accuracy on the out-of-sample test data as compared to the validation data, even though the validation data was not used for learning parameters. Do you have any recommendations for Bob on using the results of his 1000 validations?

10. Does the classification accuracy on the training data generally improve with increasing training data size? How about the point-wise average of the loss on training instances? At what point do training and testing accuracy become similar? Explain your answer.

11. What is the effect of increasing the regularization parameter on the training and testing accuracy? At what point do training and testing accuracy become similar?

Chapter 5

Radial Basis Function Networks

"Two birds disputed about a kernel, when a third swooped down and carried it off."—African Proverb

5.1 Introduction

Radial basis function (RBF) networks represent a fundamentally different architecture from what we have seen in the previous chapters. All the previous chapters use a feed-forward network in which the inputs are transmitted forward from layer to layer in a similar fashion in order to create the final outputs. A feed-forward network might have many layers, and the nonlinearity is typically created by the repeated composition of activation functions. On the other hand, an RBF network typically uses only an input layer, a single hidden layer (with a special type of behavior defined by RBF functions), and an output layer. Although it is possible to replace the output layer with multiple feed-forward layers (like a conventional network), the resulting network is still quite shallow, and its behavior is strongly influenced by the nature of the special hidden layer. For simplicity in discussion, we will work with only a single output layer. As in feed-forward networks, the input layer is not really a computational layer, and it only carries the inputs forward. The nature of the computations in the hidden layer are very different from what we have seen so far in feed-forward networks. In particular, the hidden layer performs a computation based on a comparison with a *prototype vector*, which has no exact counterpart in feed-forward networks. The structure and the computations performed by the special hidden layer is the key to the power of the RBF network.

One can characterize the difference in the functionality of the hidden and output layers as follows:

1. The hidden layer takes the input points, in which the class structure might not be linearly separable, and transforms them into a new space that is (often) linearly separable. The hidden layer often has higher dimensionality than the input layer, because transformation to a higher-dimensional space is often required in order to ensure linear separability. This principle is based on *Cover's theorem on separability of patterns* [84], which states that pattern classification problems are more likely to be linearly separable when cast into a high-dimensional space with a nonlinear transformation. Furthermore, certain types of transformations in which features represent small localities in the space are more likely to lead to linear separability. Although the dimensionality of the hidden layer is typically greater than the input dimensionality, it is always less than or equal to the number of training points. An extreme case in which the dimensionality of the hidden layer is equal to the number of training points can be shown to be roughly equivalent to *kernel learners*. Examples of such models include kernel regression and kernel support vector machines.

2. The output layer uses linear classification or regression modeling with respect to the inputs from the hidden layer. The connections from the hidden to the output layer have weights attached to them. The computations in the output layer are performed in the same way as in a standard feed-forward network. Although it is also possible to replace the output layer with multiple feed-forward layers, we will consider only the case of a single feed-forward layer for simplicity.

Just as the perceptron is a variant of the linear support vector machine, the RBF network is a generalization of kernel classification and regression. Special cases of the RBF network can be used to implement kernel regression, least-squares kernel classification, and the kernel support-vector machine. The differences among these special cases is in terms of how the output layer and the loss function is structured. In feed-forward networks, increasing nonlinearity is obtained by increasing depth. However, in an RBF network, a single hidden layer is usually sufficient to achieve the required level of nonlinearity because of its special structure. Like feed-forward networks, RBF networks are universal function approximators.

The layers of the RBF network are designed as follows:

1. The input layer simply transmits from the input features to the hidden layers. Therefore, the number of input units is exactly equal to the dimensionality d of the data. As in the case of feed-forward networks, no computation is performed in the input layers. As in all feed-forward networks, the input units are fully connected to the hidden units and carry their input forward.

2. The computations in the hidden layers are based on comparisons with *prototype vectors*. Each hidden unit contains a d-dimensional prototype vector. Let the prototype vector of the ith hidden unit be denoted by $\overline{\mu}_i$. In addition, the ith hidden unit contains a bandwidth denoted by σ_i. Although the prototype vectors are always specific to particular units, the bandwidths of different units σ_i are often set to the same value σ. The prototype vectors and bandwidth(s) are usually learned either in an unsupervised way, or with the use of mild supervision.

Then, for any input training point $\overline{X}$, the activation $\Phi_i(\overline{X})$ of the ith hidden unit is defined as follows:

$$h_i = \Phi_i(\overline{X}) = \exp\left(-\frac{||\overline{X} - \overline{\mu}_i||^2}{2 \cdot \sigma_i^2}\right) \quad \forall i \in \{1, \dots, m\} \tag{5.1}$$

The total number of hidden units is denoted by m. Each of these m units is designed to have a high level of influence on the particular cluster of points that is closest to its prototype vector. Therefore, one can view m as the number of clusters used for modeling, and it represents an important hyper-parameter available to the algorithm. For low-dimensional inputs, it is typical for the value of m to be larger than the input dimensionality d, but smaller than the number of training points n.

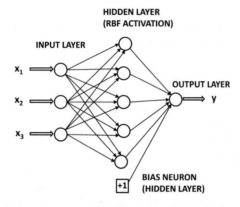

Figure 5.1: An RBF network: Note that the hidden layer is broader than the input layer, which is typical (but not mandatory).

3. For any particular training point $\overline{X}$, let h_i be the output of the ith hidden unit, as defined by Equation 5.1. The weights of the connections from the hidden to the output nodes are set to w_i. Then, the prediction $\hat{y}$ of the RBF network in the output layer is defined as follows:

$$\hat{y} = \sum_{i=1}^{m} w_i h_i = \sum_{i=1}^{m} w_i \Phi_i(\overline{X}) = \sum_{i=1}^{m} w_i \exp\left(-\frac{||\overline{X} - \overline{\mu}_i||^2}{2 \cdot \sigma_i^2}\right)$$

The variable $\hat{y}$ has a circumflex on top to indicate the fact that it is a predicted value rather than observed value. If the observed target is real-valued, then one can set up a least-squares loss function, which is much like that in a feed-forward network. The values of the weights $w_1 \dots w_m$ need to be learned in a supervised way.

An additional detail is that the hidden layer of the neural network contains bias neurons. Note that the bias neuron can be implemented by a single hidden unit in the output layer, which is always on. One can also implement this type of neuron by creating a hidden unit in which the value of σ_i is ∞. In either case, it will be assumed throughout the discussions in this chapter that this special hidden unit is absorbed among the m hidden units. Therefore, it is not treated in any special way. An example of an RBF network is illustrated in Figure 5.1.

In the RBF network, there are two sets of computations corresponding to the hidden layer and the output layer. The parameters $\overline{\mu}_i$ and σ_i of the hidden layer are learned in an unsupervised way, whereas those of the output layer are learned in a supervised way with gradient descent. The latter is similar to the case of the feed-forward network. The prototypes $\overline{\mu}_i$ may either be sampled from the data, or be set to be the m centroids of an m-way clustering algorithm. The latter solution is used frequently. The different ways of training the neural network are discussed in Section 5.2.

RBF networks can be shown to be direct generalizations of the class of kernel methods. This is primarily because the prediction in the output node can be shown to be equivalent to a weighted nearest neighbor estimator, where the weights are products of the coefficients w_i and Gaussian RBF similarities to *prototypes*. The prediction function in almost all kernel methods can also be shown to be equivalent to a weighted nearest neighbor estimator, where the weights are learned in a supervised way. Therefore, kernel methods represent a special case of RBF methods in which the number of hidden nodes is equal to the number of training points, the prototypes are set to the training points, and each σ_i has the same value. This suggests that RBF networks have greater power and flexibility than do kernel methods; this relationship will be discussed in detail in Section 5.4.

When to Use RBF Networks

A key point is that the hidden layer of the RBF network is created in an unsupervised way, tending to make it robust to all types of noise (including adversarial noise). Indeed, this property of RBF networks is shared by support vector machines. At the same time, there are limitations with respect to how much structure in the data an RBF network can learn. Deep feed-forward networks are effective at learning from data with a rich structure because the multiple layers of nonlinear activations force the data to follow specific types of patterns. Furthermore, by adjusting the structure of connections, one can incorporate domain-specific insights in feed-forward networks. Examples of such settings include recurrent and convolutional neural networks. The single layer of an RBF network limits the amount of structure that one can learn. Although both RBF networks and deep feed-forward networks are known to be universal function approximators, there are differences in terms of their generalization performance on different types of data sets.

Chapter Organization

This chapter is organized as follows. The next section discusses the various training methods for RBF networks. The use of RBF networks in classification and interpolation is discussed in Section 5.3. The relationship of the RBF method to kernel regression and classification is discussed in Section 5.4. A summary is provided in Section 5.5.

5.2   Training an RBF Network

The training of an RBF network is very different from that of a feed-forward network, which is fully integrated across different layers. In an RBF network, the training of the hidden layer is typically done in an unsupervised manner. While it is possible, in principle, to train the prototype vectors and the bandwidths using backpropagation, the problem is that there are more local minima on the loss surface of RBF networks compared to feed-forward networks. Therefore, the supervision in the hidden layer (when used) is often relatively gentle, or it is restricted only to fine-tuning weights that have already been learned. Nevertheless, since overfitting seems to be a pervasive problem with the supervised training of the hidden layer, our discussion will be restricted to unsupervised methods. In the following, we will first discuss the training of the hidden layer of an RBF network, and then discuss the training of the output layer.

5.2.1 Training the Hidden Layer

The hidden layer of the RBF network contains several parameters, including the prototype vectors $\overline{\mu}_1 \ldots \overline{\mu}_m$, and the bandwidths $\sigma_1 \ldots \sigma_m$. The hyperparameter m controls the number of hidden units. In practice, a separate value of σ_i is not set for each unit, and all units have the same bandwidth σ. However, the mean values $\overline{\mu}_i$ for the various hidden units are different because they define the all-important prototype vectors. The complexity of the model is regulated by the number of hidden units and the bandwidth. The combination of a small bandwidth and a large number of hidden units increases the model complexity, and is a useful setting when the amount of data is large. Smaller data sets require fewer units and larger bandwidths to avoid overfitting. The value of m is typically larger than the input data dimensionality, but it is never larger than the number of training points. Setting the value of m equal to the number of training points, and using each training point as a prototype in a hidden node, makes the approach equivalent to traditional kernel methods.

The bandwidth also depends on the chosen prototype vectors $\overline{\mu}_1 \ldots \overline{\mu}_m$. Ideally, the bandwidths should be set in a way that each point should be (significantly) influenced by only a small number of prototype vectors, which correspond to its closest clusters. Setting the bandwidth too large or too small compared to the inter-prototype distance will lead to under-fitting and over-fitting, respectively. Let d_{max} be maximum distance between pairs of prototype centers, and d_{ave} be the average distance between them. Then, two heuristic ways of setting the bandwidth are as follows:

$$\sigma = \frac{d_{max}}{\sqrt{m}}$$

$$\sigma = 2 \cdot d_{ave}$$

One problem with this choice of σ is that the optimal value of the bandwidth might vary in different parts of the input space. For example, the bandwidth in a dense region in the data space should be smaller than the bandwidth in a sparse region of the space. The bandwidth should also depend on how the prototype vectors are distributed in the space. Therefore, one possible solution is to choose the bandwidth σ_i of the ith prototype vector to be equal to its distance to its rth nearest neighbor among the prototypes. Here, r is a small value like 5 or 10.

However, these are only heuristic rules. It is possible to fine-tune these values by using a held-out portion of data set. In other words, candidate values of σ are generated in the neighborhood of the above recommended values of σ (as an initial reference point). Then, multiple models are constructed using these candidate values of σ (including the training of the output layer). The choice of σ that provides the least error on the held-out portion of the training data set is used. This type of approach does use a certain level of supervision in the selection of the bandwidth, without getting stuck in local minima. However, the nature of the supervision is quite gentle, which is particularly important when dealing with the parameters of the first layer in an RBF network. It is noteworthy that this type of tuning of the bandwidth is also performed when using the Gaussian kernel with a kernel support-vector machine. This similarity is not a coincidence because the kernel support-vector machine is a special case of RBF networks (cf. Section 5.4).

The selection of the prototype vectors is somewhat more complex. In particular, the following choices are often made:

1. The prototype vectors can be randomly sampled from the n training points. A total of $m < n$ training points are sampled in order to create the prototype vectors. The main problem with this approach is that it will over-represent prototypes from dense regions of the data, whereas sparse regions might get few or no prototypes. As a result, the prediction accuracy in such regions will suffer.

2. A k-means clustering algorithm can be used in order to create m clusters. The centroid of each of these m clusters can be used as a prototype. The use of the k-means algorithm is the most common choice for learning the prototype vectors.

3. Variants of clustering algorithms that partition the data *space* (rather than the points) are also used. A specific example is the use of decision trees to create the prototypes.

4. An alternative method for training the hidden layer is by using the *orthogonal least-squares algorithm*. This approach uses a certain level of supervision. In this approach, the prototype vectors are selected one by one from the training data in order to minimize the residual error of prediction on an out-of-sample test set. Since this approach requires understanding of the training of the output layer, its discussion will be deferred to a later section.

In the following, we briefly describe the k-means algorithm for creating the prototypes because it is the most common choice in real implementations. The k-means algorithm is a classical technique in the clustering literature. It uses the cluster prototypes as the prototypes for the hidden layer in the RBF method. Broadly speaking, the k-means algorithm proceeds as follows. At initialization, the m cluster prototypes are set to m random training points. Subsequently, each of the n data points is assigned to the prototype to which it has the smallest Euclidean distance. The assigned points of each prototype are averaged in order to create a new cluster center. In other words, the centroid of the created clusters is used to replace its old prototype with a new prototype. This process is repeated iteratively to convergence. Convergence is reached when the cluster assignments do not change significantly from one iteration to the next.

5.2.2 Training the Output Layer

The output layer is trained after the hidden layer has been trained. The training of the output layer is quite straightforward, because it uses only a single layer with linear activation. For ease in discussion, we will first consider the case in which the target of the output layer is real-valued. Later, we will discuss other settings. The output layer contains an m-dimensional vector of weights $\overline{W} = [w_1 \dots w_m]$ that needs to be learned. Assume that the vector $\overline{W}$ is a row vector.

Consider a situation in which the training data set contains n points $\overline{X_1} \dots \overline{X_n}$, which create the representations $\overline{H_1} \dots \overline{H_n}$ in the hidden layer. Therefore, each $\overline{H_i}$ is an m-dimensional row vector. One could stack these n row vectors on top of one another to create an $n \times m$ matrix H. Furthermore, the observed targets of the n training points are denoted by $y_1, y_2, \dots y_n$, which can be written as the n-dimensional column vector $\overline{y} = [y_1 \dots y_n]^T$.

The predictions of the n training points are given by the elements of the n-dimensional column vector $H\overline{W}^T$. Ideally, we would like these predictions to be as close to the observed vector $\overline{y}$ as possible. Therefore, the loss function L for learning the output-layer weights is as follows:

$$L = \frac{1}{2}||H\overline{W}^T - \overline{y}||^2$$

In order to reduce overfitting, one can add Tikhonov regularization to the objective function:

$$L = \frac{1}{2}||H\overline{W}^T - \overline{y}||^2 + \frac{\lambda}{2}||\overline{W}||^2 \tag{5.2}$$

Here, $\lambda > 0$ is the regularization parameter. By computing the partial derivative of L with respect to the elements of the weight vector, we obtain the following:

$$\frac{\partial L}{\partial \overline{W}} = H^T(H\overline{W}^T - \overline{y}) + \lambda\overline{W}^T = 0$$

The above derivative is written in matrix calculus notation where $\frac{\partial L}{\partial \overline{W}}$ refers to the following:

$$\frac{\partial L}{\partial \overline{W}} = \left(\frac{\partial L}{\partial w_1} \cdots \frac{\partial L}{\partial w_d}\right)^T \tag{5.3}$$

By re-adjusting the above condition, we obtain the following:

$$(H^T H + \lambda I)\overline{W}^T = H^T \overline{y}$$

When $\lambda > 0$, the matrix $H^T H + \lambda I$ is positive-definite and is therefore invertible. In other words, one obtains a simple solution for the weight vector in closed form:

$$\overline{W}^T = (H^T H + \lambda I)^{-1} H^T \overline{y} \tag{5.4}$$

Therefore, a simple matrix inversion is sufficient to find the weight vector, and backpropagation is completely unnecessary.

However, the reality is that the use of a closed-form solution is not viable in practice because the size of the matrix $H^T H$ is $m \times m$, which can be large. For example, in kernel methods, we set $m = n$, in which the matrix is too large to even materialize, let alone invert. Therefore, one uses stochastic gradient descent to update the weight vector in practice. In such a case, the gradient-descent updates (with all training points) are as follows:

$$\overline{W}^T \Leftarrow \overline{W}^T - \alpha\frac{\partial L}{\partial \overline{W}}$$
$$= \overline{W}^T(1 - \alpha\lambda) - \alpha H^T \underbrace{(H\overline{W}^T - \overline{y})}_{\text{Current Errors}}$$

One can also choose to use mini-batch gradient descent in which the matrix H in the above update can be replaced with a random subset of rows H_r from H, corresponding to the mini-batch. This approach is equivalent to what would normally be used in a traditional neural network with mini-batch stochastic gradient descent. However, it is applied only to the weights of the connections incident on the output layer in this case.

5.2.2.1   Expression with Pseudo-Inverse

In the case in which the regularization parameter λ is set to 0, the weight vector $\overline{W}$ is defined as follows:

$$\overline{W}^T = (H^T H)^{-1} H^T \overline{y} \tag{5.5}$$

The matrix $(H^T H)^{-1} H^T$ is said to be the *pseudo-inverse* of the matrix H. The pseudo-inverse of the matrix H is denoted by H^+. Therefore, one can write the weight vector $\overline{W}^T$ as follows:

$$\overline{W}^T = H^+ \overline{y} \tag{5.6}$$

The pseudo-inverse is a generalization of the notion of an inverse for non-singular or rectangular matrices. In this particular case, $H^T H$ is assumed to be invertible, although the pseudo-inverse of H can be computed even in cases where $H^T H$ is not invertible. In the case where H is square and invertible, the pseudo-inverse is the same as its inverse.

5.2.3   Orthogonal Least-Squares Algorithm

We revisit the training phase of the hidden layer. The training approach discussed in this section will use the predictions of the output layer in choosing the prototypes. Therefore, the training process of the hidden layer is supervised, although the supervision is restricted to iterative selections from the original training points. The orthogonal least-squares algorithm chooses the prototype vector one by one from the training points in order to minimize the error of prediction.

The algorithm starts by building an RBF network with a single hidden node and trying each possible training point as a prototype in order to compute the prediction error. One then selects the prototype from the training points that minimizes the error of prediction. In the next iteration, one more prototype is added to the selected prototype in order to build an RBF network with two prototypes. As in the previous iteration, all $(n-1)$ remaining training points are tried as possible prototypes in order to add to the current bag of prototypes, and the criterion for adding to the bag is the minimization of prediction error. In the $(r+1)$th iteration, one tries all the $(n-r)$ remaining training points, and adds one of them to the bag of prototypes so that the prediction error is minimized. Some of the training points in the data are held out, and are not used in the computations of the predictions or as candidates for prototypes. These out-of-sample points are used in order to test the effect of adding a prototype to the error. At some point, the error on this held-out set begins to rise as more prototypes as added. An increase in error on the held-out test set is a sign of the fact that further increase in prototypes will increase overfitting. This is the point at which one terminates the algorithm.

The main problem with this approach is that it is extremely inefficient. In each iteration, one must run n training procedures, which is computationally prohibitive for large training data sets. An interesting procedure in this respect is the *orthogonal least-squares algorithm* [65], which is known to be efficient. This algorithm is similar to the one described above in the sense that the prototype vectors are added iteratively from the original training data set. However, the procedure with which the prototype is added is far more efficient. A set of orthogonal vectors are constructed in the space spanned by the hidden unit activations from the training data set. These orthogonal vectors can be used to directly compute which prototype should be selected from the training data set.

5.2.4   Fully Supervised Learning

The orthogonal least-squares algorithm represents a type of mild supervision in which the prototype vector is selected from one of the training points based on the effect to the overall prediction error. It is also possible to perform stronger types of supervision in which one can backpropagate in order to update the prototype vectors and the bandwidth. Consider the loss function L over the various training points:

$$L = \frac{1}{2} \sum_{i=1}^{n} (\overline{H_i} \cdot \overline{W} - y_i)^2 \tag{5.7}$$

Here, $\overline{H_i}$ represents the m-dimensional vector of activations in the hidden layer for the ith training point $\overline{X_i}$.

The partial derivative with respect to each bandwidth σ_j can be computed as follows:

$$\frac{\partial L}{\partial \sigma_j} = \sum_{i=1}^{n} (\overline{H_i} \cdot \overline{W} - y_i) w_j \frac{\partial \Phi_j(\overline{X_i})}{\partial \sigma_j}$$

$$= \sum_{i=1}^{n} (\overline{H_i} \cdot \overline{W} - y_i)\, w_j \Phi_j(\overline{X_i}) \frac{||\overline{X_i} - \overline{\mu}_j||^2}{\sigma_j^3}$$

If all bandwidths σ_j are fixed to the same value σ, as is common in RBF networks, then the derivative can be computed using the same trick commonly used for handling shared weights:

$$\frac{\partial L}{\partial \sigma} = \sum_{j=1}^{m} \frac{\partial L}{\partial \sigma_j} \cdot \underbrace{\frac{\partial \sigma_j}{\partial \sigma}}_{=1}$$

$$= \sum_{j=1}^{m} \frac{\partial L}{\partial \sigma_j}$$

$$= \sum_{j=1}^{m} \sum_{i=1}^{n} (\overline{H_i} \cdot \overline{W} - y_i)\, w_j \Phi_j(\overline{X_i}) \frac{||\overline{X_i} - \overline{\mu}_j||^2}{\sigma^3}$$

One can also compute a partial derivative with respect to each element of the prototype vector. Let μ_{jk} represent the kth element of $\overline{\mu}_j$. Similarly, let x_{ik} represent the kth element of the ith training point $\overline{X_i}$. The partial derivative with respect to μ_{jk} is computed as follows:

$$\frac{\partial L}{\partial \mu_{jk}} = \sum_{i=1}^{n} (\overline{H_i} \cdot \overline{W} - y_i)\, w_j \Phi_j(\overline{X_i}) \frac{(x_{ik} - \mu_{jk})}{\sigma_j^2} \tag{5.8}$$

Using these partial derivatives, one can update the bandwidth and the prototype vectors together with the weights. Unfortunately, this type of strong approach to supervision does not seem to work very well. There are two main drawbacks with this approach:

1. An attractive characteristic of RBFs is that they are efficient to train, if unsupervised methods are used. Even the orthogonal least-squares method can be run in a reasonably amount of time. However, this advantage is lost, if one resorts to full backpropagation. In general, the two-stage training of RBF is an efficiency feature of RBF networks.

2. The loss surface of RBFs has many local minima. This type of approach tends to get stuck in local minima from the point of view of generalization error.

Because of these characteristics of RBF networks, supervised training is rarely used. In fact, it has been shown in [342] that supervised training tends to increase the bandwidths and encourage generalized responses. When supervision is used, it should be used in a very controlled way by repeatedly testing performance on out-of-sample data in order to reduce the risk of overfitting.

5.3   Variations and Special Cases of RBF Networks

The above discussion only considers the case in which the supervised training is designed for numeric target variables. In practice, it is possible for the target variables to be binary. One possibility is to treat binary class labels in $\{-1, +1\}$ as numeric responses, and use the same approach of setting the weight vector according to Equation 5.4:

$$\overline{W}^T = (H^T H + \lambda I)^{-1} H^T \overline{y}$$

As discussed in Section 2.2.2.1 of Chapter 2, this solution is also equivalent to the Fisher discriminant and the Widrow-Hoff method. The main difference is that these methods are being applied on a hidden layer of increased dimensionality, which promotes better results in more complex distributions. It is also helpful to examine other loss functions that are commonly used in feed-forward neural networks for classification.

5.3.1   Classification with Perceptron Criterion

Using the notations introduced in the previous section, the prediction of the ith training instance is given by $\overline{W} \cdot \overline{H_i}$. Here, $\overline{H_i}$ represents the m-dimensional vector of activations in the hidden layer for the ith training instance $\overline{X_i}$. Then, as discussed in Section 1.2.1.1 of Chapter 1, the perceptron criterion corresponds to the following loss function:

$$L = \max\{-y_i(\overline{W} \cdot \overline{H_i}), 0\} \tag{5.9}$$

In addition, a Tikhonov regularization term with parameter $\lambda > 0$ is often added to the loss function.

Then, for each mini-batch S of training instances, let S^+ represent the misclassified instances. The misclassified instances are defined as those for which the loss L is non-zero. For such instances, applying the sign function to $\overline{H_i} \cdot \overline{W}$ will yield a prediction with opposite sign to the observed label y_i.

Then, for each mini-batch S of training instances, the following updates are used for the misclassified instances in S^+:

$$\overline{W} \Leftarrow \overline{W}(1 - \alpha\lambda) + \alpha \sum_{(\overline{H_i}, y_i) \in S^+} y_i \overline{H_i} \tag{5.10}$$

Here, $\alpha > 0$ is the learning rate.

5.3.2 Classification with Hinge Loss

The hinge loss is used frequently in the support vector machine. Indeed, the use of hinge loss in the Gaussian RBF network can be viewed as a generalization of the support-vector machine. The hinge loss is a shifted version of the perceptron criterion:

$$L = \max\{1 - y_i(\overline{W} \cdot \overline{H_i}), 0\} \tag{5.11}$$

Because of the similarity in loss functions between the hinge loss and the perceptron criterion, the updates are also very similar. The main difference is that S^+ includes only misclassified points in the case of the perceptron criterion, whereas S^+ includes both misclassified points and marginally classified points in the case of hinge loss. This is because S^+ is defined by the set of points for which the loss function is non-zero, but (unlike the perceptron criterion) the hinge loss function is non-zero even for marginally classified points. Therefore, with this modified definition of S^+, the following updates are used:

$$\overline{W} \Leftarrow \overline{W}(1 - \alpha\lambda) + \alpha \sum_{(\overline{H_i}, y_i) \in S^+} y_i \overline{H_i} \tag{5.12}$$

Here, $\alpha > 0$ is the learning rate, and $\lambda > 0$ is the regularization parameter. Note that one can easily define similar updates for the logistic loss function (cf. Exercise 2).

5.3.3 Example of Linear Separability Promoted by RBF

The main goal of the hidden layer is to perform a transformation that promotes linear separability, so that even linear classifiers work well on the transformed data. Both the perceptron and the linear support vector machine with hinge loss are known to perform poorly when the classes are not linearly separable. The Gaussian RBF classifier is able to separate out classes that are not linearly separable in the input space when loss functions such as the perceptron criterion and hinge loss are used. The key to this separability is the local transformation created by the hidden layer. An important point is that a Gaussian kernel with a small bandwidth often results in a situation where only a small number of hidden units in particular local regions get activated to significant non-zero values, whereas the other values are almost zeros. This is because of the exponentially decaying nature of the Gaussian function, which takes on near-zero values outside a particular locality. The identification of prototypes with cluster centers often divides the space into local regions, in which significant non-zero activation is achieved only in small portions of the space. As a practical matter, each local region of the space is assigned its own feature, corresponding to the hidden unit that is activated most strongly by it.

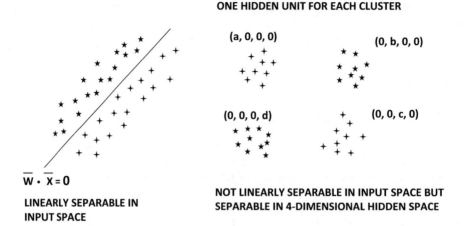

Figure 5.2: Revisiting Figure 1.4: The Gaussian RBF promotes separability because of the transformation to the hidden layer.

Examples of two data sets are illustrated in Figure 5.2. These data sets were introduced in Chapter 1 to illustrate cases that the (traditional) perceptron can or cannot solve. The traditional perceptron of Chapter 1 is able to find a solution for the data set on the left, but does not work well for the data set on the right. However, the transformation used by the Gaussian RBF method is able to address this issue of separability for the clustered data set on the right. Consider a case in which each of the centroids of the four clusters in Figure 5.2 is used as a prototype. This will result in a 4-dimensional hidden representation of the data. Note that the hidden dimensionality is higher than the input dimensionality, which is common in these settings. With appropriate choice of bandwidth, only one hidden unit will be activated strongly corresponding to the cluster identifier to which the point belongs. The other hidden units will be activated quite weakly, and will be close to 0. This will result in a rather sparse representation, as shown in Figure 5.2. We have shown the approximate 4-dimensional representations for the points in each cluster. The values of a, b, c, and d in Figure 5.2 will vary over the different points in the corresponding cluster, although they will always be strongly non-zero compared to the other coordinates. Note that one of the classes is defined by strongly non-zero values in the first and third dimensions, whereas the second class is defined by strongly non-zero values in the second and fourth dimensions. As a result, the weight vector $\overline{W} = [1, -1, 1, -1]$ will provide excellent non-linear separation between the two classes. The key point to understand is that the Gaussian RBF creates *local* features that result in separable distributions of the classes. This is exactly how a kernel support-vector machine achieves linear separability.

5.3.4   Application to Interpolation

One of the earliest applications of the Gaussian RBF was its use in interpolation of the value of a function over a set of points. The goal here is to perform *exact* interpolation of the provided points, so that the resulting function passes through all the input points. One can view interpolation as a special case of regression in which each training point is a prototype, and therefore the number of weights m in $\overline{W}$ is exactly equal to the number of training examples n. In such cases, it is possible to find a n-dimensional weight vector

$\overline{W}$ with zero error. In such a case, the activations $\overline{H_1} \ldots \overline{H_n}$ represent n-dimensional row vectors. Therefore, the matrix H obtained by stacking these row vectors on top of each other has a size of $n \times n$. Let $\overline{y} = [y_1, y_2, \ldots y_n]^T$ be the n-dimensional column vector of observed variables.

In linear regression, one attempts to minimize the loss function $||H\overline{W}^T - \overline{y}||^2$ in order to determine $\overline{W}$. This is because the matrix H is not square, and the system of equations $H\overline{W}^T = \overline{y}$ is over-complete. However, in the case of linear interpolation, the matrix H is square, and the system of equations is no longer over-complete. Therefore, it is possible to find an exact solution (with zero loss) satisfying the following system of equations:

$$H\overline{W}^T = \overline{y} \tag{5.13}$$

It can be shown that this system of equations has a unique solution when the training points are distinct from one another [323]. The value of the weight vector $\overline{W}^T$ can then be computed as follows:

$$\overline{W}^T = H^{-1}\overline{y} \tag{5.14}$$

It is noteworthy that this equation is a special case of Equation 5.6 because the pseudo-inverse of a square and non-singular matrix is the same as its inverse. In the case where the matrix H is non-singular, one can simplify the pseudo-inverse as follows:

$$H^+ = (H^T H)^{-1} H^T$$
$$= H^{-1} \underbrace{(H^T)^{-1} H^T}_{I}$$
$$= H^{-1}$$

Therefore, the case of linear interpolation is a special case of least-squares regression. Stated in another way, least-squares regression is a form of noisy interpolation, where it is impossible to fit the function through all the training points because of the limited degrees of freedom in the hidden layer. Relaxing the size of the hidden layer to the training data size allows exact interpolation. Exact interpolation is not necessarily better for computing the function value of out-of-sample points, because it might be the result of overfitting.

5.4 Relationship with Kernel Methods

The RBF network gains its power by mapping the input points into a high-dimensional hidden space in which linear models are sufficient to model nonlinearities. This is the same principle used by kernel methods like kernel regression and kernel SVMs. In fact, it can be shown that certain special cases of the RBF network reduce to kernel regression and kernel SVMs.

5.4.1 Kernel Regression as a Special Case of RBF Networks

The weight vector $\overline{W}$ in RBF networks is trained to minimize the squared loss of the following prediction function:

$$\hat{y}_i = \overline{H_i}\,\overline{W}^T = \sum_{j=1}^{m} w_j \Phi_j(\overline{X_i}) \tag{5.15}$$

Now consider the case in which the prototypes are the same as the training points, and therefore we set $\overline{\mu}_j = \overline{X}_j$ for each $j \in \{1 \ldots n\}$. Note that this approach is the same as that used in function interpolation, in which the prototypes are set to all the training points. Furthermore, each bandwidth σ is set to the same value. In such a case, one can write the above prediction function as follows:

$$\hat{y}_i = \sum_{j=1}^{n} w_j \exp\left(-\frac{||\overline{X}_i - \overline{X}_j||^2}{2\sigma^2}\right) \tag{5.16}$$

The exponentiated term on the right-hand side of Equation 5.16 can be written as the Gaussian kernel similarity between points $\overline{X}_i$ and $\overline{X}_j$. This similarity is denoted by $K(\overline{X}_i, \overline{X}_j)$. Therefore, the prediction function becomes the following:

$$\hat{y}_i = \sum_{j=1}^{n} w_j K(\overline{X}_i, \overline{X}_j) \tag{5.17}$$

This prediction function is exactly the same as that used in kernel regression with bandwidth σ, where the prediction function $\hat{y}_i^{kernel}$ is defined[1] in terms of the *Lagrange multipliers* λ_j instead of weight w_j (see, for example, [6]):

$$\hat{y}_i^{kernel} = \sum_{j=1}^{n} \lambda_j y_j K(\overline{X}_i, \overline{X}_j) \tag{5.18}$$

Furthermore, the (squared) loss function is the same in the two cases. Therefore, a one-to-one correspondence will exist between the Gaussian RBF solutions and the kernel regression solutions, so that setting $w_j = \lambda_j y_j$ leads to the same value of the loss function. Therefore, their optimal values will be the same as well. In other words, the Gaussian RBF network provides the same results as kernel regression in the special case where the prototype vectors are set to the training points. However, the RBF network is more powerful and general because it can choose different prototype vectors; therefore, the RBF network can model cases that are not possible with kernel regression. In this sense, it is helpful to view the RBF network as a flexible neural variant of kernel methods.

5.4.2   Kernel SVM as a Special Case of RBF Networks

Like kernel regression, the kernel support vector machine (SVM) is also a special case of RBF networks. As in the case of kernel regression, the prototype vectors are set to the training points, and the bandwidths of all hidden units are set to the same value of σ. Furthermore, the weights w_j are learned in order to minimize the hinge loss of the prediction.

In such a case, it can be shown that the prediction function of the RBF network is as follows:

$$\hat{y}_i = \text{sign}\left\{\sum_{j=1}^{n} w_j \exp\left(-\frac{||\overline{X}_i - \overline{X}_j||^2}{2\sigma^2}\right)\right\} \tag{5.19}$$

$$\hat{y}_i = \text{sign}\left\{\sum_{j=1}^{n} w_j K(\overline{X}_i, \overline{X}_j)\right\} \tag{5.20}$$

---

[1] A full explanation of the kernel regression prediction of Equation 5.18 is beyond the scope of this book. Readers are referred to [6].

It is instructive to compare this prediction function with that used in kernel SVMs (see, for example, [6]) with the Lagrange multipliers λ_j:

$$\hat{y}_i^{kernel} = \text{sign} \left\{ \sum_{j=1}^{n} \lambda_j y_j K(\overline{X_i}, \overline{X_j}) \right\} \tag{5.21}$$

This prediction function is of a similar form as that used in kernel SVMs, with the exception of a slight difference in the variables used. The hinge-loss is used as the objective function in both cases. By setting $w_j = \lambda_j y_j$ one obtains the same result in both cases in terms of the value of the loss function. Therefore, the optimal solutions in the kernel SVM and the RBF network will also be related according to the condition $w_j = \lambda_j y_j$. In other words, the kernel SVM is also a special case of RBF networks. Note that the weight w_j can also be considered the coefficient of each data point, when the *representer theorem* is used in kernel methods [6].

5.4.3 Observations

One can extend the arguments above to other linear models, such as the kernel Fisher discriminant and kernel logistic regression, by changing the loss function. In fact, the kernel Fisher discriminant can be obtained by simply using the binary variables as the targets and then applying kernel regression technique. However, since the Fisher discriminant works under the assumption of centered data, a bias needs to be added to the output layer to absorb any offsets from uncentered data. Therefore, the RBF network can simulate virtually any kernel method by choosing an appropriate loss function. A key point is that the RBF network provides more flexibility than kernel regression or classification. For example, one has much more flexibility in choosing the number of nodes in the hidden layer, as well as the number of prototypes. Choosing the prototypes wisely in a more economical way helps in both accuracy and efficiency. There are a number of key trade-offs associated with these choices:

1. Increasing the number of hidden units increases the complexity of the modeled function. It can be useful for modeling difficult functions, but it can cause overfitting, if the modeled function is not truly complex.

2. Increasing the number of hidden units increases the complexity of training.

One way of choosing the number of hidden units is to hold out a portion of the data, and estimate the accuracy of the model on the held-out set with different numbers of hidden units. The number of hidden units is then set to a value that optimizes this accuracy.

5.5 Summary

This chapter introduces radial basis function (RBF) networks, which represent a fundamentally different way of using the neural network architecture. Unlike feed-forward networks, the hidden layer and output layer are trained in a somewhat different way. The training of the hidden layer is unsupervised, whereas that of the output layer is supervised. The hidden layer usually has a larger number of nodes than the input layer. The key idea is to transform the data points into high-dimensional space with the use of locality-sensitive transformations, so that the transformed points become linearly separable. The approach can be used for classification, regression, and linear interpolation by changing the nature of the loss function. In classification, one can use different types of loss functions such as the Widrow-Hoff loss, the hinge loss, and the logistic loss. Special cases of different loss functions specialize to well-known kernel methods such as kernel SVMs and kernel regression. The RBF network has rarely been used in recent years, and it has become a forgotten category of neural architectures. However, it has significant potential to be used in any scenario where kernel methods are used. Furthermore, it is possible to combine this approach with feed-forward architectures by using multi-layered representations following the first hidden layer.

5.6   Bibliographic Notes

RBF networks were proposed by Broomhead and Lowe [51] in the context of function interpolation. The separability of high-dimensional transformations is shown in Cover's work [84]. A review of RBF networks may be found in [363]. The books by Bishop [41] and Haykin [182] also provide good treatments of the topic. An overview of radial basis functions is provided in [57]. The proof of universal function approximation with RBF networks is provided in [173, 365]. An analysis of the approximation properties of RBF networks is provided in [366].

Efficient training algorithms for RBF networks are described in [347, 423]. An algorithm for learning the center locations in RBF networks is proposed in [530]. The use of decision trees to initialize RBF networks is discussed in [256]. The orthogonal least-squares algorithm was proposed in [65]. Early comparisons of supervised and unsupervised training of RBF networks are provided in [342]. According to this analysis, full supervision seems to increase the likelihood of the network getting trapped in local minima. Some ideas on improving the generalization power of RBF networks are provided in [43]. Incremental RBF networks are discussed in [125]. A detailed discussion of the relationship between RBF networks and kernel methods is provided in [430].

5.7   Exercises

Some exercises require additional knowledge about machine learning that is not discussed in this book. Exercises 5, 7, and 8 require additional knowledge of kernel methods, spectral clustering, and outlier detection.

1. Consider the following variant of radial basis function networks in which the hidden units take on either 0 or 1 values. The hidden unit takes on the value of 1, if the distance to a prototype vector is less than σ. Otherwise it takes on the value of 0. Discuss the relationship of this method to RBF networks, and its relative advantages/disadvantages.

2. Suppose that you use the sigmoid activation in the final layer to predict a binary class label as a probability in the output node of an RBF network. Set up a negative log-likelihood loss for this setting. Derive the gradient-descent updates for the weights in the final layer. How does this approach relate to the logistic regression methods discussed in Chapter 2? In which case will this approach perform better than logistic regression?

3. Discuss why an RBF network is a supervised variant of a nearest-neighbor classifier.

4. Discuss how you can extend the three multi-class models discussed in Chapter 2 to RBF networks. In particular discuss the extension of the (a) multi-class perceptron, (b) Weston-Watkins SVM, and (c) softmax classifier with RBF networks. Discuss how these models are more powerful than the ones discussed in Chapter 2.

5. Propose a method to extend RBF networks to unsupervised learning with autoencoders. What will you reconstruct in the output layer? A special case of your approach should be able to roughly simulate kernel singular value decomposition.

6. Suppose that you change your RBF network so that you keep only the top-k activations in the hidden layer, and set the remaining activations to 0. Discuss why such an approach will provide improved classification accuracy with limited data.

7. Combine the top-k method of constructing the RBF layer in Exercise 6 with the RBF autoencoder in Exercise 5 for unsupervised learning. Discuss why this approach will create representations that are better suited to clustering. Discuss the relationship of this method with spectral clustering.

8. The manifold view of outliers is to define them as points that do not naturally fit into the nonlinear manifolds of the training data. Discuss how you can use RBF networks for unsupervised outlier detection.

9. Suppose that instead of using the RBF function in the hidden layer, you use dot products between prototypes and data points for activation. Show that a special case of this setting reduces to a linear perceptron.

10. Discuss how you can modify the RBF autoencoder in Exercise 5 to perform semi-supervised classification, when you have a lot of unlabeled data, and a limited amount of labeled data.

Chapter 6

Restricted Boltzmann Machines

"Available energy is the main object at stake in the struggle for existence and the evolution of the world."—Ludwig Boltzmann

6.1   Introduction

The restricted Boltzmann machine (RBM) is a fundamentally different model from the feed-forward network. Conventional neural networks are input-output mapping networks where a set of inputs is mapped to a set of outputs. On the other hand, RBMs are networks in which the probabilistic states of a network are learned for a set of inputs, which is useful for *unsupervised* modeling. While a feed-forward network minimizes a loss function of a prediction (computed from *observed* inputs) with respect to an *observed* output, a restricted Boltzmann machine models the joint probability distribution of the observed attributes together with some hidden attributes. Whereas traditional feed-forward networks have *directed* edges corresponding to the flow of computation from input to output, RBMs are *undirected* networks because they are designed to learn probabilistic *relationships* rather than input-output mappings. Restricted Boltzmann machines are probabilistic models that create latent representations of the underlying data points. Although an autoencoder can also be used to construct latent representations, a Boltzmann machine creates a *stochastic* hidden representation of each point. Most autoencoders (except for the variational autoencoder) create *deterministic* hidden representations of the data points. As a result, the RBM requires a fundamentally different way of training and using it.

C. C. Aggarwal, *Neural Networks and Deep Learning*,
https://doi.org/10.1007/978-3-319-94463-0_6

At their core, RBMs are unsupervised models that generate latent feature representations of the data points; however, the learned representations can be combined with traditional backpropagation in a closely related feed-forward network (to the specific RBM at hand) for supervised applications. This type of combination of unsupervised and supervised learning is similar to the pretraining that is performed with a traditional autoencoder architecture (cf. Section 4.7 of Chapter 4). In fact, RBMs are credited for the popularization of pretraining in the early years. The idea was soon adapted to autoencoders, which are simpler to train because of their deterministic hidden states.

6.1.1   Historical Perspective

Restricted Boltzmann machines have evolved from a classical model in the neural networks literature, which is referred to as the *Hopfield network*. This network contains nodes containing binary states, which represent binary attribute values in the training data. The Hopfield network creates a *deterministic* model of the relationships among the different attributes by using weighted edges between nodes. Eventually, the Hopfield network evolved into the notion of a Boltzmann machine, which uses *probabilistic* states to represent the Bernoulli distributions of the binary attributes. The Boltzmann machine contains both visible states and hidden states. The visible states model the distributions of the observed data points, whereas the hidden states model the distribution of the latent (hidden) variables. The parameters of the connections among the various states regulate their joint distribution. The goal is to learn the model parameters so that the likelihood of the model is maximized. The Boltzmann machine is a member of the family of (undirected) probabilistic graphical models. Eventually, the Boltzmann machine evolved into the *restricted* Boltzmann Machine (RBM). The main difference between the Boltzmann machine and the restricted Boltzmann machine is that the latter only allows connections between hidden units and visible units. This simplification is very useful from a practical point of view, because it allows the design of more efficient training algorithms. The RBM is a special case of the class of probabilistic graphical models known as *Markov random fields*.

In the initial years, RBMs were considered too slow to train and were therefore not very popular. However, at the turn of the century, faster algorithms were proposed for this class of models. Furthermore, they received some prominence as one of the ensemble components of the entry [414] winning the Netflix prize contest [577]. RBMs are generally used for unsupervised applications like matrix factorization, latent modeling, and dimensionality reduction, although there are many ways of extending them to the supervised case. It is noteworthy that RBMs usually work with binary states in their most natural form, although it is possible to work with other data types. Most of the discussion in this chapter will be restricted to units with binary states. The successful training of deep networks with RBMs preceded successful training experiences with conventional neural networks. In other words, it was shown how multiple RBMs could be stacked to create deep networks and train them effectively, before similar ideas were generalized to conventional networks.

Chapter Organization

This chapter is organized as follows. The next section will introduce Hopfield networks, which was the precursor to the Boltzmann family of models. The Boltzmann machine is introduced in Section 6.3. Restricted Boltzmann machines are introduced in Section 6.4. Applications of restricted Boltzmann machines are discussed in Section 6.5. The use of RBMs for generalized data types beyond binary representations is discussed in Section 6.6.

The process of stacking multiple restricted Boltzmann machines in order to create deep networks is discussed in Section 6.7. A summary is given in Section 6.8.

6.2 Hopfield Networks

Hopfield networks were proposed in 1982 [207] as a model to store memory. A Hopfield network is an undirected network, in which the d units (or neurons) are indexed by values drawn from $\{1 \ldots d\}$. Each connection is of the form (i, j), where each i and j is a neuron drawn from $\{1 \ldots d\}$. Each connection (i, j) is undirected, and is associated with a weight $w_{ij} = w_{ji}$. Although all pairs of nodes are assumed to have connections between them, setting w_{ij} to 0 has the effect of dropping the connection (i, j). The weight w_{ii} is set to 0, and therefore there are no self-loops. Each neuron i is associated with state s_i. An important assumption in the Hopfield network is that each s_i is a binary value drawn from $\{0, 1\}$, although one can use other conventions such as $\{-1, +1\}$. The ith node also has a bias b_i associated with it; large values of b_i encourage the ith state to be 1. The Hopfield network is an undirected model of symmetric relationships between attributes, and therefore the weights always satisfy $w_{ij} = w_{ji}$.

Each binary state in the Hopfield network corresponds to a dimension in the (binary) training data set. Therefore, if a d-dimensional training data set needs to be memorized, we need a Hopfield network with d units. The ith state in the network corresponds to the ith bit in a particular training example. The values of the states represent the binary attribute values from a training example. The weights in the Hopfield network are its parameters; large positive weights between pairs of states are indicative of high degree of positive correlation in state values, whereas large negative weights are indicative of high negative correlation. An example of a Hopfield network with an associated training data set is shown in Figure 6.1. In this case, the Hopfield network is fully connected, and the six visible states correspond to the six binary attributes in the training data.

The Hopfield network uses an optimization model to learn the weight parameters so that the weights can capture that positive and negative relationships among the attributes of the training data set. The objective function of a Hopfield network is also referred to as its *energy function*, which is analogous to the loss function of a traditional feed-forward neural network. The energy function of a Hopfield network is set up in such a way that minimizing this function encourages nodes pairs connected with large positive weights to have similar states, and pairs connected with large negative weights to have different states. The training phase of a Hopfield network, therefore, learns the weights of edges in order to minimize the energy when the states in the Hopfield network are fixed to the binary attribute values in the individual training points. Therefore, learning the weights of the Hopfield network implicitly builds an unsupervised *model* of the training data set. The energy E of a particular combination of states $\overline{s} = (s_1, \ldots s_d)$ of the Hopfield network can be defined as follows:

$$E = -\sum_i b_i s_i - \sum_{i,j:i<j} w_{ij} s_i s_j \tag{6.1}$$

The term $-b_i s_i$ encourages units with large biases to be on. Similarly, the term $-w_{ij} s_i s_j$ encourages s_i and s_j to be similar when $w_{ij} > 0$. In other words, positive weights will cause state "attraction" and negative weights will cause state "repulsion." For a small training data set, this type of modeling results in memorization, which enables one to retrieve training data points from similar, incomplete, or corrupted query points by exploring local minima of the energy function near these query points. In other words, by learning the weights of a Hopfield network, one is implicitly memorizing the training examples, although there is a relatively conservative limit of the number of examples that can be memorized from a Hopfield network containing d units. This limit is also referred to as the *capacity* of the model.

6.2.1   Optimal State Configurations of a Trained Network

A trained Hopfield contains many local optima, each of which corresponds to either a memorized point from the training data, or a representative point in a dense region of the training data. Before discussing the training of the weights of the Hopfield network, we will discuss the methodology for finding the local energy minimum of a Hopfield network when the trained weights are already given. A local minimum is defined as a combination of states in which flipping any particular bit of the network does not reduce the energy further. The training process sets the weights in such a way that the instances in the training data tend to be local minima in the Hopfield network.

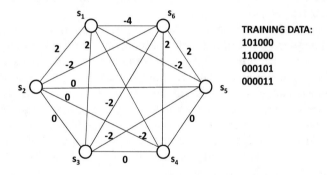

Figure 6.1: A Hopfield network with 6 visible states corresponding to 6-dimensional training data.

Finding the optimal state configuration helps the Hopfield network in recalling memories. The Hopfield network inherently learns *associative memories* because, given an input set of states (i.e., input pattern of bits), it repeatedly flips bits to improve the objective function until it finds a pattern where one cannot improve the objective function further. This local minimum (final combination of states) is often only a few bits away from the starting pattern (initial set of states), and therefore one *recalls* a closely related pattern at which a local minimum is found. Furthermore, this final pattern is often a member of the training data set (because the weights were learned using that data). In a sense, Hopfield networks provide a route towards *content-addressable memory*.

Given a starting combination of states, how can one learn the closest local minimum once the weights have already been fixed? One can use a threshold update rule to update each state in the network in order to move it towards the global energy minimum. In order to understand this point, let us compare the energy of the network between the cases when the state s_i is set to 1, and the one in which s_i is set to 0. Therefore, one can substitute two different values of s_i into Equation 6.1 to obtain the following value of the *energy gap*:

$$\Delta E_i = E_{s_i=0} - E_{s_i=1} = b_i + \sum_{j:j\neq i} w_{ij}s_j \qquad (6.2)$$

This value must be larger than 0 in order for a flip of state s_i from 0 to 1 to be attractive. Therefore, one obtains the following update rule for each state s_i:

$$s_i = \begin{cases} 1 & \text{if } \sum_{j:j\neq i} w_{ij}s_j + b_i \geq 0 \\ 0 & \text{otherwise} \end{cases} \qquad (6.3)$$

The above rule is iteratively used to test each state s_i and then flip the state if needed to satisfy the condition. If one is given the weights and the biases in the network at any particular time, it is possible to find a local energy minimum in terms of the states by repeatedly using the update rule above.

The local minima of a Hopfield network depend on its trained weights. Therefore, in order to "recall" a memory, one only has to provide a d-dimensional vector similar to the stored memory, and the Hopfield network will find the local minimum that is similar to this point by using it as a starting state. This type of associative memory recall is also common in humans, who often retrieve memories through a similar process of association. One can also provide a partial vector of initial states and use it to recover other states. Consider the Hopfield network shown in Figure 6.1. Note that the weights are set in such a way that each of the four training vectors in the figure will have low energy. However, there are some spurious minima such as 111000 as well. Therefore, it is not guaranteed that the local minima will always correspond to the points in the training data. However, the local minima do correspond to some key characteristics of the training data. For example, consider the spurious minimum corresponding to 111000. It is noteworthy that the first three bits are positively correlated, whereas the last three bits are also positively correlated. As a result, this minimum value of 111000 does reflect a broad pattern in the underlying data even though it is not explicitly present in the training data. It is also noteworthy that the weights of this network are closely related to the patterns in the training data. For example, the elements within the first three bits and last three bits are each positively correlated within that particular group of three bits. Furthermore, there are negative correlations *across* the two sets of elements. Consequently, the edges *within* each of the sets $\{s_1, s_2, s_3\}$ and $\{s_4, s_5, s_6\}$ tend to be positive, and those *across* these two sets are negative. Setting the weights in this data-specific way is the task of the training phase (cf. Section 6.2.2).

The iterative state update rule will arrive at one of the many local minima of the Hopfield network, depending on the initial state vector. Each of these local minima can be one of the learned "memories" from the training data set, and the closest memory to the initial state vector will be reached. These memories are implicitly stored in the weights learned during the training phase. However, it is possible for the Hopfield network to make mistakes, where closely related training patterns are merged into a single (deeper) minimum. For example, if the training data contains 1110111101 and 1110111110, the Hopfield network might learn 1110111111 as a local minimum. Therefore, in some queries, one might recover a pattern that is a small number of bits away from a pattern actually present in the training data. However, this is only a form of model generalization in which the Hopfield network is storing representative "cluster" centers instead of individual training points. In other words, the model starts generalizing instead of memorizing when the amount of data exceeds the capacity of the model; after all, Hopfield networks build unsupervised models from training data.

The Hopfield network can be used for recalling associative memories, correcting corrupted data, or for attribute completion. The tasks of recalling associative memories and cleaning corrupted data are similar. In both cases, one uses the corrupted input (or target input for associative recall) as the starting state, and uses the final state as the cleaned output (or recalled output). In attribute completion, the state vector is initialized by setting observed states to their known values and unobserved states randomly. At this point, only the unobserved states are updated to convergence. The bit values of these states at convergence provide the completed representation.

6.2.2   Training a Hopfield Network

For a given training data set, one needs to learn the weights, so that the local minima of this network lie near instances (or dense regions) of the training data set. Hopfield networks are trained with the *Hebbian learning rule*. According to the biological motivation of Hebbian learning, a synapse between two neurons is strengthened when the neurons on either side of the synapse have highly correlated outputs. Let $x_{ij} \in \{0, 1\}$ represent the jth bit of the ith training point. The number of training instances is assumed to be n. The Hebbian learning rule sets the weights of the network as follows:

$$w_{ij} = 4 \frac{\sum_{k=1}^{n} (x_{ki} - 0.5) \cdot (x_{kj} - 0.5)}{n} \tag{6.4}$$

One way of understanding this rule is that if two bits, i and j, in the training data are positively correlated, then the value $(x_{ki} - 0.5) \cdot (x_{kj} - 0.5)$ will usually be positive. As a result, the weights between the corresponding units will also be set to positive values. On the other hand, if two bits generally disagree, then the weights will be set to negative values. One can also use this rule without normalizing the denominator:

$$w_{ij} = 4 \sum_{k=1}^{n} (x_{ki} - 0.5) \cdot (x_{kj} - 0.5) \tag{6.5}$$

In practice, one often wants to develop incremental learning algorithms for point-specific updates. One can update w_{ij} with only the kth training data point as follows:

$$w_{ij} \Leftarrow w_{ij} + 4(x_{ki} - 0.5) \cdot (x_{kj} - 0.5) \quad \forall i, j$$

The bias b_i can be updated by assuming that a single dummy state is always on, and the bias represents the weight between the dummy and the ith state:

$$b_i \Leftarrow b_i + 2(x_{ki} - 0.5) \quad \forall i$$

In cases where the convention is to draw the state vectors from $\{-1, +1\}$, the above rule simplifies to the following:

$$w_{ij} \Leftarrow w_{ij} + x_{ki} x_{kj} \quad \forall i, j$$
$$b_i \Leftarrow b_i + x_{ki} \quad \forall i$$

There are other learning rules, such as the *Storkey learning rule*, that are commonly used. Refer to the bibliographic notes.

Capacity of a Hopfield Network

What is the size of the training data that a Hopfield network with d visible units can store without causing errors in associative recall? It can be shown that the *storage capacity* of a Hopfield network with d units is only about $0.15 \cdot d$ training examples. Since each training example contains d bits, it follows that the Hopfield network can store only about $0.15\,d^2$ bits. This is not an efficient form of storage because the number of weights in the network is given by $d(d-1)/2 = O(d^2)$. Furthermore, the weights are not binary and they can be shown to require $O(\log(d))$ bits. When the number of training examples is large, many errors will be made (in associative recall). These errors represent the *generalized* predictions from more data. Although it might seem that this type of generalization is useful for machine learning, there are limitations in using Hopfield networks for such applications.

6.2.3 Building a Toy Recommender and Its Limitations

Hopfield networks are often used for memorization-centric applications rather than the typical machine-learning applications requiring generalization. In order to understand the limits of a Hopfield network, we will consider an application associated with binary collaborative filtering. Since Hopfield networks work with binary data, we will assume the case of *implicit feedback* data in which user is associated with a set of binary attributes corresponding to whether or not they have watched the corresponding movies. Consider a situation in which the user Bob has watched movies *Shrek* and *Aladdin*, whereas the user Alice has watched *Gandhi*, *Nero*, and *Terminator*. It is easy to construct a fully connected Hopfield network on the universe of all movies and set the watched states to 1 and all other states to 0. This configuration can be used for each training point in order to update the weights. Of course, this approach can be extremely expensive if the base number of states (movies) is very large. For a database containing 10^6 movies, we would have 10^{12} edges, most of which will connect states containing zero values. This is because such type of implicit feedback data is often sparse, and most states will take on zero values.

One way of addressing this problem is to use *negative sampling*. In this approach, each user has their own Hopfield network containing their watched movies and a small sample of the movies that were not watched by them. For example, one might randomly sample 20 unwatched movies (of Alice) and create a Hopfield network containing $20 + 3 = 23$ states (including the watched movies). Bob's Hopfield network will containing $20 + 2 = 22$ states, and the unwatched samples might also be quite different. However, for pairs of movies that are common between the two networks, the weights will be shared. During training, all edge weights are initialized to 0. One can use repeated iterations of training over the different Hopfield networks to learn their shared weights (with the same algorithm discussed earlier). The main difference is that iterating over the different training points will lead to iterating over different Hopfield networks, each of which contains a small subset of the base network. Typically, only a small subset of the 10^{12} edges will be present in each of these networks, and most edges will never be encountered in any network. Such edges will implicitly be assumed to have weights of zero.

Now imagine a user Mary, who has watched *E.T.* and *Shrek*. We would like to recommend movies to this user. We use the full Hopfield network with only the non-zero edges present. We initialize the states for *E.T.* and *Shrek* to 1, and all other states to 0. Subsequently, we allow the updates of all states (other than *E.T.* and *Shrek*) in order to identify the minimum energy configuration of the Hopfield network. All states that are set to 1 during the updates can be recommended to the user. However, we would ideally like to have an *ordering* of the top recommended movies. One way of providing an ordering of all movies is to use the *energy gap* between the two states of each movie in order to rank the movies. The energy gap is computed only after the minimum energy configuration has been found. This approach is, however, quite naive because the final configuration of the Hopfield network is a deterministic one containing binary values, whereas the extrapolated values can only be estimated in terms of *probabilities*. For example, it would be much more natural to use some function of the energy gap (e.g., sigmoid) in order to create probabilistic estimations. Furthermore, it would be helpful to be able to capture correlated sets of movies with some notion of latent (or hidden) states. Clearly, we need techniques in order to increase the expressive power of the Hopfield network.

6.2.4   Increasing the Expressive Power of the Hopfield Network

Although it is not standard practice, one can add *hidden units* to a Hopfield network to increase its expressive power. The hidden states serve the purpose of capturing the latent structure of the data. The weights of connections between hidden and visible units will capture the relationship between the latent structure and the training data. In some cases, it is possible to approximately represent the data only in terms of a small number of hidden states. For example, if the data contains two tightly knit clusters, one can capture this setting in two hidden states. Consider the case in which we enhance the Hopfield network of Figure 6.1 and add two hidden units. The resulting network is shown in Figure 6.2. The edges with near-zero weights have been dropped from the figure for clarity. Even though the original data is defined in terms of six bits, the two hidden units provide a *hidden* representation of the data in terms of two bits. This hidden representation is a compressed version of the data, which tells us something about the pattern at hand. In essence, all patterns are compressed to the pattern 10 or 01, depending on whether the first three bits or the last three bits dominate the training pattern. If one fixes the hidden states of the Hopfield network to 10 and randomly initializes the visible states, then one would often obtain the pattern 111000 on repeatedly using the state-wise update rule of Equation 6.3. One also obtains the pattern 0001111 as the final resting point when one starts with the hidden state 01. Notably, the patterns 000111 and 111000 are close approximations of the two types of patterns in the data, which is what one would expect from a compression technique. If we provide an incomplete version of the visible units, and then iteratively update the other states with the update rule of Equation 6.3, one would often arrive at either 000111 and 111000 depending on how the bits in the incomplete representation are distributed. If we add hidden units to a Hopfield network *and* allow the states to be probabilistic (rather than deterministic), we obtain a Boltzmann machine. This is the reason that Boltzmann machines can be viewed as *stochastic Hopfield networks with hidden units*.

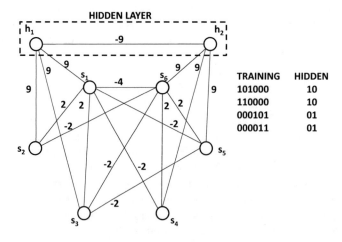

Figure 6.2: The Hopfield network with two hidden nodes

6.3 The Boltzmann Machine

Throughout this section, we assume that the Boltzmann machine contains a total of $q = (m+d)$ states, where d is the number of visible states and m is the number of hidden states. A particular state configuration is defined by the value of the state vector $\overline{s} = (s_1 \ldots s_q)$. If one explicitly wants to demarcate the visible and hidden states in $\overline{s}$, then the state vector $\overline{s}$ can be written as the pair $(\overline{v}, \overline{h})$, where $\overline{v}$ denotes the set of visible units and $\overline{h}$ denotes the set of hidden units. The states in $(\overline{v}, \overline{h})$ represent exactly the same set as $\overline{s} = \{s_1 \ldots s_q\}$, except that the visible and hidden units are explicitly demarcated in the former.

The Boltzmann machine is a probabilistic generalization of a Hopfield network. A Hopfield network *deterministically* sets each state s_i to either 1 or 0, depending on whether the energy gap ΔE_i of the state s_i is positive or negative. Recall that the energy gap of the ith unit is defined as the difference in energy between its two configurations (with other states being fixed to pre-defined values):

$$\Delta E_i = E_{s_i=0} - E_{s_i=1} = b_i + \sum_{j:j\neq i} w_{ij}s_j \tag{6.6}$$

The Hopfield network deterministically sets the value of s_i to 1, when the energy gap is positive. On the other hand, a Boltzmann machine assigns a *probability* to s_i depending on the energy gap. Positive energy gaps are assigned probabilities that are larger than 0.5. The probability of state s_i is defined by applying the sigmoid function to the energy gap:

$$P(s_i = 1|s_1, \ldots s_{i-1}, s_{i+1}, s_q) = \frac{1}{1 + \exp(-\Delta E_i)} \tag{6.7}$$

Note that the state s_i is now a Bernoulli random variable and a zero energy gap leads to a probability of 0.5 for each binary outcome of the state.

For a particular set of parameters w_{ij} and b_i, the Boltzmann machine defines a probability distribution over various state configurations. The energy of a particular configuration $\overline{s} = (\overline{v}, \overline{h})$ is denoted by $E(\overline{s}) = E([\overline{v}, \overline{h}])$, and is defined in a similar way to the Hopfield network as follows:

$$E(\overline{s}) = -\sum_i b_i s_i - \sum_{i,j:i<j} w_{ij}s_is_j \tag{6.8}$$

However, these configurations are only probabilistically known in the case of the Boltzmann machine (according to Equation 6.7). The conditional distribution of Equation 6.7 follows from a more fundamental definition of the unconditional probability $P(\overline{s})$ of a particular configuration $\overline{s}$:

$$P(\overline{s}) \propto \exp(-E(\overline{s})) = \frac{1}{Z}\exp(-E(\overline{s})) \tag{6.9}$$

The normalization factor Z is defined so that the probabilities over all possible configurations sum to 1:

$$Z = \sum_{\overline{s}} \exp(-E(\overline{s})) \tag{6.10}$$

The normalization factor Z is also referred to as the *partition function*. In general, the explicit computation of the partition function is hard, because it contains an exponential number of terms corresponding to all possible configurations of states. Because of the intractability of the partition function, exact computation of $P(\overline{s}) = P(\overline{v}, \overline{h})$ is not possible. Nevertheless, the computation of many types of conditional probabilities (e.g., $P(\overline{v}|\overline{h})$) is possible, because such conditional probabilities are ratios and the intractable normalization factor gets canceled out from the computation. For example, the conditional probability of Equation 6.7 follows from the more fundamental definition of the probability of a configuration (cf. Equation 6.9) as follows:

$$P(s_i = 1|s_1, \ldots s_{i-1}, s_{i+1}, s_q) = \frac{P(s_1, \ldots s_{i-1}, \overbrace{1}^{s_i}, s_{i+1}, s_q)}{P(s_1, \ldots s_{i-1}, \underbrace{1}_{s_i}, s_{i+1}, s_q) + P(s_1, \ldots s_{i-1}, \underbrace{0}_{s_i}, s_{i+1}, s_q)}$$

$$= \frac{\exp(-E_{s_i=1})}{\exp(-E_{s_i=1}) + \exp(-E_{s_i=0})} = \frac{1}{1 + \exp(E_{s_i=1} - E_{s_i=0})}$$

$$= \frac{1}{1 + \exp(-\Delta E_i)} = \text{Sigmoid}(\Delta E_i)$$

This is the same condition as Equation 6.9. One can also see that the logistic sigmoid function finds its roots in notions of energy from statistical physics.

One way of thinking about the benefit of setting these states probabilistically is that we can now sample from these states to create new data points that look like the original data. This makes Boltzmann machines probabilistic models rather than deterministic ones. Many generative models in machine learning (e.g., Gaussian mixture models for clustering) use a sequential process of first sampling the hidden state(s) from a prior, and then generating visible observations conditionally on the hidden state(s). This is not the case in the Boltzmann machine, in which the dependence between all pairs of states is *undirected*; the visible states depend as much on the hidden states as the hidden states depend on visible states. As a result, the generation of data with a Boltzmann machine can be more challenging than in many other generative models.

6.3.1   How a Boltzmann Machine Generates Data

In a Boltzmann machine, the dynamics of the data generation is complicated by the circular dependencies among the states based on Equation 6.7. Therefore, we need an iterative process to generate sample data points from the Boltzmann machine so that Equation 6.7 is satisfied for all states. A Boltzmann machine iteratively samples the states using a conditional distribution generated from the state values in the previous iteration until *thermal equilibrium* is reached. The notion of thermal equilibrium means that we start at a random set of states, use Equation 6.7 to compute their conditional probabilities, and then sample the values of the states again using these probabilities. Note that we can iteratively generate s_i by using $P(s_i|s_1 \ldots s_{i-1}, s_{i+1}, \ldots s_q)$ in Equation 6.7. After running this process for a long time, the sampled values of the visible states provide us with random samples of generated data points. The time required to reach thermal equilibrium is referred to as the *burn-in time* of the procedure. This approach is referred to as *Gibbs sampling* or *Markov Chain Monte Carlo (MCMC) sampling*.

At thermal equilibrium, the generated points will represent the model captured by the Boltzmann machine. Note that the dimensions in the generated data points will be correlated with one another depending on the weights between various states. States with large weights between them will tend to be heavily correlated. For example, in a text-mining application in which the states correspond to the presence of words, there will be correlations among words belonging to a topic. Therefore, if a Boltzmann machine has been trained properly on a text data set, it will generate vectors containing these types of word correlations at thermal equilibrium, even when the states are randomly initialized. It is noticeable that even generating a set of data points with the Boltzmann machine is a more complicated process compared to many other probabilistic models. For example, generating data points from a Gaussian mixture model only requires to sample points directly from the probability distribution of a sampled mixture component. On the other hand, the undirected nature of the Boltzmann machine forces us to run the process to thermal equilibrium just to generate samples. It is, therefore, an even more difficult to task to learn the weights between states for a given training data set.

6.3.2 Learning the Weights of a Boltzmann Machine

In a Boltzmann machine, we want to learn the weights in such a way so as to maximize the log-likelihood of the specific training data set at hand. The log-likelihoods of individual states are computed by using the logarithm of the probabilities in Equation 6.9. Therefore, by taking the logarithm of Equation 6.9, we obtain the following:

$$\log[P(\overline{s})] = -E(\overline{s}) - \log(Z) \tag{6.11}$$

Therefore, computing $\frac{\partial \log[P(\overline{s})]}{\partial w_{ij}}$ requires the computation of the negative derivative of the energy, although we have an additional term involving the partition function. The energy function of Equation 6.8 is linear in the weight w_{ij} with coefficient of $-s_i s_j$. Therefore, the partial derivative of the energy with respect to the weight w_{ij} is $-s_i s_j$. As a result, one can show the following:

$$\frac{\partial \log[P(\overline{s})]}{\partial w_{ij}} = \langle s_i, s_j \rangle_{data} - \langle s_i, s_j \rangle_{model} \tag{6.12}$$

Here, $\langle s_i, s_j \rangle_{data}$ represents the averaged value of $s_i s_j$ obtained by running the generative process of Section 6.3.1, when the visible states are clamped to attribute values in a training point. The averaging is done over a mini-batch of training points. Similarly, $\langle s_i, s_j \rangle_{model}$ represents the averaged value of $s_i s_j$ at thermal equilibrium without fixing visible states to training points and simply running the generative process of Section 6.3.1. In this case, the averaging is done over multiple instances of running the process to thermal equilibrium. Intuitively, we want to strengthen the weights of edges between states, which tend to be *differentially* turned on together (compared to the unrestricted model), when the visible states are fixed to the training data points. This is precisely what is achieved by the update above, which uses the data- and model-centric difference in the value of $\langle s_i, s_j \rangle$. From the above discussion, it is clear that two types of samples need to be generated in order to perform the updates:

1. **Data-centric samples:** The first type of sample fixes the visible states to a randomly chosen vector from the training data set. The hidden states are initialized to random values drawn from Bernoulli distribution with probability 0.5. Then the probability of each hidden state is recomputed according to Equation 6.7. Samples of the hidden states are regenerated from these probabilities. This process is repeated for a while, so that thermal equilibrium is reached. The values of the hidden variables at this point provide the required samples. Note that the visible states are clamped to the corresponding attributes of the relevant training data vector, and therefore they do not need to be sampled.

2. **Model samples:** The second type of sample does not put any constraints on states, and one simply wants samples from the unrestricted model. The approach is the same as discussed above, except that both the visible and hidden states are initialized to random values, and updates are continuously performed until thermal equilibrium is reached.

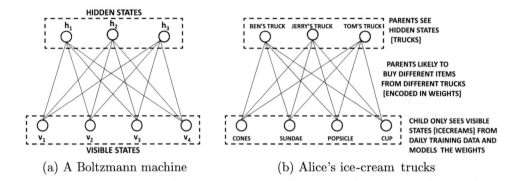

(a) A Boltzmann machine   (b) Alice's ice-cream trucks

Figure 6.3: A Restricted Boltzmann machine. Note the *restriction* of there being no interactions among either visible or hidden units.

These samples help us create an update rule for the weights. From the first type of sample, one can compute $\langle s_i, s_j \rangle_{data}$, which represents the correlations between the states of nodes i and j, when the visible vectors are fixed to a vector in the training data $\mathcal{D}$ and the hidden states are allowed to vary. Since a mini-batch of training vectors is used, one obtains multiple samples of the state vectors. The value of $\langle s_i, s_j \rangle$ is computed as the average product over all such state vectors that are obtained from Gibbs sampling. Similarly, one can estimate the value of $\langle s_i, s_j \rangle_{model}$ using the average product of s_i and s_j from the model-centric samples obtained from Gibbs sampling. Once these values have been computed, the following update is used:

$$w_{ij} \Leftarrow w_{ij} + \alpha \quad \underbrace{(\langle s_i, s_j \rangle_{data} - \langle s_i, s_j \rangle_{model})}_{\text{Partial derivative of log probability}} \tag{6.13}$$

The update rule for the bias is similar, except that the state s_j is set to 1. One can achieve this by using a dummy bias unit that is visible and is connected to all states:

$$b_i \Leftarrow b_i + \alpha \left(\langle s_i, 1 \rangle_{data} - \langle s_i, 1 \rangle_{model} \right) \tag{6.14}$$

Note that the value of $\langle s_i, 1 \rangle$ is simply the average of the sampled values of s_i for a mini-batch of training examples from either the data-centric samples or the model-centric samples.

This approach is similar to the Hebbian update rule of a Hopfield net, except that we are also removing the effect of model-centric correlations in the update. The removal of model-centric correlations is required to account for the effect of the partition function within the expression of the log probability in Equation 6.11. The main problem with the aforementioned update rule is that it is slow in practice. This is because of the Monte Carlo sampling procedure, which requires a large number of samples in order to reach thermal equilibrium. There are faster approximations to this tedious process. In the next section, we will discuss this approach in the context of a simplified version of the Boltzmann machine, which is referred to as the *restricted* Boltzmann machine.

6.4 Restricted Boltzmann Machines

In the Boltzmann machine, the connections among hidden and visible units can be arbitrary. For example, two hidden states might contain edges between them, and so might two visible states. This type of generalized assumption creates unnecessary complexity. A natural special case of the Boltzmann machine is the *restricted* Boltzmann machine (RBM), which is bipartite, and the connections are allowed only between hidden and visible units. An example of a restricted Boltzmann machine is shown in Figure 6.3(a). In this particular example, there are three hidden nodes and four visible nodes. Each hidden state is connected to one or more visible states, although there are no connections between pairs of hidden states, and between pairs of visible states. The restricted Boltzmann machine is also referred to as a *harmonium* [457].

We assume that the hidden units are $h_1 \ldots h_m$ and the visible units are $v_1 \ldots v_d$. The bias associated with the visible node v_i be denoted by $b_i^{(v)}$, and the bias associated with hidden node h_j is denoted by $b_j^{(h)}$. Note the superscripts in order to distinguish between the biases of visible and hidden nodes. The weight of the edge between visible node v_i and hidden node h_j is denoted by w_{ij}. The notations for the weights are also slightly different for the restricted Boltzmann machine (compared to the Boltzmann machine) because the hidden and visible units are indexed separately. For example, we no longer have $w_{ij} = w_{ji}$ because the first index i always belongs to a visible node and the second index j belongs to a hidden node. It is important to keep these notational differences in mind while extrapolating the equations from the previous section.

In order to provide better interpretability, we will use a running example throughout this section, which we refer to as the example of "Alice's ice-cream trucks" based on the Boltzmann machine in Figure 6.3(b). Imagine a situation in which the training data corresponds to four bits representing the ice-creams received by Alice from her parents each day. These represent the visible states in our example. Therefore, Alice can collect 4-dimensional training points, as she receives (between 0 and 4) ice-creams of different types each day. However, the ice-creams are bought for Alice by her parents from one[1] or more of three trucks shown as the hidden states in the same figure. The identity of these trucks is hidden from Alice, although she knows that there are three trucks from which her parents procure the ice-creams (and more than one truck can be used to construct a single day's ice-cream set). Alice's parents are indecisive people, and their decision-making process is unusual because they change their mind about the selected ice-creams after selecting the trucks and vice versa. The likelihood of a particular ice-cream being picked depends on the trucks selected as well as the weights to these trucks. Similarly, the likelihood of a truck being selected depends on the ice-creams that one intends to buy and the same weights. Therefore, Alice's parents can keep changing their mind about selecting ice-creams after selecting trucks and about selecting trucks after selecting ice-creams (for a while) until they reach a final decision each day. As we will see, this *circular* relationship is the characteristic of undirected models, and process used by Alice's parents is similar to Gibb's sampling.

The use of the bipartite restriction greatly simplifies inference algorithms in RBMs, while retaining the application-centric power of the approach. If we know all the values of the visible units (as is common when a training data point is provided), the probabilities of the hidden units can be computed in one step without having to go through the laborious process of Gibbs sampling. For example, the probability of each hidden unit taking on the

---

[1] This example is tricky in terms of semantic interpretability for the case in which no trucks are selected. Even in that case, the probabilities of various ice-creams turn out to be non-zero depending on the bias. One can explain such cases by adding a dummy truck that is always selected.

value of 1 can be written directly as a logistic function of the values of visible units. In other words, we can apply Equation 6.7 to the restricted Boltzmann machine to obtain the following:

$$P(h_j = 1|\overline{v}) = \frac{1}{1 + \exp(-b_j^{(h)} - \sum_{i=1}^{d} v_i w_{ij})} \tag{6.15}$$

This result follows directly from Equation 6.7, which relates the state probabilities to the energy gap ΔE_j between $h_j = 0$ and $h_j = 1$. The value of ΔE_j is $b_j + \sum_i v_i w_{ij}$ when the visible states are observed. The main difference from an unrestricted Boltzmann machine is that the right-hand side of the above equation does not contain any (unknown) hidden variables and only the hidden variables. This relationship is also useful in creating a reduced representation of each training vector, once the weights have been learned. Specifically, for a Boltzmann machine with m hidden units, one can set the value of the jth hidden value to the probability computed in Equation 6.15. Note that such an approach provides a real-valued reduced representation of the binary data. One can also write the above equation using a sigmoid function:

$$P(h_j = 1|\overline{v}) = \text{Sigmoid}\left(b_j^{(h)} + \sum_{i=1}^{d} v_i w_{ij}\right) \tag{6.16}$$

One can also use a sample of the hidden states to generate the data points in one step. This is because the relationship between the visible units and the hidden units is similar in the undirected and bipartite architecture of the RBM. In other words, we can use Equation 6.7 to obtain the following:

$$P(v_i = 1|\overline{h}) = \frac{1}{1 + \exp(-b_i^{(v)} - \sum_{j=1}^{m} h_j w_{ij})} \tag{6.17}$$

One can also express this probability in terms of the sigmoid function:

$$P(v_i = 1|\overline{h}) = \text{Sigmoid}\left(b_i^{(v)} + \sum_{j=1}^{m} h_j w_{ij}\right) \tag{6.18}$$

One nice consequence of using the sigmoid is that it is often possible to create a closely related feed-forward network with sigmoid activation units in which the weights learned by the Boltzmann machine are leveraged in a directed computation with input-output mappings. The weights of this network are then fine-tuned with backpropagation. We will give examples of this approach in the application section.

Note that the weights encode the affinities between the visible and hidden states. A large positive weight implies that the two states are likely to be on together. For example, in Figure 6.3(b), it might be possible that the parents are more likely to buy cones and sundae from Ben's truck, whereas they are more likely to buy popsicles and cups from Tom's truck. These propensities are encoded in the weights, which regulate both visible state selection and hidden state selection in a circular way. The *circular* nature of the relationship creates challenges, because the relationship between ice-cream choice and truck choice runs both ways; it is the raison d'etre for Gibb's sampling. Although Alice might not know which trucks the ice-creams are coming from, she will notice the resulting correlations among the bits in the training data. In fact, if the weights of the RBM are known by Alice, she can use Gibb's sampling to generate 4-bit points representing "typical" examples of ice-creams she will receive on future days. Even the weights of the model can be learned by Alice from examples, which is the essence of an unsupervised generative model. Given the fact that there are 3 hidden states (trucks) and enough examples of 4-dimensional training data points, Alice can learn the relevant weights and biases between the visible ice-creams and hidden trucks. An algorithm for doing this is discussed in the next section.

6.4.1 Training the RBM

Computation of the weights of the RBM is achieved using a similar type of learning rule as that used for Boltzmann machines. In particular, it is possible to create an efficient algorithm based on mini-batches. The weights w_{ij} are initialized to small values. For the current set of weights w_{ij}, they are updated as follows:

- *Positive phase:* The algorithm uses a mini-batch of training instances, and computes the probability of the state of each hidden unit in exactly one step using Equation 6.15. Then a single sample of the state of each hidden unit is generated from this probability. This process is repeated for each element in a mini-batch of training instances. The correlation between these different training instances of v_i and generated instances of h_j is computed; it is denoted by $\langle v_i, h_j \rangle_{pos}$. This correlation is essentially the average product between each such pair of visible and hidden units.

- *Negative phase:* In the negative phase, the algorithm starts with a mini-batch of training instances. Then, for each training instance, it goes through a phase of Gibbs sampling after starting with randomly initialized states. This is achieved by repeatedly using Equations 6.15 and 6.17 to compute the probabilities of the visible and hidden units, and using these probabilities to draw samples. The values of v_i and h_j at thermal equilibrium are used to compute $\langle v_i, h_j \rangle_{neg}$ in the same way as the positive phase.

- One can then use the same type of update as is used in Boltzmann machines:

$$w_{ij} \Leftarrow w_{ij} + \alpha \left(\langle v_i, h_j \rangle_{pos} - \langle v_i, h_j \rangle_{neg} \right)$$
$$b_i^{(v)} \Leftarrow b_i^{(v)} + \alpha \left(\langle v_i, 1 \rangle_{pos} - \langle v_i, 1 \rangle_{neg} \right)$$
$$b_j^{(h)} \Leftarrow b_j^{(h)} + \alpha \left(\langle 1, h_j \rangle_{pos} - \langle 1, h_j \rangle_{neg} \right)$$

Here, $\alpha > 0$ denotes the learning rate. Each $\langle v_i, h_j \rangle$ is estimated by averaging the product of v_i and h_j over the mini-batch, although the values of v_i and h_j are computed in different ways in the positive and negative phases, respectively. Furthermore, $\langle v_i, 1 \rangle$ represents the average value of v_i in the mini-batch, and $\langle 1, h_j \rangle$ represents the average value of h_j in the mini-batch.

It is helpful to interpret the updates above in terms of Alice's trucks in Figure 6.3(b). When the weights of certain visible bits (e.g., cones and sundae) are highly correlated, the above updates will tend to push the weights in directions that these correlations can be explained by the weights between the trucks and the ice-creams. For example, if the cones and sundae are highly correlated but all other correlations are very weak, it can be explained by high weights between each of these two types of ice-creams and a single truck. In practice, the correlations will be far more complex, as will the patterns of the underlying weights.

An issue with the above approach is that one would need to run the Monte Carlo sampling for a while in order to obtain thermal equilibrium and generate the negative samples. However, it turns out that it is possible to run the Monte Carlo sampling for only a short time *starting by fixing the visible states to a training data point from the mini-batch* and still obtain a good approximation of the gradient.

6.4.2   Contrastive Divergence Algorithm

The fastest variant of the contrastive divergence approach uses a *single* additional iteration of Monte Carlo sampling (over what is done in the positive phase) in order to generate the samples of the hidden and visible states. First, the hidden states are generated by fixing the visible units to a training point (which is already accomplished in the positive phase), and then the visible units are generated again (exactly once) from these hidden states using Monte Carlo sampling. The values of the visible units are used as the sampled states in lieu of the ones obtained at thermal equilibrium. The hidden units are generated again using these visible units. Thus, the main difference between the positive and negative phase is only of the number of iterations that one runs the approach starting with the same initialization of visible states to training points. In the positive phase, we use only half an iteration of simply computing the hidden states. In the negative phase, we use at least one *additional* iteration (so that visible states are recomputed from hidden states and hidden states generated again). This difference in the number of iterations is what causes the contrastive divergence between the state distributions in the two cases. The intuition is that an increased number of iterations causes the distribution to move away (i.e., diverge) from the data-conditioned states to what is proposed by the current weight vector. Therefore, the value of $(\langle v_i, h_j \rangle_{pos} - \langle v_i, h_j \rangle_{neg})$ in the update quantifies the amount of contrastive divergence. This fastest variant of the contrastive divergence algorithm is referred to as CD_1 because it uses a single (additional) iteration in order to generate the negative samples. Of course, using such an approach is only an approximation to the true gradient. One can improve the accuracy of contrastive divergence by increasing the number of additional iterations to k, in which the data is reconstructed k times. This approach is referred to as CD_k. Increased values of k lead to better gradients at the expense of speed.

   In the early iterations, using CD_1 is good enough, although it might not be helpful in later phases. Therefore, a natural approach is to progressively increase the value of k, while applying CD_k in training. One can summarize this process as follows:

1. In the early phase of gradient-descent, the weights are initialized to small values. In each iteration, only one additional step of contrastive divergence is used. One step is sufficient at this point because the difference between the weights are very inexact in early iterations and only a rough direction of descent is needed. Therefore, even if CD_1 is executed, one will be able to obtain a good direction in most cases.

2. As the gradient descent nears a better solution, higher accuracy is needed. Therefore, two or three steps of contrastive divergence are used (i.e., CD_2 or CD_3). In general, one can double the number of Markov chain steps after a fixed number of gradient descent steps. Another approach advocated in [469] is to create the value of k in CD_k by 1 after every 10,000 steps. The maximum value of k used in [469] was 20.

The contrastive divergence algorithm can be extended to many other variations of the RBM. An excellent practical guide for training restricted Boltzmann machines may be found in [193]. This guide discusses several practical issues such as initialization, tuning, and updates. In the following, we provide a brief overview of some of these practical issues.

6.4.3 Practical Issues and Improvisations

There are several practical issues in training the RBM with contrastive divergence. Although we have always assumed that the Monte Carlo sampling procedure generates binary samples, this is not quite the case. Some of the iterations of the Monte Carlo sampling directly use *computed* probabilities (cf. Equations 6.15 and 6.17), rather than *sampled* binary values. This is done in order to reduce the noise in training, because probability values retain more information than binary samples. However, there are some differences between how hidden states and visible states are treated:

- *Improvisations in sampling hidden states:* The final iteration of CD_k computes hidden states as probability values according to Equation 6.15 for positive and negative samples. Therefore, the value of h_j used for computing $\langle v_i, h_j \rangle_{pos} - \langle v_i, h_j \rangle_{neg}$ would always be a real value for both positive and negative samples. This real value is a fraction because of the use of the sigmoid function in Equation 6.15.

- *Improvisations in sampling visible states:* Therefore, the improvisations for Monte Carlo sampling of visible states are always associated with the computation of $\langle v_i, h_j \rangle_{neg}$ rather than $\langle v_i, h_j \rangle_{pos}$ because visible states are always fixed to the training data. For the negative samples, the Monte Carlo procedure *always* computes probability values of visible states according to Equation 6.17 over *all* iterations rather than using 0-1 values. This is not the case for the hidden states, which are always binary until the very last iteration.

Using probability values iteratively rather than sampled binary values is technically incorrect, and does not reach correct thermal equilibrium. However, the contrastive divergence algorithm is an approximation anyway, and this type of approach reduces significant noise at the expense of some theoretical incorrectness. Noise reduction is a result of the fact that the probabilistic outputs are closer to expected values.

The weights can be initialized from a Gaussian distribution with zero mean and a standard deviation of 0.01. Large values of the initial weights can speed up the learning, but might lead to a model that is slightly worse in the end. The visible biases are initialized to $\log(p_i/(1 - p_i))$, where p_i is the fraction of data points in which the ith dimension takes on the value of 1. The values of the hidden biases are initialized to 0.

The size of the mini-batch should be somewhere between 10 and 100. The order of the examples should be randomized. For cases in which class labels are associated with examples, the mini-batch should be selected in such a way that the proportion of labels in the batch is approximately the same as the whole data.

6.5 Applications of Restricted Boltzmann Machines

In this section, we will study several applications of restricted Boltzmann machines. These methods have been very successful for a variety of unsupervised applications, although they are also used for supervised applications. When using an RBM in a real-world application, a mapping from input to output is often required, whereas a vanilla RBM is only designed to learn probability distributions. The input-to-output mapping is often achieved by constructing a feed-forward network with weights derived from the learned RBM. In other words, one can often derive a traditional neural network that is *associated* with the original RBM.

Here, we will like to discuss the differences between the notions of the *state* of a node in the RBM, and the *activation* of that node in the associated neural network. The state of a node is a binary value sampled from the Bernoulli probabilities defined by Equations 6.15 and 6.17. On the other hand, the activation of a node in the associated neural network is the probability value derived from the use of the sigmoid function in Equations 6.15 and 6.17. Many applications use the activations in the nodes of the associated neural network, rather than the states in the original RBM after the training. Note that the final step in the contrastive divergence algorithm also leverages the activations of the nodes rather than the states while updating the weights. In practical settings, the activations are more information-rich and are therefore useful. The use of activations is consistent with traditional neural network architectures, in which backpropagation can be used. The use of a final phase of backpropagation is crucial in being able to apply the approach to supervised applications. In most cases, the critical role of the RBM is to perform unsupervised feature learning. Therefore, the role of the RBM is often only one of pretraining in the case of supervised learning. In fact, pretraining is one of the important historical contributions of the RBM.

6.5.1 Dimensionality Reduction and Data Reconstruction

The most basic function of the RBM is that of dimensionality reduction and unsupervised feature engineering. The hidden units of an RBM contain a reduced representation of the data. However, we have not yet discussed how one can reconstruct the original representation of the data with the use of an RBM (much like an autoencoder). In order to understand the reconstruction process, we first need to understand the equivalence of the undirected RBM with directed graphical models [251], in which the computation occurs in a particular direction. Materializing a directed probabilistic graph is the first step towards materializing a traditional neural network (derived from the RBM) in which the discrete probabilistic sampling from the sigmoid can be replaced with real-valued sigmoid activations.

Although an RBM is an undirected graphical model, one can "unfold" an RBM in order to create a directed model in which the inference occurs in a particular direction. In general, an undirected RBM can be shown to be equivalent to a directed graphical model with an infinite number of layers. The unfolding is particularly useful when the visible units are fixed to specific values because the number of layers in the unfolding collapses to exactly twice the number of layers in the original RBM. Furthermore, by replacing the discrete probabilistic sampling with continuous sigmoid units, this directed model functions as a virtual autoencoder, which has both an encoder portion and a decoder portion. Although the weights of an RBM have been trained using discrete probabilistic sampling, they can also be used in this related neural network with some fine tuning. This is a heuristic approach to convert what has been learned from a Boltzmann machine (i.e., the weights) into the initialized weights of a traditional neural network with sigmoid units.

An RBM can be viewed as an undirected graphical model that uses the same weight matrix to learn $\overline{h}$ from $\overline{v}$ as it does from $\overline{v}$ to $\overline{h}$. If one carefully examines Equations 6.15 and 6.17, one can see that they are very similar. The main difference is that these equations uses different biases, and they use the transposes of each other's weight matrices. In other words, one can rewrite Equations 6.15 and 6.17 in the following form for some function $f(\cdot)$:

$$\overline{h} \sim f(\overline{v}, \overline{b}^{(h)}, W)$$
$$\overline{v} \sim f(\overline{h}, \overline{b}^{(v)}, W^T)$$

The function $f(\cdot)$ is typically defined by the sigmoid function in binary RBMs, which constitute the predominant variant of this class of models. Ignoring the biases, one can replace

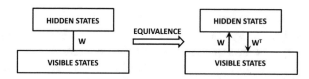

(a) Equivalence of directed and undirected relationships

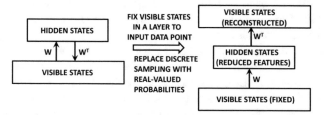

(b) Discrete graphical model to approximate real-valued neural network

Figure 6.4: Using trained RBM to approximate trained autoencoder

the undirected graph of the RBM with two directed links, as shown in Figure 6.4(a). Note that the weight matrices in the two directions are W and W^T, respectively. However, if we fix the visible states to the training points, we can perform just two iterations of these operations to reconstruct the visible states with *real-valued* approximations. In other words, we approximate this trained RBM with a traditional neural network by replacing discrete sampling with continuous-valued sigmoid activations (as a heuristic). This conversion is shown in Figure 6.4(b). In other words, instead of using the sampling operation of "$\sim$," we replace the samples with the probability values:

$$\overline{h} = f(\overline{v}, \overline{b}^{(h)}, W)$$

$$\overline{v}' = f(\overline{h}, \overline{b}^{(v)}, W^T)$$

Note that $\overline{v}'$ is the reconstructed version of $\overline{v}$ and it will contain real values (unlike the binary states in $\overline{v}$). In this case, we are working with real-valued activations rather than discrete samples. Because sampling is no longer used and all computations are performed in terms of expectations, we need to perform only one iteration of Equation 6.15 in order to learn the reduced representation. Furthermore, only one iteration of Equation 6.17 is required to learn the reconstructed data. The prediction phase works only in a single direction from the input point to the reconstructed data, and is shown on the right-hand side of Figure 6.4(b). We modify Equations 6.15 and 6.17 to define the states of this traditional neural network as real values:

$$\hat{h}_j = \frac{1}{1 + \exp(-b_j^{(h)} - \sum_{i=1}^{d} v_i w_{ij})} \tag{6.19}$$

For a setting with a total of $m \ll d$ hidden states, the real-valued reduced representation is given by $(\hat{h}_1 \ldots \hat{h}_m)$. This first step of creating the hidden states is equivalent to the encoder portion of an autoencoder, and these values are the expected values of the binary states. One can then apply Equation 6.17 to these *probabilistic values* (without creating Monte-Carlo instantiations) in order to reconstruct the visible states as follows:

$$\hat{v}_i = \frac{1}{1 + \exp(-b_i^{(v)} - \sum_j \hat{h}_j w_{ij})} \tag{6.20}$$

Although $\hat{h}_j$ does represent the expected value of the jth hidden unit, applying the sigmoid function again to this real-valued version of $\hat{h}_j$ only provides a rough approximation to the expected value of v_i. Nevertheless, the real-valued prediction $\hat{v}_i$ is an approximate reconstruction of v_i. Note that in order to perform this reconstruction we have used similar operations as traditional neural networks with sigmoid units rather than the troublesome discrete samples of probabilistic graphical models. Therefore, we can now use this related neural network as a good starting point for fine-tuning the weights with traditional backpropagation. This type of reconstruction is similar to the reconstruction used in the autoencoder architecture discussed in Chapter 2.

On first impression, it makes little sense to train an RBM when similar goals can be achieved with a traditional autoencoder. However, this broad approach of deriving a traditional neural network with a trained RBM is particularly useful when working with stacked RBMs (cf. Section 6.7). The training of a stacked RBM does not face the same challenges as those associated with deep neural networks, especially the ones related with the vanishing and exploding gradient problems. Just as the simple RBM provides an excellent initialization point for the shallow autoencoder, the stacked RBM also provides an excellent starting point for a deep autoencoder [198]. This principle led to the development of the idea of pretraining with RBMs before conventional pretraining methods were developed without the use of RBMs. As discussed in this section, one can also use RBMs for other reduction-centric applications such as collaborative filtering and topic modeling.

6.5.2 RBMs for Collaborative Filtering

The previous section shows how restricted Boltzmann machines are used as alternatives to the autoencoder for unsupervised modeling and dimensionality reduction. However, as discussed in Section 2.5.7 of Chapter 2, dimensionality reduction methods are also used for a variety of related applications like collaborative filtering. In the following, we will provide an RBM-centric alternative to the recommendation technique described in Section 2.5.7 of Chapter 2. This approach is based on the technique proposed in [414], and it was one of the ensemble components of the winning entry in the Netflix prize contest.

One of the challenges in working with ratings matrices is that they are incompletely specified. This tends to make the design of a neural architecture for collaborative filtering more difficult than traditional dimensionality reduction. Recall from the discussion in Section 2.5.7 that modeling such incomplete matrices with a traditional neural network also faces the same challenge. In that section, it was shown how one could create a different training instance *and* a different neural network for each user, depending on which ratings are observed by that user. All these different neural networks share weights. An exactly similar approach is used with the restricted Boltzmann machine, in which one training case and one RBM is defined for each user. However, in the case of the RBM, one additional problem is that the units are binary, whereas ratings can take on values from 1 to 5. Therefore, we need some way of working with the additional constraint.

In order to address this issue, the hidden units in the RBM are allowed to be 5-way softmax units in order to correspond to rating values from 1 to 5. In other words, the hidden units are defined in the form of a one-hot encoding of the rating. One-hot encodings are naturally modeled with softmax, which defines the probabilities of each possible position. The ith softmax unit corresponds to the ith movie and the probability of a particular rating being given to that movie is defined by the distribution of softmax probabilities. Therefore, if there are d movies, we have a total of d such one-hot encoded ratings. The values of the corresponding binary values of the one-hot encoded visible units are denoted by $v_i^{(1)}, \ldots v_i^{(5)}$.

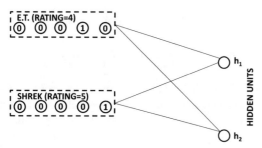

(a) RBM architecture for user Sayani (Observed Ratings: *E.T.* and *Shrek*)

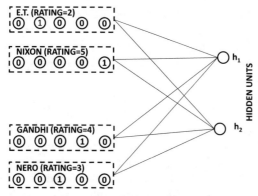

(b) RBM architecture for user Bob (Observed Ratings: *E.T.*, *Nixon*, *Gandhi*, and *Nero*)

Figure 6.5: The RBM architectures of two users are shown based on their observed ratings. It is instructive to compare this figure with the conventional neural architecture shown in Figure 2.14 in Chapter 2. In both cases, weights are shared by user-specific networks.

Note that only one of the values of $v_i^{(k)}$ can be 1 over fixed i and varying k. The hidden layer is assumed to contain m units. The weight matrix has a separate parameter for each of the multinomial outcomes of the softmax unit. Therefore, the weight between visible unit i and hidden unit j for the outcome k is denoted by $w_{ij}^{(k)}$. In addition, we have 5 biases for the visible unit i, which are denoted by $b_i^{(k)}$ for $k \in \{1, \ldots, 5\}$. The hidden units only have a single bias, and the bias of the jth hidden unit is denoted by b_j (without a superscript). The architecture of the RBM for collaborative filtering is illustrated in Figure 6.5. This example contains $d = 5$ movies and $m = 2$ hidden units. In this case, the RBM architectures of two users, Sayani and Bob, are shown in the figure. In the case of Sayani, she has specified ratings for only two movies. Therefore, a total of $2 \times 2 \times 5 = 20$ connections will be present in her case, even though we have shown only a subset of them to avoid clutter in the figure. In the case of Bob, he has four observed ratings, and therefore his network will contain a total of $4 \times 2 \times 5 = 40$ connections. Note that both Sayani and Bob have rated the movie *E.T.*, and therefore the connections from this movie to the hidden units will share weights between the corresponding RBMs.

The states of the hidden units, which are binary, are defined with the use of the sigmoid function:

$$P(h_j = 1 | \overline{v}^{(1)} \ldots \overline{v}^{(5)}) = \frac{1}{1 + \exp(-b_j - \sum_{i,k} v_i^{(k)} w_{ij}^k)} \qquad (6.21)$$

The main difference from Equation 6.15 is that the visible units also contain a superscript to correspond to the different rating outcomes. Otherwise, the condition is virtually identical. However, the probabilities of the visible units are defined differently from the traditional RBM model. In this case, the visible units are defined using the softmax function:

$$P(v_i^{(k)} = 1 | \overline{h}) = \frac{\exp(b_i^{(k)} + \sum_j h_j w_{ij}^{(k)})}{\sum_{r=1}^{5} \exp(b_i^{(r)} + \sum_j h_j w_{ij}^{(r)})} \qquad (6.22)$$

The training is done in a similar way as the unrestricted Boltzmann machine with Monte Carlo sampling. The main difference is that the visible states are generated from a multinomial model. Therefore, the MCMC sampling should also generate the negative samples from the multinomial model of Equation 6.22 to create each $v_i^{(k)}$. The corresponding updates for training the weights are as follows:

$$w_{ij}^{(k)} \Leftarrow w_{ij}^{(k)} + \alpha \left(\langle v_i^{(k)}, h_j \rangle_{pos} - \langle v_i^{(k)}, h_j \rangle_{neg} \right) \quad \forall k \qquad (6.23)$$

Note that only the weights of the *observed* visible units to all hidden units are updated for a single training example (i.e., user). In other words, the Boltzmann machine that is used is different for each user in the data, although the weights are shared across the different users. Examples of the Boltzmann machines for two different training examples are illustrated in Figure 6.5, and the architectures for Bob and Sayani are different. However, the weights for the units representing *E.T.* are shared. This type of approach is also used in the traditional neural architecture of Section 2.5.7 in which the neural network used for each training example is different. As discussed in that section, the traditional neural architecture is equivalent to a matrix factorization technique. The Boltzmann machine tends to give somewhat different ratings predictions from matrix factorization techniques, although the accuracy is similar.

Making Predictions

Once the weights have been learned, they can be used for making predictions. However, the predictive phase works with real-valued activations rather than binary states, much like a traditional neural network with sigmoid and softmax units. First, one can use Equation 6.21 in order to learn the probabilities of the hidden units. Let the probability that the jth hidden unit is 1 be denoted by $\hat{p}_j$. Then, the probabilities of *unobserved* visible units are computed using Equation 6.22. The main problem in computing Equation 6.22 is that it is defined in terms of the values of the hidden units, which are only known in the form of probabilities according to Equation 6.21. However, one can simply replace each h_j with $\hat{p}_j$ in Equation 6.22 in order to compute the probabilities of the visible units. Note that these predictions provide the probabilities of each possible rating value of each item. These probabilities can also be used to compute the expected value of the rating if needed. Although this approach is approximate from a theoretical point of view, it works well in practice and is extremely fast. By using these real-valued computations, one is effectively converting the RBM into a traditional neural network architecture with logistic units for hidden layers and softmax units for the input and output layers. Although the original paper [414] does not mention it, it is even possible to tune the weights of this network with backpropagation (cf. Exercise 1).

The RBM approach works as well as the traditional matrix factorization approach, although it tends to give different types of predictions. This type of diversity is an advantage from the perspective of using an ensemble-centric approach. Therefore, the results can be combined with the matrix factorization approach in order to yield the improvements that are naturally associated with an ensemble method. Ensemble methods generally show better improvements when diverse methods of similar accuracy are combined.

Conditional Factoring: A Neat Regularization Trick

A neat regularization trick is buried inside the RBM-based collaborative filtering work of [414]. This trick is not specific to the collaborative filtering application, but can be used in any application of an RBM. This approach is not necessary in traditional neural networks, where it can be simulated by incorporating an additional hidden layer, but it is particularly useful for RBMs. Here, we describe this trick in a more general way, without its specific modifications for the collaborative filtering application. In some applications with a large number of hidden units and visible units, the size of the parameter matrix $W = [w_{ij}]$ might be large. For example, in a matrix with $d = 10^5$ visible units, and $m = 100$ hidden units, we will have ten million parameters. Therefore, more than ten million training points will be required to avoid overfitting. A natural approach is to assume a low-rank parameter structure of the weight matrix, which is a form of regularization. The idea is to assume that the matrix W can be expressed as the product of two low-rank factors U and V, which are of sizes $d \times k$ and $m \times k$, respectively. Therefore, we have the following:

$$W = UV^T \tag{6.24}$$

Here, k is the rank of the factorization, which is typically much less than both d and m. Then, instead of learning the parameters of the matrix W, one can learn the parameters of U and V, respectively. This type of trick is used often in various machine learning applications, where parameters are represented as a matrix. A specific example is that of factorization machines, which are also used for collaborative filtering [396]. This type of approach is not required in traditional neural networks, because one can simulate it by incorporating an additional linear layer with k units between two layers with a weight matrix of W between them. The weight matrices of the two layers will be U and V^T, respectively.

6.5.3 Using RBMs for Classification

The most common way to use RBMs for classification is as a pretraining procedure. In other words, a Boltzmann machine is first used to perform unsupervised feature engineering. The RBM is then unrolled into a related encoder-decoder architecture according to the approach described in Section 6.5.1. This is a traditional neural network with sigmoid units, whose weights are derived from the unsupervised RBM rather than backpropagation. The encoder portion of this neural network is topped with an output layer for class prediction. The weights of this neural network are then fine-tuned with backpropagation. Such an approach can even be used with *stacked RBMs* (cf. Section 6.7) to yield a deep classifier. This methodology of initializing a (conventional) deep neural network with an RBM was one of the first approaches for pretraining deep networks.

There is, however, another alternative approach to perform classification with the RBM, which integrates RBM training and inference more tightly with the classification process. This approach is somewhat similar to the collaborative filtering methodology discussed in the previous section. The collaborative-filtering problem is also referred to as *matrix completion* because the missing entries of an incompletely specified matrix are predicted. The use of RBMs for recommender systems provides some useful hints about their use in classification. This is because classification can be viewed as a simplified version of the matrix completion problem in which we create a single matrix out of both the training and test rows, and the missing values belong to a particular column of the matrix. This column corresponds to the class variable. Furthermore, all the missing values are present in the test rows in the case of classification, whereas the missing values could be present anywhere in the matrix in the case of recommender systems. This relationship between classification and the generic matrix completion problem is illustrated in Figure 6.6. In classification, all features are observed for the rows corresponding to training points, which simplifies the modeling (compared to collaborative filtering in which a complete set of features is typically not observed for any row).

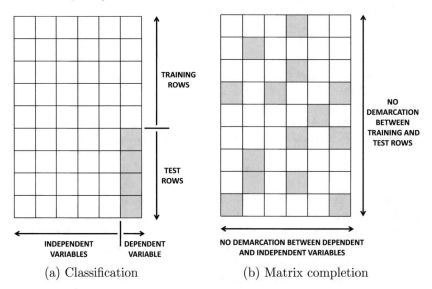

Figure 6.6: The classification problem is a special case of matrix completion. Shaded entries are missing and need to be predicted.

We assume that the input data contains d binary features. The class label has k discrete values, which corresponds to the multiway classification problem. The classification problem can be modeled by the RBM by defining the hidden and visible features as follows:

1. The visible layer contains two types of nodes corresponding to the features and the class label, respectively. There are d binary units corresponding to features, and there are k binary units corresponding to the class label. However, only one of these k binary units can take on the value of 1, which corresponds to a one-hot encoding of the class labels. This encoding of the class label is similar to the approach used for encoding the ratings in the collaborative-filtering application. The visible units for the features are denoted by $v_1^{(f)} \ldots v_d^{(f)}$, whereas the visible units for the class labels are denoted by $v_1^{(c)} \ldots v_k^{(c)}$. Note that the symbolic superscripts denote whether the visible units corresponds to a feature or a class label.

2. The hidden layer contains m binary units. The hidden units are denoted by $h_1 \ldots h_m$.

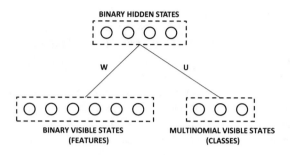

Figure 6.7: The RBM architecture for classification

The weight of the connection between the ith feature-specific visible unit $v_i^{(f)}$ and the jth hidden unit h_j is given by w_{ij}. This results in a $d \times m$ connection matrix $W = [w_{ij}]$. The weight of the connection between the ith class-specific visible unit $v_i^{(c)}$ and the jth hidden unit h_j is given by u_{ij}. This results in a $k \times m$ connection matrix $U = [u_{ij}]$. The relationships between different types of nodes and matrices for $d = 6$ features, $k = 3$ classes, and $m = 5$ hidden features is shown in Figure 6.7. The bias for the ith feature-specific visible node is denoted by $b_i^{(f)}$, and the bias for the ith class-specific visible node is denoted by $b_i^{(c)}$. The bias for the jth hidden node is denoted by b_j (with no superscript). The states of the hidden nodes are defined in terms of all visible nodes using the sigmoid function:

$$P(h_j = 1 | \overline{v}^{(f)}, \overline{v}^{(c)}) = \frac{1}{1 + \exp(-b_j - \sum_{i=1}^{d} v_i^{(f)} w_{ij} - \sum_{i=1}^{k} v_i^{(c)} u_{ij})} \qquad (6.25)$$

Note that this is the standard way in which the probabilities of hidden units are defined in a Boltzmann machine. There are, however, some differences between how the probabilities of the feature-specific visible units and the class-specific visible units are defined. In the case of the feature-specific visible units, the relationship is not very different from a standard Boltzmann machine:

$$P(v_i^{(f)} = 1 | \overline{h}) = \frac{1}{1 + \exp(-b_i^{(f)} - \sum_{j=1}^{m} h_j w_{ij})} \qquad (6.26)$$

The case of the class units is, however, slightly different because we must use the soft-max function instead of the sigmoid. This is because of the one-hot encoding of the class. Therefore, we have the following:

$$P(v_i^{(c)} = 1 | \overline{h}) = \frac{\exp(b_i^{(c)} + \sum_j h_j u_{ij})}{\sum_{l=1}^{k} \exp(b_l^{(c)} + \sum_j h_j u_{lj})} \qquad (6.27)$$

A naive approach to training the Boltzmann machine would use a similar generative model to previous sections. The multinomial model is used to generate the visible states $v_i^{(c)}$ for the classes. The corresponding updates of the contrastive divergence algorithm are as follows:

$$w_{ij} \Leftarrow w_{ij} + \alpha \left(\langle v_i^{(f)}, h_j \rangle_{pos} - \langle v_i^{(f)}, h_j \rangle_{neg} \right) \quad \text{if } i \text{ is feature unit}$$

$$u_{ij} \Leftarrow u_{ij} + \alpha \left(\langle v_i^{(c)}, h_j \rangle_{pos} - \langle v_i^{(c)}, h_j \rangle_{neg} \right) \quad \text{if } i \text{ is class unit}$$

This approach is a direct extension from collaborative filtering. However, the main problem is that this *generative* approach does not fully optimize for classification accuracy. To provide an analogy with autoencoders, one would not necessarily perform significantly better dimensionality reduction (in a supervised sense) by simply including the class variable among the inputs. The reduction would often be dominated by the unsupervised relationships among the features. Rather, the *entire focus* of the learning should be on optimizing the accuracy of classification. Therefore, a *discriminative* approach to training the RBM is often used in which the weights are learned to maximize the conditional class likelihood of the true class. Note that it is easy to set up the conditional probability of the class variable, given the visible states by using the probabilistic dependencies between the hidden features and classes/features. For example, in the traditional form of a restrictive Boltzmann machine, we are maximizing the *joint* probability of the feature variables $v_i^{(f)}$ and the class variables v_i^c. However, in the discriminative variant, the objective function is set up to maximize the *conditional* probability of the class variable $y \in \{1 \dots k\}$ $P(v_y^{(c)} = 1|\overline{v}^{(f)})$. Such an approach has a more focused effect of maximizing classification accuracy. Although it is possible to train a discriminative restricted Boltzmann machine using contrastive divergence, the problem is simplified because one can estimate $P(v_y^{(c)} = 1|\overline{v}^{(f)})$ in closed form without having to use an iterative approach. This form can be shown to be the following [263, 414]:

$$P(v_y^{(c)} = 1|\overline{v}^{(f)}) = \frac{\exp(b_y^{(c)}) \prod_{j=1}^m [1 + \exp(b_j^{(h)} + u_{yj} + \sum_i w_{ij} v_i^{(f)})]}{\sum_{l=1}^k \exp(b_l^{(c)}) \prod_{j=1}^m [1 + \exp(b_j^{(h)} + u_{lj} + \sum_i w_{ij} v_i^{(f)})]} \qquad (6.28)$$

With this differentiable closed form, it is a simple matter to differentiate the negative logarithm of the above expression for stochastic gradient descent. If $\mathcal{L}$ is the negative logarithm of the above expression and θ is any particular parameter (e.g., weight or bias) of the Boltzmann machine, one can show the following:

$$\frac{\partial \mathcal{L}}{\partial \theta} = \sum_{j=1}^m \text{Sigmoid}(o_{yj})\frac{\partial o_{yj}}{\partial \theta} - \sum_{l=1}^k \sum_{j=1}^m \text{Sigmoid}(o_{lj})\frac{\partial o_{lj}}{\partial \theta} \qquad (6.29)$$

Here, we have $o_{yj} = b_j^{(h)} + u_{yj} + \sum_i w_{ij} v_i^{(f)}$. The above expression can be easily computed for each training point and for each parameter in order to perform the stochastic gradient descent process. It is a relatively simple matter to make probabilistic predictions for unseen test instances using Equation 6.28. More details and extensions are discussed in [263].

6.5.4   Topic Models with RBMs

Topic modeling is a form of dimensionality reduction that is specific to text data. The earliest topic models, which correspond to Probabilistic Latent Semantic Analysis (PLSA), were proposed in [206]. In PLSA, the basis vectors are not orthogonal to one another, as is the case with SVD. On the other hand, both the basis vectors and the transformed representations are constrained to be nonnegative values. The nonnegativity in the value of each transformed feature is semantically useful, because it represents the strength of a topic in a particular document. In the context of the RBM, this strength corresponds to the probability that a particular hidden unit takes on the value of 1, given that the words in a particular document have been observed. Therefore, one can use the vector of conditional probabilities of the hidden states (when visible states are fixed to document words) in order to create a reduced representation of each document. It is assumed that the lexicon size is d, whereas the number of hidden units is $m \ll d$.

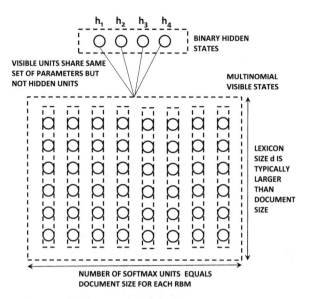

Figure 6.8: The RBM for each document is illustrated. The number of visible units is equal to the number of words in each document

This approach shares some similarities with the technique used for collaborative filtering in which a single RBM is created for each user (row of the matrix). In this case, a single RBM is created for each document. A group of visible units is created for each word, and therefore the number of groups of visible units is equal to the number of words in the document. In the following, we will concretely define how the visible and hidden states of the RBM are fixed in order to describe the concrete workings of the model:

1. For the tth document containing n_t words, a total of n_t softmax groups are retained. Each softmax group contains d nodes corresponding to the d words in the lexicon. Therefore, the RBM for each document is different, because the number of units depends on the length of the document. However, all the softmax groups within a document and across multiple documents share weights of their connections to the hidden units. The ith position in the document corresponds to the ith group of visible softmax units. The ith group of visible units is denoted by $v_i^{(1)} \ldots v_i^{(d)}$. The bias associated with $v_i^{(k)}$ is $b^{(k)}$. Note that the bias of the ith visible node depends only on k (word identity) and not on i (position of word in document). This is because the model uses a bag-of-words approach in which the positions of the words are irrelevant.

2. There are m hidden units denoted by $h_1 \ldots h_m$. The bias of the jth hidden unit is b_j.

3. Each hidden unit is connected to each of the $n_t \times d$ visible units. All softmax groups within a single RBM as well as across different RBMs (corresponding to different documents) share the same set of d weights. The kth hidden unit is connected to a group of d softmax units with a vector of d weights denoted by $\overline{W}^{(k)} = (w_1^{(k)} \ldots w_d^{(k)})$. In other words, the kth hidden unit *is connected to each of the n_t groups of d softmax units with the same set of weights $\overline{W}^{(k)}$.*

The architecture of the RBM is illustrated in Figure 6.8. Based on the architecture of the RBM, one can express the probabilities associated with the states of the hidden units with the use of the sigmoid function:

$$P(h_j = 1|\overline{v}^{(1)}, \dots \overline{v}^{(d)}) = \frac{1}{1 + \exp(-b_j - \sum_{i=1}^{n_t} \sum_{k=1}^{d} v_i^{(k)} w_j^{(k)})} \tag{6.30}$$

One can also express the visible states with the use of the multinomial model:

$$P(v_i^{(k)} = 1|\overline{h}) = \frac{\exp(b^{(k)} + \sum_{j=1}^{m} w_j^{(k)} h_j)}{\sum_{l=1}^{d} \exp(b^{(l)} + \sum_{j=1}^{m} w_j^{(l)} h_j)} \tag{6.31}$$

The normalization factor in the denominator ensures that the sum of the probabilities of visible units over all the words always sums to 1. Furthermore, the right-hand side of the above equation is independent of the index i of the visible unit. This is because this model does not depend on the position of words in the document, and the modeling treats a document as a bag of words.

With these relationships, one can apply MCMC sampling to generate samples of the hidden and visible states for the contrastive divergence algorithm. Note that the RBMs are different for different documents, although these RBMs share weights. As in the case of the collaborative filtering application, each RBM is associated with only a single training example corresponding to the relevant document. The weight update used for gradient descent is the same as used for the traditional RBM. The only difference is that the weights across different visible units are shared. This approach is similar to what is performed in collaborative filtering. We leave the derivation of the weight updates as an exercise for the reader (see Exercise 5).

After the training has been performed, the reduced representation of each document is computed by applying Equation 6.30 to the words of a document. The real-valued value of the probabilities of the hidden units provides the m-dimensional reduced representation of the document. The approach described in this section is a simplification of a multilayer approach described in the original work [469].

6.5.5   RBMs for Machine Learning with Multimodal Data

Boltzmann machines can also be used for machine learning with *multimodal* data. Multimodal data refers to a setting in which one is trying to extract information from data points with multiple modalities. For example, an image with a text description can be considered multimodal data. This is because this data object has both image and text modalities.

The main challenge in processing multimodal data is that it is often difficult to use machine learning algorithms on such heterogeneous features. Multimodal data is often processed by using a shared representation in which the two modes are mapped into a joint space. A common approach for this goal is *shared* matrix factorization. Numerous methods for using shared matrix factorization with text and image data are discussed in [6]. Since RBMs provide alternative representations to matrix factorization methods in many settings, it is natural to explore whether one can use this architecture to create a shared latent representation of the data.

An example [468] of an architecture for multimodal modeling is shown in Figure 6.9(a). In this example, it is assumed that the two modes correspond to text and image data. The image and the text data are used to create hidden states that are specific to images and

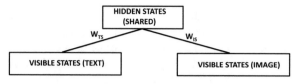

(a) A simple RBM for multimodal data

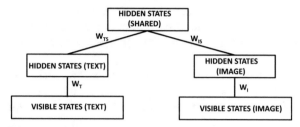

(b) A multimodal RBM with an added hidden layer

Figure 6.9: RBM architecture for multimodal data processing

text, respectively. These hidden states then feed into a single shared representation. The similarity of this architecture with the classification architecture of Figure 6.7 is striking. This is because both architectures try to map two types of features into a set of shared hidden states. These hidden states can then be used for different types of inference, such as using the shared representation for classification. As shown in Section 6.7, one can even enhance such unsupervised representations with backpropagation to fine-tune the approach. Missing data modalities can also be generated using this model.

One can optionally improve the expressive power of this model by using depth. An additional hidden layer has been added between the visible states and the shared representation in Figure 6.9(b). Note that one can add multiple hidden layers in order to create a deep network. However, we have not yet described how one can actually train a multilayer RBM. This issue is discussed in Section 6.7.

An additional challenge with the use of multimodal data is that the features are often not binary. There are several solutions to this issue. In the case of text (or data modalities with small cardinalities of discrete attributes), one can use a similar approach as used in the RBM for topic modeling where the count c of a discrete attribute is used to create c instances of the one-hot encoded attribute. The issue becomes more challenging when the data contains arbitrary real values. One solution is to discretize the data, although such an approach can lose useful information about the data. Another solution is to make changes to the energy function of the Boltzmann machine. A discussion of some of these issues is provided in the next section.

6.6 Using RBMs Beyond Binary Data Types

The entire discussion so far in this chapter has focussed on the use of RBMs for binary data types. Indeed the vast majority of RBMs are designed for binary data types. For some types of data, such as categorical data or ordinal data (e.g., ratings), one can use the softmax approach described in Section 6.5.2. For example, the use of softmax units for word-count data is discussed in Section 6.5.4. One can make the softmax approach work with an ordered attribute, when the number of discrete values of that attribute is small. However, these methods are not quite as effective for real-valued data. One possibility is to use discretization in order to convert real-valued data into discrete data, which can be handled with softmax units. Using such an approach does have the disadvantage of losing a certain amount of representational accuracy.

The approach described in Section 6.5.2 does provide some hints about how different data types can be addressed. For example, categorical or ordinal data is handled *by changing the probability distribution* of visible units to be more appropriate to the problem at hand. In general, one might need to change the distribution of not only the visible units, but also the hidden units. This is because the nature of the hidden units is dependent on the visible units.

For real-valued data, a natural solution is to use Gaussian visible units. Furthermore, the hidden units are real-valued as well, and are assumed to contain a ReLU activation function. The energy for a particular combination $(\overline{v}, \overline{h})$ of visible and hidden units is given by the following:

$$E(\overline{v}, \overline{h}) = \underbrace{\sum_i \frac{(v_i - b_i)^2}{2\sigma_i^2}}_{\text{Containment function}} - \sum_j b_j h_j - \sum_{i,j} \frac{v_i}{\sigma_i} h_j w_{ij} \qquad (6.32)$$

Note that the energy contribution of the bias of visible units is given by a *parabolic containment function*. The effect of using this containment function is to keep the value of the ith visible unit close to b_i. As is the case for other types of Boltzmann machines, the derivatives of the energy function with respect to the different variables also provide the derivatives of the log-likelihoods. This is because the probabilities are always defined by exponentiating the energy function.

There are several challenges associated with the use of this approach. An important issue is that the approach is rather unstable with respect to the choice of the variance parameter σ. In particular, updates to the visible layer tend to be too small, whereas updates to the hidden layer tend to be too large. One natural solution to this dilemma is to use more hidden units than visible units. It is also common to normalize the input data to unit variance so that the standard deviation σ of the visible units can be set to 1. The ReLU units are modified to create a noisy version. Specifically, Gaussian noise with zero mean and variance $\log(1+\exp(v))$ is added to the value of the unit before thresholding it to nonnegative values. The motivation behind using such an unusual activation function is that it can be shown to be equivalent to a *binomial unit* [348, 495], which encodes more information than the binary unit that is normally used. It is important to enable this ability when working with real-valued data. The Gibbs sampling of the real-valued RBM is similar to a binary RBM, as are the updates to the weights once the MCMC samples are generated. It is important to keep the learning rates low to prevent instability.

6.7 Stacking Restricted Boltzmann Machines

Most of the power of conventional neural architectures arises from having multiple layers of units. Deeper networks are known to be more powerful, and can model more complex functions at the expense of fewer parameters. A natural question arises concerning whether similar goals can be achieved by putting together multiple RBMs. It turns out that the RBM is well suited to creating deep networks, and was used *earlier* than conventional neural networks for creating deep models with pretraining. In other words, the RBM is trained

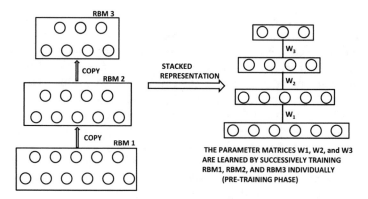

(a) The stacked RBMs are trained sequentially in pretraining

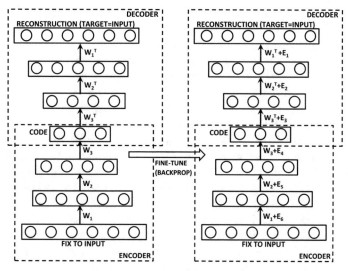

(b) Pretraining is followed by fine-tuning with backpropagation

Figure 6.10: Training a multi-layer RBM

with Gibbs sampling, and the resulting weights are grandfathered into a conventional neural network with continuous sigmoid activations (instead of sigmoid-based discrete sampling). Why should one go through the trouble to train an RBM in order to train a conventional network at all? This is because of the fact that Boltzmann machines are trained in a fundamentally different way from the backpropagation approach in conventional neural networks. The contrastive divergence approach tends to train all layers jointly, which does not cause the same problems with the vanishing and exploding gradient problems, as is the case in conventional neural networks.

At first glance, the goal of creating deep networks from RBMs seems rather difficult. First, RBMs are not quite like feed-forward units that perform the computation in a particular direction. RBMs are symmetric models in which the visible units and hidden units are connected in the form of an undirected graphical model. Therefore, one needs to define a concrete way in which multiple RBMs interact with one another. In this context, a useful observation is that even though RBMs are symmetric and discrete models, the learned weights can be used to define a related neural network that performs directed computation in the continuous space of activations. These weights are already quite close to the final solution because of how they have been learned with discrete sampling. Therefore, these weights can be fine-tuned with a relatively modest effort of traditional backpropagation. In order to understand this point, consider the single-layer RBM illustrated in Figure 6.4, which shows that even the single-layer RBM is equivalent to a directed graphical model of infinite length. However, once the visible states have been fixed, it suffices to keep only three layers of this computational graph, and perform the computations with the continuous values derived from sigmoid activations. This approach already provides a good approximate solution. The resulting network is a traditional autoencoder, although its weights have been (approximately) learned in a rather unconventional way. This section will show how this type of approach can also be applied to stacked RBMs.

What is a stacked set of RBMs? Consider a data set with d dimensions, for which the goal is to create a reduced representation with m_1 dimensions. One can achieve this goal with an RBM containing d visible units and m_1 hidden units. By training this RBM, one will obtain an m_1-dimensional representation of the data set. Now consider a second RBM that has m_1 visible units and m_2 hidden units. We can simply *copy* the m_1 outputs of the first RBM as the inputs to the second RBM, which has $m_1 \times m_2$ weights. As a result, one can train this new RBM to create an m_2-dimensional representation by using the outputs from the first RBM as its inputs. Note that we can repeat this process for k times, so that the last RBM is of size $m_{k-1} \times m_k$. Therefore, we *sequentially* train each of these RBMs by copying the output of one RBM into the input of another.

An example of a stacked RBM is shown on the left-hand side of Figure 6.10(a). This type of RBM is often shown with the concise diagram on the right-hand side of Figure 6.10(a). Note that the copying between two RBMs is a simple one-to-one copying between corresponding nodes, because the output layer of the rth RBM has exactly the same number of nodes as the input layer of the $(r+1)$th RBM. The resulting representations are *unsupervised* because they do not depend on a specific target. Another point is that the Boltzmann machine is an undirected model. However, by stacking the Boltzmann machine, we no longer have an undirected model because the upper layers receive feedback from the lower layers, but not vice versa. In fact, one can treat each Boltzmann machine as a single computational unit with many inputs and outputs, and the copying from one machine to another as the data transmission between two computational units. From this particular view of the stack of Boltzmann machines as a computational graph, it is even possible to perform backpropagation if one reverts to using the sigmoid units to create real-valued activations rather than to create the parameters needed for drawing binary samples. Although the use of real-valued activations is only an approximation, it already provides an excellent approximation because of the way in which the Boltzmann machine has been trained. This initial set of weights can be fine-tuned with backpropagation. After all, backpropagation can be performed on any computational graph, irrespective of the nature of the function computed inside the graph as long as a continuous function is computed. The fine tuning of backpropagation approach is particularly essential in the case of supervised learning, because the weights learned from a Boltzmann machine are always unsupervised.

6.7.1 Unsupervised Learning

Even in the case of unsupervised learning, the stacked RBM will generally provide reductions of better quality than a single RBM. However, the training of this RBM has to be performed carefully because results of high quality are not obtained by simply training all the layers together. Better results are obtained by using a pretraining approach. Each of the three RBMs in Figure 6.10(a) are trained sequentially. First, RBM1 is trained using the provided training data as the values of the visible units. Then, the outputs of the first RBM are used to train RBM2. This approach is repeated to train RBM3. Note that one can greedily train as many layers as desired using this approach. Assume that the weight matrices for the three learned RBMs are W_1, W_2, and W_3, respectively. Once these weight matrices have been learned, one can put together an encoder-decoder pair with these three weight matrices as shown in Figure 6.10(b). The three decoders have weight matrices W_1^T, W_2^T, and W_3^T, because they perform the inverse operations of encoders. As a result, one now has a directed encoder-decoder network that can be trained with backpropagation like any conventional neural network. The states in this network are computed using directed probabilistic operations, rather than sampled with the use of Monte-Carlo methods. One can perform backpropagation through the layers in order to fine-tune the learning. Note that the weight matrices on the right-hand side of Figure 6.10(b) have been adjusted as a result of this fine tuning. Furthermore, the weight matrices of the encoder and the decoder are no longer related in a symmetric way as a result of the fine tuning. Such stacked RBMs provide reductions of higher quality compared to those with shallower RBMs [414], which is analogous to the behavior of conventional neural networks.

6.7.2 Supervised Learning

How can one learn the weights in such a way that the Boltzmann machine is encouraged to produce a particular type of output such a class labels? Imagine that one wants to perform a k-way classification with a stack of RBMs. The use of a single-layer RBM for classification has already been discussed in Section 6.5.3, and the corresponding architecture is illustrated in Figure 6.7. This architecture can be modified by replacing the single hidden layer with a stack of hidden layers. The final layer of hidden features are then connected to the visible softmax layer that outputs the k probabilities corresponding to the different classes. As in the case of dimensionality reduction, pretraining is helpful Therefore, the first phase is completely unsupervised in which the class labels are not used. In other words, we train the weights of each hidden layer separately. This is achieved by training the weights of the lower layers first and then the higher layers, as in any stacked RBM. After the initial weights have been set in an unsupervised way, one can perform the initial training of weights between the final hidden layer and visible layer of softmax units. One can then create a directed computational graph with these initial weights, as in the case of the unsupervised setting. Backpropagation is performed on this computational graph in order to perform fine tuning of the learned weights.

6.7.3 Deep Boltzmann Machines and Deep Belief Networks

One can stack the different layers of the RBM in various ways to achieve different types of goals. In some forms of stacking, the interactions between different Boltzmann machines are bi-directional. This variation is referred to as a *deep Boltzmann machine*. In other forms of stacking, some of the layers are uni-directional, whereas others are bi-directional. An example is a *deep belief network* in which only the upper RBM is bi-directional, whereas the lower layers are uni-directional. Some of these methods can be shown to be equivalent to various types of probabilistic graphical models like *sigmoid belief nets* [350].

A deep Boltzmann machine is particularly noteworthy because of the bi-directional connections between each pair of units. The fact that the copying occurs both ways means that we can merge the nodes in adjacent nodes of two RBMs into a single layer of nodes. Furthermore, observe that one could rearrange the RBM into a bipartite graph by putting all the odd layers in one set and the even layers in another set. In other words, the deep RBM is equivalent to a single RBM. The difference from a single RBM is that the visible units form only a small subset of the units in one layer, and all pairs of nodes are not connected. Because of the fact that all pairs of nodes are not connected, the nodes in the upper layers tend to receive smaller weights than the nodes in the lower layers. As a result, pretraining again becomes necessary in which the lower layers are trained first, and then followed up with the higher layers in a greedy way. Subsequently, all layers are trained together in order to fine-tune the method. Refer to the bibliographic notes for details of these advanced models.

6.8   Summary

The earliest variant of the Boltzmann machine was the Hopfield network. The Hopfield network is an energy-based model, which stores the training data instances in its local minima. The Hopfield network can be trained with the Hebbian learning rule. A stochastic variant of the Hopfield network is the Boltzmann machine, which uses a probabilistic model to achieve greater generalization. Furthermore, the hidden states of the Boltzmann machine hold a reduced representation of the data. The Boltzmann machine can be trained with a stochastic variant of the Hebbian learning rule. The main challenge in the case of the Boltzmann machine is that it requires Gibbs sampling, which can be slow in practice. The restricted Boltzmann machine allows connections only between hidden nodes and visible nodes, which eases the training process. More efficient training algorithms are available for the restricted Boltzmann machine. The restricted Boltzmann machine can be used as a dimensionality reduction method; it can also be used in recommender systems with incomplete data. The restricted Boltzmann machine has also been generalized to count data, ordinal data, and real-valued data. However, the vast majority of RBMs are still constructed under the assumption of binary units. In recent years, several deep variants of the restricted Boltzmann machine have been proposed, which can be used for conventional machine learning applications like classification.

6.9   Bibliographic Notes

The earliest variant of the Boltzmann family of models was the Hopfield network [207]. The Storkey learning rule is proposed in [471]. The earliest algorithms for learning Boltzmann machines with the use of Monte Carlo sampling were proposed in [1, 197]. Discussions of Markov Chain Monte Carlo methods are provided in [138, 351], and many of these methods are useful for Boltzmann machines as well. RBMs were originally invented by Smolensky, and referred to as the harmonium. A tutorial on energy-based models is provided in [280]. Boltzmann machines are hard to train because of the interdependent stochastic nature of the units. The intractability of the partition function also makes the learning of the Boltzmann machine hard. However, one can estimate the partition function with *annealed importance sampling* [352]. A variant of the Boltzmann machine is the *mean-field Boltzmann machine* [373], which uses deterministic real units rather than stochastic units. However, the approach is a heuristic and hard to justify. Nevertheless, the use of real-valued approximations is popular at inference time. In other words, a traditional neural network with real-valued activations and derived weights from the trained Boltzmann machine is often used for prediction. Other variations of the RBM, such as the neural autoregressive distribution estimator [265], can be viewed as autoencoders.

The efficient mini-batch algorithm for Boltzmann machines is described in [491]. The contrastive divergence algorithm, which is useful for RBMs, is described in [61, 191]. A variation referred to as *persistent contrastive divergence* is proposed in [491]. The idea of gradually increasing the value of k in CD_k over the progress of training was proposed in [61]. The work in [61] showed that even a single iteration of the Gibbs sampling approach (which greatly reduces burn-in time) produces only a small bias in the final result, which can be reduced by gradually increasing the value of k in CD_k over the course of training. This insight was key to the efficient implementation of the RBM. An analysis of the bias in the contrastive divergence algorithm may be found in [29]. The work in [479] analyzes the convergence properties of the RBM. It is also shows that the contrastive divergence algorithm is a heuristic, which does not really optimize any objective function. A discussion and practical suggestions for training Boltzmann machines may be found in [119, 193]. The universal approximation property of RBMs is discussed in [341].

RBMs have been used for a variety of applications like dimensionality reduction, collaborative filtering, topic modeling and classification. The use of the RBM for collaborative filtering is discussed in [414]. This approach is instructive because it also shows how one can use an RBM for categorical data containing a small number of values. The application of discriminative restricted Boltzmann machines to classification is discussed in [263, 264]. The topic modeling of documents with Boltzmann machines with softmax units (as discussed in the chapter) is based on [469]. Advanced RBMs for topic modeling with a Poisson distribution are discussed in [134, 538]. The main problem with these methods is that they are unable to work well with documents of varying lengths. The use of replicated softmax is discussed in [199]. This approach is closely connected to ideas from *semantic hashing* [415].

Most of the RBMs are proposed for binary data. However, in recent years, RBMs have also been generalized to other data types. The modeling of count data with softmax units is discussed in the context of topic modeling in [469]. The challenges associated with this type of modeling are discussed in [86]. The use of the RBM for the exponential distribution family is discussed in [522], and discussion for real-valued data is provided in [348]. The introduction of binomial units to encode more information than binary units was proposed in [495]. This approach was shown to be a noisy version of the ReLU [348]. The replacement of binary units with linear units containing Gaussian noise was first proposed in [124]. The modeling of documents with deep Boltzmann machines is discussed in [469]. Boltzmann machines have also been used for multimodal learning with images and text [357, 468].

Training of deep variations of Boltzmann machines provided the first deep learning algorithms that worked well [196]. These algorithms were the first pretraining methods, which were later generalized to other types of neural networks. A detailed discussion of pretraining may be found in Section 4.7 of Chapter 4. Deep Boltzmann machines are discussed in [417], and efficient algorithms are discussed in [200, 418].

Several architectures that are related to the Boltzmann machine provide different types of modeling capabilities. The Helmholtz machine and a wake-sleep algorithm are proposed in [195]. RBMs and their multilayer variants can be shown to be equivalent to different types of probabilistic graphical models such as sigmoid belief nets [350]. A detailed discussion of probabilistic graphical models may be found in [251]. In higher-order Boltzmann machines, the energy function is defined by groups of k nodes for $k > 2$. For example, an order-3 Boltzmann machine will contain terms of the form $w_{ijk}s_i s_j s_k$. Such higher-order machines are discussed in [437]. Although these methods are potentially more powerful that traditional Boltzmann machines, they have not found much popularity because of the large amount of data they require to train.

6.10   Exercises

1. This chapter discusses how Boltzmann machines can be used for collaborative filtering. Even though discrete sampling of the contrastive divergence algorithm is used for learning the model, the final phase of inference is done using real-valued sigmoid and softmax activations. Discuss how you can use this fact to your advantage in order to fine-tune the learned model with backpropagation.

2. Implement the contrastive divergence algorithm of a restricted Boltzmann machine. Also implement the inference algorithm for deriving the probability distribution of the hidden units for a given test example. Use Python or any other programming language of your choice.

3. Consider a Boltzmann machine without a bipartite restriction (of the RBM), but with the restriction that all units are visible. Discuss how this restriction simplifies the training process of the Boltzmann machine.

4. Propose an approach for using RBMs for outlier detection.

5. Derive the weight updates for the RBM-based topic modeling approach discussed in the chapter. Use the same notations.

6. Show how you can extend the RBM for collaborative filtering (discussed in Section 6.5.2 of the chapter) with additional layers to make it more powerful.

7. A discriminative Boltzmann machine is introduced for classification towards the end of Section 6.5.3. However, this approach is designed for binary classification. Show how you can extend the approach to multi-way classification.

8. Show how you can modify the topic modeling RBM discussed in the chapter in order to create a hidden representation of each node drawn from a large, sparse graph (like a social network).

9. Discuss how you can enhance the model of Exercise 8 to include data about an unordered list of keywords associated with each node. (For example, social network nodes are associated with wall-post and messaging content.)

10. Discuss how you can enhance the topic modeling RBM discussed in the chapter with multiple layers.

Chapter 7

Recurrent Neural Networks

"Democracy is the recurrent suspicion that more than half the people are right more than half the time."—*The New Yorker*, July 3, 1944.

7.1   Introduction

All the neural architectures discussed in earlier chapters are inherently designed for multi-dimensional data in which the attributes are largely independent of one another. However, certain data types such as time-series, text, and biological data contain sequential dependencies among the attributes. Examples of such dependencies are as follows:

1. In a time-series data set, the values on successive time-stamps are closely related to one another. If one uses the values of these time-stamps as independent features, then key information about the relationships among the values of these time-stamps is lost. For example, the value of a time-series at time t is closely related to its values in the previous window. However, this information is lost when the values at individual time-stamps are treated independently of one another.

2. Although text is often processed as a bag of words, one can obtain better semantic insights when the ordering of the words is used. In such cases, it is important to construct models that take the sequencing information into account. Text data is the most common use case of recurrent neural networks.

3. Biological data often contains sequences, in which the symbols might correspond to amino acids or one of the nucleobases that form the building blocks of DNA.

C. C. Aggarwal, *Neural Networks and Deep Learning*,
https://doi.org/10.1007/978-3-319-94463-0_7

The individual values in a sequence can be either real-valued or symbolic. Real-valued sequences are also referred to as time-series. Recurrent neural networks can be used for either type of data. In practical applications, the use of symbolic values is more common. Therefore, this chapter will primarily focus on symbolic data in general, and on text data in particular. Throughout this chapter, the default assumption will be that the input to the recurrent network will be a text segment in which the corresponding symbols of the sequence are the word identifiers of the lexicon. However, we will also examine other settings, such as cases in which the individual elements are characters or in which they are real values.

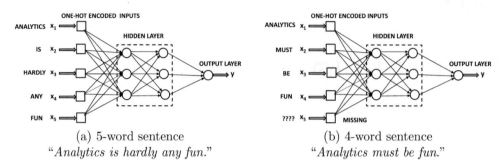

(a) 5-word sentence   (b) 4-word sentence
"*Analytics is hardly any fun.*"   "*Analytics must be fun.*"

Figure 7.1: An attempt to use a conventional neural network for sentiment analysis faces the challenge of variable-length inputs. The network architecture also does not contain any helpful information about sequential dependencies among successive words.

Many sequence-centric applications like text are often processed as bags of words. Such an approach ignores the ordering of words in the document, and works well for documents of reasonable size. However, in applications where the semantic interpretation of the sentence is important, or in which the size of the text segment is relatively small (e.g., a single sentence), such an approach is simply inadequate. In order to understand this point, consider the following pair of sentences:

> The cat chased the mouse.
> The mouse chased the cat.

The two sentences are clearly very different (and the second one is unusual). However, the bag-of-words representation would deem them identical. Hence, this type of representation works well for simpler applications (such as classification), but a greater degree of linguistic intelligence is required for more sophisticated applications in difficult settings such as *sentiment analysis, machine translation,* or *information extraction.*

One possible solution is to avoid the bag-of-words approach and create one input for each position in the sequence. Consider a situation in which one tried to use a conventional neural network in order to perform sentiment analysis on sentences with one input for each position in the sentence. The sentiment can be a binary label depending on whether it is positive or negative. The first problem that one would face is that the length of different sentences is different. Therefore, if we used a neural network with 5 sets of one-hot encoded word inputs (cf. Figure 7.1(a)), it would be impossible to enter a sentence with more than five words. Furthermore, any sentence with less than five words would have missing inputs (cf. Figure 7.1(b)). In some cases, such as Web log sequences, the length of the input sequence might run into the hundreds of thousands. More importantly, small changes in word ordering can lead to semantically different connotations, and *it is important to somehow encode information about the word ordering more directly within the architecture of the network.* The goal of such an approach would be to reduce the parameter requirements with increasing sequence length; recurrent neural networks provide an excellent example of (parameter-wise) *frugal architectural design* with the help of domain-specific insights. Therefore, the two main desiderata for the processing of sequences include (i) the ability to receive and process inputs in the same order as they are present in the sequence, and (ii) the treatment of inputs at each time-stamp in a similar manner in relation to previous history of inputs. A key challenge is that we somehow need to construct a neural network with a fixed number of parameters, but with the ability to process a variable number of inputs.

These desiderata are naturally satisfied with the use of *recurrent neural networks (RNNs)*. In a recurrent neural network, there is a one-to-one correspondence between the layers in the network and the specific positions in the sequence. The position in the sequence is also referred to as its *time-stamp*. Therefore, instead of a variable number of inputs in a single input layer, the network contains a variable number of layers, and each layer has a single input corresponding to that time-stamp. Therefore, the inputs are allowed to directly interact with down-stream hidden layers depending on their positions in the sequence. Each layer uses the same set of parameters to ensure similar modeling at each time stamp, and therefore the number of parameters is fixed as well. In other words, the same layer-wise architecture is repeated in time, and therefore the network is referred to as *recurrent*. Recurrent neural networks are also feed-forward networks with a specific structure based on the notion of *time layering*, so that they can take a *sequence* of inputs and produce a sequence of outputs. Each temporal layer can take in an input data point (either single attribute or multiple attributes), and optionally produce a multidimensional output. Such models are particularly useful for sequence-to-sequence learning applications like machine translation or for predicting the next element in a sequence. Some examples of applications include the following:

1. The input might be a sequence of words, and the output might be the same sequence shifted by 1, so that we are predicting the next word at any given point. This is a classical *language model* in which we are trying the predict the next word based on the sequential history of words. Language models have a wide variety of applications in text mining and information retrieval [6].

2. In a real-valued time-series, the problem of learning the next element is equivalent to *autoregressive analysis*. However, a recurrent neural network can learn far more complex models than those obtained with traditional time-series modeling.

3. The input might be a sentence in one language, and the output might be a sentence in another language. In this case, one can hook up two recurrent neural networks to learn the translation models between the two languages. One can even hook up a recurrent network with a different type of network (e.g., convolutional neural network) to learn captions of images.

4. The input might be a sequence (e.g., sentence), and the output might be a vector of class probabilities, which is triggered by the end of the sentence. This approach is useful for sentence-centric classification applications like sentiment analysis.

From these four examples, it can be observed that a wide variety of basic architectures have been employed or studied within the broader framework of recurrent neural networks.

There are significant challenges in learning the parameters of a recurrent neural network. One of the key problems in this context is that of the vanishing and the exploding gradient problem. This problem is particularly prevalent in the context of deep networks like recurrent neural networks. As a result, a number of variants of the recurrent neural network, such as long short-term memory (LSTM) and gated recurrent unit (GRU), have been proposed. Recurrent neural networks and their variants have been used in the context of a variety of applications like sequence-to-sequence learning, image captioning, machine translation, and sentiment analysis. This chapter will also study the use of recurrent neural networks in the context of these different applications.

7.1.1   Expressiveness of Recurrent Networks

Recurrent neural networks are known to be *Turing complete* [444]. Turing completeness means that a recurrent neural network can simulate any algorithm, given enough data and computational resources [444]. This property is, however, not very useful in practice because the amount of data and computational resources required to achieve this goal in arbitrary settings can be unrealistic. Furthermore, there are practical issues in training a recurrent neural network, such as the vanishing and exploding gradient problems. These problems increase with the length of the sequence, and more stable variations such as long short-term memory can address this issue only in a limited way. The neural Turing machine is discussed in Chapter 10, which uses external memory to improve the stability of neural network learning. A neural Turing machine can be shown to be equivalent to a recurrent neural network, and it often uses a more traditional recurrent network, referred to as the *controller*, as an important action-deciding component. Refer to Section 10.3 of Chapter 10 for a detailed discussion.

Chapter Organization

This chapter is organized as follows. The next section will introduce the basic architecture of the recurrent neural network along with the associated training algorithm. The challenges of training recurrent networks are discussed in Section 7.3. Because of these challenges, several variations of the recurrent neural network architecture have been proposed. This chapter will study several such variations. Echo-state networks are introduced in Section 7.4. Long short-term memory networks are discussed in Section 7.5. The gated recurrent unit is discussed in Section 7.6. Applications of recurrent neural networks are discussed in Section 7.7. A summary is given in Section 7.8.

7.2   The Architecture of Recurrent Neural Networks

In the following, the basic architecture of a recurrent network will be described. Although the recurrent neural network can be used in almost any sequential domain, its use in the text domain is both widespread and natural. We will assume the use of the text domain throughout this section in order to enable intuitively simple explanations of various concepts. Therefore, the focus of this chapter will be mostly on discrete RNNs, since that is the most popular use case. Note that exactly the same neural network can be used both for building a word-level RNN and a character-level RNN. The only difference between the two is the set of base symbols used to define the sequence. For consistency, we will stick to the word-level RNN while introducing the notations and definitions. However, variations of this setting are also discussed in this chapter.

The simplest recurrent neural network is shown in Figure 7.2(a). A key point here is the presence of the self-loop in Figure 7.2(a), which will cause the hidden state of the neural network to change after the input of each word in the sequence. In practice, one only works with sequences of finite length, and it makes sense to unfold the loop into a "time-layered" network that looks more like a feed-forward network. This network is shown in Figure 7.2(b). Note that in this case, we have a different node for the hidden state at each time-stamp and the self-loop has been unfurled into a feed-forward network. This representation is mathematically equivalent to Figure 7.2(a), but is much easier to comprehend because of its similarity to a traditional network. The weight matrices in different temporal layers *are shared* to ensure that the same function is used at each time-stamp. The annotations W_{xh}, W_{hh}, and W_{hy} of the weight matrices in Figure 7.2(b) make the sharing evident.

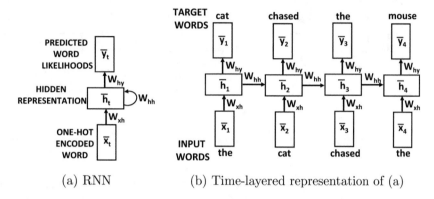

(a) RNN   (b) Time-layered representation of (a)

Figure 7.2: A recurrent neural network and its time-layered representation

It is noteworthy that Figure 7.2 shows a case in which each time-stamp has an input, output, and hidden unit. In practice, it is possible for either the input or the output units to be missing at any particular time-stamp. Examples of cases with missing inputs and outputs are shown in Figure 7.3. The choice of missing inputs and outputs would depend on the specific application at hand. For example, in a time-series forecasting application, we might need outputs at each time-stamp in order to predict the next value in the time-series. On the other hand, in a sequence-classification application, we might only need a single output label at the end of the sequence corresponding to its class. In general, it is possible for any subset of inputs or outputs to be missing in a particular application. The following discussion will assume that all inputs and outputs are present, although it is easy to generalize it to the case where some of them are missing by simply removing the corresponding terms or equations.

The particular architecture shown in Figure 7.2 is suited to language modeling. A language model is a well-known concept in natural language processing that predicts the next word, given the previous history of words. Given a sequence of words, their one-hot encoding is fed one at a time to the neural network in Figure 7.2(a). This temporal process is equivalent to feeding the individual words to the inputs at the relevant time-stamps in Figure 7.2(b). A time-stamp corresponds to the position in the sequence, which starts at 0 (or 1), and increases by 1 by moving forward in the sequence by one unit. In the setting of language modeling, the output is a vector of probabilities predicted for the next word in the sequence. For example, consider the sentence:

The cat chased the mouse.

When the word "*The*" is input, the output will be a vector of probabilities of the entire lexicon that includes the word "*cat*," and when the word "*cat*" is input, we will again get a

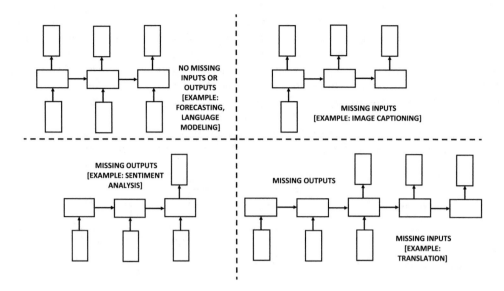

Figure 7.3: The different variations of recurrent networks with missing inputs and outputs

vector of probabilities predicting the next word. This is, of course, the classical definition of a language model in which the probability of a word is estimated based on the immediate history of previous words. In general, the input vector at time t (e.g., one-hot encoded vector of the tth word) is $\overline{x}_t$, the hidden state at time t is $\overline{h}_t$, and the output vector at time t (e.g., predicted probabilities of the $(t+1)$th word) is $\overline{y}_t$. Both $\overline{x}_t$ and $\overline{y}_t$ are d-dimensional for a lexicon of size d. The hidden vector $\overline{h}_t$ is p-dimensional, where p regulates the complexity of the embedding. For the purpose of discussion, we will assume that all these vectors are column vectors. In many applications like classification, the output is not produced at each time unit but is only triggered at the last time-stamp in the end of the sentence. Although output and input units may be present only at a subset of the time-stamps, we examine the simple case in which they are present in all time-stamps. Then, the hidden state at time t is given by a function of the input vector at time t and the hidden vector at time $(t-1)$:

$$\overline{h}_t = f(\overline{h}_{t-1}, \overline{x}_t) \qquad (7.1)$$

This function is defined with the use of weight matrices and activation functions (as used by all neural networks for learning), and *the same weights are used at each time-stamp*. Therefore, even though the hidden state evolves over time, the weights and the underlying function $f(\cdot, \cdot)$ remain fixed over all time-stamps (i.e., sequential elements) after the neural network has been trained. A separate function $\overline{y}_t = g(\overline{h}_t)$ is used to learn the output probabilities from the hidden states.

Next, we describe the functions $f(\cdot, \cdot)$ and $g(\cdot)$ more concretely. We define a $p \times d$ input-hidden matrix W_{xh}, a $p \times p$ hidden-hidden matrix W_{hh}, and a $d \times p$ hidden-output matrix W_{hy}. Then, one can expand Equation 7.1 and also write the condition for the outputs as follows:

$$\overline{h}_t = \tanh(W_{xh}\overline{x}_t + W_{hh}\overline{h}_{t-1})$$
$$\overline{y}_t = W_{hy}\overline{h}_t$$

Here, the "tanh" notation is used in a relaxed way, in the sense that the function is applied to the p-dimensional column vector in an element-wise fashion to create a p-dimensional vector with each element in $[-1, 1]$. Throughout this section, this relaxed notation will be used for several activation functions such as tanh and sigmoid. In the very first time-stamp, $\overline{h}_{t-1}$ is assumed to be some default constant vector (such as 0), because there is no input from the hidden layer at the beginning of a sentence. One can also learn this vector, if desired. Although the hidden states change at each time-stamp, the weight matrices stay fixed over the various time-stamps. Note that the output vector $\overline{y}_t$ is a set of continuous values with the same dimensionality as the lexicon. A softmax layer is applied on top of $\overline{y}_t$ so that the results can be interpreted as probabilities. *The p-dimensional output $\overline{h}_t$ of the hidden layer at the end of a text segment of t words yields its embedding, and the p-dimensional columns of W_{xh} yield the embeddings of individual words.* The latter provides an alternative to *word2vec* embeddings (cf. Chapter 2).

Because of the recursive nature of Equation 7.1, the recurrent network has the *ability to compute a function of variable-length inputs.* In other words, one can expand the recurrence of Equation 7.1 to define the function for $\overline{h}_t$ in terms of t inputs. For example, starting at $\overline{h}_0$, which is typically fixed to some constant vector (such as the zero vector), we have $\overline{h}_1 = f(\overline{h}_0, \overline{x}_1)$ and $\overline{h}_2 = f(f(\overline{h}_0, \overline{x}_1), \overline{x}_2)$. Note that $\overline{h}_1$ is a function of only $\overline{x}_1$, whereas $\overline{h}_2$ is a function of both $\overline{x}_1$ and $\overline{x}_2$. In general, $\overline{h}_t$ is a function of $\overline{x}_1 \ldots \overline{x}_t$. Since the output $\overline{y}_t$ is a function of $\overline{h}_t$, these properties are inherited by $\overline{y}_t$ as well. In general, we can write the following:

$$\overline{y}_t = F_t(\overline{x}_1, \overline{x}_2, \ldots \overline{x}_t) \tag{7.2}$$

Note that the function $F_t(\cdot)$ varies with the value of t although its relationship to its immediately previous state is always the same (based on Equation 7.1). Such an approach is particularly useful for variable-length inputs. This setting occurs often in many domains like text in which the sentences are of variable length. For example, in a language modeling application, the function $F_t(\cdot)$ indicates the probability of the next word, taking into account all the previous words in the sentence.

7.2.1 Language Modeling Example of RNN

In order to illustrate the workings of the RNN, we will use a toy example of a single sequence defined on a vocabulary of four words. Consider the sentence:

The cat chased the mouse.

In this case, we have a lexicon of four words, which are { *"the," "cat," "chased," "mouse"*}. In Figure 7.4, we have shown the probabilistic prediction of the next word at each of time-stamps from 1 to 4. Ideally, we would like the probability of the next word to be predicted correctly from the probabilities of the previous words. Each one-hot encoded input vector $\overline{x}_t$ has length four, in which only one bit is 1 and the remaining bits are 0s. The main flexibility here is in the dimensionality p of the hidden representation, which we set to 2 in this case. As a result, the matrix W_{xh} will be a 2×4 matrix, so that it maps a one-hot encoded input vector into a hidden vector $\overline{h}_t$ vector of size 2. As a practical matter, each column of W_{xh} corresponds to one of the four words, and one of these columns is copied by the expression $W_{xh}\overline{x}_t$. Note that this expression is added to $W_{hh}\overline{h}_t$ and then transformed with the tanh function to produce the final expression. The final output $\overline{y}_t$ is defined by $W_{hy}\overline{h}_t$. Note that the matrices W_{hh} and W_{hy} are of sizes 2×2 and 4×2, respectively.

In this case, the outputs are continuous values (not probabilities) in which larger values indicate greater likelihood of presence. These continuous values are eventually converted

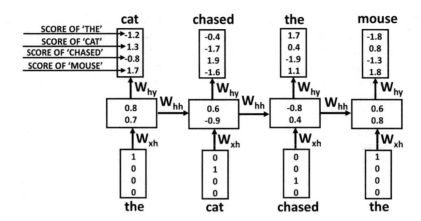

Figure 7.4: Example of language modeling with a recurrent neural network

to probabilities with the softmax function, and therefore one can treat them as substitutes to log probabilities. The word "*cat*" is predicted in the first time-stamp with a value of 1.3, although this value seems to be (incorrectly) outstripped by "*mouse*" for which the corresponding value is 1.7. However, the word "*chased*" seems to be predicted correctly at the next time-stamp. As in all learning algorithms, one cannot hope to predict every value exactly, and such errors are more likely to be made in the early iterations of the backpropagation algorithm. However, as the network is repeatedly trained over multiple iterations, it makes fewer errors over the training data.

7.2.1.1 Generating a Language Sample

Such an approach can also be used to generate an arbitrary sample of a language, once the training has been completed. How does one use such a language model at testing time, since each state requires an input word, and none is available during language generation? The likelihoods of the tokens at the first time-stamp can be generated using the <START> token as input. Since the <START> token is also available in the training data, the model will typically select a word that often starts text segments. Subsequently, the idea is to sample one of the tokens generated at each time-stamp (based on the predicted likelihood), and then use it as an input to the next time-stamp. To improve the accuracy of the sequentially predicted token, one might use beam search to expand on the most likely possibilities by always keeping track of the b best sequence prefixes of any particular length. The value of b is a user-driven parameter. By recursively applying this operation, one can generate an arbitrary sequence of text that reflects the particular training data at hand. If the <END> token is predicted, it indicates the end of that particular segment of text. Although such an approach often results in syntactically correct text, it might be nonsensical in meaning. For example, a character-level RNN[1] authored by Karpathy, Johnson, and Fei Fei [233, 580] was trained on William Shakespeare's plays. A character-level RNN requires the neural network to learn both syntax *and* spelling. After only five iterations of learning across the full data set, the following was a sample of the output:

---

[1] A long-short term memory network (LSTM) was used, which is a variation on the vanilla RNN discussed here.

KING RICHARD II:
Do cantant,-'for neight here be with hand her,-
Eptar the home that Valy is thee.

NORONCES:
Most ma-wrow, let himself my hispeasures;
An exmorbackion, gault, do we to do you comforr,
Laughter's leave: mire sucintracce shall have theref-Helt.

Note that there are a large number of misspellings in this case, and a lot of the words are gibberish. However, when the training was continued to 50 iterations, the following was generated as a part of the sample:

KING RICHARD II:
Though they good extremit if you damed;
Made it all their fripts and look of love;
Prince of forces to uncertained in conserve
To thou his power kindless. A brives my knees
In penitence and till away with redoom.

GLOUCESTER:
Between I must abide.

This generated piece of text is largely consistent with the syntax and spelling of the archaic English in William Shakespeare's plays, although there are still some obvious errors. Furthermore, the approach also indents and formats the text in a manner similar to the plays by placing new lines at reasonable locations. Continuing to train for more iterations makes the output almost error-free, and some impressive samples are also available at [235].

Of course, the semantic meaning of the text is limited, and one might wonder about the usefulness of generating such nonsensical pieces of text from the perspective of machine learning applications. The key point here is that by providing an additional *contextual* input, such as the neural representation of an image, the neural network can be made to give intelligent outputs such as a grammatically correct description (i.e., caption) of the image. In other words, language models are best used by generating *conditional* outputs.

The primary goal of the language-modeling RNN is not to create arbitrary sequences of the language, but to provide an architectural base that can be modified in various ways to incorporate the effect of the specific context. For example, applications like machine translation and image captioning learn a language model that is *conditioned* on another input such as a sentence in the source language or an image to be captioned. Therefore, the precise design of the application-dependent RNN will use the same principles as the language-modeling RNN, but will make small changes to this basic architecture in order to incorporate the specific context. In all these cases, the key is in choosing the input and output values of the recurrent units in a judicious way, so that one can backpropagate the output errors and learn the weights of the neural network in an application-dependent way.

7.2.2   Backpropagation Through Time

The negative logarithms of the softmax probability of the correct words at the various time-stamps are aggregated to create the loss function. The softmax function is described in Section 3.2.5.1 of Chapter 3, and we directly use those results here. If the output vector $\bar{y}_t$ can be written as $[\hat{y}_t^1 \ldots \hat{y}_t^d]$, it is first converted into a vector of d probabilities using the softmax function:

$$[\hat{p}_t^1 \ldots \hat{p}_t^d] = \text{Softmax}([\hat{y}_t^1 \ldots \hat{y}_t^d])$$

The softmax function above can be found in Equation 3.20 of Chapter 3. If j_t is the index of the ground-truth word at time t in the training data, then the loss function L for all T time-stamps is computed as follows:

$$L = -\sum_{t=1}^{T} \log(\hat{p}_t^{j_t}) \tag{7.3}$$

This loss function is a direct consequence of Equation 3.21 of Chapter 3. The derivative of the loss function with respect to the raw outputs may be computed as follows (cf. Equation 3.22 of Chapter 3):

$$\frac{\partial L}{\partial \hat{y}_t^k} = \hat{p}_t^k - I(k, j_t) \tag{7.4}$$

Here, $I(k, j_t)$ is an indicator function that is 1 when k and j_t are the same, and 0, otherwise. Starting with this partial derivative, one can use the straightforward backpropagation update of Chapter 3 (on the unfurled temporal network) to compute the gradients with respect to the weights in different layers. The main problem is that the weight sharing across different temporal layers will have an effect on the update process. An important assumption in correctly using the chain rule for backpropagation (cf. Chapter 3) is that the weights in different layers are distinct from one another, which allows a relatively straightforward update process. However, as discussed in Section 3.2.9 of Chapter 3, it is not difficult to modify the backpropagation algorithm to handle shared weights.

The main trick for handling shared weights is to first "pretend" that the parameters in the different temporal layers are independent of one another. For this purpose, we introduce the temporal variables $W_{xh}^{(t)}$, $W_{hh}^{(t)}$ and $W_{hy}^{(t)}$ for time-stamp t. Conventional backpropagation is first performed by working under the pretense that these variables are distinct from one another. Then, the contributions of the different temporal avatars of the weight parameters to the gradient are added to create a unified update for each weight parameter. This special type of backpropagation algorithm is referred to as *backpropagation through time (BPTT)*. We summarize the BPTT algorithm as follows:

(i) We run the input sequentially in the forward direction through time and compute the errors (and the negative-log loss of softmax layer) at each time-stamp.

(ii) We compute the gradients of the edge weights in the backwards direction on the unfurled network without any regard for the fact that weights in different time layers are shared. In other words, it is assumed that the weights $W_{xh}^{(t)}$, $W_{hh}^{(t)}$ and $W_{hy}^{(t)}$ in time-stamp t are distinct from other time-stamps. As a result, one can use conventional backpropagation to compute $\frac{\partial L}{\partial W_{xh}^{(t)}}$, $\frac{\partial L}{\partial W_{hh}^{(t)}}$, and $\frac{\partial L}{\partial W_{hy}^{(t)}}$. Note that we have used matrix calculus notations where the derivative with respect to a matrix is defined by a corresponding matrix of element-wise derivatives.

(iii) We add all the (shared) weights corresponding to different instantiations of an edge
in time. In other words, we have the following:

$$\frac{\partial L}{\partial W_{xh}} = \sum_{t=1}^{T} \frac{\partial L}{\partial W_{xh}^{(t)}}$$

$$\frac{\partial L}{\partial W_{hh}} = \sum_{t=1}^{T} \frac{\partial L}{\partial W_{hh}^{(t)}}$$

$$\frac{\partial L}{\partial W_{hy}} = \sum_{t=1}^{T} \frac{\partial L}{\partial W_{hy}^{(t)}}$$

The above derivations follow from a straightforward application of the multivariate chain
rule. As in all backpropagation methods with shared weights (cf. Section 3.2.9 of Chapter 3),
we are using the fact that the partial derivative of a temporal copy of each parameter
(such as an element of $W_{xh}^{(t)}$) with respect to the original copy of the parameter (such
as the corresponding element of W_{xh}) can be set to 1. Here, it is noteworthy that the
computation of the partial derivatives with respect to the temporal copies of the weights
is not different from traditional backpropagation at all. Therefore, one only needs to wrap
the temporal aggregation around conventional backpropagation in order to compute the
update equations. The original algorithm for backpropagation through time can be credited
to Werbos's seminal work in 1990 [526], long before the use of recurrent neural networks
became more popular.

Truncated Backpropagation Through Time

One of the computational problems in training recurrent networks is that the underlying
sequences may be very long, as a result of which the number of layers in the network may also
be very large. This can result in computational, convergence, and memory-usage problems.
This problem is solved by using *truncated backpropagation through time*. This technique
may be viewed as the analog of stochastic gradient descent for recurrent neural networks.
In the approach, the state values are computed correctly during forward propagation, but
the backpropagation updates are done only over segments of the sequence of modest length
(such as 100). In other words, only the portion of the loss over the relevant segment is used to
compute the gradients and update the weights. The segments are processed in the same order
as they occur in the input sequence. The forward propagation does not need to be performed
in a single shot, but it can also be done over the relevant segment of the sequence as long as
the values in the final time-layer of the segment are used for computing the state values in
the next segment of layers. The values in the final layer in the current segment are used to
compute the values in the first layer of the next segment. Therefore, forward propagation is
always able to accurately maintain state values, although the backpropagation uses only a
small portion of the loss. Here, we have described truncated BPTT using non-overlapping
segments for simplicity. In practice, one can update using overlapping segments of inputs.

Practical Issues

The entries of each weight matrix are initialized to small values in $[-1/\sqrt{r}, 1/\sqrt{r}]$, where
r is the number of columns in that matrix. One can also initialize each of the d columns
of the input weight matrix W_{xh} to the *word2vec* embedding of the corresponding word

(cf. Chapter 2). This approach is a form of pretraining. The specific advantage of using this type of pretraining depends on the amount of training data. It can be helpful to use this type of initialization when the amount of available training data is small. After all, pretraining is a form of regularization (see Chapter 4).

Another detail is that the training data often contains a special <START> and an <END> token at the beginning and end of each training segment. These types of tokens help the model to recognize specific text units such as sentences, paragraphs, or the beginning of a particular module of text. The distribution of the words at the beginning of a segment of text is often very different than how it is distributed over the whole training data. Therefore, after the occurrence of <START>, the model is more likely to pick words that begin a particular segment of text.

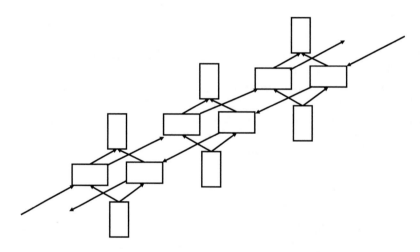

Figure 7.5: Showing three time-layers of a bidirectional recurrent network

There are other approaches that are used for deciding whether to end a segment at a particular point. A specific example is the use of a binary output that decides whether or not the sequence should continue at a particular point. Note that the binary output is in addition to other application-specific outputs. Typically, the sigmoid activation is used to model the prediction of this output, and the cross-entropy loss is used on this output. Such an approach is useful with real-valued sequences. This is because the use of <START> and <END> tokens is inherently designed for symbolic sequences. However, one disadvantage of this approach is that it changes the loss function from its application-specific formulation to one that provides a balance between end-of-sequence prediction and application-specific needs. Therefore, the weights of different components of the loss function would be yet another hyper-parameter that one would have to work with.

There are also several practical challenges in training an RNN, which make the design of various architectural enhancements of the RNN necessary. It is also noteworthy that multiple hidden layers (with long short-term memory enhancements) are used in all practical applications, which will be discussed in Section 7.2.4. However, the application-centric exposition will use the simpler single-layer model for clarity. The generalization of each of these applications to enhanced architectures is straightforward.

7.2.3 Bidirectional Recurrent Networks

One disadvantage of recurrent networks is that the state at a particular time unit only has knowledge about the past inputs up to a certain point in a sentence, but it has no knowledge about future states. In certain applications like language modeling, the results are vastly improved with knowledge about both past and future states. A specific example is handwriting recognition in which there is a clear advantage in using knowledge about both the past and future symbols, because it provides a better idea of the underlying context.

In the bidirectional recurrent network, we have separate hidden states $\overline{h}_t^{(f)}$ and $\overline{h}_t^{(b)}$ for the forward and backward directions. The forward hidden states interact only with each other and the same is true for the backward hidden states. The main difference is that the forward states interact in the forwards direction, while the backwards states interact in the backwards direction. Both $\overline{h}_t^{(f)}$ and $\overline{h}_t^{(b)}$, however, receive input from the same vector $\overline{x}_t$ (e.g., one-hot encoding of word) and they interact with the same output vector $\hat{y}_t$. An example of three time-layers of the bidirectional RNN is shown in Figure 7.5.

There are several applications in which one tries to predict the properties of the current tokens, such as the recognition of the characters in a handwriting sample, a the parts of speech in a sentence, or the classification of each token of the natural language. In general, any property of the *current* word can be predicted more effectively using this approach, because it uses the context on both sides. For example, the ordering of words in several languages is somewhat different depending on grammatical structure. Therefore, a bidirectional recurrent network often models the hidden representations of any specific point in the sentence in a more robust way with the use of backwards and forwards states, irrespective of the specific nuances of language structure. In fact, it has increasingly become more common to use bidirectional recurrent networks in various language-centric applications like speech recognition.

In the case of the bidirectional network, we have separate forward and backward parameter matrices. The forward matrices for the input-hidden, hidden-hidden, and hidden-output interactions are denoted by $W_{xh}^{(f)}$, $W_{hh}^{(f)}$, and $W_{hy}^{(f)}$, respectively. The backward matrices for the input-hidden, hidden-hidden, and hidden-output interactions are denoted by $W_{xh}^{(b)}$, $W_{hh}^{(b)}$, and $W_{hy}^{(b)}$, respectively.

The recurrence conditions can be written as follows:

$$\overline{h}_t^{(f)} = \tanh(W_{xh}^{(f)}\overline{x}_t + W_{hh}^{(f)}\overline{h}_{t-1}^{(f)})$$
$$\overline{h}_t^{(b)} = \tanh(W_{xh}^{(b)}\overline{x}_t + W_{hh}^{(b)}\overline{h}_{t+1}^{(b)})$$
$$\overline{y}_t = W_{hy}^{(f)}\overline{h}_t^{(f)} + W_{hy}^{(b)}\overline{h}_t^{(b)}$$

It is easy to see that the bidirectional equations are simple generalizations of the conditions used in a single direction. It is assumed that there are a total of T time-stamps in the neural network shown above, where T is the length of the sequence. One question is about the forward input at the boundary conditions corresponding to $t = 1$ and the backward input at $t = T$, which are not defined. In such cases, one can use a default constant value of 0.5 in each case, although one can also make the determination of these values as a part of the learning process.

An immediate observation about the hidden states in the forward and backwards direction is that they do not interact with one another at all. Therefore, one could first run the sequence in the forward direction to compute the hidden states in the forward direction, and then run the sequence in the backwards direction to compute the hidden states in the backwards direction. At this point, the output states are computed from the hidden states in the two directions.

After the outputs have been computed, the backpropagation algorithm is applied to compute the partial derivatives with respect to various parameters. First, the partial derivatives are computed with respect to the output states because both forward and backwards states point to the output nodes. Then, the backpropagation pass is computed only for the forward hidden states starting from $t = T$ down to $t = 1$. The backpropagation pass is finally computed for the backwards hidden states from $t = 1$ to $t = T$. Finally, the partial derivatives with respect to the shared parameters are aggregated. Therefore, the BPTT algorithm can be modified easily to the case of bidirectional networks. One can summarize the steps as follows:

1. Compute forward and backwards hidden states in independent and separate passes.

2. Compute output states from backwards and forward hidden states.

3. Compute partial derivatives of loss with respect to output states and each copy of the output parameters.

4. Compute partial derivatives of loss with respect to forward states and backwards states independently using backpropagation. Use these computations to evaluate partial derivatives with respect to each copy of the forwards and backwards parameters.

5. Aggregate partial derivatives over shared parameters.

Bidirectional recurrent neural networks are appropriate for applications in which the predictions are not causal based on a historical window. A classical example of a causal setting is a stream of symbols in which an event is predicted on the basis of the history of previous symbols. Even though language-modeling applications are formally considered causal applications (i.e., based on immediate history of *previous* words), the reality is that a given word can be predicted with much greater accuracy through the use of the contextual words on each side of it. In general, bidirectional RNNs work well in applications where the predictions are based on bidirectional context. Examples of such applications include handwriting recognition and speech recognition, in which the properties of individual elements in the sequence depend on those on either side of it. For example, if a handwriting is expressed in terms of the strokes, the strokes on either side of a particular position are helpful in recognizing the particular character being synthesized. Furthermore, certain characters are more likely to be adjacent than others.

A bidirectional neural network achieves almost the same quality of results as using an ensemble of two separate recurrent networks, one in which the input is presented in original form and the other in which the input is reversed. The main difference is that the parameters of the forwards and backwards states are trained jointly in this case. However, this integration is quite weak because the two types of states do not interact directly with one another.

7.2.4   Multilayer Recurrent Networks

In all the aforementioned applications, a single-layer RNN architecture is used for ease in understanding. However, in practical applications, a multilayer architecture is used in order to build models of greater complexity. Furthermore, this multilayer architecture can be used in combination with advanced variations of the RNN, such as the LSTM architecture or the gated recurrent unit. These advanced architectures are introduced in later sections.

An example of a deep network containing three layers is shown in Figure 7.6. Note that nodes in higher-level layers receive input from those in lower-level layers. The relationships among the hidden states can be generalized directly from the single-layer network. First, we rewrite the recurrence equation of the hidden layers (for single-layer networks) in a form that can be adapted easily to multilayer networks:

$$\overline{h}_t = \tanh(W_{xh}\overline{x}_t + W_{hh}\overline{h}_{t-1})$$

$$= \tanh W \left[\begin{array}{c} \overline{x}_t \\ \hline \overline{h}_{t-1} \end{array} \right]$$

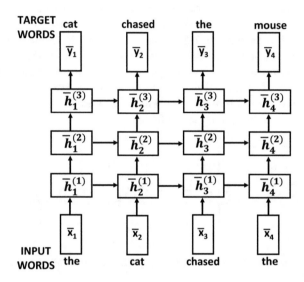

Figure 7.6: Multi-layer recurrent neural networks

Here, we have put together a larger matrix $W = [W_{xh}, W_{hh}]$ that includes the columns of W_{xh} and W_{hh}. Similarly, we have created a larger column vector that stacks up the state vector in the first hidden layer at time $t-1$ and the input vector at time t. In order to distinguish between the hidden nodes for the upper-level layers, let us add an additional superscript to the hidden state and denote the vector for the hidden states at time-stamp t and layer k by $\overline{h}_t^{(k)}$. Similarly, let the weight matrix for the kth hidden layer be denoted by $W^{(k)}$. It is noteworthy that the weights are shared across different time-stamps (as in the single-layer recurrent network), but they are not shared across different layers. Therefore, the weights are superscripted by the layer index k in $W^{(k)}$. The first hidden layer is special because it receives inputs both from the input layer at the current time-stamp and the adjacent hidden state at the previous time-stamp. Therefore, the matrices $W^{(k)}$ will have a size of $p \times (d+p)$ only for the first layer (i.e., $k = 1$), where d is the size of the input vector $\overline{x}_t$ and p is the size of the hidden vector $\overline{h}_t$. Note that d will typically not be the same as p. The recurrence condition for the first layer is already shown above by setting $W^{(1)} = W$. Therefore, let us focus on all the hidden layers k for $k \geq 2$. It turns out that the recurrence condition for the layers with $k \geq 2$ is also in a very similar form as the equation shown above:

$$\overline{h}_t^{(k)} = \tanh W^{(k)} \left[\begin{array}{c} \overline{h}_t^{(k-1)} \\ \hline \overline{h}_{t-1}^{(k)} \end{array} \right]$$

In this case, the size of the matrix $W^{(k)}$ is $p \times (p + p) = p \times 2p$. The transformation from hidden to output layer remains the same as in single-layer networks. It is easy to see that this approach is a straightforward multilayer generalization of the case of single-layer networks. It is common to use two or three layers in practical applications. In order to use a larger number of layers, it is important to have access to more training data in order to avoid overfitting.

7.3   The Challenges of Training Recurrent Networks

Recurrent neural networks are very hard to train because of the fact that the time-layered network is a very deep network, especially if the input sequence is long. In other words, the depth of the temporal layering is input-dependent. As in all deep networks, the loss function has highly varying sensitivities of the loss function (i.e., loss gradients) to different temporal layers. Furthermore, even though the loss function has highly varying gradients to the variables in different layers, the same parameter matrices are shared by different temporal layers. This combination of varying sensitivity and shared parameters in different layers can lead to some unusually unstable effects.

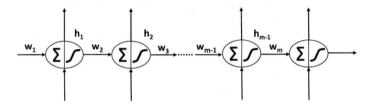

Figure 7.7: The vanishing and exploding gradient problems

The primary challenge associated with a recurrent neural network is that of the *vanishing* and *exploding gradient problems*. This point is explained in detail in Section 3.4 of Chapter 3. In this section, we will revisit this issue in the context of recurrent neural networks. It is easiest to understand the challenges associated with recurrent networks by examining the case of a recurrent network with a single unit in each layer.

Consider a set of T consecutive layers, in which the tanh activation function, $\Phi(\cdot)$, is applied between each pair of layers. The shared weight between a pair of hidden nodes is denoted by w. Let $h_1 \ldots h_T$ be the hidden values in the various layers. Let $\Phi'(h_t)$ be the derivative of the activation function in hidden layer t. Let the copy of the shared weight w in the tth layer be denoted by w_t so that it is possible to examine the effect of the backpropagation update. Let $\frac{\partial L}{\partial h_t}$ be the derivative of the loss function with respect to the hidden activation h_t. The neural architecture is illustrated in Figure 7.7. Then, one derives the following update equations using backpropagation:

$$\frac{\partial L}{\partial h_t} = \Phi'(h_{t+1}) \cdot w_{t+1} \cdot \frac{\partial L}{\partial h_{t+1}} \tag{7.5}$$

Since the shared weights in different temporal layers are the same, the gradient is multiplied with the same quantity $w_t = w$ for each layer. Such a multiplication will have a consistent bias towards vanishing when $w < 1$, and it will have a consistent bias towards exploding when $w > 1$. However, the choice of the activation function will also play a role because the derivative $\Phi'(h_{t+1})$ is included in the product. For example, the presence of the tanh activation function, for which the derivative $\Phi'(\cdot)$ is almost always less than 1, tends to increase the chances of the vanishing gradient problem.

Although the above discussion only studies the simple case of a hidden layer with one unit, one can generalize the argument to a hidden layer with multiple units [220]. In such a case, it can be shown that the update to the gradient boils down to a repeated multiplication with the same matrix A. One can show the following result:

Lemma 7.3.1 *Let A be a square matrix, the **magnitude** of whose largest eigenvalue is λ. Then, the entries of A^t tend to 0 with increasing values of t, when we have $\lambda < 1$. On the other hand, the entries of A^t diverge to large values, when we have $\lambda > 1$.*

The proof of the above result is easy to show by diagonalizing $A = P\Delta P^{-1}$. Then, it can be shown that $A^t = P\Delta^t P^{-1}$, where Δ is a diagonal matrix. The magnitude of the largest diagonal entry of Δ^t either vanishes with increasing t or it grows to an increasingly large value (in absolute magnitude) depending on whether than eigenvalue is less than 1 or larger than 1. In the former case, the matrix A^t tends to 0, and therefore the gradient vanishes. In the latter case, the gradient explodes. Of course, this does not yet include the effect of the activation function, and one can change the threshold on the largest eigenvalue to set up the conditions for the vanishing or exploding gradients. For example, the largest possible value of the sigmoid activation derivative is 0.25, and therefore the vanishing gradient problem will definitely occur when the largest eigenvalue is less that $1/0.25 = 4$. One can, of course, combine the effect of the matrix multiplication and activation function into a single *Jacobian* matrix (cf. Table 3.1 of Chapter 3), whose eigenvalues can be tested.

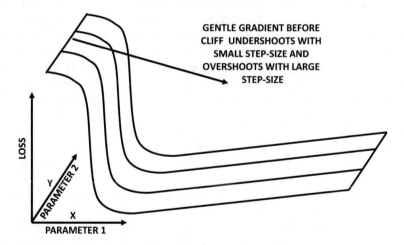

Figure 7.8: Revisiting Figure 3.13 of Chapter 3: An example of a cliff in the loss surface

In the particular case of recurrent neural networks, the *combination of the vanishing/exploding gradient and the parameter tying across different layers causes the recurrent neural network to behave in an unstable way with gradient-descent step size.* In other words, if we choose a step size that is too small, then the effect of some of the layers will cause little progress. On the other hand, if we choose a step size that is too large, then the effect of some of the layers will cause the step to overshoot the optimal point in an unstable way. An important issue here is that the gradient only tells us the best direction of movement for infinitesimally small steps; for finite steps, the behavior of the update could be substantially different from what is predicted by the gradient. The optimal points in recurrent networks are often hidden near cliffs or other regions of unpredictable change in the topography of the loss function, which causes the best directions of *instantaneous* movement to be extremely poor predictors of the best directions of *finite* movement. Since any practical learning algorithm is required to make finite steps of reasonable sizes to make good progress towards the optimal solution, this makes training rather hard. An example of a cliff is illustrated in Figure 7.8. The challenges associated with cliffs are discussed in Section 3.5.4 of Chapter 3. A detailed discussion of the exploding gradient problem and its geometric interpretation may be found in [369].

There are several solutions to the vanishing and exploding gradient problems, not all of which are equally effective. For example, the simplest solution is to use strong regularization on the parameters, which tends to reduce some of the problematic instability caused by the vanishing and exploding gradient problems. However, very strong levels of regularization can lead to models that do not achieve the full potential of a particular architecture of the neural network. A second solution that is discussed in Section 3.5.5 of Chapter 3 is *gradient clipping*. Gradient clipping is well suited to solving the exploding gradient problem. There are two types of clipping that are commonly used. The first is value-based clipping, and the second is norm-based clipping. In value-based clipping, the largest temporal components of the gradient are clipped before adding them. This was the original form of clipping that was proposed by Mikolov in his Ph.D. thesis [324]. The second type of clipping is norm-based clipping. The idea is that when the entire gradient vector has a norm that increases beyond a particular threshold, it is re-scaled back to the threshold. Both types of clipping perform in a similar way, and an analysis is provided in [368].

One observation about suddenly changing curvatures (like cliffs) is that first-order gradients are generally inadequate to fully model local error surfaces. Therefore, a natural solution is to use higher-order gradients. The main challenge with higher-order gradients is that they are computationally expensive. For example, the use of second-order methods (cf. Section 3.5.6 of Chapter 3) requires the inversion of a Hessian matrix. For a network with 10^6 parameters, this would require the inversion of a $10^6 \times 10^6$ matrix. As a practical matter, this is impossible to do with the computational power available today. However, some clever tricks for implementing second-order methods with Hessian-free methods have been proposed recently [313, 314]. The basic idea is to never compute the Hessian matrix exactly, but always work with rough approximations. A brief overview of many of these methods is provided in Section 3.5.6 of Chapter 3. These methods have also met with some success in training recurrent neural networks.

The type of instability faced by the optimization process is sensitive to the specific point on the loss surface at which the current solution resides. Therefore, choosing good initialization points is crucial. The work in [140] discusses several types of initialization that can avoid instability in the gradient updates. Using momentum methods (cf. Chapter 3) can also help in addressing some of the instability. A discussion of the power of initialization and momentum in addressing some of these issues is provided in [478]. Often simplified variants of recurrent neural networks, like *echo-state networks*, are used for creating a robust initialization of recurrent neural networks.

Another useful trick that is often used to address the vanishing and exploding gradient problems is that of batch normalization, although the basic approach requires some modifications for recurrent networks [81]. Batch normalization methods are discussed in Section 3.6 of Chapter 3. However, a variant known as *layer normalization* is more effective in recurrent networks. Layer normalization methods have been so successful that they have become a standard option while using a recurrent neural network or its variants.

Finally, a number of variants of recurrent neural networks are used to address the vanishing and exploding gradient problems. The first simplification is the use of echo-state networks in which the hidden-to-hidden matrices are randomly chosen, but only the output layers are trained. In the early years, echo-state networks were used as viable alternatives to recurrent neural networks, when it was considered too hard to train recurrent neural networks. However, these methods are too simplified to used in very complex settings. Nevertheless, these methods can still be used for robust initialization in recurrent neural networks [478]. A more effective approach for dealing with the vanishing and exploding gradient problems is to arm the recurrent network with internal memory, which lends more stability to the states of the network. The use of long short-term memory (LSTM) has become an effective way of handing the vanishing and exploding gradient problems. This approach introduces some additional states, which can be interpreted as a kind of long-term memory. The long-term memory provides states that are more stable over time, and also provide a greater level of stability to the gradient-descent process. This approach is discussed in Section 7.5.

7.3.1 Layer Normalization

The batch normalization technique discussed in Section 3.6 of Chapter 3 is designed to address the vanishing and exploding gradient problems in deep neural networks. In spite of its usefulness in most types of neural networks, the approach faces some challenges in recurrent neural networks. First, the batch statistics vary with the time-layer of the neural network, and therefore different statistics need to be maintained for different time-stamps. Furthermore, the number of layers in a recurrent network is *input-dependent*, depending on the length of the input sequence. Therefore, if a test sequence is longer than any of the training sequences encountered in the data, mini-batch statistics may not be available for some of the time-stamps. In general, the computation of the mini-batch statistics is not equally reliable for different time-layers (irrespective of mini-batch size). Finally, batch normalization cannot be applied to online learning tasks. One of the problematic issues is that batch normalization is a relatively unconventional neural network operation (compared to traditional neural networks) because the activations of the units depend on other training instances in the batch, and not just the current instance. Although batch-normalization can be adapted to recurrent networks [81], a more effective approach is *layer normalization.*

In layer normalization, the normalization is performed only over a single training instance, although the normalization factor is obtained by using all the current activations *in that layer of only the current instance.* This approach is closer to a conventional neural network operation, and we no longer have the problem of maintaining mini-batch statistics. All the information needed to compute the activations for an instance can be obtained from that instance only!

In order to understand how layer-wise normalization works, we repeat the hidden-to-hidden recursion of page 276:

$$\overline{h}_t = \tanh(W_{xh}\overline{x}_t + W_{hh}\overline{h}_{t-1})$$

This recursion is prone to unstable behavior because of the multiplicative effect across time-layers. We will show how to modify this recurrence with layer-wise normalization. As in the case of conventional batch normalization of Chapter 3, the normalization is applied to *pre-activation* values before applying the tanh activation function. Therefore, the pre-activation value at the tth time-stamp is computed as follows:

$$\overline{a}_t = W_{xh}\overline{x}_t + W_{hh}\overline{h}_{t-1}$$

Note that $\overline{a}_t$ is a vector with as many components as the number of units in the hidden layer (which we have consistently denoted as p in this chapter). We compute the mean μ_t and standard σ_t of the pre-activation values in $\overline{a}_t$:

$$\mu_t = \frac{\sum_{i=1}^{p} a_{ti}}{p}, \qquad \sigma_t = \sqrt{\frac{\sum_{i=1}^{p} a_{ti}^2}{p} - \mu_t^2}$$

Here, a_{ti} denotes the ith component of the vector $\overline{a}_t$.

As in batch normalization, we have additional learning parameters, associated with each unit. Specifically, for the p units in the tth layer, we have a p-dimensional vector of *gain parameters* $\overline{\gamma}_t$, and a p-dimensional vector of *bias parameters* denoted by $\overline{\beta}_t$. These parameters are analogous to the parameters γ_i and β_i in Section 3.6 on batch normalization. The purpose of these parameters is to re-scale the normalized values and add bias in a learnable way. The hidden activations $\overline{h}_t$ of the next layer are therefore computed as follows:

$$\overline{h}_t = \tanh\left(\frac{\overline{\gamma}_t}{\sigma_t} \odot (\overline{a}_t - \overline{\mu}_t) + \overline{\beta}_t\right) \tag{7.6}$$

Here, the notation $\odot$ indicates elementwise multiplication, and the notation $\overline{\mu}_t$ refers to a vector containing p copies of the scalar μ_t. The effect of layer normalization is to ensure that the magnitudes of the activations do not continuously increase or decrease with time-stamp (causing vanishing and exploding gradients), although the learnable parameters allow some flexibility. It has been shown in [14] that layer normalization provides better performance than batch normalization in recurrent neural networks. Some related normalizations can also be used for streaming and online learning [294].

7.4 Echo-State Networks

Echo-state networks represent a simplification of recurrent neural networks. They work well when the dimensionality of the input is small; this is because echo-state networks scale well with the number of temporal units but not with the dimensionality of the input. Therefore, these networks would be a solid option for regression-based modeling of a single or small number of real-valued time series over a relatively long time horizon. However, they would be a poor choice for modeling text in which the input dimensionality (based on one-hot encoding) would be the size of the lexicon in which the documents are represented. Nevertheless, even in this case, echo-state networks are practically useful in the initialization of weights within the network. Echo-state networks are also referred to as *liquid-state machines* [304], except that the latter uses spiking neurons with binary outputs, whereas echo-state networks use conventional activations like the sigmoid and the tanh functions.

Echo-state networks use *random weights* in the hidden-to-hidden layer and even the input-to-hidden layer, although the dimensionality of the hidden states is almost always much larger than the dimensionality of input states. For a single input series, it is not uncommon to use hidden states of dimensionality about 200. Therefore, only the output layer is trained, which is typically done with a linear layer for real-valued outputs. Note that the training of the output layer simply aggregates the errors at different output nodes, although the weights at different output nodes are still shared. Nevertheless, the objective function would still evaluate to a case of linear regression, which can be trained very simply without the need for backpropagation. Therefore, the training of the echo-state network is very fast.

As in traditional recurrent networks, the hidden-to-hidden layers have nonlinear activations such as the logistic sigmoid function, although tanh activations are also possible. A very important caveat in the initialization of the hidden-to-hidden units is that the largest eigenvector of the weight matrix W_{hh} should be set to 1. This can be easily achieved by first sampling the weights of the matrix W_{hh} randomly from a standard normal distribution, and then dividing each entry by the largest absolute eigenvalue $|\lambda_{max}|$ of this matrix.

$$W_{hh} \Leftarrow W_{hh}/|\lambda_{max}| \tag{7.7}$$

After this normalization, the largest eigenvalue of this matrix will be 1, which corresponds to its *spectral radius*. However, using a spectral radius of 1 can be too conservative because the nonlinear activations will have a dampening effect on the values of the states. For example, when using the sigmoid activation, the *largest* possible partial derivative of the sigmoid is always 0.25, and therefore using a spectral radius much larger than 4 (say, 10) is okay. When using the tanh activation function it would make sense to have a spectral radius of about 2 or 3. These choices would often still lead to a certain level of dampening over time, which is actually a useful regularization because very long-term relationships are generally much weaker than short-term relationships in time-series. One can also tune the spectral radius based on performance by trying different values of the scaling factor γ on held-out data to set $W_{hh} = \gamma W_0$. Here, W_0 is a randomly initialized matrix.

It is recommended to use sparse connectivity in the hidden-to-hidden connections, which is not uncommon in settings involving transformations with random projections. In order to achieve this goal, a number of connections in W_{hh} can be sampled to be non-zero and others are set to 0. This number of connections is typically linear in the number of hidden units. Another key trick is to divide the hidden units into groups indexed $1 \ldots K$ and only allow connectivity between hidden states belonging to with the same index. Such an approach can be shown to be equivalent to training an ensemble of echo-state networks (see. Exercise 2).

Another issue is about setting the input-to-hidden matrices W_{xh}. One needs to be careful about the scaling of this matrix as well, or else the effect of the inputs in each time-stamp can seriously damage the information carried in the hidden states from the previous time-stamp. Therefore, the matrix W_{xh} is first chosen randomly to W_1, and then it is scaled with different values of the hyper-parameter β in order to determine the final matrix $W_{xh} = \beta W_1$ that gives the best accuracy on held-out data.

The core of the echo-state network is based on a very old idea that expanding the number of features of a data set with a nonlinear transformation can often increase the expressive power of the input representation. For example, the RBF network (cf. Chapter 5) and the kernel support-vector machine both gain their power from expansion of the underlying feature space according to Cover's theorem on separability of patterns [84]. The only difference is that the echo-state network performs the feature expansion with random projection; such an approach is not without precedent because various types of random transformations are also used in machine learning as fast alternatives to kernel methods [385, 516]. It is noteworthy that feature expansion is primarily effective through nonlinear transformations, and these are provided through the activations in the hidden layers. In a sense, the echo-state method works using a similar principle to the RBF network in the temporal domain, just as the recurrent neural network is the replacement of feed-forward networks in the temporal domain. Just as the RBF network uses very little training for extracting the hidden features, the echo-state network uses little training for extracting the hidden features and instead relies on the randomized expansion of the feature space.

When used on time-series data, the approach provides excellent results on predicting values far out in the future. The key trick is to choose target output values at a time-stamp

t that correspond to the time-series input values at $t+k$, where k is the lookahead required for forecasting. In other words, an echo-state network is an excellent nonlinear autoregressive technique for modeling time-series data. One can even use this approach for forecasting multivariate time-series, although it is inadvisable to use the approach when the number of time series is very large. This is because the dimensionality of hidden states required for modeling would be simply too large. A detailed discussion on the application of the echo-state network for time-series modeling is provided in Section 7.7.5. A comparison with respect to traditional time-series forecasting models is also provided in the same section.

Although the approach cannot be realistically used for very high-dimensional inputs (like text), it is still very useful for initialization [478]. The basic idea is to initialize the recurrent network by using its echo-state variant to train the output layer. Furthermore, a proper scaling of the initialized values W_{hh} and W_{xh} can be set by trying different values of the scaling factors β and γ (as discussed above). Subsequently, traditional backpropagation is used to train the recurrent network. This approach can be viewed as a lightweight pretraining for recurrent networks.

A final issue is about the sparsity of the weight connections. Should the matrix W_{hh} be sparse? This is generally a matter of some controversy and disagreement; while sparse connectivity of echo-state networks has been recommended since the early years [219], the reasons for doing so are not very clear. The original work [219] states that sparse connectivity leads to a decoupling of the individual subnetworks, which encourages the development of individual dynamics. This seems to be an argument for increased diversity of the features learned by the echo-state network. If decoupling is indeed the goal, it would make a lot more sense to do so explicitly, and divide the hidden states into disconnected groups. Such an approach has an ensemble-centric interpretation. It is also often recommended to increase sparsity in methods involving random projections for improved efficiency of the computations. Having dense connections can cause the activations of different states to be embedded in the multiplicative noise of a large number of Gaussian random variables, and therefore more difficult to extract.

7.5 Long Short-Term Memory (LSTM)

As discussed in Section 7.3, recurrent neural networks have problems associated with vanishing and exploding gradients [205, 368, 369]. This is a common problem in neural network updates where successive multiplication by the matrix $W^{(k)}$ is inherently unstable; it either results in the gradient disappearing during backpropagation, or in it blowing up to large values in an unstable way. This type of instability is the direct result of successive multiplication with the (recurrent) weight matrix at various time-stamps. One way of viewing this problem is that a neural network that uses only multiplicative updates is good only at learning over short sequences, and is therefore inherently endowed with good short-term memory but poor long-term memory [205]. To address this problem, a solution is to change the recurrence equation for the hidden vector with the use of the LSTM with the use of long-term memory. The operations of the LSTM are designed to have fine-grained control over the data written into this long-term memory.

As in the previous sections, the notation $\overline{h}_t^{(k)}$ represents the hidden states of the kth layer of a multi-layer LSTM. For notational convenience, we also assume that the input layer $\overline{x}_t$ can be denoted by $\overline{h}_t^{(0)}$ (although this layer is obviously not hidden). As in the case of the recurrent network, the input vector $\overline{x}_t$ is d-dimensional, whereas the hidden states are p-dimensional. The LSTM is an enhancement of the recurrent neural network architecture of Figure 7.6 in which we change the recurrence conditions of how the hidden states $\overline{h}_t^{(k)}$ are propagated. In order to achieve this goal, we have an additional hidden vector of p dimensions, which is denoted by $\overline{c}_t^{(k)}$ and referred to as the *cell state*. One can view the cell state as a kind of long-term memory that retains at least a part of the information in earlier states by using a combination of partial "forgetting" and "increment" operations on the previous cell states. It has been shown in [233] that the nature of the memory in $\overline{c}_t^{(k)}$ is occasionally interpretable when it is applied to text data such as literary pieces. For example, one of the p values in $\overline{c}_t^{(k)}$ might change in sign after an opening quotation and then revert back only when that quotation is closed. The upshot of this phenomenon is that the resulting neural network is able to model long-range dependencies in the language or even a specific pattern (like a quotation) extended over a large number of tokens. This is achieved by using a gentle approach to update these cell states over time, so that there is greater persistence in information storage. Persistence in state values avoids the kind of instability that occurs in the case of the vanishing and exploding gradient problems. One way of understanding this intuitively is that if the states in different temporal layers share a greater level of similarity (through long-term memory), it is harder for the gradients with respect to the incoming weights to be drastically different.

As with the multilayer recurrent network, the update matrix is denoted by $W^{(k)}$ and is used to premultiply the column vector $[\overline{h}_t^{(k-1)}, \overline{h}_{t-1}^{(k)}]^T$. However, this matrix is of size[2] $4p \times 2p$, and therefore pre-multiplying a vector of size $2p$ with $W^{(k)}$ results in a vector of size $4p$. In this case, the updates use four intermediate, p-dimensional vector variables $\overline{i}$, $\overline{f}$, $\overline{o}$, and $\overline{c}$ that correspond to the $4p$-dimensional vector. The intermediate variables $\overline{i}$, $\overline{f}$, and $\overline{o}$ are respectively referred to as *input*, *forget*, and *output* variables, because of the roles they play in updating the cell states and hidden states. The determination of the hidden state vector $\overline{h}_t^{(k)}$ and the cell state vector $\overline{c}_t^{(k)}$ uses a multi-step process of first computing these intermediate variables and then computing the hidden variables from these intermediate variables. Note the difference between intermediate variable vector $\overline{c}$ and primary cell state $\overline{c}_t^{(k)}$, which have completely different roles. The updates are as follows:

$$
\begin{array}{ll}
\text{Input Gate:} \\
\text{Forget Gate:} \\
\text{Output Gate:} \\
\text{New C.-State:}
\end{array}
\begin{bmatrix} \overline{i} \\ \overline{f} \\ \overline{o} \\ \overline{c} \end{bmatrix}
=
\begin{pmatrix} \text{sigm} \\ \text{sigm} \\ \text{sigm} \\ \text{tanh} \end{pmatrix}
W^{(k)}
\begin{bmatrix} \overline{h}_t^{(k-1)} \\ \overline{h}_{t-1}^{(k)} \end{bmatrix}
\quad [\textbf{Setting up intermediates}]
$$

$$
\overline{c}_t^{(k)} = \overline{f} \odot \overline{c}_{t-1}^{(k)} + \overline{i} \odot \overline{c} \quad [\textbf{Selectively forget and add to long-term memory}]
$$

$$
\overline{h}_t^{(k)} = \overline{o} \odot \tanh(\overline{c}_t^{(k)}) \quad [\textbf{Selectively leak long-term memory to hidden state}]
$$

---

[2]In the first layer, the matrix $W^{(1)}$ is of size $4p \times (p+d)$ because it is multiplied with a vector of size $(p+d)$.

Here, the element-wise product of vectors is denoted by "$\odot$," and the notation "sigm" denotes a sigmoid operation. For the very first layer (i.e., $k = 1$), the notation $\overline{h}_t^{(k-1)}$ in the above equation should be replaced with $\overline{x}_t$ and the matrix $W^{(1)}$ is of size $4p \times (p + d)$. In practical implementations, biases are also used[3] in the above updates, although they are omitted here for simplicity. The aforementioned update seems rather cryptic, and therefore it requires further explanation.

The first step in the above sequence of equations is to set up the intermediate variable vectors $\overline{i}$, $\overline{f}$, $\overline{o}$, and $\overline{c}$, of which the first three should *conceptually* be considered binary values, although they are continuous values in $(0, 1)$. Multiplying a pair of binary values is like using an AND gate on a pair of boolean values. We will henceforth refer to this operation as gating. The vectors $\overline{i}$, $\overline{f}$, and $\overline{o}$ are referred to as input, forget, and output gates. In particular, these vectors are conceptually used as boolean gates for deciding (i) whether to add to a cell-state, (ii) whether to forget a cell state, and (iii) whether to allow leakage into a hidden state from a cell state. The use of the binary abstraction for the input, forget, and output variables helps in understanding the types of decisions being made by the updates. In practice, a continuous value in $(0, 1)$ is contained in these variables, which can enforce the effect of the binary gate in a probabilistic way if the output is seen as a probability. In the neural network setting, it is essential to work with continuous functions in order to ensure the differentiability required for gradient updates. The vector $\overline{c}$ contains the newly proposed contents of the cell state, although the input and forget gates regulate how much it is allowed to change the previous cell state (to retain long-term memory).

The four intermediate variables $\overline{i}$, $\overline{f}$, $\overline{o}$, and $\overline{c}$, are set up using the weight matrices $W^{(k)}$ for the kth layer in the first equation above. Let us now examine the second equation that updates the cell state with the use of some of these intermediate variables:

$$\overline{c}_t^{(k)} = \underbrace{\overline{f} \odot \overline{c}_{t-1}^{(k)}}_{\text{Reset?}} + \underbrace{\overline{i} \odot \overline{c}}_{\text{Increment?}}$$

This equation has two parts. The first part uses the p forget bits in $\overline{f}$ to decide which of the p cell states from the previous time-stamp to reset[4] to 0, and it uses the p input bits in $\overline{i}$ to decide whether to add the corresponding components from $\overline{c}$ to each of the cell states. Note that such updates of the cell states are in additive form, which is helpful in avoiding the vanishing gradient problem caused by multiplicative updates. One can view the cell-state vector as a continuously updated long-term memory, where the forget and input bits respectively decide (i) whether to reset the cell states from the previous time-stamp and forget the past, and (ii) whether to increment the cell states from the previous time-stamp to incorporate new information into long-term memory from the current word. The vector $\overline{c}$ contains the p amounts with which to increment the cell states, and these are values in $[-1, +1]$ because they are all outputs of the tanh function.

---

[3]The bias associated with the forget gates is particularly important. The bias of the forget gate is generally initialized to values greater than 1 [228] because it seems to avoid the vanishing gradient problem at initialization.

[4]Here, we are treating the forget bits as a vector of binary bits, although it contains continuous values in $(0, 1)$, which can be viewed as probabilities. As discussed earlier, the binary abstraction helps us understand the conceptual nature of the operations.

Finally, the hidden states $\overline{h}_t^{(k)}$ are updated using leakages from the cell state. The hidden state is updated as follows:

$$\overline{h}_t^{(k)} = \underbrace{\overline{o} \odot \tanh(\overline{c}_t^{(k)})}_{\text{Leak } \overline{c}_t^{(k)} \text{ to } \overline{h}_t^{(k)}}$$

Here, we are copying a functional form of each of the p cell states into each of the p hidden states, depending on whether the output gate (defined by $\overline{o}$) is 0 or 1. Of course, in the continuous setting of neural networks, partial gating occurs and only a fraction of the signal is copied from each cell state to the corresponding hidden state. It is noteworthy that the final equation does not always use the tanh activation function. The following alternative update may be used:

$$\overline{h}_t^{(k)} = \overline{o} \odot \overline{c}_t^{(k)}$$

As in the case of all neural networks, the backpropagation algorithm is used for training purposes.

In order to understand why LSTMs provide better gradient flows than vanilla RNNs, let us examine the update for a simple LSTM with a single layer and $p = 1$. In such a case, the cell update can be simplified to the following:

$$c_t = c_{t-1} * f + i * c \tag{7.8}$$

Therefore, the partial derivative c_t with respect to c_{t-1} is f, which means that the backward gradient flows for c_t are multiplied with the value of the forget gate f. Because of elementwise operations, this result generalizes to arbitrary values of the state dimensionality p. The biases of the forget gates are often set to high values initially, so that the gradient flows decay relatively slowly. The forget gate f can also be different at different time-stamps, which reduces the propensity of the vanishing gradient problem. The hidden states can be expressed in terms of the cell states as $h_t = o * \tanh(c_t)$, so that one can compute the partial derivative with respect to h_t with the use of a single tanh derivative. In other words, the long-term cell states function as gradient super-highways, which leak into hidden states.

7.6 Gated Recurrent Units (GRUs)

The Gated Recurrent Unit (GRU) can be viewed as a simplification of the LSTM, which does not use explicit cell states. Another difference is that the LSTM directly controls the amount of information changed in the hidden state using separate forget and output gates. On the other hand, a GRU uses a single reset gate to achieve the same goal. However, the basic idea in the GRU is quite similar to that of an LSTM, in terms of how it partially resets the hidden states. As in the previous sections, the notation $\overline{h}_t^{(k)}$ represents the hidden states of the kth layer for $k \geq 1$. For notational convenience, we also assume that the input layer $\overline{x}_t$ can be denoted by $\overline{h}_t^{(0)}$ (although this layer is obviously not hidden). As in the case of LSTM, we assume that the input vector $\overline{x}_t$ is d-dimensional, whereas the hidden states are p-dimensional. The sizes of the transformation matrices in the first layer are accordingly adjusted to account for this fact.

In the case of the GRU, we use two matrices $W^{(k)}$ and $V^{(k)}$ of sizes[5] $2p \times 2p$ and $p \times 2p$, respectively. Pre-multiplying a vector of size $2p$ with $W^{(k)}$ results in a vector of size $2p$, which will be passed through the sigmoid activation to create two intermediate, p-dimensional vector variables $\overline{z}_t$ and $\overline{r}_t$, respectively. The intermediate variables $\overline{z}_t$ and $\overline{r}_t$ are respectively referred to as update and reset gates. The determination of the hidden state vector $\overline{h}_t^{(k)}$ uses a two-step process of first computing these gates, then using them to decide how much to change the hidden vector with the weight matrix $V^{(k)}$:

$$\begin{matrix} \text{Update Gate:} \\ \text{Reset Gate:} \end{matrix} \quad \left[\begin{matrix} \overline{z} \\ \overline{r} \end{matrix} \right] = \left(\begin{matrix} \text{sigm} \\ \text{sigm} \end{matrix} \right) W^{(k)} \left[\begin{matrix} \overline{h}_t^{(k-1)} \\ \overline{h}_{t-1}^{(k)} \end{matrix} \right] \quad \textbf{[Set up gates]}$$

$$\overline{h}_t^{(k)} = \overline{z} \odot \overline{h}_{t-1}^{(k)} + (1 - \overline{z}) \odot \tanh V^{(k)} \left[\begin{matrix} \overline{h}_t^{(k-1)} \\ \overline{r} \odot \overline{h}_{t-1}^{(k)} \end{matrix} \right] \quad \textbf{[Update hidden state]}$$

Here, the element-wise product of vectors is denoted by "$\odot$," and the notation "sigm" denotes a sigmoid operation. For the very first layer (i.e., $k = 1$), the notation $\overline{h}_t^{(k-1)}$ in the above equation should be replaced with $\overline{x}_t$. Furthermore, the matrices $W^{(1)}$ and $V^{(1)}$ are of sizes $2p \times (p + d)$ and $p \times (p + d)$, respectively. We have also omitted the mention of biases here, but they are usually included in practical implementations. In the following, we provide a further explanation of these updates and contrast them with those of the LSTM.

Just as the LSTM uses input, output, and forget gates to decide how much of the information from the previous time-stamp to carry over to the next step, the GRU uses the update and the reset gates. The GRU does not have a separate internal memory and also requires fewer gates to perform the update from one hidden state to another. Therefore, a natural question arises about the precise role of the update and reset gates. The reset gate $\overline{r}$ decides how much of the hidden state to carry over from the previous time-stamp for a matrix-based update (like a recurrent neural network). The update gate $\overline{z}$ decides the *relative* strength of the contributions of this matrix-based update and a more direct contribution from the hidden vector $\overline{h}_{t-1}^{(k)}$ at the previous time-stamp. By allowing a direct (partial) copy of the hidden states from the previous layer, the gradient flow becomes more stable during backpropagation. The update gate of the GRU simultaneously performs the role of the input and forget gates in the LSTM in the form of $\overline{z}$ and $1 - \overline{z}$, respectively. However, the mapping between the GRU and the LSTM is not precise, because it performs these updates directly on the hidden state (and there is no cell state). Like the input, output, and forget gates in the LSTM, the update and reset gates are intermediate "scratch-pad" variables.

In order to understand why GRUs provide better performance than vanilla RNNs, let us examine a GRU with a single layer and single state dimensionality $p = 1$. In such a case, the update equation of the GRU can be written as follows:

$$h_t = z \cdot h_{t-1} + (1 - z) \cdot \tanh[v_1 \cdot x_t + v_2 \cdot r \cdot h_{t-1}] \tag{7.9}$$

Note that layer superscripts are missing in this single-layer case. Here, v_1 and v_2 are the two elements of the 2×1 matrix V. Then, it is easy to see the following:

$$\frac{\partial h_t}{\partial h_{t-1}} = z + (\text{Additive Terms}) \tag{7.10}$$

---

[5]In the first layer ($k = 1$), these matrices are of sizes $2p \times (p + d)$ and $p \times (p + d)$.

Backward gradient flow is multiplied with this factor. Here, the term $z \in (0,1)$ helps in passing *unimpeded* gradient flow and makes computations more stable. Furthermore, since the additive terms heavily depend on $(1-z)$, the overall multiplicative factor that tends to be closer to 1 even when z is small. Another point is that the value of z and the multiplicative factor $\frac{\partial h_t}{\partial h_{t-1}}$ is *different* for each time stamp, which tends to reduce the propensity for vanishing or exploding gradients.

Although the GRU is a closely related simplification of the LSTM, it should not be seen as a special case of the LSTM. A comparison of the LSTM and the GRU is provided in [71, 228]. The two models are shown to be roughly similar in performance, and the relative performance seems to depend on the task at hand. The GRU is simpler and enjoys the advantage of greater ease of implementation and efficiency. It might generalize slightly better with less data because of a smaller parameter footprint [71], although the LSTM would be preferable with an increased amount of data. The work in [228] also discusses several practical implementation issues associated with the LSTM. The LSTM has been more extensively tested than the GRU, simply because it is an older architecture and enjoys widespread popularity. As a result, it is generally seen as a safer option, particularly when working with longer sequences and larger data sets. The work in [160] also showed that none of the variants of the LSTM can reliably outperform it in a consistent way. This is because of the explicit internal memory and the greater gate-centric control in updating the LSTM.

7.7 Applications of Recurrent Neural Networks

Recurrent neural networks have numerous applications in machine learning applications, which are associated with information retrieval, speech recognition, and handwriting recognition. Text data forms the predominant setting for applications of RNNs, although there are several applications to computational biology as well. Most of the applications of RNNs fall into one of two categories:

1. *Conditional language modeling:* When the output of a recurrent network is a language model, one can enhance it with context in order to provide a relevant output to the context. In most of these cases, the context is the neural output of another neural network. To provide one example, in image captioning the context is the neural representation of an image provided by a convolutional network, and the language model provides a caption for the image. In machine translation, the context is the representation of a sentence in a source language (produced by another RNN), and the language model in the target language provides a translation.

2. *Leveraging token-specific outputs:* The outputs at the different tokens can be used to learn other properties than a language model. For example, the labels output at different time-stamps might correspond to the properties of the tokens (such as their parts of speech). In handwriting recognition, the labels might correspond to the characters. In some cases, all the time-stamps might not have an output, but the end-of-sentence marker might output a label for the entire sentence. This approach is referred to as sentence-level classification, and is often used in sentiment analysis. In some of these applications, bidirectional recurrent networks are used because the context on both sides of a word is helpful.

The following material will provide an overview of the numerous applications of recurrent neural networks. In most of these cases, we will use a single-layer recurrent network for ease in explanation and pictorial illustration. However, in most cases, a multi-layer LSTM is used. In other cases, a bidirectional LSTM is used, because it provides better performance. Replacing a single-layer RNN with a multi-layer/bidirectional LSTM in any of the following applications is straightforward. Out broader goal is to illustrate how this *family* of architectures can be used in these settings.

7.7.1 Application to Automatic Image Captioning

In image captioning, the training data consists of image-caption pairs. For example, the image[6] in the left-hand side of Figure 7.9 is obtained from the National Aeronautics and Space Administration Web site. This image is captioned *"cosmic winter wonderland."* One might have hundreds of thousands of such image-caption pairs. These pairs are used to train the weights in the neural network. Once the training has been completed, the captions are predicted for unknown test instances. Therefore, one can view this approach as an instance of image-to-sequence learning.

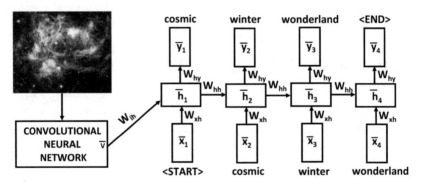

Figure 7.9: Example of image captioning with a recurrent neural network. An additional convolutional neural network is required for representational learning of the images. The image is represented by the vector $\overline{v}$, which is the output of the convolutional neural network. The inset image is by courtesy of the National Aeronautics and Space Administration (NASA).

One issue in the automatic captioning of images is that a separate neural network is required to learn the representation of the images. A common architecture to learn the representation of images is the *convolutional neural network*. A detailed discussion of convolutional neural networks is provide in Chapter 8. Consider a setting in which the convolutional neural network produces the q-dimensional vector $\overline{v}$ as the output representation. This vector is then used as an input to the neural network, but only[7] at the first time-stamp. To account for this additional input, we need another $p \times q$ matrix W_{ih}, which maps the image representation to the hidden layer. Therefore, the update equations for the various layers now need to be modified as follows:

$$\overline{h}_1 = \tanh(W_{xh}\overline{x}_1 + W_{ih}\overline{v})$$

---

[6]https://www.nasa.gov/mission_pages/chandra/cosmic-winter-wonderland.html

[7]In principle, one can also allow it to be input at all time-stamps, but it only seems to worsen performance.

$$\overline{h}_t = \tanh(W_{xh}\overline{x}_t + W_{hh}\overline{h}_{t-1}) \quad \forall t \geq 2$$
$$\overline{y}_t = W_{hy}\overline{h}_t$$

An important point here is that the convolutional neural network and the recurrent neural network are not trained in isolation. Although one might train them in isolation in order to create an initialization, the final weights are always trained jointly by running each image through the network and matching up the predicted caption with the true caption. In other words, for each image-caption pair, the weights in both networks are updated when errors are made in predicting any particular token of the caption. In practice, the errors are soft because the tokens at each point are predicted probabilistically. Such an approach ensures that the learned representation $\overline{v}$ of the images is sensitive to the specific application of predicting captions.

After all the weights have been trained, a test image is input to the entire system and passed through both the convolutional and recurrent neural network. For the recurrent network, the input at the first time-stamp is the <START> token and the representation of the image. At later time-stamps, the input is the most likely token predicted at the previous time-stamp. One can also use beam search to keep track of the b most likely sequence prefixes to expand on at each point. This approach is not very different from the language generation approach discussed in Section 7.2.1.1, except that it is conditioned on the image representation that is input to the model in the first time-stamp of the recurrent network. This results in the prediction of a relevant caption for the image.

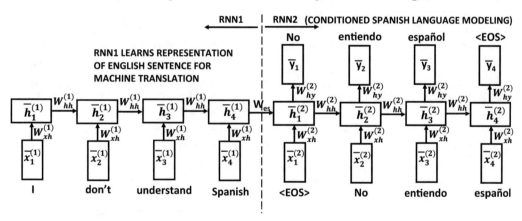

Figure 7.10: Machine translation with recurrent neural networks. Note that there are two separate recurrent networks with their own sets of shared weights. The output of $\overline{h}_4^{(1)}$ is a fixed length encoding of the 4-word English sentence.

7.7.2 Sequence-to-Sequence Learning and Machine Translation

Just as one can put together a convolutional neural network and a recurrent neural network to perform image captioning, one can put together two recurrent networks to translate one language into another. Such methods are also referred to as *sequence-to-sequence* learning because a sequence in one language is mapped to a sequence in another language. In principle, sequence-to-sequence learning can have applications beyond machine translation. For example, even question-answering (QA) systems can be viewed as sequence-to-sequence learning applications.

In the following, we provide a simple solution to machine translation with recurrent neural networks, although such applications are rarely addressed directly with the simple forms of recurrent neural networks. Rather, a variation of the recurrent neural network, referred to as the long short-term memory (LSTM) model is used. Such a model is much better in learning long-term dependencies, and can therefore work well with longer sentences. Since the general approach of using an RNN applies to an LSTM as well, we will provide the discussion of machine translation with the (simple) RNN. A discussion of the LSTM is provided in Section 7.5, and the generalization of the machine translation application to the LSTM is straightforward.

In the machine translation application, two different RNNs are hooked end-to-end, just as a convolutional neural network and a recurrent neural network are hooked together for image captioning. The first recurrent network uses the words from the source language as input. No outputs are produced at these time-stamps and the successive time-stamps accumulate knowledge about the source sentence in the hidden state. Subsequently, the end-of-sentence symbol is encountered, and the second recurrent network starts by outputting the first word of the target language. The next set of states in the second recurrent network output the words of the sentence in the target language one by one. These states also use the words of the target language as input, which is available for the case of the training instances but not for test instances (where predicted values are used instead). This architecture is shown in Figure 7.10.

The architecture of Figure 7.10 is similar to that of an autoencoder, and can even be used with pairs of identical sentences in the same language to create fixed-length representations of sentences. The two recurrent networks are denoted by RNN1 and RNN2, and their weights are not the same. For example, the weight matrix between two hidden nodes at successive time-stamps in RNN1 is denoted by $W_{hh}^{(1)}$, whereas the corresponding weight matrix in RNN2 is denoted by $W_{hh}^{(2)}$. The weight matrix W_{es} of the link joining the two neural networks is special, and can be independent of either of the two networks. This is necessary if the sizes of the hidden vectors in the two RNNs are different because the dimensions of the matrix W_{es} will be different from those of both $W_{hh}^{(1)}$ and $W_{hh}^{(2)}$. As a simplification, one can use[8] the same size of the hidden vector in both networks, and set $W_{es} = W_{hh}^{(1)}$. The weights in RNN1 are devoted to learning an encoding of the input in the source language, and the weights in RNN2 are devoted to using this encoding in order to create an output sentence in the target language. One can view this architecture in a similar way to the image captioning application, except that we are using two recurrent networks instead of a convolutional-recurrent pair. The output of the final hidden node of RNN1 is a fixed-length encoding of the source sentence. Therefore, irrespective of the length of the sentence, the encoding of the source sentence depends on the dimensionality of the hidden representation.

The grammar and length of the sentence in the source and target languages may not be the same. In order to provide a grammatically correct output in the target language, RNN2 needs to learn its language model. It is noteworthy that the units in RNN2 associated with the target language have both inputs and outputs arranged in the same way as a language-modeling RNN. At the same time, the output of RNN2 is conditioned on the input it receives from RNN1, which effectively causes language translation. In order to achieve this goal, training pairs in the source and target languages are used. The approach passes the source-target pairs through the architecture of Figure 7.10 and learns the model parameters

---

[8]The original work in [478] seems to use this option. In the Google Neural Machine Translation system [579], this weight is removed. This system is now used in Google Translate.

with the use of the backpropagation algorithm. Since only the nodes in RNN2 have outputs, only the errors made in predicting the target language words are backpropagated to train the weights in both neural networks. The two networks are jointly trained, and therefore the weights in both networks are optimized to the errors in the translated outputs of RNN2. As a practical matter, this means that the internal representation of the source language learned by RNN1 is highly optimized to the machine translation application, and is very different from one that would be learned if one had used RNN1 to perform language modeling of the source sentence. After the parameters have been learned, a sentence in the source language is translated by first running it through RNN1 to provide the necessary input to RNN2. Aside from this contextual input, another input to the first unit of RNN2 is the <EOS> tag, which causes RNN2 to output the likelihoods of the first token in the target language. The most likely token using beam search (cf. Section 7.2.1.1) is selected and used as the input to the recurrent network unit in the next time-stamp. This process is recursively applied until the output of a unit in RNN2 is also <EOS>. As in Section 7.2.1.1, we are generating a sentence from the target language using a language-modeling approach, except that the specific output is conditioned on the internal representation of the source sentence.

The use of neural networks for machine translation is relatively recent. Recurrent neural network models have a sophistication that greatly exceeds that of traditional machine translation models. The latter class of methods uses phrase-centric machine learning, which is often not sophisticated enough to learn the subtle differences between the grammars of the two languages. In practice, deep models with multiple layers are used to improve the performance.

One weakness of such translation models is that they tend to work poorly when the sentences are long. Numerous solutions have been proposed to solve the problem. A recent solution is that the sentence in the source language is input in the *opposite order* [478]. This approach brings the first few words of the sentences in the two languages closer in terms of their time-stamps within the recurrent neural network architecture. As a result, the first few words in the target language are more likely to be predicted correctly. The correctness in predicting the first few words is also helpful in predicting the subsequent words, which are also dependent on a neural language model in the target language.

7.7.2.1 Question-Answering Systems

A natural application of sequence-to-sequence learning is that of question answering (QA). Question-answering systems are designed with different types of training data. In particular, two types of question-answering systems are common:

1. In the first type, the answers are directly inferred based on the phrases and clue words in the question.

2. In the second type, the question is first transformed into a database query, and is used to query a structured knowledge base of facts.

Sequence-to-sequence learning can be helpful in both settings. Consider the first setting, in which we have training data containing question-answer pairs like the following:

What is the capital of China? <EOQ> The capital is Beijing. <EOA>

These types of training pairs are not very different from those available in the case of machine translation, and the same techniques can be used in these cases. However, note that one key difference between machine translation and question-answering systems is that there is a greater level of reasoning in the latter, which typically requires an understanding of the relationships between various entities (e.g., people, places, and organizations). This problem is related to the quintessential problem of *information extraction.* Since questions are often crafted around various types of named entities and relationships among them, information extraction methods are used in various ways. The utility of entities and information extraction is well known in answering "what/who/where/when" types of questions (e.g., entity-oriented search), because *named entities* are used to represent persons, locations, organizations, dates, and events, and *relationship extraction* provides information about the interactions among them. One can incorporate the meta-attributes about tokens, such as entity types, as additional inputs to the learning process. Specific examples of such input units are shown in Figure 7.12 of Section 7.7.4, although the figure is designed for the different application of token-level classification.

An important difference between question-answering and machine translation systems is that the latter is seeded with a large corpus of documents (e.g., a large knowledge base like Wikipedia). The query resolution process can be viewed as a kind of entity-oriented search. From the perspective of deep learning, an important challenge of QA systems is that a much larger capacity to store the knowledge is required than is typically available in recurrent neural networks. A deep learning architecture that works well in these settings is that of *memory networks* [528]. Question-answering systems pose many different settings in which the training data may be presented, and the ways in which various types of questions may be answered and evaluated. In this context, the work in [527] discusses a number of template tasks that can be useful for evaluating question-answering systems.

A somewhat different approach is to convert natural language questions into queries that are properly posed in terms of entity-oriented search. Unlike machine translation systems, question answering is often considered a multi-stage process in which understanding what is being asked (in terms of a properly represented query) is sometimes more difficult than answering the query itself. In such cases, the training pairs will correspond to the informal and formal representations of questions. For example, one might have a pair as follows:

$$\underbrace{\text{What is the capital of China? <EOQ1>}}_{\text{Natural language question}} \quad \underbrace{\textbf{CapitalOf}(\ \textit{China},\ ?)\ \text{<EOQ2>}}_{\text{Formal Representation}}$$

The expression on the right-hand side is a structured question, which queries for entities of different types such as persons, places, and organizations. The first step would be to convert the question into an internal representation like the one above, which is more prone to query answering. This conversion can be done using training pairs of questions and their internal representations in conjunction with an recurrent network. Once the question is understood as an entity-oriented search query, it can be posed to the indexed corpus, from which relevant relationships might already have been extracted up front. Therefore, the knowledge base is also preprocessed in such cases, and the question resolution boils down to matching the query with the extracted relations. It is noteworthy that this approach is limited by the complexity of the syntax in which questions are expressed, and the answers might also be simple one-word responses. Therefore, this type of approach is often used for more restricted domains. In some cases, one learns how to paraphrase questions by rewording a more complex question as a simpler question before creating the query representation [115, 118]:

$$\underbrace{\text{How can you tell if you have the flu? <EOQ1>}}_{\text{Complex question}} \quad \underbrace{\text{What are the signs of the flu? <EOQ2>}}_{\text{Paraphrased}}$$

The paraphrased question can be learned with sequence-to-sequence learning, although the work in [118] does not seem to use this approach. Subsequently, it is easier to convert the paraphrased question into a structured query. Another option is to provide the question in structured form to begin with. An example of a recurrent neural network that supports factoid question answering from QA training pairs is provided in [216]. However, unlike pure sequence-to-sequence learning, it uses the dependency parse trees of questions as the input representation. Therefore, a part of the formal understanding of the question is already encoded into the input.

7.7.3 Application to Sentence-Level Classification

In this problem, each sentence is treated as a training (or test) instance for classification purposes. Sentence-level classification is generally a more difficult problem than document-level classification because sentences are short, and there is often not enough evidence in the vector space representation to perform the classification accurately. However, the sequence-centric view is more powerful and can often be used to perform more accurate classification. The RNN architecture for sentence-level classification is shown in Figure 7.11. Note that the only difference from Figure 7.11(b) is that we no longer care about the outputs at each node but defer the class output to the end of the sentence. In other words, a single class label is predicted at the very last time-stamp of the sentence, and it is used to backpropagate the class prediction errors.

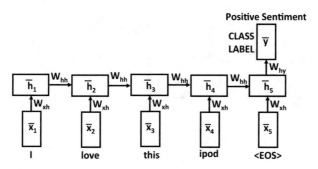

Figure 7.11: Example of sentence-level classification in a sentiment analysis application with the two classes *"positive sentiment"* and *"negative sentiment."*

Sentence-level classification is often leveraged in *sentiment analysis*. This problem attempts to discover how positive or negative users are about specific topics by analyzing the content of a sentence [6]. For example, one can use sentence-level classification to determine whether or not a sentence expresses a positive sentiment by treating the sentiment polarity as the class label. In the example shown in Figure 7.11, the sentence clearly indicates a positive sentiment. Note, however, that one cannot simply use a vector space representation containing the word *"love"* to infer the positive sentiment. For example, if words such as *"don't"* or *"hardly"* occur before *"love"*, the sentiment would change from positive to negative. Such words are referred to as *contextual valence shifters* [377], and their effect can be modeled only in a sequence-centric setting. Recurrent neural networks can handle such settings because they use the accumulated evidence over the specific sequence of words in order to predict the class label. One can also combine this approach with linguistic features. In the next section, we show how to use linguistic features for token-level classification; similar ideas also apply to the case of sentence-level classification.

7.7.4　Token-Level Classification with Linguistic Features

The numerous applications of token-level classification include information extraction and text segmentation. In information extraction, specific words or combinations of words are identified that correspond to persons, places, or organizations. The linguistic features of the word (capitalization, part-of-speech, orthography) are more important in these applications than in typical language modeling or machine translation applications. Nevertheless, the methods discussed in this section for incorporating linguistic features can be used for any of the applications discussed in earlier sections. For the purpose of discussion, consider a *named-entity recognition application* in which every entity is to be classified as one of the categories corresponding to person (P), location (L), and other (O). In such cases, each token in the training data has one of these labels. An example of a possible training sentence is as follows:

$$\underbrace{\text{William}}_{P}\ \underbrace{\text{Jefferson}}_{P}\ \underbrace{\text{Clinton}}_{P}\ \underbrace{\text{lives}}_{O}\ \underbrace{\text{in}}_{O}\ \underbrace{\text{New}}_{L}\ \underbrace{\text{York}}_{L}.$$

In practice, the tagging scheme is often more complex because it encodes information about the beginning and end of a set of contiguous tokens with the same label. For test instances, the tagging information about the tokens is not available.

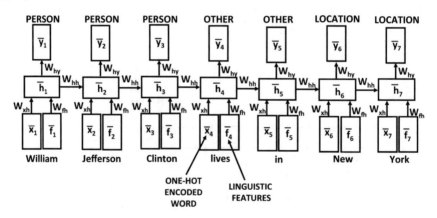

Figure 7.12: Token-wise classification with linguistic features

The recurrent neural network can be defined in a similar way as in the case of language modeling applications, except that the outputs are defined by the tags rather than the next set of words. The input at each time-stamp t is the one-hot encoding $\overline{x}_t$ of the token, and the output $\overline{y}_t$ is the tag. Furthermore, we have an additional set of q-dimensional linguistic features $\overline{f}_t$ associated with the tokens at time-stamp t. These linguistic features might encode information about the capitalization, orthography, capitalization, and so on. The hidden layer, therefore, receives two separate inputs from the tokens and from the linguistic features. The corresponding architecture is illustrated in Figure 7.12. We have an additional $p \times q$ matrix W_{fh} that maps the features $\overline{f}_t$ to the hidden layer. Then, the recurrence condition at each time-stamp t is as follows:

$$\overline{h}_t = \tanh(W_{xh}\overline{x}_t + W_{fh}\overline{f}_t + W_{hh}\overline{h}_{t-1})$$
$$\overline{y}_t = W_{hy}\overline{h}_t$$

The main innovation here is in the use of an additional weight matrix for the linguistic features. The change in the type of output tag does not affect the overall model significantly.

In some variations, it might also be helpful to *concatenate* the linguistic and token-wise features into as separate *embedding layer*, rather than adding them. The work in [565] provides an example in the case of recommender systems, although the principle can also be applied here. The overall learning process is also not significantly different. In token-level classification applications, it is sometimes helpful to use bidirectional recurrent networks in which recurrence occurs in both temporal directions [434].

7.7.5   Time-Series Forecasting and Prediction

Recurrent neural networks present a natural choice for time-series forecasting and prediction. The main difference from text is that the input units are real-valued vectors rather than (discrete) one-hot encoded vectors. For real-valued prediction, the output layer always uses linear activations, rather than the softmax function. In the event that the output is a discrete value (e.g., identifier of a specific event), it is also possible to use discrete outputs with softmax activation. Although any of the variants of the recurrent neural network (e.g., LSTM or GRU) can be used, one of the common problems in time-series analysis is that such sequences can be extremely long. Even though the LSTM and the GRU provide a certain level of protection with increased time-series length, there are limitations to the performance. This is because LSTMs and GRUs do degrade for series beyond certain lengths. Many time-series can have a very large number of time-stamps with various types of short- and long-term dependencies. The prediction and forecasting problems present unique challenges in these cases.

However, a number of useful solutions exist, at least in cases where the number of time-series to be forecasted is not too large. The most effective method is the use of the echo-state network (cf. Section 7.4), in which it is possible to effectively forecast and predict both real-valued and discrete observations with a *small* number of time-series. The caveat that the number of inputs is small is an important one, because echo-state networks rely on randomized expansion of the feature space via the hidden units (see Section 7.4). If the number of original time series is too large, then it may not turn out to be practical to expand the dimensionality of the hidden space sufficiently to capture this type of feature engineering. It is noteworthy that the vast majority of forecasting models in the time-series literature are, in fact, univariate models. A classical example is the *autoregressive model* (AR), which uses the immediate window of history in order to perform forecasting.

The use of an echo-state network in order to perform time-series regression and forecasting is straightforward. At each time-stamp, the input is a vector of d values corresponding to the d different time series that are being modeled. It is assumed that the d time series are synchronized, and this is often accomplished by preprocessing and interpolation. The output at each time-stamp is the predicted value. In forecasting, the predicted value is simply the value(s) of the different time-series at k units ahead. One can view this approach as the time-series analog of language models with discrete sequences. It is also possible to choose an output corresponding to a time-series not present in the data (e.g., predicting one stock price from another) or to choose an output corresponding to a discrete event (e.g., equipment failure). The main differences among all these cases lie in the specific choice of the loss function for the output at hand. In the specific case of time-series forecasting, a neat relationship can be shown between autoregressive models and echo-state networks.

Relationship with Autoregressive Models

An *autoregressive model* models the values of a time-series as a linear function of its immediate history of length p. The p coefficients of this model are learned with linear regression. Echo-state networks can be shown to be closely related to autoregressive models, in which the connections of the hidden-to-hidden matrix are sampled in a particular way. The additional power of the echo-state network over an autoregressive model arises from the nonlinearity used in the hidden-to-hidden layer. In order to understand this point, we will consider the special case of an echo-state network in which its input corresponds to a single time series and the hidden-to-hidden layers have linear activations. Now imagine that we could somehow choose the hidden-to-hidden connections in such a way that the values of the hidden state in each time-stamp is exactly equal to the values of the time-series in the last p ticks. What kind of sampled weight matrix would achieve this goal?

First, the hidden state needs to have p units, and therefore the size of W_{hh} is $p \times p$. It is easy to show that a weight matrix W_{hh} that shifts the hidden state by one unit and copies the input value to the vacated state caused by the shifting will result in a hidden state, which is exactly the same as the last window of p points. In other words, the matrix W_{hh} will have exactly $(p-1)$ non-zero entries of the form $(i, i+1)$ for each $i \in \{1 \ldots p-1\}$. As a result, pre-multiplying any p-dimensional column vector $\overline{h}_t$ with W_{hh} will shift the entries of $\overline{h}_t$ by one unit. For a 1-dimensional time-series, the element x_t is a 1-dimensional input into the tth hidden state of the echo state network, and W_{xh} is therefore of size $p \times 1$. Setting only the entry $(p, 0)$ of W_{xh} to 1 and all other entries to 0 will result in copying x_t into the first element of $\overline{h}_t$. The matrix W_{hy} is a $1 \times p$ matrix of *learned weights*, so that $W_{hy}\overline{h}_t$ yields the prediction $\hat{y}_t$ of the observed value y_t. In autoregressive modeling, the value of y_t is simply set to x_{t+k} for some lookahead k, and the value of k is often set to 1. It is noteworthy that the matrices W_{hh} and W_{xh} are fixed, and only W_{hy} needs to learned. This process leads to the development of a model that is identical to the time-series autoregressive model [3].

The main difference of the time-series autoregressive model from the echo-state network is that the latter fixes W_{hh} and W_{xh} randomly, and uses much larger dimensionalities of the hidden states. Furthermore, nonlinear activations are used in the hidden units. As long as the spectral radius of W_{hh} is (slightly) less than 1, a random choice of the matrices W_{hh} and W_{xh} with linear activations can be viewed as a decay-based variant of the autoregressive model. This is because the matrix W_{hh} only performs a random (but slightly decaying) transformation of the previous hidden state. Using a decaying random projection of the previous hidden state intuitively achieves similar goals as a sliding window-shifted copy of the previous state. The precise spectral radius of W_{hh} governs the rate of decay. With a sufficient number of hidden states, the matrix W_{hy} provides enough degrees of freedom to model any decay-based function of recent history. Furthermore, the proper scaling of the W_{xh} ensures that the most recent entry is not given too much or too little weight. Note that echo-state networks do test different scalings of the matrix W_{xh} to ensure that the effect of this input does not wipe out the contributions from the hidden states. The nonlinear activations in the echo-state network give greater power to this approach over a time-series autoregressive model. In a sense, echo-state networks can model complex nonlinear dynamics of the time-series, unlike an off-the-shelf autoregressive model.

7.7.6 Temporal Recommender Systems

Several solutions [465, 534, 565] have been proposed in recent years for temporal modeling of recommender systems. Some of these methods use temporal aspects of users, whereas others use temporal aspects of users and items. One observation is that the properties of items tend to be more strongly fixed in time than the properties of users. Therefore, solutions that use the temporal modeling only at the user level are often sufficient. However, some methods [534] perform the temporal modeling both at the user level and at the item level.

In the following, we discuss a simplification of the model discussed in [465]. In temporal recommender systems, the time-stamps associated with user ratings are leveraged for the recommendation process. Consider a case in which the observed rating of user i for item j at time-stamp t is denoted by r_{ijt}. For simplicity, we assume that the time-stamp t is simply the index of the rating in the sequential order it was received (although many models use the wall-clock time). Therefore, the sequence being modeled by the RNN is a sequence of rating values associated with the content-centric representations of the users and items to which the rating belongs. Therefore, we want to model the value of the rating as a function of content-centric inputs at each time-stamp.

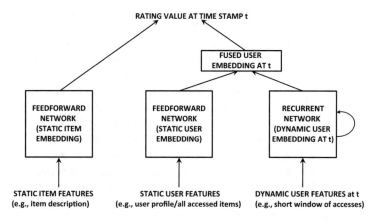

Figure 7.13: Recommendations with recurrent neural networks. At each time-stamp, the static/dynamic user features and static item features are input, and a rating value is output for that user-item combination.

We describe these content-centric representations below. The prediction of the rating r_{ijt} is assumed to be depend on (i) static features associated with the item, (ii) static features associated with the user, and (iii) the dynamic features associated with the user. The static features associated with the item might be item titles or descriptions, and one can create a bag-of-words representation of the item. The static features associated with the user might be a user-specific profile or a fixed history of accesses of this user, which does not change over the data set. The static features associated with the users are also typically represented as a bag of words, and one can even consider item-rating pairs as pseudo-keywords in order to combine user-specified keywords with ratings activity. In the case where ratings activity is used, a fixed history of accesses of the user is always leveraged for designing static features. The dynamic user features are more interesting because they are based on the dynamically changing user access history. In this case, a short history of item-rating pairs can be used as pseudo-keywords, and a bag-of-words representation can be created at time-stamp t.

In several cases, explicit ratings are not available, but implicit feedback data is available corresponding to a user clicking on an item. In the event that implicit feedback is used, negative sampling becomes necessary in which user-item pairs for which activity has not occurred are included in the sequence at random. This approach can be viewed as a hybrid between a content-based and collaborative recommendation approach. While it does use the user-item-rating triplets like a traditional recommender model, the content-centric representations of the users and items are input at each time-stamp. However, the inputs at different time-stamps correspond to different user-item pairs, and therefore the collaborative power of the patterns of ratings among different users and items is used as well.

The overall architecture of this recommender system is illustrated in Figure 7.13. It is evident that this architecture contains three different subnetworks to create feature embeddings out of static item features, static user features, and dynamic user features. The first two of these three are feed-forward networks, whereas the last of them is a recurrent neural network. First, the embeddings from the two user-centric networks are fused using either concatenation or element-wise multiplication. In the latter case, it is necessary to create embeddings of the same dimensionality for static and dynamic user features. Then, this fused user embedding at time-stamp t and the static item embedding is used to predict the rating at time-stamp t. For implicit feedback data, one can predict probabilities of positive activity for a particular user-item pair. The chosen loss function depends on the nature of the rating being predicted. The training algorithm needs to work with a consecutive sequence of training triplets (of some fixed mini-batch size) and backpropagate to the static and dynamic portions of the network simultaneously.

The aforementioned presentation has simplified several aspects of the training procedure presented in [465]. For example, it is assumed that a single rating is received at each time-stamp t, and that a fixed time-horizon is sufficient for temporal modeling. In reality, different settings might required different levels of granularity at which temporal aspects are handled. Therefore, the work in [465] proposes methods to address varying levels of granularity in the modeling process. It is also possible to perform the recommendation under a pure collaborative filtering regime without using content-centric features in any way. For example, it is possible[9] to adapt the recommender system discussed in Section 2.5.7 of Chapter 2 by using a recurrent neural network (cf. Exercise 3).

Another recent work [565] treats the problem as that of working with product-action-time triplets at an e-commerce site. The idea is that a site logs sequential actions performed by each user to various products, such as visiting a product page from a homepage, category page, or sales page, and that of actually buying the product. Each action has a *dwell time*, which indicates the amount of time that the user spends in performing that action. The dwell time is discretized into a set of intervals, which would be uniform or geometric, depending on the application at hand. It makes sense to discretize the time into geometrically increasing intervals.

One sequence is collected for each user, corresponding to the actions performed by the user. One can represent the rth element of the sequence as $(\overline{p}_r, \overline{a}_r, \overline{t}_r)$, where $\overline{p}_r$ is the one-hot encoded product, $\overline{a}_r$ is the one-hot encoded action, and $\overline{t}_r$ is the one-hot encoded discretized value of the time interval. Each of $\overline{p}_r$, $\overline{a}_r$, and $\overline{t}_r$ is a one-hot encoded vector. An embedding layer with weight matrices W_p, W_a, and W_t is used to create the representation $\overline{e}_r = (W_p \overline{p}_r, W_a \overline{a}_r, W_t \overline{t}_r)$. These matrices were pretrained with *word2vec* training applied to sequences extracted from the e-commerce site. Subsequently, the input to the recurrent

---

[9]Even though the adaptation from Section 2.5.7 is the most natural and obvious one, we have not seen it elsewhere in the literature. Therefore, it might be an interesting exercise for the reader to implement the adaptation of Exercise 3.

neural network is $\overline{e}_1 \ldots \overline{e}_T$, which was used to predict the outputs $\overline{o}_1 \ldots \overline{o}_T$. The output at the time-stamp t corresponds to the next action of the user at that time-stamp. Note that the embedding layer is also attached to the recurrent network, and it is fine-tuned during backpropagation (beyond its *word2vec* initialization). The original work [565] also adds an attention layer, although good results can be obtained even without this layer.

7.7.7 Secondary Protein Structure Prediction

In protein structure prediction, the elements of the sequence are the symbols representing one of the 20 amino acids. The 20 possible amino acids are akin to the vocabulary used in the text setting. Therefore, a one-hot encoding of the input is effective in these cases. Each position is associated with a class label corresponding to the secondary protein structure. This secondary structure can be either the alpha-helix, beta-sheet, or coil. Therefore, this problem can be reduced to token-level classification. A three-way softmax is used in the output layer. The work in [20] used a bidirectional recurrent neural network for prediction. This is because protein structure prediction is a problem that benefits from the context on both sides of a particular position. In general, the choice between using a uni-directional network and a bidirectional network is highly regulated by whether or not the prediction is causal to a historical segment or whether it depends on the context on both sides.

7.7.8 End-to-End Speech Recognition

In end-to-end speech recognition, one attempts to transcribe the raw audio files into character sequences while going through as few intermediate steps as possible. A small amount of preprocessing is still needed in order to make the data presentable as an input sequence. For example, the work in [157] presents the data as *spectrograms* derived from raw audio files using the *specgram* function of the *matplotlib* python toolkit. The width used was 254 Fourier windows with an overlap of 127 frames and 128 inputs per frame. The output is a character in the transcription sequence, which could include a character, a punctuation mark, a space, or even a null character. The label could be different depending on the application at hand. For example, the labels could be characters, phonemes, or musical notes. A bidirectional recurrent neural network is most appropriate to this setting, because the context on both sides of a character helps in improving accuracy.

One challenge associated with this type of setting is that we need the alignment between the frame representation of the audios and the transcription sequence. This type of alignment is not available a priori, and is in fact one of the outputs of the system. This leads to the problem of circular dependency between segmentation and recognition, which is also referred to as *Sayre's paradox*. This problem is solved with the use of *connectionist temporal classification*. In this approach, a dynamic programming algorithm [153] is combined with the (softmax) probabilistic outputs of the recurrent network in order to determine the alignment that maximizes the overall probability of generation. The reader is referred to [153, 157] for details.

7.7.9 Handwriting Recognition

A closely related application to speech recognition is that of handwriting recognition [154, 156]. In handwriting recognition, the input consists of a sequence of (x, y) coordinates, which represents the position of the tip of the pen at each time-stamp. The output corresponds to a sequence of characters written by the pen. These coordinates are then used to extract further features such as a feature indicating whether the pen is touching the writing surface, the angles between nearby line segments, the velocity of the writing, and normalized values of the coordinates. The work in [154] extracts a total of 25 features. It is evident that multiple coordinates will create a character. However, it is hard to know exactly how many coordinates will create each character because it may vary significantly over the handwriting and style of different writers. Much like speech recognition, the issue of proper segmentation creates numerous challenges. This is the same Sayre's paradox that is encountered in speech recognition.

In unconstrained handwriting recognition, the handwriting contains a set of *strokes*, and by putting them together one can obtain characters. One possibility is to identify the strokes up front, and then use them to build characters. However, such an approach leads to inaccurate results, because the identification of stroke boundaries is an error-prone task. Since the errors tend to be additive over different phases, breaking up the task into separate stages is generally not a good idea. At a basic level, the task of handwriting recognition is no different from speech recognition. The only difference is in terms of the specific way in which the inputs and outputs are represented. As in the case of speech recognition, connectionist temporal classification is used in which a dynamic programming approach is combined with the softmax outputs of a recurrent neural network. Therefore, the alignment and the label-wise classification is performed simultaneously with dynamic programming in order to maximize the probability that a particular output sequence is generated for a particular input sequence. Readers are referred to [154, 156].

7.8   Summary

Recurrent neural networks are a class of neural networks that are used for sequence modeling. They can be expressed as time-layered networks in which the weights are shared between different layers. Recurrent neural networks can be hard to train, because they are prone to the vanishing and the exploding gradient problems. Some of these problems can be addressed with the use of enhanced training methods as discussed in Chapter 3. However, there are other ways of training more robust recurrent networks. A particular example that has found favor is the use of long short-term memory network. This network uses a gentler update process of the hidden states in order to avoid the vanishing and exploding gradient problems. Recurrent neural networks and their variants have found use in many applications such as image captioning, token-level classification, sentence classification, sentiment analysis, speech recognition, machine translation, and computational biology.

7.9   Bibliographic Notes

One of the earliest forms of the recurrent network was the Elman network [111]. This network was a precursor to modern recurrent networks. Werbos proposed the original version of backpropagation through time [526]. Another early algorithm for backpropagation in recurrent neural networks is provided in [375]. The vast majority of work on recurrent networks has been on symbolic data, although there is also some work on real-valued time series [80, 101, 559]. The regularization of recurrent neural networks is discussed in [552].

The effect of the spectral radius of the hidden-hidden matrix on the vanishing/exploding gradient problem is discussed in [220]. A detailed discussion of the exploding gradient problem and other problems associated with recurrent neural networks may be found in [368, 369]. Recurrent neural networks (and their advanced variations) began to become more attractive after about 2010, when hardware advancements, increased data, and algorithmic tweaks made these methodologies far more attractive. The vanishing and exploding gradient problems in different types of deep networks, including recurrent networks, are discussed in [140, 205, 368]. The gradient clipping rule was discussed by Mikolov in his Ph.D. thesis [324]. The initialization of recurrent networks containing ReLUs is discussed in [271].

Early variants of the recurrent neural network included the echo-state network [219], which is also referred to as the *liquid-state machine* [304]. This paradigm is also referred to as *reservoir computing*. An overview of echo-state networks in the context of reservoir computing principles is provided in [301]. The use of batch normalization is discussed in [214]. Teacher forcing methods are discussed in [105]. Initialization strategies that reduce the effect of the vanishing and exploding gradient problems are discussed in [140].

The LSTM was first proposed in [204], and its use for language modeling is discussed in [476]. The challenges associated with training recurrent neural networks are discussed in [205, 368, 369]. It has been shown [326] that it is also possible to address some of the problems associated with the vanishing and exploding gradient problems by imposing constraints on the hidden-to-hidden matrix. Specifically, a block of the matrix is constrained to be close to the identity matrix, so that the corresponding hidden variables are updated slowly in much the same way as the memory of the LSTM is updated slowly. Several variations of recurrent neural networks and LSTMs for language modeling are discussed in [69, 71, 151, 152, 314, 328]. Bidirectional recurrent neural networks are proposed in [434]. The particular discussion of LSTMs in this chapter is based on [151], and an alternative gated recurrent unit (GRU) is presented in [69, 71]. A guide to understanding recurrent neural networks is available in [233]. Further discussions on the sequence-centric and natural language applications of recurrent neural networks are available in [143, 298]. LSTM networks are also used for sequence labeling [150], which is useful in sentiment analysis [578]. The use of a combination of convolutional neural networks and recurrent neural networks for image captioning is discussed in [225, 509]. Sequence-to-sequence learning methods for machine translation are discussed in [69, 231, 480]. Bidirectional recurrent networks and LSTMs for protein structure prediction, handwriting recognition, translation, and speech recognition are discussed in [20, 154, 155, 157, 378, 477]. In recent years, neural networks have also been used in temporal collaborative filtering, which was first introduced in [258]. Numerous methods for temporal collaborative filtering are discussed in [465, 534, 560]. A generative model for dialogues with recurrent networks is discussed in [439, 440]. The use of recurrent neural networks for action recognition is discussed in [504].

Recurrent neural networks have also been generalized to recursive neural networks for modeling arbitrary structural relationships in the data [379]. These methods generalize the use of the recurrent neural networks to trees (rather than sequences) by considering a tree-like computational graph. Their use for discovering task-dependent representations is discussed in [144]. These methods can be applied to cases in which data structures are considered as inputs to the neural network [121]. Recurrent neural networks are a special case of recursive neural network in which the structure corresponds to a linear chain of dependencies. The use of recursive neural networks for various types of natural-language and scene-processing applications is discussed in [459, 460, 461].

7.9.1 Software Resources

Recurrent neural networks and their variants are supported by numerous software frameworks like *Caffe* [571], *Torch* [572], *Theano* [573], and *TensorFlow* [574]. Several other frameworks like **DeepLearning4j** provide implementations of LSTMs [617]. Implementations of sentiment analysis with LSTM networks are available at [578]. This approach is based on the sequence labeling technique presented in [152]. A notable piece of code [580] is a character-level RNN, and it is particularly instructive for learning purposes. The conceptual description of this code is provided in [233, 618].

7.10   Exercises

1. Download the character-level RNN in [580], and train it on the *"tiny Shakespeare"* data set available at the same location. Create outputs of the language model after training for (i) 5 epochs, (ii) 50 epochs, and (iii) 500 epochs. What significant differences do you see between the three outputs?

2. Consider an echo-state network in which the hidden states are partitioned into K groups with p/K units each. The hidden states of a particular group are only allowed to have connections within their own group in the next time-stamp. Discuss how this approach is related to an ensemble method in which K independent echo-state networks are constructed and the predictions of the K networks are averaged.

3. Show how you can modify the feed-forward architecture discussed in Section 2.5.7 of Chapter 2 in order to create a recurrent neural network that can handle temporal recommender systems. Implement this adaptation and compare its performance to the feed-forward architecture on the Netflix prize data set.

4. Consider a recurrent network in which the hidden states have a dimensionality of 2. Every entry of the 2×2 matrix W_{hh} of transformations between hidden states is 3.5. Furthermore, sigmoid activation is used between hidden states of different temporal layers. Would such a network be more prone to the vanishing or the exploding gradient problem?

5. Suppose that you have a large database of biological strings containing sequences of nucleobases drawn from $\{A, C, T, G\}$. Some of these strings contain unusual mutations representing changes in the nucleobases. Propose an unsupervised method (i.e., neural architecture) using RNNs in order to detect these mutations.

6. How would your architecture for the previous question change if you were given a training database in which the mutation positions in each sequence were tagged, and the test database was untagged?

7. Recommend possible methods for pre-training the input and output layers in the machine translation approach with sequence-to-sequence learning.

8. Consider a social network with a large volume of messages sent between sender-receiver pairs, and we are interested only in the messages containing an identifying keyword, referred to as a *hashtag*. Create a real-time model using an RNN, which has the capability to recommend hashtags of interest to each user, together with potential followers of that user who might be interested in messages related to that hashtag. Assume that you have enough computational resources to incrementally train an RNN.

9. If the training data set is re-scaled by a particular factor, do the learned weights of either batch normalization or layer normalization change? What would be your answer

if only a small subset of points in the training data set are re-scaled? Would the learned weights in either normalization method be affected if the data set is re-centered?

10. Consider a setting in which you have a large database of pairs of sentences in different languages. Although you have sufficient representation of each language, some *pairs* might not be well represented in the database. Show how you can use this training data to (i) create the same universal code for a particular sentence across all languages, and (ii) have the ability to translate even between pairs of languages not well represented in the database.

Chapter 8

Convolutional Neural Networks

"The soul never thinks without a picture."—Aristotle

8.1 Introduction

Convolutional neural networks are designed to work with grid-structured inputs, which have strong spatial dependencies in local regions of the grid. The most obvious example of grid-structured data is a 2-dimensional image. This type of data also exhibits spatial dependencies, because adjacent spatial locations in an image often have similar color values of the individual pixels. An additional dimension captures the different colors, which creates a 3-dimensional input *volume*. Therefore, the features in a convolutional neural network have dependencies among one another based on spatial distances. Other forms of sequential data like text, time-series, and sequences can also be considered special cases of grid-structured data with various types of relationships among adjacent items. The vast majority of applications of convolutional neural networks focus on image data, although one can also use these networks for all types of temporal, spatial, and spatiotemporal data.

An important property of image data is that it exhibits a certain level of *translation invariance*, which is not the case in many other types of grid-structured data. For example, a banana has the same interpretation, whether it is at the top or the bottom of an image. Convolutional neural networks tend to create similar feature values from local regions with similar patterns. One advantage of image data is that the effects of specific inputs on the feature representations can often be described in an intuitive way. Therefore, this chapter will primarily work with the image data setting. A brief discussion will also be devoted to the applications of convolutional neural networks to other settings.

An important defining characteristic of convolutional neural networks is an operation, which is referred to as *convolution*. A convolution operation is a dot-product operation between a grid-structured set of weights and similar grid-structured inputs drawn from different spatial localities in the input volume. This type of operation is useful for data with a high level of spatial or other locality, such as image data. Therefore, convolutional neural networks are defined as networks that use the convolutional operation in at least one layer, although most convolutional neural networks use this operation in multiple layers.

8.1.1   Historical Perspective and Biological Inspiration

Convolutional neural networks were one of the first success stories of deep learning, well before recent advancements in training techniques led to improved performance in other types of architectures. In fact, the eye-catching successes of some convolutional neural network architectures in image-classification contests after 2011 led to broader attention to the field of deep learning. Long-standing benchmarks like *ImageNet* [581] with a top-5 classification error-rate of more than 25% were brought down to less than 4% in the years between 2011 and 2015. Convolutional neural networks are well suited to the process of hierarchical feature engineering with depth; this is reflected in the fact that the deepest neural networks in all domains are drawn from the field of convolutional networks. Furthermore, these networks also represent excellent examples of how biologically inspired neural networks can sometimes provide ground-breaking results. The best convolutional neural networks today reach or exceed human-level performance, a feat considered impossible by most experts in computer vision only a couple of decades back.

The early motivation for convolutional neural networks was derived from experiments by Hubel and Wiesel on a cat's visual cortex [212]. The visual cortex has small regions of cells that are sensitive to specific regions in the visual field. In other words, if specific areas of the visual field are excited, then those cells in the visual cortex will be activated as well. Furthermore, the excited cells also depend on the shape and orientation of the objects in the visual field. For example, vertical edges cause some neuronal cells to be excited, whereas horizontal edges cause other neuronal cells to be excited. The cells are connected using a layered architecture, and this discovery led to the conjecture that mammals use these different layers to construct portions of images at different levels of abstraction. From a machine learning point of view, this principle is similar to that of hierarchical feature extraction. As we will see later, convolutional neural networks achieve something similar by encoding primitive shapes in earlier layers, and more complex shapes in later layers.

Based on these biological inspirations, the earliest neural model was the *neocognitron* [127]. However, there were several differences between this model and the modern convolutional neural network. The most prominent of these differences was that the notion of weight sharing was not used. Based on this architecture, one of the first fully convolutional architectures, referred to as *LeNet-5* [279], was developed. This network was used by banks to identify hand-written numbers on checks. Since then, the convolutional neural network has not evolved much; the main difference is in terms of using more layers and stable activation functions like the ReLU. Furthermore, numerous training tricks and powerful hardware options are available to achieve better success in training when working with deep networks and large data sets.

A factor that has played an important role in increasing the prominence of convolutional neural networks has been the annual *ImageNet* competition [582] (also referred to as *"ImageNet Large Scale Visual Recognition Challenge [ILSVRC]"*). The ILSVRC competition uses the *ImageNet* data set [581], which is discussed in Section 1.8.2 of Chapter 1. Convolutional neural networks have been consistent winners of this contest since 2012. In fact, the dominance of convolutional neural networks for image classification is so well recognized today that almost all entries in recent editions of this contest have been convolutional neural networks. One of the earliest methods that achieved success in the 2012 *ImageNet* competition by a large margin was *AlexNet* [255]. Furthermore, the improvements in accuracy have been so extraordinarily large in the last few years that it has changed the landscape of research in the area. In spite of the fact that the vast majority of eye-catching performance gains have occurred from 2012 to 2015, the architectural differences between recent winners and some of the earliest convolutional neural networks are rather small at least at a conceptual level. Nevertheless, small details seem to matter a lot when working with almost all types of neural networks.

8.1.2 Broader Observations About Convolutional Neural Networks

The secret to the success of any neural architecture lies in tailoring the structure of the network with a semantic understanding of the domain at hand. Convolutional neural networks are heavily based on this principle, because they use sparse connections with a high-level of parameter-sharing in a domain-sensitive way. In other words, not all states in a particular layer are connected to those in the previous layer in an indiscriminate way. Rather, the value of a feature in a particular layer is connected only to a local spatial region in the previous layer with a consistent set of shared parameters across the full spatial footprint of the image. This type of architecture can be viewed as a domain-aware regularization, which was derived from the biological insights in Hubel and Wiesel's early work. In general, the success of the convolutional neural network has important lessons for other data domains. A carefully designed architecture, in which the relationships and dependencies among the data items are used in order to reduce the parameter footprint, provides the key to results of high accuracy.

A significant level of domain-aware regularization is also available in recurrent neural networks, which share the parameters from different temporal periods. This sharing is based on the assumption that temporal dependencies remain invariant with time. Recurrent neural networks are based on intuitive understanding of temporal relationships, whereas convolutional neural networks are based on an intuitive understanding of spatial relationships. The latter intuition was directly extracted from the organization of biological neurons in a cat's visual cortex. This outstanding success provides a motivation to explore how neuroscience may be leveraged to design neural networks in clever ways. Even though artificial neural networks are only caricatures of the true complexity of the biological brain, one should not underestimate the intuition that one can obtain by studying the basic principles of neuroscience [176].

Chapter Organization

This chapter is organized as follows. The next section will introduce the basics of a convolutional neural network, the various operations, and the way in which they are organized. The training process for convolutional networks is discussed in Section 8.3. Case studies with some typical convolutional neural networks that have won recent competitions are discussed in Section 8.4. The convolutional autoencoder is discussed in Section 8.5. A variety of applications of convolutional networks are discussed in Section 8.6. A summary is given in Section 8.7.

8.2   The Basic Structure of a Convolutional Network

In convolutional neural networks, the states in each layer are arranged according to a spatial grid structure. These spatial relationships are inherited from one layer to the next because each feature value is based on a small local spatial region in the previous layer. It is important to maintain these spatial relationships among the grid cells, because the convolution operation and the transformation to the next layer is critically dependent on these relationships. Each layer in the convolutional network is a 3-dimensional grid structure, which has a *height*, *width*, and *depth*. The depth of a layer in a convolutional neural network should not be confused with the depth of the network itself. The word "depth" (when used in the context of a single layer) refers to the number of *channels* in each layer, such as the number of primary color channels (e.g., blue, green, and red) in the input image or the number of feature maps in the hidden layers. The use of the word "depth" to refer to both the number of feature maps in each layer as well as the number of layers is an unfortunate overloading of terminology used in convolutional networks, but we will be careful while using this term, so that it is clear from its context.

The convolutional neural network functions much like a traditional feed-forward neural network, except that the operations in its layers are spatially organized with sparse (and carefully designed) connections between layers. The three types of layers that are commonly present in a convolutional neural network are *convolution*, *pooling*, and *ReLU*. The ReLU activation is no different from a traditional neural network. In addition, a final set of layers is often fully connected and maps in an application-specific way to a set of output nodes. In the following, we will describe each of the different types of operations and layers, and the typical way in which these layers are interleaved in a convolutional neural network.

Why do we need depth in each layer of a convolutional neural network? To understand this point, let us examine how the input to the convolutional neural network is organized. The input data to the convolutional neural network is organized into a 2-dimensional grid structure, and the values of the individual grid points are referred to as *pixels*. Each pixel, therefore, corresponds to a spatial location within the image. However, in order to encode the precise color of the pixel, we need a multidimensional array of values at each grid location. In the RGB color scheme, we have an intensity of the three primary colors, corresponding to red, green, and blue, respectively. Therefore, if the spatial dimensions of an image are 32×32 pixels and the depth is 3 (corresponding to the RGB color channels), then the overall number of pixels in the image is $32 \times 32 \times 3$. This particular image size is quite common, and also occurs in a popularly used data set for benchmarking, known as CIFAR-10 [583]. An example of this organization is shown in Figure 8.1(a). It is natural to represent the input layer in this 3-dimensional structure because two dimensions are devoted to spatial relationships and a third dimension is devoted to the independent properties along these channels. For example, the intensities of the primary colors are the independent properties in the first layer. In the hidden layers, these independent properties correspond to various types of shapes extracted from local regions of the image. For the purpose of discussion, assume that the input in the qth layer is of size $L_q \times B_q \times d_q$. Here, L_q refers to the *height* (or length), B_q refers to the width (or breadth), and d_q is the depth. In almost all image-centric applications, the values of L_q and B_q are the same. However, we will work with separate notations for height and width in order to retain generality in presentation.

For the first (input) layer, these values are decided by the nature of the input data and its preprocessing. In the above example, the values are $L_1 = 32$, $B_1 = 32$, and $d_1 = 3$. Later layers have exactly the same 3-dimensional organization, except that each of the d_q 2-dimensional grid of values for a particular input can no longer be considered a grid of raw pixels. Furthermore, the value of d_q is much larger than three for the hidden layers because the number of independent properties of a given local region that are relevant to classification can be quite significant. For $q > 1$, these grids of values are referred to as *feature maps* or *activation maps*. These values are analogous to the values in the hidden layers in a feed-forward network.

In the convolutional neural network, the parameters are organized into sets of 3-dimensional structural units, known as *filters* or *kernels*. The filter is usually square in terms of its spatial dimensions, which are typically much smaller than those of the layer the filter is applied to. On the other hand, *the depth of a filter is always same is the same as that of the layer to which it is applied.* Assume that the dimensions of the filter in the qth layer are $F_q \times F_q \times d_q$. An example of a filter with $F_1 = 5$ and $d_1 = 3$ is shown in Figure 8.1(a). It is common for the value of F_q to be small and odd. Examples of commonly used values of F_q are 3 and 5, although there are some interesting cases in which it is possible to use $F_q = 1$.

The *convolution operation* places the filter at each possible position in the image (or hidden layer) so that the filter fully overlaps with the image, and performs a dot product between the $F_q \times F_q \times d_q$ parameters in the filter and the matching grid in the input volume (with same size $F_q \times F_q \times d_q$). The dot product is performed by treating the entries in the relevant 3-dimensional region of the input volume and the filter as vectors of size $F_q \times F_q \times d_q$, so that the elements in both vectors are ordered based on their corresponding positions in the grid-structured volume. How many possible positions are there for placing the filter? This question is important, because each such position therefore defines a spatial "pixel" (or, more accurately, a *feature*) in the next layer. In other words, the number of alignments between the filter and image defines the spatial height and width of the next hidden layer. The relative spatial positions of the features in the next layer are defined based on the relative positions of the upper left corners of the corresponding spatial grids in the previous layer. When performing convolutions in the qth layer, one can align the filter at $L_{q+1} = (L_q - F_q + 1)$ positions along the height and $B_{q+1} = (B_q - F_q + 1)$ along the width of the image (without having a portion of the filter "sticking out" from the borders of the image). This results in a total of $L_{q+1} \times B_{q+1}$ possible dot products, which defines the size of the next hidden layer. In the previous example, the values of L_2 and B_2 are therefore defined as follows:

$$L_2 = 32 - 5 + 1 = 28$$
$$B_2 = 32 - 5 + 1 = 28$$

The next hidden layer of size 28×28 is shown in Figure 8.1(a). However, this hidden layer also has a depth of size $d_2 = 5$. Where does this depth come from? This is achieved by using 5 different filters with their own independent sets of parameters. Each of these 5 sets of spatially arranged features obtained from the output of a single filter is referred to as a *feature map*. Clearly, an increased number of feature maps is a result of a larger number of filters (i.e., parameter footprint), which is $F_q^2 \cdot d_q \cdot d_{q+1}$ for the qth layer. *The number of filters used in each layer controls the capacity of the model because it directly controls the number of parameters.* Furthermore, increasing the number of filters in a particular layer increases the number of feature maps (i.e., depth) of the next layer. It is possible for different layers to have very different numbers of feature maps, depending on the number of filters we use for the convolution operation in the previous layer. For example, the input layer typically only has three color channels, but it is possible for the each of the later hidden layers to have depths (i.e., number of feature maps) of more than 500. The idea here is that each filter tries to identify a particular type of spatial pattern in a small rectangular region of the image, and therefore a large number of filters is required to capture a broad variety of the possible shapes that are combined to create the final image (unlike the case of the input layer, in which three RGB channels are sufficient). Typically, the later layers tend to have a smaller spatial footprint, but greater depth in terms of the number of feature maps. For example, the filter shown in Figure 8.1(b) represents a horizontal edge detector on a grayscale image with one channel. As shown in Figure 8.1(b), the resulting feature will have high activation at each position where a horizontal edge is seen. A perfectly vertical edge will give zero activation, whereas a slanted edge might give intermediate activation. Therefore, sliding the filter everywhere in the image will already detect several key outlines of the image in a single feature map of the output volume. Multiple filters are used to create an output volume with more than one feature map. For example, a different filter might create a spatial feature map of vertical edge activations.

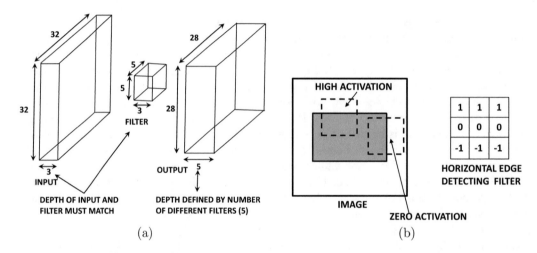

Figure 8.1: (a) The convolution between an input layer of size $32 \times 32 \times 3$ and a filter of size $5 \times 5 \times 3$ produces an output layer with spatial dimensions 28×28. The depth of the resulting output depends on the number of distinct filters and not on the dimensions of the input layer or filter. (b) Sliding a filter around the image tries to look for a particular feature in various windows of the image.

We are now ready to formally define the convolution operation. The pth filter in the qth layer has parameters denoted by the 3-dimensional tensor $W^{(p,q)} = [w_{ijk}^{(p,q)}]$. The indices i, j, k indicate the positions along the height, width, and depth of the filter. The feature maps in the qth layer are represented by the 3-dimensional tensor $H^{(q)} = [h_{ijk}^{(q)}]$. When the value of q is 1, the special case corresponding to the notation $H^{(1)}$ simply represents the input layer (which is not hidden). Then, the convolutional operations from the qth layer to the $(q+1)$th layer are defined as follows:

$$h_{ijp}^{(q+1)} = \sum_{r=1}^{F_q} \sum_{s=1}^{F_q} \sum_{k=1}^{d_q} w_{rsk}^{(p,q)} h_{i+r-1,j+s-1,k}^{(q)} \quad \forall i \in \{1 \ldots, L_q - F_q + 1\}$$

$$\forall j \in \{1 \ldots B_q - F_q + 1\}$$
$$\forall p \in \{1 \ldots d_{q+1}\}$$

The expression above seems notationally complex, although the underlying convolutional operation is really a simple dot product over the entire volume of the filter, which is repeated over all valid spatial positions (i, j) and filters (indexed by p). It is intuitively helpful to understand a convolution operation by placing the filter at each of the 28×28 possible spatial positions in the first layer of Figure 8.1(a) and performing a dot product between the vector of $5 \times 5 \times 3 = 75$ values in the filter and the corresponding 75 values in $H^{(1)}$. Even though the size of the input layer in Figure 8.1(a) is 32×32, there are only $(32 - 5 + 1) \times (32 - 5 + 1)$ possible spatial alignments between an input volume of size 32×32 and a filter of size 5×5.

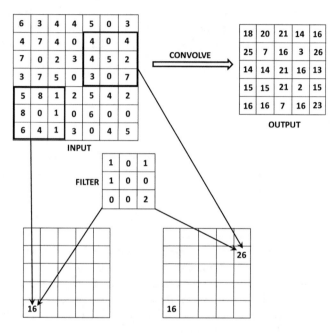

Figure 8.2: An example of a convolution between a $7 \times 7 \times 1$ input and a $3 \times 3 \times 1$ filter with stride of 1. A depth of 1 has been chosen for the filter/input for simplicity. For depths larger than 1, the contributions of each input feature map will be added to create a single value in the feature map. A single filter will always create a single feature map irrespective of its depth.

The convolution operation brings to mind Hubel and Wiesel's experiments that use the activations in small regions of the visual field to activate particular neurons. In the case of convolutional neural networks, this visual field is defined by the filter, which is applied to all locations of the image in order to detect the presence of a shape at each spatial location. Furthermore, the filters in earlier layers tend to detect more primitive shapes, whereas the filters in later layers create more complex compositions of these primitive shapes. This is not particularly surprising because most deep neural networks are good at hierarchical feature engineering.

One property of convolution is that it shows *equivariance to translation*. In other words, if we shifted the pixel values in the input in any direction by one unit and then applied convolution, the corresponding feature values will shift with the input values. This is because of the shared parameters of the filter across the entire convolution. The reason for sharing parameters across the entire convolution is that the presence of a particular shape in any part of the image should be processed in the same way irrespective of its specific spatial location.

In the following, we provide an example of the convolution operation. In Figure 8.2, we have shown an example of an input layer and a filter with depth 1 for simplicity (which does occur in the case of grayscale images with a single color channel). Note that the depth of a layer must exactly match that of its filter/kernel, and the contributions of the dot products over all the feature maps in the corresponding grid region of a particular layer will need to be added (in the general case) to create a single output feature value in the next layer. Figure 8.2 depicts two specific examples of the convolution operations with a layer of size $7 \times 7 \times 1$ and a $3 \times 3 \times 1$ filter in the bottom row. Furthermore, the entire feature map of the next layer is shown on the upper right-hand side of Figure 8.2. Examples of two convolution operations are shown in which the outputs are 16 and 26, respectively. These values are arrived at by using the following multiplication and aggregation operations:

$$5 \times 1 + 8 \times 1 + 1 \times 1 + 1 \times 2 = 16$$
$$4 \times 1 + 4 \times 1 + 4 \times 1 + 7 \times 2 = 26$$

The multiplications with zeros have been omitted in the above aggregation. In the event that the depths of the layer and its corresponding filter are greater than 1, the above operations are performed for each spatial map and then aggregated across the entire depth of the filter.

A convolution in the qth layer increases the *receptive field* of a feature from the qth layer to the $(q+1)$th layer. In other words, each feature in the next layer captures a larger spatial region in the input layer. For example, when using a 3×3 filter convolution successively in three layers, the activations in the first, second, and third hidden layers capture pixel regions of size 3×3, 5×5, and 7×7, respectively, in the *original input image*. As we will see later, other types of operations increase the receptive fields further, as they reduce the size of the spatial footprint of the layers. This is a natural consequence of the fact that features in later layers capture complex characteristics of the image over larger spatial regions, and then combine the simpler features in earlier layers.

When performing the operations from the qth layer to the $(q + 1)$th layer, the depth d_{q+1} of the computed layer depends on the *number* of filters in the qth layer, and it is independent of the *depth* of the qth layer or any of its other dimensions. In other words, the depth d_{q+1} in the $(q + 1)$th layer is always equal to the number of filters in the qth layer. For example, the depth of the second layer in Figure 8.1(a) is 5, because a total of five filters are used in the first layer for the transformation. However, in order to perform the convolutions in the second layer (to create the third layer), one must now use filters of depth 5 in order to match the new depth of this layer, even though filters of depth 3 were used in the convolutions of the first layer (to create the second layer).

8.2.1   Padding

One observation is that the convolution operation reduces the size of the $(q + 1)$th layer in comparison with the size of the qth layer. This type of reduction in size is not desirable in general, because it tends to lose some information along the borders of the image (or of the feature map, in the case of hidden layers). This problem can be resolved by using *padding*. In padding, one adds $(F_q - 1)/2$ "pixels" all around the borders of the feature map in order to maintain the spatial footprint. Note that these pixels are really feature values in the case of padding hidden layers. The value of each of these padded feature values is set

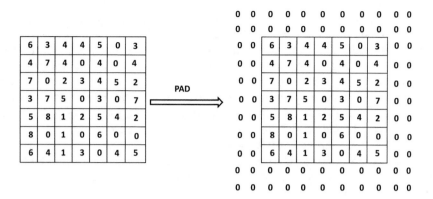

Figure 8.3: An example of padding. Each of the d_q activation maps in the entire depth of the qth layer are padded in this way.

to 0, irrespective of whether the input or the hidden layers are being padded. As a result, the spatial height and width of the input volume will both increase by $(F_q - 1)$, which is exactly what they reduce by (in the output volume) after the convolution is performed. The padded portions do not contribute to the final dot product because their values are set to 0. In a sense, what padding does is to allow the convolution operation with a portion of the filter "sticking out" from the borders of the layer and then performing the dot product only over the portion of the layer where the values are defined. This type of padding is referred to as *half-padding* because (almost) half the filter is sticking out from all sides of the spatial input in the case where the filter is placed in its extreme spatial position along the edges. Half-padding is designed to maintain the spatial footprint exactly.

When padding is not used, the resulting "padding" is also referred to as a *valid padding*. Valid padding generally does not work well from an experimental point of view. Using half-padding ensures that some of the critical information at the borders of the layer is represented in a standalone way. In the case of valid padding, the contributions of the pixels on the borders of the layer will be under-represented compared to the central pixels in the next hidden layer, which is undesirable. Furthermore, this under-representation will be compounded over multiple layers. Therefore, padding is typically performed in all layers, and not just in the first layer where the spatial locations correspond to input values. Consider a situation in which the layer has size $32 \times 32 \times 3$ and the filter is of size $5 \times 5 \times 3$. Therefore, $(5 - 1)/2 = 2$ zeros are padded on all sides of the image. As a result, the 32×32 spatial footprint first increases to 36×36 because of padding, and then it reduces back to 32×32 after performing the convolution. An example of the padding of a single feature map is shown in Figure 8.3, where two zeros are padded on all sides of the image (or feature map). This is a similar situation as discussed above (in terms of addition of two zeros), except that the spatial dimensions of the image are much smaller than 32×32 in order to enable illustration in a reasonable amount of space.

Another useful form of padding is *full-padding*. In full-padding, we allow (almost) the *full* filter to stick out from various sides of the input. In other words, a portion of the filter of size $F_q - 1$ is allowed to stick out from any side of the input with an overlap of only one spatial feature. For example, the kernel and the input image might overlap at a single pixel at an extreme corner. Therefore, the input is padded with $(F_q - 1)$ zeros on each side. In other words, each spatial dimension of the input increases by $2(F_q - 1)$. Therefore, if the input dimensions in the original image are L_q and B_q, the padded spatial dimensions in the input volume become $L_q + 2(F_q - 1)$ and $B_q + 2(F_q - 1)$. After performing the convolution, the feature-map dimensions in layer $(q+1)$ become $L_q + F_q - 1$ and $B_q + F_q - 1$, respectively. While convolution normally reduces the spatial footprint, full padding *increases* the spatial footprint. Interestingly, full-padding increases each dimension of the spatial footprint by the same value $(F_q - 1)$ that no-padding decreases it. *This relationship is not a coincidence because a "reverse" convolution operation can be implemented by applying another convolution on the fully padded output (of the original convolution) with an appropriately defined kernel of the same size.* This type of "reverse" convolution occurs frequently in the backpropagation and autoencoder algorithms for convolutional neural networks. Fully padded inputs are useful because they increase the spatial footprint, which is required in several types of convolutional autoencoders.

8.2.2   Strides

There are other ways in which convolution can reduce the spatial footprint of the image (or hidden layer). The above approach performs the convolution at every position in the spatial location of the feature map. However, it is not necessary to perform the convolution at every spatial position in the layer. One can reduce the level of granularity of the convolution by using the notion of *strides*. The description above corresponds to the case when a stride of 1 is used. When a stride of S_q is used in the qth layer, the convolution is performed at the locations 1, $S_q + 1$, $2\,S_q + 1$, and so on along both spatial dimensions of the layer. The spatial size of the output on performing this convolution[1] has height of $(L_q - F_q)/S_q + 1$ and a width of $(B_q - F_q)/S_q + 1$. As a result, the use of strides will result in a reduction of each spatial dimension of the layer by a factor of approximately S_q and the area by S_q^2, although the actual factor may vary because of edge effects. It is most common to use a stride of 1, although a stride of 2 is occasionally used as well. It is rare to use strides more than 2 in normal circumstances. Even though a stride of 4 was used in the input layer of the winning architecture [255] of the ILSVRC competition of 2012, the winning entry in the subsequent year reduced the stride to 2 [556] to improve accuracy. Larger strides can be helpful in memory-constrained settings or to reduce overfitting if the spatial resolution is unnecessarily high. Strides have the effect of rapidly increasing the receptive field of each feature in the hidden layer, while reducing the spatial footprint of the entire layer. An increased receptive field is useful in order to capture a complex feature in a larger spatial region of the image. As we will see later, the hierarchical feature engineering process of a convolutional neural network captures more complex shapes in later layers. Historically, the receptive fields have been increased with another operation, known as the *max-pooling* operation. In recent years, larger strides have been used in lieu [184, 466] of max-pooling operations, which will be discussed later.

8.2.3   Typical Settings

It is common to use stride sizes of 1 in most settings. Even when strides are used, small strides of size 2 are used. Furthermore, it is common to have $L_q = B_q$. In other words, it is desirable to work with square images. In cases where the input images are not square, preprocessing is used to enforce this property. For example, one can extract square patches

---

[1]Here, it is assumed that $(L_q - F_q)$ is exactly divisible by S_q in order to obtain a clean fit of the convolution filter with the original image. Otherwise, some ad hoc modifications are needed to handle edge effects. In general, this is not a desirable solution.

of the image to create the training data. The number of filters in each layer is often a power of 2, because this often results in more efficient processing. Such an approach also leads to hidden layer depths that are powers of 2. Typical values of the spatial extent of the filter size (denoted by F_q) are 3 or 5. In general, small filter sizes often provide the best results, although some practical challenges exist in using filter sizes that are too small. Small filter sizes typically lead to deeper networks (for the same parameter footprint) and therefore tend to be more powerful. In fact, one of the top entries in an ILSVRC contest, referred to as *VGG* [454], was the first to experiment with a spatial filter dimension of only $F_q = 3$ for all layers, and the approach was found to work very well in comparison with larger filter sizes.

Use of Bias

As in all neural networks, it is also possible to add biases to the forward operations. Each unique filter in a layer is associated with its own bias. Therefore, the pth filter in the qth layer has bias $b^{(p,q)}$. When any convolution is performed with the pth filter in the qth layer, the value of $b^{(p,q)}$ is added to the dot product. The use of the bias simply increases the number of parameters in each filter by 1, and therefore it is not a significant overhead. Like all other parameters, the bias is learned during backpropagation. One can treat the bias as a weight of a connection whose input is always set to +1. This special input is used in all convolutions, irrespective of the spatial location of the convolution. Therefore, one can assume that a special pixel appears in the input whose value is always set to 1. Therefore, the number of input features in the qth layer is $1 + L_q \times B_q \times d_q$. This is a standard feature-engineering trick that is used for handling bias in all forms of machine learning.

8.2.4 The ReLU Layer

The convolution operation is interleaved with the pooling and ReLU operations. The ReLU activation is not very different from how it is applied in a traditional neural network. For each of the $L_q \times B_q \times d_q$ values in a layer, the ReLU activation function is applied to it to create $L_q \times B_q \times d_q$ thresholded values. These values are then passed on to the next layer. Therefore, applying the ReLU does not change the dimensions of a layer because it is a simple one-to-one mapping of activation values. In traditional neural networks, the activation function is combined with a linear transformation with a matrix of weights to create the next layer of activations. Similarly, a ReLU typically follows a convolution operation (which is the rough equivalent of the linear transformation in traditional neural networks), and the ReLU layer is often not explicitly shown in pictorial illustrations of the convolution neural network architectures.

It is noteworthy that the use of the ReLU activation function is a recent evolution in neural network design. In the earlier years, saturating activation functions like sigmoid and tanh were used. However, it was shown in [255] that the use of the ReLU has tremendous advantages over these activation functions both in terms of speed and accuracy. Increased speed is also connected to accuracy because it allows one to use deeper models and train them for a longer time. In recent years, the use of the ReLU activation function has replaced the other activation functions in convolutional neural network design to an extent that this chapter will simply use the ReLU as the default activation function (unless otherwise mentioned).

8.2.5   Pooling

The pooling operation is, however, quite different. The pooling operation works on small grid regions of size $P_q \times P_q$ in each layer, and produces another layer *with the same depth* (unlike filters). For each square region of size $P_q \times P_q$ in each of the d_q activation maps, the *maximum* of these values is returned. This approach is referred to as *max-pooling*. If a stride of 1 is used, then this will produce a new layer of size $(L_q - P_q + 1) \times (B_q - P_q + 1) \times d_q$. However, it is more common to use a stride $S_q > 1$ in pooling. In such cases, the length of the new layer will be $(L_q - P_q)/S_q + 1$ and the breadth will be $(B_q - P_q)/S_q + 1$. Therefore, pooling drastically reduces the spatial dimensions of each activation map.

Unlike with convolution operations, pooling is done at the level of *each* activation map. Whereas a convolution operation simultaneously uses all d_q feature maps in combination with a filter to produce a single feature value, pooling independently operates on each feature map to produce another feature map. Therefore, the operation of pooling does not change the number of feature maps. In other words, the depth of the layer created using pooling is the same as that of the layer on which the pooling operation was performed. Examples of pooling with strides of 1 and 2 are shown in Figure 8.4. Here, we use pooling over 3×3 regions. The typical size P_q of the region over which one performs pooling is 2×2. At a stride of 2, there would be no overlap among the different regions being pooled, and it is quite common to use this type of setting. However, it has sometimes been suggested that it is desirable to have at least some overlap among the spatial units at which the pooling is performed, because it makes the approach less likely to overfit.

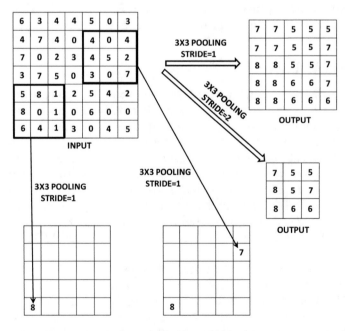

Figure 8.4: An example of a max-pooling of one activation map of size 7×7 with strides of 1 and 2. A stride of 1 creates a 5×5 activation map with heavily repeating elements because of maximization in overlapping regions. A stride of 2 creates a 3×3 activation map with less overlap. Unlike convolution, each activation map is independently processed and therefore the number of output activation maps is exactly equal to the number of input activation maps.

Other types of pooling (like average-pooling) are possible but rarely used. In the earliest convolutional network, referred to as *LeNet-5*, a variant of average pooling was used and was referred[2] to as *subsampling*. In general, max-pooling remains more popular than average pooling. The max-pooling layers are interleaved with the convolutional/ReLU layers, although the former typically occurs much less frequently in deep architectures. This is because pooling drastically reduces the spatial size of the feature map, and only a few pooling operations are required to reduce the spatial map to a small constant size.

It is common to use pooling with 2×2 filters and a stride of 2, when it is desired to reduce the spatial footprint of the activation maps. Pooling results in (some) invariance to translation because shifting the image slightly does not change the activation map significantly. This property is referred to as *translation invariance*. The idea is that similar images often have very different relative locations of the distinctive shapes within them, and translation invariance helps in being able to classify such images in a similar way. For example, one should be able to classify a bird as a bird, irrespective of where it occurs in the image.

Another important purpose of pooling is that it increases the size of the receptive field while reducing the spatial footprint of the layer because of the use of strides larger than 1. Increased sizes of receptive fields are needed to be able to capture larger regions of the image within a complex feature in later layers. Most of the rapid reductions in spatial footprints of the layers (and corresponding increases in receptive fields of the features) are caused by the pooling operations. Convolutions increase the receptive field only gently unless the stride is larger than 1. In recent years, it has been suggested that pooling is not always necessary. One can design a network with only convolutional and ReLU operations, and obtain the expansion of the receptive field by using larger strides within the convolutional operations [184, 466]. Therefore, there is an emerging trend in recent years to get rid of the max-pooling layers altogether. However, this trend has not been fully established and validated, as of the writing of this book. There seem to be at least some arguments in favor of max-pooling. Max-pooling introduces nonlinearity and a greater amount of translation invariance, as compared to strided convolutions. Although nonlinearity can be achieved with the ReLU activation function, the key point is that the effects of max-pooling cannot be exactly replicated by strided convolutions either. At the very least, the two operations are not fully interchangeable.

8.2.6 Fully Connected Layers

Each feature in the final spatial layer is connected to each hidden state in the first fully connected layer. This layer functions in exactly the same way as a traditional feed-forward network. In most cases, one might use more than one fully connected layer to increase the power of the computations towards the end. The connections among these layers are exactly structured like a traditional feed-forward network. Since the fully connected layers are densely connected, the vast majority of parameters lie in the fully connected layers. For example, if each of two fully connected layers has 4096 hidden units, then the connections between them have more than 16 million weights. Similarly, the connections from the last spatial layer to the first fully connected layer will have a large number of parameters. Even though the convolutional layers have a larger number of *activations* (and a larger memory footprint), the fully connected layers often have a larger number of *connections* (and parameter footprint). The reason that activations contribute to the memory footprint

---

[2]In recent years, subsampling also refers to other operations that reduce the spatial footprint. Therefore, there is some difference between the classical usage of this term and modern usage.

more significantly is that the number of activations are multiplied by mini-batch size while tracking variables in the forward and backward passes of backpropagation. These trade-offs are useful to keep in mind while choosing neural-network design based on specific types of resource constraints (e.g., data versus memory availability). It is noteworthy that the nature of the fully-connected layer can be sensitive to the application at hand. For example, the nature of the fully-connected layer for a classification application would be somewhat different from the case of a segmentation application. The aforementioned discussion is for the most common use-case of a classification application.

The output layer of a convolutional neural network is designed in an application-specific way. In the following, we will consider the representative application of classification. In such a case, the output layer is fully connected to every neuron in the penultimate layer, and has a weight associated with it. One might use the logistic, softmax, or linear activation depending on the nature of the application (e.g., classification or regression).

One alternative to using fully connected layers is to use average pooling across the whole spatial area of the final set of activation maps to create a single value. Therefore, the number of features created in the final spatial layer will be exactly equal to the number of filters. In this scenario, if the final activation maps are of size $7 \times 7 \times 256$, then 256 features will be created. Each feature will be the result of aggregating 49 values. This type of approach greatly reduces the parameter footprint of the fully connected layers, and it has some advantages in terms of generalizability. This approach was used in *GoogLeNet* [485]. In some applications like image segmentation, each pixel is associated with a class label, and one does not use fully connected layers. Fully convolutional networks with 1×1 convolutions are used in order to create an output spatial map.

8.2.7   The Interleaving Between Layers

The convolution, pooling, and ReLU layers are typically interleaved in a neural network in order to increase the expressive power of the network. The ReLU layers often follow the convolutional layers, just as a nonlinear activation function typically follows the linear dot product in traditional neural networks. Therefore, the convolutional and ReLU layers are typically stuck together one after the other. Some pictorial illustrations of neural architectures like *AlexNet* [255] do not explicitly show the ReLU layers because they are assumed to be always stuck to the end of the linear convolutional layers. After two or three sets of convolutional-ReLU combinations, one might have a max-pooling layer. Examples of this basic pattern are as follows:

CRCRP

CRCRCRP

Here, the convolutional layer is denoted by C, the ReLU layer is denoted by R, and the max-pooling layer is denoted by P. This entire pattern (including the max-pooling layer) might be repeated a few times in order to create a deep neural network. For example, if the first pattern above is repeated three times and followed by a fully connected layer (denoted by F), then we have the following neural network:

CRCRPCRCRPCRCRPF

The description above is not complete because one needs to specify the number/size/padding of filters/pooling layers. The pooling layer is the key step that tends to reduce the spatial footprint of the activation maps because it uses strides that are larger than 1. It is also possible to reduce the spatial footprints with strided convolutions instead of max-pooling. These networks are often quite deep, and it is not uncommon to have convolutional networks with more than 15 layers. Recent architectures also use *skip connections* between layers, which become increasingly important as the depth of the network increases (cf. Section 8.4.5).

LeNet-5

Early networks were quite shallow. An example of one of the earliest neural networks is *LeNet-5* [279]. The input data is in grayscale, and there is only one color channel. The input is assumed to be the ASCII representation of a character. For the purpose of discussion, we will assume that there are ten types of characters (and therefore 10 outputs), although the approach can be used for any number of classes.

The network contained two convolution layers, two pooling layers, and three fully connected layers at the end. However, later layers contain multiple feature maps because of the use of multiple filters in each layer. The architecture of this network is shown in Figure 8.5. The first fully connected layer was also referred to as a convolution layer (labeled as $C5$) in the original work because the ability existed to generalize it to spatial features for larger input maps. However, the specific implementation of *LeNet-5* really used $C5$ as a fully connected layer, because the filter spatial size was the same as the input spatial size. This is why we are counting $C5$ as a fully connected layer in this exposition. It is noteworthy that two versions of *LeNet-5* are shown in Figure 8.5(a) and (b). The upper diagram of Figure 8.5(a) explicitly shows the subsampling layers, which is how the architecture was presented in the original work. However, deeper architectural diagrams like *AlexNet* [255] often do not show the subsampling or max-pooling layers explicitly in order to accommodate the large number of layers. Such a concise architecture for *LeNet-5* is illustrated in Figure 8.5(b). The activation function layers are also not explicitly shown in either figure. In the original work in *LeNet-5*, the sigmoid activation function occurs immediately after the subsampling operations, although this ordering is relatively unusual in recent architectures. In most modern architectures, subsampling is replaced by max-pooling, and the max-pooling layers occur less frequently than the convolution layers. Furthermore, the activations are typically performed immediately after each convolution (rather than after each max-pooling).

The number of layers in the architecture is often counted in terms of the number of layers with weighted spatial filters and the number of fully connected layers. In other words, subsampling/max-pooling and activation function layers are often not counted separately. The subsampling in *LeNet-5* used 2×2 spatial regions with stride 2. Furthermore, unlike max-pooling, the values were averaged, scaled with a trainable weight and then a bias was added. In modern architectures, the linear scaling and bias addition operations have been dispensed with. The concise architectural representation of Figure 8.5(b) is sometimes confusing to beginners because it is missing details such as the size of the max-pooling/subsampling filters. In fact, there is no unique way of representing these architectural details, and many variations are used by different authors. This chapter will show several such examples in the case studies.

This network is extremely shallow by modern standards; yet the basic principles have not changed since then. The main difference is that the ReLU activation had not appeared at that point, and sigmoid activation was often used in the earlier architectures. Furthermore, the use of average pooling is extremely uncommon today compared to max-pooling. Recent years have seen a move away from both max-pooling and subsampling, with strided convolutions as the preferred choice. *LeNet-5* also used ten radial basis function (RBF) units in the final layer (cf. Chapter 5), in which the prototype of each unit was compared to its input vector and the squared Euclidean distance between them was output. This is the same as using the negative log-likelihood of the Gaussian distribution represented by that RBF unit. The parameter vectors of the RBF units were chosen by hand, and correspond to a stylized 7×12 bitmap image of the corresponding character class, which were flattened into a $7 \times 12 = 84$-dimensional representation. Note that the size of the penultimate layer is exactly 84 in order to enable the computation of the Euclidean distance between the vector corresponding to that layer and the parameter vector of the RBF unit. The ten outputs in the final layer provide the scores of the classes, and the smallest score among the ten units provides the prediction. This type of use of RBF units is now anachronistic in modern convolutional network design, and one generally tends to work with softmax units with log-likelihood loss on multinomial label outputs. *LeNet-5* was used extensively for character recognition, and was used by many banks to read checks.

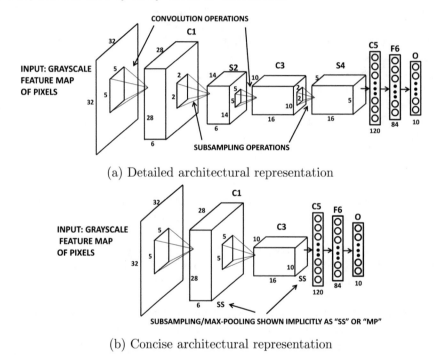

(a) Detailed architectural representation

(b) Concise architectural representation

Figure 8.5: LeNet-5: One of the earliest convolutional neural networks.

8.2.8   Local Response Normalization

A trick that is introduced in [255] is that of *local response normalization*, which is always used immediately after the ReLU layer. The use of this trick aids generalization. The basic idea of this normalization approach is inspired from biological principles, and it is intended to create competition among different filters. First, we describe the normalization formula using *all* filters, and then we describe how it is actually computed using only a subset of filters. Consider a situation in which a layer contains N filters, and the activation values of these N filters at a particular spatial position (x, y) are given by $a_1 \ldots a_N$. Then, each a_i is converted into a normalized value b_i using the following formula:

$$b_i = \frac{a_i}{(k + \alpha \sum_j a_i^2)^\beta} \tag{8.1}$$

The values of the underlying parameters used in [255] are $k = 2$, $\alpha = 10^{-4}$, and $\beta = 0.75$. However, in practice, one does not normalize over all N filters. Rather the filters are ordered arbitrarily up front to define "adjacency" among filters. Then, the normalization is performed over each set of n "adjacent" filters for some parameter n. The value of n used in [255] is 5. Therefore, we have the following formula:

$$b_i = \frac{a_i}{(k + \alpha \sum_{j=i-\lfloor n/2 \rfloor}^{i+\lfloor n/2 \rfloor} a_i^2)^\beta} \tag{8.2}$$

In the above formula, any value of $i - n/2$ that is less than 0 is set to 0, and any value of $i + n/2$ that is greater than N is set to N. The use of this type of normalization is no obsolete, and its discussion has been included here for historical reasons.

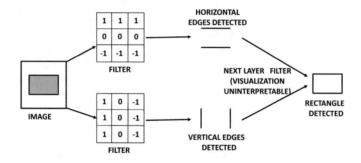

Figure 8.6: Filters detect edges and combine them to create rectangle.

8.2.9 Hierarchical Feature Engineering

It is instructive to examine the activations of the filters created by real-world images in different layers. In Section 8.5, we will discuss a concrete way in which the features extracted in various layers can be visualized. For now, we provide a subjective interpretation. The activations of the filters in the early layers are low-level features like edges, whereas those in later layers put together these low-level features. For example, a mid-level feature might put together edges to create a hexagon, whereas a higher-level feature might put together the mid-level hexagons to create a honeycomb. It is fairly easy to see why a low-level filter might detect edges. Consider a situation in which the color of the image changes along an edge. As a result, the difference between neighboring pixel values will be non-zero only across the edge. This can be achieved by choosing the appropriate weights in the corresponding low-level filter. Note that the filter to detect a horizontal edge will not be the same as that to detect a vertical edge. This brings us back to Hubel and Weisel's experiments in which different neurons in the cat's visual cortex were activated by different edges. Examples of filters detecting horizontal and vertical edges are illustrated in Figure 8.6. The next layer filter works on the hidden features and therefore it is harder to interpret. Nevertheless, the next layer filter is able to detect a rectangle by combining the horizontal and vertical edges.

In a later section, we will show visualizations of how smaller portions of real-world image activate different hidden features, much like the biological model of Hubel and Wiesel in which different shapes seem to activate different neurons. Therefore, the power of convolutional neural networks rests in the ability to put together these primitive shapes into more complex shapes layer by layer. Note that it is impossible for the first convolution layer to learn any feature that is larger than $F_1 \times F_1$ pixels, where the value of F_1 is typically a small number like 3 or 5. However, the next convolution layer will be able to put together many of these patches together to create a feature from an area of the image that is larger. The primitive features learned in earlier layers are put together in a semantically coherent way to learn increasingly complex and interpretable visual features. The choice of learned features is affected by how backpropagation adapts the features to the needs of the loss function at hand. For example, if an application is training to classify images as cars, the approach might learn to put together arcs to create a circle, and then it might put together circles with other shapes to create a car wheel. All this is enabled by the hierarchical features of a deep network.

Recent *ImageNet* competitions have demonstrated that much of the power in image recognition lies in increased depth of the network. Not having enough layers effectively prevents the network from learning the hierarchical regularities in the image that are combined to create its semantically relevant components. Another important observation is that the nature of the features learned will be sensitive to the specific data set at hand. For example, the features learned to recognize trucks will be different from those learned to recognize carrots. However, some data sets (like *ImageNet*) are diverse enough that the features learned by training on these data sets have general-purpose significance across many applications.

8.3   Training a Convolutional Network

The process of training a convolutional neural network uses the backpropagation algorithm. There are primarily three types of layers, corresponding to the convolution, ReLU, and max-pooling layers. We will separately describe the backpropagation algorithm through each of these layers. The ReLU is relatively straightforward to backpropagate through because it is no different than a traditional neural network. For max-pooling with no overlap between pools, one only needs to identify which unit is the maximum value in a pool (with ties broken arbitrarily or divided proportionally). The partial derivative of the loss with respect to the pooled state flows back to the unit with maximum value. All entries other than the maximum entry in the grid will be assigned a value of 0. Note that the backpropagation through a maximization operation is also described in Table 3.1 of Chapter 3. For cases in which the pools are overlapping, let $P_1 \ldots P_r$ be the pools in which the unit h is involved, with corresponding activations $h_1 \ldots h_r$ in the next layer. If h is the maximum value in pool P_i (and therefore $h_i = h$), then the gradient of the loss with respect to h_i flows back to h (with ties broken arbitrarily or divided proportionally). The contributions of the different overlapping pools (from $h_1 \ldots h_r$ in the next layer) are added in order to compute the gradient with respect to the unit h. Therefore, the backpropagation through the maximization and the ReLU operations are not very different from those in traditional neural networks.

8.3.1 Backpropagating Through Convolutions

The backpropagation through convolutions is also not very different from the backpropagation with linear transformations (i.e., matrix multiplications) in a feed-forward network. This point of view will become particularly clear when we present convolutions as a form of matrix multiplication. Just as backpropagation in feed-forward networks from layer $(i + 1)$ to layer i is achieved by multiplying the error derivatives with respect to layer $(i + 1)$ with the transpose of the forward propagation matrix between layers i and $(i + 1)$ (cf. Table 3.1 of Chapter 3), backpropagation in convolutional networks can also be seen as a form of transposed convolution.

First, we describe a simple element-wise approach to backpropagation. Assume that the loss gradients of the cells in layer $(i + 1)$ have already been computed. The loss derivative with respect to a cell in layer $(i + 1)$ is defined as the partial derivative of the loss function with respect to the hidden variable in that cell. Convolutions multiply the activations in layer i with filter elements to create elements in the next layer. Therefore, a cell in layer $(i + 1)$ receives aggregated contributions from a 3-dimensional volume of elements in the previous layer of filter size $F_i \times F_i \times d_i$. At the same time, a cell c in layer i contributes to multiple elements (denoted by set S_c) in layer $(i + 1)$, although the number of elements to which it contributes depends on the depth of the next layer and the stride. Identifying this "forward set" is the key to the backpropagation. A key point is that the cell c contributes to each element in S_c in an additive way after multiplying the activation of cell c with a filter element. Therefore, backpropagation simply needs to multiply the loss derivative of each element in S_c with respect to the corresponding filter element and aggregate in the backwards direction at c. For any particular cell c in layer i, the following pseudo-code can be used to backpropagate the existing derivatives in layer-$(i+1)$ to cell c in layer-i:

Identify all cells S_c in layer $(i + 1)$ to which cell c in layer i contributes;
For each cell $r \in S_c$, let δ_r be its (already backpropagated) loss-derivative with respect to cell r;
For each cell $r \in S_c$, let w_r be weight of filter element used for contributing from cell c to r;
$\delta_c = \sum_{r \in S_c} \delta_r \cdot w_r$;

After the loss gradients have been computed, the values are multiplied with those of the hidden units of the $(i - 1)$th layer to obtain the gradients with respect to the weights between the $(i - 1)$th and ith layer. In other words, the hidden value at one end point of a weight is multiplied with the loss gradient at the other end in order to obtain the partial derivative with respect to the weight. However, this computation assumes that all weights are distinct, whereas the weights in the filter are shared across the entire spatial extent of the layer. Therefore, one has to be careful to account for shared weights, and sum up the partial derivatives of all copies of a shared weight. In other words, we first pretend that the filter used in each position is distinct in order to compute the partial derivative with respect to each copy of the shared weight, and then add up the partial derivatives of the loss with respect to all copies of a particular weight.

Note that the approach above uses simple linear accumulation of gradients like traditional backpropagation. However, one has to be slightly careful in terms of keeping track of the cells that influence other cells in the next layer. One can implement backpropagation with the help of tensor multiplication operations, which can further be simplified into simple matrix multiplications of derived matrices from these tensors. This point of view will be discussed in the next two sections because it provides many insights on how many aspects of feedforward networks can be generalized to convolutional neural networks.

8.3.2   Backpropagation as Convolution with Inverted/Transposed Filter

In conventional neural networks, a backpropagation operation is performed by multiplying a vector of gradients at layer $(q+1)$ with the transposed weight matrix between the layers q and $(q+1)$ in order to obtain the vector of gradients at layer q (cf. Table 3.1). In convolution neural networks, the backpropagated derivatives are also associated with spatial positions in the layers. Is there an analogous convolution we can apply to the spatial footprint of backpropagated derivatives in a layer to obtain those of the previous layer? It turns out that this is indeed possible.

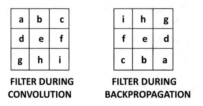

Figure 8.7: The inverse of a kernel for backpropagation

Let us consider the case in which the activations in layer q are convolved with a filter to create those in layer $(q+1)$. For simplicity, consider the case in which depth d_q of the input layer and the depth d_{q+1} of the output layer are both 1; furthermore, we use convolutions with stride 1. In such a case, the convolution filter is inverted both horizontally and vertically for backpropagation. An example of such an inverted filter is illustrated in Figure 8.7. The intuitive reason for this inversion is that the *filter* is "moved around" the spatial area of the input volume to perform the dot product, whereas the backpropagated derivatives are with respect to the *input volume*, whose relative movement with respect to the filter is the opposite of the filter movement during convolutions. Note that the entry in the extreme upper-left of the convolution filter might not even contribute to the extreme upper-left entry in the output volume (because of padding), but it will almost always contribute to the extreme lower-right entry of the output volume. This is consistent with the inversion of the filter. The backpropagated derivative set of the $(q + 1)$th layer is convolved with this inverted filter to obtain the backpropagated derivative set of the qth layer. How are the paddings of the forward convolution and backward convolution related? For a stride of 1, the sum of the paddings during forward propagation and backward propagation is $F_q - 1$, where F_q is the side length of the filter for qth layer.

Now consider the case in which the depths d_q and d_{q+1} are no longer 1, but are arbitrary values. In this case, an additional tensor transposition needs to occur. The weight of the (i, j, k)th position of the pth filter in the qth layer is $\mathcal{W} = [w_{ijk}^{(p,q)}]$. Note that i and j refer to spatial positions, whereas k refers to the depth-centric position of the weight. In such a case, let the 5-dimensional tensor corresponding to the backpropagation filters from layer $q + 1$ to layer q be denoted by $\mathcal{U} = [u_{ijk}^{(p,q+1)}]$. Then, the entries of this tensor are as follows:

$$u_{rsp}^{(k,q+1)} = w_{ijk}^{(p,q)} \tag{8.3}$$

Here, we have $r = F_q - i + 1$ and $s = F_q - j + 1$. Note that the index p of the filter identifier and depth k within a filter have been interchanged between $\mathcal{W}$ and $\mathcal{U}$ in Equation 8.3. This is a tensor-centric transposition.

In order to understand the transposition above, consider a situation in which we use 20 filters on the 3-channel RGB volume in order to create an output volume of depth 20. While backpropagating, we will need to take a *gradient volume* of depth 20 and transform to a *gradient volume* of depth 3. Therefore, we need to create 3 filters for backpropagation, each of which is for the red, green, and blue colors. We pull out the 20 spatial slices from the 20 filters that are applied to the red color, invert them using the approach of Figure 8.7, and then create a single 20-depth filter for backpropagating gradients with respect to the red slice. Similar approaches are used for the green and blue slices. The transposition and inversion in Equation 8.3 correspond to these operations.

8.3.3 Convolution/Backpropagation as Matrix Multiplications

It is helpful to view convolution as a matrix multiplication because it helps us define various related notions such as *transposed convolution, deconvolution,* and *fractional convolution*. These concepts are helpful not just in understanding backpropagation, but also in developing the machinery necessary for convolutional autoencoders. In traditional feed-forward networks, matrices that are used to transform hidden states in the forward phase are transposed in the backwards phase (cf. Table 3.1) in order to backpropagate partial derivatives across layers. Similarly, the matrices used in encoders are often transposed in the decoders when working with autoencoders in traditional settings. Although the spatial structure of the convolutional neural network does mask the nature of the underlying matrix multiplication, one can "flatten" this spatial structure to perform the multiplication and reshape back to a spatial structure using the known spatial positions of the elements of the flattened matrix. This somewhat indirect approach is helpful in understanding the fact that the convolution operation is similar to the matrix multiplication in feed-forward networks at a very fundamental level. Furthermore, real-world implementations of convolution are often accomplished with matrix multiplication.

For simplicity, let us first consider the case in which the qth layer and the corresponding filter used for convolution both have unit depth. Furthermore, assume that we are using a stride of 1 with zero padding. Therefore, the input dimensions are $L_q \times B_q \times 1$, and the output dimensions are $(L_q - F_q + 1) \times (B_q - F_q + 1) \times 1$. In the common setting in which the spatial dimensions are square (i.e., $L_q = B_q$), one can assume that the spatial dimensions of the input $A_I = L_q \times L_q$ and the spatial dimensions of the output are $A_O = (L_q - F_q + 1) \times (L_q - F_q + 1)$. Here, A_I and A_O are the spatial areas of the input and output matrices, respectively. The input can be representing by flatting the area A_I into an A_I-dimensional column vector in which the rows of the spatial area are concatenated from top to bottom. This vector is denoted by $\overline{f}$. An example of a case in which we use a 2×2 filter on a 3×3 input is shown in Figure 8.8. Therefore, the output is of size 2×2, and we have $A_I = 3 \times 3 = 9$, and $A_O = 2 \times 2 = 4$. The 9-dimensional column vector for the 3×3 input is shown in Figure 8.8. A sparse matrix C is defined in lieu of the filter, which is the key in representing the convolution as a matrix multiplication. A matrix of size $A_O \times A_I$ is defined in which each row corresponds to the convolution at one of the A_O convolution locations. These rows are associated with the spatial location of the top-left corner of the convolution region in the input matrix from which they were derived. The value of each entry in the row corresponds to one of the A_I positions in the input matrix, but this value is 0, if that input position is not involved in the convolution for that row. Otherwise, the value is set to the corresponding value of the filter, which is used for multiplication. The ordering of the entries in a row is based on the same spatially sensitive ordering of the input matrix locations as was used to flatten the input matrix into an A_I-dimensional vector. Since the filter size is usually much smaller than the input size, most of the entries in the matrix C are 0s, and each entry of the filter occurs in every row of C. Therefore, every entry in the filter is repeated A_O times in C, because it is used for A_O multiplications.

An example of a 4×9 matrix C is shown in Figure 8.8. Subsequent multiplication of C with $\overline{f}$ yields an A_O-dimensional vector. The corresponding 4-dimensional vector is shown in Figure 8.8. Since each of the A_O rows of C is associated with a spatial location, these locations are inherited by $C\overline{f}$. These spatial locations are used to reshape $C\overline{f}$ to a spatial matrix. The reshaping of the 4-dimensional vector to a 2×2 matrix is also shown in Figure 8.8.

This particular exposition uses the simplified case with a depth of 1. In the event that the depth is larger than 1, the same approach is applied for each 2-dimensional slice, and the results are added. In other words, we aggregate $\sum_p C_p \overline{f}_p$ over the various slice indices p and then the results are re-shaped into a 2-dimensional matrix. This approach amounts to a *tensor* multiplication, which is a straightforward generalization of a matrix multiplication. The tensor multiplication approach is how convolution is actually implemented in practice. In general, one will have multiple filters, which correspond to multiple output maps. In such a case, the kth filter will be converted into the sparsified matrix $C_{p,k}$, and the kth feature map of the output volume will be $\sum_p C_{p,k} \overline{f}_p$.

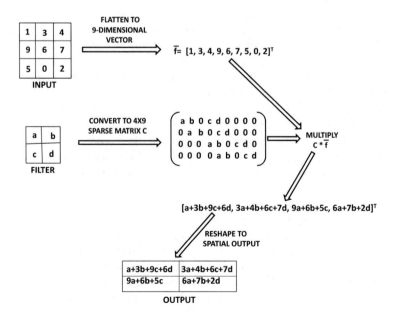

Figure 8.8: Convolution as matrix multiplication

The matrix-centric approach is very useful for performing backpropagation because one can also propagate gradients backwards by using the same approach in the backwards direction, except that the *transposed* matrix C^T is used for multiplication with the flattened vector version of a 2-dimensional slice of the output gradient. Note that the flattening of a gradient with respect to a spatial map can be done in a similar way as the flattened vector $\overline{f}$ is created in the forward phase. Consider the simple case in which both the input and output volumes have a depth of 1. If $\overline{g}$ is the flattened vector gradient of the loss with respect to the output spatial map, then the flattened gradient with respect to the input spatial map is obtained as $C^T\overline{g}$. This approach is consistent with the approach used in feed-forward networks, in which the transpose of the forward matrix is used in backpropagation. The above result is for the simple case when both input and output volumes have depth of 1. What happens in the general case? When the depth of the output volume is $d > 1$, the gradients with respect to the output maps are denoted by $\overline{g}_1 \ldots \overline{g}_d$. The corresponding gradient with respect to the features in the pth spatial slice of the input volume is given by $\sum_{k=1}^{d} C_{p,k}^T \overline{g}_k$. Here, the matrix $C_{p,k}$ is obtained by converting the pth spatial slice of the kth filter into the sparsified matrix as discussed above. This approach is a consequence of Equation 8.3. This type of transposed convolution is also useful for the deconvolution operation in convolution autoencoders, which will be discussed later in this chapter (cf. Section 8.5).

8.3.4 Data Augmentation

A common trick to reduce overfitting in convolutional neural networks is the idea of *data augmentation*. In data augmentation, new training examples are generated by using transformations on the original examples. This idea was briefly discussed in Chapter 4, although it works better in some domains than others. Image processing is one domain to which data augmentation is very well suited. This is because many transformations such as translation, rotation, patch extraction, and reflection do not fundamentally change the properties of the object in an image. However, they do increase the generalization power of the data set when trained with the augmented data set. For example, if a data set is trained with mirror images and reflected versions of all the bananas in it, then the model is able to better recognize bananas in different orientations.

Many of these forms of data augmentation require very little computation, and therefore the augmented images do not need to be explicitly generated up front. Rather, they can be created at training time, when an image is being processed. For example, while processing an image of a banana, it can be reflected into a modified banana at training time. Similarly, the same banana might be represented in somewhat different color intensities in different images, and therefore it might be helpful to create representations of the same image in different color intensities. In many cases, creating the training data set using image patches can be helpful. An important neural network that rekindled interest in deep learning by winning the ILSVRC challenge was *AlexNet*. This network was trained by extracting $224 \times 224 \times 3$ patches from the images, which also defined the input sizes for the networks. The neural networks, which were entered into the ILSVRC contest in subsequent years, used a similar methodology of extracting patches.

Although most data augmentation methods are quite efficient, some forms of transformation that use principal component analysis (PCA) can be more expensive. PCA is used in order to change the color intensity of an image. If the computational costs are high, it becomes important to extract the images up front and store them. The basic idea here is to use the 3×3 covariance matrix of each pixel value and compute the principal components. Then, Gaussian noise is added to each principal component with zero mean and variance of 0.01. This noise is fixed over all the pixels of a particular image. The approach is dependent on the fact that object identity is invariant to color intensity and illumination. It is reported in [255] that data set augmentation reduces error rate by 1%.

One must be careful not to apply data augmentation blindly without regard to the data set and application at hand. For example, applying rotations and reflections on the MNIST data set [281] of handwritten digits is a bad idea because the digits in the data set are all presented in a similar orientation. Furthermore, the mirror image of an asymmetric digit is not a valid digit, and a rotation of a '6' is a '9.' The key point in deciding what types of data augmentation are reasonable is to account for the natural distribution of images in the full data set, as well as the effect of a specific type of data set augmentation on the class labels.

8.4   Case Studies of Convolutional Architectures

In the following, we provide some case studies of convolutional architectures. These case studies were derived from successful entries to the ILSVRC competition in recent years. These are instructive because they provide an understanding of the important factors in neural network design that can make these networks work well. Even though recent years have seen some changes in architectural design (like ReLU activation), it is striking how similar the modern architectures are to the basic design of *LeNet-5*. The main changes from *LeNet-5* to modern architectures are in terms of the explosion of depth, the use of ReLU activation, and the training efficiency enabled by modern hardware/optimization enhancements. Modern architectures are deeper, and they use a variety of computational, architectural, and hardware tricks to efficiently train these networks with large amounts of data. Hardware advancements should not be underestimated; modern GPU-based platforms are 10,000 times faster than the (similarly priced) systems available at the time *LeNet-5* was proposed. Even on these modern platforms, it often takes a week to train a convolutional neural network that is accurate enough to be competitive at ILSVRC. The hardware, data-centric, and algorithmic enhancements are connected to some extent. It is difficult to try new algorithmic tricks if enough data and computational power is not available to experiment with complex/deeper models in a reasonable amount of time. Therefore, the recent revolution in deep convolutional networks could not have been possible, had it not been for the large amounts of data and increased computational power available today.

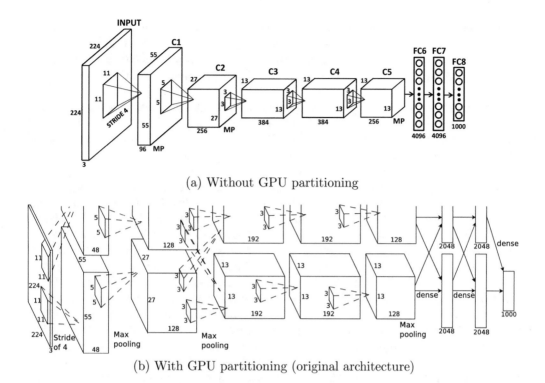

(a) Without GPU partitioning

(b) With GPU partitioning (original architecture)

Figure 8.9: The *AlexNet* architecture. The ReLU activations follow each convolution layer, and are not explicitly shown. Note that the max-pooling layers are labeled as MP, and they follow only a subset of the convolution-ReLU combination layers. The architectural diagram in (b) is from [A. Krizhevsky, I. Sutskever, and G. Hinton. Imagenet classification with deep convolutional neural networks. *NIPS Conference*, pp. 1097–1105. 2012.] ©2012 A. Krizhevsky, I. Sutskever, and G. Hinton.

In the following sections, we provide an overview of some of the well-known models that are often used for designing training algorithms for image classification. It is worth mentioning that some of these models are available as pretrained models over *ImageNet*, and the resulting features can be used for applications beyond classification. Such an approach is a form of transfer learning, which is discussed later in this section.

8.4.1 AlexNet

AlexNet was the winner of the 2012 ILSVRC competition. The architecture of *AlexNet* is shown in Figure 8.9(a). It is worth mentioning that there were two parallel pipelines of processing in the original architecture, which are not shown in Figure 8.9(a). These two pipelines are caused by two GPUs working together to build the training model with a faster speed and memory sharing. The network was originally trained on a GTX 580 GPU with 3 GB of memory, and it was impossible to fit the intermediate computations in this amount of space. Therefore, the network was partitioned across two GPUs. The original architecture is shown in Figure 8.9(b), in which the work is partitioned into two GPUs. We also show the architecture without the changes caused by the GPUs, so that it can be more easily compared with other convolutional neural network architectures discussed in this chapter. It is noteworthy that the GPUs are inter-connected in only a subset of the layers in Figure 8.9(b), which leads to some differences between Figure 8.9(a) and (b) in terms of the actual model constructed. Specifically, the GPU-partitioned architecture has fewer weights because not all layers have interconnections. Dropping some of the interconnections reduces the communication time between the processors and therefore helps in efficiency.

AlexNet starts with $224 \times 224 \times 3$ images and uses 96 filters of size $11 \times 11 \times 3$ in the first layer. A stride of 4 is used. This results in a first layer of size $55 \times 55 \times 96$. After the first layer has been computed, a max-pooling layer is used. This layer is denoted by 'MP' in Figure 8.9(a). Note that the architecture of Figure 8.9(a) is a simplified version of the architecture shown in Figure 8.9(b), which explicitly shows the two parallel pipelines. For example, Figure 8.9(b) shows a depth of the first convolution layer of only 48, because the 96 feature maps are divided among the GPUs for parallelization. On the other hand, Figure 8.9(a) does not assume the use of GPUs, and therefore the width is explicitly shown as 96. The ReLU activation function was applied after each convolutional layer, which was followed by response normalization and max-pooling. Although max-pooling has been annotated in the figure, it has not been assigned a block in the architecture. Furthermore, the ReLU and response normalization layers are not explicitly shown in the figure. These types of concise representations are common in pictorial depictions of neural architectures.

The second convolutional layer uses the response-normalized and pooled output of the first convolutional layer and filters it with 256 filters of size $5 \times 5 \times 96$. No intervening pooling or normalization layers are present in the third, fourth, or fifth convolutional layers. The sizes of the filters of the third, fourth, and fifth convolutional layers are $3 \times 3 \times 256$ (with 384 filters), $3 \times 3 \times 384$ (with 384 filters), and $3 \times 3 \times 384$ (with 256 filters). All max-pooling layers used 3×3 filters at stride 2. Therefore, there was some overlap among the pools. The fully connected layers have 4096 neurons. The final set of 4096 activations can be treated as a 4096-dimensional representation of the image. The final layer of *AlexNet* uses a 1000-way softmax in order to perform the classification. It is noteworthy that the final layer of 4096 activations (labeled by FC7 in Figure 8.9(b)) is often used to create a flat 4096 dimensional representation of an image for applications beyond classification. One can extract these features for any out-of-sample image by simply passing it through the trained neural network. These features often generalize well to other data sets and other tasks. Such features are referred to as FC7 features. In fact, the use of the extracted features from the penultimate layer as FC7 was popularized after *AlexNet*, even though the approach was known much earlier. As a result, such extracted features from the penultimate layer of a convolutional neural network are often referred to as *FC7 features*, irrespective of the number of layers in that network. It is noteworthy that the number of feature maps in middle layers is far larger than the initial depth of the volume in the input layer (which is only 3 corresponding to RGB colors) although their spatial dimensions are smaller. This is because the initial depth only contains the RGB color components, whereas the later layers capture different types of semantic features in the features maps.

Many design choices used in the architecture became standard in later architectures. A specific example is the use of ReLU activation in the architecture (instead of sigmoid or tanh units). The choice of the activation function in most convolutional neural networks today is almost exclusively focused on the ReLU, although this was not the case before *AlexNet*. Some other training tricks were known at the time, but their use in *AlexNet* popularized them. One example was the use of data augmentation, which turned out to be very useful in improving accuracy. *AlexNet* also underlined the importance of using specialized hardware like GPUs for training on such large data sets. Dropout was used with L_2-weight decay in order to improve generalization. The use of Dropout is common in virtually all types of architectures today because it provides an additional booster in most cases. The use of local response normalization was eventually discarded by later architectures.

We also briefly mention the parameter choices used in *AlexNet*. The interested reader can find the full code and parameter files of *AlexNet* at [584]. L_2-regularization was used with a parameter of 5×10^{-4}. *Dropout* was used by sampling units at a probability of 0.5. Momentum-based (mini-batch) stochastic gradient descent was used for training *AlexNet* with parameter value of 0.8. The batch-size was 128. The learning rate was 0.01, although it was eventually reduced a couple of times as the method began to converge. Even with the use of the GPU, the training time of *AlexNet* was of the order of a week.

The final top-5 error rate, which was defined as the fraction of cases in which the correct image was not included in the top-5 images, was about 15.4%. This error rate[3] was in comparison with the previous winners with an error rate of more than 25%. The gap with respect to the second-best performer in the contest was also similar. The use of single convolutional network provided a top-5 error rate of 18.2%, although using an ensemble of seven models provided the winning error-rate of 15.4%. Note that these types of ensemble-based tricks provide a consistent improvement of between 2% and 3% with most architectures. Furthermore, since the executions of most ensemble methods are embarrassingly parallelizable, it is relatively easy to perform them, as long as sufficient hardware resources are available. *AlexNet* is considered a fundamental advancement within the field of computer vision because of the large margin with which it won the ILSVRC contest. This success rekindled interest in deep learning in general, and convolutional neural networks in particular.

8.4.2 ZFNet

A variant of *ZFNet* [556] was the winner of the ILSVRC competition in 2013. Its architecture was heavily based on *AlexNet*, although some changes were made to further improve the accuracy. Most of these changes were associated with differences in hyperparameter choices, and therefore *ZFNet* is not very different from *AlexNet* at a fundamental level. One change from *AlexNet* to *ZFNet* was that the initial filters of size $11 \times 11 \times 3$ were changed to $7 \times 7 \times 3$. Instead of strides of 4, strides of 2 were used. The second layer used 5×5 filters at stride 2 as well. As in *AlexNet*, there are three max-pooling layers, and the same sizes of max-pooling filters were used. However, the first pair of max-pooling layers were performed after the first and second convolutions (rather than the second and third convolutions). As a result, the spatial footprint of the third layer changed to 13×13 rather than 27×27, although all other spatial footprints remained unchanged from *AlexNet*. The sizes of various layers in *AlexNet* and *ZFNet* are listed in Table 8.1.

The third, fourth, and fifth convolutional layers use a larger number of filters in *ZFNet* as compared to *AlexNet*. The number of filters in these layers were changed from $(384, 384, 256)$

---

[3]The top-5 error rate makes more sense in image data where a single image might contain objects of multiple classes. Throughout this chapter, we use the term "error rate" to refer to the top-5 error rate.

Table 8.1: Comparison of *AlexNet* and *ZFNet*

	AlexNet	*ZFNet*
Volume:	$224 \times 224 \times 3$	$224 \times 224 \times 3$
Operations:	Conv 11×11 (stride 4)	Conv 7×7 (stride 2), MP
Volume:	$55 \times 55 \times 96$	$55 \times 55 \times 96$
Operations:	Conv 5×5, MP	Conv 5×5 (stride 2), MP
Volume:	$27 \times 27 \times 256$	$13 \times 13 \times 256$
Operations:	Conv 3×3, MP	Conv 3×3
Volume:	$13 \times 13 \times 384$	$13 \times 13 \times 512$
Operations:	Conv 3×3	Conv 3×3
Volume:	$13 \times 13 \times 384$	$13 \times 13 \times 1024$
Operations:	Conv 3×3	Conv 3×3
Volume:	$13 \times 13 \times 256$	$13 \times 13 \times 512$
Operations:	MP, Fully connect	MP, Fully connect
FC6:	4096	4096
Operations:	Fully connect	Fully connect
FC7:	4096	4096
Operations:	Fully connect	Fully connect
FC8:	1000	1000
Operations:	Softmax	Softmax

to $(512, 1024, 512)$. As a result, the spatial footprints of *AlexNet* and *ZFNet* are the same in most layers, although the depths are different in the final three convolutional layers with similar spatial footprints. From an overall perspective, *ZFNet* used similar principles to *AlexNet*, and the main gains were obtained by changing the architectural parameters of *AlexNet*. This architecture reduced the top-5 error rate to 14.8% from 15.4%, and further increases in width/depth from the same author(s) reduced the error to 11.1%. Since most of the differences between *AlexNet* and *ZFNet* were those of minor design choices, this emphasizes the fact that small details are important when working with deep learning algorithms. Thus, extensive experimentation with neural architectures are sometimes important in order to obtain the best performance. The architecture of *ZfNet* was made wider and deeper, and the results were submitted to ILSVRC in 2013 under the name *Clarifai*, which was a company[4] founded by the first author of [556]. The difference[5] between *Clarifai* and *ZFNet* was one of width/depth of the network, although exact details of these differences are not available. This entry was the winning entry of the ILSVRC competition in 2013. Refer to [556] for details and a pictorial illustration of the architecture.

8.4.3 VGG

VGG [454] further emphasized the developing trend in terms of increased depth of networks. The tested networks were designed with various configurations with sizes between 11 and 19 layers, although the best-performing versions had 16 or more layers. *VGG* was a top-performing entry on ISLVRC in 2014, but it was not the winner. The winner was *GoogLeNet*, which had a top-5 error rate of 6.7% in comparison with the top-5 error rate of 7.3% for *VGG*. Nevertheless, *VGG* was important because it illustrated several important design principles that eventually became standard in future architectures.

---

[4]http://www.clarifai.com
[5]Personal communication from Matthew Zeiler.

An important innovation of *VGG* is that it reduced filter sizes but increased depth. It is important to understand that *reduced filter size necessitates increased depth.* This is because a small filter can capture only a small region of the image unless the network is deep. For example, a single feature that is a result of three sequential convolutions of size 3×3 will capture a region in the input of size 7×7. Note that using a single 7×7 filter directly on the input data will also capture the visual properties of a 7×7 input region. In the first case, we are using $3 \times 3 \times 3 = 27$ parameters, whereas we are using $7 \times 7 \times 1 = 49$ parameters in the second case. Therefore, the parameter footprint is smaller in the case when three sequential convolutions are used. However, three successive convolutions can often capture more interesting and complex features than a single convolution, and the resulting activations with a single convolution will look like primitive edge features. Therefore, the network with 7×7 filters will be unable to capture sophisticated shapes in smaller regions.

In general, greater depth forces more nonlinearity and greater regularization. A deeper network will have more nonlinearity because of the presence of more ReLU layers, and more regularization because the increased depth forces a structure on the layers through the use of repeated composition of convolutions. As discussed above, architectures with greater depth and reduced filter size require fewer parameters. This occurs in part because the number of parameters in each layer is given by the square of the filter size, whereas the number of parameters depend linearly on the depth. Therefore, one can drastically reduce the number of parameters by using smaller filter sizes, and instead "spend" these parameters by using increased depth. Increased depth also allows the use of a greater number of nonlinear activations, which increases the discriminative power of the model. Therefore *VGG* always uses filters with spatial footprint 3×3 and pooling of size 2×2. The convolution was done with stride 1, and a padding of 1 was used. The pooling was done at stride 2. Using a 3×3 filter with a padding of 1 maintains the spatial footprint of the output volume, although pooling always compresses the spatial footprint. Therefore, the pooling was done on non-overlapping spatial regions (unlike the previous two architectures), and always reduced the spatial footprint (i.e., both height and width) by a factor of 2. Another interesting design choice of *VGG* was that the number of filters was often increased by a factor of 2 after each max-pooling. The idea was to always increase the depth by a factor of 2 whenever the spatial footprint reduced by a factor of 2. This design choice results in some level of balance in the computational effort across layers, and was inherited by some of the later architectures like *ResNet*.

One issue with using deep configurations was that increased depth led to greater sensitivity with initialization, which is known to cause instability. This problem was solved by using pretraining, in which a shallower architecture was first trained, and then further layers were added. However, the pretraining was not done on a layer-by-layer basis. Rather, an 11-layer subset of the architecture was first trained. These trained layers were used to initialize a subset of the layers in the deeper architecture. *VGG* achieved a top-5 error of only 7.3% in the ISLVRC contest, which was one of the top performers but not the winner. The different configurations of *VGG* are shown in Table 8.2. Among these, the architecture denoted by column D was the winning architecture. Note that the number of filters increase by a factor of 2 after each max-pooling. Therefore, max-pooling causes the spatial height and width to reduce by a factor of 2, but this is compensated by increasing depth by a factor of 2. Performing convolutions with 3×3 filters and padding of 1 does not change the spatial footprint. Therefore, the sizes of each spatial dimension (i.e., height and width) in the regions between different max-pooling layers in column D of Table 8.2 are 224, 112, 56, 28, and 14, respectively. A final max-pooling is performed just before creating the fully connected layer, which reduces the spatial footprint further to 7. Therefore, the first fully

Table 8.2: Configurations used in *VGG*. The term C3D64 refers to the case in which convolutions are performed with 64 filters of spatial size 3×3 (and occasionally 1×1). The depth of the filter matches the corresponding layer. The padding of each filter is chosen in order to maintain the spatial footprint of the layer. All convolutions are followed by ReLU. The max-pool layer is referred to as M, and local response normalization as LRN. The softmax layer is denoted by S, and FC4096 refers to a fully connected layer with 4096 units. Other than the final set of layers, the number of filters always increases after each max-pooling. Therefore, reduced spatial footprint is often accompanied with increased depth.

Name:	A	A-LRN	B	C	D	E
# Layers	11	11	13	16	16	19
	C3D64	C3D64	C3D64	C3D64	C3D64	C3D64
		LRN	C3D64	C3D64	C3D64	C3D64
	M	M	M	M	M	M
	C3D128	C3D128	C3D128	C3D128	C3D128	C3D128
			C3D128	C3D128	C3D128	C3D128
	M	M	M	M	M	M
	C3D256	C3D256	C3D256	C3D256	C3D256	C3D256
	C3D256	C3D256	C3D256	C3D256	C3D256	C3D256
				C1D256	C3D256	C3D256
						C3D256
	M	M	M	M	M	M
	C3D512	C3D512	C3D512	C3D512	C3D512	C3D512
	C3D512	C3D512	C3D512	C3D512	C3D512	C3D512
				C1D512	C3D512	C3D512
						C3D512
	M	M	M	M	M	M
	C3D512	C3D512	C3D512	C3D512	C3D512	C3D512
	C3D512	C3D512	C3D512	C3D512	C3D512	C3D512
				C1D512	C3D512	C3D512
						C3D512
	M	M	M	M	M	M
	FC4096	FC4096	FC4096	FC4096	FC4096	FC4096
	FC4096	FC4096	FC4096	FC4096	FC4096	FC4096
	FC1000	FC1000	FC1000	FC1000	FC1000	FC1000
	S	S	S	S	S	S

connected layer has dense connections between 4096 neurons and a $7 \times 7 \times 512$ volume. As we will see later, most of the parameters of the neural network are hidden in these connections.

An interesting exercise has been shown in [236] about where most of the parameters and the memory of the activations is located. In particular, the vast majority of the *memory* required for storing the activations and gradients in the forward and backward phases are required by the early part of the convolutional neural network with the largest spatial footprint. This point is significant because the memory required by a mini-batch is scaled by the size of the mini-batch. For example, it is has been shown in [236] that about 93MB are required for each image. Therefore, for a mini-batch size of 128, the total memory requirement would be about 12GB. Although the early layers require the most memory because of their large spatial footprints, they do not have a large parameter footprint because of the sparse connectivity and weight sharing. In fact, most of the parameters are required by the fully connected layers at the end. The connection of the final $7 \times 7 \times 512$ spatial layer (cf. column D in Table 8.2) to the 4096 neurons required $7 \times 7 \times 512 \times 4096 = 102,760,448$ parameters. The total number of parameters in *all* layers was about $138,000,000$. Therefore, *nearly 75% of the parameters are in a single layer of connections.* Furthermore, the majority of the remaining parameters are in the final two fully connected layers. In all, dense connectivity accounts for 90% of the parameter footprint in the neural network. This point is significant, as *GoogLeNet* uses some innovations to reduce the parameter footprint in the final layers.

It is notable that some of the architectures allow 1×1 convolutions. Although a 1×1 convolution does not combine the activations of spatially adjacent features, it does combine the feature values of different channels when the depth of a volume is greater than 1. Using a 1×1 convolution is also a way to incorporate additional nonlinearity into the architecture without making fundamental changes at the spatial level. This additional nonlinearity is incorporated via the ReLU activations attached to each layer. Refer to [454] for more details.

8.4.4 GoogLeNet

GoogLeNet proposed a novel concept referred to as an *inception architecture*. An inception architecture is a *network within a network*. The initial part of the architecture is much like a traditional convolutional network, and is referred to as the *stem*. The key part of the network is an intermediate layer, referred to as an *inception module*. An example of an inception module is illustrated in Figure 8.10(a). The basic idea of the inception module is that key information in the images is available at different levels of detail. If we use a large filter, we can capture information in a bigger area containing limited variation; if we use a smaller filter, we can capture detailed information in a smaller area. While one solution would be to pipe together many small filters, this would be wasteful of parameters and depth when it would suffice to use the broader patterns in a larger area. The problem is that we do not know up front which level of detail is appropriate for each region of the image. Why not give the neural network the flexibility to model the image at different levels of granularities? This is achieved with an inception module, which convolves with three different filter sizes in parallel. These filter sizes are 1×1, 3×3, and 5×5. A purely sequential piping of filters of the same size is inefficient when one is faced with objects of different scales in different images. Since all filters on the inception layer are learnable, the neural network can decide which ones will influence the output the most. By choosing filters of different sizes along different paths, different regions are represented at a different level of granularity. *GoogLeNet* is made up of nine inception modules that are arranged sequentially. Therefore, one can choose many alternative paths through the architecture, and the resulting features will represent very different spatial regions. For example, passing through four 3×3 filters

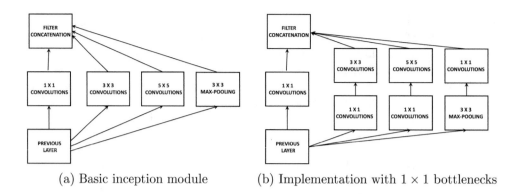

(a) Basic inception module   (b) Implementation with 1×1 bottlenecks

Figure 8.10: The inception module of *GoogLeNet*

followed by only 1×1 filters will capture a relatively small spatial area. On the other hand, passing through many 5×5 filters will result in a much larger spatial footprint. In other words, the differences in the scales of the shapes captured in different hidden features will be magnified in later layers. In recent years, batch normalization has been used in conjunction with the inception architecture, which simplifies[6] the network structure from its original form.

One observation is that the inception module results in some computational inefficiency because of the large number of convolutions of different sizes. Therefore, an efficient implementation is shown in Figure 8.10(b), in which 1×1 convolutions are used to first reduce the depth of the feature map. This is because the number of 1×1 convolution filters is a modest factor less than the depth of the input volume. For example, one might first reduce an input depth of 256 to 64 by using 64 different 1×1 filters. These additional 1×1 convolutions are referred to as the *bottleneck operations* of the inception module. Initially reducing the depth of the feature map (with cheap 1×1 convolutions) saves computational efficiency with the larger convolutions because of the reduced depth of the layers after applying the bottleneck convolutions. One can view the 1×1 convolutions as a kind of supervised dimensionality reduction before applying the larger spatial filters. The dimensionality reduction is supervised because the parameters in the bottleneck filters are learned during backpropagation. The bottleneck also helps in reducing the depth after the pooling layer. The trick of bottleneck layers is also used in some other architectures, where it is helpful for improving efficiency and output depth.

The output layer of *GoogLeNet* also illustrates some interesting design principles. It is common to use fully connected layers near the output. However, *GoogLeNet* uses average pooling across the whole spatial area of the final set of activation maps to create a single value. Therefore, the number of features created in the final layer will be exactly equal to the number of filters. An important observation is that the vast majority of parameters are spent in connecting the final convolution layer to the first fully connected layer. This type of detailed connectivity is not required for applications in which only a class label needs to be predicted. Therefore, the average pooling approach is used. However, the average pooled representation completely loses all spatial information, and one must be careful of the types of applications it is used for. An important property of *GoogLeNet* was that it is extremely compact in terms of the number of parameters in comparison with *VGG*, and the number of

---

[6]The original architecture also contained auxiliary classifiers, which have been ignored in recent years.

parameters in the former is less by an order of magnitude. This is primarily because of the use of average pooling, which eventually became standard in many later architectures. On the other hand, the overall architecture of *GoogLeNet* is computationally more expensive.

The flexibility of *GoogLeNet* is inherent in the 22-layered inception architecture, in which objects of different scales are handled with the appropriate filter sizes. This flexibility of multigranular decomposition, which is enabled by the inception modules, was one of the keys to its performance. In addition, the replacement of the fully connected layer with average pooling greatly reduced the parameter footprint. This architecture was the winner of the ILSVRC contest in 2014, and *VGG* placed a close second. Even though *GoogLeNet* outperformed *VGG*, the latter does have the advantage of simplicity, which is sometimes appreciated by practitioners. Both architectures illustrated important design principles for convolution neural networks. The inception architecture has been the focus of significant research since then [486, 487], and numerous changes have been suggested to improve performance. In later years, a version of this architecture, referred to as *Inception-v4* [487], was combined with some of the ideas in *ResNet* (see next section) to create a 75-layer architecture with only 3.08% error.

8.4.5 ResNet

ResNet [184] used 152 layers, which was almost an order of magnitude greater than previously used by other architectures. This architecture was the winner of the ILSVRC competition in 2015, and it achieved a top-5 error of 3.6%, which resulted in the first classifier with human-level performance. This accuracy is achieved by an ensemble of *ResNet* networks; even a single model achieves 4.5% accuracy. Training an architecture with 152 layers is generally not possible unless some important innovations are incorporated.

The main issue in training such deep networks is that the gradient flow between layers is impeded by the large number of operations in deep layers that can increase or decrease the size of the gradients. As discussed in Chapter 3, problems such as the vanishing and exploding gradients are caused by increased depth. However, the work in [184] suggests that the main training problem in such deep networks might not necessarily be caused by these problems, especially if batch normalization is used. The main problem is caused by the difficulty in getting the learning process to converge properly in a reasonable amount of time. Such convergence problems are common in networks with complex loss surfaces. Although some deep networks show large gaps between training and test error, the error on both the training ad test data is high in many deep networks. This implies that the optimization process has not made sufficient progress.

Although hierarchical feature engineering is the holy grail of learning with neural networks, its layer-wise implementations force all concepts in the image to require the same level of abstraction. Some concepts can be learned by using shallow networks, whereas others require fine-grained connections. For example, consider a circus elephant standing on a square frame. Some of the intricate features of the elephant might require a large number of layers to engineer, whereas the features of the square frame might require very few layers. Convergence will be unnecessarily slow when one is using a very deep network with a fixed depth across all paths to learn concepts, many of which can also be learned using shallow architectures. Why not let the neural network decide how many layers to use to learn each feature?

ResNet uses *skip connections* between layers in order to enable copying between layers and introduces an *iterative view* of feature engineering (as opposed to a hierarchical view). Long short-term memory networks and gated recurrent units leverage similar principles in sequence data by allowing portions of the states to be copied from one layer to the

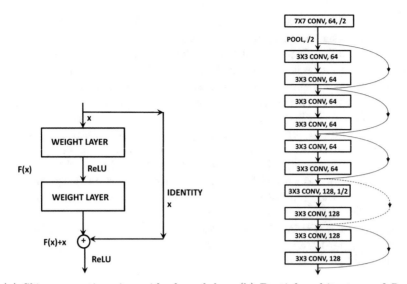

(a) Skip-connections in residual module   (b) Partial architecture of *ResNet*

Figure 8.11: The residual module and the first few layers of *ResNet*

next with the use of adjustable *gates*. In the case of *ResNet*, the non-existent "gates" are assumed to be always fully open. Most feed-forward networks only contain connections between layers i and $(i + 1)$, whereas *ResNet* contains connections between layers i and $(i + r)$ for $r > 1$. Examples of such skip connections, which form the basic unit of *ResNet*, are shown in Figure 8.11(a) with $r = 2$. This skip connection simply copies the input of layer i and adds it to the output of layer $(i+r)$. Such an approach enables effective gradient flow because the backpropagation algorithm now has a super-highway for propagating the gradients backwards using the skip connections. This basic unit is referred to as a *residual module*, and the entire network is created by putting together many of these basic modules. In most layers, an appropriately padded filter[7] is used with a stride of 1, so that the spatial size and depth of the input does not change from layer to layer. In such cases, it is easy to simply add the input of the ith layer to that of $(i + r)$. However, some layers do use strided convolutions to reduce each spatial dimension by a factor of 2. At the same time, depth is increased by a factor of 2 by using a larger number of filters. In such a case, one cannot use the identity function over the skip connection. Therefore, a linear projection matrix might need to be applied over the skip connection in order to adjust the dimensionality. This projection matrix defines a set of 1×1 convolution operations with stride of 2 in order to reduce spatial extent by factor of 2. The parameters of the projection matrix need to be learned during backpropagation.

In the original idea of *ResNet*, one only adds connections between layers i and $(i+r)$. For example, if we use $r = 2$, only skip connections only between successive odd layers are used. Later enhancements like *DenseNet* showed improved performance by adding connections between all pairs of layers. The basic unit of Figure 8.11(a) is repeated in *ResNet*, and therefore one can traverse the skip connections repeatedly in order to propagate input to the output after performing very few forward computations. An example of the first few

---

[7]Typically, a 3×3 filter is used at a stride/padding of 1. This trend started with the principles in *VGG*, and was adopted by *ResNet*.

layers of the architecture is shown in Figure 8.11(b). This particular snapshot is based on the first few layers of the 34-layer architecture. Most of the skip connections are shown in solid lines in Figure 8.11(b), which corresponds to the use of the identity function with an unchanged filter volume. However, in some layers, a stride of 2 is used, which causes the spatial and depth footprint to change. In these layers, a projection matrix needs to be used, which is denoted by a dashed skip connection. Four different architectures were tested in the original work [184], which contained 34, 50, 101, and 152 layers, respectively. The 152-layer architecture had the best performance, but even the 34-layer architecture performed better than did the best-performing ILSVRC entry from the previous year.

The use of skip connections provides paths of unimpeded gradient flow and therefore has important consequences for the behavior of the backpropagation algorithm. The skip connections take on the function of super-highways in enabling gradient flow, creating a situation where multiple paths of variable lengths exist from the input to the output. In such cases, the shortest paths enable the most learning, and the longer paths can be viewed as residual contributions. This gives the learning algorithm the flexibility of choosing the appropriate level of nonlinearity for a particular input. Inputs that can be classified with a small amount of nonlinearity will skip many connections. Other inputs with a more complex structure might traverse a larger number of connections in order to extract the relevant features. Therefore, the approach is also referred to as residual learning, in which learning along longer paths is a kind of fine tuning of the easier learning along shorter paths. In other words, the approach is well suited to cases in which different aspects of the image have different levels of complexity. The work in [184] shows that the residual responses from deeper layers are often relatively small, which validates the intuition that fixed depth is an impediment to proper learning. In such cases, the convergence is often not a problem, because the shorter paths enable a significant portion of the learning with unimpeded gradient flows. An interesting insight in [505] is that *ResNet* behaves like an ensemble of shallow networks because many alternative paths of shorter length are enabled by this type of architecture. Only a small amount of learning is enabled by the deeper paths, and only when it is absolutely necessary. The work in [505] in fact provides a pictorial depiction of an unraveled architecture of *ResNet* in which the different paths are explicitly shown in a parallel pipeline. This unraveled view provides a clear understanding of why *ResNet* has some similarities with ensemble-centric design principles. A consequence of this point of view is that dropping some of the layers from a trained *ResNet* at prediction time does not degrade accuracy as significantly as other networks like *VGG*.

More insights can be obtained by reading the work on *wide residual networks* [549]. This work suggests that increased depth of the residual network does not always help because most of the extremely deep paths are not used anyway. The skip connections do result in alternative paths and effectively increase the width of the network. The work in [549] suggests that better results can be obtained by limiting the total number of layers to some extent (say, 50 instead of 150), and using an increased number of filters in each layer. Note that a depth of 50 is still quite large from pre-*ResNet* standards, but is low compared to the depth used in recent experiments with residual networks. This approach also helps in parallelizing operations.

Variations of Skip Architectures

Since the architecture of *ResNet* was proposed, several variations were suggested to further improve performance. For example, the independently proposed *highway networks* [161]

Table 8.3: The number of layers in various top-performing ILSVRC contest entries

Name	Year	Number of Layers	Top-5 Error
–	Before 2012	≤ 5	$> 25\%$
AlexNet	2012	8	15.4%
ZfNet/Clarifai	2013	8/$>$ 8	14.8% / 11.1%
VGG	2014	19	7.3%
GoogLeNet	2014	22	6.7%
ResNet	2015	152	3.6%

introduced the notion of gated skip connections, and can be considered a more general architecture. In highway networks, gates are used in lieu of the identity mapping, although a closed gate does not pass a lot of information through. In such cases, gating networks do not behave like residual networks. However, residual networks can be considered special cases of gating networks in which the gates are always fully open. Highway networks are closely related to both LSTMs and *ResNets*, although *ResNets* still seem to perform better in the image recognition task because of their focus on enabling gradient flow with multiple paths. The original *ResNet* architecture uses a simple block of layers between skip connections. However, the *ResNext* architecture varies on this principle by using inception modules between skip connections [537].

Instead of using skip connections, one can use convolution transformations between every pair of layers [211]. Therefore, instead of the L transformations in a feed-forward network with L layers, one is using $L(L-1)/2$ transformations. In other words, the concatenation of all the feature maps of the previous $(l-1)$ layers is used by the lth layer. This architecture is referred to as *DenseNet*. Note that the goal of such an architecture is similar to that of skip connections by allowing each layer to learn from whatever level of abstraction is useful.

An interesting variant that seems to work well is the use of *stochastic depth* [210] in which some of the blocks between skip connections are randomly dropped during training time, but the full network is used during testing time. Note that this approach seems similar to *Dropout*, which makes the network thinner rather than shallower by dropping nodes. However, *Dropout* has somewhat different motivations from layer-wise node dropping, because the latter is more focused on improving gradient flow rather than preventing feature co-adaptation.

8.4.6   The Effects of Depth

The significant advancements in performance in recent years in the ILSVRC contest are mostly a result of improved computational power, greater data availability, and changes in architectural design that have enabled the effective training of neural networks with increased depth. These three aspects also support each other, because experimentation with better architectures is only possible with sufficient data and improved computational efficiency. This is also one of the reasons why the fine-tuning and tweaks of relatively old architectures (like recurrent neural networks) with known problems were not performed until recently.

The number of layers and the error rates of various networks are shown in Table 8.3. The rapid increase in accuracy in the short period from 2012 to 2015 is quite remarkable, and is unusual for most machine learning applications that are as well studied as image recognition. Another important observation is that increased depth of the neural network is closely correlated with improved error rates. Therefore, an important focus of the research in recent years has been to enable algorithmic modifications that support increased depth of the neural architecture. It is noteworthy that convolutional neural networks are among the deepest of all classes of neural networks. Interestingly, traditional feed-forward networks in other domains do not need to be very deep for most applications like classification. Indeed, the coining of the term "deep learning" owes a lot of its origins to the impressive performances of convolutional neural networks and specific improvements observed with increased depth.

8.4.7 Pretrained Models

One of the challenges faced by analysts in the image domain is that *labeled* training data may not even be available for a particular application. Consider the case in which one has a set of images that need to be used for image retrieval. In retrieval applications, labels are not available but it is important for the features to be semantically coherent. In some other cases, one might wish to perform classification on a data set with a particular set of labels, which might be limited in availability and different from large resources like *ImageNet*. These settings cause problems because neural networks require a lot of training data to build from scratch.

However, a key point about image data is that the extracted features from a particular data set are highly reusable across data sources. For example, the way in which a cat is represented will not vary a lot if the same number of pixels and color channels are used in different data sources. In such cases, generic data sources, which are representative of a wide spectrum of images, are useful. For example, the *ImageNet* data set [581] contains more than a million images drawn from 1000 categories encountered in everyday life. The chosen 1000 categories and the large diversity of images in the data set are representative and exhaustive enough that one can use them to extract features of images for general-purpose settings. For example, the features extracted from the *ImageNet* data can be used to represent a completely different image data set by passing it through a pretrained convolutional neural network (like *AlexNet*) and extracting the multidimensional features from the fully connected layers. This new representation can be used for a completely different application like clustering or retrieval. This type of approach is so common, that *one rarely trains convolutional neural networks from scratch*. The extracted features from the penultimate layer are often referred to as FC7 features, which is an inheritance from the name of the layer in *AlexNet*. Of course, an arbitrary convolutional network might not have the same number of layers as *AlexNet*; however, the name FC7 has stuck.

This type of off-the-shelf feature extraction approach [390] can be viewed as a kind of *transfer learning*, because we are using a public resource like *ImageNet* to extract features to solve different problems in settings where enough training data is not available. Such an approach has become standard practice in many image recognition tasks, and many software frameworks like *Caffe* provide ready access to these features [585, 586]. In fact, *Caffe* provides a "zoo" of such pretrained models, which can be downloaded and used [586]. If some additional training data is available, one can use it to fine-tune only the deeper layers (i.e., layers closer to the output layer). The weights of the early layers (closer to the input) are fixed. The reason for training only the deeper layers, while keeping the early layers fixed, is that the earlier layers capture only primitive features like edges, whereas the deeper layers capture more complex features. The primitive features do not change too much with the application at hand, whereas the deeper features might be sensitive to the application at hand. For example, all types of images will require edges of different orientation to represent them (captured in early layers), but a feature corresponding to the wheel of a truck will be relevant to a data set containing images of trucks. In other words, early layers tend to capture highly generalizable features (across different computer vision data sets), whereas later layers tend to capture data-specific features. A discussion of the transferability of features derived from convolutional neural networks across data sets and tasks is provided in [361].

8.5   Visualization and Unsupervised Learning

An interesting property of convolutional neural networks is that they are highly interpretable in terms of the types of features they can learn. However, it takes some effort to actually interpret these features. The first approach that comes to mind is to simply visualize the 2-dimensional (spatial) components of the filters. Although this type of visualization can provide some interesting visualizations of the primitive edges and lines learned in the first layer of the neural network, it is not very useful for later layers. In the first layer, it is possible to visualize these filters because they operate directly on the input image, and often tend to look like primitive parts of the image (such as edges). However, it is not quite as simple a matter to visualize these filters in later layers because they operate on input volumes that have already been scrambled with convolution operations. In order to obtain any kind of interpretability one must find a way to map the impacts of all operations all the way back to the input layer. Therefore, the goal of visualization is often to identify and highlight the portions of the input image to which a particular hidden feature is responding. For example, the value of one hidden feature might be sensitive to changes in the portion of the image corresponding to the wheel of a truck, and a different hidden feature might be sensitive to its hood. This is naturally achieved by computing the sensitivity (i.e., gradient) of a hidden feature with respect to each pixel of the input image. As we will see, these types of visualizations are closely related to backpropagation, unsupervised learning, and transposed convolutional operations (used for creating the decoder portions of autoencoders). Therefore, this chapter will discuss these closely related topics in an integrated way.

There are two primary settings in which one can encode and decode an image. In the first setting, the compressed feature maps are learned by using any of the supervised models discussed in earlier sections. Once the network has been trained in a supervised way, one can attempt to reconstruct the portions of the image that most activate a given feature. Furthermore, the portions of an image that are most likely to activate a particular hidden feature or a class are identified. As we will see later, this goal can be achieved with various types of backpropagation and optimization formulations. The second setting is purely unsupervised, in which a convolutional network (encoder) is hooked up to a deconvolutional network (decoder). As we will see later, the latter is also a form of transposed convolution, which is similar to backpropagation. However, in this case, the weights of the encoder and decoder are learned jointly to minimize the reconstruction error. The first setting is obviously simpler because the encoder is trained in a supervised way, and one only has to learn the effect of different portions of the input field on various hidden features. In the second setting, the entire training and learning of weights of the network has to be done from scratch.

8.5.1   Visualizing the Features of a Trained Network

Consider a neural network that has already been trained using a large data set like *ImageNet*. The goal is to visualize and understand the impact of the different portions of the input image (i.e., receptive field) on various features in the hidden layers and the output layer (e.g., the 1000 softmax outputs in *AlexNet*). We would like to answer the following questions:

1. Given an activation of a feature anywhere in the neural network for a *particular* input image, visualize the portions of the input to which that feature is responding the most. Note that the feature might be one of the hidden features in the spatially arranged layers, in the fully connected hidden layers (e.g., FC7), or even one of the softmax outputs. In the last of these cases, one obtains some insight of the specific relationship of a particular input image to a class. For example, if an input image is activating the label for *"banana,"* we hope to see the parts of the specific input image that look most like a banana.

2. Given a particular feature anywhere in the neural network, find a fantasy image that is likely to activate that feature the most. As in the previous case, the feature might be one of the hidden features or even one of the features from the softmax outputs. For example, one might want to know what type of fantasy image is most likely to classify to a *"banana"* in the trained network at hand.

In both these cases, the easiest approach to visualize the impact of specific features is to use gradient-based methods. The second of the above goals is rather hard, and one often does not obtain satisfactory visualizations without careful regularization.

Gradient-Based Visualization of Activated Features

The backpropagation algorithm that is used to train the neural network is also helpful for gradient-based visualization. It is noteworthy that backpropagation-based gradient computation is a form of transposed convolution. In traditional autoencoders, transposed weight matrices (of those used in the encoder layer) are often used in the decoder. Therefore, the connections between backpropagation and feature reconstruction are deep and are applicable across all types of neural networks. The main difference from the traditional backpropagation setting is that our end-goal is to determine the sensitivity of the hidden/output features with respect to *different pixels of the input image* rather than with respect to the weights. However, even traditional backpropagation does compute the sensitivity of the outputs with respect to various layers as an intermediate step, and therefore almost exactly the same approach can be used in both cases.

When the sensitivity of an output o is computed with respect to the input pixels, the visualization of this sensitivity over the corresponding pixels is referred to as a *saliency map* [456]. For example, the output o might be the softmax probability (or unnormalized score before applying softmax) of the class *"banana."* Then, for each pixel x_i in the image, we would like to determine the value of $\frac{\partial o}{\partial x_i}$. This value can be computed by straightforward backpropagation all the way[8] to the input layer. The softmax probability of *"banana"* will be relatively insensitive to small changes in those portions of the image that are irrelevant to the recognition of a banana. Therefore, the values of $\frac{\partial o}{\partial x_i}$ will be close to 0 for such

---

[8]Under normal circumstances, one only backpropagates to hidden layers as an intermediate step to compute gradients with respect to incoming weights in that hidden layer. Therefore, backpropagation to input layer is never really needed in traditional training. However, backpropagation to the input layer is identical to that with respect to the hidden layers.

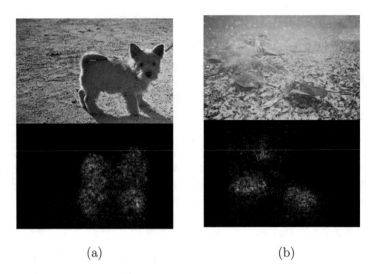

(a)   (b)

Figure 8.12: Examples of portions of specific images activated by particular class labels. These images appear in the work by Simonyan, Vedaldi, and Zisserman [456]. Reproduced with permission. (©2014 Simonyan, Vedaldi, and Zisserman)

irrelevant regions, whereas the portions of the image that define a banana will have large magnitudes. For example, in the case of *AlexNet*, the entire $224 \times 224 \times 3$ volume defined by $\frac{\partial o}{\partial x_i}$ of *backpropagated gradients* will have portions with large magnitudes corresponding to the banana in the image. To visualize this volume, we first convert it to grayscale by taking the *maximum of the absolute magnitude of the gradient* over the three RGB channels to create a $224 \times 224 \times 1$ map with only non-negative values. The bright portions of this grayscale visualization will tell us which portion of the input image are relevant to the banana. Examples of grayscale visualizations of the portions of the image that excite relevant classes are shown in Figure 8.12. For example, the bright portion of the image in Figure 8.12(a) excites the animal in the image, which also represents its class label. As discussed in Section 2.4 of Chapter 2, this type of approach can also be used for interpretability and feature selection in traditional neural networks (and not just convolutional methods).

   This general approach has also been used for visualizing the activations of specific hidden features. Consider the value h of a hidden variable for a particular input image. How is this variable responding to the input image at its current activation level? The idea is that if we slightly increase or decrease the color intensity of some pixels, the value of h will be affected more than if we increase or decrease other pixels. First, the hidden variable h will be affected by a small rectangular portion of the image (i.e., receptive field), which is very small when h is present in early layers but much larger in later layers. For example, the receptive field of h might only be of size 3×3 when it is selected from the first hidden layer in the case of *VGG*. Examples of the image crops corresponding to specific images in which a particular neuron in a hidden layer is highly activated are shown in each row on the right-hand side of Figure 8.13. Note that each row contains a somewhat similar image. This is not a coincidence because that row corresponds to a particular hidden feature, and the variations in that row are caused by the different choices of image. Note that the choices of the image for a row is also not random, because we are selecting the images that most activate that feature. Therefore, all the images will contain the same visual characteristic that cause this hidden feature to be activated. The grayscale portion of the visualization corresponds to the sensitivity of the feature to the pixel-specific values in the corresponding image crop.

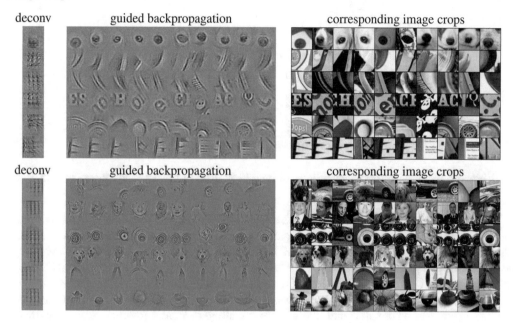

Figure 8.13: Examples of activation visualizations in different layers in Springenberg *et al.*'s work [466]. Reprinted from [466] with permission (©2015 Springenberg, Dosovitskiy, Brox, Riedmiller).

At a high level of activation level of h, some of the pixels in that receptive field will be more sensitive to h than others. By isolating the pixels to which the hidden variable h has the greatest sensitivity and visualizing the corresponding rectangular regions, one can get an idea of what part of the input map most affects a particular hidden feature. Therefore, any particular pixel x_i, we want to compute $\frac{\partial h}{\partial x_i}$, and then visualize those pixels with large values of this gradient. However, instead of backpropagation, the notions of *"deconvnet"* [556] and *guided backpropagation* [466] are sometimes used. The notion of "deconvent" is also used in convolutional autoencoders. The main difference is in terms of how the gradient of the ReLU nonlinearity is propagated backwards. As discussed in Table 3.1 of Chapter 3, the partial derivative of a ReLU unit is copied backwards during backpropagation if the *input* to the ReLU is positive, and is otherwise set to 0. However, in "deconvnet," the partial derivative of a ReLU unit is copied backwards, if this partial derivative is itself larger than 0. This is like using a ReLU on the propagated gradient in the backward pass. In other words, we replace $\overline{g}_i = \overline{g}_{i+1} \odot I(\overline{z}_i > 0)$ in Table 3.1 with $\overline{g}_i = \overline{g}_{i+1} \odot I(\overline{g}_{i+1} > 0)$. Here $\overline{z}_i$ represents the forward activations, and $\overline{g}_i$ represents the backpropagated gradients with respect to the ith layer containing only ReLU units. The function $I(\cdot)$ is an element-wise indicator function, which takes on the value of 1 for each element in the vector argument when the condition is true for that element. In guided backpropagation, we *combine* the conditions used in traditional backpropagation and ReLU by using $\overline{g}_i = \overline{g}_{i+1} \odot I(\overline{z}_i > 0) \odot I(\overline{g}_{i+1} > 0)$. A pictorial illustration of the three variations of backpropagation is shown in Figure 8.14. It is suggested in [466] that guided backpropagation gives better visualizations than "deconvnet," which in turn gives better results than traditional backpropagation.

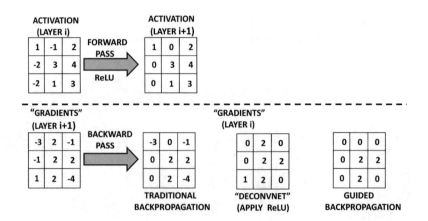

Figure 8.14: The different variations of backpropagation of ReLU for visualization

One way of interpreting the difference between traditional backpropagation and "deconvnet" is by interpreting backwards propagation of gradients as the operations of a decoder with transposed convolutions with respect to the encoder [456]. However, in this decoder, we are again using the ReLU function rather than the gradient-based transformation implied by the ReLU. After all, all forms of decoders use the same activation functions as the encoder. Another feature of the visualization approach in [466] is that it omits the use of pooling layers in the convolutional neural network altogether, and instead relies on strided convolutions. The work in [466] identified several highly activated neurons in specific layers corresponding to specific input images and provided visualizations of the rectangular regions of those images corresponding to the receptive fields of those hidden neurons. We have already discussed earlier that the right-hand side of Figure 8.13 contains the input regions corresponding to specific neurons in hidden layers. The left-hand side of Figure 8.13 also shows the specific characteristics of each image that excite that particular neuron. The visualization on the left-hand side is obtained with guided backpropagation. Note that the upper set of images correspond to the sixth layer, whereas the lower set of images corresponds to the ninth layer of the convolutional network. As a result, the images in the lower set typically corresponds to larger regions of the input image containing more complex shapes.

Another excellent set of visualizations from [556] is shown in Figure 8.15. The main difference is that the work in [556] also uses max-pooling layers, and is based on deconvolutions rather than guided backpropagation. The specific hidden variables chosen are the top-9 largest activations in each feature map. In each case, the relevant square region of the image is shown together with the corresponding visualization. It is evident that the hidden features in early layers correspond to primitive lines, which become increasingly more complex in later layers. This is one of the reasons that convolutional neural networks are viewed as methods that create hierarchical features. The features in early layers tend to be more generic, and they can be used across a wider variety of data sets. The features in later layers tend to be more specific to individual data sets. This is a key property exploited in transfer learning applications, in which pretrained networks are broadly used, and only the later layers are fine-tuned in a manner that's specific to data set and application.

Synthesized Images that Activate a Feature

The above examples tell us the portions of a *particular* image that most affect a particular neuron. A more general question is to ask what kind of image patch would maximally activate a particular neuron. For ease in discussion, we will discuss the case in which the neuron is an output value o of a particular class (i.e., unnormalized output before applying softmax). For example, the value of o might be the unnormalized score for "*banana*." Note that one can also apply a similar approach to intermediate neurons rather than the class score. We would like to learn the input image $\overline{x}$ that maximizes the output o, while applying regularization to $\overline{x}$:

$$\text{Maximize}_{\overline{x}} \ J(\overline{x}) = (o - \lambda||\overline{x}||^2)$$

Here, λ is the regularization parameter, and is important in order to extract semantically interpretable images. One can use gradient ascent in conjunction with backpropagation in order to learn the input image $\overline{x}$ that maximizes the above objective function. Therefore, we start with a zero image $\overline{x}$ and update $\overline{x}$ using gradient ascent in conjunction with backpropagation with respect to the above objective function. In other words, the following update is used:

$$\overline{x} \Leftarrow \overline{x} + \alpha \nabla_{\overline{x}} J(\overline{x}) \tag{8.4}$$

Here, α is the learning rate. The key point is that backpropagation is being leveraged in an unusual way to update the *image pixels* while keeping the (already learned) weights fixed. Examples of synthesized images for three classes are shown in Figure 8.16. Other advanced methods for generating more realistic images on the basis of class labels are discussed in [358].

8.5.2 Convolutional Autoencoders

The use of the autoencoder in traditional neural networks is discussed in Chapters 2 and 4. Recall that the autoencoder reconstructs data points after passing them through a compression phase. In some cases, the data is not compressed although the representations are sparse. The portion before the most compressed layer of the architecture is referred to as the encoder, and the portion after the compressed portion is referred to as the decoder. We repeat the pictorial view of the encoder-decoder architecture for the traditional case in Figure 8.17(a). The convolutional autoencoder has a similar principle, which reconstructs images after passing them through a compression phase. The main difference between a traditional autoencoder and a convolutional autoencoder is that the latter is focused on using spatial relationships between points in order to extract features that have a visual interpretation. The spatial convolution operations in the intermediate layers achieve precisely this goal. An illustration of the convolutional autoencoder is shown in Figure 8.17(b) in comparison with the traditional autoencoder in Figure 8.17(a). Note the 3-dimensional spatial shape of the encoder and decoder in the second case. However, it is possible to conceive of several variations to this basic architecture. For example, the codes in the middle can either be spatial or they can be flattened with the use of fully connected layers, depending on the application at hand. The fully connected layers would be necessary to create a multidimensional code that can be used with arbitrary applications (without worrying about spatial constraints among features). In the following, we will simplify the discussion by assuming that the compressed code in the middle is spatial in nature.

Just as the compression portion of the encoder uses a convolution operation, the decompression operation uses a *deconvolution* operation. Similarly, pooling is matched with an

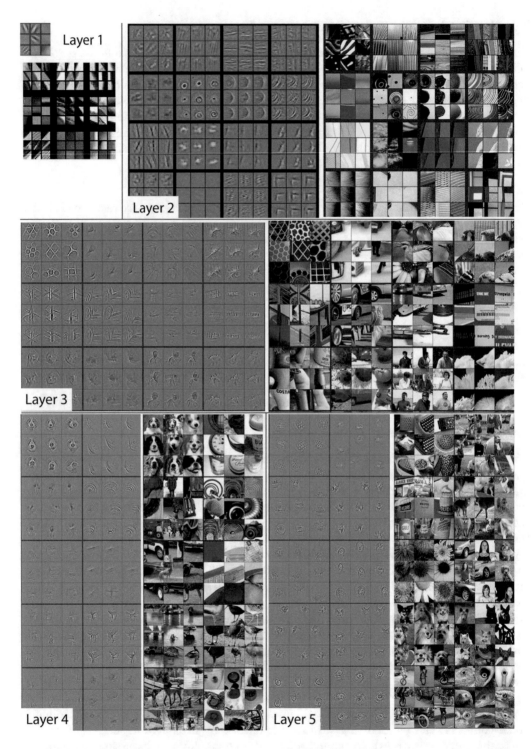

Figure 8.15: Examples of activation visualizations in different layers based on Zeiler and Fergus's work [556]. Reprinted from [556] with permission. ©Springer International Publishing Switzerland, 2014.

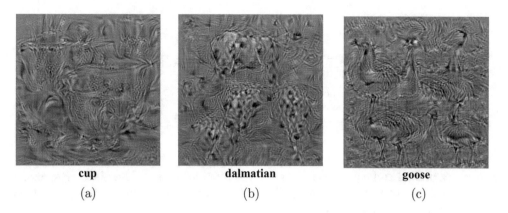

cup   dalmatian   goose

(a)   (b)   (c)

Figure 8.16: Examples of synthesized images with respect to particular class labels. These examples appear in the work by Simonyan, Vedaldi, and Zisserman [456]. Reproduced with permission (©2014 Simonyan, Vedaldi, and Zisserman)

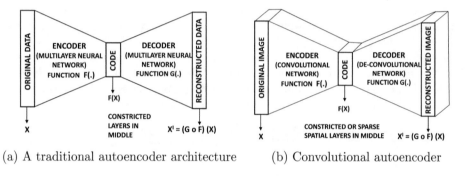

(a) A traditional autoencoder architecture   (b) Convolutional autoencoder

Figure 8.17: A traditional autoencoder and a convolutional autoencoder.

unpooling operation. Deconvolution is also referred to as *transposed convolution*. Interestingly, the transposed convolution operation is the same as that used for backpropagation. The term "deconvolution" is perhaps a bit misleading because every deconvolution is in actuality a convolution with a filter that is derived by transposing and inverting the tensor representing the original convolution filter (cf. Figure 8.7 and Equation 8.3). We can already see that deconvolution uses similar principles to that of backpropagation. The main difference is in terms of how the ReLU function is handled, which makes deconvolution more similar to "deconvnet" or *guided* backpropagation. In fact, the decoder in a convolutional autoencoder performs similar operations to the backpropagation phase of gradient-based visualization. Some architectures do away with the pooling and unpooling operations, and work with only convolution operations (together with activation functions). A notable example is the design of *fully convolutional networks* [449, 466].

The fact that the deconvolution operation is really not much different from a convolution operation is not surprising. Even in traditional feed-forward networks, the decoder part of the network performs the same types of matrix multiplications as the encoder part of the network, except that the transposed weight matrices are used. One can summarize the analogy between traditional autoencoders and convolutional autoencoders in Table 8.4. Note that the relationship between forward backpropagation and backward propagation is

Table 8.4: The relationship between backpropagation and decoders

Linear Operation	Traditional neural networks	Convolutional neural networks
Forward Propagation	Matrix multiplication	Convolution
Backpropagation	Transposed matrix multiplication	Transposed convolution
Decoder layer	Transposed matrix multiplication (Identical to backpropagation)	Transposed convolution (Identical to backpropagation)

similar in traditional and convolutional neural networks in terms of how the corresponding matrix operations are performed. A similar observation is true about the nature of the relationship between encoders and decoders.

There are three operations corresponding to the convolution, max-pooling, and the ReLU nonlinearity. The goal is to perform the inversion of the operations in the decoder layer that have been performed in the encoder layer. There is no easy way to exactly invert some of the operations (such as max-pooling and ReLU). However, excellent image reconstruction can still be achieved with the proper design choices. First, we describe the case of an autoencoder with a single layer with convolution, ReLU, and max-pooling. Then, we discuss how to generalize it to multiple layers.

Although one typically wants to use the inverse of the encoder operations in the decoder, the ReLU is not an invertible function because a value of 0 has many possible inversions. Therefore, a ReLU is replaced by another ReLU in the decoder layer (although other options are possible). Therefore, the architecture of this simple autoencoder is as follows:

$$\underbrace{\text{Convolve} \Rightarrow \text{ReLU} \Rightarrow \text{Max-Pool}}_{\text{Encoder}} \Rightarrow \text{Code} \Rightarrow \underbrace{\text{Unpool} \Rightarrow \text{ReLU} \Rightarrow \text{De-Convolve}}_{\text{Decoder}}$$

Note that the layers are symmetrically arranged in terms of how a matching layer in the decoder undoes the effect of a corresponding layer in the encoder. However, there are many variations to this basic theme. For example, the ReLU might be placed after the deconvolution. Furthermore, in some variations [310], it is recommended to use deeper encoders than the decoders with an asymmetric architecture. However, with a stacked variation of the symmetric architecture above, it is possible to train just the encoder with a classification output layer (and a supervised data set like *ImageNet*) and then use its symmetric decoder (with transposed/inverted filters) to perform "deconvnet" visualization [556]. Although one can always use this approach to initialize the autoencoder, we will discuss enhancements of this concept where the encoder and decoder are jointly trained in an unsupervised way.

We will count each layer like convolution and ReLU as a separate layer here, and therefore we have a total of seven layers including the input. This architecture is simplistic because it uses a single convolution layer in each of the encoders and decoders. In more generalized architectures, these layers are stacked to create more powerful architectures. However, it is helpful to illustrate the relationship of the basic operations like unpooling and deconvolution to their encoding counterparts (like pooling and convolution). Another simplification is that the code is contained in a spatial layer, whereas one could also insert fully connected layers in the middle. Although this example (and Figure 8.17(b)) uses a spatial code, the use of fully connected layers in the middle is more useful for practical applications. On the other hand, the spatial layers in the middle can be used for visualization.

Consider a situation in which the encoder uses d_2 square filters of size $F_1 \times F_1 \times d_1$ in the first layer. Also assume that the first layer is a (spatially) square volume of size $L_1 \times L_1 \times d_1$.

The (i, j, k)th entry of the pth filter in the first layer has weight $w_{ijk}^{(p,1)}$. This notations are consistent with those used in Section 8.2, where the convolution operation is defined. It is common to use the precise level of padding required in the convolution layer, so that the feature maps in the second layer are also of size L_1. This level of padding is $F_1 - 1$, which is referred to as *half-padding*. However, it is also possible to use no padding in the convolution layer, if one uses full padding in the corresponding deconvolution layer. In general, the sum of the paddings between the convolution and its corresponding deconvolution layer must sum to $F_1 - 1$ in order to maintain the spatial size of the layer in a convolution-deconvolution pair.

Here, it is important to understand that although each $W^{(p,1)} = [w_{ijk}^{(p,1)}]$ is a 3-dimensional tensor, one can create a 4-dimensional tensor by including the index p in the tensor. The deconvolution operation uses a transposition of this tensor, which is similar to the approach used in backpropagation (cf. Section 8.3.3). The counter-part deconvolution operation occurs from the sixth to the seventh layer (by counting the ReLU/pooling/unpooling layers in the middle). Therefore, we will define the (deconvolution) tensor $U^{(s,6)} = [u_{ijk}^{(s,6)}]$ in relation to $W^{(p,1)}$. Layer 5 contains d_2 feature maps, which were inherited from the convolution operation in the first layer (and unchanged by pooling/unpooling/ReLU operations). These d_2 feature maps need to be mapped into d_1 layers, where the value of d_1 is 3 for RGB color channels. Therefore, the number of filters in the deconvolution layer is equal to the depth of the filters in the convolution layer and vice vera. One can view this change in shape as a result of the transposition and spatial inversion of the 4-dimensional tensor created by the filters. Furthermore, the entries of the two 4-dimensional tensors are related as follows:

$$u_{ijk}^{(s,6)} = w_{rms}^{(k,1)} \quad \forall s \in \{1 \ldots d_1\}, \forall k \in \{1 \ldots d_2\} \tag{8.5}$$

Here, $r = n - i + 1$ and $m = n - j + 1$, where the spatial footprint in the first layer is $n \times n$. Note the transposition of the indices s and k in the above relationship. This relationship is identical to Equation 8.3. It is not necessary to tie the weights in the encoder and decoder, or even use a symmetric architecture between encoder and decoder [310].

The filters $U^{(s,6)}$ in the sixth layer are used just like any other convolution to reconstruct the RGB color channels of the images from the activations in layer 6. Therefore, a deconvolution operation is really a convolution operation, except that it is done with a transposed and spatially inverted filter. As discussed in Section 8.3.2, this type of deconvolution operation is also used in backpropagation. Both the convolution/deconvolution operations can also be executed with the use of matrix multiplications, as described in that section.

The pooling operations, however, irreversibly lose some information and are therefore impossible to invert exactly. This is because the non-maximal values in the layer are permanently lost by pooling. The max-unpooling operation is implemented with the help of *switches*. When pooling is performed, the precise positions of the maximal values are stored. For example, consider the common situation in which 2×2 pooling is performed at stride 2. In such a case, pooling reduces both spatial dimensions by a factor of 2, and it picks the maximum out of $2 \times 2 = 4$ values in each (non-overlapping) pooled region. The exact coordinate of the (maximal) value is stored, and is referred to as the switch. When unpooling, the dimensions are increased by a factor of 2, and the values at the switch positions are copied from the previous layer. The other values are set to 0. Therefore, after max-unpooling, exactly 75% of the entries in the layer will have uncopied values of 0 in the case of non-overlapping 2×2 pooling.

Like traditional autoencoders, the loss function is defined by the reconstruction error over all $L_1 \times L_1 \times d_1$ pixels. Therefore, if $h_{ijk}^{(1)}$ represents the values of the pixels in the first (input) layer, and $h_{ijk}^{(7)}$ represents the values of the pixels in the seventh (output) layer, the reconstruction loss E is defined as follows:

$$E = \sum_{i=1}^{L_1} \sum_{j=1}^{L_1} \sum_{k=1}^{d_1} (h_{ijk}^{(1)} - h_{ijk}^{(7)})^2 \tag{8.6}$$

Other types of error functions (such as L_1-loss and negative log-likelihood) are also used.

One can use traditional backpropagation with the autoencoder. Backpropagating through deconvolutions or the ReLU is no different than in the case of convolutions. In the case of max-unpooling, the gradient flows only through the switches in an unchanged way. Since the parameters of the encoder and the decoder are tied, one needs to sum up the gradients of the matching parameters in the two layers during gradient descent. Another interesting point is that backpropagating through deconvolutions uses almost identical operations to forward propagation through convolutions. This is because both backpropagation and deconvolution cause successive transpositions of the 4-dimensional tensor used for transformation.

This basic autoencoder can easily be extended to the case where multiple convolutions, poolings, and ReLUs are used. The work in [554] discusses the difficulty with multilayer autoencoders, and proposes several tricks to improve performance. There are several other architectural design choices that are often used to improve performance. One key point is that strided convolutions are often used (in lieu of max-pooling) to reduce the spatial footprint in the encoder, which must be balanced in the decoder with *fractionally* strided convolutions. Consider a situation in which the encoder uses a stride of S with some padding to reduce the size of the spatial footprint. In the decoder, one can increase the size of the spatial footprint by the same factor by using the following trick. While performing the convolution, we stretch the input volume by placing $S - 1$ rows of zeros[9] between every pair of rows, and $S - 1$ columns of zeros between every pair of columns before applying the filter. As a result, the input volume already stretches by a factor of approximately S in each spatial dimension. Additional padding along the borders can be applied before performing the convolution with the transposed filter. Such an approach has the effect of providing a fractional stride and expanding the output size in the decoder. An alternative approach for stretching the input volume of a convolution is to insert interpolated values (instead of zeros) between the original entries of the input volume. The interpolation is done using a convex combination of the nearest four values, and a decreasing function of the distance to each of these values is used as the proportionality factor of the interpolation [449]. The approach of stretching the inputs is sometimes combined with that of stretching the filters as well by inserting zeros within the filter [449]. Stretching the filter results in an approach, referred to as *dilated convolution*, although its use is not universal for fractionally strided convolutions. A detailed discussion of convolution arithmetic (included fractionally strided convolution) is provided in [109]. Compared to the traditional autoencoder, the convolutional autoencoder is somewhat more tricky to implement, with many different variations for better performance. Refer to the bibliographic nodes.

Unsupervised methods also have applications to improving supervised learning. The most obvious method among them is *pretraining*, which was discussed in Section 4.7 of Chapter 4. In convolutional neural networks, the methodology for pretraining is not very different in principle from what is used in traditional neural networks. Pretraining can also

---

[9]Example available at http://deeplearning.net/software/theano/tutorial/conv_arithmetic.html.

Figure 8.18: Example of image classification/localization in which the class *"fish"* is identified together with its bounding box. The image is illustrative only.

be performed by deriving the weights from a trained *deep-belief convolutional network* [285]. This is analogous to the approach in traditional neural networks, where stacked Boltzmann machines were among the earliest models used for pretraining.

8.6 Applications of Convolutional Networks

Convolutional neural networks have several applications in object detection, localization, video, and text processing. Many of these applications work on the basic principle of using convolutional neural networks to provide engineered features, on top of which multidimensional applications can be constructed. The success of convolutional neural networks remains unmatched by almost any class of neural networks. In recent years, competitive methods have even been proposed for sequence-to-sequence learning, which has traditionally been the domain of recurrent networks.

8.6.1 Content-Based Image Retrieval

In content-based image retrieval, each image is first engineered into a set of multidimensional features by using a pretrained classifier like *AlexNet*. The pretraining is typically done up front using a large data set like *ImageNet*. A huge number of choices of such pretrained classifiers is available at [586]. The features from the fully connected layers of the classifier can be used to create a multidimensional representation of the images. The multidimensional representations of the images can be used in conjunction with any multidimensional retrieval system to provide results of high quality. The use of neural codes for image retrieval is discussed in [16]. The reason that this approach works is because the features extracted from *AlexNet* have semantic significance to the different types of shapes present in the data. As a result, the quality of the retrieval is generally quite high when working with these features.

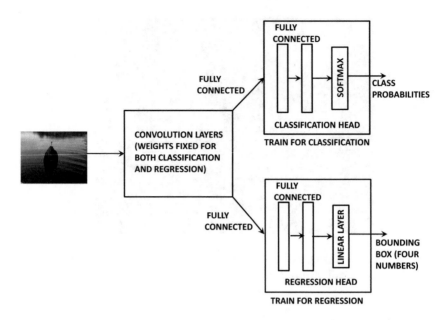

Figure 8.19: The broad framework of classification and localization

8.6.2   Object Localization

In object localization, we have a fixed set of objects in an image, and we would like to identify the rectangular regions in the image in which the object occurs. The basic idea is to take an image with a *fixed* number of objects and encase each of them in a bounding box. In the following, we will consider the simple case in which a single object exists in the image. Image localization is usually integrated with the classification problem, in which we first wish to classify the object in the image and draw a bounding box around it. For simplicity, we consider the case in which there is a single object in the image. We have shown an example of image classification and localization in Figure 8.18, in which the class *"fish"* is identified, and a bounding box is drawn around the portion of the image that delineates that class.

The bounding box of an image can be uniquely identified with four numbers. A common choice is to identify the top-left corner of the bounding box, and the two dimensions of the box. Therefore, one can identify a box with four unique numbers. This is a regression problem with multiple targets. Here, the key is to understand that one can train almost the same model for both classification and regression, which vary only in terms of the final two fully connected layers. This is because the semantic nature of the features extracted from the convolution network are often highly generalizable across a wide variety of tasks. Therefore, one can use the following approach:

1. First, we train a neural network classifier like *AlexNet* or use a pretrained version of this classifier. In the first phase, it suffices to train the classifier only with image-class pairs. One can even use an off-the-shelf pretrained version of the classifier, which was trained on *ImageNet*.

2. The last two fully connected layers and softmax layers are removed. This removed set of layers is referred to as the *classification head*. A new set of two fully connected

Figure 8.20: Example of object detection. Here, four objects are identified together with their bounding boxes. The four objects are *"fish,"* *"girl,"* *"bucket,"* and *"seat."* The image is illustrative only.

layers and a linear regression layer is attached. Only these layers are then trained with training data containing images and their bounding boxes. This new set of layers is referred to as the *regression head*. Note that the weights of the convolution layers are fixed, and are not changed. Both the classification and regression heads are shown in Figure 8.19. Since the classification and regression heads are not connected to one another in any way, these two layers can be trained independently. The convolution layers play the role of creating visual features for both classification and regression.

3. One can optionally fine-tune the convolution layers to be sensitive to both classification and regression (since they were originally trained only for classification). In such a case, both classification and regression heads are attached, and the training data for images, their classes, and bounding boxes are shown to the network. Backpropagation is used to fine-tune all layers. This full architecture is shown in Figure 8.19.

4. The entire network (with both classification and regression heads attached) is then used on the test images. The outputs of the classification head provide the class probabilities, whereas the outputs of the regression head provide the bounding boxes.

One can obtain results of superior quality by using a sliding-window approach. The basic idea in the sliding-window approach is to perform the localization at multiple locations in the image with the use of a sliding window, and then integrate the results of the different runs. An example of this approach is the *Overfeat* method [441]. Refer to the bibliographic notes for pointers to other localization methods.

8.6.3 Object Detection

Object detection is very similar to object localization, except that there is a *variable* number of objects of different classes in the image. In this case, one wishes to identify all the objects in the image together with their classes. We have shown an example of object detection in Figure 8.20, in which there are four objects corresponding to the classes *"fish,"* *"girl,"* *"bucket,"* and *"seat."* The bounding boxes of these classes are also shown in the figure.

Object detection is generally a more difficult problem than that of localization because of the variable number of outputs. In fact, one does not even know a priori how many objects there are in the image. For example, one cannot use the architecture of the previous section, where it is not clear how many classification or regression heads one might attach to the convolutional layers.

The simplest approach to this problem is to use a sliding window approach. In the sliding window approach, one tries all possible bounding boxes in the image, on which the object localization approach is applied to detect a single object. As a result, one might detect different objects in different bounding boxes, or the same object in overlapping bounding boxes. The detections from the different bounding boxes can then be integrated in order to provide the final result. Unfortunately, the approach can be rather expensive. For an image of size $L \times L$, the number of possible bounding boxes is L^4. Note that one would have to perform the classification/regression for each of these L^4 possibilities for each image at test time. This is a problem, because one generally expects the testing times to be modest enough to provide real-time responses.

In order to address this issue *region proposal methods* were advanced. The basic idea of a region proposal method is that it can serve as a general-purpose object detector that merges regions with similar pixels together to create larger regions. Therefore, the region proposal methods are used to first create a set of candidate bounding boxes, and then the object classification/localization method is run in each of them. Note that some candidate regions might not have valid objects, and others might have overlapping objects. These are then used to integrate and identify all the objects in the image. This broader approach has been used in various techniques like *MCG* [172], *EdgeBoxes* [568], and *SelectiveSearch* [501].

8.6.4 Natural Language and Sequence Learning

While the preferred way of machine learning with text sequences is that of recurrent neural networks, the use of convolutional neural networks has become increasingly popular in recent years. At first sight, convolutional neural networks do not seem like a natural fit for text-mining tasks. First, image shapes are interpreted in the same way, irrespective of where they are in the image. This is not quite the case for text, where the position of a word in a sentence seems to matter quite a bit. Second, issues such as position translation and shift cannot be treated in the same way in text data. Neighboring pixels in an image are usually very similar, whereas neighboring words in text are almost never the same. In spite of these differences, the systems based on convolutional networks have shown improved performance in recent years.

Just as an image is represented as a 2-dimensional object with an additional depth dimension defined by the number of color channels, a text sequence is represented as 1-dimensional object with depth defined by its dimensionality of representation. The dimensionality of representation of a text sentence is equal to the lexicon size for the case of one-hot encoding. Therefore, instead of 3-dimensional boxes with a spatial extent and a depth (color channels/feature maps), the filters for text data are 2-dimensional boxes with a window (sequence) length for sliding along the sentence and a depth defined by the lexicon. In later layers of the convolutional network, the depth is defined by the number of feature maps rather than the lexicon size. Furthermore, the number of filters in a given layer defines the number of feature maps in the next layer (as in image data). In image data, one performs convolutions at all 2-dimensional locations, whereas in text data one performs convolutions at all 1-dimensional points in the sentence with the same filter. One challenge with this approach is that the use of one-hot encoding increases the number of channels, and therefore blows up the number of parameters in the filters in the first layer. The lexicon size of a typical corpus may often be of the order of 10^6. Therefore, various types of pretrained embeddings of words, such as *word2vec* or *GLoVe* [371] are used (cf. Chapter 2) in lieu of the one-hot encodings of the individual words. Such word encodings are semantically rich, and the dimensionality of the representation can be reduced to a few thousand (from a hundred-thousand). This approach can provide an order of magnitude reduction in the number of parameters in the first layer, in addition to providing a semantically rich representation. All other operations (like max-pooling or convolutions) in the case of text data are similar to those of image data.

8.6.5 Video Classification

Videos can be considered generalizations of image data in which a temporal component is inherent to a sequence of images. This type of data can be considered *spatio-temporal data*, which requires us to generalize the 2-dimensional spatial convolutions to 3-dimensional spatio-temporal convolutions. Each frame in a video can be considered an image, and one therefore receives a sequence of images in time. Consider a situation in which each image is of size $224 \times 224 \times 3$, and a total of 10 frames are received. Therefore, the size of the video segment is $224 \times 224 \times 10 \times 3$. Instead of performing spatial convolutions with a 2-dimensional spatial filter (with an additional depth dimension capturing 3 color channels), we perform spatiotemporal convolutions with a 3-dimensional spatiotemporal filter (and a depth dimension capturing the color channels). Here, it is interesting to note that the nature of the filter depends on the data set at hand. A purely sequential data set (e.g., text) requires 1-dimensional convolutions with windows, an image data set requires 2-dimensional convolutions, and a video data set requires 3-dimensional convolutions. We refer to the bibliographic notes for pointers to several papers that use 3-dimensional convolutions for video classification.

An interesting observation is that 3-dimensional convolutions add only a limited amount to what one can achieve by averaging the classifications of individual frames by image classifiers. A part of the problem is that motion adds only a limited amount to the information that is available in the individual frames for classification purposes. Furthermore, sufficiently large video data sets are hard to come by. For example, even a data set containing a million videos is often not sufficient because the amount of data required for 3-dimensional convolutions is much larger than that required for 2-dimensional convolutions. Finally, 3-dimensional convolutional neural networks are good for relatively short segments of video (e.g., half a second), but they might not be so good for longer videos.

For the case of longer videos, it makes sense to combine recurrent neural networks (or LSTMs) with convolutional neural networks. For example, we can use 2-dimensional convolutions over individual frames, but a recurrent network is used to carry over states from one frame to the next. One can also use 3-dimensional convolutional neural networks over short segments of video, and then hook them up with recurrent units. Such an approach helps in identifying actions over longer time horizons. Refer to the bibliographic notes for pointers to methods that combine convolutional and recurrent neural networks.

8.7   Summary

This chapter discusses the use of convolutional neural networks with a primary focus on image processing. These networks are biologically inspired and are among the earliest success stories of the power of neural networks. An important focus of this chapter is the classification problem, although these methods can be used for additional applications such as unsupervised feature learning, object detection, and localization. Convolutional neural networks typically learn hierarchical features in different layers, where the earlier layers learn primitive shapes, whereas the later layers learn more complex shapes. The backpropagation methods for convolutional neural networks are closely related to the problems of deconvolution and visualization. Recently, convolutional neural networks have also been used for text processing, where they have shown competitive performance with recurrent neural networks.

8.8   Bibliographic Notes

The earliest inspiration for convolutional neural networks came from Hubel and Wiesel's experiments with the cat's visual cortex [212]. Based on many of these principles, the notion of the neocognitron was proposed in early work. These ideas were then generalized to the first convolutional network, which was referred to as *LeNet-5* [279]. An early discussion on the best practices and principles of convolutional neural networks may be found in [452]. An excellent overview of convolutional neural networks may be found in [236]. A tutorial on convolution arithmetic is available in [109]. A brief discussion of applications may be found in [283].

The earliest data set that was used popularly for training convolutional neural networks was the MNIST database of handwritten digits [281]. Later, larger datasets like *ImageNet* [581] became more popular. Competitions such as the *ImageNet* challenge (*ILSVRC*) [582] have served as sources of some of the best algorithms over the last five years. Examples of neural networks that have done well at various competitions include *AlexNet* [255], *ZFNet* [556], *VGG* [454], *GoogLeNet* [485], and *ResNet* [184]. The *ResNet* is closely related to highway networks [505], and it provides an iterative view of feature engineering. A useful precursor to *GoogLeNet* was the Network-in-Network (NiN) architecture [297], which illustrated some useful design principles of the inception module (such as the use of bottleneck operations). Several explanations of why *ResNet* works well are provided in [185, 505]. The use of inception modules between skip connections is proposed in [537]. The use of stochastic depth in combination with residual networks is discussed in [210]. Wide residual networks are proposed in [549]. A related architecture, referred to as *FractalNet* [268], uses both short and long paths in the network, but does not use skip connections. Training is done by dropping subpaths in the network, although prediction is done on the full network.

Off-the-shelf feature extraction methods with pretrained models are discussed in [223, 390, 585]. In cases where the nature of the application is very different from *ImageNet* data, it might make sense to extract features only from the lower layers of the pretrained model. This is because lower layers often encode more generic/primitive features like edges and basic shapes, which tend to work across an array of settings. The local-response normalization approach is closely related to the contrast normalization discussed in [221].

The work in [466] proposes that it makes sense to replace the max-pooling layer with a convolutional layer with increased stride. Not using a max-pooling layer is an advantage in the construction of an autoencoder because one can use a convolutional layer with a fractional stride within the decoder [384]. Fractional strides place zeros within the rows and columns of the input volume, when it is desired to increase the spatial footprint from the convolution operation. The notion of *dilated convolutions* [544] in which zeros are placed within the rows/columns of the filter (instead of input volume) is also sometimes used. The connections between deconvolution networks and gradient-based visualization are discussed in [456, 466]. Simple methods for inverting the features created by a convolutional neural network are discussed in [104]. The work in [308] discuss how to reconstruct an image optimally from a given feature representation. The earliest use the convolutional autoencoder is discussed in [387]. Several variants of the basic autoencoder architecture were proposed in [318, 554, 555]. One can also borrow ideas from restricted Boltzmann machines to perform unsupervised feature learning. One of the earliest such ideas that uses Deep Belief Nets (DBNs) is discussed in [285]. The use of different types of deconvolution, visualization, and reconstruction is discussed in [130, 554, 555, 556]. A very large-scale study for unsupervised feature extraction from images is reported in [270].

There are some ways of learning feature representations in an unsupervised way, which seem to work quite well. The work in [76] clusters on small image patches with a k-means algorithm in order to generate features. The centroids of the clusters can be used to extract features. Another option is use random weights as filters in order to extract features [85, 221, 425]. Some insight on this issue is provided in [425], which shows that a combination of convolution and pooling becomes frequency selective and translation invariant, even with random weights.

A discussion of neural feature engineering for image retrieval is provided in [16]. Numerous methods have been proposed in recent years for image localization. A particularly prominent system in this regard was *Overfeat* [441], which was the winner of the 2013 *ImageNet* competition. This method used a sliding-window approach in order to obtain results of superior quality. Variations of *AlexNet*, *VGG*, and *ResNet* have also done well in the *ImageNet* competition. Some of the earliest methods for object detection were proposed in [87, 117]. The latter is also referred to as the *deformable parts model* [117]. These methods did not use neural networks or deep learning, although some connections have been drawn [163] between deformable parts models and convolutional neural networks. In the deep learning era, numerous methods like *MCG* [172], *EdgeBoxes* [568], and *SelectiveSearch* [501] have been proposed. The main problem with these methods is that they are somewhat slow. Recently, the *Yolo* method, which is a fast object detection method, was proposed in [391]. However, some of the speed gains are at the expense of accuracy. Nevertheless, the overall effectiveness of the method is still quite high. The use of convolutional neural networks for image segmentation is discussed in [180]. Texture synthesis and style transfer methods with convolutional neural networks are proposed in [131, 132, 226]. Tremendous advances have been made in recent years in facial recognition with neural networks. The early work [269, 407] showed how convolutional networks can be used for face recognition. Deep variants are discussed in [367, 474, 475].

Convolutional neural networks for natural language processing are discussed in [78, 79, 102, 227, 240, 517]. These methods often leverage on *word2vec* or GloVe methods to start with a richer set of features [325, 371]. The notion of recurrent and convolutional neural networks has also been combined for text classification [260]. The use of character-level convolutional networks for text classification is discussed in [561]. Methods for image captioning by combining convolutional and recurrent neural networks are discussed in [225, 509]. The use of convolutional neural networks for processing graph-structured data is discussed in [92, 188, 243]. A discussion of the use of convolutional neural networks in time-series and speech is provided [276].

Video data can be considered the spatiotemporal generalization of image data from the perspective of convolutional networks [488]. The use of 3-dimensional convolutional neural networks for large-scale video classification is discussed in [17, 222, 234, 500], and the works in [17, 222] proposed the earliest methods for 3-dimensional convolutional neural networks in video classification. All the neural networks for image classification have natural 3-dimensional counterparts. For example, a generalization of *VGG* to the video domain with 3-dimensional convolutional networks is discussed in [500]. Surprisingly, the results from 3-dimensional convolutional networks are only slightly better than single-frame methods, which perform classifications from individual frames of the video. An important observation is that individual frames already contain a lot of information for classification purposes, and the addition of motion often does not help for classification, unless the motion characteristics are essential for distinguishing classes. Another issue is that the data sets for video classification are often limited in scale compared to what is really required for building large-scale systems. Even though the work in [234] collected a relatively large-scale data set of over a million *YouTube* videos, this scale seems to be insufficient in the context of video processing. After all, video processing requires 3-dimensional convolutions that are far more complex than the 2-dimensional convolutions in image processing. As a result, it is often beneficial to combine hand-crafted features with the convolutional neural network [514]. Another useful feature that has found applicability in recent years is the notion of optical flow [53]. The use of 3-dimensional convolutional neural networks is helpful for classification of videos over shorter time scales. Another common idea for video classification is to combine convolutional neural networks with recurrent neural networks [17, 100, 356, 455]. The work in [17] was the earliest method for combining recurrent and convolutional neural networks. The use of recurrent neural networks is helpful when one has to perform the classification over longer time scales. A recent method [21] combines recurrent and convolutional neural networks in a homogeneous way. The basic idea is to make every neuron in the convolution neural network to be recurrent. One can view this approach to be a direct recurrent extension of convolutional neural networks.

8.8.1   Software Resources and Data Sets

A variety of packages are available for deep learning with convolutional neural networks like *Caffe* [571], *Torch* [572], *Theano* [573], and *TensorFlow* [574]. Extensions of *Caffe* to Python and MATLAB are available. A discussion of feature extraction from *Caffe* may be found in [585]. A "model zoo" of pretrained models from *Caffe* may be found in [586]. *Theano* is Python-based, and it provides high-level packages like *Keras* [575] and *Lasagne* [576] as interfaces. An open-source implementation of convolutional neural networks in MATLAB, referred to as *MatConvNet*, may be found in [503]. The code and parameter files for *AlexNet* are available at [584].

The two most popular data sets for testing convolutional neural networks are *MNIST* and *ImageNet*. Both these data sets are described in detail in Chapter 1. The *MNIST* data set is quite well behaved because its images have been centered and normalized. As a result, the images in *MNIST* can be classified accurately even with conventional machine learning methods, and therefore convolutional neural networks are not necessary. On the other hand, the images in *ImageNet* contain images from different perspectives, and do require convolutional neural networks. Nevertheless, the 1000-category setting of *ImageNet*, together with its large size, makes it a difficult candidate for testing in a computationally efficient way. A more modestly sized data set is *CIFAR-10* [583]. This data set contains only 60,000 instances divided into ten categories, and contains 6,000 color images. Each image in the data set has size $32 \times 32 \times 3$. It is noteworthy that the *CIFAR-10* data set is a small subset of the *tiny images data set* [642], which originally contains 80 million images. The *CIFAR-10* data set is often used for smaller scale testing, before a more large-scale training is done with *ImageNet*. The *CIFAR-100* data set is just like the *CIFAR-10* data set, except that it has 100 classes, and each class contains 600 instances. The 100 classes are grouped into 10 super-classes.

8.9 Exercises

1. Consider a 1-dimensional time-series with values 2, 1, 3, 4, 7. Perform a convolution with a 1-dimensional filter 1, 0, 1 and zero padding.

2. For a one-dimensional time series of length L and a filter of size F, what is the length of the output? How much padding would you need to keep the output size to a constant value?

3. Consider an activation volume of size $13 \times 13 \times 64$ and a filter of size $3 \times 3 \times 64$. Discuss whether it is possible to perform convolutions with strides 2, 3, 4, and 5. Justify your answer in each case.

4. Work out the sizes of the spatial convolution layers for each of the columns of Table 8.2. In each case, we start with an input image volume of $224 \times 224 \times 3$.

5. Work out the number of parameters in each spatial layer for column D of Table 8.2.

6. Download an implementation of the *AlexNet* architecture from a neural network library of your choice. Train the network on subsets of varying size from the *ImageNet* data, and plot the top-5 error with data size.

7. Compute the convolution of the input volume in the upper-left corner of Figure 8.2 with the horizontal edge detection filter of Figure 8.1(b). Use a stride of 1 without padding.

8. Perform a 4×4 pooling at stride 1 of the input volume in the upper-left corner of Figure 8.4.

9. Discuss the various type of pretraining that one can use in the image captioning application discussed in Section 7.7.1 of Chapter 7.

10. You have a lot of data containing ratings of users for different images. Show how you can combine a convolutional neural network with the collaborative filtering ideas discussed in Chapter 2 to create a hybrid between a collaborative and content-centric recommender system.

Chapter 9

Deep Reinforcement Learning

"The reward of suffering is experience."—Harry S. Truman

9.1 Introduction

Human beings do not learn from a concrete notion of training data. Learning in humans is a continuous experience-driven process in which decisions are made, and the reward/punishment received from the *environment* are used to guide the learning process for future decisions. In other words, learning in intelligent beings is by reward-guided *trial and error*. Furthermore, much of human intelligence and instinct is encoded in genetics, which has evolved over millions of years with another environment-driven process, referred to as *evolution*. Therefore, almost all of biological intelligence, as we know it, originates in one form or other through an interactive process of trial and error with the environment. In his interesting book on artificial intelligence [453], Herbert Simon proposed the *ant hypothesis*:

> "Human beings, viewed as behaving systems, are quite simple. The apparent complexity of our behavior over time is largely a reflection of the complexity of the environment in which we find ourselves."

Human beings are considered simple because they are one-dimensional, selfish, and reward-driven entities (when viewed as a whole), and all of biological intelligence is therefore attributable to this simple fact. Since the goal of artificial intelligence is to simulate biological intelligence, it is therefore natural to draw inspirations from the successes of biological greed in simplifying the design of highly complex learning algorithms.

A reward-driven trial-and-error process, in which a system learns to interact with a complex environment to achieve rewarding outcomes, is referred to in machine learning parlance as *reinforcement learning*. In reinforcement learning, the process of trial and error is driven by the need to maximize the expected rewards over time. Reinforcement learning can be a gateway to the quest for creating truly intelligent *agents* such as game-playing algorithms, self-driving cars, and even intelligent robots that interact with the environment. Simply speaking, it is a gateway to general forms of artificial intelligence. We are not quite there yet. However, we have made huge strides in recent years with exciting results:

1. Deep learners have been trained to play video games by using only the raw pixels of the video console as feedback. A classical example of this setting is the Atari 2600 console, which is a platform supporting multiple games. The input to the deep learner from the Atari platform is the display of pixels from the current state of the game. The reinforcement learning algorithm predicts the actions based on the display and inputs them into the Atari console. Initially, the computer algorithm makes many mistakes, which are reflected in the virtual rewards given by the console. As the learner gains experience from its mistakes, it makes better decisions. This is exactly how humans learn to play video games. The performance of a recent algorithm on the Atari platform has been shown to surpass human-level performance for a large number of games [165, 335, 336, 432]. Video games are excellent test beds for reinforcement learning algorithms, because they can be viewed as highly simplified representations of the choices one has to make in various decision-centric settings. Simply speaking, video games represent toy microcosms of real life.

2. DeepMind has trained a deep learning algorithm *AlphaGo* [445] to play the game of *Go* by using the reward-outcomes in the moves of games drawn from both human and computer self-play. *Go* is a complex game that requires significant human intuition, and the large tree of possibilities (compared to other games like chess) makes it an incredibly difficult candidate for building a game-playing algorithm. *AlphaGo* has not only convincingly defeated all top-ranked *Go* players it has played against [602, 603], but has contributed to innovations in the style of human play by using unconventional strategies in defeating these players. These innovations were a result of the reward-driven experience gained by *AlphaGo* by playing itself over time. Recently, the approach has also been generalized to chess, and it has convincingly defeated one of the top conventional engines [447].

3. In recent years, deep reinforcement learning has been harnessed in self-driving cars by using the feedback from various sensors around the car to make decisions. Although it is more common to use supervised learning (or *imitation learning*) in self-driving cars, the option of using reinforcement learning has always been recognized as a viable possibility [604]. During the course of driving, these cars now consistently make fewer errors than do human beings.

4. The quest for creating self-learning robots is a task in reinforcement learning [286, 296, 432]. For example, robot locomotion turns out to be surprisingly difficult in nimble configurations. Teaching a robot to walk can be couched as a reinforcement learning task, if we do not show a robot what walking looks like. In the reinforcement learning paradigm, we only incentivize the robot to get from point A to point B as efficiently as possible using its available limbs and motors [432]. Through reward-guided trial and error, robots learn to roll, crawl, and eventually walk.

Reinforcement learning is appropriate for tasks *that are simple to evaluate but hard to specify*. For example, it is easy to evaluate a player's performance at the end of a complex game like chess, but it is hard to specify the precise action in every situation. As in biological organisms, reinforcement learning provides a path to the *simplification of learning complex behaviors* by only defining the reward and letting the algorithm learn reward-maximizing behaviors. The complexity of these behaviors is automatically inherited from that of the environment. This is the essence of Herbert Simon's ant hypothesis [453] at the beginning of this chapter. Reinforcement learning systems are inherently *end-to-end systems* in which a complex task is not broken up into smaller components, but viewed through the lens of a simple reward.

The simplest example of a reinforcement learning setting is the *multi-armed bandit problem*, which addresses the problem of a gambler choosing one of many slot machines in order to maximize his payoff. The gambler suspects that the (expected) rewards from the various slot machines are not the same, and therefore it makes sense to play the machine with the largest expected reward. Since the expected payoffs of the slot machines are not known in advance, the gambler has to *explore* different slot machines by playing them and also *exploit* the learned knowledge to maximize the reward. Although exploration of a particular slot machine might gain some additional knowledge about its payoff, it incurs the risk of the (potentially fruitless) cost of playing it. Multi-armed bandit algorithms provide carefully crafted strategies to optimize the trade-off between exploration and exploitation. However, in this simplified setting, each decision of choosing a slot machine is identical to the previous one. This is not quite the case in settings such as video games and self-driving cars with raw sensory inputs (e.g., video game screen or traffic conditions), which define the *state* of the system. Deep learners are excellent at distilling these sensory inputs into *state-sensitive* actions by wrapping their learning process within the exploration/exploitation framework.

Chapter Organization

This chapter is organized as follows. The next section introduces multi-armed bandits, which constitutes one of the simplest stateless settings in reinforcement learning. The notion of states is introduced in Section 9.3. The Q-learning method is introduced in Section 9.4. Policy gradient methods are discussed in Section 9.5. The use of Monte Carlo tree search strategies is discussed in Section 9.6. A number of case studies are discussed in Section 9.7. The safety issues associated with deep reinforcement learning methods are discussed in Section 9.8. A summary is given in Section 9.9.

9.2 Stateless Algorithms: Multi-Armed Bandits

We revisit the problem of a gambler who repeatedly plays slot machines based on previous experience. The gambler suspects that one of the slot machines has a better expected reward than others and attempts to both explore and exploit his experience with the slot machines. Trying the slot machines randomly is wasteful but helps in gaining experience. Trying the slot machines for a very small number of times and then always picking the best machine might lead to solutions that are poor in the long-term. How should one navigate this trade-off between exploration and exploitation? Note that every trial provides the same probabilistically distributed reward as previous trials for a given action, and therefore there is no notion of *state* in such a system. This is a simplified case of traditional reinforcement learning in which the notion of state is important. In a computer video game, moving the cursor in a particular direction has a reward that heavily depends on the *state* of the video game.

There are a number of strategies that the gambler can use to regulate the trade-off between exploration and exploitation of the search space. In the following, we will briefly describe some of the common strategies used in multi-armed bandit systems. All these methods are instructive because they provide the basic ideas and framework, which are used in generalized settings of reinforcement learning. In fact, some of these stateless algorithms are also used as subroutines in general forms of reinforcement learning. Therefore, it is important to explore this simplified setting.

9.2.1 Naïve Algorithm

In this approach, the gambler plays each machine for a fixed number of trials in the exploration phase. Subsequently, the machine with the highest payoff is used forever in the exploitation phase. Although this approach might seem reasonable at first sight, it has a number of drawbacks. The first problem is that it is hard to determine the number of trials at which one can confidently predict whether a particular slot machine is better than another machine. The process of estimation of payoffs might take a long time, especially in cases where the payoff events are rare compared to non-payoff events. Using many exploratory trials will waste a significant amount of effort on suboptimal strategies. Furthermore, if the wrong strategy is selected in the end, the gambler will use the wrong slot machine forever. Therefore, the approach of fixing a particular strategy forever is unrealistic in real-world problems.

9.2.2 ϵ-Greedy Algorithm

The ϵ-greedy algorithm is designed to use the best strategy as soon as possible, without wasting a significant number of trials. The basic idea is to choose a random slot machine for a fraction ϵ of the trials. These exploratory trials are also chosen at random (with probability ϵ) from all trials, and are therefore fully interleaved with the exploitation trials. In the remaining $(1 - \epsilon)$ fraction of the trials, the slot machine with the best average payoff so far is used. An important advantage of this approach is that one is guaranteed to not be trapped in the wrong strategy forever. Furthermore, since the exploitation stage starts early, one is often likely to use the best strategy a large fraction of the time.

The value of ϵ is an algorithm parameter. For example, in practical settings, one might set $\epsilon = 0.1$, although the best choice of ϵ will vary with the application at hand. It is often difficult to know the best value of ϵ to use in a particular setting. Nevertheless, the value of ϵ needs to be reasonably small in order to gain significant advantages from the exploitation portion of the approach. However, at small values of ϵ it might take a long time to identify the correct slot machine. A common approach is to use *annealing*, in which large values of ϵ are initially used, with the values declining with time.

9.2.3 Upper Bounding Methods

Even though the ϵ-greedy strategy is better than the naïve strategy in dynamic settings, it is still quite inefficient at learning the payoffs of new slot machines. In upper bounding strategies, the gambler does not use the mean payoff of a slot machine. Rather, the gambler takes a more optimistic view of slot machines that have not been tried sufficiently, and therefore uses a slot machine with the best *statistical upper bound* on the payoff. Therefore, one can consider the upper bound U_i of testing a slot machine i as the sum of expected reward Q_i and one-sided confidence interval length C_i:

$$U_i = Q_i + C_i \tag{9.1}$$

The value of C_i is like a bonus for increased uncertainty about that slot machine in the mind of the gambler. The value C_i is proportional to the standard deviation of the *mean* reward of the tries so far. According to the central limit theorem, this standard deviation is inversely proportional to the square-root of the number of times the slot machine i is tried (under the i.i.d. assumption). One can estimate the mean μ_i and standard deviation σ_i of the ith slot machine and then set C_i to be $K \cdot \sigma_i / \sqrt{n_i}$, where n_i is the number of times the ith slot machine has been tried. Here, K decides the level of confidence interval. Therefore, rarely tested slot machines will tend to have larger upper bounds (because of larger confidence intervals C_i) and will therefore be tried more frequently.

Unlike ϵ-greedy, the trials are no longer divided into two categories of exploration and exploitation; the process of selecting the slot machine with the largest upper bound has the dual effect of encoding both the exploration and exploitation aspects within each trial. One can regulate the trade-off between exploration and exploitation by using a specific level of statistical confidence. The choice of $K = 3$ leads to a 99.99% confidence interval for the upper bound under the Gaussian assumption. In general, increasing K will give large bonuses C_i for uncertainty, thereby causing exploration to comprise a larger proportion of the plays compared to an algorithm with smaller values of K.

9.3 The Basic Framework of Reinforcement Learning

The bandit algorithms of the previous section are stateless. In other words, the decision made at each time stamp has an identical environment, and the actions in the past only affect the knowledge of the agent (not the environment itself). This is not the case in generic reinforcement learning settings like video games or self-driving cars, which have a notion of *state*.

In generic reinforcement learning settings, each action is associated with a reward *in isolation*. While playing a video game, you do not get a reward only because you made a particular move. The reward of a move depends on all the other moves you made in the past, which are incorporated in the *state* of the environment. In a video game or self-driving car, we would need a different way of performing the credit assignment in a particular system state. For example, in a self-driving car, the reward for violently swerving a car in a normal state would be different from that of performing the same action in a state that indicates the danger of a collision. In other words, we need a way to quantify the reward of each action in a way that is specific to a particular system state.

In reinforcement learning, we have an *agent* that interacts with the *environment* with the use of *actions*. For example, the player is the agent in a video game, and moving the joystick in a certain direction in a video game is an action. The environment is the entire set up of the video game itself. These actions change the environment and lead to a new *state*. In a video game, the state represents all the variables describing the current position of the player at a particular point. The environment gives the agent rewards, depending on how well the goals of the learning application are being met. For example, scoring points in a video game is a reward. Note that the rewards may sometimes not be directly associated with a particular action, but with a combination of actions taken some time back. For example, the player might have cleverly positioned a cursor at a particularly convenient point a few movies back, and actions since then might have had no bearing on the reward. Furthermore, the reward for an action might itself not be deterministic in a particular state (e.g., pulling the lever of a slot machine). *One of the primary goals of reinforcement learning is to identify the inherent values of actions in different states, irrespective of the timing and stochasticity of the reward.*

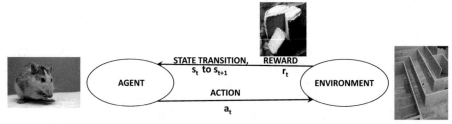

1. **AGENT (MOUSE) TAKES AN ACTION a_t (LEFT TURN IN MAZE) FROM STATE (POSITION) s_t**
2. **ENVIRONMENT GIVES MOUSE REWARD r_t (CHEESE/NO CHEESE)**
3. **THE STATE OF AGENT IS CHANGED TO s_{t+1}**
4. **MOUSE'S NEURONS UPDATE SYNAPTIC WEIGHTS BASED ON WHETHER ACTION EARNED CHEESE**

OVERALL: AGENT LEARNS OVER TIME TO TAKE STATE-SENSITIVE ACTIONS THAT EARN REWARDS

Figure 9.1: The broad framework of reinforcement learning

The learning process helps the agent choose actions based on the inherent values of the actions in different states. This general principle applies to all forms of reinforcement learning in biological organisms, such as a mouse learning a path through a maze to earn a reward. The rewards earned by the mouse depend on an entire sequence of actions, rather than on only the latest action. When a reward is earned, the synaptic weights in the mouse's brain adjust to reflect how sensory inputs should be used to decide future actions in the maze. This is exactly the approach used in deep reinforcement learning, where a neural network is used to predict actions from sensory inputs (e.g., pixels of video game). This relationship between the agent and the environment is shown in Figure 9.1.

The entire set of states and actions and rules for transitioning from one state to another is referred to as a *Markov decision process.* The main property of a Markov decision process is that the state at any particular time stamp encodes all the information needed by the environment to make state transitions and assign rewards based on agent actions. Finite Markov decision processes (e.g., tic-tac-toe) terminate in a finite number of steps, which is referred to as an *episode.* A particular episode of this process is a finite sequence of actions, states, and rewards. An example of length $(n + 1)$ is the following:

$$s_0 a_0 r_0 s_1 a_1 r_1 \ldots s_t a_t r_t \ldots s_n a_n r_n$$

Note that s_t is the state *before* performing action a_t, and performing the action a_t causes a reward of r_t and transition to state s_{t+1}. This is the time-stamp convention used throughout this chapter (and several other sources), although the convention in Sutton and Barto's book [483] outputs r_{t+1} in response to action a_t in state s_t (which slightly changes the subscripts in all the results). Infinite Markov decision processes (e.g., continuously working robots) do not have finite length episodes and are referred to as *non-episodic.*

Examples

Although a system state refers to a complete description of the environment, many practical approximations are often made. For example, in an Atari video game, the system state might be defined by a fixed-length window of game snapshots. Some examples are as follows:

1. *Game of tic-tac-toe, chess, or Go:* The state is the position of the board at any point, and the actions correspond to the moves made by the agent. The reward is +1, 0, or −1 (depending on win, draw, or loss), *which is received at the end of the game.* Note that rewards are often not received immediately after strategically astute actions.

2. *Robot locomotion:* The state corresponds to the current configuration of robot joints and its position. The actions correspond to the torques applied to robot joints. The reward at each time stamp is a function of whether the robot stays upright and the amount of forward movement from point A to point B.

3. *Self-driving car:* The states correspond to the sensor inputs from the car, and the actions correspond to the steering, acceleration, and braking choices. The reward is a hand-crafted function of car progress and safety.

Some effort usually needs to be invested in defining the state representations and corresponding rewards. However, once these choices have been made, reinforcement learning frameworks are end-to-end systems.

9.3.1 Challenges of Reinforcement Learning

Reinforcement learning is more difficult than traditional forms of supervised learning for the following reasons:

1. When a reward is received (e.g., winning a game of chess), it is not exactly known how much each action has contributed to that reward. This problem lies at the heart of reinforcement learning, and is referred to as the *credit-assignment problem.* Furthermore, rewards may be probabilistic (e.g., pulling the lever of a slot machine), which can only be *estimated* approximately in a data-driven manner.

2. The reinforcement learning system might have a very large number of states (such as the number of possible positions in a board game), and must be able to make sensible decisions in states it has not seen before. This task of model generalization is the primary function of deep learning.

3. A specific choice of action affects the collected data in regard to future actions. As in multi-armed bandits, there is a natural trade-off between exploration and exploitation. If actions are taken only to learn their reward, then it incurs a cost to the player. On the other hand, sticking to known actions might result in suboptimal decisions.

4. Reinforcement learning merges the notion of data collection with learning. Realistic simulations of large physical systems such as robots and self-driving cars are limited by the need to physically perform these tasks and gather responses to actions in the presence of the practical dangers of failures. In many cases, the early portion of learning in a task may have few successes and many failures. *The inability to gather sufficient data in real settings beyond simulated and game-centric environments is arguably the single largest challenge to reinforcement learning.*

In the following sections, we will introduce a simple reinforcement learning algorithm and discuss the role of deep learning methods.

9.3.2   Simple Reinforcement Learning for Tic-Tac-Toe

One can generalize the stateless ϵ-greedy algorithm in the previous section to learn to play the game of tic-tac-toe. In this case, each board position is a state, and the action corresponds to placing 'X' or 'O' at a valid position. The number of valid states of the 3×3 board is bounded above by $3^9 = 19683$, which corresponds to three possibilities ('X', 'O', and blank) for each of 9 positions. Instead of estimating the value of each (stateless) action in multi-armed bandits, we now estimate the value of each state-action *pair* (s, a) based on the historical performance of action a in state s against a fixed opponent. Shorter wins are preferred at discount factor $\gamma < 1$, and therefore the *unnormalized* value of action a in state s is increased with γ^{r-1} in case of wins and $-\gamma^{r-1}$ in case of losses after r moves (including the current move). Draws are credited with 0. The discount also reflects the fact that the significance of an action decays with time in real-world settings. In this case, the table is updated only after all moves are made for a game (although later methods in this chapter allow *online* updates after each move). The normalized values of the actions in the table are obtained by dividing the unnormalized values with the number of times the state-action pair was updated (which is maintained separately). The table starts with small random values, and the action a in state s is chosen greedily to be the action with the highest normalized value with probability $1 - \epsilon$, and is chosen to be a random action otherwise. All moves in a game are credited after the termination of each game. Over time, the values of all state-action pairs will be learned and the resulting moves will also adapt to the play of the fixed opponent. Furthermore, one can even use self-play to generate these tables optimally. When self-play is used, the table is updated from a value in $\{-\gamma^r, 0, \gamma^r\}$ depending on win/draw/loss *from the perspective of the player for whom moves are made*. At inference time, the move with the highest normalized value from the perspective of the player are made.

9.3.3   Role of Deep Learning and a Straw-Man Algorithm

The aforementioned algorithm for tic-tac-toe did not use neural networks or deep learning, and this is also the case in many traditional algorithms for reinforcement learning [483]. The overarching goal of the ϵ-greedy algorithm for tic-tac-toe was to learn the inherent *long-term* value of each state-action pair, since the rewards are received long after valuable actions are performed. The goal of the training process is to perform the *value discovery* task of identifying which actions are truly beneficial in the long-term at a particular state. For example, making a clever move in tic-tac-toe might set a trap, which eventually results in assured victory. Examples of two such scenarios are shown in Figure 9.2(a) (although the trap on the right is somewhat less obvious). Therefore, one needs to credit a *strategically* good move favorably in the table of state-action pairs and not just the final winning move. The trial-and-error technique based on the ϵ-greedy method of Section 9.3.2 will indeed assign high values to clever traps. Examples of typical values from such a table are shown in Figure 9.2(b). Note that the less obvious trap of Figure 9.2(a) has a slightly lower value because moves assuring wins after longer periods are discounted by γ, and ϵ-greedy trial-and-error might have a harder time finding the win after setting the trap.

The main problem with this approach is that the number of states in many reinforcement learning settings is too large to tabulate explicitly. For example, the number of possible states in a game of chess is so large that the set of all known positions by humanity is

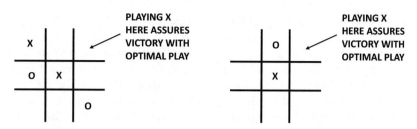

(a) Two examples from tic-tac-toe assuring victory down the road.

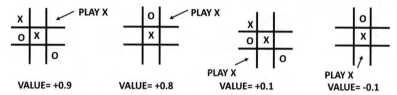

(b) Four entries from the table of state-action values in tic-tac-toe. Trial-and-error learns that moves assuring victory have high value.

(c) Positions from two different games between *Alpha Zero* (white) and *Stockfish* (black) [447]: On the left, white sacrifices a pawn and concedes a passed pawn in order to trap black's light-square bishop behind black's own pawns. This strategy eventually resulted in a victory for white after many more moves than the horizon of a conventional chess-playing program like *Stockfish*. In the second game on the right, white has sacrificed material to incrementally cramp black to a position where all moves worsen the position. Incrementally improving positional advantage is the hallmark of the very best human players rather than chess-playing software like *Stockfish*, whose hand-crafted evaluations sometimes fail to accurately capture subtle differences in positions. The neural network in reinforcement learning, which uses the board state as input, evaluates positions in an integrated way without any prior assumptions. The data generated by trial-and-error provides the only experience for training a very complex evaluation function that is indirectly encoded within the parameters of the neural network. The trained network can therefore *generalize* these learned experiences to new positions. This is similar to how humans learn from previous games to better evaluate board positions.

Figure 9.2: Deep learners are needed for large state spaces like (c).

a minuscule fraction of the valid positions. In fact, the algorithm of Section 9.3.2 is a refined form of *rote learning* in which Monte Carlo simulations are used to refine and remember the long-term values of *seen* states. One learns about the value of a trap in tic-tac-toe only because previous Monte Carlo simulations have experienced victory many times *from that exact board position*. In most challenging settings like chess, one must *generalize* knowledge learned from prior experiences to a state that the learner has not seen before. All forms of learning (including reinforcement learning) are most useful when they are used to generalize known experiences to unknown situations. In such cases, the table-centric forms of reinforcement learning are woefully inadequate. Deep learning models serve the role of *function approximators*. Instead of learning and *tabulating* the values of all moves in all positions (using reward-driven trial and error), one learns the value of each move as a *function* of the input state, based on a *trained model* using the outcomes of prior positions. Without this approach, reinforcement learning cannot be used beyond toy settings like tic-tac-toe.

For example, a straw-man (but not very good) algorithm for chess might use the same ϵ-greedy algorithm of Section 9.3.2, but the values of actions are computed by using the board state as input to a convolutional neural network. The output is the evaluation of the board position. The ϵ-greedy algorithm is simulated to termination with the output values, and the discounted ground-truth value of each move in the simulation is selected from the set $\{\gamma^{r-1}, 0, -\gamma^{r-1}\}$ depending on win/draw/loss and number of moves r to game completion (including the current move). Instead of updating a table of state-action pairs, the parameters of the neural network are updated by treating each move as a training point. The board position is input, and the output of the neural network is compared with the ground-truth value from $\{\gamma^{r-1}, 0, -\gamma^{r-1}\}$ to update the parameters. At inference time, the move with the best output score (with some minimax lookahead) can be used.

Although the aforementioned approach is too naive, a sophisticated system with Monte Carlo tree search, known as *Alpha Zero*, has recently been trained [447] to play chess. Two examples of positions [447] from different games in the match between *Alpha Zero* and a conventional chess program, *Stockfish-8.0*, are provided in Figure 9.2(c). In the chess position on the left, the reinforcement learning system makes a *strategically* astute move of cramping the opponent's bishop at the expense of immediate material loss, which most hand-crafted computer evaluations would not prefer. In the position on the right, *Alpha Zero* has sacrificed two pawns and a piece exchange in order to incrementally constrict black to a point where all its pieces are completely paralyzed. Even though *Alpha Zero* (probably) never encountered these specific positions during training, its deep learner has the ability to extract relevant features and patterns from previous trial-and-error experience in other board positions. In this particular case, the neural network seems to recognize the primacy of spatial patterns representing subtle positional factors over tangible material factors (much like a human's neural network).

In real-life settings, states are often described using sensory inputs. The deep learner uses this input representation of the state to learn the values of specific actions (e.g., making a move in a game) in lieu of the table of state-action pairs. Even when the input representation of the state (e.g., pixels) is quite primitive, neural networks are masters at squeezing out the relevant insights. This is similar to the approach used by humans to process primitive sensory inputs to define the *state* of the world and make decisions about *actions* using our biological neural network. We do not have a table of pre-memorized state-action pairs for every possible real-life situation. The deep-learning paradigm converts the forbiddingly large table of state-action values into a parameterized model mapping states-action pairs to values, which can be trained easily with backpropagation.

9.4 Bootstrapping for Value Function Learning

The simple generalization of the ϵ-greedy algorithm to tic-tac-toe (cf. Section 9.3.2) is a rather naive approach that does not work for *non-episodic settings*. In episodic settings like tic-tac-toe, a fixed-length sequence of at most nine moves can be used to characterize the full and final reward. In non-episodic settings like robots, the Markov decision process may not be finite or might be very long. Creating a sample of the ground-truth reward by Monte Carlo sampling becomes difficult and *online* updating might be desirable. This is achieved with the methodology of *bootstrapping*.

Intuition 9.4.1 (Bootstrapping) *Consider a Markov decision process in which we are predicting values (e.g., long-term rewards) at each time-stamp. We do not need the ground-truth at each time-stamp, as long as we can use a partial simulation of the future to improve the prediction at the current time-stamp. This improved prediction can be used as the ground-truth at the current time stamp for a model without knowledge of the future.*

For example, Samuel's checkers program [421] used the difference in evaluation at the current position and the minimax evaluation obtained by looking several moves ahead with the same function as a "prediction error" in order to update the evaluation function. The idea is that the minimax evaluation from looking ahead is stronger than the one without lookahead and can therefore be used as a "ground truth" to compute the error.

Consider a Markov decision process with the following sequence of states, actions, and rewards:

$$s_0 a_0 r_0 s_1 a_1 r_1 \ldots s_t a_t r_t \ldots$$

For example, in a video game, each state s_t might represent a historical window of pixels [335] with a feature representation $\overline{X}_t$. In order to account for the (possibly) delayed rewards of actions, the cumulative reward R_t at time t is given by the discounted sum of the immediate rewards $r_t, r_{t+1}, r_{t+2}, \ldots r_\infty$ at all future time stamps:

$$R_t = r_t + \gamma \cdot r_{t+1} + \gamma^2 \cdot r_{t+2} + \gamma^3 \cdot r_{t+3} \ldots = \sum_{i=0}^{\infty} \gamma^i r_{t+i} \qquad (9.2)$$

The discount factor $\gamma \in (0, 1)$ regulates how myopic we want to be in allocating rewards. The value of γ is less than 1 because future rewards are worth less than immediate rewards. Choosing $\gamma = 0$ will result in myopically setting the full reward R_t to r_t and nothing else. Therefore, it will be impossible to learn a long-term trap in tic-tac-toe. Values of γ that are too close to 1 will result in modeling instability for very long Markov decision processes.

The *Q-function* or *Q-value* for the state-action pair (s_t, a_t) is denoted by $Q(s_t, a_t)$, and is a measure of the *inherent* (i.e., long-term) value of performing the action a_t in state s_t. The Q-function $Q(s_t, a_t)$ represents the best possible reward obtained till the end of the game on performing the action a_t in state s_t. In other words, $Q(s_t, a_t)$ is equal to $\max\{E[R_{t+1}|a_t]\}$. Therefore, if A is the set of all possible actions, then the chosen action at time t is given by the action a_t^* that maximizes $Q(s_t, a_t)$. In other words, we have:

$$a_t^* = \text{argmax}_{a_t \in A} Q(s_t, a_t) \qquad (9.3)$$

This predicted action is a good choice for the next move, although it is often combined with an exploratory component (e.g., ϵ-greedy policy) to improve long-term training outcomes.

9.4.1   Deep Learning Models as Function Approximators

For ease in discussion, we will work with the Atari setting [335] in which a fixed window of the last few snapshots of pixels provides the state s_t. Assume that the feature representation of s_t is denoted by $\overline{X}_t$. The neural network uses $\overline{X}_t$ as the input and outputs $Q(s_t, a)$ for each possible legal action a from the universe of actions denoted by the set A.

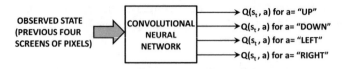

Figure 9.3: The Q-Network for the Atari video game setting

Assume that the neural network is parameterized by the vector of weights $\overline{W}$, and it has $|A|$ outputs containing the Q-values corresponding to the various actions in A. In other words, for each action $a \in A$, the neural network is able to compute the function $F(\overline{X}_t, \overline{W}, a)$, which is defined to be the *learned estimate* of $Q(s_t, a)$:

$$F(\overline{X}_t, \overline{W}, a) = \hat{Q}(s_t, a) \tag{9.4}$$

Note the circumflex on top of the Q-function in order to indicate that it is a predicted value using the learned parameters $\overline{W}$. Learning $\overline{W}$ is the key to using the model for deciding which action to use at a particular time-stamp. For example, consider a video game in which the possible moves are up, down, left, and right. In such a case, the neural network will have four outputs as shown in Figure 9.3. In the specific case of the Atari 2600 games, the input contains $m = 4$ spatial pixel maps in grayscale, representing the window of the last m moves [335, 336]. A convolutional neural network is used to convert pixels into Q-values. This network is referred to as a *Q-network*. We will provide more details of the specifics of the architecture later.

The Q-Learning Algorithm

The weights $\overline{W}$ of the neural network need to be learned via training. Here, we encounter an interesting problem. We can learn the vector of weights only if we have *observed* values of the Q-function. With observed values of the Q-function, we could easily set up a loss in terms of $Q(s_t, a) - \hat{Q}(s_t, a)$ in order to perform the learning after each action. The problem is that the Q-function represents the maximum discounted reward over all *future* combinations of actions, and there is no way of observing it at the current time.

Here, there is an interesting trick for setting up the neural network loss function. According to Intuition 9.4.1, *we do not really need the observed Q-values in order to set up a loss function as long as we know an improved estimate of the Q-values by using partial knowledge from the future.* Then, we can use this improved estimate to create a surrogate "observed" value. This "observed" value is defined by the *Bellman equation* [26], which is a dynamic programming relationship satisfied by the Q-function, and the partial knowledge is the reward observed at the current time-stamp for each action. According to the Bellman equation, we set the "ground-truth" by looking ahead one step and predicting at s_{t+1}:

$$Q(s_t, a_t) = r_t + \gamma \max_a \hat{Q}(s_{t+1}, a) \tag{9.5}$$

The correctness of this relationship follows from the fact that the Q-function is designed to maximize the discounted future payoff. We are essentially looking at all actions one step ahead in order to create an improved estimate of $Q(s_t, a_t)$. It is important to set $\hat{Q}(s_{t+1}, a)$ to 0 in case the process terminates after performing a_t for episodic sequences. We can write this relationship in terms of our neural network predictions as well:

$$F(\overline{X}_t, \overline{W}, a_t) = r_t + \gamma \max_a F(\overline{X}_{t+1}, \overline{W}, a) \tag{9.6}$$

Note that one must first wait to observe the state $\overline{X}_{t+1}$ and reward r_t by performing the action a_t, before we can compute the "observed" value at time-stamp t on the right-hand side of the above equation. This provides a natural way to express the loss L_t of the neural network at time stamp t by comparing the (surrogate) observed value to the predicted value at time stamp t:

$$L_t = \left\{ \underbrace{[r_t + \gamma \max_a F(\overline{X}_{t+1}, \overline{W}, a)]}_{\text{Treat as constant ground-truth}} - F(\overline{X}_t, \overline{W}, a_t) \right\}^2 \tag{9.7}$$

Therefore, we can now update the vector of weights $\overline{W}$ using backpropagation on this loss function. Here, it is important to note that the target values estimated using the inputs at $(t+1)$ are treated as constant ground-truths by the backpropagation algorithm. Therefore, the derivative of the loss function will treat these estimated values as constants, even though they were obtained from the parameterized neural network with input $\overline{X}_{t+1}$. Not treating $F(\overline{X}_{t+1}, \overline{W}, a)$ as a constant will lead to poor results. This is because we are treating the prediction at $(t+1)$ as an improved estimate of the ground-truth (based on the bootstrapping principle). Therefore, the backpropagation algorithm will compute the following:

$$\overline{W} \Leftarrow \overline{W} + \alpha \left\{ \underbrace{[r_t + \gamma \max_a F(\overline{X}_{t+1}, \overline{W}, a)]}_{\text{Treat as constant ground-truth}} - F(\overline{X}_t, \overline{W}, a_t) \right\} \frac{\partial F(\overline{X}_t, \overline{W}, a_t)}{\partial \overline{W}} \tag{9.8}$$

In matrix-calculus notation, the partial derivative of a function $F()$ with respect to the vector $\overline{W}$ is essentially the gradient $\nabla_{\overline{W}} F$. At the beginning of the process, the Q-values estimated by the neural network are random because the vector of weights $\overline{W}$ is initialized randomly. However, the estimation gradually becomes more accurate with time, as the weights are constantly changed to maximize rewards.

Therefore, at any given time-stamp t at which action a_t and reward r_t has been observed, the following training process is used for updating the weights $\overline{W}$:

1. Perform a forward pass through the network with input $\overline{X}_{t+1}$ to compute $\hat{Q}_{t+1} = \max_a F(\overline{X}_{t+1}, \overline{W}, a)$. The value is 0 in case of termination after performing a_t. *Treating the terminal state specially is important.* According to the Bellman equations, the Q-value at previous time-stamp t should be $r_t + \gamma \hat{Q}_{t+1}$ for observed action a_t at time t. Therefore, instead of using observed values of the target, we have created a *surrogate* for the target value at time t, and we pretend that this surrogate is an observed value given to us.

2. Perform a forward pass through the network with input $\overline{X}_t$ to compute $F(\overline{X}_t, \overline{W}, a_t)$.

3. Set up a loss function in $L_t = (r_t + \gamma Q_{t+1} - F(\overline{X}_t, \overline{W}, a_t))^2$, and backpropagate in the network with input $\overline{X}_t$. Note that this loss is associated with neural network output node corresponding to action a_t, and the loss for all other actions is 0.

4. One can now use backpropagation on this loss function in order to update the weight vector $\overline{W}$. Even though the term $r_t + \gamma Q_{t+1}$ in the loss function is also obtained as a prediction from input $\overline{X}_{t+1}$ to the neural network, it is treated as a (constant) observed value during gradient computation by the backpropagation algorithm.

Both the training and the prediction are performed simultaneously, as the values of actions are used to update the weights and select the next action. It is tempting to select the action with the largest Q-value as the relevant prediction. However, such an approach might perform inadequate exploration of the search space. Therefore, one couples the optimality prediction with a policy such as the ϵ-greedy algorithm in order to select the next action. The action with the largest predicted payoff is selected with probability $(1 - \epsilon)$. Otherwise, a random action is selected. The value of ϵ can be annealed by starting with large values and reducing them over time. Therefore, the *target prediction value* for the neural network is computed using the best possible action in the Bellman equation (which might eventually be different from observed action a_{t+1} based on the ϵ-greedy policy). This is the reason that Q-learning is referred to as an *off-policy algorithm* in which the target prediction values for the neural network update are computed using actions that might be different from the actually observed actions in the future.

There are several modifications to this basic approach in order to make the learning more stable. Many of these are presented in the context of the Atari video game setting [335]. First, presenting the training examples *exactly* in the sequence they occur can lead to local minima because of the strong similarity among training examples. Therefore, a fixed-length history of actions/rewards is used as a pool. One can view this as a history of experiences. Multiple experiences are sampled from this pool to perform mini-batch gradient descent. In general, it is possible to sample the same action multiple times, which leads to greater efficiency in leveraging the learning data. Note that the pool is updated over time as old actions drop out of the pool and newer ones are added. Therefore, the training is still temporal in an approximate sense, but not strictly so. This approach is referred to as *experience replay*, as experiences are replayed multiple times in a somewhat different order than the original actions.

Another modification is that the network used for estimating the target Q-values with Bellman equations (step 1 above) is not the same as the network used for predicting Q-values (step 2 above). The network used for estimating the target Q-values is updated more slowly in order to encourage stability. Finally, one problem with these systems is the sparsity of the rewards, especially at the initial stage of the learning when the moves are random. For such cases, a variety of tricks such as *prioritized experience replay* [428] can be used. The basic idea is to make more efficient use of the training data collected during reinforcement learning by prioritizing actions from which more can be learned.

9.4.2 Example: Neural Network for Atari Setting

For the convolutional neural network [335, 336], the screen sizes were set to 84×84 pixels, which also defined the spatial footprints of the first layer in the convolutional network. The input was in grayscale, and therefore each screen required only a single spatial feature map, although a depth of 4 was required in the input layer to represent the previous four windows of pixels. Three convolutional layers were used with filters of size 8×8, 4×4, and 3×3, respectively. A total of 32 filters were used in the first convolutional layer, and 64 filters were used in each of the other two, with the strides used for convolution being 4, 2, and 1, respectively. The convolutional layers were followed by two fully connected layers. The number of neurons in the penultimate layer was equal to 512, and that in the final layer was equal to the number of outputs (possible actions). The number of output layers varied between 4 and 18, and was game-specific. The overall architecture of the convolutional network is illustrated in Figure 9.4.

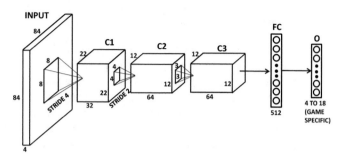

Figure 9.4: The convolutional neural network for the Atari setting

All hidden layers used the ReLU activation, and the output used linear activation in order to predict the real-valued Q-value. No pooling was used, and the strides in the convolution provided spatial compression. The Atari platform supports many games, and the same broader architecture was used across different games in order to showcase its generalizability. There was some variation in performance across different games, although human performance was exceeded in many cases. The algorithm faced the greatest challenges in games in which longer-term strategies were required. Nevertheless, the robust performance of a relatively homogeneous framework across many games was encouraging.

9.4.3   On-Policy Versus Off-Policy Methods: SARSA

The Q-Learning methodology belongs to the class of methods, referred to as *temporal difference learning*. In Q-learning, the actions are chosen according to an ϵ-greedy policy. However, the parameters of the neural network are updated based on the best possible action at each step with the Bellman equation. The best possible action at each step is not quite the same as the ϵ-greedy policy used to perform the simulation. Therefore, Q-learning is an *off-policy reinforcement learning method*. Choosing a different policy for executing actions from those for performing updates does not worsen the ability to find the optimum solutions that are goals of the updates. In fact, since more exploration is performed with a randomized policy, local optima are avoided.

In *on-policy methods*, the actions are consistent with the updates, and therefore the updates can be viewed as policy *evaluation* rather than *optimization*. In order to understand this point, we will describe the updates for the SARSA (State-Action-Reward-State-Action) algorithm, in which the optimal reward in the next step is not used for computing updates. Rather, the next step is updated using the same ϵ-greedy policy to obtain the action a_{t+1} for computing the target values. Then, the loss function for the next step is defined as follows:

$$L_t = \left\{ r_t + \gamma F(\overline{X}_{t+1}, \overline{W}, a_{t+1}) - F(\overline{X}_t, \overline{W}, a_t) \right\}^2 \qquad (9.9)$$

The function $F(\cdot, \cdot, \cdot)$ is defined in the same way as the previous section. The weight vector is updated based on this loss, and then the action a_{t+1} is executed:

$$\overline{W} \Leftarrow \overline{W} + \alpha \left\{ \underbrace{[r_t + \gamma F(\overline{X}_{t+1}, \overline{W}, a_{t+1})]}_{\text{Treat as constant ground-truth}} - F(\overline{X}_t, \overline{W}, a_t) \right\} \frac{\partial F(\overline{X}_t, \overline{W}, a_t)}{\partial \overline{W}} \qquad (9.10)$$

Here, it is instructive to compare this update with those used in Q-learning according to Equation 9.8. In Q-learning, one is using the *best possible* action at each state in order to update the parameters, even though the policy that is actually executed might be ϵ-greedy (which encourages exploration). In SARSA, we are using the action that was actually selected by the ϵ-greedy method in order to perform the update. Therefore, the approach is an *on-policy method*. Off-policy methods like Q-learning are able to decouple exploration from exploitation, whereas on-policy methods are not. Note that if we set the value of ϵ in the ϵ-greedy policy to 0 (i.e., vanilla greedy), then both Q-Learning and SARSA would specialize to the same algorithm. However, such an approach would not work very well because there is no exploration. SARSA is useful when learning cannot be done separately from prediction. Q-learning is useful when the learning can to be done offline, which is followed by exploitation of the learned policy with a vanilla-greedy method at $\epsilon = 0$ (and no need for further model updates). Using ϵ-greedy at inference time would be dangerous in Q-learning, because the policy never pays for its exploratory component and therefore does not learn how to keep exploration safe. For example, a Q-learning based robot will take the shortest path to get from point A to point B even if it is along the edge of the cliff, whereas a SARSA-trained robot will not.

Learning Without Function Approximators

It is possible to also learn Q-values without using function approximators *in cases where the state-space is very small*. For example, in a toy game like tic-tac-toe, one can learn $Q(s_t, a_t)$ explicitly by using trial-and-error play against a strong opponent. In this case, the Bellman equations (cf. Equation 9.5) are used at each move to update an *array* containing the explicit value of $Q(s_t, a_t)$. Using Equation 9.5 directly is too aggressive. More generally, gentle updates are performed for learning rate $\alpha < 1$:

$$Q(s_t, a_t) \Leftarrow Q(s_t, a_t)(1 - \alpha) + \alpha(r_t + \gamma \max_a Q(s_{t+1}, a)) \qquad (9.11)$$

Using $\alpha = 1$ will result in Equation 9.5. Updating the array continually will result in a table containing the correct *strategic* value of each move; see, for example, Figure 9.2(a) for an understanding of the notion of strategic value. Figure 9.2(b) contains examples of four entries from such a table.

One can also use the SARSA algorithm without function approximators by using the action a_{t+1} based on the ϵ-greedy policy. We use a superscript p in $Q^p(\cdot, \cdot)$ to indicate that it is a policy evaluation operator of the policy p (which is ϵ-greedy in this case):

$$Q^p(s_t, a_t) \Leftarrow Q^p(s_t, a_t)(1 - \alpha) + \alpha(r_t + \gamma Q(s_{t+1}, a_{t+1})) \qquad (9.12)$$

This approach is a more sophisticated alternative to the ϵ-greedy method discussed in Section 9.3.2. Note that if action a_t at state s_t leads to termination (for episodic processes), then $Q^p(s_t, a_t)$ is simply set to r_t.

9.4.4 Modeling States Versus State-Action Pairs

A minor variation of the theme in the previous sections is to learn the value of a particular state (rather than state-action pair). One can implement all the methods discussed earlier by maintaining values of states rather than state-action pairs. For example, SARSA can be implemented by evaluating all the values of states resulting from each possible action and selecting a good one based on a pre-defined policy like ϵ-greedy. In fact, the earliest methods for temporal difference learning (or *TD-learning*) maintained values on states rather than state-action pairs. From an efficiency perspective, it is more convenient to output the values of all actions in one shot (rather than repeatedly evaluate each forward state) for value-based decision making. Working with state values rather that state-action pairs becomes useful only when the policy cannot be expressed neatly in terms of state-action pairs. For example, we might evaluate a forward-looking tree of promising moves in chess, and report some averaged value for bootstrapping. In such cases, it is desirable to evaluate states rather than state-action pairs. This section will therefore discuss a variation of temporal difference learning in which states are directly evaluated.

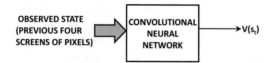

Figure 9.5: Estimating the value of a state with temporal difference learning

Let the value of the state s_t be denoted by $V(s_t)$. Now assume that you have a parameterized neural network that uses the observed attributes $\overline{X}_t$ (e.g., pixels of last four screens in Atari game) of state s_t to estimate $V(s_t)$. An example of this neural network is shown in Figure 9.5. Then, if the function computed by the neural network is $G(\overline{X}_t, \overline{W})$ with parameter vector $\overline{W}$, we have the following:

$$G(\overline{X}_t, \overline{W}) = \hat{V}(s_t) \tag{9.13}$$

Note that the policy being followed to decide the actions might use some arbitrary evaluation of forward-looking states to decide actions. For now, we will assume that we have some reasonable heuristic policy for choosing the actions that uses the forward-looking state values in some way. For example, if we evaluate each forward state resulting from an action and select one of them based on a pre-defined policy (e.g., ϵ-greedy), the approach discussed below is the same as SARSA.

If the action a_t is performed with reward r_t, the resulting state is s_{t+1} with value $V(s_{t+1})$. Therefore, the bootstrapped ground-truth estimate for $V(s_t)$ can be obtained with the help of this lookahead:

$$V(s_t) = r_t + \gamma V(s_{t+1}) \tag{9.14}$$

This estimate can also be stated in terms of the neural network parameters:

$$G(\overline{X}_t, \overline{W}) = r_t + \gamma G(\overline{X}_{t+1}, \overline{W}) \tag{9.15}$$

During the training phase, one needs to shift the weights so as to push $G(\overline{X}_t, \overline{W})$ towards the improved "ground truth" value of $r_t + \gamma G(\overline{X}_{t+1}, \overline{W})$. As in the case of Q-learning, we work with the boot-strapping pretension that the value $r_t + \gamma G(\overline{X}_{t+1}, \overline{W})$ is an observed value given to us. Therefore, we want to minimize the *TD-error* defined by the following:

$$\delta_t = \underbrace{r_t + \gamma G(\overline{X}_{t+1}, \overline{W})}_{\text{"Observed" value}} - G(\overline{X}_t, \overline{W}) \tag{9.16}$$

Therefore, the loss function L_t is defined as follows:

$$L_t = \delta_t^2 = \left\{ \underbrace{r_t + \gamma G(\overline{X}_{t+1}, \overline{W})}_{\text{"Observed" value}} - G(\overline{X}_t, \overline{W}) \right\}^2 \tag{9.17}$$

As in Q-learning, one would first compute the "observed" value of the state at time stamp t using the input $\overline{X}_{t+1}$ into the neural network to compute $r_t + \gamma G(\overline{X}_{t+1}, \overline{W})$. Therefore, one would have to wait till the action a_t has been observed, and therefore the observed features $\overline{X}_{t+1}$ of state s_{t+1} are available. This "observed" value (defined by $r_t + \gamma G(\overline{X}_{t+1}, \overline{W})$) of state s_t is then used as the (constant) target to update the weights of the neural network, when the input $\overline{X}_t$ is used to predict the value of the state s_t. Therefore, one would need to move the weights of the neural network based on the gradient of the following loss function:

$$\overline{W} \Leftarrow \overline{W} - \alpha \frac{\partial L_t}{\partial \overline{W}}$$

$$= \overline{W} + \alpha \left\{ \underbrace{[r_t + \gamma G(\overline{X}_{t+1}, \overline{W})]}_{\text{"Observed" value}} - G(\overline{X}_t, \overline{W}) \right\} \frac{\partial G(\overline{X}_t, \overline{W})}{\partial \overline{W}}$$

$$= \overline{W} + \alpha \delta_t (\nabla G(\overline{X}_t, \overline{W}))$$

This algorithm is a special case of the $TD(\lambda)$ algorithm with λ set to 0. This special case only updates the neural network by creating a bootstrapped "ground-truth" for the current time-stamp based on the evaluations of the next time-stamp. This type of ground-truth is an inherently myopic *approximation*. For example, in a chess game, the reinforcement learning system might have inadvertently made some mistake many steps ago, and it is suddenly showing high errors in the bootstrapped predictions without having shown up earlier. The errors in the bootstrapped predictions are indicative of the fact that we have received new information about each past state $\overline{X}_k$, which we can use to alter its prediction. One possibility is to bootstrap by looking ahead for multiple steps (see Exercise 7). Another solution is the use of $TD(\lambda)$, which explores the continuum between perfect Monte Carlo ground truth and single-step approximation with smooth decay. The adjustments to older predictions are increasingly discounted at the rate $\lambda < 1$. In such a case, the update can be shown to be the following [482]:

$$\overline{W} \Leftarrow \overline{W} + \alpha \delta_t \underbrace{\sum_{k=0}^{t} (\lambda \gamma)^{t-k} (\nabla G(\overline{X}_k, \overline{W}))}_{\text{Alter prediction of } \overline{X}_k} \tag{9.18}$$

At $\lambda = 1$, the approach can be shown to be equivalent to a method in which Monte-Carlo evaluations (i.e., rolling out an episodic process to the end) are used to compute the ground-truth [482]. This is because we are always using new information about errors to fully correct

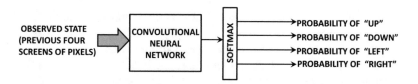

Figure 9.6: The policy network for the Atari video game setting. It is instructive to compare this configuration with the Q-network of Figure 9.3.

our past mistakes without discount at $\lambda = 1$, thereby creating an unbiased estimate. Note that λ is only used for discounting the steps, whereas γ is also used in computing the TD-error δ_t according to Equation 9.16. The parameter λ is *algorithm-specific*, whereas γ is *environment-specific*. Using $\lambda = 1$ or Monte Carlo sampling leads to lower bias and higher variance. For example, consider a chess game in which agents Alice and Bob each make three errors in a single game but Alice wins in the end. This single Monte Carlo roll out will not be able to distinguish the impact of each specific error and will assign the discounted credit for final game outcome to each board position. On the other hand, an n-step temporal difference method (i.e., n-ply board evaluation) might see a temporal difference error for each board position in which the agent made a mistake and was detected by the n-step lookahead. It is only with sufficient data (i.e., more games) that the Monte Carlo method will distinguish between different types of errors. However, choosing very small values of λ will have difficulty in learning openings (i.e., greater bias) because errors with long-term consequences will not be detected. Such problems with openings are well documented [22, 496].

Temporal difference learning was used in Samuel's celebrated checkers program [421], and also motivated the development of TD-Gammon for Backgammon by Tesauro [492]. A neural network was used for state value estimation, and its parameters were updated using temporal-difference bootstrapping over successive moves. The final inference was performed with minimax evaluation of the improved evaluation function over a shallow depth such as 2 or 3. TD-Gammon was able to defeat several expert players. It also exhibited some unusual strategies of game play that were eventually adopted by top-level players.

9.5 Policy Gradient Methods

The value-based methods like Q-learning attempt to predict the value of an action with the neural network and couple it with a generic policy (like ϵ-greedy). On the other hand, policy gradient methods estimate the *probability* of each action at each step with the goal of maximizing the overall reward. Therefore, the policy is itself parameterized, rather than using the value estimation as an intermediate step for choosing actions.

The neural network for estimating the policy is referred to as a *policy network* in which the input is the current state of the system, and the output is a set of probabilities associated with the various actions in the video game (e.g., moving up, down, left, or right). As in the case of the Q-network, the input can be an observed representation of the agent state. For example, in the Atari video game setting, the observed state can be the last four screens of pixels. An example of a policy network is shown in Figure 9.6, which is relevant for the Atari setting. It is instructive to compare this policy network with the Q-network of Figure 9.3. Given an output of probabilities for various actions, we throw a biased die with the faces associated with these probabilities, and select one of these actions. Therefore, for each action a, observed state representation $\overline{X}_t$, and current parameter $\overline{W}$, the neural network is able to compute the function $P(\overline{X}_t, \overline{W}, a)$, which is the probability that the action a should be performed. One of the actions is sampled, and a reward is observed for that action. If the policy is poor, the action will more likely be a mistake and the reward will be poor as well. Based on the reward obtained from executing the action, the weight vector $\overline{W}$ is updated for the next iteration. The update of the weight vector is based on the notion of policy gradient with respect to the weight vector $\overline{W}$. One challenge in estimating the policy gradient is that the reward of an action is often not observed immediately, but is tightly integrated into the future sequence of rewards. Often *Monte Carlo policy roll-outs* must be used in which the neural network is used to follow a particular policy to estimate the discounted rewards over a longer horizon.

We want to update the weight vector of the neural network along the gradient of increasing the reward. As in Q-Learning, the expected discounted rewards over a given horizon H are computed as follows:

$$J = E[r_0 + \gamma \cdot r_1 + \gamma^2 \cdot r_2 + \ldots + \gamma^H \cdot r_H] = \sum_{i=0}^{H} E[\gamma^i r_i] \qquad (9.19)$$

Therefore, the goal is to update the weight vector as follows:

$$\overline{W} \Leftarrow \overline{W} + \alpha \nabla J \qquad (9.20)$$

The main problem in estimating the gradient ∇J is that the neural network only outputs probabilities. The observed rewards are only Monte Carlo samples of these outputs, whereas we want to compute the gradients of *expected* rewards (cf. Equation 9.19). Common policy gradients methods include *finite difference methods*, *likelihood ratio methods*, and *natural policy gradients*. In the following, we will only discuss the first two methods.

9.5.1 Finite Difference Methods

The method of finite differences side-steps the problem of stochasticity with empirical simulations that provide estimates of the gradient. Finite difference methods use weight perturbations in order to estimate gradients of the reward. The idea is to use s different perturbations of the neural network weights, and examine the expected change ΔJ in the reward. Note that this will require us to run the perturbed policy for the horizon of H moves in order to estimate the change in reward. Such a sequence of H moves is referred to as a *roll-out*. For example, in the case of the Atari game, we will need to play it for a trajectory of H moves for each of these s different sets of perturbed weights in order to estimate the changed reward. In games where an opponent of sufficient strength is not available to train against, it is possible to play a game against a version of the opponent based on parameters learned a few iterations back.

In general, the value of H might be large enough that we might reach the end of the game, and therefore the score used will be the one at the end of the game. In some games like *Go*, the score is available only at the end of the game, with a $+1$ for a win and -1 for a loss. In such cases, it becomes more important to choose H large enough so as to play till the end of the game. As a result, we will have s different weight (change) vectors $\Delta \overline{W}_1 \ldots \Delta \overline{W}_s$, together with corresponding changes $\Delta J_1 \ldots \Delta J_s$ in the total reward. Each of these pairs roughly satisfies the following relationship:

$$(\Delta \overline{W}_r) \nabla J^T \approx \Delta J_r \quad \forall r \in \{1 \ldots s\} \qquad (9.21)$$

We can create an s-dimensional column vector $\overline{y} = [\Delta J_1 \ldots \Delta J_s]^T$ of the changes in the objective function and an $N \times s$ matrix D by stacking the rows $\Delta \overline{W}_r$ on top of each other, where N is the number of parameters in the neural network. Therefore, we have the following:

$$D[\nabla J]^T \approx \overline{y} \qquad (9.22)$$

Then, the policy gradient is obtained by performing a straightforward linear regression of the change in objective functions with respect to the change in weight vectors. By using the formula for linear regression (cf. Section 2.2.2.2 of Chapter 2), we obtain the following:

$$\nabla J^T = (D^T D)^{-1} D^T \overline{y} \qquad (9.23)$$

This gradient is used for the update in Equation 9.20. It is required to run the policy for a sequence of H moves for each of the s samples to estimate the gradients. This process can sometimes be slow.

9.5.2 Likelihood Ratio Methods

Likelihood-ratio methods were proposed by Williams [533] in the context of the REIN-FORCE algorithm. Consider the case in which we are following the policy with probability vector $\overline{p}$ and we want to maximize $E[Q^p(s,a)]$, which is the long-term expected value of state s and each sampled action a from the neural network. Consider the case in which the probability of action a is $p(a)$ (which is output by the neural network). In such a case, we want to find the gradient of $E[Q^p(s,a)]$ with respect to the weight vector $\overline{W}$ of the neural network for stochastic gradient ascent. Finding the gradient of an expectation from sampled events is non-obvious. However, the log-probability trick allows us to convert it into the expectation of a gradient, which is additive over the samples of state-action pairs:

$$\nabla E[Q^p(s,a)] = E[Q^p(s,a)\nabla \log(p(a))] \qquad (9.24)$$

We show the proof of the above result in terms of the partial derivative with respect to a single neural network weight w under the assumption that a is a discrete variable:

$$\frac{\partial E[Q^p(s,a)]}{\partial w} = \frac{\partial \left[\sum_a Q^p(s,a)p(a)\right]}{\partial w} = \sum_a Q^p(s,a)\frac{\partial p(a)}{\partial w} = \sum_a Q^p(s,a)\left[\frac{1}{p(a)}\frac{\partial p(a)}{\partial w}\right]p(a)$$

$$= \sum_a Q^p(s,a)\left[\frac{\partial \log(p(a))}{\partial w}\right]p(a) = E\left[Q^p(s,a)\frac{\partial \log(p(a))}{\partial w}\right]$$

The above result can also be shown for the case in which a is a continuous variable (cf. Exercise 1). Continuous actions occur frequently in robotics (e.g., distance to move arm).

It is easy to use this trick for neural network parameter estimation. Each action a sampled by the simulation is associated with the long-term reward $Q^p(s,a)$, which is obtained by Monte Carlo simulation. Based on the relationship above, the gradient of the expected advantage is obtained by multiplying the gradient of the log-probability $\log(p(a))$ of that action (computable from the neural network in Figure 9.6 using backpropagation) with the long-term reward $Q^p(s,a)$ (obtained by Monte Carlo simulation).

Consider a simple game of chess with a win/loss/draw at the end and discount factor γ In this case, the long-term reward of each move is simply obtained as a value from $\{+\gamma^{r-1}, 0, -\gamma^{r-1}\}$, when r moves remain to termination. The value of the reward depends on the final outcome of the game, and number of remaining moves (because of reward discount). Consider a game containing at most H moves. Since multiple roll-outs are used, we get a whole bunch of training samples for the various input states and corresponding outputs in the neural network. For example, if we ran the simulation for 100 roll-outs, we would get at most $100 \times H$ different samples. Each of these would have a long-term reward drawn from $\{+\gamma^{r-1}, 0, -\gamma^{r-1}\}$. For each of these samples, the reward serves as a weight during a gradient-ascent update of the log-probability of the sampled action.

$$\overline{W} \Leftarrow \overline{W} + Q^p(s,a)\nabla\log(p(a)) \qquad (9.25)$$

Here, $p(a)$ is the neural network's output probability of the sampled action. The gradients are computed using backpropagation, and these updates are similar to those in Equation 9.20. This process of sampling and updating is carried through to convergence.

Note that the gradient of the log-probability of the ground-truth class is often used to update softmax classifiers with cross-entropy loss in order to increase the probability of the correct class (which is intuitively similar to the update here). The difference here is that we are weighting the update with the Q-values because we want to push the parameters more aggressively in the direction of highly rewarding actions. One could also use mini-batch gradient ascent over the actions in the sampled roll-outs. Randomly sampling from different roll-outs can be helpful in avoiding the local minima arising from correlations because the successive samples from each roll-out are closely related to one another.

Reducing Variance with Baselines: Although we have used the long-term reward $Q^p(s,a)$ as the quantity to be optimized, it is more common to subtract a baseline value from this quantity in order to obtain its *advantage* (i.e, differential impact of the action over expectation). The baseline is ideally state-specific, but can be a constant as well. In the original work of REINFORCE, a constant baseline was used (which is typically some measure of average long-term reward over all states). Even this type of simple measure can help in speeding up learning because it reduces the probabilities of less-than-average performers and increases the probabilities of more-than-average performers (rather than increasing both at differential rates). A constant choice of baseline does not affect the bias of the procedure, but it reduces the variance. A *state-specific* option for the baseline is the value $V^p(s)$ of the state s immediately *before* sampling action a. Such a choice results in the advantage $(Q^p(s,a) - V^p(s))$ becoming identical to the temporal difference error. This choice makes intuitive sense, because the temporal difference error contains *additional* information about the differential reward of an action beyond what we would know before choosing the action. Discussions on baseline choice may be found in [374, 433].

Consider an example of an Atari game-playing agent, in which a roll-out samples the move UP and output probability of UP was 0.2. Assume that the (constant) baseline is 0.17, and the long-term reward of the action is +1, since the game results in win (and there is no reward discount). Therefore, the score of every action in that roll-out is 0.83 (after subtracting the baseline). Then, the gain associated with all actions (output nodes of the neural network) other than UP at that time-step would be 0, and the gain associated with the output node corresponding to UP would be $0.83 \times \log(0.2)$. One can then backpropagate this gain in order to update the parameters of the neural network.

Adjustment with a state-specific baseline is easy to explain intuitively. Consider the example of a chess game between agents Alice and Bob. If we use a baseline of 0, then each move will only be credited with a reward corresponding to the final result, and the difference between good moves and bad moves will not be evident. In other words, we need to simulate a lot more games to differentiate positions. On the other hand, if we use the value of the state (before performing the action) as the baseline, then the (more refined) temporal difference error is used as the advantage of the action. In such a case, moves that have greater state-specific impact will be recognized with a higher advantage (within a single game). As a result, fewer games will be required for learning.

9.5.3 Combining Supervised Learning with Policy Gradients

Supervised learning is useful for initializing the weights of the policy network before applying reinforcement learning. For example, in a game of chess, one might have prior examples of expert moves that are already known to be good. In such a case, we simply perform gradient ascent with the same policy network, except that each expert move is assigned the fixed credit of 1 for evaluating the gradient according to Equation 9.24. This problem becomes identical to that of softmax classification, where the goal of the policy network is to predict the same move as the expert. One can sharpen the quality of the training data with some examples of bad moves with a negative credit obtained from computer evaluations. This approach would be considered supervised learning rather than reinforcement learning because we are simply using prior data, and not generating/simulating the data that we learn from (as is common in reinforcement learning). This general idea can be extended to any reinforcement learning setting, where some prior examples of actions and associated rewards are available. Supervised learning is extremely common in these settings for initialization because of the difficultly in obtaining high-quality data in the early stages of the process. Many published works also interleave supervised learning and reinforcement learning in order to achieve greater data efficiency [286].

9.5.4 Actor-Critic Methods

So far, we have discussed methods that are either dominated by *critics* or by *actors* in the following way:

1. The Q-learning and $TD(\lambda)$ methods work with the notion of a value function that is optimized. This value function is a critic, and the policy (e.g., ϵ-greedy) of the actor is directly derived from this critic. Therefore, the actor is subservient to the critic, and such methods are considered *critic-only* methods.

2. The policy-gradient methods do not use a value function at all, and they directly learn the probabilities of the policy actions. The values are often estimated using Monte Carlo sampling. Therefore, these methods are considered *actor-only* methods.

Note that the policy-gradient methods do need to evaluate the advantage of intermediate actions, and this estimation has so far been done with the use of Monte Carlo simulations. The main problem with Monte Carlo simulations is its high complexity and inability to use in an online setting.

However, it turns out that one can learn the advantage of intermediate actions using value function methods. As in the previous section, we use the notation $Q^p(s_t, a)$ to denote the value of action a, when the policy p followed by the policy network is used. Therefore, we would now have two coupled neural networks– a policy network and a Q-network. The policy network learns the probabilities of actions, and the Q-network learns the values $Q^p(s_t, a)$ of various actions in order to provide an estimation of the advantage to the policy network. Therefore, the policy network uses $Q^p(s_t, a)$ (with baseline adjustments) to weight its gradient ascent updates. The Q-network is updated using an on-policy update as in SARSA, where the policy is controlled by the policy network (rather than ϵ-greedy). The Q-network, however, does not directly decide the actions as in Q-learning, because the policy decisions are outside its control (beyond its role as a critic). Therefore, the policy network is the actor and the value network is the critic. To distinguish between the policy network and the Q-network, we will denote the parameter vector of the policy network by $\overline{\Theta}$, and that of the Q-network by $\overline{W}$.

We assume that the state at time stamp t is denoted by s_t, and the observable features of the state input to the neural network are denoted by $\overline{X}_t$. Therefore, we will use s_t and $\overline{X}_t$ interchangeably below. Consider a situation at the tth time-stamp, where the action a_t has been observed after state s_t with reward r_t. Then, the following sequence of steps is applied for the $(t+1)$th step:

1. Sample the action a_{t+1} using the current state of the parameters in the policy network. Note that the current state is s_{t+1} because the action a_t is already observed.

2. Let $F(\overline{X}_t, \overline{W}, a_t) = \hat{Q}^p(s_t, a_t)$ represent the estimated value of $Q^p(s_t, a_t)$ by the Q-network using the observed representation $\overline{X}_t$ of the states and parameters $\overline{W}$. Estimate $Q^p(s_t, a_t)$ and $Q^p(s_{t+1}, a_{t+1})$ using the Q-network. Compute the TD-error δ_t as follows:

$$\delta_t = r_t + \gamma \hat{Q}^p(s_{t+1}, a_{t+1}) - \hat{Q}^p(s_t, a_t)$$
$$= r_t + \gamma F(\overline{X}_{t+1}, \overline{W}, a_{t+1}) - F(\overline{X}_t, \overline{W}, a_t)$$

3. **[Update policy network parameters]:** Let $P(\overline{X}_t, \overline{\Theta}, a_t)$ be the probability of the action a_t predicted by policy network. Update the parameters of the policy network as follows:

$$\overline{\Theta} \leftarrow \overline{\Theta} + \alpha \hat{Q}^p(s_t, a_t) \nabla_{\Theta} \log(P(\overline{X}_t, \overline{\Theta}, a_t))$$

Here, α is the learning rate for the policy network and the value of $\hat{Q}^p(s_t, a_t) = F(\overline{X}_t, \overline{W}, a_t)$ is obtained from the Q-network.

4. **[Update Q-Network parameters]:** Update the Q-network parameters as follows:

$$\overline{W} \Leftarrow \overline{W} + \beta \delta_t \nabla_W F(\overline{X}_t, \overline{W}, a_t)$$

Here, β is the learning rate for the Q-network. A caveat is that the learning rate of the Q-network is generally higher than that of the policy network.

The action a_{t+1} is then executed in order to observe state s_{t+2}, and the value of t is incremented. The next iteration of the approach is executed (by repeating the above steps) at this incremented value of t. The iterations are repeated, so that the approach is executed to convergence. The value of $\hat{Q}^p(s_t, a_t)$ is the same as the value $\hat{V}^p(s_{t+1})$.

If we use $\hat{V}^p(s_t)$ as the baseline, the advantage $\hat{A}^p(s_t, a_t)$ is defined by the following:

$$\hat{A}^p(s_t, a_t) = \hat{Q}^p(s_t, a_t) - \hat{V}^p(s_t)$$

This changes the updates as follows:

$$\overline{\Theta} \leftarrow \overline{\Theta} + \alpha \hat{A}^p(s_t, a_t) \nabla_{\Theta} \log(P(\overline{X}_t, \overline{\Theta}, a_t))$$

Note the replacement of $\hat{Q}(s_t, a_t)$ in the original algorithm description with $\hat{A}(s_t, a_t)$. In order to estimate the value $\hat{V}^p(s_t)$, one possibility is to maintain another set of parameters representing the value network (which is different from the Q-network). The TD-algorithm can be used to update the parameters of the value network. However, it turns out that a single value-network is enough. This is because we can use $r_t + \gamma \hat{V}^p(s_{t+1})$ in lieu of $\hat{Q}(s_t, a_t)$. This results in an advantage function, which is the same as the TD-error:

$$\hat{A}^p(s_t, a_t) = r_t + \gamma \hat{V}^p(s_{t+1}) - \hat{V}^p(s_t)$$

In other words, we need the single value-network (cf. Figure 9.5), which serves as the critic. The above approach can also be generalized to use the $TD(\lambda)$ algorithm at any value of λ.

9.5.5 Continuous Action Spaces

The methods discussed to this point were all associated with discrete action spaces. For example, in a video game, one might have a discrete set of choices such as whether to move the cursor up, down, left, and right. However, in a robotics application, one might have continuous action spaces, in which we wish to move the robot's arm a certain distance. One possibility is to discretize the action into a set of fine-grained intervals, and use the midpoint of the interval as the representative value. One can then treat the problem as one of discrete choice. However, this is not a particularly satisfying design choice. First, the ordering among the different choices will be lost by treating inherently ordered (numerical) values as categorical values. Second, it blows up the space of possible actions, especially if the action space is multidimensional (e.g., separate dimensions for distances moved by the robot's arm and leg). Such an approach can cause overfitting, and greatly increase the amount of data required for learning.

A commonly used approach is to allow the neural network to output the parameters of a continuous distribution (e.g., mean and standard deviation of Gaussian), and then sample from the parameters of that distribution in order to compute the value of the action in the next step. Therefore, the neural network will output the mean μ and standard deviation σ for the distance moved by the robotic arm, and the actual action a will be sampled from the Gaussian $\mathcal{N}(\mu, \sigma)$ with this parameter:

$$a \sim \mathcal{N}(\mu, \sigma) \tag{9.26}$$

In this case, the action a represents the distance moved by the robot arm. The values of μ and σ can be learned using backpropagation. In some variations, σ is fixed up front as a hyper-parameter, with only the mean μ needing to be learned. The likelihood ratio trick also applies to this case, except that we use the logarithm of the density at a, rather than the discrete probability of the action a.

9.5.6 Advantages and Disadvantages of Policy Gradients

Policy gradient methods represent the most natural choice in applications like robotics that have continuous sequences of states and actions. For cases in which there are multidimensional and continuous action spaces, the number of possible combinations of actions can be very large. Since Q-learning methods require the computation of the maximum Q-value over all such actions, this step can turn out to be computationally intractable. Furthermore, policy gradient methods tend to be stable and have good convergence properties. However, policy gradient methods are susceptible to local minima. While Q-learning methods are less stable in terms of convergence behavior than are policy-gradient methods, and can sometimes oscillate around particular solutions, they have better capacity to reach near global optima.

Policy-gradient methods do possess one additional advantage in that they can learn stochastic policies, leading to better performance in settings where deterministic policies are known to be suboptimal (such as guessing games) due to being able to be exploited by the opponent. Q-learning provides deterministic policies, and so policy gradients are preferable in these settings because they provide a probability distribution on the possible actions from which the action is sampled.

9.6   Monte Carlo Tree Search

Monte Carlo tree search is a way of improving the strengths of learned policies and values at inference time by combining them with lookahead-based exploration. This improvement also provides a basis for lookahead-based bootstrapping like temporal difference learning. It is also leveraged as a probabilistic alternative to the deterministic minimax trees that are used by conventional game-playing software (although the applicability is not restricted to games). Each node in the tree corresponds to a state, and each branch corresponds to a possible action. The tree grows over time during the search as new states are encountered. The goal of the tree search is to select the best branch to recommend the predicted action of the agent. Each branch is associated with a value based on previous outcomes in tree search from that branch as well as an upper bound "bonus" that reduces with increased exploration. This value is used to set the priority of the branches during exploration. The learned goodness of a branch is adjusted after each exploration, so that branches leading to positive outcomes are favored in later explorations.

In the following, we will describe the Monte Carlo tree search used in *AlphaGo* as a case study for exposition. Assume that the probability $P(s, a)$ of each action (move) a at state (board position) s can be estimated using a policy network. At the same time, for each move we have a quantity $Q(s, a)$, which is the quality of the move a at state s. For example, the value of $Q(s, a)$ increases with increasing number of wins by following action a from state s in simulations. The *AlphaGo* system uses a more sophisticated algorithm that also incorporates some neural evaluations of the board position after a few moves (cf. Section 9.7.1). Then, in each iteration, the "upper bound" $u(s, a)$ of the quality of the move a at state s is given by the following:

$$u(s, a) = Q(s, a) + K \cdot \frac{P(s, a) \sqrt{\sum_b N(s, b)}}{N(s, a) + 1} \tag{9.27}$$

Here, $N(s, a)$ is the number of times that the action a was followed from state s over the course of the Monte Carlo tree search. In other words, the upper bound is obtained by starting with the quality $Q(s, a)$, and adding a "bonus" to it that depends on $P(s, a)$ and the number of times that branch is followed. The idea of scaling $P(s, a)$ by the number of visits is to discourage frequently visited branches and encourage greater exploration. The Monte Carlo approach is based on the strategy of selecting the branch with the largest upper bound, as in multi-armed bandit methods (cf. Section 9.2.3). Here, the second term on the right-hand side of Equation 9.27 plays the role of providing the confidence interval for computing the upper bound. As the branch is played more and more, the exploration "bonus" for that branch is reduced, because the width of its confidence interval drops. The hyperparameter K controls the degree of exploration.

At any given state, the action a with the largest value of $u(s, a)$ is followed. This approach is applied recursively until following the optimal action does not lead to an existing node. This new state s' is now added to the tree as a leaf node with initialized values of each $N(s', a)$ and $Q(s', a)$ set to 0. Note that the simulation up to a leaf node is fully deterministic, and no randomization is involved because $P(s, a)$ and $Q(s, a)$ are deterministically computable. Monte Carlo simulations are used to estimate the value of the newly added leaf node s'. Specifically, Monte Carlo rollouts from the policy network (e.g., using $P(s,a)$ to sample actions) return either $+1$ or -1, depending on win or loss. In Section 9.7.1, we will discuss some alternatives for leaf-node evaluation that use a value network as well. After evaluating the leaf node, the values of $Q(s'', a'')$ and $N(s'', a'')$ on all edges (s'', a'') on the path from the current state s to the leaf s' are updated. The value of $Q(s'', a'')$ is maintained as the average value of all the evaluations at leaf nodes reached from that branch during the Monte Carlo tree search. After multiple searches have been performed from s, the most visited edge is selected as the relevant one, and is reported as the desired action.

Use in Bootstrapping

Traditionally, Monte Carlo tree search has been used during inference rather than during training. However, since Monte Carlo tree search provides an improved estimate $Q(s,a)$ of the value of a state-action pair (as a result of lookaheads), it can also be used for bootstrapping (Intuition 9.4.1). Monte Carlo tree search provides an excellent alternative to n-step temporal-difference methods. One point about on-policy n-step temporal-difference methods is that they explore a single sequence of n-moves with the ϵ-greedy policy, and therefore tend to be too weak (with increased depth but not width of exploration). One way to strengthen them is to examine all possible n-sequences and use the optimal one with an off-policy technique (i.e., generalizing Bellman's 1-step approach). In fact, this was the approach used in Samuel's checkers program [421], which used the best option in the mini-max tree for bootstrapping (and later referred to as *TD-Leaf* [22]). This results in increased complexity of exploring all possible n-sequences. Monte Carlo tree search can provide a robust alternative for bootstrapping, because it can explore multiple branches from a node to generate averaged target values. For example, the lookahead-based ground truth can use the averaged performance over all the explorations starting at a given node.

AlphaGo Zero [447] bootstraps policies rather than state values, which is extremely rare. *AlphaGo Zero* uses the relative visit probabilities of the branches at each node as *posterior* probabilities of the actions at that state. These posterior probabilities are improved over the probabilistic outputs of the policy network by virtue of the fact that the visit decisions use knowledge about the future (i.e., evaluations at deeper nodes of the Monte Carlo tree). The posterior probabilities are therefore bootstrapped as ground-truth values with respect to the policy network probabilities and used to update the weight parameters (cf. Section 9.7.1.1).

9.7 Case Studies

In the following, we present case studies from real domains to showcase different reinforcement learning settings. We will present examples of reinforcement learning in *Go*, robotics, conversational systems, self-driving cars, and neural-network hyperparameter learning.

9.7.1 AlphaGo: Championship Level Play at Go

Go is a two-person board game like chess. The complexity of a two-person board game largely depends on the size of the board and the number of valid moves at each position. The simplest example of a board game is tic-tac-toe with a 3×3 board, and most humans can solve it optimally without the need for a computer. Chess is a significantly more complex game with an 8×8 board, although clever variations of the brute-force approach of *selectively* exploring the minimax tree of moves up to a certain depth can perform significantly better than the best human today. *Go* occurs at the extreme end of complexity because of its 19×19 board.

Players play with white or black *stones*, which are kept in bowls next to the *Go* board. An example of a *Go* board is shown in Figure 9.7. The game starts with an empty board, and it fills up as players put stones on the board. Black makes the first move and starts with 181 stones in her bowl, whereas white starts with 180 stones. The total number of junctions is equal to the total number of stones in the bowls of the two players. A player places a stone of her color in each move at a particular position (from the bowl), and does not move it once it is placed. A stone of the opponent can be captured by encircling it. The objective of the game is for the player to control a larger part of the board than her opponent by encircling it with her stones.

Figure 9.7: Example of a *Go* board with stones.

Whereas one can make about 35 possible moves (i.e., tree branch factor) in a particular position in chess, the average number of possible moves at a particular position in *Go* is 250, which is almost an order of magnitude larger. Furthermore, the average number of sequential moves (i.e., tree depth) of a game of *Go* is about 150, which is around twice as large as chess. All these aspects make *Go* a much harder candidate from the perspective of automated game-playing. The typical strategy of chess-playing software is to construct a minimax tree with all combinations of moves the players can make up to a certain depth, and then evaluate the final board positions with chess-specific heuristics (such as the amount of remaining material and the safety of various pieces). Suboptimal parts of the tree are pruned in a heuristic manner. This approach is simply a improved version of a brute-force strategy in which all possible positions are explored up to a given depth. The number of nodes in the minimax tree of *Go* is larger than the number of atoms in the observable universe, even at modest depths of analysis (20 moves for each player). As a result of the importance of spatial intuition in these settings, humans always perform better than brute force strategies at *Go*. The use of reinforcement learning in *Go* is much closer to what humans attempt to do. We rarely try to explore all possible combinations of moves; rather, we visually learn patterns on the board that are predictive of advantageous positions, and try to make moves in directions that are expected to improve our advantage.

The automated learning of spatial patterns that are predictive of good performance is achieved with a convolutional neural network. The state of the system is encoded in the board position at a particular point, although the board representation in *AlphaGo* includes some additional features about the status of junctions or the number of moves since a stone was played. Multiple such spatial maps are required in order to provide full knowledge of the state. For example, one feature map would represent the status of each intersection, another would encode the number of turns since a stone was played, and so on. Integer feature maps were encoded into multiple one-hot planes. Altogether, the game board could be represented using 48 binary planes of 19×19 pixels.

AlphaGo uses its win-loss experience with repeated game playing (both using the moves of expert players and with games played against itself) to learn good policies for moves in various positions with a policy network. Furthermore, the evaluation of each position on the *Go* board is achieved with a value network. Subsequently, Monte Carlo tree search is used for final inference. Therefore, *AlphaGo* is a multi-stage model, whose components are discussed in the following sections.

Policy Networks

The policy network takes as its input the aforementioned visual representation of the board, and outputs the probability of action a in state s. This output probability is denoted by $p(s, a)$. Note that the actions in the game of *Go* correspond to the probability of placing a stone at each legal position on the board. Therefore, the output layer uses the softmax activation. Two separate policy networks are trained using different approaches. The two networks were identical in structure, containing convolutional layers with ReLU nonlinearities. Each network contained 13 layers. Most of the convolutional layers convolve with 3×3 filters, except for the first and final convolutions. The first and final filters convolve with 5×5 and 1×1 filters, respectively. The convolutional layers were zero padded to maintain their size, and 192 filters were used. The ReLU nonlinearity was used, and no maxpooling was used in order to maintain the spatial footprint.

The networks were trained in the following two ways:

- *Supervised learning:* Randomly chosen samples from expert players were used as training data. The input was the state of the network, while the output was the action performed by the expert player. The score (advantage) of such a move was always +1, because the goal was to train the network to *imitate* expert moves, which is also referred to as *imitation learning*. Therefore, the neural network was backpropagated with the log-likelihood of the probability of the chosen move as its gain. This network is referred to as the SL-policy network. It is noteworthy that these supervised forms of imitation learning are often quite common in reinforcement learning for avoiding cold-start problems. However, subsequent work [446] showed that dispensing with this part of the learning was a better option.

- *Reinforcement learning:* In this case, reinforcement learning was used to train the network. One issue is that *Go* needs two opponents, and therefore the network was played against itself in order to generate the moves. The current network was always played against a randomly chosen network from a few iterations back, so that the reinforcement learning could have a pool of randomized opponents. The game was played until the very end, and then an advantage of +1 or −1 was associated with each move depending on win or loss. This data was then used to train the policy network. This network was referred to as the RL-policy network.

Note that these networks were already quite formidable *Go* players compared to state-of-the-art software, and they were combined with Monte Carlo tree search to strengthen them.

Value Networks

This network was also a convolutional neural network, which uses the state of the network as the input and the predicted score in $[-1, +1]$ as output, where $+1$ indicates a perfect probability of 1. The output is the predicted score of the next player, whether it is white or black, and therefore the input also encodes the "color" of the pieces in terms of "player" or "opponent" rather than white or black. The architecture of the value network was very similar to the policy network, except that there were some differences in terms of the input and output. The input contained an additional feature corresponding to whether the next player to play was white or black. The score was computed using a single tanh unit at the end, and therefore the value lies in the range $[-1, +1]$. The early convolutional layers of the value network are the same as those in the policy network, although an additional convolutional layer is added in layer 12. A fully connected layer with 256 units and ReLU activation follows the final convolutional layer. In order to train the network, one possibility is to use positions from a data set [606] of *Go* games. However, the preferred choice was to generate the data set using self-play with the SL-policy and RL-policy networks all the way to the end, so that the final outcomes were generated. The state-outcome pairs were used to train the convolutional neural network. Since the positions in a single game are correlated, using them sequentially in training causes overfitting. It was important to sample positions from different games in order to prevent overfitting caused by closely related training examples. Therefore, each training example was obtained from a distinct game of self-play.

Monte Carlo Tree Search

A simplified variant of Equation 9.27 was used for exploration, which is equivalent to setting $K = 1/\sqrt{\sum_b N(s, b)}$ at each node s. Section 9.6 described a version of the Monte Carlo tree search method in which only the RL-policy network is used for evaluating leaf nodes. In the case of *AlphaGo*, two approaches are combined. First, fast Monte Carlo rollouts were used from the leaf node to create evaluation e_1. While it is possible to use the policy network for rollout, *AlphaGo* trained a simplified softmax classifier with a database of human games and some hand-crafted features for faster speed of rollouts. Second, the value network created a separate evaluation e_2 of the leaf nodes. The final evaluation e is a convex combination of the two evaluations as $e = \beta e_1 + (1 - \beta)e_2$. The value of $\beta = 0.5$ provided the best performance, although using only the value network also provided closely matching performance (and a viable alternative). The most visited branch in Monte Carlo tree search was reported as the predicted move.

9.7.1.1 Alpha Zero: Enhancements to Zero Human Knowledge

A later enhancement of the idea, referred to as *AlphaGo Zero* [446], removed the need for human expert moves (or an SL-network). Instead of separate policy and value networks, a single network outputs both the policy (i.e., action probabilities) $p(s, a)$ and the value $v(s)$ of the position. The cross-entropy loss on the output policy probabilities and the squared loss on the value output were added to create a single loss. Whereas the original version of *AlphaGo* used Monte Carlo tree search only for inference from trained networks, the zero-knowledge versions also use the visit counts in Monte Carlo tree search for training. One can view the visit count of each branch in tree search as a policy *improvement* operator over $p(s, a)$ by virtue of its lookahead-based exploration. This provides a basis for creating boot-strapped ground-truth values (Intuition 9.4.1) for neural network learning. While temporal difference learning bootstraps state values, this approach bootstraps visit counts for learning policies. The predicted probability of Monte Carlo tree search for action a in board state s is $\pi(s,a) \propto N(s,a)^{1/\tau}$, where τ is a temperature parameter. The value of $N(s,a)$ is computed using a similar Monte Carlo search algorithm as used for *AlphaGo*, where the *prior* probabilities $p(s,a)$ output by the neural network are used for computing Equation 9.27. The value of $Q(s,a)$ in Equation 9.27 is set to the average value output $v(s')$ from the neural network of the newly created leaf nodes s' reached from state s.

AlphaGo Zero updates the neural network by bootstrapping $\pi(s,a)$ as a ground-truth, whereas ground-truth *state values* are generated with Monte Carlo simulations. At each state s, the probabilities $\pi(s,a)$, values $Q(s,a)$ and visit counts $N(s,a)$ are updated by running the Monte Carlo tree search procedure (repeatedly) starting at state s. The neural network from the previous iteration is used for selecting branches according to Equation 9.27 until a state is reached that does not exist in the tree or a terminal state is reached. For each non-existing state, a new leaf is added to the tree with its Q-values and visit values initialized to zero. The Q-values and visit counts of all edges on the path from s to the leaf node are updated based on leaf evaluation by the neural network (or by game rules for terminal states). After multiple searches starting from node s, the *posterior* probability $\pi(s,a)$ is used to sample an action for self-play and reach the next node s'. The entire procedure discussed in this paragraph is repeated at node s' to recursively obtain the next position s''. The game is recursively played to completion and the final value from $\{-1, +1\}$ is returned as the ground-truth value $z(s)$ of uniformly sampled states s on the game path. Note that $z(s)$ is defined from the perspective of the player at state s. The ground-truth values of the probabilities are already available in $\pi(s,a)$ for various values of a. Therefore, one can create a training instance for the neural network containing the input representation of state s, the bootstrapped ground-truth probabilities in $\pi(s,a)$, and the Monte Carlo ground-truth value $z(s)$. This training instance is used to update the neural network parameters. Therefore, if the probability and value outputs for the neural network are $p(s,a)$ and $v(s)$, respectively, the loss for a neural network with weight vector $\overline{W}$ is as follows:

$$L = [v(s) - z(s)]^2 - \sum_a \pi(s,a)\log[p(s,a)] + \lambda||\overline{W}||^2 \qquad (9.28)$$

Here, $\lambda > 0$ is the regularization parameter.

Further advancements were proposed in the form of *Alpha Zero* [447], which could play multiple games such as *Go*, shogi, and chess. *Alpha Zero* has handily defeated the best chess-playing software, *Stockfish*, and has also defeated the best shogi software (*Elmo*). The victory in chess was particularly unexpected by most top players, because it was always assumed that chess required too much domain knowledge for a reinforcement learning system to win over a system with hand-crafted evaluations.

Comments on Performance

AlphaGo has shown extraordinary performance against a variety of computer and human opponents. Against a variety of computer opponents, it won 494 out of 495 games [445]. Even when *AlphaGo* was handicapped by providing four free stones to the opponent, it won 77%, 86%, and 99% of the games played against (the software programs named) *Crazy Stone, Zen,* and *Pachi*, respectively. It also defeated notable human opponents, such as the European champion, the World champion, and the top-ranked player.

A more notable aspect of its performance was the way in which it achieved its victories. In several of its games, *AlphaGo* made many unconventional and brilliantly unorthodox moves, which would sometimes make sense only in hindsight after the victory of the program [607, 608]. There were cases in which the moves made by *AlphaGo* were contrary to conventional wisdom, but eventually revealed innovative insights acquired by *AlphaGo* during self-play. After this match, some top *Go* players reconsidered their approach to the entire game.

The performance of *Alpha Zero* in chess was similar, where it often made material sacrifices in order to incrementally improve its position and constrict its opponent. This type of behavior is a hallmark of human play and is very different from conventional chess software (which is already much better than humans). Unlike hand-crafted evaluations, it seemed to have no pre-conceived notions on the material values of pieces, or on when a king was safe in the center of the board. Furthermore, it discovered most well-known chess openings on its own using self-play, and seemed to have its own opinions on which ones were "better." In other words, it had the ability to discover knowledge on its own. A key difference of reinforcement learning from supervised learning is that *it has the ability to innovate beyond known knowledge through learning by reward-guided trial and error.* This behavior represents some promise in other applications.

9.7.2   Self-Learning Robots

Self-learning robots represent an important frontier in artificial intelligence, in which robots can be trained to perform various tasks such as locomotion, mechanical repairs, or object retrieval by using a reward-driven approach. For example, consider the case in which one has constructed a robot that is *physically* capable of locomotion (in terms of how it is constructed and the movement choices available to it), but it has to learn the precise *choice* of movements in order to keep itself balanced and move from point A to point B. As bipedal humans, we are able to walk and keep our balance naturally without even thinking about it, but this is not a simple matter for a bipedal robot in which an incorrect choice of joint movement could easily cause it to topple over. The problem becomes even more difficult when uncertain terrain and obstacles are placed in the way of a robot.

This type of problem is naturally suited to reinforcement learning, because it is easy to judge whether a robot is walking correctly, but it is hard to specify precise rules about what the robot should do in every possible situation. In the reward-driven approach of reinforcement learning, the robot is given (virtual) rewards every time it makes progress in locomotion from point A to point B. Otherwise, the robot is free to take any actions, and it is not pre-trained with knowledge about the specific choice of actions that would help keep it balanced and walk. In other words, the robot is not seeded with any knowledge of what walking looks like (beyond the fact that it will be rewarded for using its available actions for making progress from point A to point B). This is a classical example of reinforcement learning, because the robot now needs to learn the specific sequence of actions to take in order to earn the goal-driven rewards. Although we use locomotion as a specific example in this case, this general principle applies to any type of learning in robots. For example, a second problem is that of teaching a robot manipulation tasks such as grasping an object or screwing the cap on a bottle. In the following, we will provide a brief discussion of both cases.

9.7.2.1   Deep Learning of Locomotion Skills

In this case, locomotion skills were taught to virtual robots [433], in which the robot was simulated with the *MuJoCo* physics engine [609], which stands for *Multi-Joint Dynamics with Contact.* It is a physics engine aiming to facilitate research and development in robotics, biomechanics, graphics, and animation, where fast and accurate simulation is needed without having to construct an actual robot. Both a humanoid and a quadruped robot were used. An example of the biped model is shown in Figure 9.8. The advantage of this type of simulation is that it is inexpensive to work with a virtual simulation, and one avoids the natural safety and expense issues that arise with the physical damages in an experimentation framework that is likely to be marred by high levels of mistakes/accidents. On the flip side, a physical model provides more realistic results. In general, a simulation can often be used for smaller scale testing before building a physical model.

Figure 9.8: Example of the virtual humanoid robot. Original image is available at [609].

The humanoid model has 33 state dimensions and 10 actuated degrees of freedom, while the quadruped model has 29 state dimensions and 8 actuated degrees of freedom. Models were rewarded for forward progress, although episodes were terminated when the center of mass of the robot fell below a certain point. The actions of the robot were controlled by joint torques. A number of features were available to the robot, such as sensors providing the positions of obstacles, the joint positions, angles, and so on. These features were fed into the neural networks. Two neural networks were used; one was used for value estimation, and the other was used for policy estimation. Therefore, a policy gradient method was used in which the value network played the role of estimating the advantage. Such an approach is an instantiation of an actor-critic method.

A feed-forward neural network was used with three hidden layers, with 100, 50, and 25 tanh units, respectively. The approach in [433] requires the estimation of both a policy function and a value function, and the same architecture was used in both cases for the hidden layers. However, the value estimator required only one output, whereas the policy estimator required as many outputs as the number of actions. Therefore, the main difference between the two architectures was in terms of how the output layer and the loss function was designed. The generalized advantage estimator (GAE) was used in combination with trust-based policy optimization (TRPO). The bibliographic notes contain pointers to specific details of these methods. On training the neural network for 1000 iterations with reinforcement learning, the robot learned to walk with a visually pleasing gait. A video of the final results of the robot walking is available at [610]. Similar results were also later released by Google DeepMind with more extensive abilities of avoiding obstacles or other challenges [187].

9.7.2.2   Deep Learning of Visuomotor Skills

A second and interesting case of reinforcement learning is provided in [286], in which a robot was trained for several household tasks such as placing a coat hanger on a rack, inserting a block into a shape-sorting cube, fitting the claw of a toy hammer under a nail with various grasps, and screwing a cap onto a bottle. Examples of these tasks are illustrated in Figure 9.9(a) along with an image of the robot. The actions were 7-dimensional joint motor torque commands, and each action required a sequence of commands in order to optimally perform the task. In this case, an actual physical model of a robot was used for training. A camera image was used by the robot in order to locate the objects and manipulate them. This camera image can be considered the robot's eyes, and the convolutional neural network used by the robot works on the same conceptual principle as the visual cortex (based on Hubel and Wiesel's experiments). Even though this setting seems very different from that of the Atari video games at first sight, there are significant similarities in terms of how image frames can help in mapping to policy actions. For example, the Atari setting also works with a convolutional neural network on the raw pixels. However, there were some additional inputs here, corresponding to the robot and object positions. These tasks require a high level of learning in visual perception, coordination, and contact dynamics, all of which need to learned automatically.

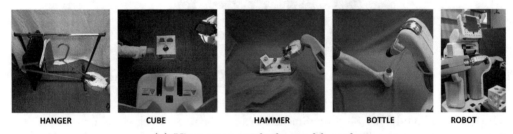

(a) Visuomotor tasks learned by robot

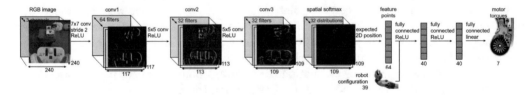

(b) Architecture of the convolutional neural network

Figure 9.9: Deep learning of visuomotor skills. These figures appear in [286]. (©2016 Sergey Levine, Chelsea Finn, Trevor Darrell, and Pieter Abbeel)

A natural approach is to use a convolutional neural network for mapping image frames to actions. As in the case of Atari games, spatial features need to be learned in the layers of the convolutional neural network that are suitable for earning the relevant rewards in a task-sensitive manner. The convolutional neural network had 7 layers and 92,000 parameters. The first three layers were convolutional layers, the fourth layer was a spatial softmax, and the fifth layer was a fixed transformation from spatial feature maps to a concise set of two coordinates. The idea was to apply a softmax function to the responses across the spatial feature map. This provides a probability of each position in the feature map. The expected position using this probability distribution provides the 2-dimensional coordinate, which is referred to as a *feature point*. Note that each spatial feature map in the convolution layer creates a feature point. The feature point can be viewed as a kind of soft argmax over the spatial probability distribution. The fifth layer was quite different from what one normally sees in a convolutional neural network, and was designed to create a precise representation of the visual scene that was suitable for feedback control. The spatial feature points are concatenated with the robot's configuration, which is an additional input occurring only after the convolution layers. This concatenated feature set is fed into two fully connected layers, each with 40 rectified units, followed by linear connections to the torques. Note that only the observations corresponding to the camera were fed to the first layer of the convolutional neural network, and the observations corresponding to the robot state were fed to the first fully connected layer. This is because the convolutional layers cannot make much use of the robot states, and it makes sense to concatenate the state-centric inputs after the visual inputs have been processed by the convolutional layers. The entire network contained about 92,000 parameters, of which 86,000 were in the convolutional layers. The architecture of the convolutional neural network is shown in Figure 9.9(b). The observations consist of the RGB camera image, joint encoder readings, velocities, and end-effector pose.

The full robot states contained between 14 and 32 dimensions, such as the joint angles, end-effector pose, object positions, and their velocities. This provided a practical notion of a state. As in all policy-based methods, the outputs correspond to the various actions (motor torques). One interesting aspect of the approach discussed in [286] is that it transforms the reinforcement learning problem into supervised learning. A *guided policy search* method was used, which is not discussed in this chapter. This approach converts portions of the reinforcement learning problem into supervised learning. Interested readers are referred to [286], where a video of the performance of the robot (trained using this system) may also be found.

9.7.3 Building Conversational Systems: Deep Learning for Chatbots

Chatbots are also referred to as *conversational systems* or *dialog systems*. The ultimate goal of a chatbot is to build an agent that can freely converse with a human about a variety of topics in a natural way. We are very far from achieving this goal. However, significant progress has been made in building chatbots for specific domains and particular applications (e.g., negotiation or shopping assistant). An example of a relatively general-purpose system is Apple's Siri, which is a digital personal assistant. One can view Siri as an open-domain system, because it is possible to have conversations with it about a wide variety of topics. It is reasonably clear to anyone using Siri that the assistant is sometimes either unable to provide satisfactory responses to difficult questions, and in some cases hilarious responses to common questions are hard-coded. This is, of course, natural because the system is relatively general-purpose, and we are nowhere close to building a human-level conversational system. In contrast, closed-domain systems have a specific task in mind, and can therefore be more easily trained in a reliable way.

In the following, we will describe a system built by *Facebook* for end-to-end learning of negotiation skills [290]. This is a closed-domain system because it is designed for the particular purpose of negotiation. As a test-bed, the following negotiation task was used. Two agents are shown a collection of items of different types (e.g., two books, one hat, three balls). The agents are instructed to divide these items among themselves by negotiating a split of the items. A key point is that the value of each of the types of items is different for the two agents, but they are not aware of the value of the items for each other. This is often the case in real-life negotiations, where users attempt to reach a mutually satisfactory outcome by negotiating for items of value to them.

The values of the items are always assumed to be non-negative and generated randomly in the test-bed under some constraints. First, the total value of all items for a user is 10. Second, each item has non-zero value to at least one user so that it makes little sense to ignore an item. Last, some items have nonzero values to both users. Because of these constraints, it is impossible for both users to achieve the maximum score of 10, which ensures a competitive negotiation process. After 10 turns, the agents are allowed the option to complete the negotiation with no agreement, which has a value of 0 points for both users. The three item types of books, hats, and balls were used, and a total of between 5 and 7 items existed in the pool. The fact that the values of the items are different for the two users (without knowledge about each other's assigned values) is significant; if both negotiators are capable, they will be able to achieve a total value of larger than 10 for the items between them. Nevertheless, the better negotiator will be able to capture the larger value by optimally negotiating for items with a high value for them.

The reward function for this reinforcement learning setting is the final value of the items attained by the user. One can use supervised learning on previous dialogs in order to maximize the likelihood of utterances. A straightforward use of recurrent networks to maximize the likelihood of utterances resulted in agents that were too eager to compromise. Therefore, the approach combined supervised learning with reinforcement learning. The incorporation of supervised learning within the reinforcement learning helps in ensuring that the models do not diverge from human language. A form of planning for dialogs called *dialog roll-out* was introduced. The approach uses an encoder-decoder recurrent architecture, in which the decoder maximizes the reward function rather than the likelihood of utterances. This encoder-decoder architecture is based on sequence-to-sequence learning, as discussed in Section 7.7.2 of Chapter 7.

To facilitate supervised learning, dialogs were collected from *Amazon Mechanical Turk*. A total of 5808 dialogs were collected in 2236 unique scenarios, where a scenario is defined by assignment of a particular set of values to the items. Of these cases, 252 scenarios corresponding to 526 dialogs were held out. Each scenario results in two training examples, which are derived from the perspective of each agent. A concrete training example could be one in which the items to be divided among the two agents correspond to 3 books, 2 hats, and 1 ball. These are part of the input to each agent. The second input could be the value of each item to the agent, which are (i) Agent A: book:1, hat:3, ball:1, and (ii) Agent B: book:2, hat:1, ball:2. Note that this means that agent A should secretly try to get as many hats as possible in the negotiation, whereas agent B should focus on books and balls. An example of a dialog in the training data is given below [290]:

Agent A: I want the books and the hats, you get the ball.
Agent B: Give me a book too and we have a deal.
Agent A: Ok, deal.
Agent B: ⟨choose⟩

The final output for agent A is 2 books and 2 hats, whereas the final output for agent B is 1 book and 1 ball. Therefore, each agent has her own set of inputs and outputs, and the dialogs for each agent are also viewed from their own perspective in terms of the portions that are reads and the portions that are writes. Therefore, each scenario generates two training examples and the same recurrent network is shared for generating the writes and the final output of each agent. The dialog x is a list of tokens $x_0 \ldots x_T$, containing the turns of each agent interleaved with symbols marking whether the turn was written by an agent or their partner. A special token at the end indicates that one agent has marked that an agreement has been reached.

The supervised learning procedure uses four different gated recurrent units (GRUs). The first gated recurrent unit GRU_g encodes the input goals, the second gated recurrent unit GRU_q generates the terms in the dialog, a forward-output gated recurrent unit $GRU_{\vec{o}}$, and a backward-output gated recurrent unit $GRU_{\overleftarrow{o}}$. The output is essentially produced by a bi-directional GRU. These GRUs are hooked up in end-to-end fashion. In the supervised learning approach, the parameters are trained using the inputs, dialogs, and outputs available from the training data. The loss for the supervised model for a weighted sum of the token-prediction loss of the dialog and the output choice prediction loss of the items.

However, for reinforcement learning, dialog roll-outs are used. Note that the group of GRUs in the supervised model is, in essence, providing probabilistic outputs. Therefore, one can adapt the same model to work for reinforcement learning by simply changing the loss function. In other words, the GRU combination can be considered a type of policy network. One can use this policy network to generate Monte Carlo roll-outs of various dialogs and their final rewards. Each of the sampled actions becomes a part of the training data, and the action is associated with the final reward of the roll-out. In other words, the approach uses *self-play* in which the agent negotiates with itself to learn better strategies. The final reward achieved by a roll-out is used to update the policy network parameters. This reward is computed based on the value of the items negotiated at the end of the dialog. This approach can be viewed as an instance of the REINFORCE algorithm [533]. One issue with self-play is that the agents tend to learn their own language, which deviates from natural human language when both sides use reinforcement learning. Therefore, one of the agents is constrained to be a supervised model.

For the final prediction, one possibility is to directly sample from the probabilities output by the GRU. However, such an approach is often not optimal when working with recurrent networks. Therefore, a two-stage approach is used. First, c candidate utterances are created by using sampling. The expected reward of each candidate utterance is computed and the one with the largest expected value is selected. In order to compute the expected reward, the output was scaled by the probability of the dialog because low-probability dialogs were unlikely to be selected by either agent.

A number of interesting observations were made in [290] about the performance of the approach. First, the supervised learning methods often tended to give up easily, whereas the reinforcement learning methods were more persistent in attempting to obtain a good deal. Second, the reinforcement learning method would often exhibit human-like negotiation tactics. In some cases, it feigned interest in an item that was not really of much value in order to obtain a better deal for another item.

9.7.4 Self-Driving Cars

As in the case of the robot locomotion task, the car is rewarded for progressing from point A to point B without causing accidents or other undesirable road incidents. The car is equipped with various types of video, audio, proximity, and motion sensors in order to record observations. The objective of the reinforcement learning system is for the car to go from point A to point B safely irrespective of road conditions.

Driving is a task for which it is hard to specify the proper rules of action in every situation; on the other hand, it is relatively easy to judge when one is driving correctly. This is precisely the setting that is well suited to reinforcement learning. Although a fully self-driving car would have a vast array of components corresponding to inputs and sensors of various types, we focus on a simplified setting in which a single camera is used [46, 47]. This system is instructive because it shows that even a single front-facing camera is sufficient to accomplish quite a lot when paired with reinforcement learning. Interestingly, this work was inspired by the 1989 work of Pomerleau [381], who built the *Autonomous Land Vehicle in a Neural Network (ALVINN)* system, and the main difference from the work done over 25 years back was one of increased data and computational power. In addition, the work uses some advances in convolutional neural networks for modeling. Therefore, this work showcases the great importance of increased data and computational power in building reinforcement learning systems.

The training data was collected by driving in a wide variety of roads and conditions. The data was collected primarily from central New Jersey, although highway data was also collected from Illinois, Michigan, Pennsylvania, and New York. Although a single front-facing camera in the driver position was used as the primary data source for making decisions, the training phase used two additional cameras at other positions in the front to collect rotated and shifted images. These auxiliary cameras, which were not used for final decision making, were however useful for collecting additional data. The placement of the additional cameras ensured that their images were shifted and rotated, and therefore they could be used to train the network to recognize cases where the car position had been compromised. In short, these cameras were useful for data augmentation. The neural network was trained to minimize the error between the steering command output by the network and the command output by the human driver. Note that this approach tends to make the approach closer to supervised learning rather than reinforcement learning. These types of learning methods are also referred to as *imitation learning* [427]. Imitation learning is often used as a first step to buffer the cold-start inherent in reinforcement learning systems.

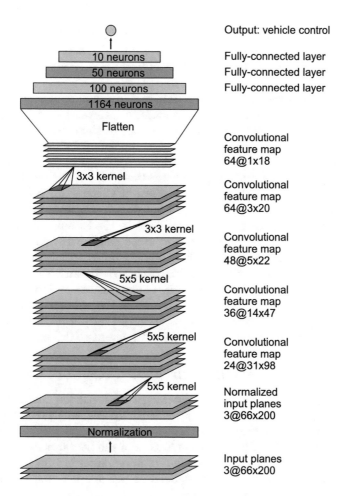

Figure 9.10: The neural network architecture of the control system in the self-driving car discussed in [46] (Courtesy NVIDIA).

Scenarios involving imitation learning are often similar to those involving reinforcement learning. It is relatively easy to use reinforcement setting in this scenario by giving a reward when the car makes progress without human intervention. On the other hand, if the car either does not make progress or requires human intervention, it is penalized. However, this does not seem to be the way in which the self-driving system of [46, 47] is trained. One issue with settings like self-driving cars is that one always has to account for safety issues during training. Although published details on most of the available self-driving cars are limited, it seems that supervised learning has been the method of choice compared to reinforcement learning in this setting. Nevertheless, the differences between using supervised learning and reinforcement learning are not significant in terms of the broader architecture of the neural network that would be useful. A general discussion of reinforcement learning in the context of self-driving cars may be found in [612].

The convolutional neural network architecture is shown in Figure 9.10. The network consists of 9 layers, including a normalization layer, 5 convolutional layers, and 3 fully connected layers. The first convolutional layer used a 5×5 filter with a stride of 2. The next two convolutional layers each used non-strided convolution with a 3×3 filter. These convolutional layers were followed with three fully connected layers. The final output value was a control value, corresponding to the inverse turning radius. The network had 27 million connections and 250, 000 parameters. Specific details of how the deep neural network performs the steering are provided in [47].

The resulting car was tested both in simulation and in actual road conditions. A human driver was always present in the road tests to perform interventions when necessary. On this basis, a measure was computed on the percentage of time that human intervention was required. It was found that the vehicle was autonomous 98% of the time. A video demonstration of this type of autonomous driving is available in [611]. Some interesting observations were obtained by visualizing the activation maps of the trained convolutional neural network (based on the methodology discussed in Chapter 8). In particular, it was observed that the features were heavily biased towards learning aspects of the image that were important to driving. In the case of unpaved roads, the feature activation maps were able to detect the outlines of the roads. On the other hand, if the car was located in a forest, the feature activation maps were full of noise. Note that this does not happen in a convolutional neural network that is trained on *ImageNet* because the feature activation maps would typically contain useful characteristics of trees, leaves, and so on. This difference in the two cases is because the convolutional network of the self-driving setting is trained in a goal-driven matter, and it learns to detect features that are relevant to driving. The specific characteristics of the trees in a forest are not relevant to driving.

9.7.5 Inferring Neural Architectures with Reinforcement Learning

An interesting application of reinforcement learning is to learn the neural network architecture for performing a specific task. For discussion purposes, let us consider a setting in which we wish to determine the structure of a convolutional neural architecture for classify a data set like CIFAR-10 [583]. Clearly, the structure of the neural network depends on a number of hyper-parameters, such as the number of filters, filter height, filter width, stride height, and stride width. These parameters depend on one another, and the parameters of later layers depend on those from earlier layers.

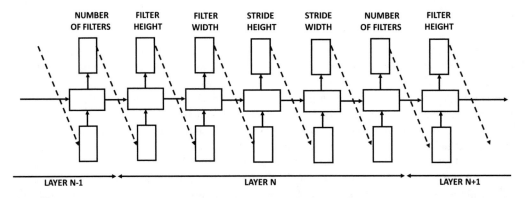

Figure 9.11: The controller network for learning the convolutional architecture of the child network [569]. The controller network is trained with the REINFORCE algorithm.

The reinforcement learning method uses a recurrent network as the *controller* to decide the parameters of the convolutional network, which is also referred to as the *child network* [569]. The overall architecture of the recurrent network is illustrated in Figure 9.11.

The choice of a recurrent network is motivated by the sequential dependence between different architectural parameters. The softmax classifier is used to predict each output as a token rather than a numerical value. This token is then used as an input into the next layer, which is shown by the dashed lines in Figure 9.11. The generation of the parameter as a token results in a discrete action space, which is generally more common in reinforcement learning as compared to a continuous action space.

The performance of the child network on a validation set drawn from CIFAR-10 is used to generate the reward signal. Note that the child network needs to be trained on the CIFAR-10 data set in order to test its accuracy. Therefore, this process requires a full training procedure of the child network, which is quite expensive. This reward signal is used in conjunction with the REINFORCE algorithm in order to train the parameters of the controller network. Therefore, the controller network is really the policy network in this case, which generates a sequence of inter-dependent parameters.

A key point is about the number of layers of the child network (which also decides the number of layers in the recurrent network). This value is not held constant but it follows a certain schedule as training progresses. In the early iterations, the number of layers is fewer, and therefore the learned architecture of the convolutional network is shallow. As training progresses, the number of layers slowly increases over time. The policy gradient method is not very different from what is discussed earlier in this chapter, except that a recurrent network is trained with the reward signal rather than a feed-forward network. Various types of optimizations are also discussed in [569], such as efficient implementations with parallelism and the learning of advanced architectural designs like skip connections.

9.8 Practical Challenges Associated with Safety

Simplifying the design of highly complex learning algorithms with reinforcement learning can sometimes have unexpected effects. By virtue of the fact that reinforcement learning systems have larger levels of freedom than other learning systems, it naturally leads to some safety related concerns. While biological greed is a powerful factor in human intelligence, it is also a source of many undesirable aspects of human behavior. The simplicity that is the greatest strength of reward-driven learning is also its greatest pitfall in biological systems. Simulating such systems therefore results in similar pitfalls from the perspective of artificial intelligence. For example, poorly designed rewards can lead to unforeseen consequences, because of the exploratory way in which the system learns its actions. Reinforcement learning systems can frequently learn unknown "cheats" and "hacks" in imperfectly designed video games, which tells us a cautionary tale of what might happen in a less-than-perfect real world. Robots learn that simply pretending to screw caps on bottles can earn faster rewards, as long as the human or automated evaluator is fooled by the action. In other words, the design of the reward function is sometimes not a simple matter.

Furthermore, a system might try to earn virtual rewards in an "unethical" way. For example, a cleaning robot might try to earn rewards by first creating messes and then cleaning them [10]. One can imagine even darker scenarios for robot nurses. Interestingly, these types of behaviors are sometimes also exhibited by humans. These undesirable similarities are a direct result of simplifying the learning process in machines by leveraging the simple greed-centric principles with which biological organisms learn. Striving for simplicity results in ceding more control to the machine, which can have unexpected effects. In some cases, there are ethical dilemmas in even designing the reward function. For example, if it becomes inevitable that an accident is going to occur, should a self-driving car save its driver or two pedestrians? Most humans would save themselves in this setting as a matter of reflexive biological instinct; however, it is an entirely different matter to incentivize a learning system to do so. At the same time, it would be hard to convince a human operator to trust a vehicle where her safety is not the first priority for the learning system. Reinforcement learning systems are also susceptible to the ways in which their human operators interact with them and manipulate the effects of their underlying reward function; there have been occasions where a chatbot was taught to make offensive or racist remarks.

Learning systems have a harder time in generalizing their experiences to new situations. This problem is referred to as *distributional shift*. For example, a self-driving car trained in one country might perform poorly in another. Similarly, the exploratory actions in reinforcement learning can sometimes be dangerous. Imagine a robot trying to solder wires in an electronic device, where the wires are surrounded with fragile electronic components. Trying exploratory actions in this setting is fraught with perils. These issues tell us that we cannot build AI systems with no regard to safety. Indeed, some organizations like *OpenAI* [613] have taken the lead in these matters of ensuring safety. Some of these issues are also discussed in [10] with broader frameworks of possible solutions. In many cases, it seems that the human would have to be involved in the loop to some extent in order to ensure safety [424].

9.9 Summary

This chapter studies the problem of reinforcement learning in which agents interact with the environment in a reward-driven manner in order to learn the optimal actions. There are several classes of reinforcement learning methods, of which the Q-learning methods and the policy-driven methods are the most common. Policy-driven methods have become increasingly popular in recent years. Many of these methods are end-to-end systems that integrate deep neural networks to take in sensory inputs and learn policies that optimize rewards. Reinforcement learning algorithms are used in many settings like playing video or other types of games, robotics, and self-driving cars. The ability of these algorithms to learn via experimentation often leads to innovative solutions that are not possible with other forms of learning. Reinforcement learning algorithms also pose unique challenges associated with safety because of the oversimplification of the learning process with reward functions.

9.10 Bibliographic Notes

An excellent overview on reinforcement learning may be found in the book by Sutton and Barto [483]. A number of surveys on reinforcement learning are available at [293]. David Silver's lectures on reinforcement learning are freely available on *YouTube* [619]. The method of temporal differences was proposed by Samuel in the context of a checkers program [421] and formalized by Sutton [482]. Q-learning was proposed by Watkins in [519], and a convergence proof is provided in [520]. The SARSA algorithm was introduced in [412]. Early methods for using neural networks in reinforcement learning were proposed in [296, 349, 492, 493, 494]. The work in [492] developed TD-Gammon, which was a backgammon playing program.

A system that used a convolutional neural network to create a deep Q-learning algorithm with raw pixels was pioneered in [335, 336]. It has been suggested in [335] that the approach presented in the paper can be improved with other well-known ideas such as prioritized sweeping [343]. Asynchronous methods that use multiple agents in order to perform the learning are discussed in [337]. The use of multiple asynchronous threads avoids the problem of correlation within a thread, which improves convergence to higher-quality solutions. This type of asynchronous approach is often used in lieu of the experience replay technique. Furthermore, an n-step technique, which uses a lookahead of n steps (instead of 1 step) to predict the Q-values, was proposed in the same work.

One drawback of Q-learning is that it is known to overestimate the values of actions under certain circumstances. An improvement over Q-learning, referred to as *double Q-learning*, was proposed in [174]. In the original form of Q-learning, the same values are used to both select and evaluate an action. In the case of double Q-learning, these values are decoupled, and therefore one is now learning two separate values for selection and evaluation. This change tends to make the approach less sensitive to the overestimation problem. The use of prioritized experience replay to improve the performance of reinforcement learning algorithms under sparse data is discussed in [428]. Such an approach significantly improves the performance of the system on Atari games.

In recent years, policy gradients have become more popular than Q-learning methods. An interesting and simplified description of this approach for the Atari game of *Pong* is provided in [605]. Early methods for using finite difference methods for policy gradients are discussed in [142, 355]. Likelihood methods for policy gradients were pioneered by the REINFORCE algorithm [533]. A number of analytical results on this class of algorithms are provided in [484]. Policy gradients have been used in for learning in the game of *Go* [445], although the overall approach combines a number of different elements. Natural policy gradients were proposed in [230]. One such method [432] has been shown to perform well at learning locomotion in robots. The use of *generalized advantage estimation (GAE)* with continuous rewards is discussed in [433]. The approach in [432, 433] uses natural policy gradients for optimization, and the approach is referred to as *trust region policy optimization* (TRPO). The basic idea is that bad steps in learning are penalized more severely in reinforcement learning (than supervised learning) because the quality of the collected data worsens. Therefore, the TRPO method prefers second-order methods with conjugate gradients (see Chapter 3), in which the updates tend to stay within good regions of trust. Surveys are also available on specific types of reinforcement learning methods like actor-critic methods [162].

Monte Carlo tree search was proposed in [246]. Subsequently, it was used in the game of *Go* [135, 346, 445, 446]. A survey on these methods may be found in [52]. Later versions of *AlphaGo* dispensed with the supervised portions of learning, adapted to chess and shogi, and performed better with zero initial knowledge [446, 447]. The *AlphaGo* approach combines several ideas, including the use of policy networks, Monte Carlo tree search, and convolutional neural networks. The use of convolutional neural networks for playing the game of *Go* has been explored in [73, 307, 481]. Many of these methods use supervised learning in order to mimic human experts at *Go*. Some TD-learning methods for chess, such as *NeuroChess* [496], *KnightCap* [22], and *Giraffe* [259] have been explored, but were not as successful as conventional engines. The pairing of convolutional neural networks and reinforcement learning for spatial games seems to be a new (and successful) recipe that distinguishes *Alpha Zero* from these methods. Several methods for training self-learning robots are presented in [286, 432, 433]. An overview of deep reinforcement learning methods for dialog generation is provided in [291]. Conversation models that use only supervised learning with recurrent networks are discussed in [440, 508]. The negotiation chatbot discussed in this chapter is described in [290]. The description of self-driving cars is based on [46, 47]. An MIT course on self-driving cars is available at [612]. Reinforcement learning has also been used to generate structured queries from natural language [563], or for learning neural architectures in various tasks [19, 569].

Reinforcement learning can also improve deep learning models. This is achieved with the notion of *attention* [338, 540], in which reinforcement learning is used to focus on selective parts of the data. The idea is that large parts of the data are often irrelevant for learning, and learning how to focus on selective portions of the data can significantly improve results. The selection of relevant portions of the data is achieved with reinforcement learning. Attention mechanisms are discussed in Section 10.2 of Chapter 10. In this sense, reinforcement learning is one of the topics in machine learning that is more tightly integrated with deep learning than seems at first sight.

9.10.1   Software Resources and Testbeds

Although significant progress has been made in designing reinforcement learning algorithms in recent years, commercial software using these methods is still relatively limited. Nevertheless, numerous software testbeds are available that can be used in order to test various algorithms. Perhaps the best source for high-quality reinforcement learning baselines is available from *OpenAI* [623]. *TensorFlow* [624] and *Keras* [625] implementations of reinforcement learning algorithms are also available.

Most frameworks for testing and development of reinforcement learning algorithms are specialized to specific types of reinforcement learning scenarios. Some frameworks are lightweight, and can be used for quick testing. For example, the ELF framework [498], created by *Facebook*, is designed for real-time strategy games, and is an open-source and light-weight reinforcement learning framework. The *OpenAI Gym* [620] provides environments for development of reinforcement learning algorithms for Atari games and simulated robots. The *OpenAI Universe* [621] can be used to turn reinforcement learning programs into Gym environments. For example, self-driving car simulations have been added to this environment. An Arcade learning environment for developing agents in the context of Atari games is described in [25]. The *MuJoCo* simulator [609], which stands for Multi-Joint dynamics with Contact, is a physics engine, and is designed for robotics simulations. An application with the use of *MuJoCo* is described in this chapter. *ParlAI* [622] is an open-source framework for dialog research by *Facebook*, and is implemented in Python. Baidu has created an open-source platform of its self-driving car project, referred to as *Apollo* [626].

9.11   Exercises

1. The chapter gives a proof of the likelihood ratio trick (cf. Equation 9.24) for the case in which the action a is discrete. Generalize this result to continuous-valued actions.

2. Throughout this chapter, a neural network, referred to as the policy network, has been used in order to implement the policy gradient. Discuss the importance of the choice of network architecture in different settings.

3. You have two slot machines, each of which has an array of 100 lights. The probability distribution of the reward from playing each machine is an unknown (and possibly machine-specific) function of the pattern of lights that are currently lit up. Playing a slot machine changes its light pattern in some well-defined but unknown way. Discuss why this problem is more difficult than the multi-armed bandit problem. Design a deep learning solution to optimally choose machines in each trial that will maximize the average reward per trial at steady-state.

4. Consider the well-known game of rock-paper-scissors. Human players often try to use the history of previous moves to guess the next move. Would you use a Q-learning or a policy-based method to learn to play this game? Why? Now consider a situation in which a human player samples one of the three moves with a probability that is an unknown function of the history of 10 previous moves of each side. Propose a deep learning method that is designed to play with such an opponent. Would a well-designed deep learning method have an advantage over this human player? What policy should a human player use to ensure probabilistic parity with a deep learning opponent?

5. Consider the game of tic-tac-toe in which a reward drawn from $\{-1, 0, +1\}$ is given at the end of the game. Suppose you learn the values of all states (assuming optimal play from both sides). Discuss why states in non-terminal positions will have non-zero value. What does this tell you about credit-assignment of intermediate moves to the reward value received at the end?

6. Write a Q-learning implementation that learns the value of each state-action pair for a game of tic-tac-toe by repeatedly playing against human opponents. No function approximators are used and therefore the entire table of state-action pairs is learned using Equation 9.5. Assume that you can initialize each Q-value to 0 in the table.

7. The two-step TD-error is defined as follows:

$$\delta_t^{(2)} = r_t + \gamma r_{t+1} + \gamma^2 V(s_{t+2}) - V(s_t)$$

(a) Propose a TD-learning algorithm for the 2-step case.

(b) Propose an on-policy n-step learning algorithm like SARSA. Show that the update is truncated variant of Equation 9.16 after setting $\lambda = 1$. What happens for the case when $n = \infty$?

(c) Propose an off-policy n-step learning algorithm like Q-learning and discuss its advantages/disadvantages with respect to (b).

Chapter 10

Advanced Topics in Deep Learning

"Instead of trying to produce a program to simulate the adult mind, why not rather try to produce one which simulates the child's? If this were then subjected to an appropriate course of education one would obtain the adult brain."—Alan Turing in *Computing Machinery and Intelligence*

10.1 Introduction

This book will cover several advanced topics in deep learning, which either do not naturally fit within the focus of the previous chapters, or because their level of complexity requires separate treatment. The topics discussed in this chapter include the following:

1. *Attention models:* Humans do not actively use all the information available to them from the environment at any given time. Rather, they focus on specific portions of the data that are relevant to the task at hand. This biological notion is referred to as *attention*. A similar principle can also be applied to artificial intelligence applications. Models with attention use reinforcement learning (or other methods) to focus on smaller portions of the data that are relevant to the task at hand. Such methods have recently been leveraged for improved performance.

2. *Models with selective access to internal memory:* These models are closely related to attention models, although the difference is that the attention is focused primarily on specific parts of the stored data. A helpful analogy is to think of how memory is accessed by humans to perform specific tasks. Humans have a huge repository of data within the memory cells of their brains. However, at any given point, only a small part of it is accessed, which is relevant to the task at hand. Similarly, modern computers have significant amounts of memory, but computer programs are designed to access it in a selective and controlled way with the use of variables, which are indirect *addressing mechanisms.* All neural networks have memory in the form of hidden states. However,

it is so tightly integrated with the computations that it is hard to separate data access from computations. By controlling reads and writes to the internal memory of the neural network more selectively and explicitly introducing the notion of addressing mechanisms, the resulting network performs computations that reflect the human style of programming more closely. Often such networks have better generalization power than more traditional neural networks when performing predictions on out-of-sample data. One can also view selective memory access as applying a form of attention *internally* to the memory of a neural network. The resulting architecture is referred to as a *memory network* or *neural Turing machine*.

3. *Generative adversarial networks:* Generative adversarial networks are designed to create generative models of data from samples. These networks can create realistic looking samples from data by using two adversarial networks. One network generates synthetic samples (generator), and the other (which is a discriminator) classifies a mixture of original instances and generated samples as either real or synthetic. An adversarial game results in an improved generator over time, until the discriminator is no longer able to distinguish between real and fake samples. Furthermore, by conditioning on a specific type of context (e.g., image caption), it is also possible to guide the creation of specific types of desired samples.

Attention mechanisms often have to make hard decisions about specific parts of the data to attend to. One can view this choice in a similar way to the choices faced by a reinforcement learning algorithm. Some of the methods used for building attention-based models are heavily based on reinforcement learning, although others are not. Therefore, it is strongly recommended to study the materials in Chapter 9 before reading this chapter.

Neural Turing machines are related to a closely related class of architectures referred to as memory networks. Recently, they have shown promise in building question-answering systems, although the results are still quite primitive. The construction of a neural Turing machine can be considered a gateway to many capabilities in artificial intelligence that have not yet been fully realized. As is common in the historical experience with neural networks, more data and computational power will play the prominent role in bringing these promises to reality.

Most of this book discusses different types of feed-forward networks, which are based on the notion of changing weights based on errors. A completely different way of learning is that of *competitive learning*, in which the neurons compete for the right to respond to a subset of the input data. The weights are modified based on the winner of this competition. This approach is a variant of Hebbian learning discussed in Chapter 6, and is useful for unsupervised learning applications like clustering, dimensionality reduction and compression. This paradigm will also be discussed in this chapter.

Chapter Organization

This chapter is organized as follows. The next section discusses attention mechanisms in deep learning. Some of these methods are closely related to deep learning models. The augmentation of neural networks with external memory is discussed in Section 10.3. Generative adversarial networks are discussed in Section 10.4. Competitive learning methods are discussed in Section 10.5. The limitations of neural networks are presented in Section 10.6. A summary is presented in Section 10.7.

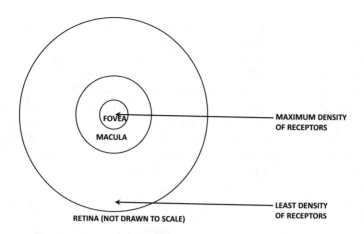

Figure 10.1: Resolutions in different regions of the eye. Most of what we focus on is captured by the macula.

10.2 Attention Mechanisms

Human beings rarely use all the available sensory inputs in order to accomplish specific tasks. Consider the problem of finding an address defined by a specific house number on a street. Therefore, an important component of the task is to identify the number written either on the door or the mailbox of a house. In this process, the retina often has an image of a broader scene, although one rarely focuses on the full image. The retina has a small portion, referred to as the *macula* with a central *fovea*, which has an extremely high resolution compared to the remainder of the eye. This region has a high concentration of color-sensitive cones, whereas most of the non-central portions of the eye have relatively low resolution with a predominance of color-insensitive rods. The different regions of the eye are shown in Figure 10.1. When reading a street number, the fovea *fixates* on the number, and its image falls on a portion of the retina that corresponds to the macula (and especially the fovea). Although one is aware of the other objects outside this central field of vision, it is virtually impossible to use images in the peripheral region to perform detail-oriented tasks. For example, it is very difficult to read letters projected on peripheral portions of the retina. The foveal region is a tiny fraction of the full retina, and it has a diameter of only 1.5 mm. The eye effectively transmits a high-resolution version of less than 0.5% of the surface area of the image that falls on the full retina. This approach is biologically advantageous, because only a carefully selected part of the image is transmitted in high resolution, and it reduces the internal processing required *for the specific task at hand*. Although the structure of the eye makes it particularly easy to understand the notion of selective attention towards visual inputs, this selectivity is not restricted only to visual aspects. Most of the other senses of the human, such as hearing or smells, are often highly focussed depending on the situation at hand. Correspondingly, we will first discuss the notion of attention in the context of computer vision, and then discuss other domains like text.

An interesting application of attention comes from the images captured by *Google Streetview*, which is a system created by Google to enable Web-based retrieval of images of various streets in many countries. This kind of retrieval requires a way to connect houses with their street numbers. Although one might record the street number during image capture, this information needs to be distilled from the image. Given a large image of the frontal part of a house, is there a way of systematically identifying the numbers corresponding to the street address? The key here is to be able to systematically focus on small parts of the image to find what one is looking for. The main challenge here is that there is no way of identifying the relevant portion of the image with the information available up front. Therefore, an iterative approach is required in searching specific parts of the image with the use of knowledge gained from previous iterations. Here, it is useful to draw inspirations from how biological organisms work. Biological organisms draw quick visual cues from whatever they are focusing on in order to identify *where to next look* to get what they want. For example, if we first focus on the door knob by chance, then we know from experience (i.e., our trained neurons tell us) to look to its upper left or right to find the street number. This type of iterative process sounds a lot like the reinforcement learning methods discussed in the previous chapter, where one iteratively obtains cues from previous steps in order to learn what to do to earn *rewards* (i.e., accomplish a task like finding the street number). As we will see later, many applications of attention are paired with reinforcement learning.

The notion of attention is also well suited to natural language processing in which the information that we are looking for is hidden in a long segment of text. This problem arises frequently in applications like machine translation and question-answering systems where the entire sentence needs to be coded up as a fixed length vector by the recurrent neural network (cf. Section 7.7.2 of Chapter 7). As a result, the recurrent neural network is often unable to focus on the appropriate portions of the source sentence for translation to the target sentence. In such cases, it is advantageous to align the target sentence with appropriate portions of the source sentence during translation. In such cases, attention mechanisms are useful in isolating the relevant parts of the source sentence while creating a specific part of the target sentence. It is noteworthy that attention mechanisms need not always be couched in the framework of reinforcement learning. Indeed, most of the attention mechanisms in natural language models do not use reinforcement learning, but they use attention to weight specific parts of the input in a soft way.

10.2.1 Recurrent Models of Visual Attention

The work on recurrent models of visual attention [338] uses reinforcement learning to focus on important parts of an image. The idea is to use a (relatively simple) neural network in which only the resolution of specific portions of the image centered at a particular location is high. This location can change with time, as one learns more about the relevant portions of the image to explore over the course of time. Selecting a particular location in a given time-stamp is referred to as a *glimpse*. A recurrent neural network is used as the controller to identify the precise location in each time-stamp; this choice is based on the feedback from the glimpse in the previous time-stamp. The work in [338] shows that using a simple neural network (called a "glimpse network") to process the image together with the reinforcement-based training can outperform a convolutional neural network for classification.

We consider a dynamic setting in which the image may be partially observable, and the portions that are observable might vary with time-stamp t. Therefore, this setting is quite general, although we can obviously use it for more specialized settings in which the image $\overline{X}_t$ is fixed in time. The overall architecture can be described in a modular way by treating specific parts of the neural network as black-boxes. These modular portions are described below:

1. *Glimpse sensor:* Given an image with representation $\overline{X}_t$, a *glimpse sensor* creates a retina-like representation of the image. The glimpse sensor is conceptually assumed

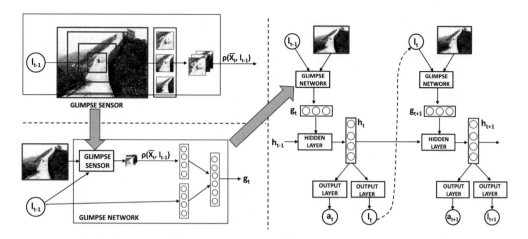

Figure 10.2: The recurrent architecture for leveraging visual attention

to not have full access to the image (because of bandwidth constraints), and is able to access only a small portion of the image in high-resolution, which is centered at l_{t-1}. This is similar to how the eye accesses an image in real life. The resolution of a particular location in the image reduces with distance from the location l_{t-1}. The reduced representation of the image is denoted by $\rho(\overline{X}_t, l_{t-1})$. The glimpse sensor, which is shown in the upper left corner of Figure 10.2, is a part of a larger glimpse network. This network is discussed below.

2. *Glimpse network:* The glimpse network contains the glimpse sensor and encodes both the glimpse location l_{t-1} and the glimpse representation $\rho(\overline{X}_t, l_{t-1})$ into hidden spaces using linear layers. Subsequently, the two are combined into a single hidden representation using another linear layer. The resulting output g_t is the input into the tth time-stamp of the hidden layer in the recurrent neural network. The glimpse network is shown in the lower-right corner of Figure 10.2.

3. *Recurrent neural network:* The recurrent neural network is the main network that is creating the action-driven outputs in each time-stamp (for earning rewards). The recurrent neural network includes the glimpse network, and therefore it includes the glimpse sensor as well (since the glimpse sensor is a part of the glimpse network). This output action of the network at time-stamp t is denoted by a_t, and rewards are associated with the action. In the simplest case, the reward might be the class label of the object or a numerical digit in the *Google Streetview* example. It also outputs a location l_t in the image for the next time-stamp, on which the glimpse network should focus. The output $\pi(a_t)$ is implemented as a probability of action a_t. This probability is implemented with the softmax function, as is common in policy networks (cf. Figure 9.6 of Chapter 9). The training of the recurrent network is done using the objective function of the REINFORCE framework to maximize the expected reward over time. The gain for each action is obtained by multiplying $\log(\pi(a_t))$ with the advantage of that action (cf. Section 9.5.2 of Chapter 9). Therefore, the overall approach is a reinforcement learning method in which the attention locations and actionable outputs are learned simultaneously. It is noteworthy that the history of actions of this recurrent network is encoded within the hidden states h_t. The overall

architecture of the neural network is illustrated on the right-hand side of Figure 10.2. Note that the glimpse network is included as a part of this overall architecture, because the recurrent network utilizes a glimpse of the image (or current state of scene) in order to perform the computations in each time-stamp.

Note that the use of a recurrent neural network architecture is useful but not necessary in these contexts.

Reinforcement Learning

This approach is couched within the framework of reinforcement learning, which allows it to be used for any type of visual reinforcement learning task (e.g., robot selecting actions to achieve a particular goal) instead of image recognition or classification. Nevertheless, supervised learning is a simple special case of this approach.

The actions a_t correspond to choosing the choosing the class label with the use of a softmax prediction. The reward r_t in the tth time-stamp might be 1 if the classification is correct after t time-stamps of that roll out, and 0, otherwise. The overall reward R_t at the tth time-stamp is given by the sum of all discounted rewards over future time stamps. However, this action can vary with the application at hand. For example, in an image captioning application, the action might correspond to choosing the next word of the caption.

The training of this setting proceeds in a similar manner to the approach discussed in Section 9.5.2 of Chapter 9. The gradient of the expected reward at time-stamp t is given by the following:

$$\nabla E[R_t] = R_t \nabla \log(\pi(a_t)) \tag{10.1}$$

Backpropagation is performed in the neural network using this gradient and policy roll-outs. In practice, one will have multiple rollouts, each of which contains multiple actions. Therefore, one will have to add the gradients with respect to all these actions (or a mini-batch of these actions) in order to obtain the final direction of ascent. As is common in policy gradient methods, a baseline is subtracted from the rewards to reduce variance. Since a class label is output at each time-stamp, the accuracy will improve as more glimpses are used. The approach performs quite well using between six and eight glimpses on various types of data.

10.2.1.1   Application to Image Captioning

In this section, we will discuss the application of the visual attention approach (discussed in the previous section) to the problem of image captioning. The problem of image captioning is discussed in Section 7.7.1 of Chapter 7. In this approach, a single feature representation $\overline{v}$ of the entire image is input to the *first time-stamp* of a recurrent neural network. When a feature representation of the entire image is input, it is only provided as input at the first time-stamp when the caption begins to be generated. However, when attention is used, we want to focus on the portion of image that corresponds to the word being generated. Therefore, it makes sense to provide different attention-centric inputs at different time-stamps. For example, consider an image with the following caption:

"Bird flying during sunset."

The attention should be on the location in the image corresponding to the wings of the bird while generating the word *"flying,"* and the attention should be on the setting sun, while generating the word *"sunset."* In such a case, each time-stamp of the recurrent neural network should receive a representation of the image in which the attention is on a specific location. Furthermore, as discussed in the previous section, the values of these locations are also generated by the recurrent network in the previous time-stamp.

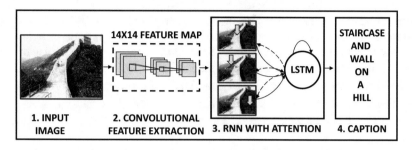

Figure 10.3: Visual attention in image captioning

Note that this approach can already be implemented with the architecture shown in Figure 10.2 by predicting one word of the caption in each time-stamp (as the action) together with a location l_t in the image, which will be the focus of attention in the next time-stamp. The work in [540] is an adaptation of this idea, but it uses several modifications to handle the higher complexity of the problem. First, the glimpse network does use a more sophisticated convolutional architecture to create a 14×14 feature map. This architecture is illustrated in Figure 10.3. Instead of using a glimpse sensor to produce the modified version of the image in each time-stamp, the work in [540] starts with L different preprocessed variants on the image. These preprocessed variants are centered at different locations in the image, and therefore the attention mechanism is restricted to selecting from one of these locations. Then, instead of producing a location l_t in the $(t-1)$th time-stamp, it produces a probability vector $\overline{\alpha}_t$ of length L indicating the relevance of each of the L locations for which representations were preprocessed in the convolutional neural network. In hard attention models, one of the L locations is sampled by using the probability vector $\overline{\alpha}_t$, and the preprocessed representation of that location is provided as input into the hidden state h_t of the recurrent network at the next time-stamp. In other words, the glimpse network in the classification application is replaced with this sampling mechanism. In soft attention models, the representation models of all L locations are averaged by using the probability vector $\overline{\alpha}_t$ as weighting. This averaged representation is provided as input to the hidden state at time-stamp t. For soft attention models, straightforward backpropagation is used for training, whereas for hard attention models, the REINFORCE algorithm (cf. Section 9.5.2 of Chapter 9) is used. The reader is referred to [540] for details, where both these types of methods are discussed.

10.2.2 Attention Mechanisms for Machine Translation

As discussed in Section 7.7.2 of Chapter 7, recurrent neural networks (and specifically their long short-term memory (LSTM) implementations) are used frequently for machine translation. In the following, we use generalized notations corresponding to any type of recurrent neural network, although the LSTM is almost always the method of choice in these settings. For simplicity, we use a single-layer network in our exposition (as well as all the illustrative figures of the neural architectures). In practice, multiple layers are used, and it is relatively easy to generalize the simplified discussion to the multi-layer case. There are several ways in which attention can be incorporated in neural machine translation. Here, we focus on a method proposed in Luong *et al.* [302], which is an improvement over the original mechanism proposed in Bahdanau *et al.* [18].

We start with the architecture discussed in Section 7.7.2 of Chapter 7. For ease in discussion, we replicate the neural architecture of that section in Figure 10.4(a). Note that there are two recurrent neural networks, of which one is tasked with the encoding of the source sentence into a fixed length representation, and the other is tasked with decoding this representation into a target sentence. This is, therefore, a straightforward case of sequence-to-sequence learning, which is used for neural machine translation. The hidden states of the source and target networks are denoted by $h_t^{(1)}$ and $h_t^{(2)}$, respectively, where $h_t^{(1)}$ corresponds to the hidden state of the tth word in the source sentence, and $h_t^{(2)}$ corresponds to the hidden state of the tth word in the target sentence. These notations are borrowed from Section 7.7.2 of Chapter 7.

In attention-based methods, the hidden states $h_t^{(2)}$ are transformed to enhanced states $H_t^{(2)}$ with some additional processing from an *attention layer*. The goal of the attention layer is to incorporate context from the source hidden states into the target hidden states to create a new and enhanced set of target hidden states.

In order to perform attention-based processing, the goal is to find a source representation that is close to the current target hidden state $h_t^{(2)}$ being processed. This is achieved by using the similarity-weighted average of the source vectors to create a context vector $\bar{c}_t$:

$$\bar{c}_t = \frac{\sum_{j=1}^{T_s} \exp(\overline{h}_j^{(1)} \cdot \overline{h}_t^{(2)}) \overline{h}_j^{(1)}}{\sum_{j=1}^{T_s} \exp(\overline{h}_j^{(1)} \cdot \overline{h}_t^{(2)})} \tag{10.2}$$

Here, T_s is the length of the source sentence. This particular way of creating the context vector is the most simplified one among all the different versions discussed in [18, 302]; however, there are several other alternatives, some of which are parameterized. One way of viewing this weighting is with the notion of an *attention variable* $a(t, s)$, which indicates the importance of source word s to target word t:

$$a(t, s) = \frac{\exp(\overline{h}_s^{(1)} \cdot \overline{h}_t^{(2)})}{\sum_{j=1}^{T_s} \exp(\overline{h}_j^{(1)} \cdot \overline{h}_t^{(2)})} \tag{10.3}$$

We refer to the vector $[a(t, 1), a(t, 2), \ldots a(t, T_s)]$ as the attention vector $\bar{a}_t$, and it is specific to the target word t. This vector can be viewed as a set of probabilistic weights summing to 1, and its length depends on the source sentence length T_s. It is not difficult to see that Equation 10.2 is created as an attention-weighted sum of the source hidden vectors, where the attention weight of target word t towards source word s is $a(t, s)$. In other words, Equation 10.2 can be rewritten as follows:

$$\bar{c}_t = \sum_{j=1}^{T_s} a(t, j) \overline{h}_j^{(1)} \tag{10.4}$$

In essence, this approach identifies a contextual representation of the source hidden states, which is most relevant to the current target hidden state being considered. Relevance is defined by using the dot product similarity between source and target hidden states, and is captured in the attention vector. Therefore, we create a new target hidden state $H_t^{(2)}$ that combines the information in the context and the original target hidden state as follows:

$$\overline{H}_t^{(2)} = \tanh\left(W_c \begin{bmatrix} \bar{c}_t \\ \overline{h}_t^2 \end{bmatrix}\right) \tag{10.5}$$

Once this new hidden representation $\overline{H}_t^{(2)}$ is created, it is used in lieu of the original hidden representation $\overline{h}_t^{(2)}$ for the final prediction. The overall architecture of the attention-sensitive system is given in Figure 10.4(b). Note the enhancements from Figure 10.4(a) with the addition of an attention mechanism. This model is referred to as the *global attention model* in [302]. This model is a *soft* attention model, because one is weighting all the source words with a probabilistic weight, and hard judgements are not made about which word is the most relevant one to a target word. The original work in [302] discusses another *local* model, which makes hard judgements about the relevance of target words. The reader is referred to [302] for details of this model.

Refinements

Several refinements can improve the basic attention model. First, the attention vector $\overline{a}_t$ is computed by exponentiating the raw dot products between $\overline{h}_t^{(1)}$ and $\overline{h}_s^{(2)}$, as shown in Equation 10.3. These dot products are also referred to as *scores*. In reality, there is no reason that similar positions in the source and target sentences should have similar hidden states. In fact, the source and target recurrent networks do not even need to use hidden representations of the same dimensionality (even though this is often done in practice). Nevertheless, it was shown in [302] that dot-product based similarity scoring tends to do very well in global attention models, and was the best option compared to parameterized alternatives. It is possible that the good performance of this simple approach might be a result of its regularizing effect on the model. The parameterized alternatives for computing the similarity performed better in local models (i.e., hard attention), which are not discussed in detail here.

Most of these alternative models for computing the similarity use parameters to regulate the computation, which provides some additional flexibility in relating the source and target positions. The different options for computing the score are as follows:

$$
\text{Score}(t, s) = \begin{cases} \overline{h}_s^{(1)} \cdot \overline{h}_t^{(2)} & \text{Dot product} \\ (\overline{h}_t^{(2)})^T W_a \overline{h}_s^{(1)} & \text{General: Parameter matrix } W_a \\ \overline{v}_a^T \tanh \left(W_a \begin{bmatrix} \overline{h}_s^{(1)} \\ \overline{h}_t^{2} \end{bmatrix} \right) & \text{Concat: Parameter matrix } W_a \text{ and vector } \overline{v}_a \end{cases}
$$

$$(10.6)$$

The first of these options is identical to the one discussed in the previous section according to Equation 10.3. The other two models are referred to as *general* and *concat*, respectively, as annotated above. Both these options are parameterized with the use of weight vectors, and the corresponding parameters are also annotated above. After the similarity scores have been computed, the attention values can be computed in an analogous way to the case of the dot-product similarity:

$$
a(t, s) = \frac{\exp(\text{Score}(t, s))}{\sum_{j=1}^{T_s} \exp(\text{Score}(t, j))} \tag{10.7}
$$

These attention values are used in the same way as in the case of dot product similarity. The parameter matrices W_a and $\bar{v}_a$ need to be learned during training. The *concat* model was proposed in earlier work [18], whereas the *general* model seemed to do well in the case of hard attention.

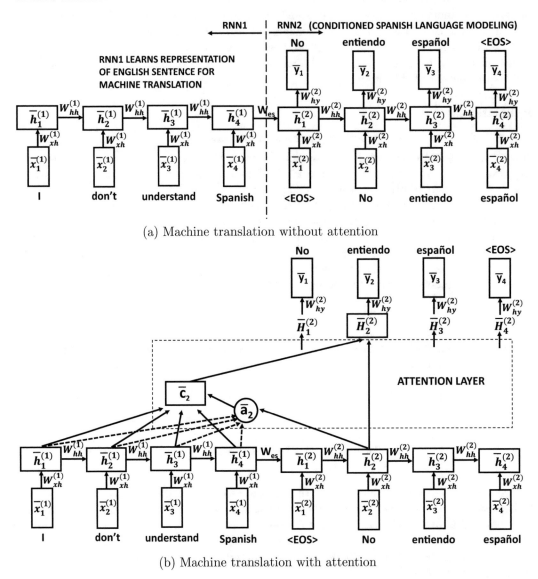

(a) Machine translation without attention

(b) Machine translation with attention

Figure 10.4: The neural architecture in (a) is the same as the one illustrated in Figure 7.10 of Chapter 7. An extra attention layer has been added to (b).

There are several differences of this model [302] from an earlier model presented in Bahdanau *et al.* [18]. We have chosen this model because it is simpler and it illustrates the basic concepts in a straightforward way. Furthermore, it also seems to provide better performance according to the experimental results presented in [302]. There are also some differences in the choice of neural network architecture. The work in Luong *et al.* used a uni-directional recurrent neural network, whereas that in Bahdanau *et al.* emphasizes the use of a bidirectional recurrent neural network.

Unlike the image captioning application of the previous section, the machine translation approach is a soft attention model. The hard attention setting seems to be inherently designed for reinforcement learning, whereas the soft attention setting is differentiable, and can be used with backpropagation. The work in [302] also proposes a local attention mechanism, which focuses on a small window of context. Such an approach shares some similarities with a hard mechanism for attention (like focusing on a small region of an image as discussed in the previous section). However, it is not completely a hard approach either because one focuses on a smaller portion of the sentence using the importance weighting generated by the attention mechanism. Such an approach is able to implement the local mechanism without incurring the training challenges of reinforcement learning.

10.3 Neural Networks with External Memory

In recent years, several related architectures have been proposed that augment neural networks with *persistent memory* in which the notion of memory is clearly separated from the computations, and one can control the ways in which computations selectively access and modify particular memory locations. The LSTM can be considered to have persistent memory, although it does not clearly separate the memory from the computations. This is because the computations in a neural network are tightly integrated with the values in the hidden states, which serve the role of storing the intermediate results of the computations.

Neural Turing machines are neural networks with *external memory*. The base neural network can read or write to the external memory and therefore plays the role of a controller in guiding the computation. With the exception of LSTMs, most neural networks do not have the concept of persistent memory over long time scales. In fact, the notions of computation and memory are not clearly separated in traditional neural networks (including LSTMs). The ability to manipulate persistent memory, when combined with a clear separation of memory from computations, leads to a *programmable computer* that can simulate algorithms from examples of the input and output. This principle has led to a number of related architectures such as *neural Turing machines* [158], *differentiable neural computers* [159], and *memory networks* [528].

Why is it useful to learn from examples of the input and output? Almost all general-purpose AI is based on the assumption of being able to simulate biological behaviors in which we only have examples of the input (e.g., sensory inputs) and outputs (e.g., actions), without a crisp definition of the algorithm/function that was actually computed by that set of behaviors. In order to understand the difficulty in learning from example, we will first begin with an example of a sorting application. Although the definitions and algorithms for sorting are both well-known and crisply defined, we explore a fantasy setting in which we do not have access to these definitions and algorithms. In other words, the algorithm starts with a setting in which it has no idea of what sorting looks like. It only has examples of inputs and their sorted outputs.

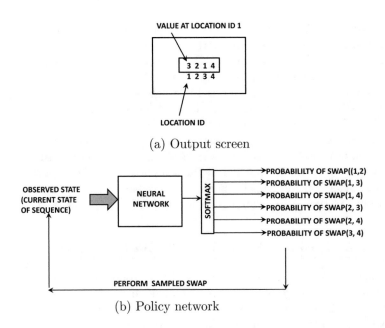

(a) Output screen

(b) Policy network

Figure 10.5: The output screen and policy network for learning the fantasy game of sorting

10.3.1   A Fantasy Video Game: Sorting by Example

Although it is a simple matter to sort a set of numbers using any known sorting algorithm (e.g., quicksort), the problem becomes more difficult if we are not told that the function of the algorithm is to sort the numbers. Rather, we are only given *examples* of pairs of scrambled inputs and sorted outputs, and we have to automatically learn *sequences of actions* for any given input, so that the output reflects what we have learned from the examples. The goal is, therefore, to learn to sort by example using a specific set of pre-defined actions. This is a generalized view of machine learning where our inputs and outputs can be in almost any format (e.g., pixels, sounds), and goal is to learn to transform from input to output by a sequence of *actions*. These actions are the elementary steps that we are allowed to perform in our algorithm. We can already see that this action-driven approach is closely related to the reinforcement learning methodologies discussed in Chapter 9.

For simplicity, consider the case in which we want to sort only sequences of four numbers, and therefore we have four positions on our "video game screen" containing the current status of the original sequence of numbers. The screen of the fantasy video game is shown in Figure 10.5(a). There are 6 possible actions that the video game player can perform, and each action is of the form SWAP(i, j), which swaps the content of locations i and j. Since there are four possible values of each of i and j, the total number of possible actions is given by $\binom{4}{2} = 6$. The objective of the video game is to sort the numbers by using as few swaps as possible. We want to construct an algorithm that plays this video game by choosing swaps judiciously. Furthermore, the machine learning algorithm is not seeded with the knowledge that the outputs are supposed to be sorted, and it only has examples of inputs and outputs in order to build a model that (ideally) learns a policy to convert inputs into their sorted versions. Further, the video game player is not shown the input-output pairs but only incentivised with rewards when they make "good swaps" that progress towards a proper sort.

This setting is almost identical to the *Atari* video game setting discussed in Chapter 9. For example, we can use a policy network in which the current sequence of four numbers as the input to the neural network and the output is a probability of each of the 6 possible actions. This architecture is shown in Figure 10.5(b). It is instructive to compare this architecture with the policy network in Figure 9.6 of Chapter 9. The advantage for each action can be modeled in a variety of heuristic ways. For example, a naive approach would be to roll out the policy for T swapping moves and set the reward to $+1$, if we are able to obtain the correct output by then, and to -1, otherwise. Using smaller values of T would tend to favor speed over accuracy. One can also define more refined reward functions in which the reward for a sequence of moves is defined by how much closer one gets to the known output.

Consider a situation in which the probability of action $a = \text{SWAP}(i, j)$ is $\pi(a)$ (as output by the softmax function of the neural network) and the advantage is $F(a)$. Then, in policy gradient methods, we set up an objective function J_a, which is the expected advantage of action a. As discussed in Section 9.5 of Chapter 9, the gradient of this advantage with respect to the parameters of the policy network is given by the following:

$$\nabla J_a = F(a) \cdot \nabla \log(\pi(a)) \tag{10.8}$$

This gradient is added up over a minibatch of actions from the various rollouts, and used to update the weights of the neural network. Here, it is interesting to note that reinforcement learning helps us in implementing a policy for an algorithm that learns from examples.

10.3.1.1 Implementing Swaps with Memory Operations

The above video game can also be implemented by a neural network in which the allowed operations are memory read/writes and we want to sort the sequence in as few memory read/writes as possible. For example, a candidate solution to this problem would be one in which the state of the sequence is maintained in an external memory with additional space to store temporary variables for swaps. As discussed below, swaps can be implemented easily with memory read/writes. A recurrent neural network can be used to copy the states from one time-stamp to the next. The operation $\text{SWAP}(i, j)$ can be implemented by first *reading* locations i and j from memory and storing them in temporary registers. The register for i can then be written to the location of j in memory, and that for j can be written to location for i. Therefore, a sequence of memory read-writes can be used to implement swaps. In other words, we could also implement a policy for sorting by training a "controller" recurrent network that decides which locations of memory to read from and write to. However, if we create a generalized architecture with memory-based operations, the controller might learn a more efficient policy than simply implementing swaps. Here, it is important to understand that it is useful to have some form of persistent memory that stores the current state of the sorted sequence. The states of a neural network, including a (vanilla) recurrent neural network, are simply too transient to store this type of information.

Greater memory availability increases the power and sophistication of the architecture. With smaller memory availability, the policy network might learn only a simple $O(n^2)$ algorithm using swaps. On the other hand, with larger memory availability, the policy network would be able to use memory reads and writes to synthesize a wider range of operations, and it might be able to learn a much faster sorting algorithm. After all, a reward function that credits a policy for getting the correct sort in T moves would tend to favor polices with fewer moves.

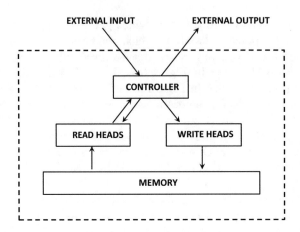

Figure 10.6: The neural Turing machine

10.3.2   Neural Turing Machines

A long-recognized weakness of neural networks is that they are unable to clearly separate the internal variables (i.e., hidden states) from the computations occurring inside the network, which causes the states to become transient (unlike biological or computer memory). A neural network in which we have an external memory and the ability to read and write to various locations in a controlled manner is very powerful, and provides a path to simulating general classes of algorithms that can be implemented on modern computers. Such an architecture is referred to as a neural Turing machine or a *differentiable neural computer*. It is referred to as a *differentiable* neural computer, because it learns to simulate algorithms (which make discrete sequences of steps) with the use of continuous optimization. Continuous optimization has the advantage of being *differentiable*, and therefore one can use backpropagation to learn optimized algorithmic steps on the input.

It is noteworthy that traditional neural networks also have memory in terms of their hidden states, and in the specific case of an LSTM, some of these hidden states are designed to be persistent. However, neural Turing machines clearly distinguish between the external memory and the hidden states within the neural network. The hidden states within the neural network can be viewed in a similar way to CPU registers that are used for transitory computation, whereas the external memory is used for persistent computation. The external memory provides the neural Turing machine to perform computations in a more similar way to how human programmers manipulate data on modern computers. This property often gives neural Turing machines much better generalizability in the learning process, as compared to somewhat similar models like LSTMs. This approach also provides a path to defining persistent data structures that are well separated from neural computations. The inability to clearly separate the program variables from computational operations has long been recognized as one of the key weaknesses of traditional neural networks.

The broad architecture of a neural Turing machine is shown in Figure 10.6. At the heart of the neural Turing machine is a controller, which is implemented using some form of a recurrent neural network (although other alternatives are possible). The recurrent architecture is useful in order to carry over the state from one time-step to the next, as the neural Turing machine implements any particular algorithm or policy. For example, in our sorting game, the current state of the sequence of numbers is carried over from one step to the next. In each time-step, it receives inputs from the environment, and writes outputs to the environment. Furthermore, it has an external memory to which it can read and write with the use of reading and writing *heads*. The memory is structured as an $N \times m$ matrix in which there are N memory cells, each of which is of length m. At the tth time-stamp, the m-dimensional vector in the ith row of the memory is denoted by $\overline{M}_t(i)$.

The heads output a special *weight* $w_t(i) \in (0,1)$ associated with each location i at time-stamp t that controls the degree to which it reads and writes to each output location. In other words, if the read head outputs a weight of 0.1, then it interprets anything read from the ith memory location after scaling it with 0.1 and adds up the weighted reads over different values of i. The weight of the write head is also defined in an analogous way for writing, and more details are given later. Note that the weight uses the time-stamp t as a subscript; therefore a separate set of weights is emitted at each time-stamp t. In our earlier example of swaps, this weight is like the softmax probability of a swap in the sorting video game, so that a discrete action is converted to a soft and differentiable value. However, one difference is that the neural Turing machine is not defined stochastically like the policy network of the previous section. In other words, we do not use the weight $w_t(i)$ to sample a memory cell stochastically; rather, it defines how much we read from or erase the contents of that cell. It is sometimes helpful to view each update as the expected amount by which a stochastic policy would have read or updated it. In the following, we provide a more formal description.

If the weights $w_t(i)$ have been defined, then the m-dimensional vector at location i can be read as a weighted combination of the vectors in different memory locations:

$$r_t = \sum_{i=1}^{N} w_t(i)\overline{M}_t(i) \tag{10.9}$$

The weights $w_t(i)$ are defined in such a way that they sum to 1 over all N memory vectors (like probabilities):

$$\sum_{i=1}^{N} w_t(i) = 1 \tag{10.10}$$

The writing is based on the principle of making changes by first erasing a portion of the memory and then adding to it. Therefore, in the ith time-stamp, the write head emits a weighting vector $w_t(i)$ together with length-m erase- and add-vectors $\overline{e}_t$ and $\overline{a}_t$, respectively. Then, the update to a cell is given by a combination of an erase and an addition. First the erase operation is performed:

$$\overline{M}'_t(i) \Leftarrow \underbrace{\overline{M}_{t-1}(i) \odot (1 - w_t(i)\overline{e}_t(i))}_{\text{Partial Erase}} \tag{10.11}$$

Here, the $\odot$ symbol indicates elementwise multiplication across the m dimensions of the ith row of the memory matrix. Each element in the erase vector $\overline{e}_t$ is drawn from $(0,1)$. The m-dimensional erase vector gives fine-grained control to the choice of the elements from the m-dimensional row that can be erased. It is also possible to have multiple write heads, and the order in which multiplication is performed using the different heads does not matter because multiplication is both commutative and associative. Subsequently, additions can be performed:

$$\overline{M}_t(i) = \underbrace{\overline{M}'_t(i) + w_t(i)\overline{a}_t}_{\text{Partial Add}} \tag{10.12}$$

If multiple write heads are present, then the order of the addition operations does not matter. However, all erases must be done before all additions to ensure a consistent result irrespective of the order of additions.

Note that the changes to the cell are extremely gentle by virtue of the fact that the weights sum to 1. One can view the above update as having an intuitively similar effect as stochastically picking one of the N rows of the memory (with probability $w_t(i)$) and then sampling individual elements (with probabilities $\overline{e}_t$) to change them. However, such updates are not differentiable (unless one chooses to parameterize them using policy-gradient tricks from reinforcement learning). Here, we settle for a soft update, where all cells are changed slightly, so that the differentiability of the updates is retained. Furthermore, if there are multiple write heads, it will lead to more aggressive updates. One can also view these weights in an analogous way to how information is selectively exchanged between the hidden states and the memory states in an LSTM with the use of sigmoid functions to regulate the amount read or written into each long-term memory location (cf. Chapter 7).

Weightings as Addressing Mechanisms

The weightings can be viewed in a similar way to how addressing mechanisms work. For example, one might have chosen to sample the ith row of the memory matrix with probability $w_t(i)$ to read or write it, which is a *hard* mechanism. The soft addressing mechanism of the neural Turing machine is somewhat different in that we are reading from and writing to all cells, but changing them by tiny amounts. So far, we have not discussed *how* this addressing mechanism of setting $w_t(i)$ works. The addressing can be done either by content or by location.

In the case of addressing by content, a vector $\overline{v}_t$ of length-m, which is the *key vector*, is used to weight locations based on their dot-product similarity to $\overline{v}_t$. An exponential mechanism is used for regulating the importance of the dot-product similarity in the weighting:

$$w_t^c(i) = \frac{\exp(\text{cosine}(\overline{v}_t, \overline{M}_t(i)))}{\sum_{j=1}^{N} \exp(\text{cosine}(\overline{v}_t \cdot \overline{M}_t(j)))} \tag{10.13}$$

Note that we have added a superscript ro $w_t^c(i)$ to indicate that it is a purely content-centric weighting mechanism. Further flexibility is obtained by using a temperature parameter within the exponents to adjust the level of sharpness of the addressing. For example, if we use the temperature parameter β_t, the weights can be computed as follows:

$$w_t^c(i) = \frac{\exp(\beta_t \text{cosine}(\overline{v}_t, \overline{M}_t(i)))}{\sum_{j=1}^{N} \exp(\beta_t \text{cosine}(\overline{v}_t \cdot \overline{M}_t(j)))} \tag{10.14}$$

Increasing β_t makes the approach more like hard addressing, while reducing β_t is like soft addressing. If one wants to use only content-based addressing, then one can use $w_t(i) = w_t^c(i)$ for the addressing. Note that pure content-based addressing is almost like random access. For example, if the content of a memory location $\overline{M}_t(i)$ includes its location, then a key-based retrieval is like soft random access of memory.

A second method of addressing is by using sequential addressing with respect to the location in the previous time-stamp. This approach is referred to as location-based addressing. In location-based addressing, the value of the content weight $w_t^c(i)$ in the current iteration, and the final weights $w_{t-1}(i)$ in the previous iteration are used as starting points. First, *interpolation* mixes a partial level of random access into the location accessed in the previous iteration (via the content weight), and then a *shifting* operation adds an element of sequential access. Finally, the softness of the addressing is *sharpened* with a temperature-like parameter. The entire process of location-based addressing uses the following steps:

$$\text{Content Weights}(\overline{v}_t, \beta_t) \Rightarrow \text{Interpolation}(g_t) \Rightarrow \text{Shift}(\overline{s}_t) \Rightarrow \text{Sharpen}(\gamma_t)$$

Each of these operations uses some outputs from the controller as input parameters, which are shown above with the corresponding operation. Since the creation of the content weights $w_t^c(i)$ has already been discussed, we explain the other three steps:

1. *Interpolation:* In this case, the vector from the previous iteration is combined with the content weights $w_t^c(i)$ created in the current iteration using a single interpolation weight $g_t \in (0,1)$ that are output by the controller. Therefore, we have:

$$w_t^g(i) = g_t \cdot w_t^c(i) + (1 - g_t) \cdot w_{t-1}(i) \tag{10.15}$$

Note that if g_t is 0, then the content is not used at all.

2. *Shift:* In this case, a rotational shift is performed in which a normalized vector over integer shifts is used. For example, consider a situation where $s_t[-1] = 0.2$, $s_t[0] = 0.5$ and $s_t[1] = 0.3$. This means that the weights should shift by -1 with gating weight 0.2, and by 1 with gating weight 0.3. Therefore, we define the shifted vector $w_t^s(i)$ as follows:

$$w_t^s(i) = \sum_{i=1}^{N} w_t^g(i) \cdot s_t[i - j] \tag{10.16}$$

Here, the index of $s_t[i - j]$ is applied in combination with the modulus function to adjust it back to between -1 and $+1$ (or other integer range in which $s_t[i - j]$ is defined).

3. *Sharpening:* The process of sharpening simply takes the current set of weights, and makes them more biased towards 0 or 1, values without changing their ordering. A parameter $\gamma_t \geq 1$ is used for the sharpening, where larger values of γ_t create shaper values:

$$w_t(i) = \frac{[w_t^s(i)]^{\gamma_t}}{\sum_{j=1}^{N} [w_t^s(j)]^{\gamma_t}} \tag{10.17}$$

The parameter γ_t plays a similar role as the temperature parameter β_t in the case of content-based weight sharpening. This type of sharpening is important because the shifting mechanism introduces a certain level of blurriness to the weights.

The purpose of these steps is as follows. First, one can use a purely content-based mechanism by using a gating weight g_t of 1. One can view a content-based mechanism as a kind of random access to memory with the key vector. Using the weight vector $w_{t-1}(i)$ in the previous iteration within the interpolation has the purpose of enabling sequential access from the reference point of the previous step. The shift vector defines how much we are willing to move from the reference point provided by the interpolation vector. Finally, sharpening helps us control the level of softness of addressing.

Architecture of Controller

An important design choice is that of the choice of the neural architecture in the controller. A natural choice is to use a recurrent neural network in which there is already a notion of temporal states. Furthermore, using an LSTM provides additional internal memory to the external memory in the neural Turing machine. The states within the neural network are like CPU registers that are used for internal computation, but they are not persistent (unlike the external memory). It is noteworthy that once we have a concept of external memory, it is not absolutely essential to use a recurrent network. This is because the memory can capture the notion of states; reading and writing from the same set of locations over successive time-stamps achieves temporal statefulness, as in a recurrent neural network. Therefore, it is also possible to use a feed-forward neural network for the controller, which offers better transparency compared to the hidden states in the controller. The main constraint in the feed-forward architecture is that the number of read and write heads constrain the number of operations in each time-stamp.

Comparisons with Recurrent Neural Networks and LSTMs

All recurrent neural networks are known to be *Turing complete* [444], which means that they can be used to simulate any algorithm. Therefore, neural Turing machines do not *theoretically* add to the inherent capabilities of any recurrent neural network (including an LSTM). However, despite the Turing completeness of recurrent networks, there are severe limitations to their practical performance as well as generalization power on data sets containing longer sequences. For example, if we train a recurrent network on sequences of a certain size, and then apply on test data with a different size distribution, the performance will be poor.

The controlled form of the external memory access in a neural Turing machine provides it with practical advantages over a recurrent neural network in which the values in the transient hidden states are tightly integrated with computations. Although an LSTM is augmented with its own internal memory, which is somewhat resistant to updates, the processes of computation and memory access are still not clearly separated (like a modern computer). In fact, the amount of computation (i.e., number of activations) and the amount of memory (i.e., number of hidden units) are also tightly integrated in all recurrent neural networks. Clean separation between memory and computations allows control on the memory operations in a more interpretable way, which is at least somewhat similar to how a human programmer accesses and writes to internal data structures. For example, in a question-answering system, we want to be able to able to read a passage and then answer questions about it; this requires much better control in terms of being able to read the story into memory in some form.

An experimental comparison in [158] showed that the neural Turing machine works better with much longer sequences of inputs as compared to the LSTM. One of these experiments provided both the LSTM and the neural Turing machine with pairs of input/output sequences that were identical. The goal was to copy the input to the output. In this case, the neural Turing machine generally performed better as compared to the LSTM, especially when the inputs were long. Unlike the un-interpretable LSTM, the operations in the memory network were far more interpretable, and the copying algorithm implicitly learned by the neural Turing machine performed steps that were similar to how a human programmer would perform the task. As a result, the copying algorithm could generalize even to longer sequences than were seen during training time in the case of the neural Turing machine (but not so much in the case of the LSTM). In a sense, the intuitive way in which a neural Turing machine handles memory updates from one time-stamp to the next provides it a helpful regularization. For example, if the copying algorithm of the neural Turing machine mimics a human coder's style of implementing a copying algorithm, it will do a better job with longer sequences at test time.

In addition, the neural Turing machine was experimentally shown to be good at the task of *associative recall,* in which the input is a sequence of items together with a randomly chosen item from this sequence. The output is the next item in the sequence. The neural Turing machine was again able to learn this task better than an LSTM. In addition, a sorting application was also implemented in [158]. Although most of these applications are relatively simple, this work is notable for its *potential* in using more carefully tuned architectures to perform complex tasks. One such enhancement was the differentiable neural computer [159], which has been used for complex tasks of reasoning in graphs and natural languages. Such tasks are difficult to accomplish with a traditional recurrent network.

10.3.3 Differentiable Neural Computer: A Brief Overview

The differentiable neural computer is an enhancement over the neural Turing machines with the use of additional structures to manage memory allocation and keeping track of temporal sequences of writes. These enhancements address two main weaknesses of neural Turing machines:

1. Even though the neural Turing machine is able to perform both content- and location-based addressing, there is no way of avoiding the fact that it writes on overlapping blocks when it uses shift-based mechanisms to address contiguous blocks of locations. In modern computers, this issue is resolved by proper memory allocation during running time. The differentiable neural computer incorporates memory allocation mechanisms within the architecture.

2. The neural Turing machine does not keep track of the order in which memory locations are written. Keeping track of the order in which memory locations are written is useful in many cases such as keeping track of a sequence of instructions.

In the following, we will discuss only a brief overview of how these two additional mechanisms are implemented. For more detailed discussions of these mechanisms, we refer the reader to [159].

The memory allocation mechanism in a differentiable neural computer is based on the concepts that (i) locations that have just been written but not read yet are probably useful, and that (ii) the reading of a location reduces its usefulness. The memory allocation mechanism keeps track of a quantity referred to as the *usage* of a location. The usage of a location is automatically increased after each write, and it is potentially decreased after a read. Before writing to memory, the controller emits a set of free gates from each read head that determine whether the most recently read locations should be freed. These are then used to update the usage vector from the previous time-stamp. The work in [159] discusses a number of algorithms for how these usage values are used to identify locations for writing.

The second issue addressed by the differentiable neural computer is in terms of how it keeps track of the sequential ordering of the memory locations at which the writes are performed. Here, it is important to understand that the writes to the memory locations are soft, and therefore one cannot define a strict ordering. Rather, a soft ordering exists between all pairs of locations. Therefore, an $N \times N$ temporal link matrix with entries $L_t[i, j]$ is maintained. The value of $L_t[i, j]$ always lie in the range $(0, 1)$ and it indicates the degree to which row i of the $N \times m$ memory matrix was written to just after row j. In order to update the temporal link matrix, a precedence weighting is defined over the locations in the memory rows. Specifically, $p_t(i)$ defines the degree to which location i was the last one written to at the tth time-stamp. This precedence relation is used to update the temporal link matrix in each time-stamp. Although the temporal link matrix potentially requires $O(N^2)$ space, it is very sparse and can therefore be stored in $O(N \cdot \log(N))$ space. The reader is referred to [159] for additional details of the maintenance of the temporal link matrix.

It is noteworthy that many of the ideas of neural Turing machines, memory networks, and attention mechanisms are closely related. The first two ideas were independently proposed at about the same time. The initial papers on these topics tested them on different tasks. For example, the neural Turing machine was tested on simple tasks like copying or sorting, whereas the memory network was tested on tasks like question-answering. However, this difference was also blurred at a later stage, when the differentiable neural computer was tested on the question-answering tasks. Broadly speaking, these applications are still in their infancy, and a lot needs to be done to bring them to a level where they can be commercially used.

10.4 Generative Adversarial Networks (GANs)

Before introducing generative adversarial networks, we will first discuss the notions of the *generative* and *discriminative* models, because they are both used for creating such networks. These two types of learning models are as follows:

1. *Discriminative models:* Discriminative models directly estimate the conditional probability $P(y|\overline{X})$ of the label y, given the feature values in $\overline{X}$. An example of a discriminative model is logistic regression.

2. *Generative models:* Generative models estimate the joint probability $P(\overline{X}, y)$, which is a generative probability of a data instance. Note that the joint probability can be used to estimate the conditional probability of y given $\overline{X}$ by using the Bayes rule as follows:

$$P(y|\overline{X}) = \frac{P(\overline{X}, y)}{P(\overline{X})} = \frac{P(\overline{X}, y)}{\sum_z P(\overline{X}, z)} \qquad (10.18)$$

An example of a generative model is the naïve Bayes classifier.

Discriminative models can only be used in supervised settings, whereas generative models are used in both supervised and unsupervised settings. For example, in a multiclass setting, one can create a generative model of only one of the classes by defining an appropriate prior distribution on that class and then sampling from the prior distribution to generate examples of the class. Similarly, one can generate each point in the entire data set from a particular distribution by using a probabilistic model with a particular prior. Such an approach is used in the variational autoencoder (cf. Section 4.10.4 of Chapter 4) in order to sample points from a Gaussian distribution (as a prior) and then use these samples as input to the decoder in order to generate samples like the data.

Generative adversarial networks work with two neural network models simultaneously. The first is a generative model that produces synthetic examples of objects that are similar to a real repository of examples. Furthermore, the goal is to create synthetic objects that are so realistic that it is impossible for a trained observer to distinguish whether a particular object belongs to the original data set, or whether it was generated synthetically. For example, if we have a repository of car images, the generative network will use the generative model to create synthetic examples of car images. As a result, we will now end up with both real and fake examples of car images. The second network is a discriminative network that has been trained on a data set which is labeled with the fact of whether the images are synthetic or fake. The discriminative model takes in inputs of either real examples from the base data or synthetic objects created by the generator network, and tries to discern as to whether the objects are real or fake. In a sense, one can view the generative network as a "counterfeiter" trying to produce fake notes, and the discriminative network as the "police" who is trying to catch the counterfeiter producing fake notes. Therefore, the two networks are adversaries, and training makes both adversaries better, until an equilibrium is reached between them. As we will see later, this adversarial approach to training boils down to formulating a minimax problem.

When the discriminative network is correctly able to flag a synthetic object as fake, the fact is used by the generative network to modify its weights, so that the discriminative network will have a harder time classifying samples generated from it. After modifying the weights of the generator network, new samples are generated from it, and the process is repeated. Over time, the generative network gets better and better at producing counterfeits. Eventually, it becomes impossible for the discriminator to distinguish between real and synthetically generated objects. In fact, it can be formally shown that the *Nash equilibrium* of this minimax game is a (generator) parameter setting in which the distribution of points created by the generator is the same as that of the data samples. For the approach to work well, it is important for the discriminator to be a high-capacity model, and also have access to a lot of data.

The generated objects are often useful for creating large amounts of synthetic data for machine learning algorithms, and may play a useful role in data augmentation. Furthermore, by adding context, it is possible to use this approach for generating objects with different properties. For example, the input might be a text caption, such as "*spotted cat with collar*," and the output will be a fantasy image matching the description [331, 392]. The generated objects are sometimes also used for artistic endeavors. Recently, these methods have also found application in image-to-image translation. In image-to-image translation, the missing characteristics of an image are completed in a realistic way. Before discussing the applications, we will first discuss the details of training a generative adversarial network.

10.4.1 Training a Generative Adversarial Network

The training process of a generative adversarial network proceeds by alternately updating the parameters of the generator and the discriminator. Both the generator and discriminator are neural networks. The discriminator is a neural network with d-dimensional inputs and a single output in $(0, 1)$, which indicates the probability whether or not the d-dimensional input example is real. A value of 1 indicates that the example is real, and a value of 0 indicates that the example is synthetic. Let the output of the discriminator for input $\overline{X}$ be denoted by $D(\overline{X})$.

The generator takes as input noise samples from a p-dimensional probability distribution, and uses it to generate d-dimensional examples of the data. One can view the generator in an analogous way to the decoder portion of a variational autoencoder (cf. Section 4.10.4 of Chapter 4), in which the input distribution is a p-dimensional point drawn from a Gaussian distribution (which is the *prior* distribution), and the output of the decoder is a d-dimensional data point with a similar distribution as the real examples. The training process here is, however, very different from that in a variational autoencoder. Instead of using the reconstruction error for training, the discriminator error is used to train the generator to create other samples like the input data distribution.

The goal for the discriminator is to correctly classify the real examples to a label of 1, and the synthetically generated examples to a label of 0. On the other hand, the goal for the generator is generate examples so that they fool the discriminator (i.e., encourage the discriminator to label such examples as 1). Let R_m be m randomly sampled examples from the real data set, and S_m be m synthetic samples that are generated by using the generator. Note that the synthetic samples are generated by first creating a set N_m of p-dimensional noise samples $\{\overline{Z}_m \ldots \overline{Z}_m\}$, and then applying the generator to these noise samples as the input to create the data samples $S_m = \{G(\overline{Z}_1) \ldots G(\overline{Z}_m)\}$. Therefore, the *maximization* objective function J_D for the discriminator is as follows:

$$\text{Maximize}_D \ J_D = \underbrace{\sum_{\overline{X} \in R_m} \log\left[D(\overline{X})\right]}_{m \text{ samples of real examples}} + \underbrace{\sum_{\overline{X} \in S_m} \log\left[1 - D(\overline{X})\right]}_{m \text{ samples of synthetic examples}}$$

It is easy to verify that this objective function will be maximized when real examples are correctly classified to 1 and synthetic examples are correctly classified to 0.

Next we define the objective function of the generator, whose goal is to fool the discriminator. For the generator, we do not care about the real examples, because the generator only cares about the sample it generates. The generator creates m synthetic samples, S_m, and the goal is to ensure that the discriminator recognizes these examples as genuine ones. Therefore, the generator objective function, J_G, *minimizes* the likelihood that these samples are flagged as synthetic, which results in the following optimization problem:

$$\text{Minimize}_G \ J_G = \underbrace{\sum_{\overline{X} \in S_m} \log\left[1 - D(\overline{X})\right]}_{m \text{ samples of synthetic examples}}$$

$$= \sum_{\overline{Z} \in N_m} \log\left[1 - D(G(\overline{Z}))\right]$$

This objective function is minimized when the synthetic examples are incorrectly classified to 1. By minimizing the objective function, we are effectively trying to learn parameters of the generator that fool the discriminator into incorrectly classifying the synthetic examples to be true samples from the data set. An alternative objective function for the generator is to maximize $\log\left[D(\overline{X})\right]$ for each $\overline{X} \in S_m$ instead of minimizing $\log\left[1 - D(\overline{X})\right]$, and this alternative objective function sometimes works better during the early iterations of optimization.

The overall optimization problem is therefore formulated as a minimax game over J_D. Note that maximizing J_G over different choices of the parameters in the generator G is the same as maximizing J_D because $J_D - J_G$ does not include any of the parameters of the generator G. Therefore, one can write the overall optimization problem (over both generator and discriminator) as follows:

$$\text{Minimize}_G \ \text{Maximize}_D \ J_D \tag{10.19}$$

The result of such an optimization is a *saddle point* of the optimization problem. Examples of what saddle points look like with respect to the topology of the loss function are shown[1] in Figure 3.17 of Chapter 3.

---

[1]The examples in Chapter 3 are given in a different context. Nevertheless, if we pretend that the loss function in Figure 3.17(b) represents J_D, then the annotated saddle point in the figure is visually instructive.

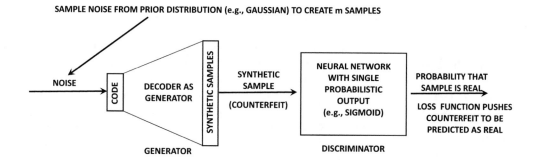

Figure 10.7: Hooked up configuration of generator and discriminator for performing gradient-descent updates on generator

Stochastic gradient ascent is used for learning the parameters of the discriminator and stochastic gradient descent is used for learning the parameters of the generator. The gradient update steps are alternated between the generator and the discriminator. In practice, however, k steps of the discriminator are used for each step of the generator. Therefore, one can describe the gradient update steps as follows:

1. **(Repeat k times):** A mini-batch of size $2 \cdot m$ is constructed with an equal number of real and synthetic examples. The synthetic examples are created by inputting noise samples to the generator from the prior distribution, whereas the real samples are selected from the base data set. Stochastic gradient ascent is performed on the parameters of the discriminator so as the maximize the likelihood that the discriminator correctly classifies both the real and synthetic examples. For each update step, this is achieved by performing backpropagation on the discriminator network with respect to the mini-batch of $2 \cdot m$ real/synthetic examples.

2. **(Perform once):** Hook up the discriminator at the end of the generator as shown in Figure 10.7. Provide the generator with m noise inputs so as to create m synthetic examples (which is the current mini-batch). Perform stochastic gradient descent on the parameters of the generator so as to minimize the likelihood that the discriminator correctly classifies the synthetic examples. The minimization of $\log\left[1 - D(\overline{X})\right]$ in the loss function explicitly encourages these counterfeits to be predicted as real.

   Even though the discriminator is hooked up to the generator, the gradient updates (during backpropagation) are performed with respect to the parameters of only the generator network. Backpropagation will automatically compute the gradients with respect to both the generator and discriminator networks for this hooked up configuration, but only the parameters of the generator network are updated.

The value of k is typically small (less than 5), although it is also possible to use $k = 1$. This iterative process is repeated to convergence until Nash equilibrium is reached. At this point, the discriminator will be unable to distinguish between the real and synthetic examples.

There are a few factors that one needs to be careful of during the training. First, if the generator is trained too much without updating the discriminator, it can lead to a situation in which the generator repeatedly produces very similar samples. In other words, there will be very little diversity between the samples produced by the generator. This is the reason that the training of the generator and discriminator are done simultaneously with interleaving.

Second, the generator will produce poor samples in early iterations and therefore $D(\overline{X})$ will be close to 0. As a result, the loss function will be close to 0, and its gradient will be quite modest. This type is saturation causes slow training of the generator parameters. In such cases, it makes sense to maximize $\log\left[D(\overline{X})\right]$ instead of minimizing $\log\left[1 - D(\overline{X})\right]$ during the early stages of training of the generator parameters. Although this approach is heuristically motivated, and one can no longer write a minimax formulation like Equation 10.19, it tends to work well in practice (especially in the early stages of the training when the discriminator rejects all samples).

10.4.2   Comparison with Variational Autoencoder

The variational autoencoder and the generative adversarial network were developed independently at around the same time. There are some interesting similarities and differences between these two models. This section will discusses a comparison of these two models.

Unlike a variational autoencoder, only a decoder (i.e., generator) is learned, and an encoder is not learned in the training process of the generative adversarial network. Therefore, a generative adversarial network is not designed to reconstruct specific input samples like a variational autoencoder. However, both models can generate images like the base data, because the hidden space has a known structure (typically Gaussian) from which points can be sampled. In general, the generative adversarial network produces samples of better quality (e.g., less blurry images) than a variational autoencoder. This is because the adversarial approach is specifically designed to produce realistic images, whereas the regularization of the variational autoencoder actually hurts the quality of the generated objects. Furthermore, when reconstruction error is used to create an output for a specific image in the variational autoencoder, it forces the model to average over all plausible outputs. Averaging over plausible outputs, which are often slightly shifted from one another, is a direct cause of blurriness. On the other hand, a method that is specifically designed to produce objects of a quality that fool the discriminator will create a single object in which the different portions are in harmony with one another (and therefore more realistic).

The variational autoencoder is methodologically quite different from the generative adversarial network. The re-parametrization approach used by the variational autoencoder is very useful for training networks with a stochastic nature. Such an approach has the potential to be used in other types of neural network settings with a generative hidden layer. In recent years, some of the ideas in the variational autoencoder have been combined with the ideas in generative adversarial networks.

10.4.3   Using GANs for Generating Image Data

GAN is commonly used is for generating image objects with varying types of context. Indeed, the image setting is, by far, the most common use case of GANs. The generator for the image setting is referred to as a *deconvolutional network*. The most popular way to design a deconvolutional network for the GAN is discussed in [384]. Therefore, the corresponding GAN is also referred to as a DCGAN. It is noteworthy that the term "deconvolution" has generally been replaced by transposed convolution in recent years, because the former term is somewhat misleading.

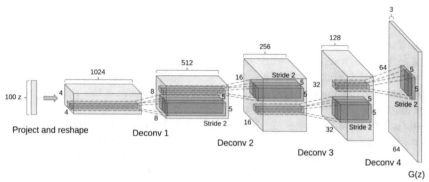

(a) Convolution architecture of DCGAN

(b) Smooth image transitions caused by changing input noise are shown in each row

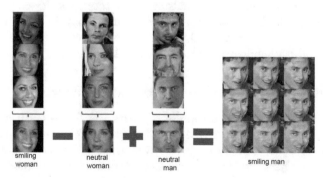

(c) Arithmetic operations on input noise have semantic significance

Figure 10.8: The convolutional architecture of DCGAN and generated images. These figures appeared in [A. Radford, L. Metz, and S. Chintala. Unsupervised representation learning with deep convolutional generative adversarial networks. *arXiv preprint arXiv:1511.06434*, 2015]. ©2015 Alec Radford. Used with permission.

The work in [384] starts with 100-dimensional Gaussian noise, which is the starting point of the decoder. This 100-dimensional Gaussian noise is reshaped into 1024 feature maps of size 4×4. This is achieved with a fully connected matrix multiplication with the 100-dimensional input, and the result is reshaped into a tensor. Subsequently, the depth of each layer reduces by a factor of 2, while increasing the lengths and widths by a factor of 2. For example, the second layer contains 512 feature maps, whereas the third layer contains 256 feature maps.

However, increasing length and width with convolution seems odd, because a convolution with even a stride of 1 tends to reduce spatial map size (unless one uses additional zero padding). So how can one use convolutions to increase lengths and widths by a factor of 2? This is achieved by using *fractionally strided convolutions* or *transposed convolutions* at a fractional value of 0.5. These types of transposed convolutions are described at the end of Section 8.5.2 of Chapter 8. The case of fractional strides is not very different from unit strides, and it can be conceptually viewed as a convolution performed after stretching the input volume spatially by either inserting zeros between rows/columns or by inserted interpolated values. Since the input volume is already stretched by a particular factor, applying convolution with stride 1 on this input is equivalent to using fractional strides on the original input. An alternative to the approach of fractionally strided convolutions is to use pooling and unpooling in order to manipulate the spatial footprints. When fractionally strided convolutions are used, no pooling or unpooling needs to be used. An overview of the architecture of the generator in DCGAN is given in Figure 10.8. A detailed discussion of the convolution arithmetic required for fractionally strided convolutions is available in [109].

The generated images are sensitive to the noise samples. Figure 10.8(b) shows examples of the images are generated using the different noise samples. An interesting example is shown in the sixth row in which a room without a window is gradually transformed into one with a large window [384]. Such smooth transitions are also observed in the case of the variational autoencoder. The noise samples are also amenable to vector arithmetic, which is semantically interpretable. For example, one would subtract a noise sample of a neutral woman from that of a smiling woman and add the noise sample of a smiling man. This noise sample is input to the generator in order to obtain an image sample of a smiling man. This example [384] is shown in Figure 10.8(c).

The discriminator also uses a convolutional neural network architecture, except that the leaky ReLU was used instead of the ReLU. The final convolutional layer of the discriminator is flattened and fed into a single sigmoid output. Fully connected layers were not used in either the generator or the discriminator. As is common in convolutional neural networks, the ReLU activation is used. Batch normalization was used in order to reduce any problems with the vanishing and exploding gradient problems [214].

10.4.4 Conditional Generative Adversarial Networks

In conditional adversarial generative networks (CGANs), both the generator and the discriminator are conditioned on an additional input object, which might be a label, a caption, or even another object of the same type. In this case, the input typically correspond to *associated pairs of target objects and contexts*. The contexts are typically related to the target objects in some domain-specific way, which is learned by the model. For example, a context such as *"smiling girl"* might provide an image of a smiling girl. Here, it is important to note that there are many possible choices of images that the CGAN can create for smiling girls, and the specific choice depends on the value of the noise input. Therefore, the CGAN can create a universe of target objects, based on its creativity and imagination. In general, if

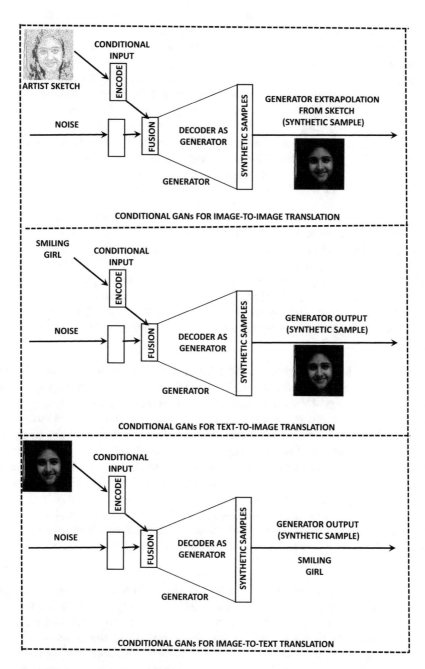

Figure 10.9: Different types of conditional generators for adversarial network. The examples are only illustrative in nature, and they do not reflect actual CGAN output.

the context is more complex than the target output, this universe of target objects tends to shrink, and it is even possible for the generator to output fixed objects irrespective of the noise input to the generator. Therefore, it is more common for the contextual inputs to be simpler than the objects being modeled. For example, it is more common for the context to be a caption and the object to be an image, rather than the converse. Nevertheless, both situations are technically possible.

Examples of different types of conditioning in conditional GANs are shown in Figure 10.9. The context provides the additional input needed for the conditioning. In general, the context may be of any object data type, and the generated output may be of any other data type. The more interesting cases of CGAN use are those in which the context contains much less complexity (e.g., a caption) as compared to the generated output (e.g., image). In such cases, CGANs show a certain level of creativity in filling in missing details. These details can change depending on the noise input to the generator. Some examples of the object-context pairs may be as follows:

1. Each object may be associated with a label. The label provides the conditioning for generating images. For example, in the MNIST data set (cf. Chapter 1), the conditioning might be a label value from 0 to 9, and the generator is expected to create an image of that digit, when provided that conditioning. Similarly, for an image data set, the conditioning might be a label like *"carrot"* and the output would be an image of a carrot. The experiments in the original work on conditional adversarial nets [331] generated a 784-dimensional representation of a digit based on a label from 0 to 9. The base examples of the digits were obtained from the MNIST data set (cf. Section 1.8.1 of Chapter 1).

2. The target object and its context might be of the same type, although the context might be missing the rich level of detail in the target object. For example, the context might be a human artist's sketch of a purse, and the target object might be an actual photograph of the same purse with all details filled in. Another example could be an artist's sketch of a criminal suspect (which is the context), and the target object (output of generator) could be an extrapolation of the actual photograph of the person. The goal is to use a given sketch to generate various realistic samples with details filled in. Such an example is illustrated in the top part of Figure 10.9. When the contextual objects have complex representations such as images or text sentences, they may need to be converted to a multidimensional representation with an encoder, so that they can be fused with multidimensional Gaussian noise. This encoder might be a convolutional network in the case of image context or a recurrent neural network or *word2vec* model in the case of text context.

3. Each object might be associated with a textual description (e.g., image with caption), and the latter provides the context. The caption provides the conditioning for the object. The idea is that by providing a context like *"blue bird with sharp claws,"* the generator should provide a fantasy image that reflects this description. An example of an illustrative image generated using the context *"smiling girl"* is illustrated in Figure 10.9. Note that it is also possible to use an image context, and generate a caption for it using a GAN, as shown in the bottom of the figure. However, it is more common to generate complex objects (e.g., images) from simpler contexts (e.g., captions) rather than the reverse. This is because a variety of more accurate supervised learning methods are available when one is trying to generate simple objects (e.g., labels or captions) from complex objects (e.g., images).

4. The base object might be a photograph or video in black and white (e.g., classic movie), and the output object might be the color version of the object. In essence, the GAN learns from examples of such pairs what is the most realistic way of coloring a black-and-white scene. For example, it will use the colors of trees in the training data to give corresponding colors in the generated object without changing its basic outline.

In all these cases, it is evident that GANs are very good at *filling in missing information.* The unconditional GAN is a special case of this setting in which all forms of context are missing, and therefore the GAN is forced to create an image without any information. The conditional case is potentially more interesting from an application-centric point of view because one often has setting where a small amount of partial information is available, and one must extrapolate in a realistic way. When the amount of available context is very small, missing data analysis methods will not work because they require significantly more context to provide reconstructions. On other hand, GANs do not promise faithful reconstructions (like autoencoders or matrix factorization methods), but they provide realistic extrapolations in which missing details are filled into the object in a realistic and harmonious way. As a result, the GAN uses this freedom to generate samples of high quality, rather than a blurred estimation of the average reconstruction. Although a given generation may not perfectly reflect a given context, one can always generate multiple samples in order to explore different types of extrapolations of the same context. For example, given the sketch of a criminal suspect, one might generate different photographs with varying details that are not present in the sketch. In this sense, generative adversarial networks exhibit a certain level of artistry/creativity that is not present in conventional data reconstruction methods. This type of creativity is essential when one is working with only a small amount of context to begin with, and therefore the model needs to be have sufficient freedom to fill in missing details in a reasonable way.

It is noteworthy that a wide variety of machine learning problems (including classification) can be viewed as missing data imputation problems. Technically, the CGAN can be used for these problems as well. However, the CGAN is more useful for specific types of missing data, where the missing portion is too large to be faithfully reconstructed by the model. Although one can even use a CGAN for classification or image captioning, this is obviously not the best use[2] of the generator model, which is tailored towards generative creativity. When the conditioning object is more complex as compared to the output object, it is possible to get into situations where the CGAN generates a fixed output irrespective of input noise.

In the case of the generator, the inputs correspond to a point generated from the noise distribution and the conditional object, which are combined to create a single hidden code. This input is fed into the generator (decoder), which creates a conditioned sample for the data. For the discriminator, the input is a sample from the base data and its context. The base object and its conditional input are first fused into a hidden representation, and the discriminator then provides a classification of whether the same is real or generated. The overall architecture for the training of the generator portion is shown in Figure 10.10. It is instructive to compare this architecture with that of the unconditional GAN in Figure 10.7. The main difference is that an additional conditional input is provided in the second case. The loss function and the overall arrangement of the hidden layers is very similar in both

---

[2]It turns out that by modifying the *discriminator* to output classes (including the *fake* class), one can obtain state-of-the-art semi-supervised classification with very few labels [420]. However, using the *generator* to output the labels is not a good choice.

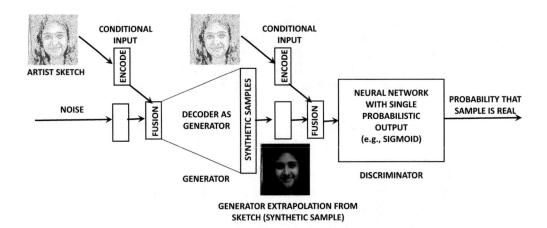

Figure 10.10: Conditional generative adversarial network for hooked up discriminator: It is instructive to compare this architecture with that of the unconditional generative adversarial network in Figure 10.7.

cases. Therefore, the change from an unconditional GAN to a conditional GAN requires only minor changes to the overall architecture. The backpropagation approach remains largely unaffected, except that there are some additional weights in the portion of the neural network associated with the conditioning inputs that one might need to update.

An important point about using GANs with various data types is that they might require some modifications in order to perform the encoding and decoding in a data-sensitive way. While we have given several examples from the image and text domain in our discussion above, most of the description of the algorithm is focussed on vanilla multidimensional data (rather than image or text data). Even when the label is used as the context, it needs to be encoded into a multidimensional representation (e.g., one-hot encoding). Therefore, both Figures 10.9 and 10.10 contain a specifically denoted component for encoding the context. In the earliest work on conditional GANs [331], the pre-trained *AlexNet* convolution network [255] is used as the encoder for image context (without the final label prediction layer). *AlexNet* was pre-trained on the *ImageNet* database. The work in [331] even uses a multimodal setting in which an image is input together with some text annotations. The output is another set of text tags further describing the image. For text annotations, a pre-trained *word2vec* (skip-gram) model is used as the encoder. It is noteworthy that it is even possible to fine-tune the weights of these pre-trained encoder networks while updating the weights of the generator (by backpropagating beyond the generator into the encoder). This is particularly useful if the nature of the data set for object generation in the GAN is very different from the data sets on which the encoders were pretrained. However, the original work in [331] fixed these encoders to their pre-trained configurations, and was still able to generate reasonably high-quality results.

Although the *word2vec* model is used in the specific example above for encoding text, several other options can be used. One option is to use a recurrent neural network, when the input is a full sentence rather than a word. For words, a character-level recurrent network can also be used. In all cases, it is possible to start with an appropriately pre-trained encoder, and then fine-tune it during CGAN training.

10.5 Competitive Learning

Most of the learning methods discussed in this book are based on updating the weights in the neural network in order to correct for errors. Competitive learning is a fundamentally different paradigm in which the goal is not to map inputs to outputs in order to correct errors. Rather, the neurons compete for the right to respond to a subset of similar input data and push their weights closer to one or more input data points. Therefore, the learning process is also very different from the backpropagation algorithm used in neural networks.

The broad idea in training is as follows. The activation of an output neuron increases with greater similarity between the weight vector of the neuron and the input. It is assumed that the weight vector of the neuron has the same dimensionality as the input. A common approach is to use the Euclidian distance between the input and the weight vector in order to compute the activation. Smaller distances lead to larger activations. The output unit that has the highest activation to a given input is declared the winner and moved closer to the input.

In the winner-take-all strategy, only the winning neuron (i.e., neurons with largest activation) is updated and the remaining neurons remain unchanged. Other variants of the competitive learning paradigm allow other neurons to participate in the update based on pre-defined neighborhood relationships. Furthermore, some mechanisms are also available that allow neurons to inhibit one another. These mechanisms are forms of regularization that can be used to learn representations with a specific type of pre-defined structure, which is useful in applications like 2-dimensional visualization. First, we discuss a simple version of the competitive learning algorithm in which the winner-take-all approach is used.

Let $\overline{X}$ be an input vector in d dimensions, and $\overline{W}_i$ be the weight vector associated with the ith neuron in the same number of dimensions. Assume that a total of m neurons is used, where m is typically much less than the size of the data set n. The following steps are used by repeatedly sampling $\overline{X}$ from the input data and making the following computations:

1. The Euclidean distance $||\overline{W}_i - \overline{X}||$ is computed for each i. If the pth neuron has the smallest value of the Euclidean distance, then it is declared as the winner. Note that the value of $||\overline{W}_i - \overline{X}||$ is treated as the activation value of the ith neuron.

2. The pth neuron is updated using the following rule:

$$\overline{W}_p \Leftarrow \overline{W}_p + \alpha(\overline{X} - \overline{W}_p) \qquad (10.20)$$

Here, $\alpha > 0$ is the learning rate. Typically, the value of α is much less than 1. In some cases, the learning rate α reduces with progression of the algorithm.

The basic idea in competitive learning is to view the weight vectors as prototypes (like the centroids in k-means clustering), and then move the (winning) prototype a small distance towards the training instance. The value of α regulates the fraction of the distance between the point and the weight vector, by which the movement of $\overline{W}_p$ occurs. Note that k-means clustering also achieves similar goals, albeit in a different way. After all, when a point is assigned to the winning centroid, it moves that centroid by a small distance towards the training instance at the end of the iteration. Competitive learning allows some natural variations of this framework, which can be used for unsupervised applications like clustering and dimensionality reduction.

10.5.1   Vector Quantization

Vector quantization is the simplest application of competitive learning. Some changes are made to the basic competitive learning paradigm with the notion of *sensitivity*. Each node has a sensitivity $s_i \geq 0$ associated with it. The sensitivity value helps in balancing the points among different clusters. The basic steps of vector quantization are similar to those in the competitive learning algorithm except for differences caused by how s_i is updated and used in the computations. The value of s_i is initialized to 0 for each point. In each iteration, the value of s_i is increased by $\gamma > 0$ for non-winners and set to 0 for the winner. Furthermore, to choose the winner, the smallest value of $||\overline{W}_i - \overline{X}|| - s_i$ is used. Such an approach tends to make the clusters more balanced, even if the different regions have widely varying density. This approach ensures that points in dense regions are typically very close to one of the weight vectors and the points in sparse regions are approximated very poorly. Such a property is common in applications like dimensionality reduction and compression. The value of γ regulates the effect of sensitivity. Setting γ to 0 reverts to pure competitive learning as discussed above.

The most common application of vector quantization is compression. In compression, each point is represented by its closest weight vector $\overline{W}_i$, where i ranges from 1 to m. Note that the value of m is much less than the number of points n in the data set. The first step is to construct a code book containing the vectors $\overline{W}_1 \ldots \overline{W}_m$, which requires a space of $m \cdot d$ for a data set of dimensionality d. Each point is stored as an index value from 1 through m, depending on its closest weight vector. However, only $\log_2(m)$ bits are required in order to store each data point. Therefore, the overall space requirement is $m \cdot d + \log_2(m)$, which is typically much less than the original space required $n \cdot d$ of the data set. For example, a data set containing 10 billion points in 100 dimensions requires space in the order of 4 Terabytes, if 4 bytes are required for each dimension. On the other hand, by quantizing with $m = 10^6$, the space required for the code-book is less than half a Gigabyte, and 20 bits are required for each point. Therefore, the space required for the points (without the code-book) is less than 3 Gigabytes. Therefore, the overall space requirement is less than 3.5 Gigabytes including the code-book. Note that this type of compression is lossy, and the error of the approximation of the point $\overline{X}$ is $||\overline{X} - \overline{W}_i||$. Points in dense regions are approximated very well, whereas outliers in sparse regions are approximated poorly.

10.5.2   Kohonen Self-Organizing Map

The Kohonen self-organizing map is a variation on the competitive learning paradigm in which a 1-dimensional string-like or 2-dimensional lattice-like structure is imposed on the neurons. For greater generality in discussion, we will consider the case in which a 2-dimensional lattice-like structure is imposed on the neurons. As we will see, this type of lattice structure enables the mapping of all points to 2-dimensional space for visualization. An example of a 2-dimensional lattice structure of 25 neurons arranged in a 5×5 rectangular grid is shown in Figure 10.11(a). A hexagonal lattice containing the same number of neurons is shown in Figure 10.11(b). The shape of the lattice affects the shape of the 2-dimensional regions in which the clusters will be mapped. The case of 1-dimensional string-like structure is similar. The idea of using the lattice structure is that the values of $\overline{W}_i$ in adjacent lattice neurons tend to be similar. Here, it is important to define separate notations to distinguish between the distance $||\overline{W}_i - \overline{W}_j||$ and the distance on the lattice. The distance between adjacent pairs of neurons on the lattice is exactly one unit. For example, the distance between the neurons i and j based on the lattice structure in Figure 10.11(a) is 1 unit, and the

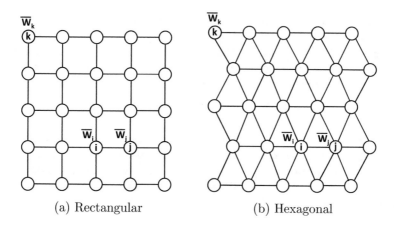

(a) Rectangular   (b) Hexagonal

Figure 10.11: An example of a 5×5 lattice structure for the self-organizing map. Since neurons i and j are close in the lattice, the learning process will bias the values of $\overline{W}_i$ and $\overline{W}_j$ to be more similar. The rectangular lattice will lead to rectangular clustered regions in the resulting 2-dimensional representation, whereas the hexagonal lattice will lead to hexagonal clustered regions in the resulting 2-dimensional representation.

distance between neurons i and k is $\sqrt{2^2 + 3^2} = \sqrt{13}$. The vector-distance in the original input space (e.g., $||\overline{X} - \overline{W}_i||$ or $||\overline{W}_i - \overline{W}_j||$) is denoted by a notation like $Dist(\overline{W}_i, \overline{W}_j)$. On the other hand, the distance between neurons i and j along the lattice structure is denoted by $LDist(i, j)$. Note that the value of $LDist(i, j)$ is dependent only on the indices (i, j), and is independent of the values of the vectors $\overline{W}_i$ and $\overline{W}_j$.

The learning process in the self-organizing map is regulated in such a way that the closeness of neurons i and j (based on lattice distance) will also bias their weight vectors to be more similar. In other words, *the lattice structure of the self-organizing maps acts as a regularizer in the learning process.* As we will see later, imposing this type of 2-dimensional structure on the learned weights is helpful for visualizing the original data points with a 2-dimensional embedding.

The overall self-organizing map training algorithm proceeds in a similar way to competitive learning by sampling $\overline{X}$ from the training data, and finding the winner neuron based on the Euclidean distance. The weights in the winner neuron are updated in a manner similar to the vanilla competitive learning algorithm. However, the main difference is that a damped version of this update is also applied to the lattice-neighbors of the winner neuron. In fact, in soft variations of this method, one can apply this update to all neurons, and the level of damping depends on the lattice distance of that neuron to the winning neuron. The damping function, which always lies in $[0, 1]$, is typically defined by a Gaussian kernel:

$$Damp(i, j) = \exp\left(-\frac{LDist(i, j)^2}{2\sigma^2}\right) \qquad (10.21)$$

Here, σ is the bandwidth of the Gaussian kernel. Using extremely small values of σ reverts to pure winner-take-all learning, whereas using larger values of σ leads to greater regularization in which lattice-adjacent units have more similar weights. For small values of σ, the damping function will be 1 only for the winner neuron, and it will be 0 for all other neurons. Therefore, the value of σ is one of the parameters available to the user for tuning. Note that many other kernel functions are possible for controlling the regularization and damping. For example, instead of the smooth Gaussian damping function, one can use a thresholded step kernel, which takes on a value of 1 when $LDist(i,j) < \sigma$, and 0, otherwise.

The training algorithm repeatedly samples $\overline{X}$ from the training data, and computes the distances of $\overline{X}$ to each weight $\overline{W}_i$. The index p of the winning neuron is computed. Rather than applying the update only to $\overline{W}_p$ (as in winner-take-all), the following update is applied to each $\overline{W}_i$:

$$\overline{W}_i \Leftarrow \overline{W}_i + \alpha \cdot Damp(i,p) \cdot (\overline{X} - \overline{W}_i) \quad \forall i \tag{10.22}$$

Here, $\alpha > 0$ is the learning rate. It is common to allow the learning rate α to reduce with time. These iterations are continued until convergence is reached. Note that weights that are lattice-adjacent will receive similar updates, and will therefore tend to become more similar over time. *Therefore, the training process forces lattice-adjacent clusters to have similar points, which is useful for visualization.*

Using the Learned Map for 2D Embeddings

The self-organizing map can be used in order to induce a 2-dimensional embedding of the points. For a $k \times k$ grid, all 2-dimensional lattice coordinates will be located in a square in the positive quadrant with vertices $(0,0)$, $(0, k-1)$, $(k-1, 0)$, and $(k-1, k-1)$. Note that each grid point in the lattice is a vertex with integer coordinates. The simplest 2-dimensional embedding is simply by representing each point $\overline{X}$ with its closest grid point (i.e., winner neuron). However, such an approach will lead to overlapping representations of points. Furthermore, a 2-dimensional representation of the data can be constructed and each coordinate is one of $k \times k$ values from $\{0 \ldots k-1\} \times \{0 \ldots k-1\}$. This is the reason that the self-organizing map is also referred to as a *discretized* dimensionality reduction method. It is possible to use various heuristics to disambiguate these overlapping points. When applied to high-dimensional document data, a visual inspection often shows documents of a particular topic being mapped to a particular local regions. Furthermore, documents of related topics (e.g., politics and elections) tend to get mapped to adjacent regions. Illustrative examples of how a self-organizing map arranges documents of four topics with rectangular and hexagonal lattices are shown in Figure 10.12(a) and (b), respectively. The regions are colored differently, depending on the majority topic of the documents belonging to the corresponding region.

Self-organizing maps have a strong neurobiological basis in terms of their relationship with how the mammalian brain is structured. In the mammalian brain, various types of sensory inputs (e.g., touch) are mapped onto a number of folded planes of cells, which are referred to as *sheets* [129]. When parts of the body that are close together receive an input (e.g., tactile input), then groups of cells that are physically close together in the brain will also fire together. Therefore, proximity in (sensory) inputs is mapped to proximity in neurons, as in the case of the self-organizing map. As with the neurobiological inspiration of convolutional neural networks, such insights are always used for some form of regularization.

Although Kohonen networks are used less often in the modern era of deep learning, they have significant potential in the unsupervised setting. Furthermore, the basic idea of competition can even be incorporated in multi-layer feed-forward networks. Many competitive principles are often combined with more traditional feed-forward networks. For example, the r-sparse and winner-take-all autoencoders (cf. Section 2.5.5.1 of Chapter 2) are both based on competitive principles. Similarly, the notion of local response normalization (cf. Section 8.2.8 of Chapter 8) is based on competition between neurons. Even the notions of attention discussed in this chapter use competitive principles in terms of focusing on a subset of the activations. Therefore, even though the self-organizing map has become

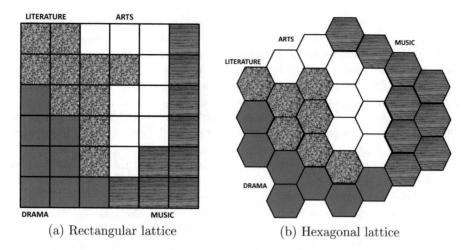

(a) Rectangular lattice   (b) Hexagonal lattice

Figure 10.12: Examples of 2-dimensional visualization of documents belonging to four topics

less popular in recent years, the basic principles of competition can also be integrated with traditional feed-forward networks.

10.6 Limitations of Neural Networks

Deep learning has made significant progress in recent years, and has even outperformed humans on many tasks like image classification. Similarly, the success of reinforcement learning to show super-human performance in some games that require sequential planning has been quite extraordinary. Therefore, it is tempting to posit that artificial intelligence might eventually come close to or even exceed the abilities of humans in a more generic way. However, there are several fundamental technical hurdles that need to be crossed before we can build machines that learn and think like people [261]. In particular, neural networks require large amounts of training data to provide high-quality results, which is significantly inferior to human abilities. Furthermore, the amount of energy required by neural networks for various tasks far exceeds that consumed by the human for similar tasks. These observations put fundamental constraints on the abilities of neural networks to exceed certain parameters of human performance. In the following, we discuss these issues along with some recent research directions.

10.6.1 An Aspirational Goal: One-Shot Learning

Although deep learning has received increasing attention in recent years because of its success on large-scale learning tasks (compared to the mediocre performance in early years on smaller data sets), this also exposes an important weakness in current deep learning technology. For tasks like image classification, where deep learning has exceeded human performance, it has done so in a *sample-inefficient fashion*. For example, the *ImageNet* database contains more than a million images, and a neural network will often require thousands of samples of a class in order to properly classify it. Humans do not require tens of thousands of images of a truck, to learn that it is a truck. If a child is shown a truck once, she will often be able to recognize another truck even when it is of a somewhat different model, shape, and color. This suggests that humans have much better ability to generalize to new settings as compared to artificial neural networks. The general principle of being able to learn from just one or very few examples is referred to as *one-shot learning*.

The ability of humans to generalize with fewer examples is not surprising because the connectivity of the neurons in the human brain is relatively sparse and has been carefully designed by nature. This architecture has evolved over millions of years, and has been passed down from generation to generation. In an indirect sense, the human neural connection structure already encodes a kind of "knowledge" gained from the "evolution experience" over millions of years. Furthermore, humans also gain knowledge over their lifetime over a variety of tasks, which helps them learn specific tasks faster. Subsequently, learning to do *specific* tasks (like recognizing a truck) is simply a fine-tuning of the encoding a person is both born with and which one gains over the course of a lifetime. In other words, humans are masters of transfer learning both within and across generations.

Developing generalized forms of transfer learning, so that the training time spent on particular tasks is not thrown away but is reused is a key area of future research. To a limited extent, the benefits of transfer learning have already been demonstrated in deep learning. As discussed in Chapter 8, convolutional neural networks like *AlexNet* [255] are often pre-trained on large image repositories like *ImageNet*. Subsequently, when the neural network needs to be applied to a new data set, the weights can be fine-tuned with the new data set. Often far fewer number of examples are required for this fine-tuning, because most of the basic features learned in earlier layers do not change with the data set at hand. In many cases, the learned features can also be generalized across tasks by removing the later layers or the network and adding additional task-specific layers. This general principle is also used in text mining. For example, many text feature learning models like *word2vec* are reused across many text mining tasks, even when they were pre-trained on different corpora. In general, the knowledge transfer can be in terms of the extracted features, the model parameters, or other contextual information.

There is another form of transfer learning, which is based on the notion of learning *across tasks*. The basic idea is to always reuse the training work that has already been done either fully or partially in one task in order to improve its ability to learn another task. This principle is referred to as *learning-to-learn*. Thrun and Platt defined [497] learning-to-learn as follows. Given a family of tasks, a training experience for each task, and a family of performance measures (one for each task), an algorithm is said to *learn-to-learn* if its performance at each task improves both with experience *and* the number of tasks. Central to the difficulty of learning-to-learn is the fact that the tasks are all somewhat different and it is therefore challenging to perform experience transfer across tasks. Therefore, the rapid learning occurs within a task, whereas the learning is guided by knowledge gained more gradually across tasks, which captures the way in which task structure varies across target domains [416]. In other words, there is a two-tiered organization of how tasks are learned. This notion is also referred to as *meta-learning*, although this term is overloaded and is used in several other concepts in machine learning. The ability of learning-to-learn is a uniquely biological quality, where living organisms tend to show improved performance even at weakly related tasks, as they gain experience over other tasks. At a weak level, even the pre-training of networks is an example of learning-to-learn, because we can use the weights of the network trained on a particular data set and task to another setting, so that learning in the new setting occurs rapidly. For example, in a convolutional neural network, the features in many of the early layers are primitive shapes (e.g., edges), and they retain their usability irrespective of the kind of task and data set that they are applied on. On the other hand, the final layer might be highly task specific. However, training a single layer requires much less data than the entire network.

Early work on one-shot learning [116] used Bayesian frameworks in order to transfer the learned knowledge from one category to the next. Some successes have been shown at meta-learning with the use of structured architectures that leverage the notions of attention, recursion, and memory. In particular, good results have been shown on the task of learning across categories with neural Turing machines [416]. The ability of memory-augmented networks to learn from limited data has been known for a long time. For example, even networks with internal memory like the LSTM have been shown to exhibit impressive performance for learning never-before seen quadratic functions with a small number of examples. The neural Turning machine is an even better architecture in this respect, and the work in [416] shows how it can be leveraged for meta-learning. Neural Turing machines have also been used to build matching networks for one-shot learning [507]. Even though these works do represent advances in the abilities to perform one-shot learning, the capabilities of these methods are still quite rudimentary compared to humans. Therefore, this topic remains an open area for future research.

10.6.2   An Aspirational Goal: Energy-Efficient Learning

Closely related to the notion of sample efficiency is that of *energy efficiency*. Deep learning systems that work on high-performance hardware are energy inefficient, and require large amounts of power to function. For example, if one uses multiple GPU units in parallel in order to accomplish a compute-intensive task, one might easily use more than a kilowatt of power. On the other hand, a human brain barely requires twenty watts to function, which is much less than the power required by a light bulb. Another point is that the human brain often does not perform detailed computations exactly, but simply makes estimates. In many learning settings, this is sufficient and can sometimes even add to generalization power. This suggests that energy-efficiency may sometimes be found in architectures that emphasize generalization over accuracy.

Several algorithms have recently been developed that trade-off accuracy in computations for improved power-efficiency of computations. Some of these methods also show improved generalization because of the noise effects of the low-precision computations. The work in [83] proposes methods for using binary weights in order to perform efficient computations. An analysis of the effect of using different representational codes on energy efficiency is provided in [289]. Certain types of neural networks, which contain *spiking neurons*, are known to be more energy-efficient [60]. The notion of spiking neurons is directly based on the biological model of the mammalian brain. The basic idea is that the neurons do not fire at each propagation cycle, but they fire only when the *membrane potential* reaches a specific value. The membrane potential is an intrinsic quality of a neuron associated with its electrical charge.

Energy efficiency is often achieved when the size of the neural network is small, and redundant connections are pruned. Removing redundant connections also helps in regularization. The work in [169] proposes to learn weights and connections in neural networks simultaneously by pruning redundant connections. In particular, weights that are close to zero can be removed. As discussed in Chapter 4, training a network to give near-zero weights can be achieved with L_1-regularization. However, the work in [169] shows that L_2-regularization gives higher accuracy. Therefore, the work in [169] uses L_2-regularization and prunes the weights that are below a particular threshold. The pruning is done in an iterative fashion, where the weights are retrained after pruning them, and then the low-weight edges are pruned again. In each iteration, the trained weights from the previous phase are used for the next phase. As a result, the dense network can be sparsified into a network with far fewer connections. Furthermore, the dead neurons that have zero input connections and output connections are pruned. Further enhancements were reported in [168], where the approach was combined with Huffman coding and quantization for compression. The goal of quantization is to reduce the number of bits representing each connection. This approach reduced the storage required by *AlexNet* [255] by a factor of 35, from about 240MB to 6.9MB with no loss of accuracy. As a result, it becomes possible to fit the model into on-chip SRAM cache rather than off-chip DRAM memory. This has advantages from the perspective of speed, energy efficiency, as well as the ability to perform mobile computation in embedded devices. In particular, a hardware accelerator has been used in [168] in order to achieve these goals, and this acceleration is enabled by the ability to fit the model on the SRAM cache.

Another direction is to develop hardware that is tailored directly to neural networks. It is noteworthy that there is no distinction between software and hardware in humans; while this distinction is helpful from the perspective of computer maintenance, it is also a source of inefficiency that is not shared by the human brain. Simply speaking, the hardware and software are tightly integrated in the brain-inspired model of computing. In recent years, progress has been made in the area of *neuromorphic computing* [114]. This notion is based on a new chip architecture containing spiking neurons, low-precision synapses, and a scalable communication network. Readers are referred to [114] for the description of a convolutional neural network architecture (based on neuromorphic computing) that provides state-of-the-art image-recognition performance.

10.7 Summary

In this chapter, several advanced topics in deep learning have been discussed. The chapter starts with a discussion of attention mechanisms. These mechanisms have been used for both image and text data. In all cases, the incorporation of attention has improved the generalization power of the underlying neural network. Attention mechanisms can also be used to augment computers with external memory. A memory-augmented network has similar theoretical properties as a recurrent neural network in terms of being Turing complete. However, it tends to perform computations in a more interpretable way, and therefore generalizes well to test data sets that are somewhat different from the training data. For example, one can accurately work with longer sequences than the training data set contains in order to perform classification. The simplest example of a memory-augmented network is a neural Turing machine, which has subsequently been generalized to the notion of a differentiable neural computer.

Generative adversarial networks are recent techniques that use an adversarial interaction process between a generative network and a discriminative network in order to generate synthetic samples that are similar to a database of real samples. Such networks can be used as generative models that create input samples for testing machine learning algorithms. In addition, by imposing a conditional on the generative process, it is possible to create samples with different types of contexts. These ideas have been used in various types of applications such as text-to-image and image-to-image translation.

Numerous advanced topics have also been explored in recent years such as one-shot learning and energy-efficient learning. These represent areas in which neural network technology greatly lags the abilities of humans. Although significant advances have been made in recent years, there is significant scope of future research in these areas.

10.8 Bibliographic Notes

Early techniques for using attention in neural network training were proposed in [59, 266]. The recurrent models of visual attention discussed in this chapter are based on the work in [338]. The recognition of multiple objects in an image with visual attention is discussed in [15]. The two most well known models are neural machine translation with attention are discussed in [18, 302]. The ideas of attention have also been extended to image captioning. For example, the work in [540] presents methods for image captioning based on both soft and hard attention models. The use of attention models for text summarization is discussed in [413]. The notion of attention is also useful for focusing on specific parts of the image to enable visual question-answering [395, 539, 542]. A useful mechanism for attention is the use of *spatial transformer networks*, which can selectively crop out or focus on portions of an image. The use of attention models for visual question answering is discussed in [299].

Neural Turing machines [158] and memory networks [473, 528] were proposed around the same time. Subsequently, the neural Turing machine was generalized to a differential neural computer with the use of better memory allocation mechanisms and those for tracking the sequence of writes. The neural Turing machine and differentiable neural computer have been applied to various tasks such as copying, associative recall, sorting, graph querying and language querying. On the other hand, the primary focus of memory networks [473, 528] has been on language understanding and question answering. However, the two architectures are quite similar. The main difference is that the model in [473] focusses on content-based addressing mechanisms rather than location-based mechanisms; doing so reduces the need for sharpening. A more focussed study on the problem of question-answering is provided in [257]. The work in [393] proposes the notion of a neural program interpreter, which is a recurrent and compositional neural network that learns to represent and execute programs. An interesting version of the Turing machine has also been designed with the use of reinforcement learning [550, 551], and it can be used for learning wider classes of complex tasks. The work in [551] shows how simple algorithms can be learned from examples. The parallelization of these methods with GPUs is discussed in [229].

Generative adversarial networks (GANs) have been proposed in [149], and an excellent tutorial on the topic may be found in [145]. An early method proposed a similar architecture for generating chairs with convolutional networks [103]. Improved training algorithms are discussed in [420]. The main challenges in training adversarial networks have to do with *instability* and *saturation*. A theoretical understanding of some of these issues, together with some principled methods for addressing them are discussed in [11, 12]. Energy-based GANs are proposed in [562], it is claimed that they have better stability. Adversarial ideas have also been generalized to autoencoder architectures [311]. Generative adversarial networks are used frequently in the image domain to generate realistic images with various properties [95, 384]. In these cases, a deconvolution network is used in the generator, and therefore the resulting GAN is referred to as a DCGAN. The idea of conditional generative networks and their use in generating objects with context is discussed in [331, 392]. The approach has also been used recently for image to image translation [215, 370, 518]. Although generative adversarial networks are often used in the image domain, they have also been extended recently to sequences [546]. The use of CGANs for predicting the next frame in a video is discussed in [319].

The earliest works on competitive learning may be found in [410, 411]. Gersho and Gray [136] provide an excellent overview of vector quantization methods. Vector quantization methods are alternatives to sparse coding techniques [75]. Kohonen's self-organizing feature map was introduced in [248], and more detailed discussions from the same author may be found in [249, 250]. Many variants of this basic architecture, such as *neural gas*, are used for incremental learning [126, 317].

A discussion of learning-to-learn methods may be found in [497]. The earliest methods in this area used Bayesian models [116]. Later methods focused on various types of neural Turing machines [416, 507]. Zero-shot learning methods are proposed in [364, 403, 462]. Evolutionary methods can also be used to perform long-term learning [543]. Numerous methods have also been proposed to make deep learning more energy-efficient, such as the use of binary weights [83, 389], specially designed chips [114], and compression mechanisms [213, 168, 169]. Specialized methods have also been developed [68] for convolutional neural networks.

10.8.1   Software Resources

The recurrent model for visual attention is available at [627]. The MATLAB code for the attention mechanism for neural machine translation discussed in this chapter (from the original authors) may be found in [628]. Implementations of the Neural Turing Machine in *TensorFlow* may be found in [629, 630]. The two implementations are related because the approach in [630] adopts some of the portions of [629]. An LSTM controller is used in the original implementation. Implementations in *Keras*, *Lasagne*, and *Torch* may be found in [631, 632, 633]. Several implementations from *Facebook* on memory networks are available at [634]. An implementation of memory networks in *TensorFlow* nay be found in [635]. An implementation of dynamic memory networks in *Theano* and *Lasagne* is available at [636].

An implementation of DCGAN in *TensorFlow* may be found in [637]. In fact, several variants of the GAN (and other topics discussed in this chapter) are available from this contributor [638]. A *Keras* implementation of the GAN may be found in [639]. Implementations of various types of GANs, including the Wasserstein GAN and the variational autoencoder may be found in [640]. These implementations are executed in *PyTorch* and *TensorFlow*. An implementation of the text-to-image GAN in *TensorFlow* is provided in [641], and this implementation is built on top of the aforementioned DCGAN implementation [637].

10.9   Exercises

1. What are the main differences in the approaches used for training hard-attention and soft-attention models?

2. Show how you can use attention models to improve the token-wise classification application of Chapter 7.

3. Discuss how the k-means algorithm is related to competitive learning.

4. Implement a Kohonen self-organizing map with (i) a rectangular lattice, and (ii) a hexagonal lattice.

5. Consider a two-player game like GANs with objective function $f(x, y)$, and we want to compute $\min_x \max_y f(x, y)$. Discuss the relationship between $\min_x \max_y f(x, y)$ and $\max_y \min_x f(x, y)$. When are they equal?

6. Consider the function $f(x, y) = \sin(x + y)$, where we are trying to minimize $f(x, y)$ with respect to x and maximize with respect to y. Implement the alternating process of gradient descent and ascent discussed in the book for GANs to optimize this function. Do you always get the same solution over different starting points?

Bibliography

[1] D. Ackley, G. Hinton, and T. Sejnowski. A learning algorithm for Boltzmann machines. *Cognitive Science*, 9(1), pp. 147–169, 1985.

[2] C. Aggarwal. Data classification: Algorithms and applications, *CRC Press*, 2014.

[3] C. Aggarwal. Data mining: The textbook. *Springer*, 2015.

[4] C. Aggarwal. Recommender systems: The textbook. *Springer*, 2016.

[5] C. Aggarwal. Outlier analysis. *Springer*, 2017.

[6] C. Aggarwal. Machine learning for text. *Springer*, 2018.

[7] R. Ahuja, T. Magnanti, and J. Orlin. Network flows: Theory, algorithms, and applications. *Prentice Hall*, 1993.

[8] E. Aljalbout, V. Golkov, Y. Siddiqui, and D. Cremers. Clustering with deep learning: Taxonomy and new methods. *arXiv:1801.07648*, 2018.
https://arxiv.org/abs/1801.07648

[9] R. Al-Rfou, B. Perozzi, and S. Skiena. Polyglot: Distributed word representations for multilingual nlp. *arXiv:1307.1662*, 2013.
https://arxiv.org/abs/1307.1662

[10] D. Amodei *at al.* Concrete problems in AI safety. *arXiv:1606.06565*, 2016.
https://arxiv.org/abs/1606.06565

[11] M. Arjovsky and L. Bottou. Towards principled methods for training generative adversarial networks. *arXiv:1701.04862*, 2017.
https://arxiv.org/abs/1701.04862

[12] M. Arjovsky, S. Chintala, and L. Bottou. Wasserstein gan. *arXiv:1701.07875*, 2017.
https://arxiv.org/abs/1701.07875

[13] J. Ba and R. Caruana. Do deep nets really need to be deep? *NIPS Conference*, pp. 2654–2662, 2014.

© Springer International Publishing AG, part of Springer Nature 2018
C. C. Aggarwal, *Neural Networks and Deep Learning*,
https://doi.org/10.1007/978-3-319-94463-0

[14] J. Ba, J. Kiros, and G. Hinton. Layer normalization. *arXiv:1607.06450*, 2016.
https://arxiv.org/abs/1607.06450

[15] J. Ba, V. Mnih, and K. Kavukcuoglu. Multiple object recognition with visual attention.
arXiv: 1412.7755, 2014.
https://arxiv.org/abs/1412.7755

[16] A. Babenko, A. Slesarev, A. Chigorin, and V. Lempitsky. Neural codes for image retrieval.
arXiv:1404.1777, 2014.
https://arxiv.org/abs/1404.1777

[17] M. Baccouche, F. Mamalet, C. Wolf, C. Garcia, and A. Baskurt. Sequential deep learning
for human action recognition. *International Workshop on Human Behavior Understanding*,
pp. 29–39, 2011.

[18] D. Bahdanau, K. Cho, and Y. Bengio. Neural machine translation by jointly learning to align
and translate. *ICLR*, 2015. Also *arXiv:1409.0473*, 2014.
https://arxiv.org/abs/1409.0473

[19] B. Baker, O. Gupta, N. Naik, and R. Raskar. Designing neural network architectures using
reinforcement learning. *arXiv:1611.02167*, 2016.
https://arxiv.org/abs/1611.02167

[20] P. Baldi, S. Brunak, P. Frasconi, G. Soda, and G. Pollastri. Exploiting the past and the future
in protein secondary structure prediction. *Bioinformatics*, 15(11), pp. 937–946, 1999.

[21] N. Ballas, L. Yao, C. Pal, and A. Courville. Delving deeper into convolutional networks for
learning video representations. *arXiv:1511.06432*, 2015.
https://arxiv.org/abs/1511.06432

[22] J. Baxter, A. Tridgell, and L. Weaver. Knightcap: a chess program that learns by combining
td (lambda) with game-tree search. *arXiv cs/9901002*, 1999.

[23] M. Bazaraa, H. Sherali, and C. Shetty. Nonlinear programming: theory and algorithms. *John
Wiley and Sons*, 2013.

[24] S. Becker, and Y. LeCun. Improving the convergence of back-propagation learning with second order methods. *Proceedings of the 1988 connectionist models summer school*, pp. 29–37,
1988.

[25] M. Bellemare, Y. Naddaf, J. Veness, and M. Bowling. The arcade learning environment:
An evaluation platform for general agents. *Journal of Artificial Intelligence Research*, 47,
pp. 253–279, 2013.

[26] R. E. Bellman. Dynamic Programming. *Princeton University Press*, 1957.

[27] Y. Bengio. Learning deep architectures for AI. *Foundations and Trends in Machine Learning*,
2(1), pp. 1–127, 2009.

[28] Y. Bengio, A. Courville, and P. Vincent. Representation learning: A review and new perspectives. *IEEE TPAMI*, 35(8), pp. 1798–1828, 2013.

[29] Y. Bengio and O. Delalleau. Justifying and generalizing contrastive divergence. *Neural Computation*, 21(6), pp. 1601–1621, 2009.

[30] Y. Bengio and O. Delalleau. On the expressive power of deep architectures. *Algorithmic
Learning Theory*, pp. 18–36, 2011.

[31] Y. Bengio, P. Lamblin, D. Popovici, and H. Larochelle. Greedy layer-wise training of deep networks. *NIPS Conference*, 19, 153, 2007.

[32] Y. Bengio, N. Le Roux, P. Vincent, O. Delalleau, and P. Marcotte. Convex neural networks. *NIPS Conference*, pp. 123–130, 2005.

[33] Y. Bengio, J. Louradour, R. Collobert, and J. Weston. Curriculum learning. *ICML Conference*, 2009.

[34] Y. Bengio, L. Yao, G. Alain, and P. Vincent. Generalized denoising auto-encoders as generative models. *NIPS Conference*, pp. 899–907, 2013.

[35] J. Bergstra *et al.* Theano: A CPU and GPU math compiler in Python. *Python in Science Conference*, 2010.

[36] J. Bergstra, R. Bardenet, Y. Bengio, and B. Kegl. Algorithms for hyper-parameter optimization. *NIPS Conference*, pp. 2546–2554, 2011.

[37] J. Bergstra and Y. Bengio. Random search for hyper-parameter optimization. *Journal of Machine Learning Research*, 13, pp. 281–305, 2012.

[38] J. Bergstra, D. Yamins, and D. Cox. Making a science of model search: Hyperparameter optimization in hundreds of dimensions for vision architectures. *ICML Confererence*, pp. 115–123, 2013.

[39] D. Bertsekas. Nonlinear programming *Athena Scientific*, 1999.

[40] C. M. Bishop. Pattern recognition and machine learning. *Springer*, 2007.

[41] C. M. Bishop. Neural networks for pattern recognition. *Oxford University Press*, 1995.

[42] C. M. Bishop. Bayesian Techniques. Chapter 10 in "Neural Networks for Pattern Recognition," pp. 385–439, 1995.

[43] C. M Bishop. Improving the generalization properties of radial basis function neural networks. *Neural Computation*, 3(4), pp. 579–588, 1991.

[44] C. M. Bishop. Training with noise is equivalent to Tikhonov regularization. *Neural computation*, 7(1),pp. 108–116, 1995.

[45] C. M. Bishop, M. Svensen, and C. K. Williams. GTM: A principled alternative to the self-organizing map. *NIPS Conference*, pp. 354–360, 1997.

[46] M. Bojarski *et al.* End to end learning for self-driving cars. *arXiv:1604.07316*, 2016.
https://arxiv.org/abs/1604.07316

[47] M. Bojarski *et al.* Explaining How a Deep Neural Network Trained with End-to-End Learning Steers a Car. *arXiv:1704.07911*, 2017.
https://arxiv.org/abs/1704.07911

[48] H. Bourlard and Y. Kamp. Auto-association by multilayer perceptrons and singular value decomposition. *Biological Cybernetics*, 59(4), pp. 291–294, 1988.

[49] L. Breiman. Random forests. *Journal Machine Learning archive*, 45(1), pp. 5–32, 2001.

[50] L. Breiman. Bagging predictors. *Machine Learning*, 24(2), pp. 123–140, 1996.

[51] D. Broomhead and D. Lowe. Multivariable functional interpolation and adaptive networks. *Complex Systems*, 2, pp. 321–355, 1988.

[52] C. Browne *et al.* A survey of monte carlo tree search methods. *IEEE Transactions on Computational Intelligence and AI in Games*, 4(1), pp. 1–43, 2012.

[53] T. Brox and J. Malik. Large displacement optical flow: descriptor matching in variational motion estimation. *IEEE TPAMI*, 33(3), pp. 500–513, 2011.

[54] A. Bryson. A gradient method for optimizing multi-stage allocation processes. *Harvard University Symposium on Digital Computers and their Applications*, 1961.

[55] C. Bucilu, R. Caruana, and A. Niculescu-Mizil. Model compression. *ACM KDD Conference*, pp. 535–541, 2006.

[56] P. Bühlmann and B. Yu. Analyzing bagging. *Annals of Statistics*, pp. 927–961, 2002.

[57] M. Buhmann. Radial Basis Functions: Theory and implementations. *Cambridge University Press*, 2003.

[58] Y. Burda, R. Grosse, and R. Salakhutdinov. Importance weighted autoencoders. *arXiv:1509.00519*, 2015.
https://arxiv.org/abs/1509.00519

[59] N. Butko and J. Movellan. I-POMDP: An infomax model of eye movement. *IEEE International Conference on Development and Learning*, pp. 139–144, 2008.

[60] Y. Cao, Y. Chen, and D. Khosla. Spiking deep convolutional neural networks for energy-efficient object recognition. *International Journal of Computer Vision*, 113(1), 54–66, 2015.

[61] M. Carreira-Perpinan and G. Hinton. On Contrastive Divergence Learning. *AISTATS*, 10, pp. 33–40, 2005.

[62] S. Chang, W. Han, J. Tang, G. Qi, C. Aggarwal, and T. Huang. Heterogeneous network embedding via deep architectures. *ACM KDD Conference*, pp. 119–128, 2015.

[63] N. Chawla, K. Bowyer, L. Hall, and W. Kegelmeyer. SMOTE: synthetic minority over-sampling technique. *Journal of Artificial Intelligence Research*, 16, pp. 321–357, 2002.

[64] J. Chen, S. Sathe, C. Aggarwal, and D. Turaga. Outlier detection with autoencoder ensembles. *SIAM Conference on Data Mining*, 2017.

[65] S. Chen, C. Cowan, and P. Grant. Orthogonal least-squares learning algorithm for radial basis function networks. *IEEE Transactions on Neural Networks*, 2(2), pp. 302–309, 1991.

[66] W. Chen, J. Wilson, S. Tyree, K. Weinberger, and Y. Chen. Compressing neural networks with the hashing trick. *ICML Confererence*, pp. 2285–2294, 2015.

[67] Y. Chen and M. Zaki. KATE: K-Competitive Autoencoder for Text. *ACM KDD Conference*, 2017.

[68] Y. Chen, T. Krishna, J. Emer, and V. Sze. Eyeriss: An energy-efficient reconfigurable accelerator for deep convolutional neural networks. *IEEE Journal of Solid-State Circuits*, 52(1), pp. 127–138, 2017.

[69] K. Cho, B. Merrienboer, C. Gulcehre, F. Bougares, H. Schwenk, and Y. Bengio. Learning phrase representations using RNN encoder-decoder for statistical machine translation. *EMNLP*, 2014.
https://arxiv.org/pdf/1406.1078.pdf

[70] J. Chorowski, D. Bahdanau, D. Serdyuk, K. Cho, and Y. Bengio. Attention-based models for speech recognition. *NIPS Conference*, pp. 577–585, 2015.

[71] J. Chung, C. Gulcehre, K. Cho, and Y. Bengio. Empirical evaluation of gated recurrent neural networks on sequence modeling. *arXiv:1412.3555*, 2014.
https://arxiv.org/abs/1412.3555

[72] D. Ciresan, U. Meier, L. Gambardella, and J. Schmidhuber. Deep, big, simple neural nets for handwritten digit recognition. *Neural Computation*, 22(12), pp. 3207–3220, 2010.

[73] C. Clark and A. Storkey. Training deep convolutional neural networks to play go. *ICML Confererence*, pp. 1766–1774, 2015.

[74] A. Coates, B. Huval, T. Wang, D. Wu, A. Ng, and B. Catanzaro. Deep learning with COTS HPC systems. *ICML Confererence*, pp. 1337–1345, 2013.

[75] A. Coates and A. Ng. The importance of encoding versus training with sparse coding and vector quantization. *ICML Confererence*, pp. 921–928, 2011.

[76] A. Coates and A. Ng. Learning feature representations with k-means. *Neural networks: Tricks of the Trade*, Springer, pp. 561–580, 2012.

[77] A. Coates, A. Ng, and H. Lee. An analysis of single-layer networks in unsupervised feature learning. *AAAI Conference*, pp. 215–223, 2011.

[78] R. Collobert, J. Weston, L. Bottou, M. Karlen, K. Kavukcuoglu, and P. Kuksa. Natural language processing (almost) from scratch. *Journal of Machine Learning Research*, 12, pp. 2493–2537, 2011.

[79] R. Collobert and J. Weston. A unified architecture for natural language processing: Deep neural networks with multitask learning. *ICML Conference*, pp. 160–167, 2008.

[80] J. Connor, R. Martin, and L. Atlas. Recurrent neural networks and robust time series prediction. *IEEE Transactions on Neural Networks*, 5(2), pp. 240–254, 1994.

[81] T. Cooijmans, N. Ballas, C. Laurent, C. Gulcehre, and A. Courville. Recurrent batch normalization. *arXiv:1603.09025*, 2016.
https://arxiv.org/abs/1603.09025

[82] C. Cortes and V. Vapnik. Support-vector networks. *Machine Learning*, 20(3), pp. 273–297, 1995.

[83] M. Courbariaux, Y. Bengio, and J.-P. David. BinaryConnect: Training deep neural networks with binary weights during propagations. *arXiv:1511.00363*, 2015.
https://arxiv.org/pdf/1511.00363.pdf

[84] T. Cover. Geometrical and statistical properties of systems of linear inequalities with applications to pattern recognition. *IEEE Transactions on Electronic Computers*, pp. 326–334, 1965.

[85] D. Cox and N. Pinto. Beyond simple features: A large-scale feature search approach to unconstrained face recognition. *IEEE International Conference on Automatic Face and Gesture Recognition and Workshops*, pp. 8–15, 2011.

[86] G. Dahl, R. Adams, and H. Larochelle. Training restricted Boltzmann machines on word observations. *arXiv:1202.5695*, 2012.
https://arxiv.org/abs/1202.5695

[87] N. Dalal and B. Triggs. Histograms of oriented gradients for human detection. *Computer Vision and Pattern Recognition*, pp. 886–893, 2005.

[88] Y. Dauphin, R. Pascanu, C. Gulcehre, K. Cho, S. Ganguli, and Y. Bengio. Identifying and attacking the saddle point problem in high-dimensional non-convex optimization. *NIPS Conference*, pp. 2933–2941, 2014.

[89] N. de Freitas. Machine Learning, University of Oxford (Course Video), 2013. https://www.youtube.com/watch?v=w2OtwL5T1ow&list=PLE6Wd9FREdyJ5lbFl8Uu–GjecvVw66F6

[90] N. de Freitas. Deep Learning, University of Oxford (Course Video), 2015. https://www.youtube.com/watch?v=PlhFWT7vAEw&list=PLjK8ddCbDMphIMSXn–1IjyYpHU3DaUYw

[91] J. Dean *et al.* Large scale distributed deep networks. *NIPS Conference*, 2012.

[92] M. Defferrard, X. Bresson, and P. Vandergheynst. Convolutional neural networks on graphs with fast localized spectral filtering. *NIPS Conference*, pp. 3844–3852, 2016.

[93] O. Delalleau and Y. Bengio. Shallow vs. deep sum-product networks. *NIPS Conference*, pp. 666–674, 2011.

[94] M. Denil, B. Shakibi, L. Dinh, M. A. Ranzato, and N. de Freitas. Predicting parameters in deep learning. *NIPS Conference*, pp. 2148–2156, 2013.

[95] E. Denton, S. Chintala, and R. Fergus. Deep Generative Image Models using a Laplacian Pyramid of Adversarial Networks. *NIPS Conference*, pp. 1466–1494, 2015.

[96] G. Desjardins, K. Simonyan, and R. Pascanu. Natural neural networks. *NIPS Congference*, pp. 2071–2079, 2015.

[97] F. Despagne and D. Massart. Neural networks in multivariate calibration. *Analyst*, 123(11), pp. 157R–178R, 1998.

[98] T. Dettmers. 8-bit approximations for parallelism in deep learning. *arXiv:1511.04561*, 2015. https://arxiv.org/abs/1511.04561

[99] C. Ding, T. Li, and W. Peng. On the equivalence between non-negative matrix factorization and probabilistic latent semantic indexing. *Computational Statistics and Data Analysis*, 52(8), pp. 3913–3927, 2008.

[100] J. Donahue, L. Anne Hendricks, S. Guadarrama, M. Rohrbach, S. Venugopalan, K. Saenko, and T. Darrell. Long-term recurrent convolutional networks for visual recognition and description. *IEEE conference on computer vision and pattern recognition*, pp. 2625–2634, 2015.

[101] G. Dorffner. Neural networks for time series processing. *Neural Network World*, 1996.

[102] C. Dos Santos and M. Gatti. Deep Convolutional Neural Networks for Sentiment Analysis of Short Texts. *COLING*, pp. 69–78, 2014.

[103] A. Dosovitskiy, J. Tobias Springenberg, and T. Brox. Learning to generate chairs with convolutional neural networks. *CVPR Conference*, pp. 1538–1546, 2015.

[104] A. Dosovitskiy and T. Brox. Inverting visual representations with convolutional networks. *CVPR Conference*, pp. 4829–4837, 2016.

[105] K. Doya. Bifurcations of recurrent neural networks in gradient descent learning. *IEEE Transactions on Neural Networks*, 1, pp. 75–80, 1993.

[106] C. Doersch. Tutorial on variational autoencoders. *arXiv:1606.05908*, 2016. https://arxiv.org/abs/1606.05908

[107] H. Drucker and Y. LeCun. Improving generalization performance using double backpropagation. *IEEE Transactions on Neural Networks*, 3(6), pp. 991–997, 1992.

[108] J. Duchi, E. Hazan, and Y. Singer. Adaptive subgradient methods for online learning and stochastic optimization. *Journal of Machine Learning Research*, 12, pp. 2121–2159, 2011.

[109] V. Dumoulin and F. Visin. A guide to convolution arithmetic for deep learning. *arXiv:1603.07285*, 2016.
https://arxiv.org/abs/1603.07285

[110] A. Elkahky, Y. Song, and X. He. A multi-view deep learning approach for cross domain user modeling in recommendation systems. *WWW Conference*, pp. 278–288, 2015.

[111] J. Elman. Finding structure in time. *Cognitive Science*, 14(2), pp. 179–211, 1990.

[112] J. Elman. Learning and development in neural networks: The importance of starting small. *Cognition*, 48, pp. 781–799, 1993.

[113] D. Erhan, Y. Bengio, A. Courville, P. Manzagol, P. Vincent, and S. Bengio. Why does unsupervised pre-training help deep learning?. *Journal of Machine Learning Research*, 11, pp. 625–660, 2010.

[114] S. Essar *et al.* Convolutional neural networks for fast, energy-efficient neuromorphic computing. *Proceedings of the National Academy of Science of the United States of America*, 113(41), pp. 11441–11446, 2016.

[115] A. Fader, L. Zettlemoyer, and O. Etzioni. Paraphrase-Driven Learning for Open Question Answering. *ACL*, pp. 1608–1618, 2013.

[116] L. Fei-Fei, R. Fergus, and P. Perona. One-shot learning of object categories. *IEEE TPAMI*, 28(4), pp. 594–611, 2006.

[117] P. Felzenszwalb, R. Girshick, D. McAllester, and D. Ramanan. Object detection with discriminatively trained part-based models. *IEEE TPAMI*, 32(9), pp. 1627–1645, 2010.

[118] A. Fader, L. Zettlemoyer, and O. Etzioni. Open question answering over curated and extracted knowledge bases. *ACM KDD Conference*, 2014.

[119] A. Fischer and C. Igel. An introduction to restricted Boltzmann machines. *Progress in Pattern Recognition, Image Analysis, Computer Vision, and Applications*, pp. 14–36, 2012.

[120] R. Fisher. The use of multiple measurements in taxonomic problems. *Annals of Eugenics*, 7: pp. 179–188, 1936.

[121] P. Frasconi, M. Gori, and A. Sperduti. A general framework for adaptive processing of data structures. *IEEE Transactions on Neural Networks*, 9(5), pp. 768–786, 1998.

[122] Y. Freund and R. Schapire. A decision-theoretic generalization of online learning and application to boosting. *Computational Learning Theory*, pp. 23–37, 1995.

[123] Y. Freund and R. Schapire. Large margin classification using the perceptron algorithm. *Machine Learning*, 37(3), pp. 277–296, 1999.

[124] Y. Freund and D. Haussler. Unsupervised learning of distributions on binary vectors using two layer networks. *Technical report*, Santa Cruz, CA, USA, 1994

[125] B. Fritzke. Fast learning with incremental RBF networks. *Neural Processing Letters*, 1(1), pp. 2–5, 1994.

[126] B. Fritzke. A growing neural gas network learns topologies. *NIPS Conference*, pp. 625–632, 1995.

[127] K. Fukushima. Neocognitron: A self-organizing neural network model for a mechanism of pattern recognition unaffected by shift in position. *Biological Cybernetics*, 36(4), pp. 193–202, 1980.

[128] S. Gallant. Perceptron-based learning algorithms. *IEEE Transactions on Neural Networks*, 1(2), pp. 179–191, 1990.

[129] S. Gallant. Neural network learning and expert systems. *MIT Press*, 1993.

[130] H. Gao, H. Yuan, Z. Wang, and S. Ji. Pixel Deconvolutional Networks. *arXiv:1705.06820*, 2017.
https://arxiv.org/abs/1705.06820

[131] L. Gatys, A. S. Ecker, and M. Bethge. Texture synthesis using convolutional neural networks. *NIPS Conference*, pp. 262–270, 2015.

[132] L. Gatys, A. Ecker, and M. Bethge. Image style transfer using convolutional neural networks. *IEEE Conference on Computer Vision and Pattern Recognition*, pp. 2414–2423, 2015.

[133] H. Gavin. The Levenberg-Marquardt method for nonlinear least squares curve-fitting problems, 2011.
http://people.duke.edu/~hpgavin/ce281/lm.pdf

[134] P. Gehler, A. Holub, and M. Welling. The Rate Adapting Poisson (RAP) model for information retrieval and object recognition. *ICML Confererence*, 2006.

[135] S. Gelly *et al.* The grand challenge of computer Go: Monte Carlo tree search and extensions. *Communcations of the ACM*, 55, pp. 106–113, 2012.

[136] A. Gersho and R. M. Gray. Vector quantization and signal compression. *Springer Science and Business Media*, 2012.

[137] A. Ghodsi. STAT 946: Topics in Probability and Statistics: Deep Learning, *University of Waterloo*, Fall 2015.
https://www.youtube.com/watch?v=fyAZszlPphs&list=PLehuLRPyt1Hyi78UOkMP–WCGRxGcA9NVOE

[138] W. Gilks, S. Richardson, and D. Spiegelhalter. Markov chain Monte Carlo in practice. *CRC Press*, 1995.

[139] F. Girosi and T. Poggio. Networks and the best approximation property. *Biological Cybernetics*, 63(3), pp. 169–176, 1990.

[140] X. Glorot and Y. Bengio. Understanding the difficulty of training deep feedforward neural networks. *AISTATS*, pp. 249–256, 2010.

[141] X. Glorot, A. Bordes, and Y. Bengio. Deep Sparse Rectifier Neural Networks. *AISTATS*, 15(106), 2011.

[142] P. Glynn. Likelihood ratio gradient estimation: an overview, *Proceedings of the 1987 Winter Simulation Conference*, pp. 366–375, 1987.

[143] Y. Goldberg. A primer on neural network models for natural language processing. *Journal of Artificial Intelligence Research (JAIR)*, 57, pp. 345–420, 2016.

[144] C. Goller and A. Küchler. Learning task-dependent distributed representations by backpropagation through structure. *Neural Networks*, 1, pp. 347–352, 1996.

[145] I. Goodfellow. NIPS 2016 tutorial: Generative adversarial networks. *arXiv:1701.00160*, 2016.
https://arxiv.org/abs/1701.00160

[146] I. Goodfellow, O. Vinyals, and A. Saxe. Qualitatively characterizing neural network optimization problems. *arXiv:1412.6544*, 2014. [Also appears in *International Conference in Learning
Representations*, 2015]
https://arxiv.org/abs/1412.6544

[147] I. Goodfellow, Y. Bengio, and A. Courville. Deep learning. *MIT Press*, 2016.

[148] I. Goodfellow, D. Warde-Farley, M. Mirza, A. Courville, and Y. Bengio. Maxout networks.
arXiv:1302.4389, 2013.

[149] I. Goodfellow *et al.* Generative adversarial nets. *NIPS Conference*, 2014.

[150] A. Graves, A. Mohamed, and G. Hinton. Speech recognition with deep recurrent neural
networks. *Acoustics, Speech and Signal Processing (ICASSP)*, pp. 6645–6649, 2013.

[151] A. Graves. Generating sequences with recurrent neural networks. *arXiv:1308.0850*, 2013.
https://arxiv.org/abs/1308.0850

[152] A. Graves. Supervised sequence labelling with recurrent neural networks *Springer*, 2012.
http://rd.springer.com/book/10.1007%2F978-3-642-24797-2

[153] A. Graves, S. Fernandez, F. Gomez, and J. Schmidhuber. Connectionist temporal classification: labelling unsegmented sequence data with recurrent neural networks. *ICML Confererence*, pp. 369–376, 2006.

[154] A. Graves, M. Liwicki, S. Fernandez, R. Bertolami, H. Bunke, and J. Schmidhuber. A
novel connectionist system for unconstrained handwriting recognition. *IEEE TPAMI*, 31(5),
pp. 855–868, 2009.

[155] A. Graves and J. Schmidhuber. Framewise Phoneme Classification with Bidirectional LSTM
and Other Neural Network Architectures. *Neural Networks*, 18(5–6), pp. 602–610, 2005.

[156] A. Graves and J. Schmidhuber. Offline handwriting recognition with multidimensional recurrent neural networks. *NIPS Conference*, pp. 545–552, 2009.

[157] A. Graves and N. Jaitly. Towards End-To-End Speech Recognition with Recurrent Neural
Networks. *ICML Conference*, pp. 1764–1772, 2014.

[158] A. Graves, G. Wayne, and I. Danihelka. Neural turing machines. *arXiv:1410.5401*, 2014.
https://arxiv.org/abs/1410.5401

[159] A. Graves *et al.* Hybrid computing using a neural network with dynamic external memory.
Nature, 538.7626, pp. 471–476, 2016.

[160] K. Greff, R. K. Srivastava, J. Koutnik, B. Steunebrink, and J. Schmidhuber. LSTM: A search
space odyssey. *IEEE Transactions on Neural Networks and Learning Systems*, 2016.
http://ieeexplore.ieee.org/abstract/document/7508408/

[161] K. Greff, R. K. Srivastava, and J. Schmidhuber. Highway and residual networks learn unrolled
iterative estimation. *arXiv:1612.07771*, 2016.
https://arxiv.org/abs/1612.07771

[162] I. Grondman, L. Busoniu, G. A. Lopes, and R. Babuska. A survey of actor-critic reinforcement learning: Standard and natural policy gradients. *IEEE Transactions on Systems, Man, and Cybernetics*, 42(6), pp. 1291–1307, 2012.

[163] R. Girshick, F. Iandola, T. Darrell, and J. Malik. Deformable part models are convolutional neural networks. *IEEE Conference on Computer Vision and Pattern Recognition*, pp. 437–446, 2015.

[164] A. Grover and J. Leskovec. node2vec: Scalable feature learning for networks. *ACM KDD Conference*, pp. 855–864, 2016.

[165] X. Guo, S. Singh, H. Lee, R. Lewis, and X. Wang. Deep learning for real-time Atari game play using offline Monte-Carlo tree search planning. *Advances in NIPS Conference*, pp. 3338–3346, 2014.

[166] M. Gutmann and A. Hyvarinen. Noise-contrastive estimation: A new estimation principle for unnormalized statistical models. *AISTATS*, 1(2), pp. 6, 2010.

[167] R. Hahnloser and H. S. Seung. Permitted and forbidden sets in symmetric threshold-linear networks. *NIPS Conference*, pp. 217–223, 2001.

[168] S. Han, X. Liu, H. Mao, J. Pu, A. Pedram, M. Horowitz, and W. Dally. EIE: Efficient Inference Engine for Compressed Neural Network. *ACM SIGARCH Computer Architecture News*, 44(3), pp. 243–254, 2016.

[169] S. Han, J. Pool, J. Tran, and W. Dally. Learning both weights and connections for efficient neural networks. *NIPS Conference*, pp. 1135–1143, 2015.

[170] L. K. Hansen and P. Salamon. Neural network ensembles. *IEEE TPAMI*, 12(10), pp. 993–1001, 1990.

[171] M. Hardt, B. Recht, and Y. Singer. Train faster, generalize better: Stability of stochastic gradient descent. *ICML Confererence*, pp. 1225–1234, 2006.

[172] B. Hariharan, P. Arbelaez, R. Girshick, and J. Malik. Simultaneous detection and segmentation. *arXiv:1407.1808*, 2014.
https://arxiv.org/abs/1407.1808

[173] E. Hartman, J. Keeler, and J. Kowalski. Layered neural networks with Gaussian hidden units as universal approximations. *Neural Computation*, 2(2), pp. 210–215, 1990.

[174] H. van Hasselt, A. Guez, and D. Silver. Deep Reinforcement Learning with Double Q-Learning. *AAAI Conference*, 2016.

[175] B. Hassibi and D. Stork. Second order derivatives for network pruning: Optimal brain surgeon. *NIPS Conference*, 1993.

[176] D. Hassabis, D. Kumaran, C. Summerfield, and M. Botvinick. Neuroscience-inspired artificial intelligence. *Neuron*, 95(2), pp. 245–258, 2017.

[177] T. Hastie, R. Tibshirani, and J. Friedman. The elements of statistical learning. *Springer*, 2009.

[178] T. Hastie and R. Tibshirani. Generalized additive models. *CRC Press*, 1990.

[179] T. Hastie, R. Tibshirani, and M. Wainwright. Statistical learning with sparsity: the lasso and generalizations. *CRC Press*, 2015.

[180] M. Havaei *et al.* Brain tumor segmentation with deep neural networks. *Medical Image Analysis*, 35, pp. 18–31, 2017.

[181] S. Hawkins, H. He, G. Williams, and R. Baxter. Outlier detection using replicator neural networks. *International Conference on Data Warehousing and Knowledge Discovery*, pp. 170–180, 2002.

[182] S. Haykin. Neural networks and learning machines. *Pearson*, 2008.

[183] K. He, X. Zhang, S. Ren, and J. Sun. Delving deep into rectifiers: Surpassing human-level performance on imagenet classification. *IEEE International Conference on Computer Vision*, pp. 1026–1034, 2015.

[184] K. He, X. Zhang, S. Ren, and J. Sun. Deep residual learning for image recognition. *IEEE Conference on Computer Vision and Pattern Recognition*, pp. 770–778, 2016.

[185] K. He, X. Zhang, S. Ren, and J. Sun. Identity mappings in deep residual networks. *European Conference on Computer Vision*, pp. 630–645, 2016.

[186] X. He, L. Liao, H. Zhang, L. Nie, X. Hu, and T. S. Chua. Neural collaborative filtering. *WWW Conference*, pp. 173–182, 2017.

[187] N. Heess *et al.* Emergence of Locomotion Behaviours in Rich Environments. *arXiv:1707.02286*, 2017.
https://arxiv.org/abs/1707.02286
Video 1 at: https://www.youtube.com/watch?v=hx_bgoTF7bs
Video 2 at: https://www.youtube.com/watch?v=gn4nRCC9TwQ&feature=youtu.be

[188] M. Henaff, J. Bruna, and Y. LeCun. Deep convolutional networks on graph-structured data. *arXiv:1506.05163*, 2015.
https://arxiv.org/abs/1506.05163

[189] M. Hestenes and E. Stiefel. Methods of conjugate gradients for solving linear systems. *Journal of Research of the National Bureau of Standards*, 49(6), 1952.

[190] G. Hinton. Connectionist learning procedures. *Artificial Intelligence*, 40(1–3), pp. 185–234, 1989.

[191] G. Hinton. Training products of experts by minimizing contrastive divergence. *Neural Computation*, 14(8), pp. 1771–1800, 2002.

[192] G. Hinton. To recognize shapes, first learn to generate images. *Progress in Brain Research*, 165, pp. 535–547, 2007.

[193] G. Hinton. A practical guide to training restricted Boltzmann machines. *Momentum*, 9(1), 926, 2010.

[194] G. Hinton. Neural networks for machine learning, *Coursera Video*, 2012.

[195] G. Hinton, P. Dayan, B. Frey, and R. Neal. The wake–sleep algorithm for unsupervised neural networks. *Science*, 268(5214), pp. 1158–1162, 1995.

[196] G. Hinton, S. Osindero, and Y. Teh. A fast learning algorithm for deep belief nets. *Neural Computation*, 18(7), pp. 1527–1554, 2006.

[197] G. Hinton and T. Sejnowski. Learning and relearning in Boltzmann machines. *Parallel Distributed Processing: Explorations in the Microstructure of Cognition*, MIT Press, 1986.

[198] G. Hinton and R. Salakhutdinov. Reducing the dimensionality of data with neural networks. *Science*, 313, (5766), pp. 504–507, 2006.

[199] G. Hinton and R. Salakhutdinov. Replicated softmax: an undirected topic model. *NIPS Conference*, pp. 1607–1614, 2009.

[200] G. Hinton and R. Salakhutdinov. A better way to pretrain deep Boltzmann machines. *NIPS Conference*, pp. 2447–2455, 2012.

[201] G. Hinton, N. Srivastava, A. Krizhevsky, I. Sutskever, and R. Salakhutdinov. Improving neural networks by preventing co-adaptation of feature detectors. *arXiv:1207.0580*, 2012.
https://arxiv.org/abs/1207.0580

[202] G. Hinton, O. Vinyals, and J. Dean. Distilling the knowledge in a neural network. *NIPS Workshop*, 2014.

[203] R. Hochberg. Matrix Multiplication with CUDA: A basic introduction to the CUDA programming model. *Unpublished manuscript*, 2012.
http://www.shodor.org/media/content/petascale/materials/UPModules/
matrixMultiplication/moduleDocument.pdf

[204] S. Hochreiter and J. Schmidhuber. Long short-term memory. *Neural Computation*, 9(8), pp. 1735–1785, 1997.

[205] S. Hochreiter, Y. Bengio, P. Frasconi, and J. Schmidhuber. Gradient flow in recurrent nets: the difficulty of learning long-term dependencies, *A Field Guide to Dynamical Recurrent Neural Networks*, IEEE Press, 2001.

[206] T. Hofmann. Probabilistic latent semantic indexing. *ACM SIGIR Conference*, pp. 50–57, 1999.

[207] J. J. Hopfield. Neural networks and physical systems with emergent collective computational abilities. *National Academy of Sciences of the USA*, 79(8), pp. 2554–2558, 1982.

[208] K. Hornik, M. Stinchcombe, and H. White. Multilayer feedforward networks are universal approximators. *Neural Networks*, 2(5), pp. 359–366, 1989.

[209] Y. Hu, Y. Koren, and C. Volinsky. Collaborative filtering for implicit feedback datasets. *IEEE International Conference on Data Mining*, pp. 263–272, 2008.

[210] G. Huang, Y. Sun, Z. Liu, D. Sedra, and K. Weinberger. Deep networks with stochastic depth. *European Conference on Computer Vision*, pp. 646–661, 2016.

[211] G. Huang, Z. Liu, K. Weinberger, and L. van der Maaten. Densely connected convolutional networks. *arXiv:1608.06993*, 2016.
https://arxiv.org/abs/1608.06993

[212] D. Hubel and T. Wiesel. Receptive fields of single neurones in the cat's striate cortex. *The Journal of Physiology*, 124(3), pp. 574–591, 1959.

[213] F. Iandola, S. Han, M. Moskewicz, K. Ashraf, W. Dally, and K. Keutzer. SqueezeNet: AlexNet-level accuracy with 50x fewer parameters and< 0.5 MB model size. *arXiv:1602.07360*, 2016.
https://arxiv.org/abs/1602.07360

[214] S. Ioffe and C. Szegedy. Batch normalization: Accelerating deep network training by reducing internal covariate shift. *arXiv:1502.03167*, 2015.

[215] P. Isola, J. Zhu, T. Zhou, and A. Efros. Image-to-image translation with conditional adversarial networks. *arXiv:1611.07004*, 2016.
https://arxiv.org/abs/1611.07004

[216] M. Iyyer, J. Boyd-Graber, L. Claudino, R. Socher, and H. Daume III. A Neural Network for Factoid Question Answering over Paragraphs. *EMNLP*, 2014.

[217] R. Jacobs. Increased rates of convergence through learning rate adaptation. *Neural Networks*, 1(4), pp. 295–307, 1988.

[218] M. Jaderberg, K. Simonyan, and A. Zisserman. Spatial transformer networks. *NIPS Conference*, pp. 2017–2025, 2015.

[219] H. Jaeger. The "echo state" approach to analysing and training recurrent neural networks – with an erratum note. *German National Research Center for Information Technology GMD Technical Report*, 148(34), 13, 2001.

[220] H. Jaeger and H. Haas. Harnessing nonlinearity: Predicting chaotic systems and saving energy in wireless communication. *Science*, 304, pp. 78–80, 2004.

[221] K. Jarrett, K. Kavukcuoglu, M. Ranzato, and Y. LeCun. What is the best multi-stage architecture for object recognition? *International Conference on Computer Vision (ICCV)*, 2009.

[222] S. Ji, W. Xu, M. Yang, and K. Yu. 3D convolutional neural networks for human action recognition. *IEEE TPAMI*, 35(1), pp. 221–231, 2013.

[223] Y. Jia *et al.* Caffe: Convolutional architecture for fast feature embedding. *ACM International Conference on Multimedia*, 2014.

[224] C. Johnson. Logistic matrix factorization for implicit feedback data. *NIPS Conference*, 2014.

[225] J. Johnson, A. Karpathy, and L. Fei-Fei. Densecap: Fully convolutional localization networks for dense captioning. *IEEE Conference on Computer Vision and Pattern Recognition*, pp. 4565–4574, 2015.

[226] J. Johnson, A. Alahi, and L. Fei-Fei. Perceptual losses for real-time style transfer and super-resolution. *European Conference on Computer Vision*, pp. 694–711, 2015.

[227] R. Johnson and T. Zhang. Effective use of word order for text categorization with convolutional neural networks. *arXiv:1412.1058*, 2014.
https://arxiv.org/abs/1412.1058

[228] R. Jozefowicz, W. Zaremba, and I. Sutskever. An empirical exploration of recurrent network architectures. *ICML Confererence*, pp. 2342–2350, 2015.

[229] L. Kaiser and I. Sutskever. Neural GPUs learn algorithms. *arXiv:1511.08228*, 2015.
https://arxiv.org/abs/1511.08228

[230] S. Kakade. A natural policy gradient. *NIPS Conference*, pp. 1057–1063, 2002.

[231] N. Kalchbrenner and P. Blunsom. Recurrent continuous translation models. *EMNLP*, 3, 39, pp. 413, 2013.

[232] H. Kandel, J. Schwartz, T. Jessell, S. Siegelbaum, and A. Hudspeth. Principles of neural science. *McGraw Hill*, 2012.

[233] A. Karpathy, J. Johnson, and L. Fei-Fei. Visualizing and understanding recurrent networks. *arXiv:1506.02078*, 2015.
https://arxiv.org/abs/1506.02078

[234] A. Karpathy, G. Toderici, S. Shetty, T. Leung, R. Sukthankar, and L. Fei-Fei. Large-scale video classification with convolutional neural networks. *IEEE Conference on Computer Vision and Pattern Recognition*, pp. 725–1732, 2014.

[235] A. Karpathy. The unreasonable effectiveness of recurrent neural networks, *Blog post*, 2015.
http://karpathy.github.io/2015/05/21/rnn-effectiveness/

[236] A. Karpathy, J. Johnson, and L. Fei-Fei. Stanford University Class CS321n: Convolutional neural networks for visual recognition, 2016.
http://cs231n.github.io/

[237] H. J. Kelley. Gradient theory of optimal flight paths. *Ars Journal*, 30(10), pp. 947–954, 1960.

[238] F. Khan, B. Mutlu, and X. Zhu. How do humans teach: On curriculum learning and teaching dimension. *NIPS Conference*, pp. 1449–1457, 2011.

[239] T. Kietzmann, P. McClure, and N. Kriegeskorte. Deep Neural Networks In Computational Neuroscience. *bioRxiv, 133504*, 2017.
https://www.biorxiv.org/content/early/2017/05/04/133504

[240] Y. Kim. Convolutional neural networks for sentence classification. *arXiv:1408.5882*, 2014.

[241] D. Kingma and J. Ba. Adam: A method for stochastic optimization. *arXiv:1412.6980*, 2014.
https://arxiv.org/abs/1412.6980

[242] D. Kingma and M. Welling. Auto-encoding variational bayes. *arXiv:1312.6114*, 2013.
https://arxiv.org/abs/1312.6114

[243] T. Kipf and M. Welling. Semi-supervised classification with graph convolutional networks. *arXiv:1609.02907*, 2016.
https://arxiv.org/pdf/1609.02907.pdf

[244] S. Kirkpatrick, C. Gelatt, and M. Vecchi. Optimization by simulated annealing. *Science*, 220, pp. 671–680, 1983.

[245] J. Kivinen and M. Warmuth. The perceptron algorithm vs. winnow: linear vs. logarithmic mistake bounds when few input variables are relevant. *Computational Learning Theory*, pp. 289–296, 1995.

[246] L. Kocsis and C. Szepesvari. Bandit based monte-carlo planning. *ECML Conference*, pp. 282–293, 2006.

[247] R. Kohavi and D. Wolpert. Bias plus variance decomposition for zero-one loss functions. *ICML Conference*, 1996.

[248] T. Kohonen. The self-organizing map. Neurocomputing, 21(1), pp. 1–6, 1998.

[249] T. Kohonen. Self-organization and associative memory. *Springer*, 2012.

[250] T. Kohonen. Self-organizing maps, *Springer*, 2001.

[251] D. Koller and N. Friedman. Probabilistic graphical models: principles and techniques. *MIT Press*, 2009.

[252] E. Kong and T. Dietterich. Error-correcting output coding corrects bias and variance. *ICML Conference*, pp. 313–321, 1995.

[253] Y. Koren. Factor in the neighbors: Scalable and accurate collaborative filtering. *ACM Transactions on Knowledge Discovery from Data (TKDD)*, 4(1), 1, 2010.

[254] A. Krizhevsky. One weird trick for parallelizing convolutional neural networks. *arXiv:1404.5997*, 2014.
https://arxiv.org/abs/1404.5997

[255] A. Krizhevsky, I. Sutskever, and G. Hinton. Imagenet classification with deep convolutional neural networks. *NIPS Conference*, pp. 1097–1105. 2012.

[256] M. Kubat. Decision trees can initialize radial-basis function networks. *IEEE Transactions on Neural Networks*, 9(5), pp. 813–821, 1998.

[257] A. Kumar *et al.* Ask me anything: Dynamic memory networks for natural language processing. *ICML Confererence*, 2016.

[258] Y. Koren. Collaborative filtering with temporal dynamics. *ACM KDD Conference*, pp. 447–455, 2009.

[259] M. Lai. Giraffe: Using deep reinforcement learning to play chess. *arXiv:1509.01549*, 2015.

[260] S. Lai, L. Xu, K. Liu, and J. Zhao. Recurrent Convolutional Neural Networks for Text Classification. *AAAI*, pp. 2267–2273, 2015.

[261] B. Lake, T. Ullman, J. Tenenbaum, and S. Gershman. Building machines that learn and think like people. *Behavioral and Brain Sciences*, pp. 1–101, 2016.

[262] H. Larochelle. Neural Networks (Course). Universite de Sherbrooke, 2013.
https://www.youtube.com/watch?v=SGZ6BttHMPw&list=PL6Xpj9I5qXYEcOhn7–
TqghAJ6NAPrNmUBH

[263] H. Larochelle and Y. Bengio. Classification using discriminative restricted Boltzmann machines. *ICML Conference*, pp. 536–543, 2008.

[264] H. Larochelle, M. Mandel, R. Pascanu, and Y. Bengio. Learning algorithms for the classification restricted Boltzmann machine. *Journal of Machine Learning Research*, 13, pp. 643–669, 2012.

[265] H. Larochelle and I. Murray. The neural autoregressive distribution estimator. *International Conference on Artificial Intelligence and Statistics*, pp. 29–37, 2011.

[266] H. Larochelle and G. E. Hinton. Learning to combine foveal glimpses with a third-order Boltzmann machine. *NIPS Conference*, 2010.

[267] H. Larochelle, D. Erhan, A. Courville, J. Bergstra, and Y. Bengio. An empirical evaluation of deep architectures on problems with many factors of variation. *ICML Conference*, pp. 473–480, 2007.

[268] G. Larsson, M. Maire, and G. Shakhnarovich. Fractalnet: Ultra-deep neural networks without residuals. *arXiv:1605.07648*, 2016.
https://arxiv.org/abs/1605.07648

[269] S. Lawrence, C. L. Giles, A. C. Tsoi, and A. D. Back. Face recognition: A convolutional neural-network approach. *IEEE Transactions on Neural Networks*, 8(1), pp. 98–113, 1997.

[270] Q. Le *et al.* Building high-level features using large scale unsupervised learning. *ICASSP*, 2013.

[271] Q. Le, N. Jaitly, and G. Hinton. A simple way to initialize recurrent networks of rectified linear units. *arXiv:1504.00941*, 2015.
https://arxiv.org/abs/1504.00941

[272] Q. Le and T. Mikolov. Distributed representations of sentences and documents. *ICML Conference*, pp. 1188–196, 2014.

[273] Q. Le, J. Ngiam, A. Coates, A. Lahiri, B. Prochnow, and A. Ng, On optimization methods for deep learning. *ICML Conference*, pp. 265–272, 2011.

[274] Q. Le, W. Zou, S. Yeung, and A. Ng. Learning hierarchical spatio-temporal features for action recognition with independent subspace analysis. *CVPR Conference*, 2011.

[275] Y. LeCun. Modeles connexionnistes de l'apprentissage. *Doctoral Dissertation*, Universite Paris, 1987.

[276] Y. LeCun and Y. Bengio. Convolutional networks for images, speech, and time series. *The Handbook of Brain Theory and Neural Networks*, 3361(10), 1995.

[277] Y. LeCun, Y. Bengio, and G. Hinton. Deep learning. *Nature*, 521(7553), pp. 436–444, 2015.

[278] Y. LeCun, L. Bottou, G. Orr, and K. Muller. Efficient backprop. in G. Orr and K. Muller (eds.) *Neural Networks: Tricks of the Trade*, Springer, 1998.

[279] Y. LeCun, L. Bottou, Y. Bengio, and P. Haffner. Gradient-based learning applied to document recognition. *Proceedings of the IEEE*, 86(11), pp. 2278–2324, 1998.

[280] Y. LeCun, S. Chopra, R. M. Hadsell, M. A. Ranzato, and F.-J. Huang. A tutorial on energy-based learning. *Predicting Structured Data*, MIT Press, pp. 191–246,, 2006.

[281] Y. LeCun, C. Cortes, and C. Burges. The MNIST database of handwritten digits, 1998.
http://yann.lecun.com/exdb/mnist/

[282] Y. LeCun, J. Denker, and S. Solla. Optimal brain damage. *NIPS Conference*, pp. 598–605, 1990.

[283] Y. LeCun, K. Kavukcuoglu, and C. Farabet. Convolutional networks and applications in vision. *IEEE International Symposium on Circuits and Systems*, pp. 253–256, 2010.

[284] H. Lee, C. Ekanadham, and A. Ng. Sparse deep belief net model for visual area V2. *NIPS Conference*, 2008.

[285] H. Lee, R. Grosse, B. Ranganath, and A. Y. Ng. Convolutional deep belief networks for scalable unsupervised learning of hierarchical representations. *ICML Conference*, pp. 609–616, 2009.

[286] S. Levine, C. Finn, T. Darrell, and P. Abbeel. End-to-end training of deep visuomotor policies. *Journal of Machine Learning Research*, 17(39), pp. 1–40, 2016.
Video at: https://sites.google.com/site/visuomotorpolicy/

[287] O. Levy and Y. Goldberg. Neural word embedding as implicit matrix factorization. *NIPS Conference*, pp. 2177–2185, 2014.

[288] O. Levy, Y. Goldberg, and I. Dagan. Improving distributional similarity with lessons learned from word embeddings. *Transactions of the Association for Computational Linguistics*, 3, pp. 211–225, 2015.

[289] W. Levy and R. Baxter. Energy efficient neural codes. *Neural Computation*, 8(3), pp. 531–543, 1996.

[290] M. Lewis, D. Yarats, Y. Dauphin, D. Parikh, and D. Batra. Deal or No Deal? End-to-End Learning for Negotiation Dialogues. *arXiv:1706.05125*, 2017.
https://arxiv.org/abs/1706.05125

[291] J. Li, W. Monroe, A. Ritter, M. Galley,, J. Gao, and D. Jurafsky. Deep reinforcement learning for dialogue generation. *arXiv:1606.01541*, 2016.
https://arxiv.org/abs/1606.01541

[292] L. Li, W. Chu, J. Langford, and R. Schapire. A contextual-bandit approach to personalized news article recommendation. *WWW Conference*, pp. 661–670, 2010.

[293] Y. Li. Deep reinforcement learning: An overview. *arXiv:1701.07274*, 2017.
https://arxiv.org/abs/1701.07274

[294] Q. Liao, K. Kawaguchi, and T. Poggio. Streaming normalization: Towards simpler and more biologically-plausible normalizations for online and recurrent learning. *arXiv:1610.06160*, 2016.
https://arxiv.org/abs/1610.06160

[295] D. Liben-Nowell, and J. Kleinberg. The link-prediction problem for social networks. *Journal of the American Society for Information Science and Technology*, 58(7), pp. 1019–1031, 2007.

[296] L.-J. Lin. Reinforcement learning for robots using neural networks. *Technical Report*, DTIC Document, 1993.

[297] M. Lin, Q. Chen, and S. Yan. Network in network. *arXiv:1312.4400*, 2013.
https://arxiv.org/abs/1312.4400

[298] Z. Lipton, J. Berkowitz, and C. Elkan. A critical review of recurrent neural networks for sequence learning. *arXiv:1506.00019*, 2015.
https://arxiv.org/abs/1506.00019

[299] J. Lu, J. Yang, D. Batra, and D. Parikh. Hierarchical question-image co-attention for visual question answering. *NIPS Conference*, pp. 289–297, 2016.

[300] D. Luenberger and Y. Ye. Linear and nonlinear programming, *Addison-Wesley*, 1984.

[301] M. Lukosevicius and H. Jaeger. Reservoir computing approaches to recurrent neural network training. *Computer Science Review*, 3(3), pp. 127–149, 2009.

[302] M. Luong, H. Pham, and C. Manning. Effective approaches to attention-based neural machine translation. *arXiv:1508.04025*, 2015.
https://arxiv.org/abs/1508.04025

[303] J. Ma, R. P. Sheridan, A. Liaw, G. E. Dahl, and V. Svetnik. Deep neural nets as a method for quantitative structure-activity relationships. *Journal of Chemical Information and Modeling*, 55(2), pp. 263–274, 2015.

[304] W. Maass, T. Natschlager, and H. Markram. Real-time computing without stable states: A new framework for neural computation based on perturbations. *Neural Computation*, 14(11), pp. 2351–2560, 2002.

[305] L. Maaten and G. E. Hinton. Visualizing data using t-SNE. *Journal of Machine Learning Research*, 9, pp. 2579–2605, 2008.

[306] D. J. MacKay. A practical Bayesian framework for backpropagation networks. *Neural Computation*, 4(3), pp. 448–472, 1992.

[307] C. Maddison, A. Huang, I. Sutskever, and D. Silver. Move evaluation in Go using deep convolutional neural networks. *International Conference on Learning Representations*, 2015.

[308] A. Mahendran and A. Vedaldi. Understanding deep image representations by inverting them. *IEEE Conference on Computer Vision and Pattern Recognition*, pp. 5188–5196, 2015.

[309] A. Makhzani and B. Frey. K-sparse autoencoders. *arXiv:1312.5663*, 2013.
https://arxiv.org/abs/1312.5663

[310] A. Makhzani and B. Frey. Winner-take-all autoencoders. *NIPS Conference*, pp. 2791–2799, 2015.

[311] A. Makhzani, J. Shlens, N. Jaitly, I. Goodfellow, and B. Frey. Adversarial autoencoders. *arXiv:1511.05644*, 2015.
https://arxiv.org/abs/1511.05644

[312] C. Manning and R. Socher. CS224N: Natural language processing with deep learning. *Stanford University School of Engineering*, 2017.
https://www.youtube.com/watch?v=OQQ-W_63UgQ

[313] J. Martens. Deep learning via Hessian-free optimization. *ICML Conference*, pp. 735–742, 2010.

[314] J. Martens and I. Sutskever. Learning recurrent neural networks with hessian-free optimization. *ICML Conference*, pp. 1033–1040, 2011.

[315] J. Martens, I. Sutskever, and K. Swersky. Estimating the hessian by back-propagating curvature. *arXiv:1206.6464*, 2016.
https://arxiv.org/abs/1206.6464

[316] J. Martens and R. Grosse. Optimizing Neural Networks with Kronecker-factored Approximate Curvature. *ICML Conference*, 2015.

[317] T. Martinetz, S. Berkovich, and K. Schulten. 'Neural-gas' network for vector quantization and its application to time-series prediction. *IEEE Transactions on Neural Network*, 4(4), pp. 558–569, 1993.

[318] J. Masci, U. Meier, D. Ciresan, and J. Schmidhuber. Stacked convolutional auto-encoders for hierarchical feature extraction. *Artificial Neural Networks and Machine Learning*, pp. 52–59, 2011.

[319] M. Mathieu, C. Couprie, and Y. LeCun. Deep multi-scale video prediction beyond mean square error. *arXiv:1511.054*, 2015.
https://arxiv.org/abs/1511.05440

[320] P. McCullagh and J. Nelder. Generalized linear models *CRC Press*, 1989.

[321] W. S. McCulloch and W. H. Pitts. A logical calculus of the ideas immanent in nervous activity. *The Bulletin of Mathematical Biophysics*, 5(4), pp. 115–133, 1943.

[322] G. McLachlan. Discriminant analysis and statistical pattern recognition *John Wiley & Sons*, 2004.

[323] C. Micchelli. Interpolation of scattered data: distance matrices and conditionally positive definite functions. *Constructive Approximations*, 2, pp. 11–22, 1986.

[324] T. Mikolov. Statistical language models based on neural networks. *Ph.D. thesis, Brno University of Technology*, 2012.

[325] T. Mikolov, K. Chen, G. Corrado, and J. Dean. Efficient estimation of word representations in vector space. *arXiv:1301.3781*, 2013.
https://arxiv.org/abs/1301.3781

[326] T. Mikolov, A. Joulin, S. Chopra, M. Mathieu, and M. Ranzato. Learning longer memory in recurrent neural networks. *arXiv:1412.7753*, 2014.
https://arxiv.org/abs/1412.7753

[327] T. Mikolov, I. Sutskever, K. Chen, G. Corrado, and J. Dean. Distributed representations of words and phrases and their compositionality. *NIPS Conference*, pp. 3111–3119, 2013.

[328] T. Mikolov, M. Karafiat, L. Burget, J. Cernocky, and S. Khudanpur. Recurrent neural network based language model. *Interspeech*, Vol 2, 2010.

[329] G. Miller, R. Beckwith, C. Fellbaum, D. Gross, and K. J. Miller. Introduction to WordNet: An on-line lexical database. *International Journal of Lexicography*, 3(4), pp. 235–312, 1990.
https://wordnet.princeton.edu/

[330] M. Minsky and S. Papert. Perceptrons. An Introduction to Computational Geometry, *MIT Press*, 1969.

[331] M. Mirza and S. Osindero. Conditional generative adversarial nets. *arXiv:1411.1784*, 2014.
https://arxiv.org/abs/1411.1784

[332] A. Mnih and G. Hinton. A scalable hierarchical distributed language model. *NIPS Conference*, pp. 1081–1088, 2009.

[333] A. Mnih and K. Kavukcuoglu. Learning word embeddings efficiently with noise-contrastive estimation. *NIPS Conference*, pp. 2265–2273, 2013.

[334] A. Mnih and Y. Teh. A fast and simple algorithm for training neural probabilistic language models. *arXiv:1206.6426*, 2012.
https://arxiv.org/abs/1206.6426

[335] V. Mnih *et al*. Human-level control through deep reinforcement learning. *Nature*, 518 (7540), pp. 529–533, 2015.

[336] V. Mnih, K. Kavukcuoglu, D. Silver, A. Graves, I. Antonoglou, D. Wierstra, and M. Riedmiller. Playing atari with deep reinforcement learning. *arXiv:1312.5602.*, 2013.
https://arxiv.org/abs/1312.5602

[337] V. Mnih *et al*. Asynchronous methods for deep reinforcement learning. *ICML Confererence*, pp. 1928–1937, 2016.

[338] V. Mnih, N. Heess, and A. Graves. Recurrent models of visual attention. *NIPS Conference*, pp. 2204–2212, 2014.

[339] H. Mobahi and J. Fisher. A theoretical analysis of optimization by Gaussian continuation. *AAAI Conference*, 2015.

[340] G. Montufar. Universal approximation depth and errors of narrow belief networks with discrete units. *Neural Computation*, 26(7), pp. 1386–1407, 2014.

[341] G. Montufar and N. Ay. Refinements of universal approximation results for deep belief networks and restricted Boltzmann machines. *Neural Computation*, 23(5), pp. 1306–1319, 2011.

[342] J. Moody and C. Darken. Fast learning in networks of locally-tuned processing units. *Neural Computation*, 1(2), pp. 281–294, 1989.

[343] A. Moore and C. Atkeson. Prioritized sweeping: Reinforcement learning with less data and less time. *Machine Learning*, 13(1), pp. 103–130, 1993.

[344] F. Morin and Y. Bengio. Hierarchical Probabilistic Neural Network Language Model. *AIS-TATS*, pp. 246–252, 2005.

[345] R. Miotto, F. Wang, S. Wang, X. Jiang, and J. T. Dudley. Deep learning for healthcare: review, opportunities and challenges. *Briefings in Bioinformatics*, pp. 1–11, 2017.

[346] M. Müller, M. Enzenberger, B. Arneson, and R. Segal. Fuego - an open-source framework for board games and Go engine based on Monte-Carlo tree search. *IEEE Transactions on Computational Intelligence and AI in Games*, 2, pp. 259–270, 2010.

[347] M. Musavi, W. Ahmed, K. Chan, K. Faris, and D. Hummels. On the training of radial basis function classifiers. *Neural Networks*, 5(4), pp. 595–603, 1992.

[348] V. Nair and G. Hinton. Rectified linear units improve restricted Boltzmann machines. *ICML Conference*, pp. 807–814, 2010.

[349] K. S. Narendra and K. Parthasarathy. Identification and control of dynamical systems using neural networks. *IEEE Transactions on Neural Networks*, 1(1), pp. 4–27, 1990.

[350] R. M. Neal. Connectionist learning of belief networks. *Artificial intelligence*, 1992.

[351] R. M. Neal. Probabilistic inference using Markov chain Monte Carlo methods. *Technical Report CRG-TR-93-1*, 1993.

[352] R. M. Neal. Annealed importance sampling. *Statistics and Computing*, 11(2), pp. 125–139, 2001.

[353] Y. Nesterov. A method of solving a convex programming problem with convergence rate $O(1/k^2)$. *Soviet Mathematics Doklady*, 27, pp. 372–376, 1983.

[354] A. Ng. Sparse autoencoder. *CS294A Lecture notes*, 2011.
https://nlp.stanford.edu/~socherr/sparseAutoencoder_2011new.pdf
https://web.stanford.edu/class/cs294a/sparseAutoencoder_2011new.pdf

[355] A. Ng and M. Jordan. PEGASUS: A policy search method for large MDPs and POMDPs. *Uncertainity in Artificial Intelligence*, pp. 406–415, 2000.

[356] J. Y.-H. Ng, M. Hausknecht, S. Vijayanarasimhan, O. Vinyals, R. Monga, and G. Toderici. Beyond short snippets: Deep networks for video classification. *IEEE Conference on Computer Vision and Pattern Recognition*, pp. 4694–4702, 2015.

[357] J. Ngiam, A. Khosla, M. Kim, J. Nam, H. Lee, and A. Ng. Multimodal deep learning. *ICML Conference*, pp. 689–696, 2011.

[358] A. Nguyen, A. Dosovitskiy, J. Yosinski, T., Brox, and J. Clune. Synthesizing the preferred inputs for neurons in neural networks via deep generator networks. *NIPS Conference*, pp. 3387–3395, 2016.

[359] J. Nocedal and S. Wright. Numerical optimization. *Springer*, 2006.

[360] S. Nowlan and G. Hinton. Simplifying neural networks by soft weight-sharing. *Neural Computation*, 4(4), pp. 473–493, 1992.

[361] M. Oquab, L. Bottou, I. Laptev, and J. Sivic. Learning and transferring mid-level image representations using convolutional neural networks. *IEEE Conference on Computer Vision and Pattern Recognition*, pp. 1717–1724, 2014.

[362] G. Orr and K.-R. Müller (editors). Neural Networks: Tricks of the Trade, *Springer*, 1998.

[363] M. J. L. Orr. Introduction to radial basis function networks, *University of Edinburgh Technical Report, Centre of Cognitive Science*, 1996.
ftp://ftp.cogsci.ed.ac.uk/pub/mjo/intro.ps.Z

[364] M. Palatucci, D. Pomerleau, G. Hinton, and T. Mitchell. Zero-shot learning with semantic output codes. *NIPS Conference*, pp. 1410–1418, 2009.

[365] J. Park and I. Sandberg. Universal approximation using radial-basis-function networks. *Neural Computation*, 3(1), pp. 246–257, 1991.

[366] J. Park and I. Sandberg. Approximation and radial-basis-function networks. *Neural Computation*, 5(2), pp. 305–316, 1993.

[367] O. Parkhi, A. Vedaldi, and A. Zisserman. Deep Face Recognition. *BMVC*, 1(3), pp. 6, 2015.

[368] R. Pascanu, T. Mikolov, and Y. Bengio. On the difficulty of training recurrent neural networks. *ICML Conference*, 28, pp. 1310–1318, 2013.

[369] R. Pascanu, T. Mikolov, and Y. Bengio. Understanding the exploding gradient problem. *CoRR, abs/1211.5063*, 2012.

[370] D. Pathak, P. Krahenbuhl, J. Donahue, T. Darrell, and A. A. Efros. Context encoders: Feature learning by inpainting. *CVPR Conference*, 2016.

[371] J. Pennington, R. Socher, and C. Manning. Glove: Global Vectors for Word Representation. *EMNLP*, pp. 1532–1543, 2014.

[372] B. Perozzi, R. Al-Rfou, and S. Skiena. Deepwalk: Online learning of social representations. *ACM KDD Conference*, pp. 701–710.

[373] C. Peterson and J. Anderson. A mean field theory learning algorithm for neural networks. *Complex Systems*, 1(5), pp. 995–1019, 1987.

[374] J. Peters and S. Schaal. Reinforcement learning of motor skills with policy gradients. *Neural Networks*, 21(4), pp. 682–697, 2008.

[375] F. Pineda. Generalization of back-propagation to recurrent neural networks. *Physical Review Letters*, 59(19), 2229, 1987.

[376] E. Polak. Computational methods in optimization: a unified approach. *Academic Press*, 1971.

[377] L. Polanyi and A. Zaenen. Contextual valence shifters. *Computing Attitude and Affect in Text: Theory and Applications*, pp. 1–10, Springer, 2006.

[378] G. Pollastri, D. Przybylski, B. Rost, and P. Baldi. Improving the prediction of protein secondary structure in three and eight classes using recurrent neural networks and profiles. *Proteins: Structure, Function, and Bioinformatics*, 47(2), pp. 228–235, 2002.

[379] J. Pollack. Recursive distributed representations. *Artificial Intelligence*, 46(1), pp. 77–105, 1990.

[380] B. Polyak and A. Juditsky. Acceleration of stochastic approximation by averaging. *SIAM Journal on Control and Optimization*, 30(4), pp. 838–855, 1992.

[381] D. Pomerleau. ALVINN, an autonomous land vehicle in a neural network. *Technical Report*, Carnegie Mellon University, 1989.

[382] B. Poole, J. Sohl-Dickstein, and S. Ganguli. Analyzing noise in autoencoders and deep networks. *arXiv:1406.1831*, 2014.
https://arxiv.org/abs/1406.1831

[383] H. Poon and P. Domingos. Sum-product networks: A new deep architecture. *Computer Vision Workshops (ICCV Workshops)*, pp. 689–690, 2011.

[384] A. Radford, L. Metz, and S. Chintala. Unsupervised representation learning with deep convolutional generative adversarial networks. *arXiv:1511.06434*, 2015.
https://arxiv.org/abs/1511.06434

[385] A. Rahimi and B. Recht. Random features for large-scale kernel machines. *NIPS Conference*, pp. 1177–1184, 2008.

[386] M.' A. Ranzato, Y-L. Boureau, and Y. LeCun. Sparse feature learning for deep belief networks. *NIPS Conference*, pp. 1185–1192, 2008.

[387] M.' A. Ranzato, F. J. Huang, Y-L. Boureau, and Y. LeCun. Unsupervised learning of invariant feature hierarchies with applications to object recognition. *Computer Vision and Pattern Recognition*, pp. 1–8, 2007.

[388] A. Rasmus, M. Berglund, M. Honkala, H. Valpola, and T. Raiko. Semi-supervised learning with ladder networks. *NIPS Conference*, pp. 3546–3554, 2015.

[389] M. Rastegari, V. Ordonez, J. Redmon, and A. Farhadi. Xnor-net: Imagenet classification using binary convolutional neural networks. *European Conference on Computer Vision*, pp. 525–542, 2016.

[390] A. Razavian, H. Azizpour, J. Sullivan, and S. Carlsson. CNN features off-the-shelf: an astounding baseline for recognition. *IEEE Conference on Computer Vision and Pattern Recognition Workshops*, pp. 806–813, 2014.

[391] J. Redmon, S. Divvala, R. Girshick, and A. Farhadi. You only look once: Unified, real-time object detection. *IEEE Conference on Computer Vision and Pattern Recognition*, pp. 779–788, 2016.

[392] S. Reed, Z. Akata, X. Yan, L. Logeswaran, B. Schiele, and H. Lee. Generative adversarial text to image synthesis. *ICML Conference*, pp. 1060–1069, 2016.

[393] S. Reed and N. de Freitas. Neural programmer-interpreters. *arXiv:1511.06279*, 2015.

[394] R. Rehurek and P. Sojka. Software framework for topic modelling with large corpora. *LREC 2010 Workshop on New Challenges for NLP Frameworks*, pp. 45–50, 2010.
https://radimrehurek.com/gensim/index.html

[395] M. Ren, R. Kiros, and R. Zemel. Exploring models and data for image question answering. *NIPS Conference*, pp. 2953–2961, 2015.

[396] S. Rendle. Factorization machines. *IEEE ICDM Conference*, pp. 995–100, 2010.

[397] S. Rifai, P. Vincent, X. Muller, X. Glorot, and Y. Bengio. Contractive auto-encoders: Explicit invariance during feature extraction. *ICML Conference*, pp. 833–840, 2011.

[398] S. Rifai, Y. Dauphin, P. Vincent, Y. Bengio, and X. Muller. The manifold tangent classifier. *NIPS Conference*, pp. 2294–2302, 2011.

[399] D. Rezende, S. Mohamed, and D. Wierstra. Stochastic backpropagation and approximate inference in deep generative models. *arXiv:1401.4082*, 2014.
https://arxiv.org/abs/1401.4082

[400] R. Rifkin. Everything old is new again: a fresh look at historical approaches in machine learning. *Ph.D. Thesis*, Massachusetts Institute of Technology, 2002.

[401] R. Rifkin and A. Klautau. In defense of one-vs-all classification. *Journal of Machine Learning Research*, 5, pp. 101–141, 2004.

[402] V. Romanuke. Parallel Computing Center (Khmelnitskiy, Ukraine) represents an ensemble of 5 convolutional neural networks which performs on MNIST at 0.21 percent error rate. Retrieved 24 November 2016.

[403] B. Romera-Paredes and P. Torr. An embarrassingly simple approach to zero-shot learning. *ICML Confererence*, pp. 2152–2161, 2015.

[404] X. Rong. word2vec parameter learning explained. *arXiv:1411.2738*, 2014.
https://arxiv.org/abs/1411.2738

[405] F. Rosenblatt. The perceptron: A probabilistic model for information storage and organization in the brain. *Psychological Review*, 65(6), 386, 1958.

[406] D. Ruck, S. Rogers, and M. Kabrisky. Feature selection using a multilayer perceptron. *Journal of Neural Network Computing*, 2(2), pp. 40–88, 1990.

[407] H. A. Rowley, S. Baluja, and T. Kanade. Neural network-based face detection. *IEEE TPAMI*, 20(1), pp. 23–38, 1998.

[408] D. Rumelhart, G. Hinton, and R. Williams. Learning representations by back-propagating errors. *Nature*, 323 (6088), pp. 533–536, 1986.

[409] D. Rumelhart, G. Hinton, and R. Williams. Learning internal representations by back-propagating errors. In *Parallel Distributed Processing: Explorations in the Microstructure of Cognition*, pp. 318–362, 1986.

[410] D. Rumelhart, D. Zipser, and J. McClelland. Parallel Distributed Processing, *MIT Press*, pp. 151–193, 1986.

[411] D. Rumelhart and D. Zipser. Feature discovery by competitive learning. *Cognitive science*, 9(1), pp. 75–112, 1985.

[412] G. Rummery and M. Niranjan. Online Q-learning using connectionist systems (Vol. 37). *University of Cambridge, Department of Engineering*, 1994.

[413] A. M. Rush, S. Chopra, and J. Weston. A Neural Attention Model for Abstractive Sentence Summarization. *arXiv:1509.00685*, 2015.
https://arxiv.org/abs/1509.00685

[414] R. Salakhutdinov, A. Mnih, and G. Hinton. Restricted Boltzmann machines for collaborative filtering. *ICML Confererence*, pp. 791–798, 2007.

[415] R. Salakhutdinov and G. Hinton. Semantic Hashing. *SIGIR workshop on Information Retrieval and applications of Graphical Models*, 2007.

[416] A. Santoro, S. Bartunov, M. Botvinick, D. Wierstra, and T. Lillicrap. One shot learning with memory-augmented neural networks. *arXiv: 1605:06065*, 2016.
https://www.arxiv.org/pdf/1605.06065.pdf

[417] R. Salakhutdinov and G. Hinton. Deep Boltzmann machines. *Artificial Intelligence and Statistics*, pp. 448–455, 2009.

[418] R. Salakhutdinov and H. Larochelle. Efficient Learning of Deep Boltzmann Machines. *AISTATs*, pp. 693–700, 2010.

[419] T. Salimans and D. Kingma. Weight normalization: A simple reparameterization to accelerate training of deep neural networks. *NIPS Conference*, pp. 901–909, 2016.

[420] T. Salimans, I. Goodfellow, W. Zaremba, V. Cheung, A. Radford, and X. Chen. Improved techniques for training gans. *NIPS Conference*, pp. 2234–2242, 2016.

[421] A. Samuel. Some studies in machine learning using the game of checkers. *IBM Journal of Research and Development*, 3, pp. 210–229, 1959.

[422] T Sanger. Neural network learning control of robot manipulators using gradually increasing task difficulty. *IEEE Transactions on Robotics and Automation*, 10(3), 1994.

[423] H. Sarimveis, A. Alexandridis, and G. Bafas. A fast training algorithm for RBF networks based on subtractive clustering. *Neurocomputing*, 51, pp. 501–505, 2003.

[424] W. Saunders, G. Sastry, A. Stuhlmueller, and O. Evans. Trial without Error: Towards Safe Reinforcement Learning via Human Intervention. *arXiv:1707.05173*, 2017.
https://arxiv.org/abs/1707.05173

[425] A. Saxe, P. Koh, Z. Chen, M. Bhand, B. Suresh, and A. Ng. On random weights and unsupervised feature learning. *ICML Confererence*, pp. 1089–1096, 2011.

[426] A. Saxe, J. McClelland, and S. Ganguli. Exact solutions to the nonlinear dynamics of learning in deep linear neural networks. *arXiv:1312.6120*, 2013.

[427] S. Schaal. Is imitation learning the route to humanoid robots? *Trends in Cognitive Sciences*, 3(6), pp. 233–242, 1999.

[428] T. Schaul, J. Quan, I. Antonoglou, and D. Silver. Prioritized experience replay. *arXiv:1511.05952*, 2015.
https://arxiv.org/abs/1511.05952

[429] T. Schaul, S. Zhang, and Y. LeCun. No more pesky learning rates. *ICML Confererence*, pp. 343–351, 2013.

[430] B. Schölkopf, K. Sung, C. Burges, F. Girosi, P. Niyogi, T. Poggio, and V. Vapnik. Comparing support vector machines with Gaussian kernels to radial basis function classifiers. *IEEE Transactions on Signal Processing*, 45(11), pp. 2758–2765, 1997.

[431] J. Schmidhuber. Deep learning in neural networks: An overview. *Neural Networks*, 61, pp. 85–117, 2015.

[432] J. Schulman, S. Levine, P. Abbeel, M. Jordan, and P. Moritz. Trust region policy optimization. *ICML Conference*, 2015.

[433] J. Schulman, P. Moritz, S. Levine, M. Jordan, and P. Abbeel. High-dimensional continuous control using generalized advantage estimation. *ICLR Conference*, 2016.

[434] M. Schuster and K. Paliwal. Bidirectional recurrent neural networks. *IEEE Transactions on Signal Processing*, 45(11), pp. 2673–2681, 1997.

[435] H. Schwenk and Y. Bengio. Boosting neural networks. *Neural Computation*, 12(8), pp. 1869–1887, 2000.

[436] S. Sedhain, A. K. Menon, S. Sanner, and L. Xie. Autorec: Autoencoders meet collaborative filtering. *WWW Conference*, pp. 111–112, 2015.

[437] T. J. Sejnowski. Higher-order Boltzmann machines. *AIP Conference Proceedings*, 15(1), pp. 298–403, 1986.

[438] G. Seni and J. Elder. Ensemble methods in data mining: Improving accuracy through combining predictions. *Morgan and Claypool*, 2010.

[439] I. Serban, A. Sordoni, R. Lowe, L. Charlin, J. Pineau, A. Courville, and Y. Bengio. A hierarchical latent variable encoder-decoder model for generating dialogues. *AAAI*, pp. 3295–3301, 2017.

[440] I. Serban, A. Sordoni, Y. Bengio, A. Courville, and J. Pineau. Building end-to-end dialogue systems using generative hierarchical neural network models. *AAAI Conference*, pp. 3776–3784, 2016.

[441] P. Sermanet, D. Eigen, X. Zhang, M. Mathieu, R. Fergus, and Y. LeCun. Overfeat: Integrated recognition, localization and detection using convolutional networks. *arXiv:1312.6229*, 2013.
https://arxiv.org/abs/1312.6229

[442] A. Shashua. On the equivalence between the support vector machine for classification and sparsified Fisher's linear discriminant. *Neural Processing Letters*, 9(2), pp. 129–139, 1999.

[443] J. Shewchuk. An introduction to the conjugate gradient method without the agonizing pain. *Technical Report, CMU-CS-94-125*, Carnegie-Mellon University, 1994.

[444] H. Siegelmann and E. Sontag. On the computational power of neural nets. *Journal of Computer and System Sciences*, 50(1), pp. 132–150, 1995.

[445] D. Silver *et al.* Mastering the game of Go with deep neural networks and tree search. *Nature*, 529.7587, pp. 484–489, 2016.

[446] D. Silver *et al.* Mastering the game of go without human knowledge. *Nature*, 550.7676, pp. 354–359, 2017.

[447] D. Silver *et al.* Mastering chess and shogi by self-play with a general reinforcement learning algorithm. *arXiv*, 2017.
https://arxiv.org/abs/1712.01815

[448] S. Shalev-Shwartz, Y. Singer, N. Srebro, and A. Cotter. Pegasos: Primal estimated sub-gradient solver for SVM. *Mathematical Programming*, 127(1), pp. 3–30, 2011.

[449] E. Shelhamer, J., Long, and T. Darrell. Fully convolutional networks for semantic segmentation. *IEEE TPAMI*, 39(4), pp. 640–651, 2017.

[450] J. Sietsma and R. Dow. Creating artificial neural networks that generalize. *Neural Networks*, 4(1), pp. 67–79, 1991.

[451] B. W. Silverman. Density Estimation for Statistics and Data Analysis. *Chapman and Hall*, 1986.

[452] P. Simard, D. Steinkraus, and J. C. Platt. Best practices for convolutional neural networks applied to visual document analysis. *ICDAR*, pp. 958–962, 2003.

[453] H. Simon. The Sciences of the Artificial. *MIT Press*, 1996.

[454] K. Simonyan and A. Zisserman. Very deep convolutional networks for large-scale image recognition. *arXiv:1409.1556*, 2014.
https://arxiv.org/abs/1409.1556

[455] K. Simonyan and A. Zisserman. Two-stream convolutional networks for action recognition in videos. *NIPS Conference*, pp. 568–584, 2014.

[456] K. Simonyan, A. Vedaldi, and A. Zisserman. Deep inside convolutional networks: Visualising image classification models and saliency maps. *arXiv:1312.6034*, 2013.

[457] P. Smolensky. Information processing in dynamical systems: Foundations of harmony theory. *Parallel Distributed Processing: Explorations in the Microstructure of Cognition*, Volume 1: Foundations. pp. 194–281, 1986.

[458] J. Snoek, H. Larochelle, and R. Adams. Practical bayesian optimization of machine learning algorithms. *NIPS Conference*, pp. 2951–2959, 2013.

[459] R. Socher, C. Lin, C. Manning, and A. Ng. Parsing natural scenes and natural language with recursive neural networks. *ICML Confererence*, pp. 129–136, 2011.

[460] R. Socher, J. Pennington, E. Huang, A. Ng, and C. Manning. Semi-supervised recursive autoencoders for predicting sentiment distributions. *Empirical Methods in Natural Language Processing (EMNLP)*, pp. 151–161, 2011.

[461] R. Socher, A. Perelygin, J. Wu, J. Chuang, C. Manning, A. Ng, and C. Potts. Recursive deep models for semantic compositionality over a sentiment treebank. *Empirical Methods in Natural Language Processing (EMNLP)*, p. 1642, 2013.

[462] Socher, Richard, Milind Ganjoo, Christopher D. Manning, and Andrew Ng. Zero-shot learning through cross-modal transfer. *NIPS Conference*, pp. 935–943, 2013.

[463] K. Sohn, H. Lee, and X. Yan. Learning structured output representation using deep conditional generative models. *NIPS Conference*, 2015.

[464] R. Solomonoff. A system for incremental learning based on algorithmic probability. *Sixth Israeli Conference on Artificial Intelligence, Computer Vision and Pattern Recognition*, pp. 515–527, 1994.

[465] Y. Song, A. Elkahky, and X. He. Multi-rate deep learning for temporal recommendation. *ACM SIGIR Conference on Research and Development in Information Retrieval*, pp. 909–912, 2016.

[466] J. Springenberg, A. Dosovitskiy, T. Brox, and M. Riedmiller. Striving for simplicity: The all convolutional net. *arXiv:1412.6806*, 2014.
https://arxiv.org/abs/1412.6806

[467] N. Srivastava, G. Hinton, A. Krizhevsky, I. Sutskever, and R. Salakhutdinov. Dropout: A simple way to prevent neural networks from overfitting. *The Journal of Machine Learning Research*, 15(1), pp. 1929–1958, 2014.

[468] N. Srivastava and R. Salakhutdinov. Multimodal learning with deep Boltzmann machines. *NIPS Conference*, pp. 2222–2230, 2012.

[469] N. Srivastava, R. Salakhutdinov, and G. Hinton. Modeling documents with deep Boltzmann machines. *Uncertainty in Artificial Intelligence*, 2013.

[470] R. K. Srivastava, K. Greff, and J. Schmidhuber. Highway networks. *arXiv:1505.00387*, 2015.
https://arxiv.org/abs/1505.00387

[471] A. Storkey. Increasing the capacity of a Hopfield network without sacrificing functionality. *Artificial Neural Networks*, pp. 451–456, 1997.

[472] F. Strub and J. Mary. Collaborative filtering with stacked denoising autoencoders and sparse inputs. *NIPS Workshop on Machine Learning for eCommerce*, 2015.

[473] S. Sukhbaatar, J. Weston, and R. Fergus. End-to-end memory networks. *NIPS Conference*, pp. 2440–2448, 2015.

[474] Y. Sun, D. Liang, X. Wang, and X. Tang. Deepid3: Face recognition with very deep neural networks. *arXiv:1502.00873*, 2013.
https://arxiv.org/abs/1502.00873

[475] Y. Sun, X. Wang, and X. Tang. Deep learning face representation from predicting 10,000 classes. *IEEE Conference on Computer Vision and Pattern Recognition*, pp. 1891–1898, 2014.

[476] M. Sundermeyer, R. Schluter, and H. Ney. LSTM neural networks for language modeling. *Interspeech*, 2010.

[477] M. Sundermeyer, T. Alkhouli, J. Wuebker, and H. Ney. Translation modeling with bidirectional recurrent neural networks. *EMNLP*, pp. 14–25, 2014.

[478] I. Sutskever, J. Martens, G. Dahl, and G. Hinton. On the importance of initialization and momentum in deep learning. *ICML Confererence*, pp. 1139–1147, 2013.

[479] I. Sutskever and T. Tieleman. On the convergence properties of contrastive divergence. *International Conference on Artificial Intelligence and Statistics*, pp. 789–795, 2010.

[480] I. Sutskever, O. Vinyals, and Q. V. Le. Sequence to sequence learning with neural networks. *NIPS Conference*, pp. 3104–3112, 2014.

[481] I. Sutskever and V. Nair. Mimicking Go experts with convolutional neural networks. *International Conference on Artificial Neural Networks*, pp. 101–110, 2008.

[482] R. Sutton. Learning to Predict by the Method of Temporal Differences, *Machine Learning*, 3, pp. 9–44, 1988.

[483] R. Sutton and A. Barto. Reinforcement Learning: An Introduction. *MIT Press*, 1998.

[484] R. Sutton, D. McAllester, S. Singh, and Y. Mansour. Policy gradient methods for reinforcement learning with function approximation. *NIPS Conference*, pp. 1057–1063, 2000.

[485] C. Szegedy, W. Liu, Y. Jia, P. Sermanet, S. Reed, D. Anguelov, D. Erhan, V. Vanhoucke, and A. Rabinovich. Going deeper with convolutions. *IEEE Conference on Computer Vision and Pattern Recognition*, pp. 1–9, 2015.

[486] C. Szegedy, V. Vanhoucke, S. Ioffe, J. Shlens, and Z. Wojna. Rethinking the inception architecture for computer vision. *IEEE Conference on Computer Vision and Pattern Recognition*, pp. 2818–2826, 2016.

[487] C. Szegedy, S. Ioffe, V. Vanhoucke, and A. Alemi. Inception-v4, Inception-ResNet and the Impact of Residual Connections on Learning. *AAAI Conference*, pp. 4278–4284, 2017.

[488] G. Taylor, R. Fergus, Y. LeCun, and C. Bregler. Convolutional learning of spatio-temporal features. *European Conference on Computer Vision*, pp. 140–153, 2010.

[489] G. Taylor, G. Hinton, and S. Roweis. Modeling human motion using binary latent variables. *NIPS Conference*, 2006.

[490] C. Thornton, F. Hutter, H. H. Hoos, and K. Leyton-Brown. Auto-WEKA: Combined selection and hyperparameter optimization of classification algorithms. *ACM KDD Conference*, pp. 847–855, 2013.

[491] T. Tieleman. Training restricted Boltzmann machines using approximations to the likelihood gradient. *ICML Conference*, pp. 1064–1071, 2008.

[492] G. Tesauro. Practical issues in temporal difference learning. *Advances in NIPS Conference*, pp. 259–266, 1992.

[493] G. Tesauro. Td-gammon: A self-teaching backgammon program. *Applications of Neural Networks*, Springer, pp. 267–285, 1992.

[494] G. Tesauro. Temporal difference learning and TD-Gammon. *Communications of the ACM*, 38(3), pp. 58–68, 1995.

[495] Y. Teh and G. Hinton. Rate-coded restricted Boltzmann machines for face recognition. *NIPS Conference*, 2001.

[496] S. Thrun. Learning to play the game of chess *NIPS Conference*, pp. 1069–1076, 1995.

[497] S. Thrun and L. Platt. Learning to learn. *Springer*, 2012.

[498] Y. Tian, Q. Gong, W. Shang, Y. Wu, and L. Zitnick. ELF: An extensive, lightweight and flexible research platform for real-time strategy games. *arXiv:1707.01067*, 2017.
https://arxiv.org/abs/1707.01067

[499] A. Tikhonov and V. Arsenin. Solution of ill-posed problems. *Winston and Sons*, 1977.

[500] D. Tran *et al.* Learning spatiotemporal features with 3d convolutional networks. *IEEE International Conference on Computer Vision*, 2015.

[501] R. Uijlings, A. van de Sande, T. Gevers, and M. Smeulders. Selective search for object recognition. *International Journal of Computer Vision*, 104(2), 2013.

[502] H. Valpola. From neural PCA to deep unsupervised learning. *Advances in Independent Component Analysis and Learning Machines*, pp. 143–171, Elsevier, 2015.

[503] A. Vedaldi and K. Lenc. Matconvnet: Convolutional neural networks for matlab. *ACM International Conference on Multimedia*, pp. 689–692, 2005.
http://www.vlfeat.org/matconvnet/

[504] V. Veeriah, N. Zhuang, and G. Qi. Differential recurrent neural networks for action recognition. *IEEE International Conference on Computer Vision*, pp. 4041–4049, 2015.

[505] A. Veit, M. Wilber, and S. Belongie. Residual networks behave like ensembles of relatively shallow networks. *NIPS Conference*, pp. 550–558, 2016.

[506] P. Vincent, H. Larochelle, Y. Bengio, and P. Manzagol. Extracting and composing robust features with denoising autoencoders. ICML Confererence, pp. 1096–1103, 2008.

[507] O. Vinyals, C. Blundell, T. Lillicrap, and D. Wierstra. Matching networks for one-shot learning. *NIPS Conference*, pp. 3530–3638, 2016.

[508] O. Vinyals and Q. Le. A Neural Conversational Model. *arXiv:1506.05869*, 2015.
https://arxiv.org/abs/1506.05869

[509] O. Vinyals, A. Toshev, S. Bengio, and D. Erhan. Show and tell: A neural image caption generator. *CVPR Conference*, pp. 3156–3164, 2015.

[510] J. Walker, C. Doersch, A. Gupta, and M. Hebert. An uncertain future: Forecasting from static images using variational autoencoders. *European Conference on Computer Vision*, pp. 835–851, 2016.

[511] L. Wan, M. Zeiler, S. Zhang, Y. LeCun, and R. Fergus. Regularization of neural networks using dropconnect. *ICML Conference*, pp. 1058–1066, 2013.

[512] D. Wang, P. Cui, and W. Zhu. Structural deep network embedding. *ACM KDD Conference*, pp. 1225–1234, 2016.

[513] H. Wang, N. Wang, and D. Yeung. Collaborative deep learning for recommender systems. *ACM KDD Conference*, pp. 1235–1244, 2015.

[514] L. Wang, Y. Qiao, and X. Tang. Action recognition with trajectory-pooled deep-convolutional descriptors. *IEEE Conference on Computer Vision and Pattern Recognition*, pp. 4305–4314, 2015.

[515] S. Wang, C. Aggarwal, and H. Liu. Using a random forest to inspire a neural network and improving on it. *SIAM Conference on Data Mining*, 2017.

[516] S. Wang, C. Aggarwal, and H. Liu. Randomized feature engineering as a fast and accurate alternative to kernel methods. *ACM KDD Conference*, 2017.

[517] T. Wang, D. Wu, A. Coates, and A. Ng. End-to-end text recognition with convolutional neural networks. *International Conference on Pattern Recognition*, pp. 3304–3308, 2012.

[518] X. Wang and A. Gupta. Generative image modeling using style and structure adversarial networks. *ECCV*, 2016.

[519] C. J. H. Watkins. Learning from delayed rewards. *PhD Thesis*, King's College, Cambridge, 1989.

[520] C. J. H. Watkins and P. Dayan. Q-learning. *Machine Learning*, 8(3–4), pp. 279–292, 1992.

[521] K. Weinberger, B. Packer, and L. Saul. Nonlinear Dimensionality Reduction by Semidefinite Programming and Kernel Matrix Factorization. *AISTATS*, 2005.

[522] M. Welling, M. Rosen-Zvi, and G. Hinton. Exponential family harmoniums with an application to information retrieval. *NIPS Conference*, pp. 1481–1488, 2005.

[523] A. Wendemuth. Learning the unlearnable. *Journal of Physics A: Math. Gen.*, 28, pp. 5423–5436, 1995.

[524] P. Werbos. Beyond Regression: New Tools for Prediction and Analysis in the Behavioral Sciences. *PhD thesis, Harvard University*, 1974.

[525] P. Werbos. The roots of backpropagation: from ordered derivatives to neural networks and political forecasting (Vol. 1). *John Wiley and Sons*, 1994.

[526] P. Werbos. Backpropagation through time: what it does and how to do it. *Proceedings of the IEEE*, 78(10), pp. 1550–1560, 1990.

[527] J. Weston, A. Bordes, S. Chopra, A. Rush, B. van Merrienboer, A. Joulin, and T. Mikolov. Towards ai-complete question answering: A set of pre-requisite toy tasks. *arXiv:1502.05698*, 2015.
https://arxiv.org/abs/1502.05698

[528] J. Weston, S. Chopra, and A. Bordes. Memory networks. *ICLR*, 2015.

[529] J. Weston and C. Watkins. Multi-class support vector machines. *Technical Report CSD-TR-98-04*, Department of Computer Science, Royal Holloway, University of London, May, 1998.

[530] D. Wettschereck and T. Dietterich. Improving the performance of radial basis function networks by learning center locations. *NIPS Conference*, pp. 1133–1140, 1992.

[531] B. Widrow and M. Hoff. Adaptive switching circuits. *IRE WESCON Convention Record*, 4(1), pp. 96–104, 1960.

[532] S. Wieseler and H. Ney. A convergence analysis of log-linear training. *NIPS Conference*, pp. 657–665, 2011.

[533] R. J. Williams. Simple statistical gradient-following algorithms for connectionist reinforcement learning. *Machine Learning*, 8(3–4), pp. 229–256, 1992.

[534] C. Wu, A. Ahmed, A. Beutel, A. Smola, and H. Jing. Recurrent recommender networks. *ACM International Conference on Web Search and Data Mining*, pp. 495–503, 2017.

[535] Y. Wu, C. DuBois, A. Zheng, and M. Ester. Collaborative denoising auto-encoders for top-n recommender systems. *Web Search and Data Mining*, pp. 153–162, 2016.

[536] Z. Wu. Global continuation for distance geometry problems. *SIAM Journal of Optimization*, 7, pp. 814–836, 1997.

[537] S. Xie, R. Girshick, P. Dollar, Z. Tu, and K. He. Aggregated residual transformations for deep neural networks. *arXiv:1611.05431*, 2016.
https://arxiv.org/abs/1611.05431

[538] E. Xing, R. Yan, and A. Hauptmann. Mining associated text and images with dual-wing harmoniums. *Uncertainty in Artificial Intelligence*, 2005.

[539] C. Xiong, S. Merity, and R. Socher. Dynamic memory networks for visual and textual question answering. *ICML Confererence*, pp. 2397–2406, 2016.

[540] K. Xu *et al.* Show, attend, and tell: Neural image caption generation with visual attention. *ICML Confererence*, 2015.

[541] O. Yadan, K. Adams, Y. Taigman, and M. Ranzato. Multi-gpu training of convnets. *arXiv:1312.5853*, 2013.
https://arxiv.org/abs/1312.5853

[542] Z. Yang, X. He, J. Gao, L. Deng, and A. Smola. Stacked attention networks for image question answering. *IEEE Conference on Computer Vision and Pattern Recognition*, pp. 21–29, 2016.

[543] X. Yao. Evolving artificial neural networks. *Proceedings of the IEEE*, 87(9), pp. 1423–1447, 1999.

[544] F. Yu and V. Koltun. Multi-scale context aggregation by dilated convolutions. *arXiv:1511.07122*, 2015.
https://arxiv.org/abs/1511.07122

[545] H. Yu and B. Wilamowski. Levenberg–Marquardt training. *Industrial Electronics Handbook*, 5(12), 1, 2011.

[546] L. Yu, W. Zhang, J. Wang, and Y. Yu. SeqGAN: Sequence Generative Adversarial Nets with Policy Gradient. *AAAI Conference*, pp. 2852–2858, 2017.

[547] W. Yu, W. Cheng, C. Aggarwal, K. Zhang, H. Chen, and Wei Wang. NetWalk: A flexible deep embedding approach for anomaly Detection in dynamic networks, *ACM KDD Conference*, 2018.

[548] W. Yu, C. Zheng, W. Cheng, C. Aggarwal, D. Song, B. Zong, H. Chen, and W. Wang. Learning deep network representations with adversarially regularized autoencoders. *ACM KDD Conference*, 2018.

[549] S. Zagoruyko and N. Komodakis. Wide residual networks. *arXiv:1605.07146*, 2016. https://arxiv.org/abs/1605.07146

[550] W. Zaremba and I. Sutskever. Reinforcement learning neural turing machines. *arXiv:1505.00521*, 2015.

[551] W. Zaremba, T. Mikolov, A. Joulin, and R. Fergus. Learning simple algorithms from examples. *ICML Confererence*, pp. 421–429, 2016.

[552] W. Zaremba, I. Sutskever, and O. Vinyals. Recurrent neural network regularization. *arXiv:1409.2329*, 2014.

[553] M. Zeiler. ADADELTA: an adaptive learning rate method. *arXiv:1212.5701*, 2012. https://arxiv.org/abs/1212.5701

[554] M. Zeiler, D. Krishnan, G. Taylor, and R. Fergus. Deconvolutional networks. *Computer Vision and Pattern Recognition (CVPR)*, pp. 2528–2535, 2010.

[555] M. Zeiler, G. Taylor, and R. Fergus. Adaptive deconvolutional networks for mid and high level feature learning. *IEEE International Conference on Computer Vision (ICCV)—*, pp. 2018–2025, 2011.

[556] M. Zeiler and R. Fergus. Visualizing and understanding convolutional networks. *European Conference on Computer Vision*, Springer, pp. 818–833, 2013.

[557] C. Zhang, S. Bengio, M. Hardt, B. Recht, and O. Vinyals. Understanding deep learning requires rethinking generalization. *arXiv:1611.03530*. https://arxiv.org/abs/1611.03530

[558] D. Zhang, Z.-H. Zhou, and S. Chen. Non-negative matrix factorization on kernels. *Trends in Artificial Intelligence*, pp. 404–412, 2006.

[559] L. Zhang, C. Aggarwal, and G.-J. Qi. Stock Price Prediction via Discovering Multi-Frequency Trading Patterns. *ACM KDD Conference*, 2017.

[560] S. Zhang, L. Yao, and A. Sun. Deep learning based recommender system: A survey and new perspectives. *arXiv:1707.07435*, 2017. https://arxiv.org/abs/1707.07435

[561] X. Zhang, J. Zhao, and Y. LeCun. Character-level convolutional networks for text classification. *NIPS Conference*, pp. 649–657, 2015.

[562] J. Zhao, M. Mathieu, and Y. LeCun. Energy-based generative adversarial network. *arXiv:1609.03126*, 2016. https://arxiv.org/abs/1609.03126

[563] V. Zhong, C. Xiong, and R. Socher. Seq2SQL: Generating structured queries from natural language using reinforcement learning. *arXiv:1709.00103*, 2017. https://arxiv.org/abs/1709.00103

[564] C. Zhou and R. Paffenroth. Anomaly detection with robust deep autoencoders. *ACM KDD Conference*, pp. 665–674, 2017.

[565] M. Zhou, Z. Ding, J. Tang, and D. Yin. Micro Behaviors: A new perspective in e-commerce recommender systems. *WSDM Conference*, 2018.

[566] Z.-H. Zhou. Ensemble methods: Foundations and algorithms. *CRC Press*, 2012.

[567] Z.-H. Zhou, J. Wu, and W. Tang. Ensembling neural networks: many could be better than all. *Artificial Intelligence*, 137(1–2), pp. 239–263, 2002.

[568] C. Zitnick and P. Dollar. Edge Boxes: Locating object proposals from edges. *ECCV*, pp. 391–405, 2014.

[569] B. Zoph and Q. V. Le. Neural architecture search with reinforcement learning. *arXiv:1611.01578*, 2016.
https://arxiv.org/abs/1611.01578

[570] https://deeplearning4j.org/

[571] http://caffe.berkeleyvision.org/

[572] http://torch.ch/

[573] http://deeplearning.net/software/theano/

[574] https://www.tensorflow.org/

[575] https://keras.io/

[576] https://lasagne.readthedocs.io/en/latest/

[577] http://www.netflixprize.com/community/topic_1537.html

[578] http://deeplearning.net/tutorial/lstm.html

[579] https://arxiv.org/abs/1609.08144

[580] https://github.com/karpathy/char-rnn

[581] http://www.image-net.org/

[582] http://www.image-net.org/challenges/LSVRC/

[583] https://www.cs.toronto.edu/~kriz/cifar.html

[584] http://code.google.com/p/cuda-convnet/

[585] http://caffe.berkeleyvision.org/gathered/examples/feature_extraction.html

[586] https://github.com/caffe2/caffe2/wiki/Model-Zoo

[587] http://scikit-learn.org/

[588] http://clic.cimec.unitn.it/composes/toolkit/

[589] https://github.com/stanfordnlp/GloVe

[590] https://deeplearning4j.org/

[591] https://code.google.com/archive/p/word2vec/

[592] https://www.tensorflow.org/tutorials/word2vec/

[593] https://github.com/aditya-grover/node2vec

[594] https://www.wikipedia.org/

[595] https://github.com/caglar/autoencoders

[596] https://github.com/y0ast

[597] https://github.com/fastforwardlabs/vae-tf/tree/master

[598] https://science.education.nih.gov/supplements/webversions/BrainAddiction/guide/
       lesson2-1.html

[599] https://www.ibm.com/us-en/marketplace/deep-learning-platform

[600] https://www.coursera.org/learn/neural-networks

[601] https://archive.ics.uci.edu/ml/datasets.html

[602] http://www.bbc.com/news/technology-35785875

[603] https://deepmind.com/blog/exploring-mysteries-alphago/

[604] http://selfdrivingcars.mit.edu/

[605] http://karpathy.github.io/2016/05/31/rl/

[606] https://github.com/hughperkins/kgsgo-dataset-preprocessor

[607] https://www.wired.com/2016/03/two-moves-alphago-lee-sedol-redefined-future/

[608] https://qz.com/639952/
       googles-ai-won-the-game-go-by-defying-millennia-of-basic-human-instinct/

[609] http://www.mujoco.org/

[610] https://sites.google.com/site/gaepapersupp/home

[611] https://drive.google.com/file/d/0B9raQzOpizn1TkRIa241ZnBEcjQ/view

[612] https://www.youtube.com/watch?v=1L0TKZQcUtA&list=PLrAXtmErZgOeiKm4sgNOkn–
       GvNjby9efdf

[613] https://openai.com/

[614] http://jaberg.github.io/hyperopt/

[615] http://www.cs.ubc.ca/labs/beta/Projects/SMAC/

[616] https://github.com/JasperSnoek/spearmint

[617] https://deeplearning4j.org/lstm

[618] http://colah.github.io/posts/2015-08-Understanding-LSTMs/

[619] https://www.youtube.com/watch?v=2pWv7GOvuf0

[620] https://gym.openai.com

[621] https://universe.openai.com

[622] https://github.com/facebookresearch/ParlAI

[623] https://github.com/openai/baselines

[624] https://github.com/carpedm20/deep-rl-tensorflow

[625] https://github.com/matthiasplappert/keras-rl

[626] http://apollo.auto/

[627] https://github.com/Element-Research/rnn/blob/master/examples/

[628] https://github.com/lmthang/nmt.matlab

[629] https://github.com/carpedm20/NTM-tensorflow

[630] https://github.com/camigord/Neural-Turing-Machine

[631] https://github.com/SigmaQuan/NTM-Keras

[632] https://github.com/snipsco/ntm-lasagne

[633] https://github.com/kaishengtai/torch-ntm

[634] https://github.com/facebook/MemNN

[635] https://github.com/carpedm20/MemN2N-tensorflow

[636] https://github.com/YerevaNN/Dynamic-memory-networks-in-Theano

[637] https://github.com/carpedm20/DCGAN-tensorflow

[638] https://github.com/carpedm20

[639] https://github.com/jacobgil/keras-dcgan

[640] https://github.com/wiseodd/generative-models

[641] https://github.com/paarthneekhara/text-to-image

[642] http://horatio.cs.nyu.edu/mit/tiny/data/

[643] https://developer.nvidia.com/cudnn

[644] http://www.nvidia.com/object/machine-learning.html

[645] https://developer.nvidia.com/deep-learning-frameworks

Index

Printed in the United States
By Bookmasters